SILVER BURDETT CHEMISTRY PROGRAM

CHEMISTRY
Pupil's Textbook
Teacher's Edition
GREGORY CHOPPIN
LEE SUMMERLIN

LABORATORY INVESTIGATIONS IN CHEMISTRY
Laboratory Guide
Student Record Book
Teacher's Edition
HAROLD FERGUSON
JOSEPH SCHMUCKLER
ALBERT CARO
ALLENE JOHNSON

TESTS FOR CHEMISTRY
LEE SUMMERLIN

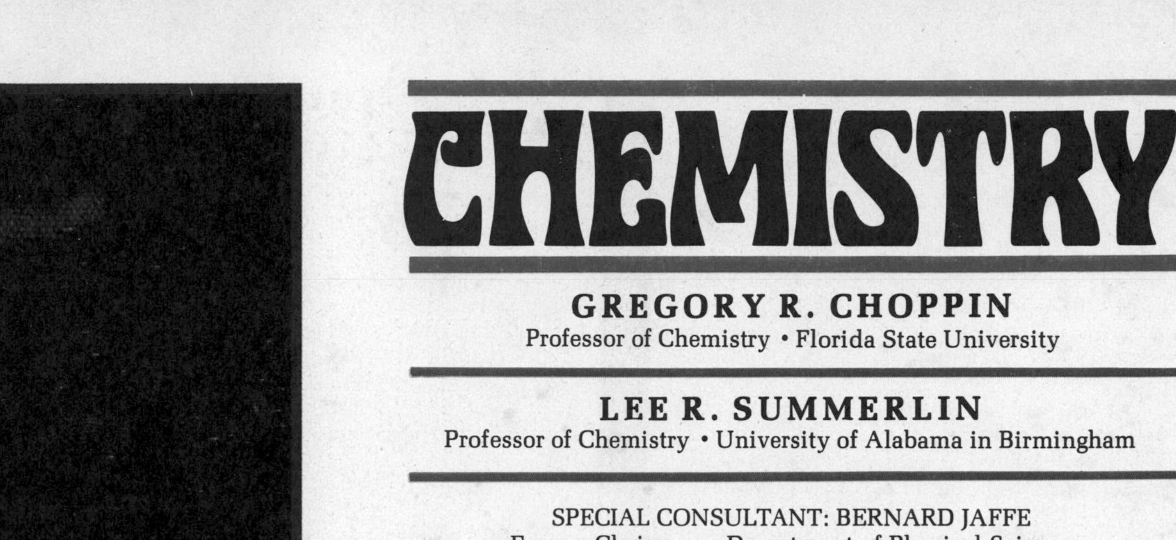

CHEMISTRY

GREGORY R. CHOPPIN
Professor of Chemistry • Florida State University

LEE R. SUMMERLIN
Professor of Chemistry • University of Alabama in Birmingham

SPECIAL CONSULTANT: BERNARD JAFFE
Former Chairman • Department of Physical Science
James Madison High School • New York City

SILVER BURDETT COMPANY

Morristown, New Jersey
Glenview, Ill. • Palo Alto • Dallas • Atlanta

ACKNOWLEDGMENTS

It is extremely difficult to acknowledge the assistance of all the people who have played an integral part in the production of a textbook. Our students, our teachers, and our teaching colleagues have all contributed more than they will ever realize to this effort. The following people, who read and criticized all aspects of the chemistry program, are acknowledged with our deep gratitude:

Mrs. Emily Beckwith
Cockeysville, High School
Cockeysville, Maryland

Dr. Hugh Cartwright
University of Victoria
Victoria, British Columbia

Mr. Peter Dahl
Lowell High School
San Fancisco, California

Mrs. JoAnn Durham
Ft. Payne High School
Ft. Payne, Alabama

Dr. Kenneth V. Fast
Kirkwood Sr. High School
Kirkwood, Missouri

Mr. James Gardner
Millburn High School
Millburn, New Jersey

Mr. Paul Green
Richards High School
Tallahassee, Florida

Mrs. Marilyn Lucas
Euclid High School
Euclid, Ohio

Mrs. Katherine E. Wichenden
Tabor Academy
Marion, Massachusettes

ISBN 0-382-04427-4

CONTENTS

INTRODUCTION

When we are very young, we must learn first to crawl, then to take the first uncertain steps. Much later a few of us may know the thrill of winning the Olympic marathon or of scaling the summit of Mount Everest. As Everest is a towering symbol of physical accomplishment, science stands as a towering symbol of human intelligence. And like the baby, we must learn to crawl and to take the first tentative steps in science. It is necessary to spend most of our time in this crawling stage on the basic aspects of chemistry. The essence of science is the excitement of being the first to learn something new about nature. The importance of technology is the central role it plays in every aspect of modern life. But first we must learn and understand the simpler facts and theories of chemistry.

The foundation of the world of matter is the structure of the atom and the particles of which it is made. However, the development of chemistry did not proceed from an understanding of the atom to the organization of the universe. Instead, knowledge that was more accessible, because it was more observable, was attained first. More abstract concepts, such as those concerning the atomic nature of matter, followed. For instance, the essential difference between compounds and elements was understood before the nature of molecules and atoms. In the same way, we discuss the differences between compounds and elements before their basic natures. The states of matter are distinguished on an observable basis, and then their molecular nature is covered. The topic of chemical periodicity is developed before details on the nature of electronic arrangement. The quantum mechanical model of the atom is presented as the result of prior developments and not simply as the most recent and useful concept of atomic structure.

Since this is the manner in which the science of chemistry actually developed, we believe it is the way in which the nature of chemistry can be most easily and clearly approached.

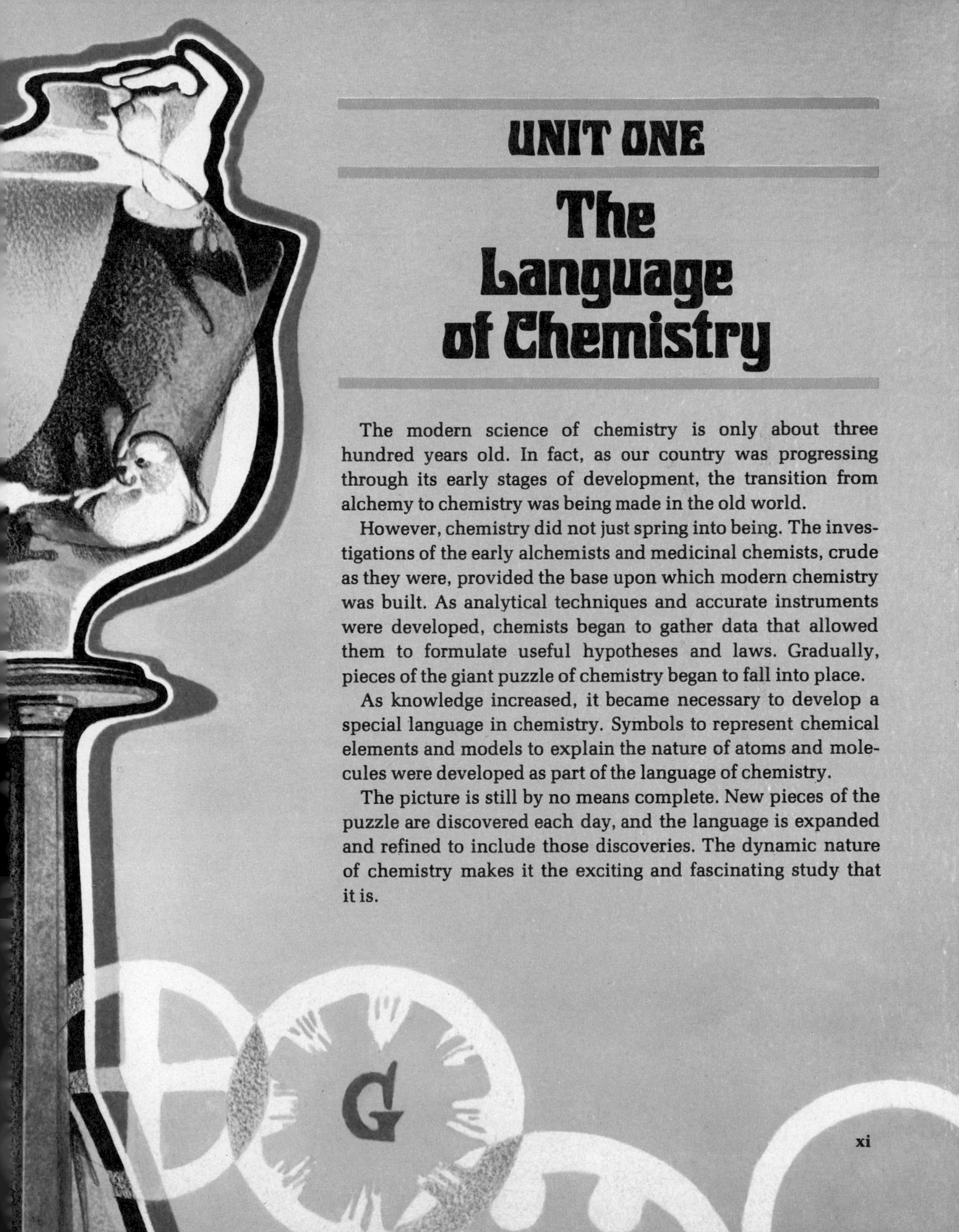

UNIT ONE

The Language of Chemistry

The modern science of chemistry is only about three hundred years old. In fact, as our country was progressing through its early stages of development, the transition from alchemy to chemistry was being made in the old world.

However, chemistry did not just spring into being. The investigations of the early alchemists and medicinal chemists, crude as they were, provided the base upon which modern chemistry was built. As analytical techniques and accurate instruments were developed, chemists began to gather data that allowed them to formulate useful hypotheses and laws. Gradually, pieces of the giant puzzle of chemistry began to fall into place.

As knowledge increased, it became necessary to develop a special language in chemistry. Symbols to represent chemical elements and models to explain the nature of atoms and molecules were developed as part of the language of chemistry.

The picture is still by no means complete. New pieces of the puzzle are discovered each day, and the language is expanded and refined to include those discoveries. The dynamic nature of chemistry makes it the exciting and fascinating study that it is.

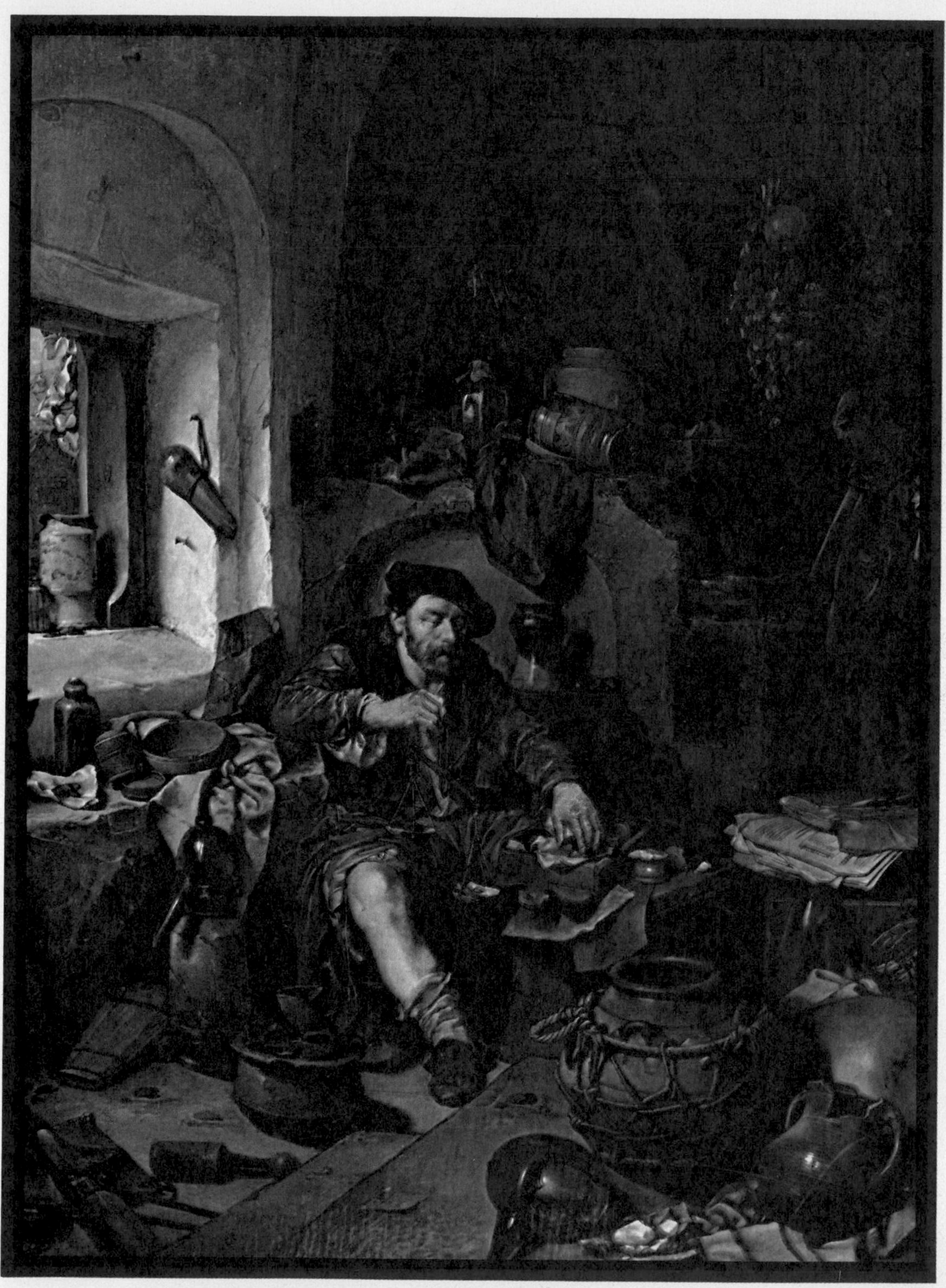

Modern chemistry grew out of the imagination and curiosity of early scientists.

CHAPTER ONE

Alchemy to Modern Chemistry

Many students face the study of chemistry with great apprehension. And it's no wonder! The very thought of memorizing complex formulas and solving difficult problems is enough to frighten anyone. Perhaps you have thumbed through your chemistry book. You probably find yourself a little awed at the thought of having to learn the strange language of the chemist. But chemistry need not be difficult. The study of chemistry can be a pleasant experience. In fact, it can even be fun.

There is another thing you should keep in mind. Your textbook represents the efforts of thousands of scientists spanning thousands of years. And the advancement in chemistry has never stopped. New discoveries in chemistry are made every day. Chemistry is a dynamic, ever-changing process in which anyone can be involved, including you. You may be just the person to provide answers to some of the problems that confront scientists today.

When your grandmother and grandfather were in high school, chemists knew of the existence of about 90 elements. Today there are 108 elements. And everything that exists is composed of some combination of these elements. Did your mother or father study chemistry in high school? If so, show them the table of elements on pages 146–147. See how many they can recognize! When your children study chemistry, perhaps there will be 110 or 120 elements. Just imagine how much more chemistry they will have to learn. In fact, it has been estimated that the total amount of scientific information doubles every ten years. By the time your children study chemistry, there will be four times as much scientific information! But let's not worry about what your children will be learning. Let's see what there is for you to learn.

ALCHEMY AND ALCHEMISTS

1–1 · The beginnings of chemistry · The first chemist was that first individual who tried to understand and adapt to the surrounding environment. That was perhaps two million years ago. People of some prehistoric cultures probably observed molten copper flowing from heated rocks. Through experiments, those early chemists learned to mold the copper into crude weapons and utensils that helped make their lives a little easier. Around 3000 B.C., early cultures probably noticed that certain strange "rocks" fell from the sky. These "rocks" were unlike any other rocks on the earth. Now, we know that these were not rocks at all. They were meteorites composed of metallic iron. Our primitive chemists experimented with the iron and learned how to put its unusual properties to work. The strange rocks were pounded, bent, and shaped into better spears and more durable tools. The art of working with metals such as copper from the earth and iron from the meteorites is now called **metallurgy.** And metallurgy played a significant role in the development of chemistry.

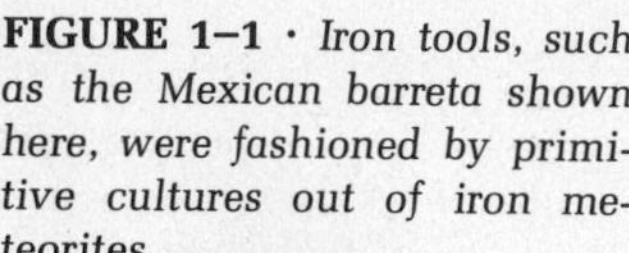

FIGURE 1–1 · *Iron tools, such as the Mexican barreta shown here, were fashioned by primitive cultures out of iron meteorites.*

1–2 · Alchemy, the basis of modern chemistry · As civilization developed, the problems of the natural world were still viewed as a whole. There was no attempt to separate the study of matter and its properties (chemistry) from any other area of human observation. However, in the third century B.C., a new science began to develop in Alexandria, Egypt. That was **alchemy.** Alchemy combined the Egyptian arts of metallurgy, dyeing, and glassmaking in a search for methods of changing matter and prolonging life. It was based on those Egyptian arts, and the philosophy of logic developed by the Greeks.

From Alexandria, alchemy began to spread throughout the world (Figure 1–2). In each country, alchemy was influenced by the prevalent culture. For example, the Arabian alchemists applied the knowledge of alchemy to their knowledge of medicine. They also developed the theory that metals were composed of the elements mercury and sulfur. That is one example of how alchemists began to lay the foundation for modern chemistry. Let's see some of the other ways that the alchemists influenced the development of modern chemistry.

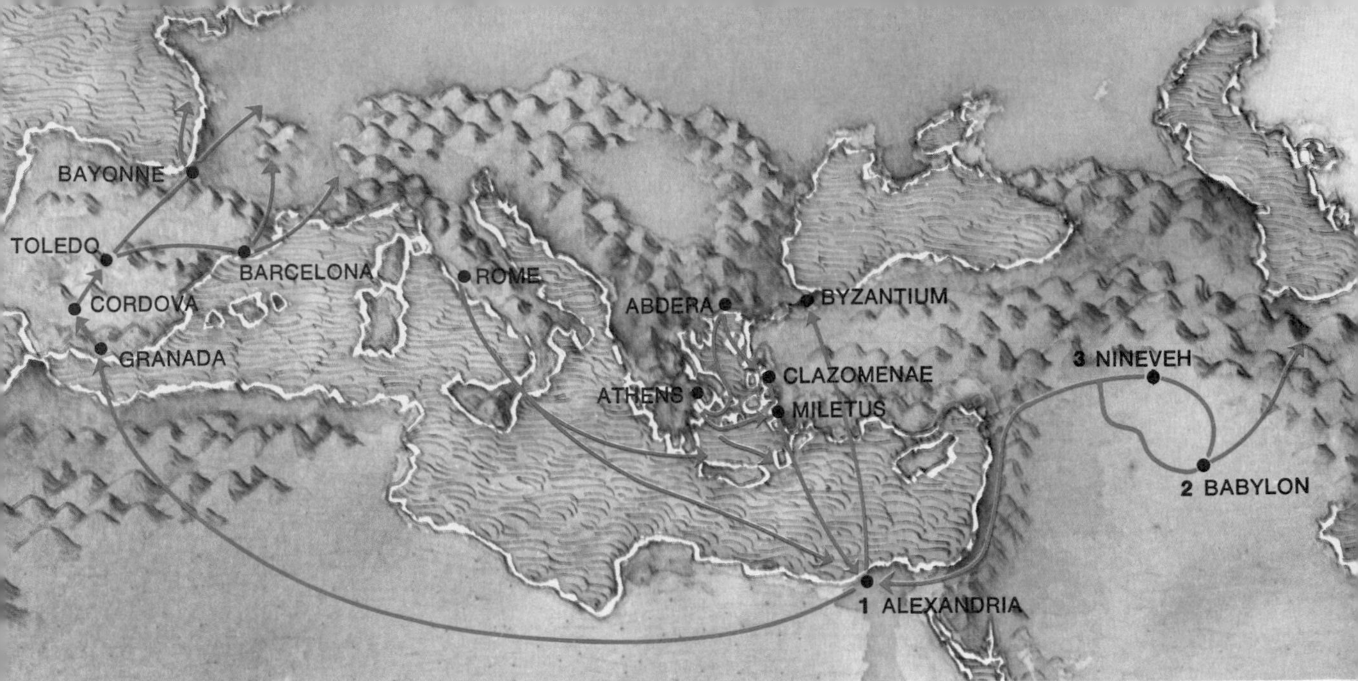

FIGURE 1–2 · *This map illustrates the spread of alchemy throughout Europe from its basic roots in the practical arts of the Egyptian (1), Mesopotamian (2), and Persian (3) cultures.*

1–3 · Early alchemists assigned symbols to substances · The early alchemists made many important contributions. For example, they developed a system of assigning symbols to the substances they used. Even though our symbols today are very different, that was a start. For example, to the alchemist, the sun symbolized sulfur, which was given the symbol 🜍. The moon symbolized mercury, which became ☿. And Saturn symbolized lead, which was represented as ♄.

Mars represented iron, ♂, and Venus represented copper, ♀. Perhaps you recognize those two symbols from biology. Iron (♂) was found to be hard and durable, but dull and lacking luster. Those were properties that alchemists thought described men, so ♂ became the symbol for male. On the other hand, alchemists observed copper as delicate, easily twisted or shaped, and bright. They felt, in those days, that those properties described women. So the symbol for female became ♀. What metals would you choose to symbolize male and female?

It is not surprising that early alchemists bestowed magical properties on certain elements and other substances. They believed all substances were made inside the earth by various combinations of the elements sulfur and mercury. These two elements were thought to have opposite qualities. The alchemists believed their proper union could yield the *philosopher's stone*. This was the magic substance that supposedly caused metals such as lead and iron to change into precious gold.

FIGURE 1–3 · *In this early lithograph, two philosophers, Senior and Adolphus, are shown discussing the tree of universal matter. Try to name the elements of which they thought all matter was made.*

While some alchemists were searching for the philosopher's stone, others were in pursuit of the mysterious *elixir of life.* This elixir would, according to the thirteenth-century alchemist Arnold of Villanova, "turn an old person into a youth, dispel poisons from the heart, fortify the lungs, regenerate the blood, and heal wounds." This search for the elixir of life continued until 1513, when the Spanish explorer Ponce de León sought the Fountain of Youth in the New World.

1–4 · Alchemist—magician or scientist? · We even find evidence that many would-be alchemists were also very good "con artists." A common trick was to take a nail of half gold and half iron and cover it with a dark paint. The would-be alchemist would produce a bottle of liquid that could "turn iron into gold." With customers looking on, the alchemist would dip the gold end of the painted nail into the solution. As the paint washed away, the unwary customer was astonished to see the half of the nail dipped into the solution turn into gold. Of course, the customer would have this magic solution at any price! And the alchemist would search for the next victim.

Another favorite trick of the alchemists involved heating the red mineral cinnabar, which is composed of mercury and sulfur. The heat would burn off the sulfur, leaving, much to the amazement of onlookers, a shiny pool of liquid mercury. To mystify the audience further, the alchemist would heat the mercury and again produce the red substance! We now know that this red substance is not cinnabar, but an oxide of mercury. (An oxide of mercury is produced when mercury is combined with oxygen.) It was produced when mercury was heated in air. But the alchemist didn't know this. The alchemists felt they had the power to break down this mineral and build it again at will.

Not all the alchemists were fakes. And, needless to say, neither the philosopher's stone nor the elixir of life was ever found. But during the search for these elusive substances, the alchemists performed many valuable experiments.

1–5 · Alchemy becomes a science · As alchemy spread through the European countries, it advanced rapidly due to the contributions of each individual society. By the middle ages, two distinct groups of alchemists evolved. The first group was known as the **puffers.** The puffers were mainly amateur alchemists who sought quick wealth and fame by trying to change ordinary metals such as lead into valuable metals like gold (Figure 1–4).

FIGURE 1–4 · *Why, do you think, were these alchemists called "Puffers"?*

The other group included the more professional alchemists known as **adepts.** They studied and experimented as a means of acquiring a greater knowledge of nature. It has been said, "The science of chemistry was born at the potter's wheel, the glazier's workshop, the blacksmith's forge, and the perfumist's salon." Each of these sources contributed to the laboratory techniques found today in chemistry. As these techniques improved, chemists began to acquire a deeper understanding of our natural world. Some equipment in modern laboratories is amazingly similar to the equipment used by the alchemists. The technology, the magic, and the art of alchemy evolved into what we know as modern science. The transition from alchemy to true science occurred sometime between the thirteenth and fifteenth centuries. But we should remember that we owe a great deal to the two thousand years of alchemy. Alchemy laid the groundwork that allowed us to reach our present, sophisticated view of our environment. The great English natural scientist Francis Bacon stressed the importance of alchemy in the seventeenth century.

Alchemy may be compared to the man who told his sons that he left them gold buried somewhere in his vineyard; where they by digging found no gold but by turning up the mold about the roots of the vines, procured a plentiful vintage.

FIGURE 1–5 · *This sixteenth-century painting by Stradanus depicts alchemical investigation being pursued for medicinal purposes. The modern pharmaceutical industry had its beginnings in such experiments.*

The chart below traces the development of alchemy and shows some of the more famous alchemists. Try to find out what these early alchemists contributed to their art. Ask your school librarian for help.

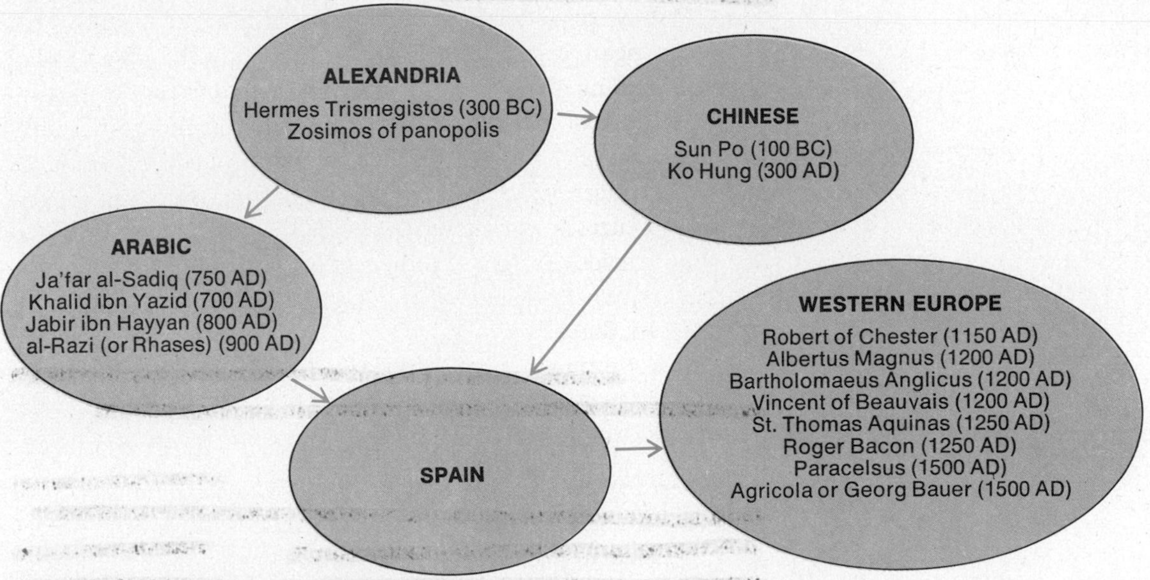

Though the alchemists' original goals, such as turning lead into gold, were never realized, the far-reaching effects of alchemy in the development of science were great.

The transition from alchemy to an experimental science opened many doors. After that transition, scientific knowledge increased rapidly. It became impossible for any one person to keep up with the ever-growing body of information. Therefore, scientists began separating the whole of science into many parts, such as physics, chemistry, biology, and geology. This separation continues even today as new sciences, such as meteorology, oceanography, and space science, develop. In the remainder of this book, we will examine briefly some of the various sciences. But our main concern will be that "vintage" to which Francis Bacon referred—**chemistry.**

REVIEW IT NOW

1. What arts were utilized in the science of alchemy?
2. Who were the puffers?
3. Who were the adepts?

WHAT IS CHEMISTRY ?

1–6 · Properties and changes · Chemistry may be defined as *the study of the properties of matter and the changes that occur in the composition of matter*. For example, we can study the properties of water in the forms of ice, liquid, and steam. We can also study the decomposition of water into the two gases of which it is composed, hydrogen and oxygen. These studies of the properties of water, its decomposition, and its reaction with other substances are in the domain of chemistry.

Chemists are also concerned with the amounts of energy that are required to cause changes in substances. For example, how much energy is required to melt ice, to boil water, or to decompose water into hydrogen and oxygen? When you seek the answers to questions like these, you are beginning to think like a chemist. So chemistry is the science of matter, of energy, and of the changes in matter that accompany the energy changes.

1–7 · Physical and chemical changes · The changes that matter undergoes may be classified into two broad categories, **physical change** and **chemical change**. In a physical change, the basic chemical nature or composition of matter is not changed. Only the physical state is altered. The freezing of water is an example of a physical change. Liquid water and ice have the same chemical composition. But they have different physical forms. When solid ice melts, its chemical composition does not change. In a chemical change (a chemical reaction), however, the basic chemical nature of the material is changed.

FIGURE 1–6 · *How many physical forms of water can you see in this photograph?*

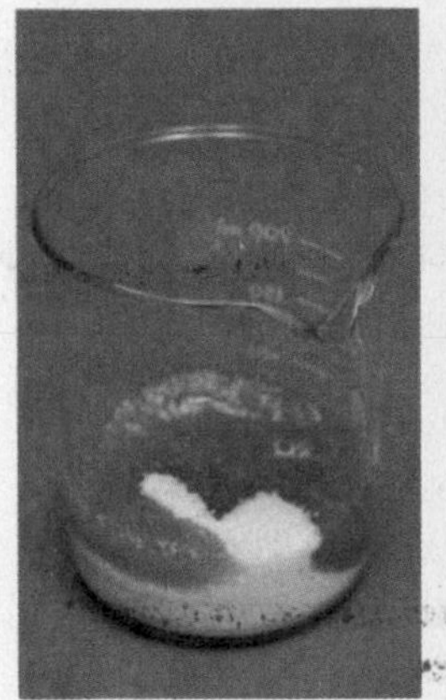

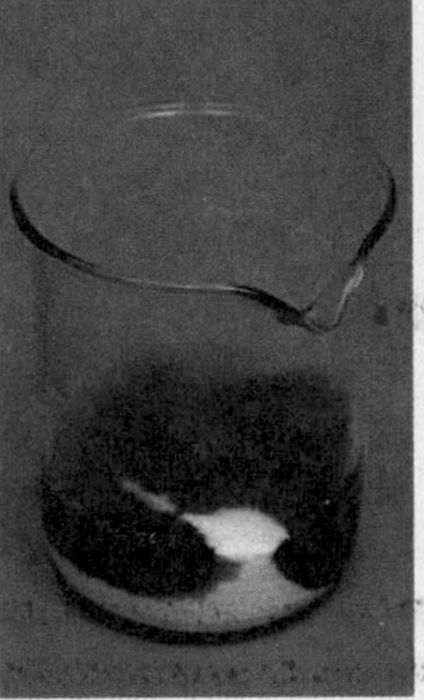

FIGURE 1–7 · *These photographs illustrate an example of a chemical change. When sulfuric acid is added to the sugar, the chemical properties of both substances change. The products of this reaction include carbon, water, carbon dioxide, sulfur dioxide, and some carbon monoxide.*

The conversion of liquid water into hydrogen gas and oxygen gas is an example of chemical change (Figure 1–8). This process involves much more than simply changing water from one physical form to another. The basic nature of water is lost in this change, and two new substances are formed—hydrogen and oxygen. Each of these gases has its own set of characteristics, many of which are not shared by water.

A major difference between a physical change and a chemical change is often the amount of energy involved. Usually, a chemical change either releases or absorbs much more energy than does a physical change. Let's use the chemical formation of 1.00

discuss picture

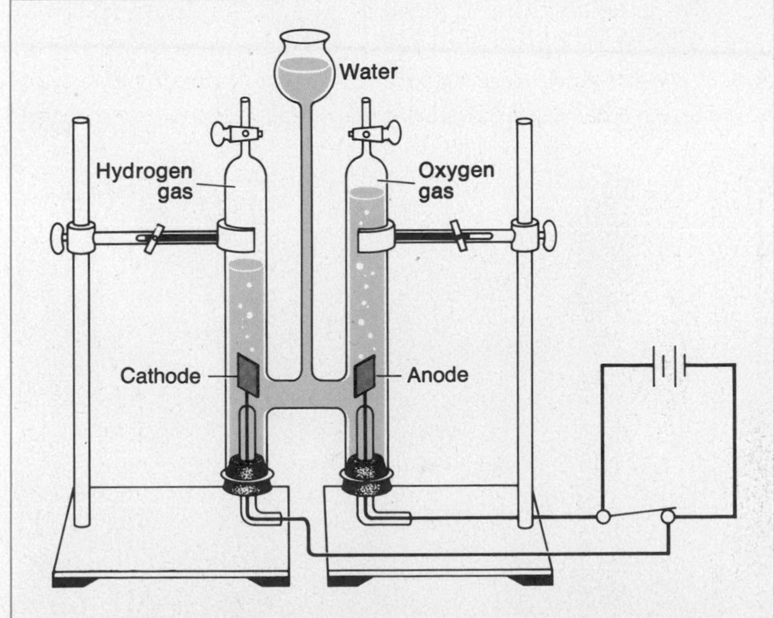

FIGURE 1–8 · *Water is chemically changed by electrolysis. What does electolysis mean? What will happen when the switch is open? (The electrolysis of pure water is a very slow process, since there is little in pure water to conduct the electric current between electrodes.)*

gram of liquid water from hydrogen and oxygen gases as an example. In this process, almost fifty times more energy is released than when 1.00 gram of ice is formed physically by freezing.

1–8 · The experimental nature of chemistry · Chemistry is an experimental science. Chemists first study the nature of substances and their changes in the laboratory. They perform a sufficient amount of experimentation to acquire a body of data. Then the chemist can attempt to correlate the data into some picture model or explanation of the behavior of the substance.

As a result of analyzing the experimental data, the chemist can begin to formulate laws and theories. It is important to understand the difference between laws and theories. *A law* is simply a statement of the observed behavior of matter. Laws do not offer any explanation for this behavior. They merely record observations. For example, a behavioral scientist might state as a law that in the United States people today are on the average taller than people of a hundred years ago. The scientist has studied a wide sampling of the present population and that of a hundred years ago. This is a large enough sample to state that people are taller today as a valid fact or law. The scientist does

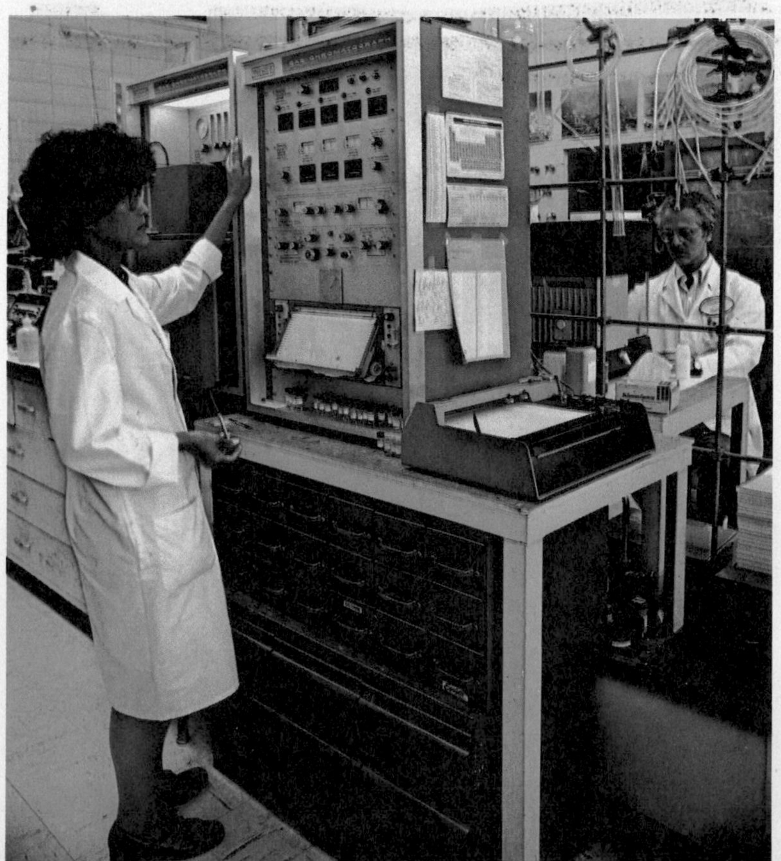

FIGURE 1–9 · *Chemistry is observation, discovery, organization, thought, creativity, and understanding. These processes begin in the laboratory.*

not explain why people are taller today than a hundred years ago. Once scientists offer such an explanation, they are then proposing a *theory*. For example, suppose the scientist went on to say that people are taller today because the diet is better than it was a hundred years ago. This is a theory, not a law, since it offers a possible explanation for the observation.

We will be using the terms *law* and *theory* throughout this book. Therefore, we must be clear in our understanding of the difference. A law is a statement of observed fact. A theory is a proposed explanation of the observed behavior of substances. Frequently, scientists propose *models* that in essence are theories. However, models are usually based on some analogy used to illustrate a theory. For example, let's look at the way scientists, at one time, tried to explain the theory about the nature of the atom. It was suggested that an atom is composed of a small, heavy, positively charged nucleus about which the electrons spin somewhat like the planets spinning about the sun. This was the planetary model of an atom. It tried to present a mental picture of the atomic theory. We no longer use this model. Experimentation has uncovered new facts that this model cannot explain so the model must be revised.

REVIEW IT NOW

1. Briefly define *chemistry*.
2. How does a chemical change differ from a physical change?
3. What is meant by the statement, "Chemistry is an experimental science"?
4. How does a law differ from a theory?
5. What is a scientific model? How does it help scientists understand nature?

CONSERVATION LAWS

1–9 · Law of the Conservation of Matter · One of the basic observations in science is that things are conserved. In other words, certain properties are not changed. For example, the total amount of matter and energy is constant. This fact is very useful in chemistry. We express this in the conservation laws of matter and energy that follow.

THE LAW OF THE CONSERVATION OF MATTER

In a chemical reaction, the total mass of the products is equal to the total mass of the reactants.

Let's look at an example. Suppose 100 grams of water are decomposed into hydrogen and oxygen. The total mass of the hydrogen and the oxygen produced equals 100 grams. This is also true in physical changes. Suppose 100 grams of water are frozen into ice. The mass of the ice will also be exactly 100 grams. Similarly, if the 100 grams of water are evaporated, the product will be exactly 100 grams of steam. A frequent statement of the Law of the Conservation of Matter is that matter can be neither created nor destroyed in physical or chemical changes (Figure 1–10).

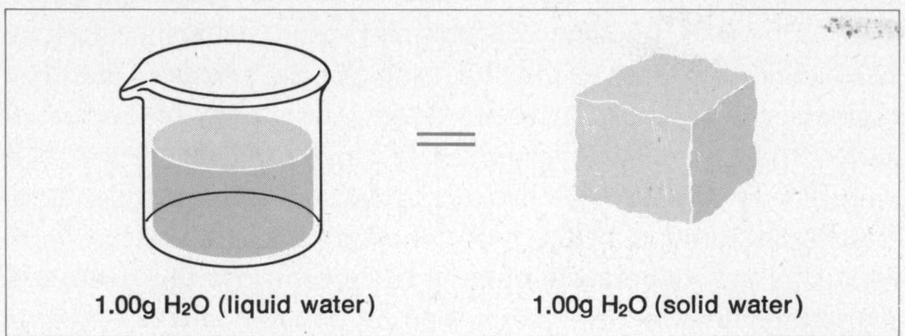

FIGURE 1–10 · *Freezing 1.00 gram of water illustrates the Law of the Conservation of Matter.*

1–10 · Law of the Conservation of Energy · Energy is defined as the capacity to do work. Energy can exist in many forms, such as heat (thermal), light (radiant), mechanical, electrical, magnetic, and chemical. Also, energy can be converted from one form to another. The combustion of gasoline in the cylinders of an engine is a good example. This combustion converts chemical energy into heat energy and mechanical energy. Another good example is the passage of electricity through the filament of a light bulb. This converts electrical energy into heat energy and light energy. In a chemical change, some chemical energy stored in chemical compounds may be released on reaction as heat energy and light energy. However, even though the energy appears in different forms, the total amount of the energy remains constant.

Let's look at an example of a physical change in which the amount of energy remains constant. Suppose we melted 18.0 grams of ice at 0°C. The same amount of heat energy is absorbed that is released when 18.0 grams of water freeze at 0°C. The amount of energy absorbed is found to be identical with the amount of energy released. This is also true in a chemical change, such as converting water to hydrogen and oxygen or vice versa. A specific amount of heat energy is absorbed by the conversion of 18.0 grams of water to 16.0 grams of oxygen and

2.00 grams of hydrogen. Exactly the same amount of heat energy is released by the formation of 18.0 grams of water from 16.0 grams of oxygen and 2.00 grams of hydrogen. Observations such as these led scientists to express the following law.

THE LAW OF THE CONSERVATION OF ENERGY

In any chemical or physical change, energy can be neither created nor destroyed.

1–11 · The combined conservation law · In 1905, Albert Einstein, one of history's most outstanding scientists, developed a startling theory. He proposed that matter and energy are actually different forms of the same thing. He also theorized that the conversion of mass to energy, and energy to mass, can occur. Careful modern research has proved that very small amounts of matter are destroyed in the spectacular nuclear fusion (combining atoms) reactions on the sun and other stars. Great amounts of energy appear in the place of those minute amounts of lost matter. This energy is millions of times greater than the energy of ordinary chemical reactions. The conversion of minute amounts of matter into tremendous amounts of energy during the process of nuclear fission (splitting atoms) has been the source of great destruction as a weapon. It may also be a source of great benefit if it can be used successfully as the basis for power production in the future.

FIGURE 1–11 · *Nuclear fission can be the source of both awesome destruction and tremendous benefit. Even the testing of nuclear weapons can cause destruction thousands of kilometers from the testing site. Recently, test explosions in China have caused harmful radioactive fallout in our country only two to three days after the test.*

Remember that a law is merely a statement of an observation. Therefore, we can state that the Law of the Conservation of Matter and the Law of the Conservation of Energy are both true for chemical reactions. In chemical reactions, the amount of matter that is transformed into energy is extremely small. In fact, it is so small that the change in mass cannot be measured experimentally. Because of this, the Law of the Conservation of Matter is valid for chemical reactions. However, if we study nuclear reactions, we find that a change in mass after the reaction can be measured. Since we can measure a change in mass in a reaction involving the nucleus, the Law of the Conservation of Matter does not conform to these observations. It appears to be invalid. However, in those situations where we can experimentally observe (and compare) a change in mass and a change in energy, we find that a combined law is convenient. This combined law is stated below.

THE LAW OF THE CONSERVATION OF MATTER PLUS ENERGY
The total amount of matter and energy of the universe can be neither increased nor decreased (created nor destroyed). But matter and energy can be transformed into each other.

REVIEW IT NOW

1. State the Law of the Conservation of Matter.
2. State the Law of the Conservation of Energy.
3. Why is it necessary to combine the conservation laws into a single law?

CHEMISTRY—THE STUDY OF MATTER

1–12 · Solid, liquid, gas · Let's consider the "stuff" of the universe. There are millions of different kinds of chemical materials. But all these chemical materials commonly exist in only three different physical forms, or states of matter: **solid, liquid,** and **gas.** Water can exist as a solid (ice) if the temperature is below 0°C. Between 0°C and 100°C, it exists mainly as a liquid. Above 100°C, water is found in the gaseous state under ordinary conditions of pressure. The state in which a substance exists is dependent on three factors. It is dependent partly on the material itself, partly on the temperature, and partly on the pressure of its surroundings. For example, water can be kept in

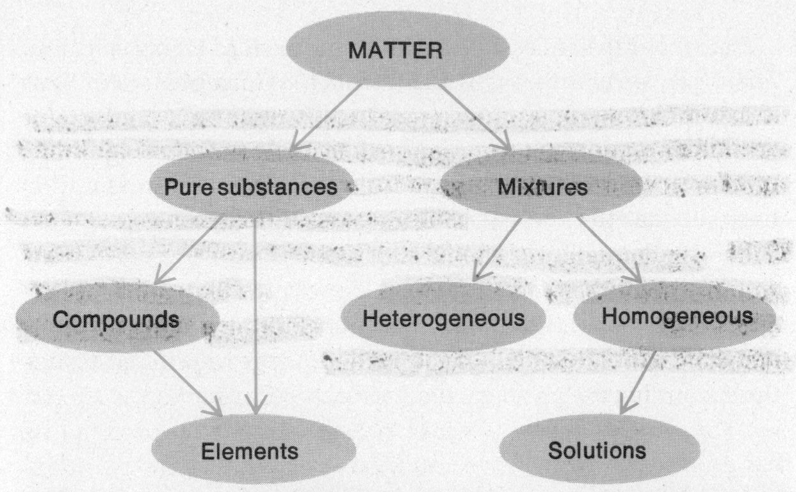

FIGURE 1–12 · *Types of matter can be classified as shown here.*

the liquid state well above 100°C if the pressure exerted on it is high. This is what we commonly observe in a pressure cooker.

Physical changes of matter from one state to another by heating or cooling are very common. Iron, which we know as a hard, gray solid, is melted in foundries and changes to a shimmering, silvery liquid. If its temperature is raised high enough, even gaseous iron vapor is formed.

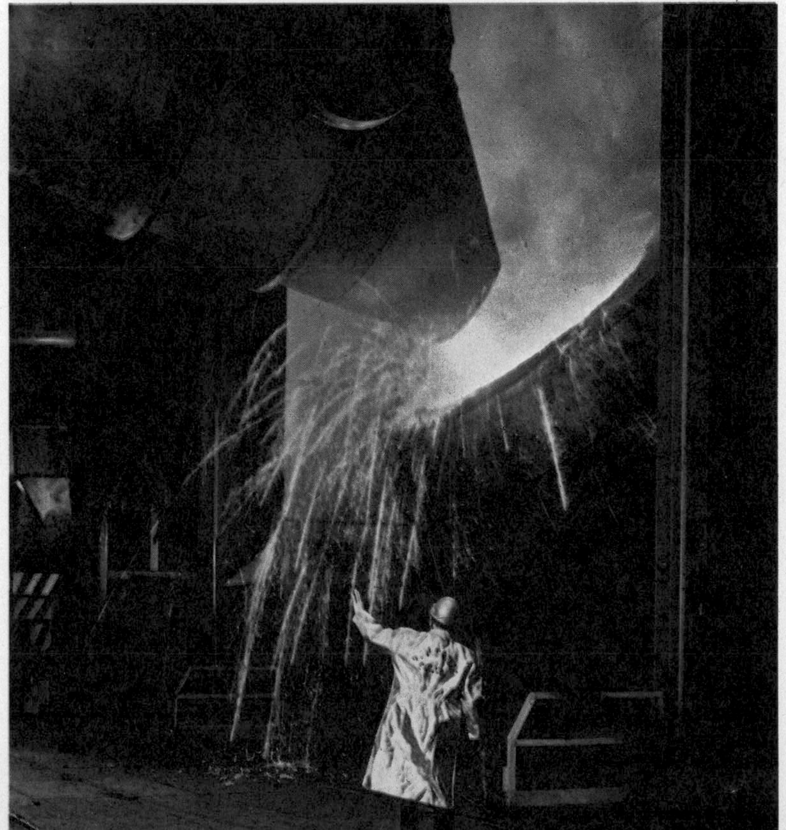

FIGURE 1–13 · *Molten iron is charged into a Basic Oxygen Furnace at Bethlehem Steel Corporation's plant in Sparrow Point, Maryland. The BOF can produce steel in less than an hour.*

For a few substances the transition from solid to gas, and vice versa, proceeds without going through the liquid state. This transition from the solid state directly to the gaseous state, without going through the liquid phase, is known as sublimation. Carbon dioxide is an example of a substance that undergoes sublimation, or that sublimes. As dry ice, it exists as a solid. At temperatures above 78.5°C it transforms directly to carbon dioxide gas. Napthalene, usually used in the form of moth balls, is another substance that sublimes. Solid napthalene goes directly to the vapor state. This vapor permeates clothes and other articles to kill moths.

FIGURE 1–14 · *Solid iodine crystals sublime directly into a purple iodine vapor during iodine sublimation.*

1–13 · The elements of the ancients · Most substances can be either decomposed or transformed by chemical changes. This idea led the ancient philosophers to speculate on the existence of a primary substance. This was thought to be a substance that could not be decomposed and from which all other substances were formed.

Thales of Miletus was the first to theorize that water is the primary substance. This philosopher, astronomer, and geometer, born about 624 B.C., came to this conclusion because water is necessary to the survival of all living things.

Later, other philosophers in the same region of western Asia Minor, the cradle of Greek science, continued to develop the concept of fundamental substances. Anaximenes of Miletus, who lived about 550 B.C., proposed that air is the primary substance. Heraclitus, a Greek philosopher and poet of the early fifth century B.C., postulated fire as the elemental substance.

Finally, the great Greek philosopher Empedocles, who was born about 500 B.C., wrote about an idea that was to dominate Western scientific thought until the eighteenth century. He was the first to express the idea that all matter is composed not of a single substance but of four elements—air, earth, fire, and water. That theory lasted for more than two thousand years. Some early scientists considered it to be correct until experimental chemistry emerged as a science in the 1700's.

☉ *Gold*
☽; *Silver*
♀ *Copper*
♃ *Tin*
♄ *Lead*
☿ *Mercury*
♂ *Iron*
Zinc
B;W *Biſmuth*
♁ *Antimony*

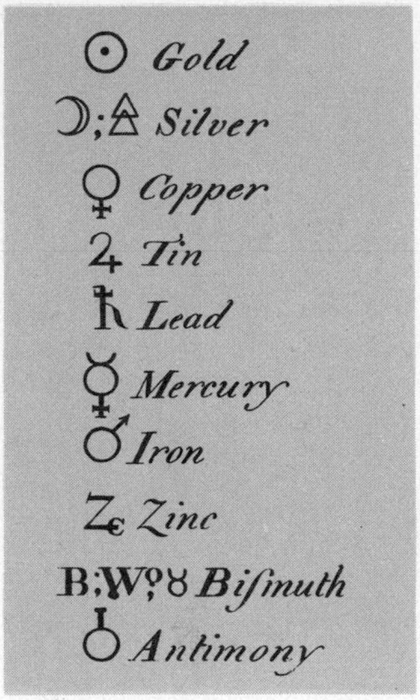

FIGURE 1–15 · *Early element symbols are shown here. Do you recognize any of these symbols?*

1–14 · Today's elements · Scientists now think everything is composed of simple substances that cannot be decomposed into simpler substances by any chemical change. These simple substances are called **elements**. Examine Tables 2–2 and 2–3 given on page 30. How many of these elements do you recognize?

1–15 · What are compounds? · There are many substances with which the chemist works that are not elements. These substances are called **compounds.** Each compound is composed of two or more elements. These elements are combined in such a way that (1) they can no longer be identified by their original, individual properties and (2) only chemical action can tear them apart.

FIGURE 1–16 · *Only six of the 108 elements known are shown in this photograph. Using their symbols, try to find out what these elements are and what their symbols stand for.*

FIGURE 1–17 · *The properties of these compounds are significantly different from the properties of the elements of which they are composed. Look at the names of these compounds. What elements do you think make up each compound?*

The properties of a compound are nearly always different from the properties of the elements of which it is composed. Cane sugar is a compound made up of the element carbon, hydrogen, and oxygen, all chemically combined. Pure cane sugar is a sweet, white, crystalline solid that dissolves in water. Compare these properties with those of the gases hydrogen and oxygen and those of solid, black, insoluble carbon.

1–16 · How does a mixture differ from a compound? · In a compound, the elements must be chemically united. But there are other kinds of materials made up of two or more elements or compounds. Even though the particles in them are thoroughly intermingled or mixed, the original substances can still be identified by their own distinguishing properties. From this we may conclude that the substances are not chemically joined, but are simply mixed together.

A pinch of salt and a pinch of white sand stirred together are an excellent example of a *mixture*. The salt can be identified by its characteristic taste. The sand can be identified by its gritty feel on the tongue and teeth. A mixture, then, is a material composed of two or more substances that are not chemically combined. Most of the materials that you use daily are mixtures. Examples of familiar mixtures are soil, air, paper, petroleum, milk, many other foods, and most metals.

The properties of a mixture are generally the same as the properties of the elements or compounds that compose it. A handful of iron powder combined with a handful of powdered sulfur is a mixture. This mixture has properties that resemble the properties of both the black iron and the yellow sulfur. If a magnet is passed through such a mixture, the iron clings to the magnet, leaving the sulfur. If a liquid called carbon disulfide is added to the mixture, the sulfur is dissolved, leaving the iron. But if the mixture of iron and sulfur is heated, those two elements combine and form a compound known as iron sulfide, FeS. Iron sulfide does not look like either iron or sulfur, and the properties of this compound do not resemble those of either sulfur or iron. It is not magnetic like iron, nor does it dissolve in carbon disulfide like sulfur. Therefore, it is no longer a mixture.

1–17 · Two types of mixtures · Some mixtures are **homogeneous.** Their component parts are evenly distributed throughout. For example, salt dissolves in water to form a homogeneous mixture. You are also familiar with homogenized peanut butter and homogenized milk. In those foods, the oil in the peanut butter and the cream in the milk are equally dispersed throughout. There is no definite or visible boundary between the various parts of a homogeneous mixture. All *solutions* are examples of homogeneous mixtures. In **heterogeneous** mixtures, the component parts are not evenly distributed. Concrete and a mixture of salt and sand are examples of heterogeneous mixtures. You can easily distinguish between the sand and the salt and between the different particles in the concrete.

Substances in a mixture can usually be easily separated from one another. A mixture of salt and sand, for example, can be separated by adding water. The salt dissolves to form a salt solution, and the sand settles to the bottom. The solution can then be poured into another container and heated to drive off the water, and the solid salt can be recovered.

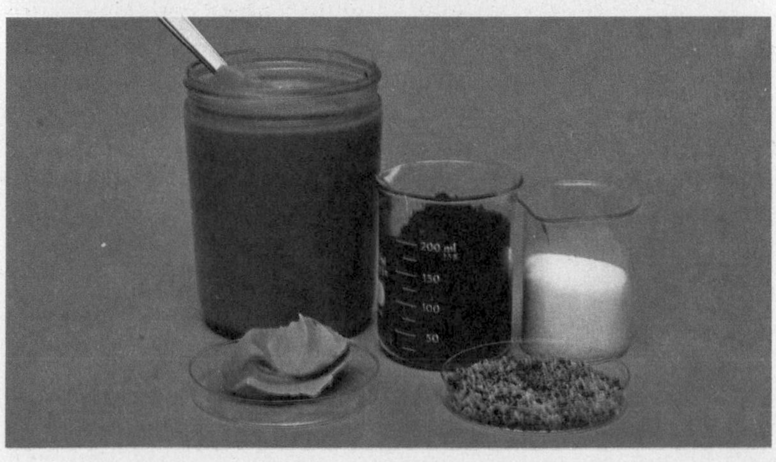

FIGURE 1–18 · *Peanut butter is a homogeneous mixture. The salt in the large beaker is a compound. The soil in the small beaker is a mixture. Combining the soil and salt produces a heterogeneous mixture (shown in the petri dish).*

Two liquids in solution, such as alcohol and water, can be separated by taking advantage of a difference in their individual properties, such as their boiling points. (Properties of substances are the different characteristics or qualities they possess.) When a mixture of alcohol and water is heated, the alcohol will boil off first. That is because alcohol has a boiling point lower than that of water. The alcohol is then cooled, or condensed, to produce liquid alcohol. This process is called distillation. Distillation plays a very important role in many major industries. Can you think of other ways of separating components of a mixture?

1–18 · Atoms and molecules and how they differ · Suppose we divide a glass of water in half. Then suppose we continue dividing the amount of water in half beyond the point of visibility. There must be a limit to this process. Eventually, a very, very small amount of water is left. This last bit of water is a

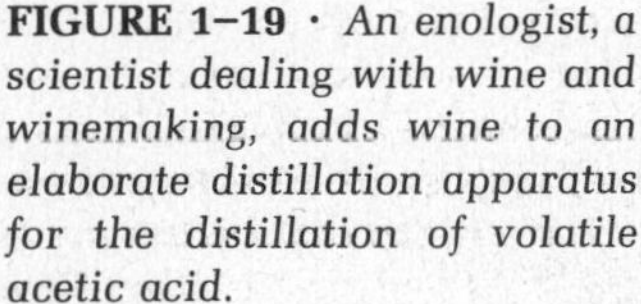

FIGURE 1–19 · *An enologist, a scientist dealing with wine and winemaking, adds wine to an elaborate distillation apparatus for the distillation of volatile acetic acid.*

molecule of water. If we attempt further division, we must use conditions that cause chemical change. And after chemical change, the molecule is no longer water. A molecule is so small that in the original glass of water we considered dividing, there would be about 10^{26} molecules. The process of dividing that amount of water would go on more than eighty times before a single molecule could be reached.

To gain a better picture of this, take any length of string you wish and begin dividing it. You will find that ten to fifteen times is about the limit of the number of times that you can divide the string before it becomes too small to handle. Now imagine dividing the string seventy more times to obtain a molecule!

A molecule can be broken down into even smaller particles. When it is divided, however, it is no longer the same substance. A molecule of water can be divided into three smaller pieces, but these pieces no longer have either the physical or the chemical properties of water. These smaller, submolecular pieces are called *atoms*. One molecule of water, H_2O, is composed of two atoms of hydrogen, H, and one atom of oxygen, O. An atom is the smallest particle that can exist as an element.

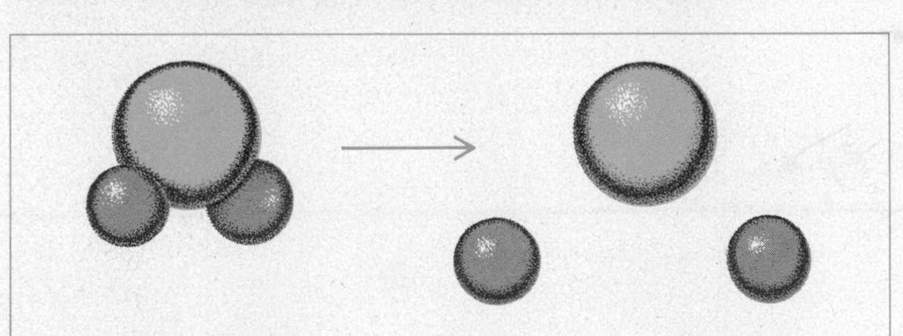

FIGURE 1–20 · *A molecule of water is composed of two atoms of hydrogen and one atom of oxygen.*

Molecules and atoms, compounds and elements—the simplest forms of matter—are at the heart of chemistry and will be the natural center of our interest throughout our study.

REVIEW IT NOW

1 What is sublimation?
2 What were the "four elements" of the ancients?
3 What is an element? What is a compound?
4 How does a mixture differ from a compound?
5 How does a homogeneous mixture differ from a heterogeneous mixture?
6 What process can be used to separate a mixture of water and alcohol?

SUMMARY

Chemistry is the branch of science concerned with the nature of matter and with the changes in the composition of matter. There are two broad categories of material change. Physical changes are those that do not involve changes in the basic composition or characteristics of substances. Chemical changes are those that do involve changes in the basic composition and properties of substances. Accompanying all material changes are energy changes. The purpose of studying all these changes is to discover the important laws that describe the behavior of matter. Through such study, scientists have evolved the fundamental natural law—the Law of the Conservation of Matter and Energy. This law represents the summation of a great deal of human experience. Like many other laws, it grew out of careful observation and clear thinking.

Chemistry is an experimental science. The chemist uses models and theories in an attempt to explain the existence of, and the relationships between, experimental facts. Models and theories arise from the interaction of experiment, ideas, and imagination. The chemist attempts to be an observant and a thoughtful person but is by no means infallible. New facts change old theories.

Matter with which the chemist works can exist in three physical states—solid, liquid, and gas. But what are the basic elements of matter—water, air, fire, and earth? We now know that there are many elements and that all compounds and mixtures are produced from them.

An atom is the smallest particle that can exist as an element. In compounds, the elements can no longer be identified by their original, individual properties. In mixtures, the component parts retain their individual properties no matter how thoroughly they are mixed. A molecule is the smallest particle that can exist as a substance and still retain the properties of that substance.

REVIEW QUESTIONS

1 What is your definition of chemistry?

2 What were some of the contributions alchemists made to the development of modern chemistry?

3 What are some differences between a physical change and a chemical change?

4 Indicate whether each of the following involves physical changes, chemical changes, or both.

a. A cake baking
b. A stick breaking
c. Water boiling
d. Wax melting
e. An egg frying
f. A bomb exploding
g. A ship corroding
h. Sulfur burning
i. Sugar dissolving
j. Leaves changing color

5 What is the difference between a law and a theory?

6 State the Law of the Conservation of Matter in your own words.

7 State the Law of the Conservation of Energy in your own words.

8 Considering your answers to questions **6** and **7**,

a. is gasoline destroyed when it is burned?

b. is food destroyed when it is eaten?

c. is a log destroyed when it decays?

9 In what three physical states does matter commonly exist?

10 Name a substance that does not normally exist in all three states.

11 What are some basic differences between a compound and a mixture?

12 What is the difference between an atom and an element?

13 What is an atom?

14 What is a molecule?

15 Indicate whether each of the following is an element, a compound, or a mixture.

a. Air	**e.** Steam	**i.** Wood	**m.** Paper
b. Seawater	**f.** Ice	**j.** Iron	**n.** Aspirin
c. Fresh water	**g.** Gasoline	**k.** Steel	**o.** Glass
d. Water	**h.** Stone	**l.** Nickel	**p.** Mercury

SUGGESTED READINGS

de France, Ellen Gerard. "Chemistry in Language and Literature." *Chemistry*, April 1970, p. 16.

Jaffe, Bernard. *Crucibles: The Story of Chemistry*, Fawcett, 1962.

Kauffman, George B., and Zie Anna Payne. "Contributions of Ancients and Alchemists." *Chemistry*, April 1973, p. 6.

Massie, Samuel P. "The George Washington Carver Story." *Chemistry*, September 1970, p. 18.

May, Ira, and William Wort. "Chemistry in Colonial America." *Chemistry*, July–August 1976, p. 6.

Rosenbaum, G. P. "The Epic of Alchemy: From Plato to Boyle." *Chemistry*, December 1972, p. 14.

Sherwood, Martin. "Sea of Chemicals." *Chemistry*, July–August 1970, p. 34.

———"Great Moments in Chemistry. Part III: Alchemy." *Chemistry*, December 1970, p. 5.

———. "Great Moments in Chemistry. Part IV: Iatrochemistry." *Chemistry*, June 1971, p. 18.

———. "Great Moments in Chemistry. Part V: Phlogiston." *Chemistry*, December 1971, p. 14.

The Crab nebula, a cloud of gas resulting from the explosion of a star.

CHAPTER TWO

The Chemical Elements

It is difficult to say exactly when modern chemistry began. Many fifteenth- and sixteenth-century scientists still held on to their beliefs in alchemy. However, they began to experiment and test their ideas and theories. Because of this, they were becoming true scientists.

TWO LEADING SCIENTISTS BUILD A FOUNDATION

2–1 · Paracelsus, one of the founders of modern chemistry · Several scientists in the 1400's and 1500's were responsible for the transition from alchemy to modern chemistry. Let's single out a few of the more important figures such as Paracelsus and Robert Boyle.

One such individual was a German-born scientist and physician named Theophrastus Bombastus von Hohenheim (1493 – 1541). You are probably saying to yourself, "Wow! Do I have to remember all that?" Fortunately, Theophrastus Bombastus von Hohenheim simplified things greatly by giving himself a nickname. He was known as a person who thought very highly of himself. He especially thought he was much greater than the great physician Celsus, who lived a thousand years earlier. In order to bring this to everyone's attention, he gave himself a nickname. This new name was *Paracelsus*, meaning "greater than Celsus."

Paracelsus is considered the founder of medical chemistry. He used some of the techniques of the alchemist. But he was the first physician to try to actually diagnose a patient's illness and to use chemicals and medicines to cure the patient. His emphasis on experimentation provided a break from alchemy.

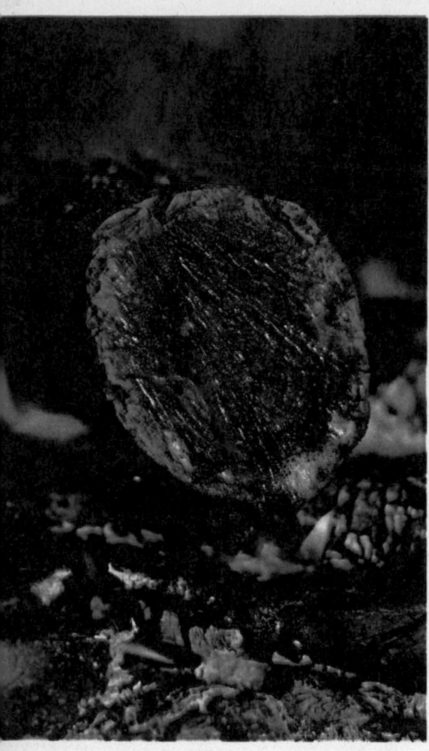

FIGURE 2–1 · *Study this photograph. Can you see why early scientists thought that substances consisted only of earth, air, fire, and water? Remember, that type of observation was the only one on which they relied. Suppose you were an early scientist who wanted to determine of what the substances around you were made. What are some of the steps you would take to discover the types of elements that make up substances?*

It led to a more fundamental understanding of nature by introducing practical application of one's discoveries.

The school of medicinal chemistry founded by Paracelsus had great influence on another important scientist, Robert Boyle (1627–1691). Robert Boyle was considered the leading authority on chemistry in his time. He firmly believed in the importance of experimentation as opposed to mere speculation in the study of science.

The early philosophers attempted to explain things by "reasoning," with very little experimentation. For example, even in Paracelsus' time, scientists believed everything consisted of four elements. These elements were earth, air, fire, and water. To those early scientists, the proof of this idea was very simple. When a green stick is burned, smoke (air) is produced, and moisture (water) seeps out of the stick. When the fire has consumed most of the stick, there is only the ash (earth) left. To early scientists, this was sufficient proof that a substance consisted of earth, air, fire, and water! Unfortunately, few of the early scientists bothered to extend the idea to substances other than a green stick. If they had, they would have found out quickly that their theory needed revision.

2–2 · Robert Boyle defined elements and compounds · Robert Boyle, like Paracelsus, rejected the four elements of the Greeks and proposed his own theory. He emphasized the distinction between pure substances and mixtures. Boyle proposed the existence of many elements and developed one of the first definitions of an element.

Certain primitive and simple or perfectly unmingled bodies; which not being made of any other bodies, or of one another, are the ingredients of which all those called perfectly mixed bodies are immediately compounded, and into which they are ultimately resolved.

Simply, what Boyle was saying is that there are elements and there are compounds. Compounds are made up of the simple and more fundamental elements. Unfortunately, it was almost a hundred years before Boyle's definition of an element became accepted. This happened with many other great ideas because quantitative experimentation did not develop until the late 1800's. That type of experimentation is necessary for the significance and validity of Boyle's concept to be understood and proved.

REVIEW IT NOW

1 What contributions did Paracelsus and Robert Boyle make to modern science?
2 Why were many great theories in science not accepted until years later?
3 On what evidence did the early scientists base their belief that the four main elements were earth, air, fire, and water?

CLASSIFYING AND NAMING ELEMENTS

2–3 · Lavoisier reduces compounds to elements · Professional scientists, as we know them today, did not exist until the middle of the nineteenth century. Before that time, the scientists were usually people of wealth or people supported by wealthy individuals. Those scientists spent their lives studying science as a fulltime avocation or as a hobby. But, there were no industrial laboratories or research institutes that paid scientists to do research.

Some of the people who could afford to be scientists, such as Robert Boyle and Antoine Lavoisier, made significant contributions. The French scientist Antoine Lavoisier (1743–1794) became wealthy as a tax collector for the king of France. It has been said that he amassed a fortune of $16 million!

Lavoisier was largely responsible for the transition from qualitative to quantitative experimentation. Qualitative experimentation means any experiments attempting to identify the components that make up a substance. Quantitative experimentation refers to experiments used to determine the amounts, or proportions, of the components of that substance. One example of Lavoisier's contribution to quantitative experimentation was his study of the process of burning. He demonstrated that combustion can only occur in the presence of oxygen, thus relating combustion (burning) to oxidation (combining with oxygen). Also, he carefully studied the **mass** relationships in chemical reactions. (Mass is the term used in the measure of the amount of matter.) In other words, he compared the mass of the chemicals being combined with the mass of the resulting products. These painstaking measurements led him to the Law of the Conservation of Matter, which we discussed in Chapter 1.

Antoine Laurent Lavoisier *(1743–1794, French). As a young man, Lavoisier abandoned the study of law for the physical sciences. Because of his brilliant quantitative studies, he is often referred to as "the founder of modern chemistry." For his membership in the Ferme Generale, which collected taxes on tobacco, salt, and imports, he was accused of treason and beheaded during the French Revolution.*

Lavoisier also discovered that the mass changes observed in various products were due to changes in the state of their chemical combination. He realized from his experiments that the mass of some substances could be reduced further by chemical reaction. Therefore, such substances could not be the simplest elemental substances. With that realization, he was able to conduct chemical experiments to isolate substances that could not be further reduced in mass. Such experimentation produced substances that supported Boyle's definition of chemical elements. Lavoisier believed a substance that was reduced as much as possible and could not be reduced further in mass by chemical reaction must be classified as the simplest elemental substance or, simply, as an element. Although there was no absolute proof of his definition, Lavoisier still described certain substances that he could not separate further in the following way: "Since we have not hitherto discovered the means of separating them, [they] act with regard to us as simple substances."

2–4 · Lavoisier's list of elements · As a result of his experimentation, Lavoisier compiled a list of thirty-three elements. Twenty-six of those elements appear in our modern table of elements. Five of his list were metallic oxides, which were decomposed some time later. The other two elements listed among the thirty-three were light and heat. This illustrates the fact that Lavoisier was not completely free of some of the older concepts about the basic elements of nature.

Lavoisier's list of the chemical elements was of great importance. It gave scientists a summary of the fundamental materials of nature as they were known in 1789. It also laid the foundation for experiments designed to seek new and as yet undiscovered elements. The list of chemical elements has grown from 26 in 1789 to 108 today. These 108 chemical elements include 18 artificial (synthetic) elements that are not usually found in nature. However, some extremely small traces of these artificial elements have been created by cosmic radiation in recent geologic time and can be found in certain minerals.

2–5 · The chemical symbols for the elements · In 1814 Jöns Berzelius, a Swedish chemist, invented a simple system of chemical notation for the elements. Today the system is used by chemists in every country. Berzelius took the first letter of the name of an element for its symbol. Thus, C represents carbon, H represents hydrogen, and U represents uranium.

TABLE 2–1 · Lavoisier's Table of Elements

LAVOISIER'S NAME	MODERN ENGLISH NAME
Lumière	Light
Calorique	Heat
Oxygène	Oxygen
Azote	Nitrogen
Hydrogène	Hydrogen
Soufre	Sulfur
Phosphore	Phosphorus
Carbone	Carbon
Radical muriatique	———
Radical fluorique	———
Radical boracique	———
Antimoine	Antimony
Argent	Silver
Arsenic	Arsenic
Bismuth	Bismuth
Cobalt	Cobalt
Cuivre	Copper
Étain	Tin
Fer	Iron
Manganèse	Manganese
Mo	Mercury
Molybdene	Molybdenum
Nickel	Nickel
Or	Gold
Platine	Platinum
Plomb	Lead
Tungstène	Tungsten
Zinc	Zinc
Chaux	Calcium oxide (lime)
Magnésie	Magnesium Oxide
Baryte	Barium oxide
Alumine	Aluminum oxide
Silice	Silicon dioxide (sand)

EXCURSION ONE
A Look at the Elements

Any discovery in science results from experience and hard work. But, scientists are not always serious and, by no means, perfect. Some discoveries are accidents or have humorous stories behind them. Excursion 1 tells the more fascinating and humorous stories about the discovery of some of the 108 elements known today.

However, one problem with this method is that all elements cannot begin with different letters, since there are only twenty-six letters in the alphabet. The first letter of the name of several of the elements is the same. Eleven elements have names beginning with the letter *C*. Most of the elements have been given two-letter symbols. The symbol usually begins with the first letter of the element's name. This is followed by a second letter from the name. The first letter is always capitalized. The second letter is never capitalized. Some examples of such symbols are Ni (nickel), He (helium), Ar (argon), and Al (aluminum). Many other examples of such symbols can be found in the **Periodic Table,** on pages 146–147. Find the eleven elements that begin with the letter *C* (Table 2–2).

TABLE 2–2 · Elements Beginning with C

ELEMENT	SYMBOL
Cadmium	Cd
Calcium	Ca
Californium	Cf
Carbon	C
Cerium	Ce
Cesium	Cs
Chlorine	Cl
Chromium	Cr
Cobalt	Co
Copper	Cu
Curium	Cm

The next to last element listed in Table 2–2 has a symbol that seems to make only partial sense. Copper does, indeed, begin with the letter *C*. But where is there a *u* in its name? The Latin name for copper, *cuprum*, is the clue to the puzzle. The symbol for copper, as well as the symbols for a number of other familiar elements, is derived from Latin. Listed in Table 2 – 3 are eleven elements, whose symbols are derived from either the Latin (L) or the German (G) name.

TABLE 2–3 · Elements and their Foreign Derivatives

ELEMENT	FOREIGN NAME	SYMBOL
Antimony	Stibium (L)	Sb
Copper	Cuprum (L)	Cu
Gold	Aurum (L)	Au
Iron	Ferrum (L)	Fe
Lead	Plumbum (L)	Pb
Mercury	Hydrargyrum (L)	Hg
Potassium	Kalium (L)	K
Silver	Argentum (L)	Ag
Sodium	Natrium (L)	Na
Tin	Stannum (L)	Sn
Tungsten	Wolfram (G)	W

REVIEW IT NOW

1 What theories and/or methods did each of the following scientists contribute to our understanding of chemistry: Robert Boyle, Paracelsus, Antoine Lavoisier?

2 Of what importance was Lavoisier's list of chemical elements?

3 Describe the system Berzelius devised for assigning symbols to the chemical elements.

ELEMENTS EXIST AROUND US IN CERTAIN AMOUNTS

2–6 · The elements of the universe · It is evident from experiments that there are a certain number of chemical elements existing in nature. But how abundant are the different elements? Are there equal amounts of each of the elements, or is there a wide variation in their relative abundance? Also, is the variation in the distribution of the elements the same throughout the universe? Or is there a difference in the distribution and amounts of specific elements in the stars and on the earth? These may seem to be straightforward questions, but it's extremely difficult to provide answers. It's very difficult to determine the distribution of those elements that are not part of our earth and its atmosphere. We can't even analyze our own sun very well. Therefore, you can imagine the difficulty in trying to analyze each of the elements in distant suns and their planets. We do not even know how many planets may exist undetected around all the stars. Another problem is that we can't determine how much material there is in interstellar space. But advances are being made (Figure 2–2.)

FIGURE 2–2 · *Scientists are learning more and more about our universe and its elements through space exploration. Just as lunar samples gathered by astronauts increase our knowledge of the moon, scientists are learning a great deal about Mars from the photographs and chemical analyses transmitted to us from Vikings 1 and 2. This photograph is one of the many photos transmitted to earth. The sample scoop (right-center) scoops up samples of rock and soil for chemical analysis. The bright reddish-orange surface of Mars is strewn with a variety of angular rocks of various shapes and sizes.*

In spite of all these difficulties, scientists have been able to propose a table of the relative abundance of the elements in the universe. They have accomplished that by using data from studies of the light emitted by the stars and the gas clouds in our galaxies and other nearby galaxies. Also, they have analyzed the chemical composition of meteorites that have struck the earth and the lunar samples gathered by astronauts. Scientists have also estimated the amount of material in the vast expanse of interstellar space. Table 2–4 lists the thirteen most abundant elements in the universe. This table is based on a relative abundance, using the measured amount of silicon as a standard. In other words, there are 35 000 atoms of hydrogen in the universe for every one atom of silicon. But there is only 1.00 atom of calcium for every 15.0 atoms of silicon. Hydrogen makes up approximately 91.0 percent of all the atoms in the universe, and helium makes up approximately 9.00 percent.

TABLE 2–4 · The Thirteen Most Abundant Elements

ELEMENT	RELATIVE ATOM ABUNDANCE
Hydrogen	3.5×10^4
Helium	3.5×10^3
Oxygen	2.2×10^1
Nitrogen	1.6×10^1
Carbon	8
Neon	2.4
Iron	1.8
Silicon	1.0
Magnesium	9×10^{-1}
Sulfur	3.5×10^{-1}
Nickel	1.3×10^{-1}
Aluminum	8.8×10^{-2}
Calcium	6.7×10^{-2}

*These abundances are estimates expressed relative to silicon taken as 1.00; in percentages, H is 91%, He 9%, and the remainder slightly over 0.1% total.

All other atoms in the universe, except hydrogen and helium, amount to 0.10 percent. In fact, we can say that our universe is really composed of hydrogen slightly contaminated by helium and very little else. The data suggests that hydrogen may be the basic substance of the universe. Most scientists also suggest that all the elements heavier than hydrogen have been synthesized from hydrogen by nuclear reactions in the stars.

2–7 · The elements of the earth · As you have seen, the elements heavier than helium are in very slight abundance on a universal basis. But that is not the case for the material existing in and on the earth. In fact, there is relatively little hydrogen found on the earth. That is because the earth's gravitational attraction is not strong enough to hold such a light atom. Table 2–5 lists the chemical composition of the earth on a percentage basis. Taking the total earth into consideration, the most abundant element is iron. The next most abundant element is oxygen, followed by magnesium and silicon. These amounts change when we consider only the thin crust of the earth and not the total earth. The earth's core is believed to be largely molten metals, mainly iron and nickel. But the most abundant elements in the crust of the earth are oxygen and silicon. This demonstrates that the silicate minerals, containing both oxygen and silicon, are predominant.

As you have read, most scientists believe all the elements heavier than hydrogen were built up, or synthesized, from hydrogen by nuclear reactions in a star. Once those elements were synthesized, the star must have exploded and ejected them into space. After some period of time, some of those elements must have condensed into the materials that formed the earth. You know that our bodies are composed of many elements, including carbon, oxygen, nitrogen, calcium, and phosphorus. The atoms of all those heavier elements must have been originally

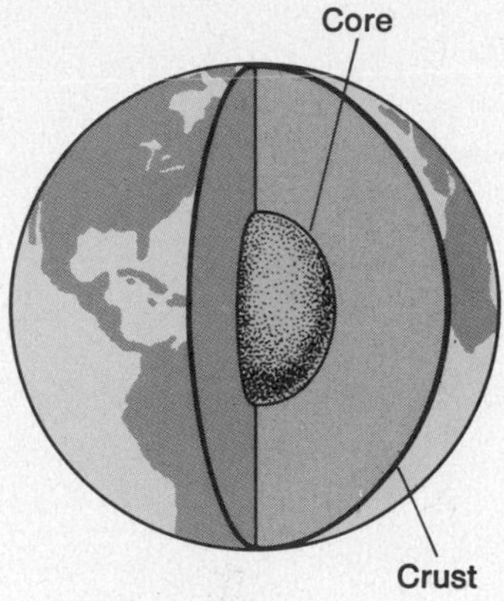

FIGURE 2–3 · *Note the thickness of the earth's crust as compared to its core.*

TABLE 2–5 · Elemental Composition of the Earth

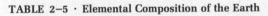

ELEMENT	BULK COMPOSITION (percent)	CRUST (percent)	OCEANS (percent)	ATMOSPHERE (percent)
Fe	35.39	5.9	—	—
O	27.79	43.8	85.79	21.0
Mg	17.00	3.2	0.14	—
Si	12.64	27.0	—	—
S	2.74	—	—	—
Ni	2.70	—	—	—
Ca	0.61	5.1	—	—
Al	0.44	10.0	—	—
Co	0.20	—	—	—
Na	0.14	2.2	1.14	—
Mn	0.09	—	—	—
K	0.07	1.7	—	—
Ti	0.04	1.0	—	—
P	0.03	—	—	—
Cr	0.01	—	—	—
H	—	0.3	10.67	—
Cl	—	0.1	2.07	—
N	—	—	—	78.1
Ar	—	—	—	0.9

synthesized in some star. It's a fascinating idea that the material of which we are made came from some long-ago, exploded star. Thus, in a real sense, each of us is a collection of star dust.

REVIEW IT NOW

1 How have scientists been able to determine the possible relative abundance of elements in the universe?
2 What are the two most abundant elements in the universe?
3 Considering the total earth, what are the four most abundant elements?
4 What is believed to be the source of all elements heavier than hydrogen?

COMPOUNDS AND ELEMENTS

2–8 · The ratios of elements in certain compounds are constant · Compounds are made up of elements. Therefore, the next logical question is, What amount of each element is present in a specific compound? And does that amount change from sample to sample of the same compound? For the moment, let's use water as a representative compound. Suppose you collect a sample of rainwater. Also, suppose you break down this rainwater into the elements of which it is composed. You will find that 88.8 grams of oxygen gas and 11.2 grams of hydrogen gas will be produced from each 100 grams of water. Let's carry this a little further. Suppose 100 grams of ice from the Arctic Ocean are melted, and the resulting 100 grams of water are decomposed. Then 88.8 grams of oxygen gas and 11.2 grams of hydrogen gas will again be produced. In fact, the decomposition, or analysis, of 100 grams of any pure water always produces 88.8 grams of oxygen gas and 11.2 grams of hydrogen gas. Therefore, we can say that the mass composition of water does not change. It is constant. For water, there is always a ratio of 88.8 to 11.2, or 7.94 times as much oxygen present by mass as hydrogen.

2–9 · The mass composition of compounds is constant · We should never draw conclusions about anything from only one set of observations. Therefore, we won't draw conclusions about the mass composition of all compounds from our observations only of water. Let's look at another example. Large deposits of elemental sulfur are found in widely separated parts of the world. Three good examples are Sicily, Texas, and Louisiana. Suppose a 100-gram sample of sulfur is taken from each

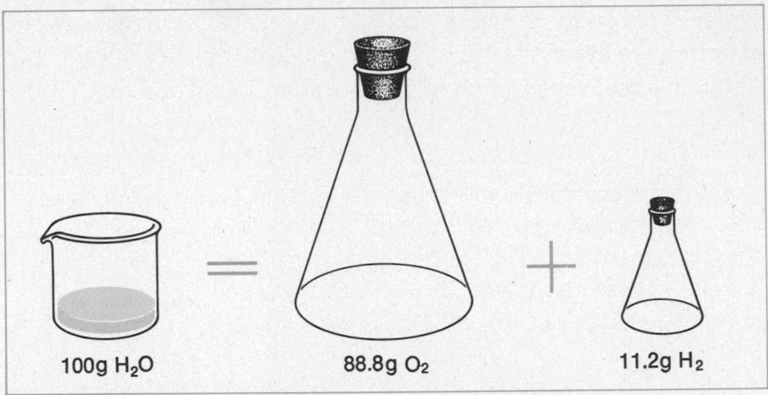

FIGURE 2–4 · *Everytime 100 grams of water are decomposed into oxygen and hydrogen, 88.8 grams of O_2 are produced, and 11.2 grams of H_2 are produced.*

different location. Also, suppose each is burned in air. This will produce 200 grams of a colorless gas called sulfur dioxide. This same gas will form every time sulfur is burned in air. You could guess from its name that sulfur dioxide is a compound consisting of sulfur and oxygen. The following reaction is a simple statement of what happens when sulfur is burned in the presence of oxygen.

$$\begin{array}{ccccc} \text{sulfur} & + & \text{oxygen} & \rightarrow & \text{sulfur dioxide} \\ 100\text{ g} & & 100\text{ g} & & 200\text{ g} \end{array}$$

The synthesis of sulfur dioxide from sulfur and oxygen can be duplicated in any laboratory.

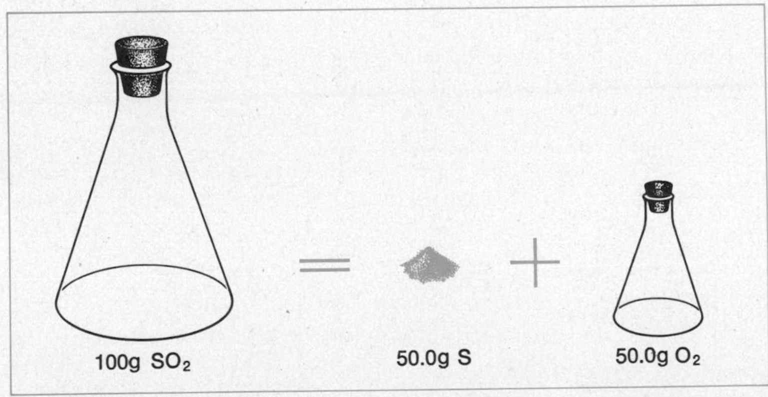

FIGURE 2–5 · *The decomposition of sulfur dioxide always results in 50 percent sulfur and 50 percent oxygen.*

Earlier, we saw that the mass composition of water is constant. The mass composition of sulfur dioxide is also constant. Tests can be performed to prove our generalizations.

Many sulfur compounds, called sulfides, when burned in air, react to produce sulfur dioxide. When a sulfide of mercury is burned in air, the element mercury and sulfur dioxide gas form.

FIGURE 2–6 · *Burning mercury sulfide in air results in liquid mercury and gaseous sulfur dioxide. The silvery droplets in the picture are mercury being formed during the reaction.*

When lead sulfide is burned in air, solid lead oxide and gaseous sulfur dioxide are formed. We can add these two equations to our list of reactions that produce sulfur dioxide.

$$\text{mercury (II) sulfide} + \text{oxygen} \rightarrow \text{mercury} + \text{sulfur dioxide (gas)}$$
$$\text{lead sulfide} + \text{oxygen} \rightarrow \text{lead oxide} + \text{sulfur dioxide (gas)}$$

Sulfur dioxide can be formed by either of the reactions above. When it is decomposed, 200 grams of sulfur dioxide will always produce 100 grams of sulfur and 100 grams of oxygen. We have discussed both the synthesis of sulfur dioxide from its elements and the analysis of sulfur dioxide into its elements. From these observations, it is evident that the constant mass composition of the compound is an experimental fact!

The mass composition has been determined for thousands of different compounds in addition to water and sulfur dioxide. The constancy of composition of those compounds, like that of water and sulfur dioxide, is also an experimental fact. The results are identical no matter where the compounds are found, synthesized, or analyzed. This important generalization, or observed regularity, is often stated as a fundamental law of chemistry.

THE LAW OF DEFINITE COMPOSITION

Elements in a compound always occur in a definite proportion by mass.

This is another way of saying that the composition of each specific compound is always the same.

2–10 · The percentage composition of compounds · We have seen that in any sample of water there is 7.94 times as much oxygen as hydrogen by mass. And in any sample of sulfur dioxide, there are equal masses of sulfur and oxygen. The chemist expresses these facts as the **percentage composition,** which is calculated in simple mathematical terms.

$$\text{Percentage composition} = \frac{\text{Mass of element}}{\text{Mass of compound}} \times 100$$

Using the preceding examples, we can calculate the percentage composition of water and sulfur dioxide.

Water:

$$\text{Percent of oxygen} = \frac{88.8 \text{ g of oxygen}}{100 \text{ g of water}} \times 100 = 88.8\%$$

$$\text{Percent of hydrogen} = \frac{11.2 \text{ g of hydrogen}}{100 \text{ g of water}} \times 100 = 11.2\%$$

Note that the percentages must total 100.

Sulfur:

$$\text{Percent of sulfur} = \frac{100 \text{ g of sulfur}}{200 \text{ g of sulfur dioxide}} \times 100 = 50.0\%$$

$$\text{Percent of oxygen} = \frac{100 \text{ g of oxygen}}{200 \text{ g of sulfur dioxide}} \times 100 = 50.0\%$$

EXERCISE

1. *Will the percent of hydrogen and oxygen change if we deal with 75.0 g of water rather than 100 g?*

$$\text{Percent of oxygen} = \frac{66.6 \text{ g of oxygen}}{75.0 \text{ g of water}} \times 100 = ?$$ 88.8%

$$\text{Percent of hydrogen} = \frac{8.40 \text{ g of hydrogen}}{75.0 \text{ g of water}} \times 100 = ?$$ 11.2%

NOTE

If the elements in compounds are always present in the same mass ratios, then the percentage compositions must be constant. That is true no matter what the size of the sample of the compound.

2. *Suppose we use a 16.8-g sample of sulfur dioxide instead of the 200-g sample. Will the percentage composition of sulfur dioxide be different?*

$$\text{Percent of sulfur} = \frac{8.40 \text{ g of sulfur}}{16.8 \text{ g of sulfur dioxide}} \times 100 = ?$$ 50%

$$\text{Percent of oxygen} = \frac{8.40 \text{ g of oxygen}}{16.8 \text{ g of sulfur dioxide}} \times 100 = ?$$ 50%

2–11 · Using percentage composition · We can use percentage composition of compounds to determine masses of elements that are present in samples of those compounds.

EXAMPLE

How much oxygen would be produced from the decomposition of 50.0 g of water?

SOLUTION

We have shown water to be 88.8% oxygen by mass. Therefore, because the mass composition of a compound is constant, 88.8% of 50.0 g of water will be oxygen.

$$\text{Mass of oxygen} = (50.0\text{ g})\ (0.888)$$
$$\text{Mass of oxygen} = 44.4\text{ g}$$

EXAMPLE

How much sulfur would be produced from 25.0 g of sulfur dioxide?

SOLUTION

The percentage composition of sulfur in sulfur dioxide is 50.0%. Therefore, one half the mass of any sample of sulfur dioxide is due to sulfur.

$$\text{Mass of sulfur} = (25.0\text{ g})\ (0.50)$$
$$\text{Mass of sulfur} = 12.50\text{ g}$$

EXERCISE

1. *What is the percentage composition of calcium in calcium carbonate, $CaCO_3$? Analysis of a 50.0-g calcium carbonate sample shows that 20.0 g are due to calcium.*
2. *How much calcium would be needed for 300 g of calcium carbonate?*

2–12 · Definite composition and atomic theory · The Law of Definite Composition is the very basis of chemical analysis. And chemical analysis is of great importance in our modern society. Scientists are constantly using chemical analysis for many purposes. Through chemical analysis, they can identify materials, measure the purity of substances, and determine the

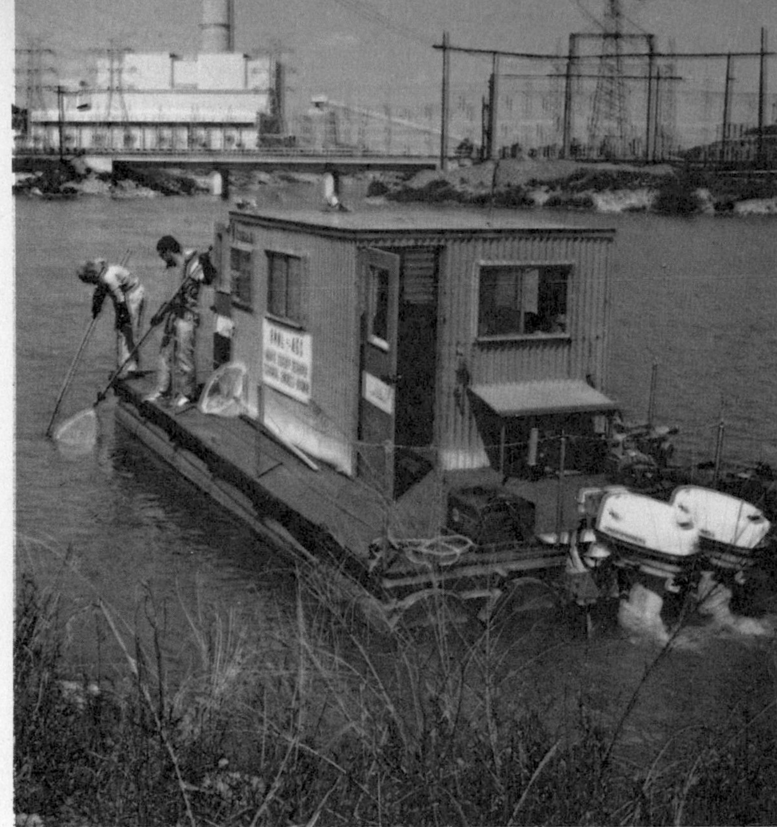

FIGURE 2–7 · *A great deal can be learned about the cause and cure of water pollution from small crafts such as this.*

degree of environmental pollution. Those are only a few examples of the law's usefulness. It also provides the fundamental quantitative basis for chemical experimentation. That is because it is a direct outgrowth of the Law of the Conservation of Matter. However, the Law of Definite Composition has still further importance in chemistry. John Dalton's realization of the full significance of the Law of Definite Composition led him to propose the first modern atomic theory. This theory is the subject of Chapter 3.

REVIEW IT NOW

1. What is the mass ratio of hydrogen to oxygen in water? What is the mass ratio of sulfur to oxygen in sulfur dioxide?
2. Using water and sulfur dioxide as examples, show that the constant mass composition is an experimental fact.
3. How do we calculate the percentage composition of a compound?
4. What practical application might there be in calculating percentage composition?
5. State the Law of Definite Composition. Of what importance to chemistry is the Law of Definite Composition?

SUMMARY

The idea that all matter consisted of earth, air, fire, and water was carried over into the fifteenth century. Robert Boyle, considered one of the most important pioneers of modern chemistry, proposed definitions of an element and a compound.

Building on the work of Robert Boyle, Antoine Lavoisier studied mass relationships in chemical reactions. His work resulted in the Law of the Conservation of Matter. Lavoisier compiled the first meaningful list of elements (although only twenty-six were known at that time).

Jöns Berzelius contributed to the advance of modern chemistry by devising a system of assigning symbols to the chemical elements.

With the improvement of experimental techniques, scientists began studying the composition of matter. The nature of elements and compounds was better understood when it was discovered that the mass composition of compounds is constant. This led to the Law of Definite Composition. Chemists learned to determine the percentage composition of compounds and to use this information as a basis for chemical analysis. Thus the chemist learned to identify materials and measure the purity of substances.

REVIEW QUESTIONS

1 Suppose a Canadian chemist discovered a new element and wished to name it Canadium after Canada. What two symbols could be appropriate for this new element? Which of those two would be more logical? Why?

2 On what basis can we make the statement that each of us is really a collection of "star dust"?

3 In what ways does the chemist use the Law of Definite Composition?

4 The chemist has determined that 70.0% of the compound Fe_2O_3 is Fe. If you decomposed 350 g of Fe_2O_3, how much Fe would result?

5 What percent of the compound in question **4** is oxygen?

6 If you decomposed 350 g of Fe_2O_3, how much oxygen would result?

7 Suppose a chemist did an experiment in which he passed an electric current through water. That decomposed the water into hydrogen gas and oxygen gas. The chemist produced 0.0623 g of hydrogen and 0.4984 g of oxygen. What is the percentage of hydrogen to oxygen in the water? What is the mass ratio of hydrogen to oxygen in the water?

8 When iron combines with sulfur to form a chemical compound, it is always found that 1.00 g of sulfur combines with 1.75 g of iron. If 10.00 g of sulfur are used in making this compound, how much iron will be needed?

9 When sulfur burns, it reacts with oxygen in the air to produce the gas sulfur dioxide. A mass ratio of 1.00:1.00 between sulfur and oxygen is always obtained. If 26.432 g of the gas are formed, how many grams of sulfur were burned?

10 State, in your own words, the Law of Definite Composition and the Law of the Conservation of Matter.

SUGGESTED READINGS

Braun, Robert, and Joseph Sapio. "Atomic Absorption Spectroscopy." *Chemistry*, June 1974, p. 9.

Cleveland, J. M. "Plutonium—The Lively Element. Part I: Historical Background." *Chcmistry*, December 1965. "Part II, Behavior in Solutions." *Chemistry*, January 1970, p. 10.

"Discovery Claim: Elements 116, 126." *Science News*, June 26, 1976, p. 404.

"Discovery of Element 106." *Science News*, September 1974, p. 164.

"Doubt Over the Discovery of Element 126." *Science News*, December, 1976, p. 357.

Flaschen, Stewart. *Search and Research—The Story of the Chemical Elements.* Boston: Allyn &Bacon, Inc., 1965.

Habashi, Fathi. "Ida Noddack, 75, and Element 75." *Chemistry*, February 1971, p. 14.

House, J. E., Jr. "Beryllium." *Chemistry*, December 1971, p. 10.

Keller, Eugenia. "Man and the Universe. Part IV: Origin of the Elements." *Chemistry*, July–August 1972, p. 17.

Navratil, James D. "Niobium: Space Age Metal." *Chemistry*, September 1970, p. 13.

———. "Magnesium." *Chemistry*, May 1971, p. 6.

Schramm, David N. "The Age of the Elements." *Scientific American*, January 1974, p. 69.

Seaborg, Glenn T. "From Mendeleev to Mendelevium—and Beyond." *Chemistry*, January 1970, p. 6.

———, and Arnold Fritsch. "The Synthetic Elements: III." *Scientific American*, April 1963, p. 68.

Weand, Barron L. "The Lightest Metal—Lithium." *Chemistry*, July–August 1971, p. 10.

Weeks, Mary, and Henry Leicester. *Discovery of the Elements*, 7th ed. Easton, Pa.: Journal of Chemical Education Inc., 1968.

Zimmerman, Joan. "The Strange World of Helium." *Chemistry*, February 1970, p. 14.

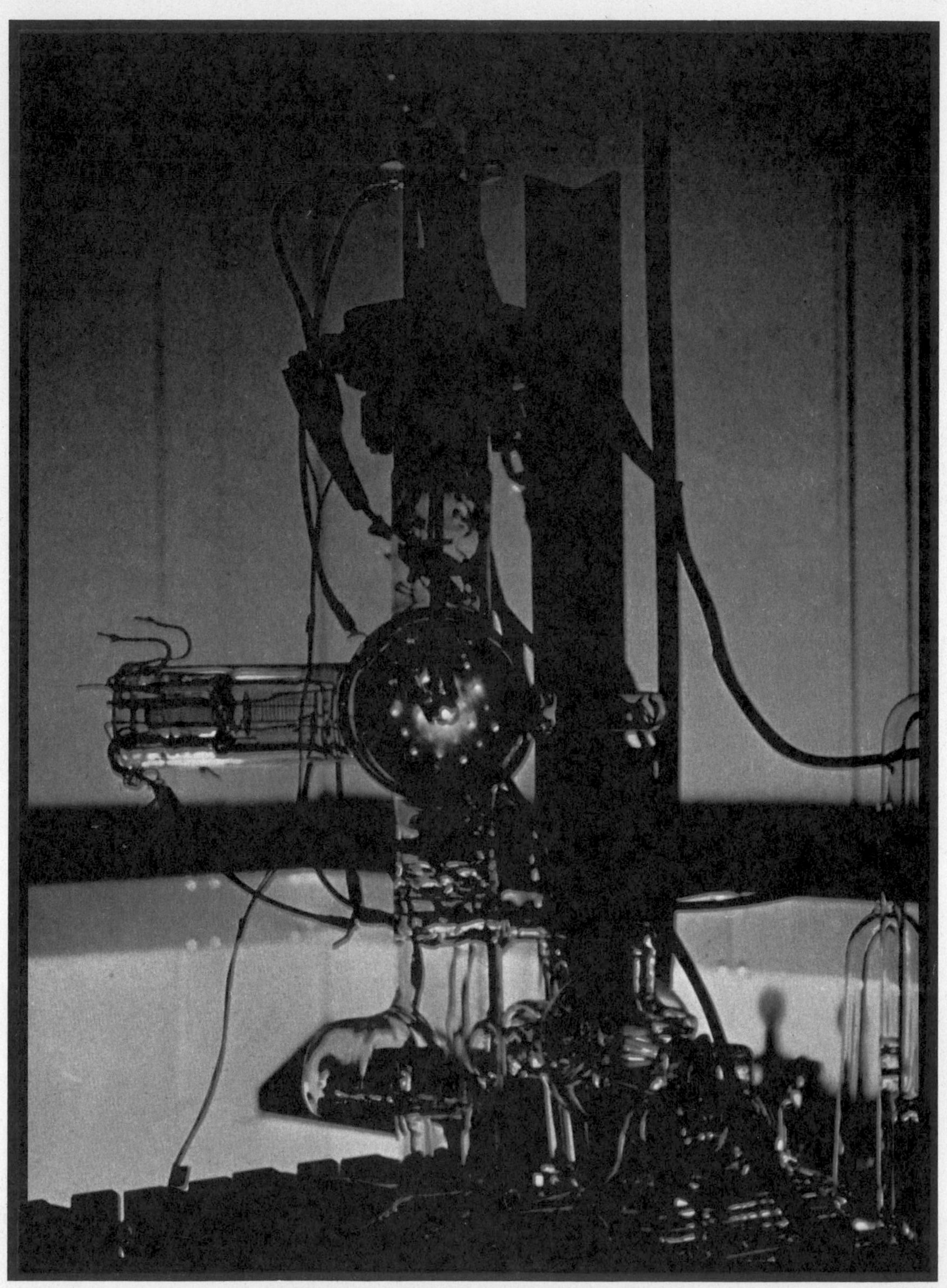

This low energy electron diffraction equipment is used to study the arrangement of atoms.

CHAPTER THREE

Atoms and Molecules

Let's begin this chaper with a simple exercise.

Tear off a strip along the edge of a sheet of notebook paper. Now tear the strip in half. Take one of the halves and tear it in half. Repeat this process until you have a tiny piece of paper that you cannot halve again. Your piece of paper has become "indivisible."

Simple, isn't it? Yet that is the way philosophers of ancient Greece demonstrated that matter can be broken down until finally a piece of matter is left that cannot be further subdivided. Even if you could put your small piece of paper under a microscope and in some way continue to halve it, you would eventually have a piece so small that it would be impossible to divide. Leucippus and Democritus, two famous Greek philosophers, spoke of this indivisible and indestructible piece of matter as being an *atom*. They suggested that matter consists of very small, definite units that are responsible for the set of properties of each particular type of matter.

Atomism has proved to be the most fruitful scientific idea passed on to us by the ancient Greeks. Even in the seventeenth century, that idea was basically unchanged. In 1661, Robert Boyle wrote an important book on chemistry, *The Sceptical Chymist*. In the book he stated that "the universal matter of the universe consists of little particles of several sizes and shapes." This idea of the atom lasted even until the end of the eighteenth century. At the end of the eighteenth century, John Dalton, an English Quaker schoolteacher, proposed the first useful atomic theory of matter.

In this chapter, we will explore Dalton's theory and see how the modern idea of atomic structure evolved.

CHYMISTA
SCEPTICUS
VEL
DUBIA
ET
PARADOXA
CHYMICO-PHYSICA
circa
Spagyricorum
Principia
Authore
ROB. BOYLE
Nobili Anglo

Rotterodami
Apud Arnoldum Leers
Anno 1668

FIGURE 3–1 · *This is the title page of Boyle's book, from the Dutch edition of 1668:* The Sceptical Chymist or Chemical and Physical Doubts and Paradoxes about the Principles of the Spagyrists. *The spagyrists believed in a sulfur-mercury-salt theory of the constitution of metals.*

ATOMS

3–1 · Dalton proposes an atomic theory · Dalton was familiar with the philosophical concept of atomism. He also understood the Law of Definite Composition. Dalton thought about the structure of matter and tried to relate that to the Law of Definite Composition. Remember, the law states that elements in a compound must always occur in definite proportion by mass. Therefore, it seemed logical to Dalton that elements must combine in definite units or portions to form compounds. Let's look at an example. In the formation of carbon dioxide, any specific mass of carbon is always combined with a definite, constant mass of oxygen. An atom of carbon with a constant fixed mass must be combined with one, two, or three atoms of oxygen of definite mass. The Law of Definite Composition implies that atoms have fixed masses. It also seemed logical to Dalton that a compound always has the same relative numbers of combined atoms.

Dalton's atomic theory, the first atomic theory proposed, contained references to an experimentally measured property, the property of mass. Dalton's measurements were rather crude. And the experimental data on combining masses available to him were not very extensive or accurate. That type of measurement had originated with Lavoisier only twenty years earlier. Nevertheless, from such fragmentary and not too accurate data, Dalton was able to suggest a useful atomic theory. Dalton's theory has been modified, and some parts have been discarded as experimental chemical science has evolved. But Dalton's theory still remains the cornerstone of the modern atomic theory of matter.

These are the principle aspects of Dalton's theory that are still useful today.

1. *All matter consists of extremely small, indivisible particles called atoms.*
2. *All atoms of any one element are similiar to one another, particularly in mass. But they are different from atoms of all other elements.*
3. *Chemical changes are changes in the combinations of atoms with one another.*
4. *Atoms remain indivisible in even the most violent chemical reaction.*

3–2 · Dalton determines atomic masses · Dalton believed the atoms of different elements had different masses. He thought that by determining the masses of the different kinds of atoms, he could learn more about how they combine. He realized, though, that he could not actually determine the mass of a single atom of an element. In fact, even today it can only be done indirectly.

However, Dalton knew that elements combine according to fixed ratios by mass. For example, 23.00 grams of sodium combine with 79.92 grams of bromine to form sodium bromide. This is a ratio of approximately 1:3.5. Dalton believed the ratios of the masses in a compound depended on the masses of the individual atoms of each element. Also, Dalton thought that studying the ratios of the masses in which elements combine could help determine the relative mass of single atoms of all the elements.

Dalton selected hydrogen, the lightest element known, as his standard. He assigned to each atom of hydrogen the atomic mass of 1.00. That meant that the atomic mass of all other elements would be greater than 1.00. He then analyzed the crude mass composition data known in his time. From those data, he determined the atomic mass of other elements relative to that of hydrogen.

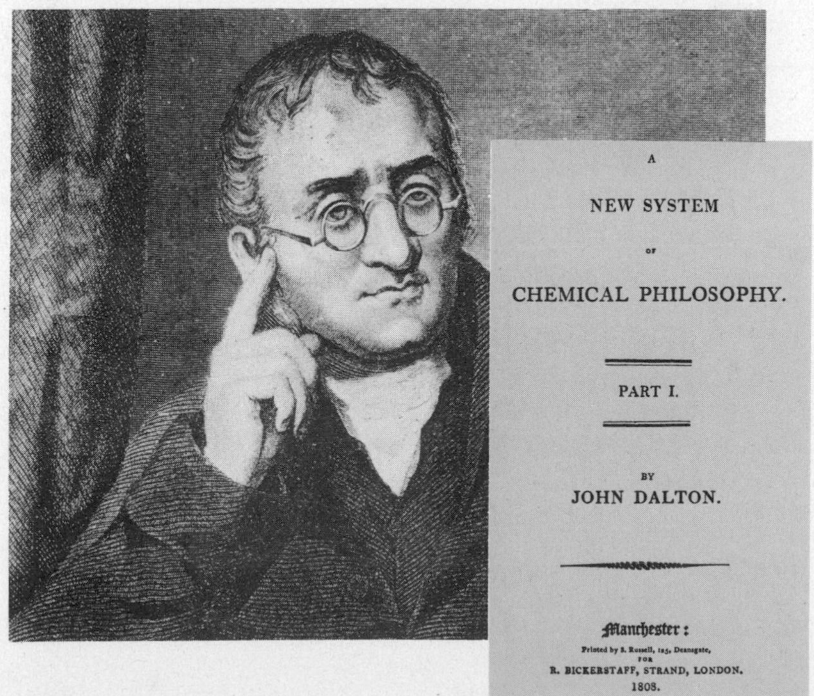
A

NEW SYSTEM

OF

CHEMICAL PHILOSOPHY.

PART I.

BY

JOHN DALTON.

Manchester:

Printed by S. Russell, 125, Deansgate,

FOR

R. BICKERSTAFF, STRAND, LONDON.

1808.

FIGURE 3–2 · John Dalton *(1766–1844, English). Though one of the most influential scientists of his time, Dalton was compelled to give private lessons in arithmetic to earn a living, even after he was over 60 years old. The title page pictured here heralded the publication of Dalton's atomic theory.*

3–3 · Dalton's dilemma · Dalton was faced with a great experimental problem in arriving at the relative atomic masses. He knew the mass composition of certain chemical compounds. But he had no experimental evidence to indicate the ratio of atoms in those compounds. For example, Dalton knew from his experiments that eight parts of oxygen are combined with one part of hydrogen, by mass, to form water. He assumed that the water molecules were composed of one atom of hydrogen and one atom of oxygen. It followed that one oxygen atom is eight times as heavy as one hydrogen atom. Then the relative atomic mass of oxygen would be 8.00. Because of those assumptions, Dalton believed the formula for water was HO.

If, however, some other ratio of oxygen and hydrogen atoms existed in water, the relative atomic mass of oxygen would not be 8.00. It would be a submultiple or multiple of 8.00. Suppose Dalton had known that the correct formula for water was H_2O – one atom of oxygen for every two hydrogen atoms. Then the relative mass of oxygen would be 16.0. Keep in mind that hydrogen was assigned the mass of 1.00. The mass ratio is 8:1 (oxygen to hydrogen). For Dalton, water might have had the formula HO_2. In that case, the relative mass of the oxygen atom would be 4.00. You probably know that water has the atom ratio H_2O. Therefore, you may be surprised to learn that it took Dalton a long time to determine his incorrect formula for water (HO). But remember, Dalton did not have any experimental evidence. Indeed, he had no experimental evidence for the atom ratios of any compounds. That was his dilemma. His solution was an arbitrary one. He proposed atom ratios according to the following scheme.

1. *Suppose only a single compound of the two elements A and B were known. Dalton assumed that they would combine in a one-to-one ratio as AB. So water was to Dalton, using modern symbols, HO, and not H_2O. To Dalton, ammonia was NH, and not NH_3 as we know it to be.*
2. *Suppose two different compounds of the same two elements were known. Then Dalton assumed the simplest atom ratios possible, AB and AB_2 or A_2B. Thus, for Dalton, CO and CO_2 were the formulas for the two known oxides of carbon.*

Dalton's formulas for the oxides of carbon and sulfur, as well as for some other compounds, are now known to be correct. But many other formulas based on his assumptions are incorrect. The lack of a firm experimental basis for chemical formulas was an unsolvable problem for John Dalton. It was only in the last years of the nineteenth century, because of improvements in experimental techniques, that a basis was firmly established to the satisfaction of most chemists.

3–4 · Dalton prepares a historic table · Dalton gathered a great deal of experimental data on the mass composition of compounds. He made many arbitrary assumptions of atom ratios for those compounds. Using his data, Dalton prepared the first table of relative atomic masses. The table was made public on October 21, 1802. But the table was inaccurate because it was based on crude data and assumptions that could not be verified. Nonetheless, Dalton's table of relative atomic masses is a monument to his brilliance and foresight. His achievement was a crucial advance in chemistry. He demonstrated the importance of the masses of atoms in distinguishing one atomic species from another. Dalton provided generations of scientists with the experimental basis for testing and modifying his theory.

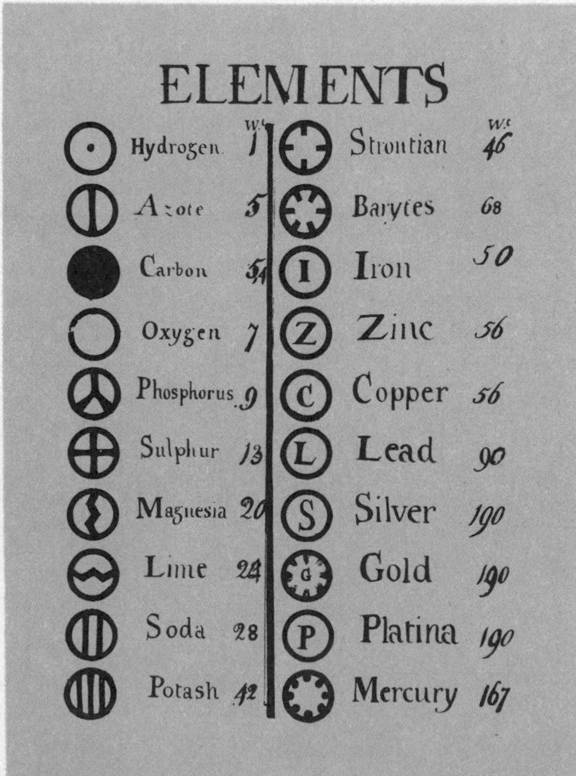

FIGURE 3–3 · *A lecture diagram used by Dalton to illustrate his atomic theory. The atomic masses that he gave to elements are shown. What inconsistencies with his own theory are evident in the diagram?*

FIGURE 3–4 · *(Left) This photograph shows the national mass standard designated to kilogram 20. This standard is composed of 90% platinum and 10% iridium. It has been a national standard since 1893. Interestingly, there has never been a national standard for the pound, which has always been defined in terms of kilograms. (Right) This photograph shows light being emitted by krypton gas in a lamp. Krypton light waves have defined the meter since 1960. The meter is 1 650 763.73 wavelengths of light emitted by the krypton isotope, Kr-86.*

3–5 · The atomic mass unit and relative atomic and molecular masses · By the late nineteenth century, chemists had far more accurate experimental data than Dalton had. Those chemists disagreed about many things. But they finally agreed to resolve their differences with respect to a single scale of relative atomic masses. At an international meeting, they agreed to use the masses of a fixed number of atoms as a standard. Initially, they used the mass of the number of atoms of oxygen in 16.0000 grams of oxygen. Thus, an oxygen atom was given the arbitrary value of 16.0000 **atomic mass units, amu.** This amu could then be compared with other atoms of other elements to determine their amu. Thus, by comparison, one carbon atom would have a relative mass of 12.011 amu. Later, it was discovered that elements usually have several kinds of atoms (isotopes). The relative scale of atomic masses was changed to be based on the mass of one type of carbon atom (^{12}C=12.0000 amu). When the standard was chosen, chemists had no means for experimentally determining the mass of single atoms. To do that, one must be able to determine the mass for a number of atoms and then determine how many atoms there are in the sample. The mass of a single atom can then be derived from those two pieces of experimental evidence. Today chemists can count atoms. But in the middle of the nineteenth century, neither the theoretical basis nor the experimental techniques for counting atoms had been discovered. Chemists had to arbitrarily pick a standard for the mass of single atoms.

The atomic mass unit is only a label for that standard, and all atomic masses are relative to that standard. It is quite obvious that a single atom of carbon cannot possibly have a mass of 12.0000 grams or kilograms. Such a large amount contains a vast number of carbon atoms.

The value of 12.0000 amu for the mass of the carbon atom was chosen as a standard for a specific reason. That value was convenient, and it led to the relative atomic masses of many of the other elements. That was true whether those atomic masses were whole numbers, or close to whole numbers.

Now we can define the relative atomic masses of the elements on the basis of a convenient and universal standard. The **relative atomic mass** of an element is *the mass of one atom of that element relative to the mass of one atom of carbon*. Remember, the mass of one atom of carbon, by convention, has the assigned mass of 12.0000 atomic mass units. Table 3–1 shows a list of the relative atomic masses of other elements, based on this definition.

TABLE 3–1 · Relative Atomic Masses of Some Elements

ELEMENT	SYMBOL	ATOMIC MASS	ELEMENT	SYMBOL	ATOMIC MASS
Aluminum	Al	26.98	Lead	Pb	207.19
Antimony	Sb	121.75	Lithium	Li	6.939
Argon	Ar	39.948	Magnesium	Mg	24.312
Arsenic	As	74.92	Manganese	Mn	54.938
Barium	Ba	137.34	Mercury	Hg	200.59
Beryllium	Be	9.012	Neon	Ne	20.183
Bismuth	Bi	208.98	Nickel	Ni	58.71
Boron	B	10.81	Nitrogen	N	14.007
Bromine	Br	79.909	Oxygen	O	15.9994
Cadmium	Cd	112.40	Phosphorus	P	30.974
Calcium	Ca	40.08	Platinum	Pt	195.09
Carbon	C	12.011	Potassium	K	39.102
Cesium	Cs	132.91	Silicon	Si	28.086
Chlorine	Cl	35.453	Silver	Ag	107.870
Chromium	Cr	51.996	Sodium	Na	22.990
Cobalt	Co	58.93	Strontium	Sr	87.62
Copper	Cu	63.54	Sulfur	S	32.064
Fluorine	F	19.00	Thorium	Th	232.04
Gold	Au	196.97	Tin	Sn	118.69
Helium	He	4.003	Tungsten	W	183.85
Hydrogen	H	1.0080	Uranium	U	238.03
Iodine	I	126.90	Vanadium	V	50.942
Iron	Fe	55.847	Xenon	Xe	131.30
Krypton	Kr	83.80	Zinc	Zn	65.37

Molecular masses of compounds must be related to the same standard. Thus, the **relative molecular mass** of a compound is determined in the same way the relative atomic mass is. It is *the mass of one molecule of that compound relative to the mass of one atom of carbon.*

REVIEW IT NOW

1 What is the basis of Dalton's atomic theory?
2 State Dalton's atomic theory.
3 What was Dalton's "dilemma" in arriving at relative atomic masses?
4 What assumptions did he make with regard to atom ratios?
5 Define the term *atomic mass unit.*
6 What is meant by *relative atomic mass?*

MOLECULES

3–6 · The mole · Chemists in the nineteenth century recognized the need for a larger unit of comparison among atoms and molecules than the atomic mass unit. They also recognized the need for a unit that has physical meaning. They chose to use a *mass* of atoms or molecules to represent a large number of atoms or molecules. This large unit of comparison (mass of atoms and molecules) is called the **mole** (mol). The mole is defined as the number of atoms of carbon in 12.0000 grams of carbon containing only the ^{12}C isotope. The atomic mass of carbon is not 12.0000. It is actually 12.011 because of the presence of two isotopes. These two isotopes are ^{12}C (=12.0000) and ^{13}C (=13.0034). They will be discussed in Chapter 19. For our purposes here, we can say that they are different forms of the same element.

If 31.998 grams of oxygen contain one mole of diatomic oxygen molecules, then 31.998 grams of oxygen must contain two moles of oxygen atoms. A mole of oxygen atoms, then, would be the number of atoms of oxygen contained in 15.999 grams of oxygen.

Using $^{12}C = 12.0000$ amu as a standard for relative atomic masses, the mole can be defined in other ways. *A mole is the number of atoms contained in the relative atomic mass of any element when that mass is measured in grams.* Thus, 23.0 grams of sodium contain a mole of sodium atoms. A mole of iron atoms has a mass of 55.8 grams. *A mole is also the number*

FIGURE 3–5 · *Approximately one mole of carbon is shown here. How many grams of carbon equal a mole of carbon?*

of molecules contained in the relative molecular mass of a compound when that mass is measured in grams. Thus, 44.0 grams of carbon dioxide contain a mole of carbon dioxide molecules. A mole of nitrogen molecules has a mass of 28.0 grams.

The actual number of atoms or molecules that constitute a mole is expressed exponentially as 6.023×10^{23}. This number is named the **Avogadro number,** or *N*.

The Avogadro number, 602 300 quintillion, is so large it is almost impossible for us to comprehend it. Perhaps an analogy will help. Suppose all the people in the world (3500 million people) were asked to count an Avogadro number of molecules. Also, suppose this task was to be accomplished by each person counting one molecule per second without a break. It would take more than six thousand years to complete the job!

FIGURE 3–6 · *This is a mole of copper sulfate. How many grams do you think are present?*

In 1875, the Avogadro number had been determined to within 30 percent of its true value. Today, several methods enable scientists to determine the Avogadro number within 0.01 percent! Later we will consider how this number is determined in the laboratory.

The important thing to remember about the Avogadro number is just that—it is a number. It is the number of particles in a mole. Just as a dozen implies twelve doughnuts, eggs, or anything else, a mole implies 6.023×10^{23}, or an Avogadro number, of atoms, molecules, bricks, people, or anything else.

FIGURE 3–7 · *These three containers demonstrate 1.00 liter, 10.0 liters, and 22.4 liters, consecutively.*

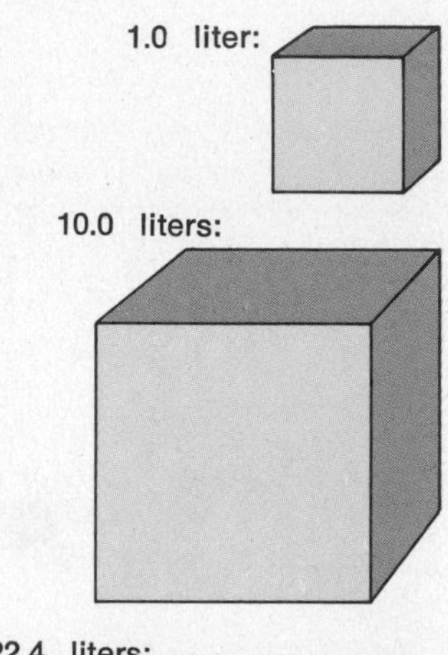

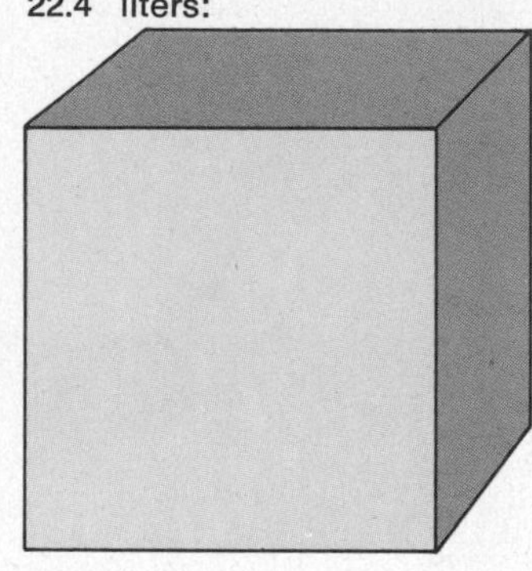

EXERCISE

1. *How many moles of bricks would you have if you had 12.046×10^{23} bricks?*
2. *How many bricks would you have if you had 0.50 mole of bricks?*

3–7 · The mole and the molar volume of gases · Early in the nineteenth century, the Italian scientist Amadeo Avogadro proposed that equal volumes of all gases contain an equal number of molecules if the gases are under the same conditions of temperature and pressure. The importance of that hypothesis was ignored for almost fifty years, until the first international congress of chemistry in 1860. Since that time, there has been a great increase in chemical knowledge. Much of that rapid increase in chemical knowledge resulted from the understanding and use of the following hypothesis.

AVOGADRO'S HYPOTHESIS

Equal volumes of gases, at the same temperature and pressure, contain equal numbers of molecules.

It was Avogadro's hypothesis that allowed a definitive scale of atomic masses to be established. He clarified for Dalton and his successors the numbers of molecules being measured for mass in any particular sample of a compound or element. A mole of a gas of 0°C and one atmosphere pressure (760 Torr) contains exactly 6.023×10^{23} molecules. This is true, no matter what gas is involved. Moreover, this number of molecules under these conditions of temperature and pressure will occupy 22.414 liters. This volume is known as the **molar gas volume.** And the number of molecules in this molar gas volume is the Avogadro number, or a mole.

NOTE

Remember, in problems involving gases, the temperature and pressure of the gas are always important. Chemists define 0°C and 760 Torr (1 atm) as standard temperature and pressure, STP.

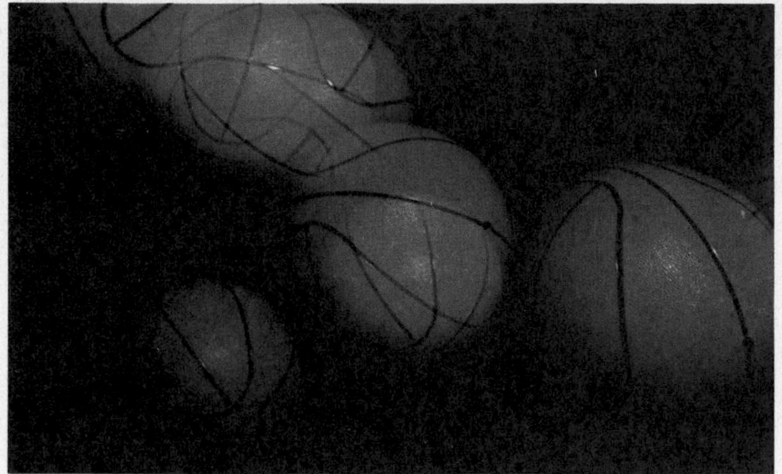

FIGURE 3–8 · *Three basketballs approximates the molar gas volume.*

3–8 · The Law of Multiple Proportions · Remember the way Dalton formulated his atomic theory? He realized that the Law of Definite Composition must have a companion law. He called this companion law the Law of Multiple Proportions. The Law of Definite Composition implied that matter is composed of atoms, and that these atoms unite in definite fixed units each with its definite mass. Now suppose two elements form more than one compound, thereby combining in different atomic ratios. Then the percentage masses of the elements in the two compounds would be different. For example, suppose carbon and oxygen form two compounds. One compound contains one atom each of carbon and oxygen. A second contains two atoms of oxygen with one atom of carbon. Each compound would follow the Law of Definite Composition. Every sample of that compound would have the same mass ratio of oxygen and carbon. However, there would also be a relationship between the two compounds. The ratios of the mass of oxygen in the first compound and the mass of oxygen in the second compound for the same mass of carbon would be 1:2.

Consider for a moment the two compounds of carbon. The first, carbon monoxide, is composed of 42.9 percent carbon and 57.1 percent oxygen by mass. The other compound, carbon dioxide, is composed of 27.3 percent carbon and 72.7 percent oxygen by mass. The ratio of oxygen to carbon in carbon monoxide is 57.1:42.9, or 1.33:1.00. The ratio in carbon dioxide is 72.7:27.3, or 2.66:1.00. In other words, 1.00 gram of carbon combines with 1.33 grams of oxygen in carbon monoxide. And 1.00 gram of carbon combines with 2.66 grams of oxygen in carbon dioxide. The ratio of the combining mass of oxygen in these two carbon-oxygen compounds is 1.33:2.66 or 1:2. This is a necessary consequence of the atomic theory. In the first compound one atom of oxygen is combining and in the second compound two atoms of oxygen, or twice as much, are combining.

FIGURE 3-9 • *There are two possible compounds of carbon and oxygen, carbon monoxide and carbon dioxide.*

When nitrogen and oxygen react with each other, they form five distinctly different compounds. In order to simplify it, we will express the mass composition for these compounds as the mass of oxygen in each of these compounds per 1.00 gram of nitrogen. In an actual laboratory analysis of these compounds, the mass of oxygen per 1.00 gram of nitrogen was found to be 0.570 gram, and 1.136, 1.734, 2.258, and 2.869 grams respectively. But you may wonder what relationship exists among these masses of oxygen that are combined with the same mass of nitrogen. If we divide each of the oxygen masses by the lowest mass, 0.570 gram, we can determine the number ratio among those masses.

$$\frac{0.570\text{ g}}{0.570\text{ g}}:\frac{1.136\text{ g}}{0.570\text{ g}}:\frac{1.734\text{ g}}{0.570\text{ g}}:\frac{2.258\text{ g}}{0.570\text{ g}}:\frac{2.869\text{ g}}{0.570\text{ g}}$$

or

$$1.00:1.99:3.04:3.96:5.03$$

Any experiment has some unavoidable error and uncertainty in its results. Therefore, we may round off these numbers in keeping with their experimental uncertainty.

$$1:2:3:4:5$$

Thus, 1.00 gram of nitrogen can combine only with 1, 2, 3, 4, or 5 times 0.570 gram of oxygen.

We can also determine the oxygen mass ratio per 1.00 gram of sulfur. We will use an arbitrary compound mass of 100 grams. Thus, our mass percentages are converted directly to masses of elements per 100 grams of compound.

In sulfur dioxide, 50.0 grams of oxygen combine with 50.0 grams of sulfur. This is a mass ratio of 50 :50, or 1:1, for these two elements in this particular compound. Sulfur combines with oxygen in a ratio of 1:1. In other words, 1.00 gram of sulfur combines with 1.00 gram of oxygen to form sulfur dioxide.

In the compound sulfur trioxide, we learned that 60.0 grams of oxygen combine with 40.0 grams of sulfur. This combination of elements is in a mass ratio of 60.0 : 40.0, or 1.50 : 1.00. In other words, in the compound sulfur trioxide, there is 1.50 times as much oxygen as sulfur, by mass. Then 1.00 gram of sulfur would combine with 1.50 grams of oxygen. If we compare our data, we find this equation.

$$\frac{\text{Mass of oxygen/1.00 g of sulfur in sulfur dioxide}}{\text{Mass of oxygen/1.00 g of sulfur in sulfur trioxide}} = \frac{1.00}{1.50}$$

The ratio of the masses of oxygen combined with a fixed mass of sulfur in sulfur dioxide and sulfur trioxide is 1.00:1.50. In small whole numbers it is 2.00:3.00. (This is true when the numbers in the ratio 1.00:1.50 are multiplied by 2; the ratio becomes 2.00:3.00.)

These results are derived from the fact that atoms combine in fixed units as proposed by Dalton in his atomic theory. Dalton expressed the following law.

THE LAW OF MULTIPLE PROPORTIONS

When two elements combine to form more than one compound with the mass of one element remaining fixed, the ratios of the masses of the other element are in small whole numbers.

EXERCISE

An analysis of a 100-g sample of nitrogen monoxide shows 46.6 g of nitrogen and 53.4 g of oxygen. An analysis of nitrogen dioxide, another compound of nitrogen and oxygen, shows 30.4 g of nitrogen for every 69.6 g of oxygen. What is the ratio of oxygen to nitrogen for these two compounds? How does your answer demonstrate the Law of Multiple Proportions?

REVIEW IT NOW

1 What is a mole?
2 What is the Avogadro number?
3 Explain Avogadro's hypothesis.

SUMMARY

The Law of Definite Composition and the Law of Multiple Proportions are summary statements of large amounts of experimental data. This summary of experience led Dalton to suspect that matter was made up of tiny, indivisible particles, called atoms. According to Dalton's atomic theory, each element is made up of atoms of that element. All the atoms in an element are alike, and all have a definite mass and definite properties. A chemical reaction involves changes in the combinations of atoms with one another. On the basis of this theory, Dalton was able to account in general for the experimental laws of chemical combination. He postulated relative masses for the atoms of each element. His dilemma, however, was that he had no way of knowing how many atoms of each element combine to make a specific compound.

Dalton's table of relative masses was revised as new data were gathered. An arbitrary unit, the atomic mass unit (amu), was established. Arbitrary standards for atomic masses were set also. Now chemists use 12.0 amu as the standard value for carbon. All other atomic masses are relative to this standard.

Recognizing the need for a larger unit than the amu, chemists defined the number of atoms of carbon in 12.0 grams of carbon as a mole. Unlike the amu, this expression has a physical meaning. The actual number of atoms or molecules that make up a mole is 6.02×10^{23}. This number is called the Avogadro number, or *N*.

REVIEW QUESTIONS

1 In Dalton's time, only one compound of hydrogen and sulfur (hydrogen sulfide) was known. How would Dalton have written a formula for hydrogen sulfide?

2 Why did Dalton select hydrogen as the standard when devising his scale of relative atomic masses?

3 Why did chemists later select carbon 12.0 as a standard?

4 According to Table 3 - 1, fluorine has an atomic mass of 19.000. What does this mean?

5 One mole of nitrogen molecules (N_2) has a mass of 28.00 g. According to this, how would you define one mole of nitrogen atoms?

6 Refer to Table 3 - 1 to answer the following.

- **a.** What is the mass of one mole of lead atoms?
- **b.** How many atoms would there be in 4.00 g of helium?
- **c.** Approximately how many moles of mercury atoms would it take to produce a mass of 400 g?
- **d.** How many moles of nitrogen atoms would there be in 14.00 g of nitrogen gas?
- **e.** How many moles of nitrogen molecules would there be in 14.00 g of nitrogen gas?

7. Nitrogen gas and hydrogen gas react according to the following equation to produce ammonia, also a gas.

1 volume nitrogen (gas) + 3 volumes hydrogen (gas) =
2 volumes ammonia (gas)

a. What is the volume ratio of the three gases in the reaction?
b. What is the molar ratio of the three gases in the reaction?

8. Suppose the following gas densities were measured at STP (Standard Temperature and Pressure).

Substance	*Density (g/l)*
A	1.08
B	1.32
C	1.46
D	1.80

If the chemist assigns C a molecular mass of 3.00, calculate the molecular masses of A, B, and D relative to C.

9. What gas volume would each of the following represent?
a. 32.0 g CH_4 (CH_4 = 16.0 amu)
b. 8.00 g O_2 (O_2 = 32.0 amu)
c. 5.60 g CO (CO = 28.0 amu)
d. 0.50 mole N_2 (N_2 = 28.0 amu)
e. 10.0 moles He (He = 4.00 amu)
f. 11.0 g CO_2 (CO_2 = 44.0 amu)

SUGGESTED READINGS

Bethe, Hans A. "What Holds the Nucleus Together?" *Scientific American Offprint*. San Francisco: W. H. Freeman and Co.

Feifer, Nathan. "Pythagoreanism and Theories of the Structure of Matter." *Chemistry*, March 1974, p. 6.

Ferreira, Ricardo, and Aymar Soriano. "Can Matter Be Converted to Energy?" *Chemistry*, October 1972, p. 19.

Hofstadter, Robert. "The Atomic Nucleus." *Scientific American Offprint*. San Francisco: W. H. Freeman and Co.

Schrödinger, Erwin. "What Is Matter?" *Scientific American Offprint*. San Francisco: W. H. Freeman and Co.

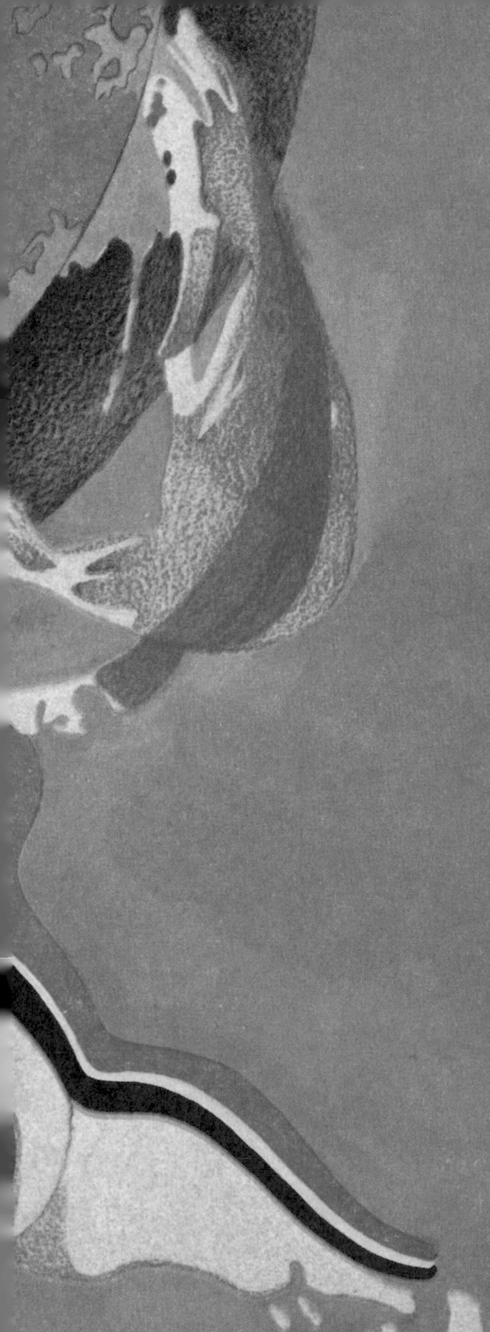

UNIT TWO

The Chemistry of Matter

Look around you. There are hundreds of different kinds of matter. Yet all of those different types of matter are made from the same building blocks—the elements. Chemical formulas and equations represent the way the elements combine and arrange themselves to form the various types of matter.

Everything in our environment falls into one of three categories—solid, liquid, and gas. There are important differences among those three physical states, and the chemist is very much concerned with those differences. How do gases behave as they do? What holds atoms and molecules together in a liquid? Why are they held closer together in a solid than in a liquid? How are atoms and molecules arranged in solids? How is energy involved when substances change from one physical state to another? Those are some of the questions to which chemists have sought, and are still seeking the answers.

To understand chemistry, we must understand the basic forms in which all matter exists. We must also seek regularities in the properties of matter and search for explanations for those regularities.

Our task in understanding chemistry can be greatly simplified if we understand the periodicity and regularities that exist among the chemical elements and the forms of matter.

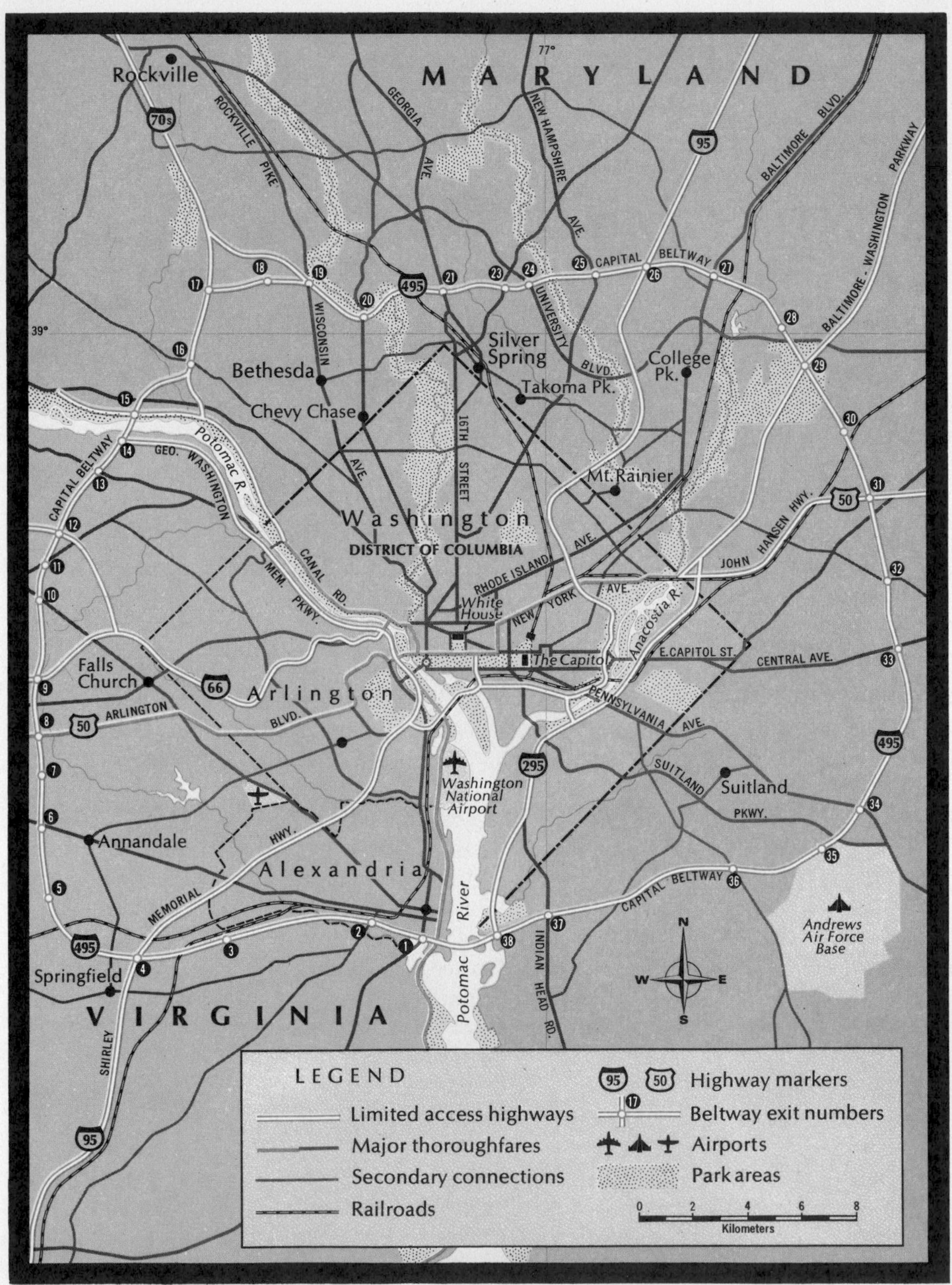

Symbols are used in a variety of ways for simplification and convenience.

CHAPTER FOUR

Formulas and Chemical Equations

Earlier you learned a simple system of shorthand notation for elements and compounds. Of course, using symbols and formulas to represent the names of elements and compounds is very convenient. But with the adoption of the Avogadro hypothesis, symbols have become more than just convenient. They are tools for communicating scientific knowledge.

CHEMICAL FORMULAS

4–1 · Chemical formulas for compounds · The Berzelius system of symbols described in Chapter 2 is also used for the shorthand notation of compounds. Just as an element is represented by its **symbol,** so a compound is represented by its **formula.** The formula for a compound contains the symbols for each of the elements in that compound. For example, the formula for zinc oxide, a compound of zinc and oxygen, is ZnO. Zinc chloride, a compound of zinc and chlorine, has the formula $ZnCl_2$. The formula for zinc nitride, a compound of zinc and nitrogen, is Zn_3N_2. These examples were chosen to indicate clearly the quantitative aspect of chemical formulas. In other words, a formula tells not only the elements that are combined in the compound, but also how many atoms of each element are in it. A number appearing below and to the right of a symbol is called a **subscript.** It represents the number of atoms of the element whose symbol it follows. Let's see what the subscripts in the formula Zn_3N_2, zinc nitride, tell us. For every three atoms of zinc in zinc nitride, there are two atoms of nitrogen. The subscript 1 is never used. Rather than write Zn_1O_1, the chemist simply writes ZnO.

4–2 · The meaning of symbols and formulas · What does the symbol Fe mean? Fe stands for the name of the element iron. Also, Fe stands for one atom of iron. However, as we mentioned earlier, chemists do not work with single atoms of elements. For example, when iron reacts chemically, large numbers of iron atoms are involved. Then the symbol Fe also stands for a standard large number of iron atoms. For chemists, Fe represents one *mole* of iron atoms. You will recall from the preceding chapter that one mole equals the Avogadro number, 6.02×10^{23}. Just as the term *dozen* refers to the quantity 12, the term *mole* refers to the quantity 6.02×10^{23}. Since one mole of iron atoms has a mass of 55.85 grams, the symbol Fe also represents 55.85 grams of iron. Perhaps you can begin to see the great significance of the chemical language!

What does the formula S_8 mean? Notice that we refer to the symbol Fe, but it is the formula S_8. Why? The notation S_8 tells us that sulfur exists naturally as a molecule consisting of eight atoms. Thus S_8 represents one mole of sulfur molecules containing eight moles of sulfur atoms. Since one mole of sulfur atoms has a mass of 32.07 grams, the formula S_8 also represents 8×32.07 grams. The symbol S_8 also represents 256.56 grams of sulfur.

4–3 · The mole and the determination of chemical formulas · The mole concept is very important in the experimental determination of chemical formulas. There is a relationship between the moles of atoms and the chemical formulas for compounds that they form. This relationship can be observed in the reaction between hydrogen and chlorine gases that forms gaseous hydrogen chloride. The reaction is described in the following manner.

1 volume of hydrogen
+ → 2 volumes of hydrogen chloride
1 volume of chlorine

or

1 molecule of hydrogen
+ → 2 molecules of hydrogen chloride
1 molecule of chlorine

or

1 mole of hydrogen
+ → 2 moles of hydrogen chloride
1 mole of chlorine

Both hydrogen and chlorine gases are diatomic molecules, H_2 and Cl_2. Thus, we can describe the reaction as:

$$H_2 + Cl_2 \rightarrow 2HCl$$

The symbol H_2 represents one mole of diatomic hydrogen gas. The symbol Cl_2 represents one mole of diatomic chlorine gas. The formula HCl represents one mole of hydrogen chloride molecules. Therefore, two moles of hydrogen chloride are represented in the equation above. Also, the formula HCl indicates clearly that one mole of hydrogen chloride contains one mole of hydrogen atoms chemically combined with one mole of chlorine atoms. Earlier we stated that a formula tells what elements and how many of those elements are combined in a compound. We now recognize that a chemical formula indicates the mole ratio of the atoms combined in a compound.

With this knowledge, we can consider the experimental determinations of chemical formulas. Such determinations rely on the Law of Definite Composition.

Knowing the mass composition and the relative atomic mass of the elements in a compound can give us the mole ratio of atoms combined in the compound. The mole ratio obtained gives us the simplest formula for the compound.

In many cases, the simplest formula for a compound is also its true formula. In other cases, the true formula for a compound is an integral multiple of that simplest formula. For example, CH_4 is the simplest formula for the compound methane. It is also the true formula for that compound. On the other hand, CH_3 is the simplest formula for the compound ethane, but the true formula for ethane is C_2H_6, or $2 \times CH_3$. Figure 4–1 shows three ways to represent the ethane molecule.

FIGURE 4–1 · *Three methods of depicting molecular structure are represented here. These show the ethane molecule.*

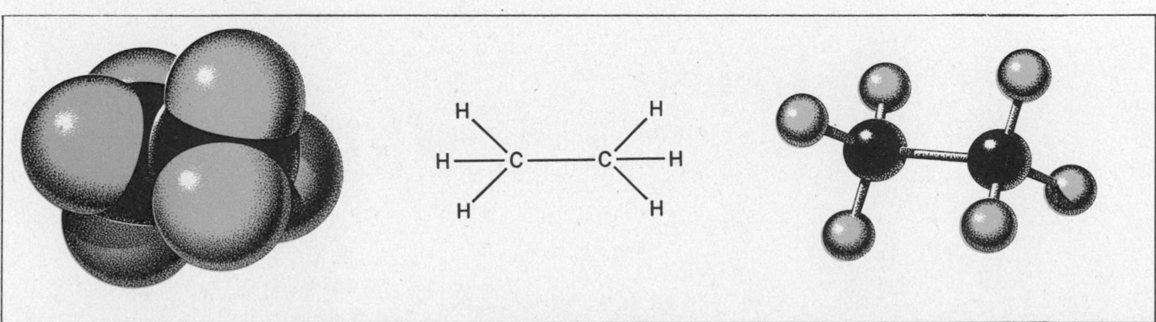

From percentage composition data, we can only derive the simplest formula for a compound. Further experimental information or data on molecular mass is needed to determine the true formula.

EXAMPLE

Find the simplest formula for the gaseous compound that contains 63.6% nitrogen and 36.4% oxygen. (N = 14.0 g/mol (grams per mole); O = 16.0 g/mol)

SOLUTION

1. *You must convert the percentages to mass, assume a 100-g sample, and divide by the atomic mass. That will determine the number of moles of each of the combined elements.*

$$\text{Moles of nitrogen atoms} = \frac{63.6\ \cancel{g}}{14.0\ \cancel{g}/\text{mol}} = 4.54\ \text{mol}$$

$$\text{Moles of oxygen atoms} = \frac{36.4\ \cancel{g}}{16.0\ \cancel{g}/\text{mol}} = 2.28\ \text{mol}$$

2. *Next you must determine the mole ratio of the different types of atoms in the compound. To do that, divide the number of moles of each element present by the smallest number of moles calculated.*

$$\text{Mole ratio for nitrogen: } \frac{4.54\ \cancel{\text{mol}}}{2.28\ \cancel{\text{mol}}} = 1.99$$

$$\text{Mole ratio for oxygen: } \frac{2.28\ \cancel{\text{mol}}}{2.28\ \cancel{\text{mol}}} = 1.00$$

3. *Finally, establish the simplest formula, recognizing the indivisibility of atoms.*
From step **2,** *the formula for this oxide of nitrogen is* N_2O, *using integral numbers of atoms.*

EXAMPLE

Find the simplest formula for the oxide of arsenic that contains 75.8% arsenic. (As = 74.9 g/mol)

SOLUTION

1. $\text{Moles of arsenic atoms} = \dfrac{75.8\ \cancel{g}}{74.9\ \cancel{g}/\text{mol}} = 1.01\ \text{mol}$

$$\text{Moles of oxygen atoms} = \frac{24.2 \text{ g}}{16.0 \text{ g/mol}} = 1.51 \text{ mol}$$

2. $$\text{Mole ratio for arsenic: } \frac{1.01 \text{ mol}}{1.01 \text{ mol}} = 1.00$$

$$\text{Mole ratio for oxygen: } \frac{1.51 \text{ mol}}{1.01 \text{ mol}} = 1.50$$

3. *From step* **2**, *the formula for this oxide of arsenic is* $As_{1.00}O_{1.50}$, *which, after multiplying by 2, becomes the whole-number ratio* As_2O_3.

EXAMPLE

What is the formula of a compound that contains 92.23% carbon and 7.77% hydrogen? (C = 12.0 g/mol; H = 1.01 g/mol)

SOLUTION

1. *Determine the simplest formula for the compound. The percentage of carbon (92.23) and the percentage of hydrogen (7.77) total 100. Therefore, a 100-g sample contains 92.23 g of carbon and 7.77 g of hydrogen.*

2. $$\text{Moles of carbon atoms} = \frac{92.23 \text{ g}}{12.0 \text{ g/mol}} = 7.69 \text{ mol}$$

$$\text{Moles of hydrogen atoms} = \frac{7.77 \text{g}}{1.01 \text{ g/mol}} = 7.69 \text{ mol}$$

$$\text{Mole ratio for carbon: } \frac{7.69 \text{ mol}}{7.69 \text{ mol}} = 1.00$$

$$\text{Mole ratio for hydrogen: } \frac{7.69 \text{ mol}}{7.69 \text{ mol}} = 1.00$$

3. *The simplest formula is* $C_{1.00}H_{1.00}$, *or CH. (Remember that the subscript 1 is never used.)*

Taking this problem one step further:

If 2.20 g of the vapor of CH occup 628 ml at STP (Standard Temperature and air Pressure, or 0°C and 760 Torr), what is its true molecular mass (M) and its true formula? (Remember, the molar volume is 22.4 l/mol at 0°C and 760 Torr).

1. 628 ml = .628 l

$$M = \frac{2.20 \text{ g}}{.628 \text{ l}} \times 22.4 \text{ l/mol} = 78.46 \text{ g/mol}$$

2. *Determine the molecular mass corresponding to the simplest formula,* M_{CH}.

$$C = 12.0 \text{ g/mol}$$
$$H = 1.01 \text{ g/mol}$$
$$M_{CH} = 13.0 \text{ g/mol}$$

3. *Compare the approximate true molecular mass (M) with that based on the simplest formula* (M_{CH})*, and arrive at the true formula. This is done by dividing the true molecular mass (M) by the molecular mass based on the simplest formula of this compound* (M_{CH}).

$$M = 78.46 \text{ g/mol} \qquad M_{CH} = 13.0 \text{ g/mol}$$

M is six times greater than M_{CH}*; therefore, the true formula for this hydrocarbon (a compound consisting of only carbon and hydrogen) is* $(CH)_6$ *or, as it usually appears,* C_6H_6 *(benzene).*

When a mixture of powdered iron, Fe, and sulfur, S_8, is heated, a reaction occurs. The product of the reaction is a black, solid compound called iron(II) sulfide. Analysis of the compound shows that it is composed of 63.5 percent iron and 36.5 percent sulfur. Knowing this, we can determine the formula for iron(II) sulfide. Assuming a 100-gram sample, we calculate the number of moles of atoms of each element present. A mole of Fe weighs 55.85 grams, and a mole of sulfur weighs 32.07 grams.

$$\text{Moles of iron atoms} = \frac{63.5 \not{g}}{55.85 \not{g}/\text{mol}} = 1.14 \text{ mol}$$

$$\text{Moles of sulfur atoms} = \frac{36.5 \not{g}}{32.07 \not{g}/\text{mol}} = 1.14 \text{ mol}$$

The numbers of moles of iron atoms and sulfur atoms in iron(II) sulfide are in the ratio of 1.14:1.14, or 1:1. Therefore, the experimentally determined simplest formula for iron(II) sulfide is FeS.

4–4 · Determining the mass of a mole of a compound from its formula · What does the formula FeS mean quantitatively? It tells us that in one mole of iron(II) sulfide, there are one mole of iron atoms and one mole of sulfur atoms. We know the mass of one mole of iron atoms and the mass of one mole of sulfur atoms. Therefore, FeS must represent 87.92 grams

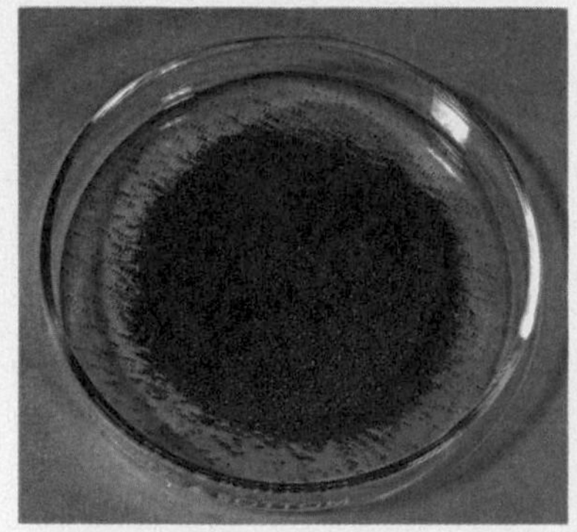

FIGURE 4–2 · *Powdered iron (left) and sulfur (center) form iron sulfide (right) when reacted together.*

(55.85 g + 32.07 g) of iron(II) sulfide. Just as we discovered with S_8, the mass of a mole of molecules is the sum of the masses of the total number of moles of atoms. Therefore, the formula for a compound allows us to calculate the mass of a mole of that compound easily.

EXAMPLE

What is the mass of one mole of potassium dichromate, $K_2Cr_2O_7$?

SOLUTION

1. *From Table 3–1, page 49, determine the mass per mole of atoms for each element in the compound.*
2. *Multiply the mass of a mole of each element by the number of moles of that element present in one mole of the compound.*
3. *Total all the masses.*

For K_2, $2 \times K = 2 \times 39.102$ g/mol = 78.204 g/mol

For Cr_2, $2 \times Cr = 2 \times 51.996$ g/mol = 103.992 g/mol

For O_7, $7 \times O = 7 \times 15.999$ g/mol = 111.993 g/mol

$K_2Cr_2O_7$ = 294.189 g/mol

EXERCISE

Calculate the mass of 1 mole of the following compounds.

1. K_2SO_4 (potassium sulfate)
2. NH_4OH (ammonium hydroxide)
3. $Al_2(SO_4)_3$ (aluminum sulfate)

REVIEW IT NOW

1 What does a formula tells us about a compound?
2 What do the subscripts tell us?
3 How can we use percentage composition to determine the simplest formula for a compound?

CHEMICAL EQUATIONS

4–5 · Chemical equations and what they mean · We have seen how chemical formulas are experimentally determined. Now we know that chemical symbols and formulas represent a fixed number of atoms. Or in other words, they represent a mole or a multiple of a mole (or a fixed volume). We can use the symbols and formulas to describe chemical reactions.

The **chemical equation** is the symbolic language used to describe a chemical reaction. The word *equation* itself is a clue to the proper writing of chemical equations. Something must be equal in a chemical reaction. Let us consider the reaction between powdered iron, Fe, and sulfur, S_8, to find the equality we seek. The reaction, written out is; Iron reacts with sulfur to form iron(II) sulfide. (The (II) indicates something about the nature of the compound formed. Do not be concerned with this now, we will discuss it later.)

It can be written more simply.

$$\text{Iron} + \text{sulfur} \rightarrow \text{iron(II) sulfide}$$

Or it can be stated even more simply.

$$Fe + S_8 \rightarrow FeS$$

Do you notice anything wrong with this last equation? As written, it states that eight moles of elemental sulfur atoms react to produce only one mole of combined sulfur atoms. That does not agree with the Law of the Conservation of Matter, which we discussed earlier. How can eight moles of elemental sulfur atoms (256.56 g) produce only one mole (32.07 g) of combined sulfur? We must account for the remaining atoms of sulfur. Therefore, the symbolic description might be changed to read in this way.

$$Fe + S_8 \rightarrow FeS_8$$

It might seem easy to write $Fe + S_8 \rightarrow FeS_8$. But this is incorrect. The formula for iron(II) sulfide is FeS. Remember that we determined that fact from mass composition data. The formula FeS may not be tampered with. It is an experimental fact!

Another possible way to write the formula is $Fe + S_8 \rightarrow 8FeS$. Now we have created eight moles of combined iron atoms, or 446.80 grams, from only one mole of elemental iron, or 55.85 grams. Again, this is not possible. Therefore, the symbolic picture must be altered again. It now reads as follows:

$$8Fe + S_8 \rightarrow 8FeS$$

This states that eight moles of iron atoms combine with eight moles of sulfur atoms (one mole of molecular sulfur) to form eight moles of iron(II) sulfide. In other words, the number of reacting iron atoms is equal to the number of combined iron atoms. Also, the number of reacting sulfur atoms is equal to the number of combined sulfur atoms. We have discovered the fundamental equality we sought. Atoms are equal in number

FIGURE 4–3 · *The chemical equation is the fundamental tool for communicating chemical information. That is so in graduate education in chemistry, in research laboratories, and in industry, just as it is in this book. The chemical formula pictured here shows the steps in the formation of the antibiotic, Terramycin.*

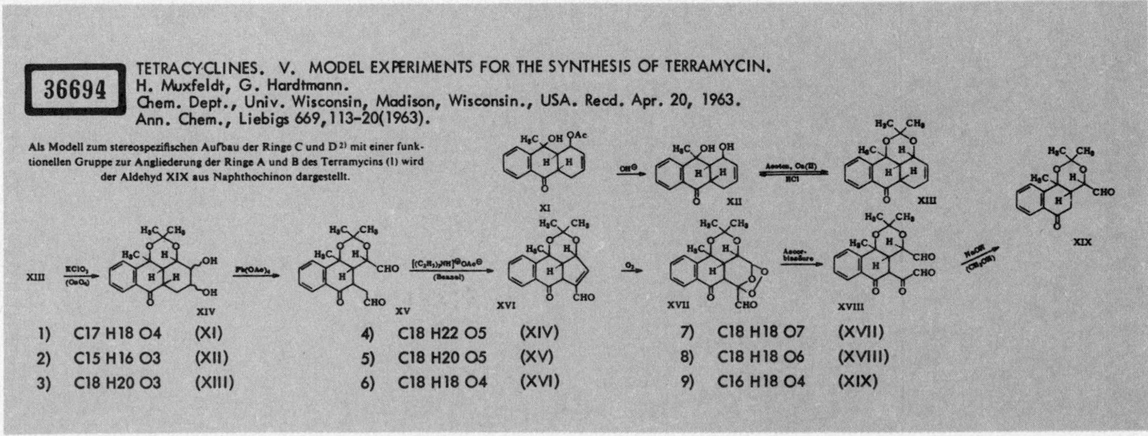

36694 TETRACYCLINES. V. MODEL EXPERIMENTS FOR THE SYNTHESIS OF TERRAMYCIN.
H. Muxfeldt, G. Hardtmann.
Chem. Dept., Univ. Wisconsin, Madison, Wisconsin., USA. Recd. Apr. 20, 1963.
Ann. Chem., Liebigs 669,113-20(1963).

Als Modell zum stereospezifischen Aufbau der Ringe C und D 2) mit einer funktionellen Gruppe zur Angliederung der Ringe A und B des Terramycins (I) wird der Aldehyd XIX aus Naphthochinon dargestellt.

1)	C17 H18 O4	(XI)	4)	C18 H22 O5	(XIV)	7)	C18 H18 O7	(XVII)
2)	C15 H16 O3	(XII)	5)	C18 H20 O5	(XV)	8)	C18 H18 O6	(XVIII)
3)	C18 H20 O3	(XIII)	6)	C18 H18 O4	(XVI)	9)	C16 H18 O4	(XIX)

and type before and after a reaction. Atoms are conserved. This fact is another statement of the Law of the Conservation of Matter.

This is the last symbolic representation we wrote.

$$8Fe + S_8 \rightarrow 8FeS$$

It is a **balanced** chemical equation. It can also be written:

$$8Fe + S_8 = 8FeS$$

It may be useful here to consider some details concerning this and all other equations. The numeral 8 that appears before the symbol Fe and before the formula FeS is called a **coefficient.** (There is an analogy between chemical and algebraic equations.) Remember that the 8 appearing after S is called a subscript. Writing a correct, balanced chemical equation involves changing coefficients. But to preserve the Law of Definite Composition, we do not change subscripts.

4–6 · Balanced chemical equations, how they are written · Writing a balanced chemical equation for a chemical reaction can be explained by two simple rules.

1. *Know the correct symbols and formulas for reactants and products.*
2. *Observe the Law of the Conservation of Matter by conserving atoms. (The total number of each kind of atom of the reactant on the left side of the equation must balance or equal the number of those atoms on the right side representing the product.)*

EXAMPLE

When the compound potassium chlorate is heated, it decomposes into potassium chloride and oxygen gas. Write the balanced chemical equation for this reaction.

SOLUTION

1. *The formulas for the reactants and products of the reaction are the following.*

$$KClO_3 = \text{potassium chlorate}$$
$$KCl = \text{potassium chloride}$$
$$O_2 = \text{oxygen gas}$$

TABLE 4–1 · Important Common Valences

	METALS		NONMETALS AND ACID RADICALS	
MONOVALENT (I)	Ammonium	(NH_4)	Acetate (from acetic acid)	(CH_3COO)
	Hydrogen	H	Bromine (*in* bromides)	Br
	Copper (I) or cuprous	Cu	Chlorate (from chloric acid)	(ClO_3)
	Lithium	Li	Chlorine (*in* chlorides)	Cl
	Potassium	K	Cyanide (from hydrocyanic acid)	CN
	Silver	Ag	Dihydrogen phosphate (from phosphoric acid)	(H_2PO_4)
	Sodium	Na	Fluorine (*in* fluorides)	F
			Hydrogen carbonate (from carbonic acid, also called bicarbonate)	(HCO_3)
			Hydrogen sulfate (from sulfuric acid, also called bisulfate)	(HSO_4)
			Hydroxyl [from water as H(OH)]	(OH)
			Iodine (*in* iodides)	I
			Nitrate (from nitric acid)	(NO_3)
			Nitrite (from nitrous acid)	(NO_2)
			Permanganate (from permanganic acid)	(MnO_4)
DIVALENT (II)	Barium	Ba	Carbonate (from carbonic acid)	(CO_3)
	Calcium	Ca	Chromate (from chromic acid)	(CrO_4)
	Copper(II) or cupric	Cu	Dichromate (from dichromic acid)	(Cr_2O_7)
	Iron(II) or ferrous	Fe	Monohydrogen phosphate (from phosphoric acid)	(HPO_4)
	Lead(II) or plumbous	Pb	Oxalate (from oxalic acid)	(OOCCOO)
	Magnesium	Mg	Oxygen (*in* oxides)	O
	Mercury(I) or mercurous	(Hg_2)*	Oxygen (*in* peroxides)	(O_2)
	Mercury(II) or mercuric	Hg	Sulfate (from sulfuric acid)	(SO_4)
	Tin(II) or stannous	Sn	Sulfite (from sulfurous acid)	(SO_3)
	Zinc	Zn	Sulfur (*in* sulfides)	(S)
TRIVALENT (III)	Aluminum	Al	Arsenate (from arsenic acid)	(AsO_4)
	Antimony(III)	Sb	Nitrogen (*in* nitrides)	N
	Arsenic(III)	As	Phosphate (from phosphoric acid)	(PO_4)
	Chromium(III)	Cr	Phosphorus (*in* phosphides)	P
	Iron(III) or ferric	Fe		

*Mercury(I) compounds contain two mercury atoms acting together with a valence of 2 – e.g., mercury(I) chloride, Hg_2Cl_2; mercury(I) nitrate, $Hg_2(NO_3)_2$; and mercury(I) chromate, Hg_2CrO_4. The corresponding mercury(II) compounds are $HgCl_2$, $Hg(NO_3)_2$, and $HgCrO_4$.

2. *The reaction may be written this way.*

$$KClO_3 \rightarrow KCl + O_2$$

The number of potassium and chlorine atoms are equal on both sides. In other words, the equation is balanced with respect to potassium and chlorine. But there are three moles of oxygen atoms as reactants and only two moles of oxygen as product. The least common multiple of 3 and 2 is 6. Therefore, multiply the reactant oxygen atoms by 2 and the product oxygen atoms by 3.

$$2KClO_3 \rightarrow KCl + 3O_2$$

Now the oxygen atoms are balanced. But there is an imbalance between the reactant potassium and chlorine atoms and the product potassium and chlorine atoms.
This is easily solved by multiplying the product KCl by 2.

$$2KClO_3 \rightarrow 2KCl + 3O_2$$

Would it also be correct to write the balanced equation in the following manner?

$$KClO_3 \rightarrow KCl + 1.5\ O_2$$

Certainly! Remember that the coefficients merely indicate the ratio between the moles of the reactants and the moles of the products. 1.5 moles of oxygen is indicated here, not 1.5 oxygen molecules. If you examine the two equations, you will find that the ratios are the same. However, chemical equations are written only with integral coefficients.

EXAMPLE

Write the balanced chemical equation for the complete combustion of benzene in air that forms carbon dioxide and water vapor.

SOLUTION

1. *The following are the formulas for the reactants and products.*

$$C_6H_6 = \text{benzene}$$
$$O_2 = \text{oxygen gas}$$
$$CO_2 = \text{carbon dioxide}$$
$$H_2O = \text{water vapor}$$

2. The reaction is written:

$$C_6H_6 + O_2 \rightarrow CO_2 + H_2O$$

There are six moles of carbon atoms, C_6, and six moles of hydrogen atoms, H_6, present in one mole of the reactant benzene, C_6H_6. Therefore, there must be six moles of carbon dioxide to account for the six moles of carbon atoms. Also, there must be three moles of water vapor in order to account for the six moles of hydrogen atoms.

$$C_6H_6 + O_2 \rightarrow 6CO_2 + 3H_2O$$

For six moles of carbon dioxide and three moles of water vapor to form, a total of fifteen moles of oxygen atoms as reactants are required. There are twelve moles of oxygen atoms in $6CO_2$ and three moles of oxygen atoms in $3H_2O$. Since elemental oxygen is diatomic, we write the following equation.

$$C_6H_6 + 15/2O_2 = 6CO_2 + 3H_2O$$

Or we can write it in this way.

$$C_6H_6 + 7.50O_2 = 6CO_2 + 3H_2O$$

Then we multiply through by 2.

$$2C_6H_6 + 15O_2 = 12CO_2 + 6H_2O$$

4–7 · Making chemical equations more informative · A great amount of information is communicated by chemical equations. Before going any further in this discussion, let's add to our understanding of chemical equations with the following discussion.

Consider again each of the two balanced chemical equations that were just studied in detail.

$$2KClO_3 = 2KCl + 3O_2$$

and

$$C_6H_6 + 7.50\ O_2 = 6CO_2 + 3H_2O$$

In addition to the information that the equations provide, it is also helpful to know the physical state of each reactant and product. Is potassium chlorate ($KClO_3$) a solid, a liquid, or a gas? What about potassium chloride (KCl) and benzene (C_6H_6)? From now on, each chemical equation given in this book will indicate the physical state of the chemical substances involved in chemical reactions. This will become very important to us in later chapters.

Immediately following each symbol or formula in a chemical equation will be one of the following abbreviations to indicate the physical state of a given substance.

(s) = *solid*
(l) = *liquid*
(g) = *gas or vapor*
(aq) = *aqueous (water) solution*

Thus, the two chemical equations we have been studying can be rewritten.

$$2KClO_3(s) = 2KCl(s) + 3O_2(g)$$

and

$$C_6H_6(l) + 7.50\ O_2(g) = 6CO_2(g) + 3H_2O(g)$$

EXERCISE

Before proceeding, a little practice in equation balancing will be useful. Try to balance the following equations.

1. $P_4(s) + O_2(g) \rightarrow P_4O_{10}(s)$
2. $Zn(s) + HCl(aq) \rightarrow ZnCl_2(aq) + H_2(g)$
3. $SiO_2(s) + C(s) \rightarrow SiC(s) + CO(g)$
4. $MgO(s) + H_2SO_4(aq) \rightarrow MgSO_4(aq) + H_2O(l)$
5. $Cu(s) + AgNO_3(aq) \rightarrow Cu(NO_3)_2(aq) + Ag(s)$
6. $C_2H_5OH(l) + O_2(g) \rightarrow CO_2(g) + H_2O(g)$
7. $BaCl_2(aq) + Na_2SO_4(aq) \rightarrow BaSO_4(s) + NaCl(aq)$
8. $HNO_3(aq) + Al(OH)_3(s) \rightarrow Al(NO_3)_3(aq) + HOH(l)$

4–8 · The quantitative meaning of chemical equations · We have seen that chemical symbols and formulas tell us "how much." Chemical equations based on those symbols and formulas, therefore, must also take on a precise quantitative meaning.

Suppose we again consider the reaction of the decomposition of potassium chlorate.

$$2KClO_3(s) = 2KCl(s) + 3O_2(g)$$

What does the equation tell us? Exactly two moles of potassium chlorate will decompose to yield exactly two moles of potassium chloride and exactly three moles of oxygen. But one mole of $KClO_3$ is 122.56 grams of that compound. One mole of KCl is 74.56 grams of that compound. And one mole of O_2 is 32.00 grams. Recall from Chapter 3 that one mole of any gas has a molar volume of 22.4 liters at STP (Standard Temperature and Pressure).

Thus, we can interpret the equation in a number of ways.

$$2KClO_3(s) = 2KCl(s) + 3O_2(g)$$

$$2 \text{ moles} \rightarrow 2 \text{ moles} + 3 \text{ moles}$$

(Note that there is no law of the conservation of moles.)

or

$$2 \times 122.56 \text{ g} \rightarrow 2 \times 74.56 \text{ g} + 3 \times 32.00 \text{ g}$$

$$245.12 \text{ g} \rightarrow 149.12 \text{ g} + 96.00 \text{ g}$$

$$245.12 \text{ g} = 245.12 \text{ g}$$

(Note, though, that the Law of the Conservation of Matter always holds.)

or

$$245.12 \text{ g} \rightarrow 149.12 \text{ g} + 3 \times 22.4 \text{ l at STP}$$

$$245.12 \text{ g} \rightarrow 149.12 \text{ g} + 67.2 \text{ l}$$

Let us take another example. A similar analysis of the reaction for the complete combustion of benzene follows.

$$C_6H_6(l) + 7.50\ O_2(g) \rightarrow 6CO_2(g) + 3H_2O(g)$$

$$1 \text{ mole} + 7.50 \text{ moles} \rightarrow 6 \text{ moles} + 3 \text{ moles}$$

or

$$78.12 \text{ g} + 7.50 \times 32.00 \text{ g} \rightarrow 6 \times 44.01 \text{ g} + 3 \times 18.02 \text{ g}$$

$$78.12 \text{ g} + 240.00 \text{ g} \rightarrow 264.06 \text{ g} + 54.06 \text{ g}$$

$$318.12 \text{ g} = 318.12 \text{ g}$$

or

$$78.12 \text{ g} + 7.50 \times 22.4 \text{ l} \rightarrow 6 \times 22.4 \text{ l} + 3 \times 22.4 \text{ l at STP}$$

$$78.12 \text{ g} + 168 \text{ l} \rightarrow 134 \text{ l} + 67.2 \text{ l at STP}$$

or

$$78.12 \text{ g} + 7.50 \text{ volumes} \rightarrow 6 \text{ volumes} + 3 \text{ volumes}$$

(Note when O_2, CO_2, and H_2O are all in the gaseous state, under the same conditions)

The detailed study just made on two different chemical equations demonstrates that chemical equations show quantitative relationships between the chemical reactants and products involved. These quantitative relationships are called **stoichiometric relationships.** Stoichiometric relationships can be divided into three classes: (1) mass–mass, (2) mass–volume, and (3) volume–volume. However, if the mole concept is used to solve stoichiometric problems, all three classes of problems are solved in a similar manner.

4–9 · Mass–mass problems · We will consider each type of stoichiometric problem in detail, but they all start in the same way.

1. *Write the correct, balanced chemical equation to establish the mole ratio for the substances involved in the problem.*
2. *Convert the given information (grams, volumes) into moles.*

EXAMPLE

What mass of water vapor can be produced from 1.60 g of oxygen gas? (O_2 = 32.0 g/mol; H_2O = 18.0 g/mol)

SOLUTION

1. *Write the balanced equation;* $2H_2(g) + O_2(g) = 2H_2O(g)$. *The mole ratio of* O_2 *to* H_2O *is 1:2; for every mole, fraction of a mole, or multiple of a mole of* O_2 *used, there will be twice as many moles of* H_2O *produced.*
2. *Determine the actual number of moles of oxygen in 1.60 g* $O_2(g)$. *(Number of moles, n = grams of substance per g/mol of substance.)*
   $n_{O_2} = 1.60 \text{ g}/32.0 \text{ g/mole} = 0.050 \text{ mol} = 5.00 \times 10^{-2} \text{ mol}$
3. *The mole ratio of* O_2:H_2O *is 1:2, or* $n_{H_2O} = 2n_{O_2}$. *Therefore,* 5.00×10^{-2} *m* O_2 *will produce* $2(5.00 \times 10^{-2})$ *mol* H_2O, *or* $n_{H_2O} = 1.00 \times 10^{-1}$ *mol.*
4. *Convert the mole notation to grams.*

$$\cancel{\text{Moles}} \times \text{grams}/\cancel{\text{mole}} = \text{grams}$$

$$1.00 \times 10^{-1}\ \cancel{m} \times 18.0\ \text{g}/\cancel{m} = 1.80\ \text{g}\ H_2O(g)$$

From 1.60 g of oxygen gas, 1.80 g of water vapor will be produced. Perhaps a road map of our operation will be helpful here. Follow and study each numbered step until the reasoning behind the steps becomes clear to you.

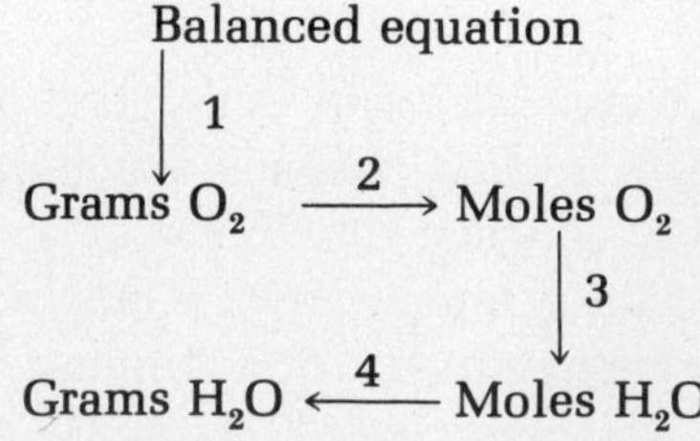

Since we are using the *Mole Concept,* we can use another method to work our mass–mass problems. This method is based on setting up the problem so that units can be cancelled.

It is often called the "Dimensional Analysis" method. This is especially convenient if you use a slide rule or calculator, since it sets up the problem as a continuous mathematical operation. Let's illustrate by repeating the same example.

What mass of water vapor will be produced from 1.60 g of oxygen gas? (O_2 = 32.0 g/mol; H_2O = 18.0 g/mol)

1. *Since we are given 1.60 g oxygen gas, we must convert this to moles of oxygen gas. We will set up an expression where "g" units cancel.*

$$1.60\ \cancel{g\,O_2} \times \frac{1 \text{ mole } O_2}{32.0\ \cancel{g\,O_2}}$$

2. *Next we must convert* moles O_2 *to* moles H_2O. *Our equation tells us that 1 mole of O_2 produces 2 moles H_2O. We will add this to our expression, making sure it is set up so that the "mole O_2" label cancels.*

$$1.60\ \cancel{g\,O_2} \times \frac{1\ \cancel{\text{mole } O_2}}{32.0\ \cancel{g\,O_2}} \times \frac{2 \text{ moles } H_2O}{1\ \cancel{\text{mole } O_2}}$$

3. *Now, following the same road map previously established, we must convert* moles H_2O *to* grams H_2O, *again being sure that units cancel.*

$$1.60\ \cancel{g\,O_2} \times \frac{1\ \cancel{\text{mole } O_2}}{32.0\ \cancel{g\,O_2}} \times \frac{2\ \cancel{\text{moles } H_2O}}{1\ \cancel{\text{mole } O_2}} \times \frac{18.0 \text{ g } H_2O}{1\ \cancel{\text{mole } H_2O}}$$

4. *Since the problem asked for an answer in "mass of water" and that is the final label in our expression, we know that all the necessary information is in our mathematical expression.*
5. *Now with a slide rule or a calculator, we can very easily perform the entire calculation by successively multiplying and dividing.*

$$1.60\ \cancel{g\,O_2} \times \frac{1\ \cancel{\text{mole } O_2}}{32.0\ \cancel{g\,O_2}} \times \frac{2\ \cancel{\text{moles } H_2O}}{1\ \cancel{\text{mole } O_2}} \times \frac{18.0 \text{ g } H_2O}{1\ \cancel{\text{mole } H_2O}} = 1.80 \text{ g } H_2O$$

4–10 · Mass–volume problem calculations · In any problem involving the measurement of the volume of a gas, a very important factor must be considered. You will learn in Chapter 6 that the conditions of temperature and pressure should be specified. For any condition other than 0°C and 760 Torr, STP (standard temperature and pressure), a calculation involving the Ideal Gas Law will usually be necessary. Until Chapter 5, all problems will be solved for STP conditions.

EXAMPLE

What volume of dry oxygen gas that is measured at STP will be required to react completely with 6.06 g H_2? ($H_2 = 2.02$ g/mol)

SOLUTION

This time, suppose we set up our road map first. Where are we going, and how do we get there?

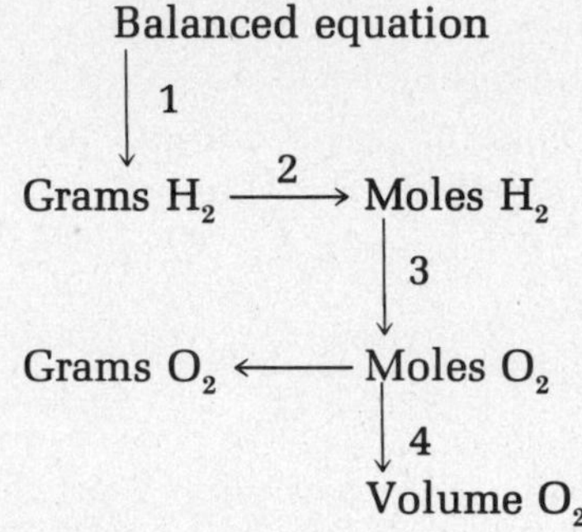

Notice that our map shows that we want to arrive at a volume of O_2 this time, and bypass "grams O_2."

1. *Write the correct, balanced chemical equation.*

$$2H_2(g) + O_2(g) \rightarrow 2H_2O(g)$$

2. *Convert grams H_2 to moles H_2.*

$$n_{H_2} = 6.06\ \text{g}/2.02\ \text{g/mol} = 3.00\ \text{mol}$$

3. *The mole ratio $n_{H2}:n_{O2} = 2:1$.*
   Therefore, for every 3.00 mol H_2, there must be half as many, or 1.50, mol O_2.

4. *Convert the mole notation to liters at STP. (The molar volume of any gas at STP is 22.4 l.)*
   Moles × Liters/mole = Liters

$$1.50\ \cancel{\text{mol}}\ O_2 \times 22.4\ \text{l}/\cancel{\text{mol}} = 33.6\ \text{l of oxygen gas at STP}$$

At STP 33.6 l O_2 will be required to react with 6.06 g H_2.
By again following our road map, we can solve the same mass–volume problem by using our method of canceling units.

1. *Convert grams H_2 to moles H_2.*

$$6.06\ \cancel{g\,H_2} \times \frac{1\ \text{mol}\ H_2}{2.02\ \cancel{g\,H_2}}$$

2. *Convert moles H_2 to moles O_2.*

$$6.06\ \cancel{g\,H_2} \times \frac{1\ \cancel{\text{mol}\ H_2}}{2.02\ \cancel{g\,H_2}} \times \frac{1\ \text{mol}\ O_2}{2\ \cancel{\text{mol}\ H_2}}$$

3. *Convert moles O_2 to volume O_2, asked for in the problem.*

$$6.06\ \cancel{g\,H_2} \times \frac{1\ \cancel{\text{mol}\ H_2}}{2.02\ \cancel{g\,H_2}} \times \frac{1\ \cancel{\text{mol}\ O_2}}{2\ \cancel{\text{moles}\ H_2}} \times \frac{22.4\ \text{l}\ O_2\ (\text{STP})}{1\ \cancel{\text{mol}\ O_2}}$$

4. *Complete the calculation, in one continuous operation.*

$$6.06\ \cancel{g\,H_2} \times \frac{1\ \cancel{\text{mol}\ H_2}}{2.02\ \cancel{g\,H_2}} \times \frac{1\ \cancel{\text{mol}\ O_2}}{2\ \cancel{\text{moles}\ H_2}} \times \frac{22.4\ \text{l}\ O_2\ (\text{STP})}{1\ \cancel{\text{mol}\ O_2}} = 33.6\ \text{l}\ O_2\ (\text{STP})$$

4–11 · Volume–volume problems · The stoichiometric calculations that involve volumes alone are the simplest of all. Avogadro's hypothesis states that under the same conditions of temperature and pressure, equal volumes of gases contain equal numbers of molecules. Therefore, the coefficients indicating the molar ratios for each gaseous substance in a chemical equation can be read directly as a general volume.

Amedeo Avogadro *(1776–1856, Italian). Avogadro was active in civil affairs as well as in teaching. Like Lavoisier, he held many public offices. He became involved with public instruction, meterology, weights and measures, and national statistics.*

EXAMPLE

What volume of oxygen will react with 11.2 l of hydrogen to form water vapor?

SOLUTION

1. *Write the correct, balanced chemical equation.*

$$2H_2(g) + O_2(g) \rightarrow 2H_2O(g)$$

2. *The ratio of the volumes of hydrogen, oxygen, and water vapor are simply 2:1:2, or the mole ratios. Our road map tells us the following.*

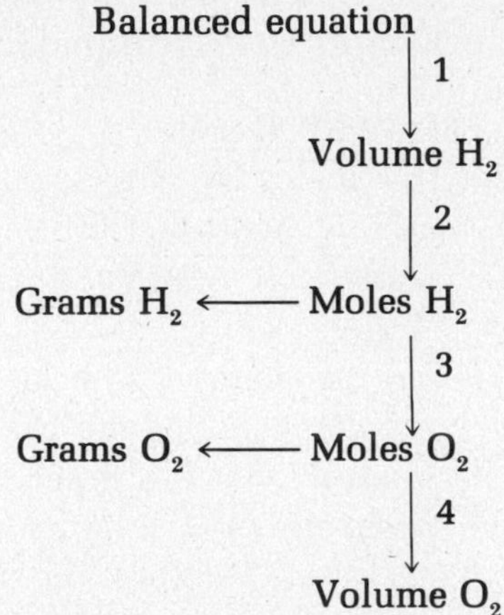

Therefore, the volume of H_2 to O_2 is 2:1.

$$V_{O_2} = 0.50\ V_{H_2}$$
$$= 0.50\ (11.2\ l)$$
$$= 5.60\ l$$

Under the same conditions of temperature and pressure, 5.60 l of oxygen gas will react with 11.2 l of hydrogen. If we set up the same problem to cancel labels, we would have the following.

1. *Convert liters H_2 to moles H_2.*
2. *Convert moles H_2 to moles O_2.*
3. *Convert moles O_2 to liters O_2.*

or,

$$11.2\ \cancel{l\,H_2} \times \frac{1\ \cancel{mol\ H_2}}{22.4\ \cancel{l\,H_2}} \times \frac{1\ \cancel{mol\ O_2}}{2\ \cancel{moles\ H_2}} \times \frac{22.4\ l\ O_2}{1\ \cancel{mol\ O_2}} = 5.60\ l\ O_2$$

Of course, it is often easy to cancel numbers, making such a calculation very simple.

Study the typical problems on the preceding pages. After you thoroughly understand the mechanism we have used, try another set of similar problems. You may find it helpful to construct your road map with arrows directing you to the quantity that you are asked to determine. Remember, regardless of where your road map directs you, you must go through "moles" to get there!

EXERCISE

1. *What mass of oxygen gas will be produced from the decomposition of 1.226 g $KClO_3$? ($KClO_3$ = 122.6 g/mol)*
2. *What volume of dry oxygen gas (measured at STP) will be produced from the decomposition of 1.226 g $KClO_3$?*
3. *What volume of oxygen gas will be required to produce 44.8 l of carbon dioxide gas, according to the following equation for the combustion of methane gas (CH_4)? (The equation must first be balanced!)*

$$CH_4\,(g) + O_2\,(g) \rightarrow CO_2\,(g) + H_2O(g)$$

REVIEW IT NOW

1. What is a chemical equation?
2. What does the coefficient indicate?
3. What does a subscript tell us?
4. State two simple rules to follow when balancing equations.
5. What can we do to change a fraction of a mole (for example, 1.50 CO_2) to a whole number?

SUMMARY

A system of symbols and formulas is necessary for chemists to communicate scientific knowledge. Such a system was developed by Jöns Berzelius. In the system, elements are represented by symbols, and compounds are represented by formulas. The formula tells the chemist what atoms are in the compound and how many atoms of each element are present.

In using formulas to demonstrate a chemical reaction, a ratio of moles of reacting substances is expressed. This allows the chemist to determine the simplest formula for a compound, if the percent of composition is known. Also, the mass of a mole of a compound can be determined from its formula. In writing chemical equations, coefficients are used to show the ratio between moles of reactants and moles of products. To make equations even more informative, we indicate if the various substances involved are a gas (g), a solid (s), or a liquid (l).

With this information, it is easy to convert the mass of one reactant compound or element into the mass of a product compound or element. Also, volumes can be converted to mass, and mass to volumes. In order to carry out such calculations, it is necessary to convert mass or volume to moles. This is similar to following a road map for the purpose of reaching a specific destination.

REVIEW QUESTIONS

1 What does the symbol Zn mean in terms of each of the following?
   a. Number of atoms of Zn
   b. Number of grams of Zn
   c. Number of moles of Zn

2 Why do we say that Zn is a "symbol," but P_4 is a "formula"?

3 **a.** How many moles of *molecules* are represented in the formula P_4?
   b. How many moles of *atoms* are represented in the formula P_4?

4 Consider the formula for sucrose (table sugar), $C_{12}H_{22}O_{11}$. What does this formula tell you in regard to the following?
   a. Types of atoms present
   b. Moles of each type of atom present
   c. Moles of molecules present
   d. Arrangement of the atoms within the molecules
   e. Weight in grams of one mole of sugar molecules

5 When the sucrose mentioned in question **4** is used in the body, it reacts with O_2 to produce energy. The products are CO_2 and water. Express this reaction as a balanced equation.

6 Find the simplest formula for a bromide of calcium if the compound contains 20.0% calcium and 80.0% bromine. (Ca = 40 g/mol; Br = 80 g/mol)

7 A certain compound contains 53.73% iron (Fe) and 46.27% sulfur.
   a. Determine the simplest formula for this compound.
   b. How do you know that your answer in **a** represents the simplest formula?

8 Using the relative atomic weights listed in Table 3 – 1, determine the mass in grams of each of the following.
   a. 1.00 mole of $Na_2S_2O_3$
   b. 0.50 mole of CO_2
   c. 1.00×10^{-3} mole of $C_{254}H_{377}N_{65}O_{75}S_6$
   d. 3.60 moles of $Pb(NO_3)_2$

9 Balance the following chemical equations.
   a. $As_4(s) + O_2(g) \rightarrow As_4O_6(s)$
   b. $H_2S(g) + O_2(g) \rightarrow H_2O(g) + SO_2(g)$
   c. $Al_2O_3(s) + HCl(aq) \rightarrow AlCl_3(aq) + H_2O(l)$
   d. $Na(s) + H_2O(l) \rightarrow NaOH(aq) + H_2(g)$
   e. $AgNO_3(aq) + MgCl_2(aq) \rightarrow AgCl(s) + Mg(NO_3)_2(aq)$
   f. $CaCO_3(s) \rightarrow CaO(s) + CO_2(g)$

g. $HCl(aq) + NaOH(aq) \rightarrow H_2O(l) + NaCl(aq)$
h. $Al(s) + Fe_2O_3(s) \rightarrow Al_2O_3(s) + Fe(s)$
i. $NaNO_3(s) \rightarrow NaNO_2(s) + O_2(g)$
j. $Ca(OH)_2(aq) + CO_2(g) \rightarrow Ca(HCO_3)(aq)$
k. $Al(s) + H_3PO_4(aq) \rightarrow H_2(g) + AlPO_4(s)$
l. $MnO_2(s) \rightarrow Mn_3O_4(s) + O_2(g)$

10 Interpret the equations below in terms of each of the following.
Number of moles of each reactant and product
Weight in grams of each reactant and product
Volume at STP if the reactant or product is a gas
a. $P_4(s) + 3O_2(g) = P_4O_6(s)$
b. $Fe(OH)_3(s) + 3HCl(aq) = FeCl_3(aq) + 3H_2O(l)$
c. $NH_3(g) + 5/4\ O_2(g) = NO(g) + 3/2\ H_2O(g)$
d. $Pb(CH_3)_4(g) + 15/2\ O_2(g) = PbO(s) + 4CO_2(g) + 6H_2O(g)$

11 Phosphorus trichloride, PCl_3, is made when white phosphorus, P_4, reacts with chlorine gas according to the following equation.

$$P_4(s) + 6Cl_2(g) \rightarrow 4PCl_3(s)$$

a. How many grams of phosphorus are required to produce 5.49 g PCl_3?
b. What volume of chlorine, measured at STP, will be used in the process?

12 **a.** What volume of oxygen, measured at STP, is needed for the complete combustion of 20.0 g of hydrogen?
b. What weight of water will be produced?

13 **a.** How many moles of oxygen are required to prepare 142 g P_4O_{10} from elemental white phosphorus?
b. What mass of oxygen is this?

14 Suppose 2.17 g HgO are thermally decomposed to elemental mercury and oxygen.
a. What weight of mercury will be produced?
b. How many oxygen molecules will be produced?

SUGGESTED READINGS

Fabishak, Vernon L. "A Matrix Method for Balancing Chemical Equations." *Chemistry*, December 1967.

Greene, G. S. David. "An Algebraic Method for Balancing Chemical Equations." *Chemistry*, March 1975, p. 19.

Kieffer, William F. *The Mole Concept in Chemistry*, 2nd ed. New York: D. Van Nostrand Co., 1973.

"New Avogadro's Number." *Chemistry*, March 1975, p. 23.

Strong, Laurence E. "Balancing Chemical Equations." *Chemistry*, January 1974, p. 13.

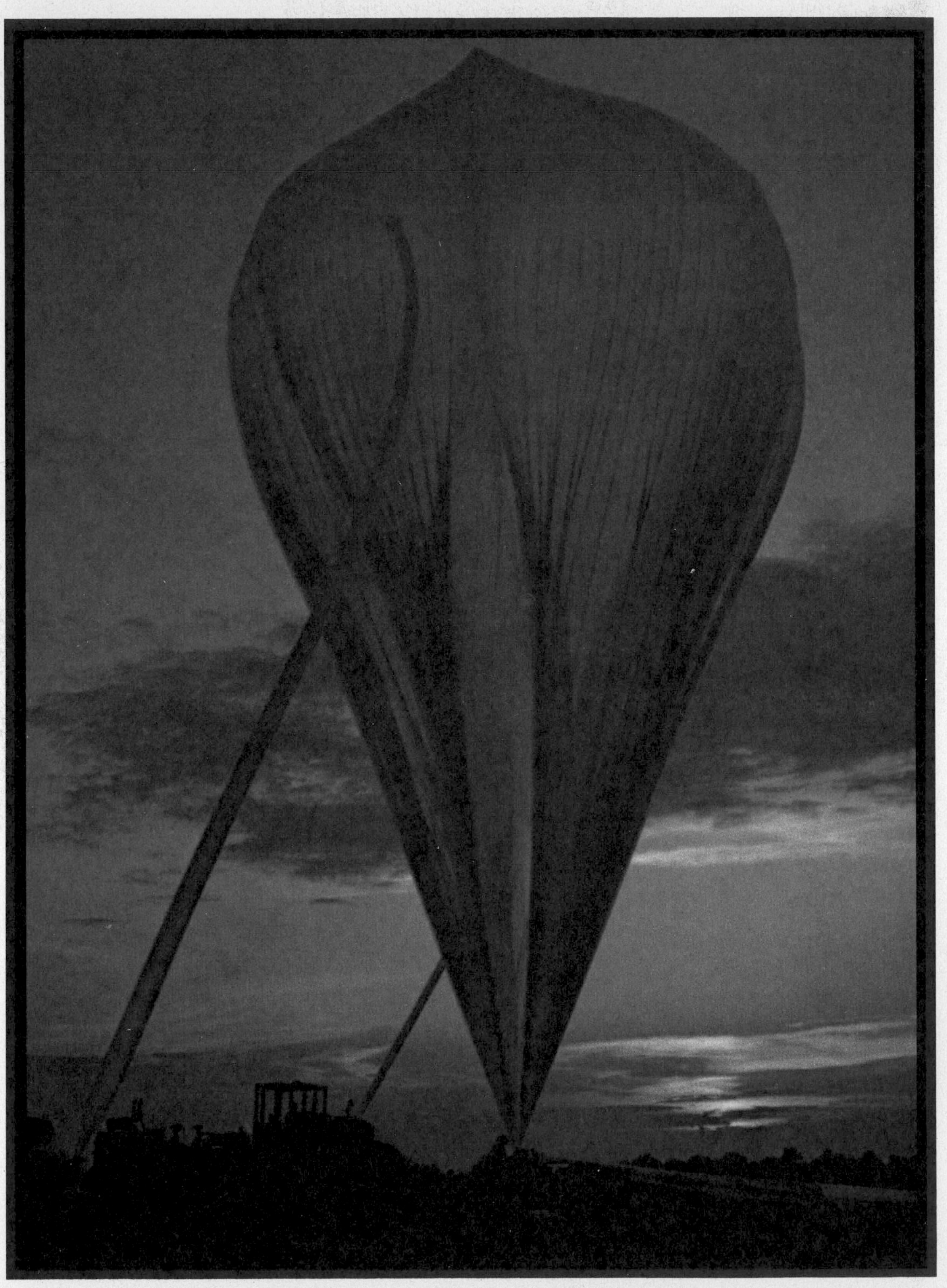

Helium-filled research balloons evaluate the impact of fluorocarbons on the ozone layer.

CHAPTER FIVE

The Gaseous State

So far we have discussed elements and compounds. We have also discussed the quantitative aspects of the composition of compounds. That led Dalton to the formulation of his atomic theory. From experience, you are aware that matter exists in three physical states—gas, liquid, and solid. Let us study these physical states with a particular emphasis on explaining them in terms of atoms and molecules. Then we can consider more details of atoms and molecules. We begin in Chapter 5 with what is, in many respects, the simplest physical state—the gaseous state.

FIGURE 5–1 · *Solids retain their shape.*

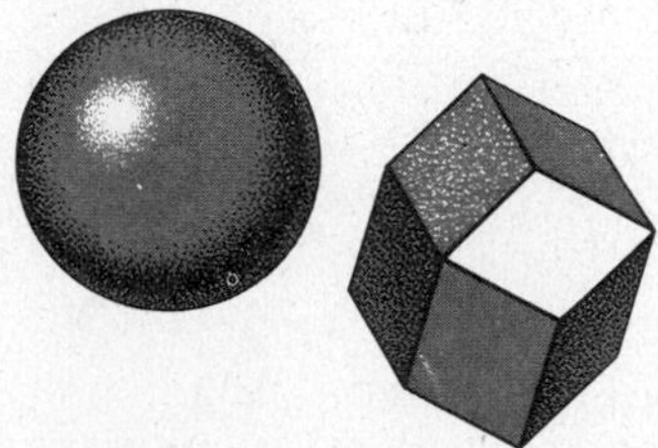

FIGURE 5–2 · *Liquids take the shape of their containers.*

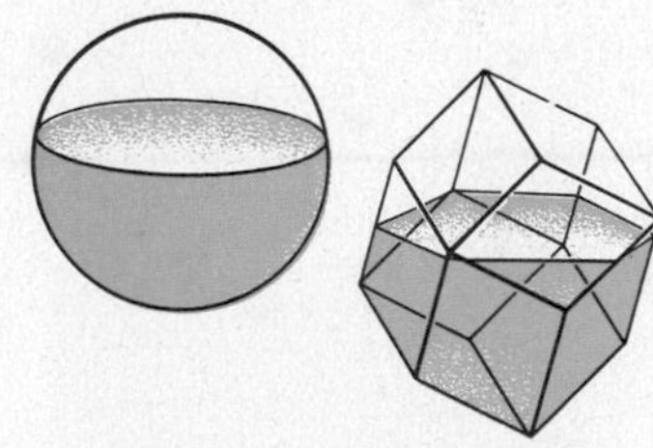

FIGURE 5–3 · *Gases fill the entire volume available to them.*

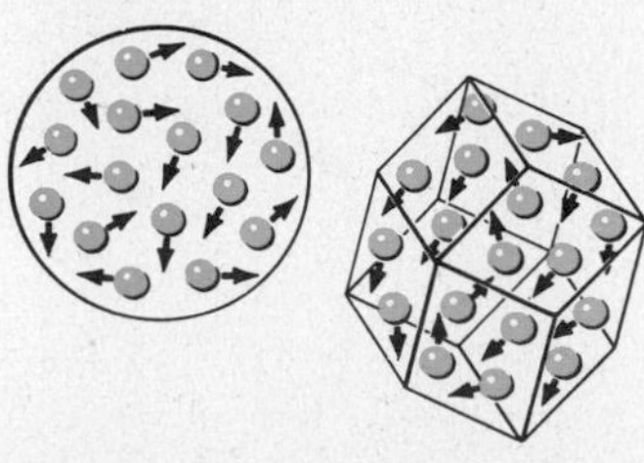

THE BEHAVIOR OF GASES

5–1 · Gases have no definite shape · Dalton's model of the atom shows it as a hard, tiny sphere of fixed mass. His model accounts well for the Law of Definite Composition and the Law of Multiple Proportions. That atomic model was soon applied to gases to help explain their experimental behavior.

Consider carefully our common observations of solid, liquid, and gaseous matter. Certain similarities and differences in properties become apparent. All solid objects have definite shapes and definite volumes (Figure 5–1). All liquids have definite volumes, but take the shape of the containers that hold them. Unlike solids, liquids have indefinite shapes (Figure 5–2). Gases, unlike solids and liquids, have no definite shape or volume. They completely fill any volume open to them, regardless of shape (Figure 5–3). Atoms or molecules in the gaseous state are greatly separated from one another, have little effect on one another, and are in constant motion.

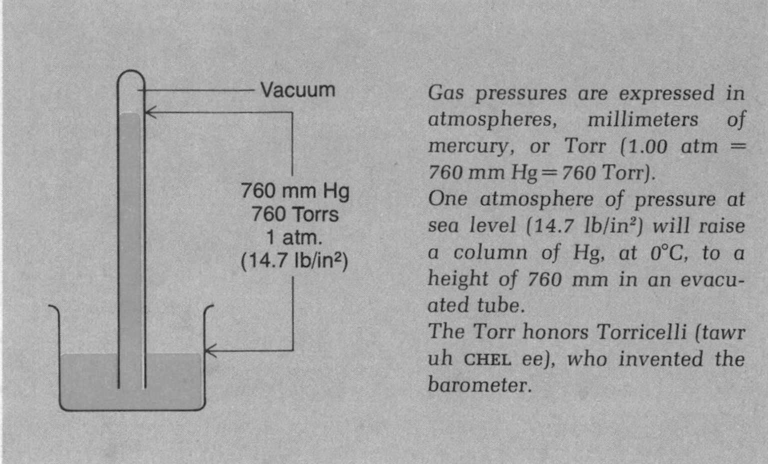

Gas pressures are expressed in atmospheres, millimeters of mercury, or Torr (1.00 atm = 760 mm Hg = 760 Torr).
One atmosphere of pressure at sea level (14.7 lb/in²) will raise a column of Hg, at 0°C, to a height of 760 mm in an evacuated tube.
The Torr honors Torricelli (tawr uh CHEL *ee), who invented the barometer.*

The best model for explaining the physical behavior of gases is derived from the Daltonian model of the atom. To that model of a tiny, hard, indivisible sphere, we add our assumption that gas particles are widely separated and in constant motion. Let us also assume, for the moment, that the gas particles have no effect on one another as they whiz about in space (Figure 5–3). We know that gases do not behave exactly like that. We know that gas particles must somehow attract one another or else gases could not condense into liquids. However, the attraction of gas molecules is usually small, so we can assume that they don't attract one another in an ideal situation. This assumption makes it simpler to explain gas behavior. We will call the gas just described an *ideal* gas. After we have dealt with ideal gases, we can consider how we might alter our model to include real gases.

FIGURE 5–4 · *The three states of matter are demonstrated by this burning candle.*

5–2 · The effect of the concentration of a gas in a container · Suppose we place ten marbles in a large, rectangular box and shake that box at a constant rate. The marbles will bounce around and strike the walls of the box with a certain frequency. This frequency, or rate, will depend on how vigorously we shake the box. Let us suppose that any one wall is struck at an average rate of thirty times per minute. Now suppose we add ten more marbles to the box, doubling the number of marbles. If we shake the box at the same constant rate, we will observe an average of sixty hits per minute on each wall. The number of times the marbles hit the wall per minute is the pressure on the wall.

A gas in a container consists of many small particles bouncing around like the marbles in a box. The pressure of the gas is due to the impacts of the gas particles on the container walls. What does the behavior of the marbles suggest? If we double the number, or concentration, of the gas particles in the container, the pressure should double if all other conditions remain constant (Figure 5 – 5). Experimentally, suppose 1.00 gram of nitrogen gas exerts a pressure of 1.00 atmosphere in a certain container. Then 2.00 grams of nitrogen gas will exert a pressure of 2.00 atmospheres in the same container at the same temperature. 1.00 gram of nitrogen represents a certain number of gaseous particles. According to Dalton's theory, 2.00 grams represents twice that number of particles. By doubling the concentration of nitrogen molecules in a given volume, the pressure exerted by the gas molecules is doubled (Figure 5 – 6 on page 88).

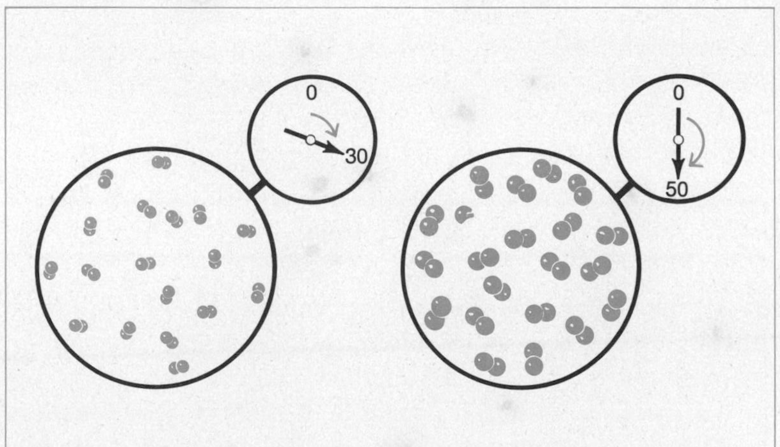

FIGURE 5–5 · *This ideal-gas model depicts the relationship between gas concentration and gas pressure. The pressure gauges show how much pressure is being exerted by the gases.*

5–3 · The effect of temperature · The agreement of experimental observation with the prediction of our model is encouraging. Now suppose we keep ten marbles in the box but change the rate of shaking. As we increase the rate of shaking, the marbles bounce around faster. The average number of wall collisions per minute is increased, and therefore the pressure is increased. We can increase the rate of movement in a gas by giving the molecules more energy. That is done by raising the temperature. Therefore, we expect the pressure of a gas to increase as its temperature is increased (Figure 5 – 9 on page 91). Again experimental observation of gases agrees with this prediction.

FIGURE 5–6 · *This graph illustrates the effect of pressure on the volume of a gas.*

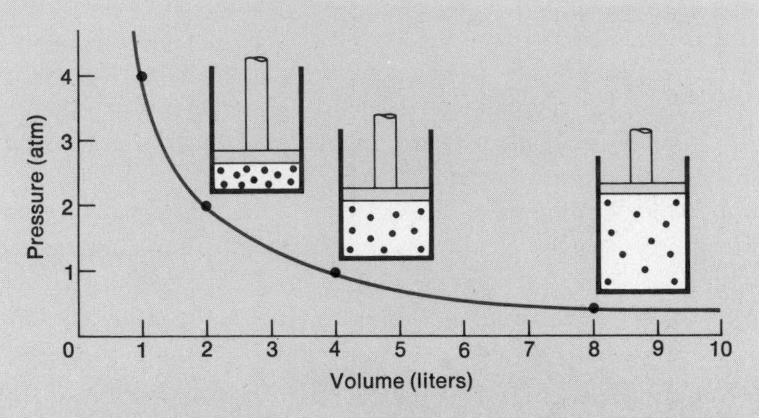

REVIEW IT NOW

1 What is an *ideal* gas?
2 Describe the model we use to explain the behavior of an ideal gas.
3 How does the concentration of gas molecules affect the pressure of a gas in a container?
4 How is gas pressure defined?
5 What effect does increasing the temperature have on the gas pressure?

GAS LAWS

5–4 · The effect of altering the volume of the container: Boyle's Law · Instead of doubling the number of marbles, we now put the original ten marbles in a box only half as big as the first box. With the same rate of shaking, the number of wall impacts would again double. This leads us to expect that the pressure of a gas would double if its volume were halved (Figures 5–6 and 5–7). Also, the pressure of a gas would be halved if its volume were doubled. If the pressure of a gas is 1.00 atmosphere for a volume of 1.00 liter, we expect a pressure of 2.00 atmospheres for a volume of 0.50 liter or conversely, 0.50 atmosphere for 2.00 liters. Notice that in all three cases, pressure multiplied by the volume equals 1.00. This means that our model predicts that pressure (P) times volume (V) equals a constant (k) for a given sample of gas at a given temperature. In Table 5–1, the pressure-volume relationship for oxygen at several different pressures confirms this prediction. The slight variations in the $P \times V$ product are due to the experimental uncertainties present in scientific measurements.

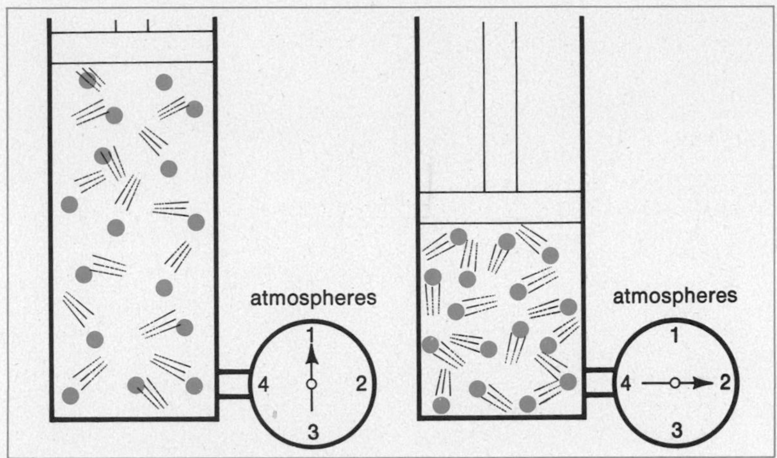

FIGURE 5–7 · *This ideal-gas model depicts the relationship between gas pressure and gas volume.*

TABLE 5–1 · Pressure and Volume of 16.0 grams of oxygen at 25°C

PRESSURE (atm) ×	VOLUME (a) =	k
0.60	20.70	12.0
0.80	15.30	12.0
1.00	12.50	12.5
1.20	10.10	12.1
1.40	8.80	12.3

In 1660, Robert Boyle first discovered the relationship predicted by our model. He stated his findings in a law. The pressure-volume relationship of a gas is known as **Boyle's Law.**

BOYLE'S LAW

The volume of a constant mass of gas varies inversely with the pressure exerted on it, if the temperature remains constant.

Carefully examine the data presented in Table 5 – 1. Note that multiplying the pressure by the volume produces a constant (within the limits of experimental uncertainty). Mathematically, then, Boyle's Law can be expressed by the following equation.

$$PV = k$$

Since a constant does not change, it is easy to understand the relationship between pressure and volume. If P decreases, V must increase, so that when the two are multiplied together, the same product will result.

FIGURE 5–8 · *This picture shows an observation balloon taking off. How do you think its appearance will change as it rises higher into the atmosphere? Why?*

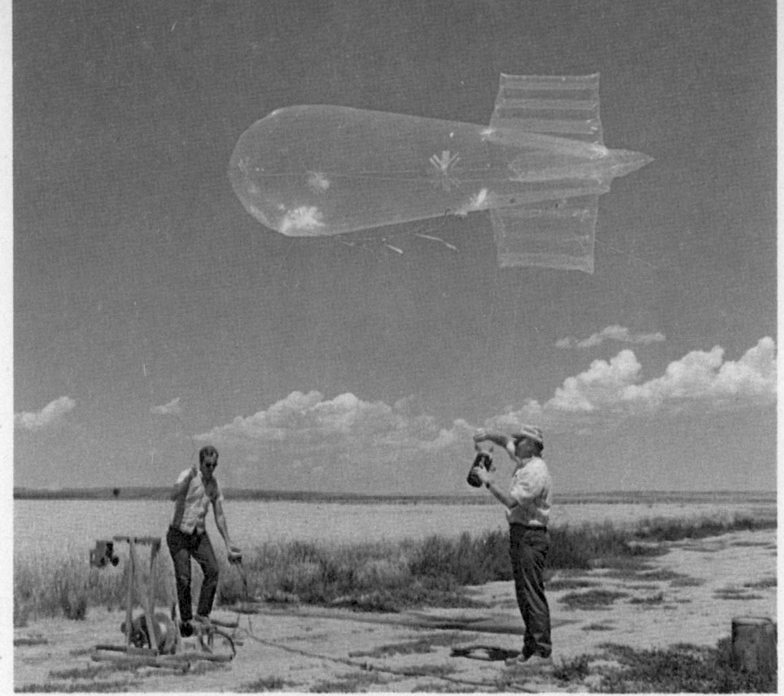

Boyle's Law can also be expressed in a slightly different form. For the same amount of a gas at a constant temperature, the previous equation can be used for different pressures (P_1, P_2, P_3, etc.) and their volumes (V_1, V_2, V_3, etc.).

$$P_1V_1 = P_2V_2 = P_3V_3 = \cdots = k$$

or

$$P_1V_1 = P_2V_2$$

EXAMPLE

A sample of nitrogen gas occupies 20.0 ml at 27.0°C at a pressure of 800 Torr. What volume will the sample occupy at 27.0°C and 760 Torr?

SOLUTION A

$$P_1 = 800 \text{ Torr} \qquad P_2 = 760 \text{ Torr}$$
$$V_1 = 20.0 \text{ ml} \qquad V_2 = ?$$

Since the temperature is constant, Boyle's Law tells us that:

$$P_1V_1 = P_2V_2$$
$$(800 \text{ Torr})(20.0 \text{ ml}) = (760 \text{ Torr})(V_2)$$
$$\frac{(800 \not{\text{Torr}})(20.0 \text{ ml})}{760 \not{\text{Torr}}} = V_2$$
$$21.0 \text{ ml} = V_2$$

SOLUTION B

It is neither necessary nor wise to depend solely on memorized formulas to solve problems. For example, observation helps you recognize that a gas expands if the pressure on it is decreased. Therefore, the original volume of 20.0 ml of nitrogen gas will increase if the pressure changes from 800 Torr to 760 Torr. The new volume of nitrogen gas will be greater than 20.0 ml. Therefore, you multiply the original 20.0 ml volume by a factor greater than one.

$$V_2 = 20.0 \text{ ml} \left(\frac{800 \cancel{\text{Torr}}}{760 \cancel{\text{Torr}}}\right)$$

$$V_2 = 21.0 \text{ ml}$$

5–5 · The effect of temperature and Charles's Law · A common observation concerning gases is that they expand as their temperatures increase. Jacques Charles (1746–1823) was a French scientist. He noticed that for a constant mass of gas at a constant pressure, the volume of the gas is proportional to the absolute temperature of the gas. Data showing this relationship, **Charles's Law,** are plotted in Figure 5–9.

FIGURE 5–9 · *The graph below indicates the volume of a gas as a function of Celsius temperature.*

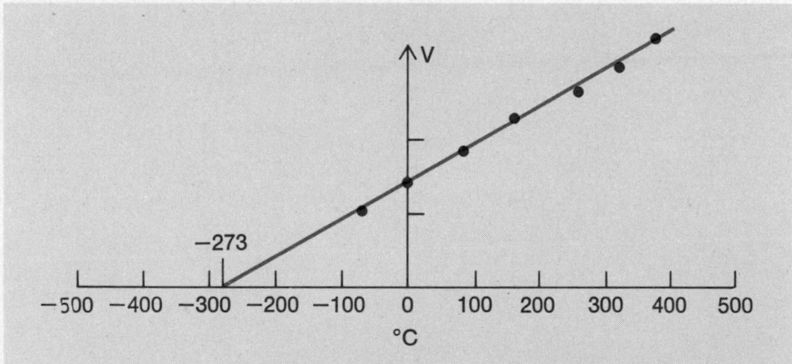

Examine the graph carefully. The straight line indicates that the two variables, gas volume and gas temperature, are proportional. That is, as temperature increases, volume also increases. However, note that the gas volume does not double when the Celsius temperature doubles. The two variables, therefore, are not directly proportional.

5–6 · The absolute temperature scale and Charles's Law · Try to imagine what will happen to our model ideal gas if we continue to cool it. Extending the line in Figure 5–9 beyond 0°C (the broken line in the graph) would lead us to predict that at −273°C our ideal-gas volume should disappear. In order for the volume to disappear, all motion of the gas particles would have to cease at −273°C. And the particles would have no volume of their own—obviously an unreal situation.

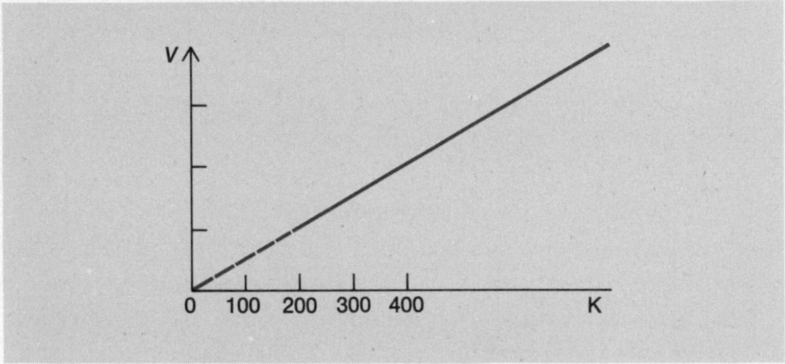

FIGURE 5–10 · *The graph illustrates the volume of a gas as a function of absolute temperature.*

However, if we could cool a gas to −273°C, it would be at the lowest temperature possible. And this lowest temperature might be taken as the zero point of the temperature scale. That is why the temperature of −273°C is called **absolute zero.** This temperature is the logical one from which to start a new temperature scale. In such a new temperature scale, all temperatures are positive. Temperatures below 0 K (−273°C) are not possible.

About sixty years after Charles's discovery, William Thompson (1824–1907), titled Lord Kelvin, reexamined Charles's Law. From that examination, he invented the absolute temperature scale (Figure 5–11). On this scale, all temperature values are positive and are related to the Celsius scale by the following equation.

$$K = {}^{\circ}C + 273^{\circ}$$

Replotting the Charles's Law data that are given in Figure 5–9 in terms of absolute temperatures results in Figure 5–10. Now the proportionality between gas volume and gas temperature is a direct one. Double the absolute temperature of a gas sample at a constant pressure, and the gas volume will double. It is much easier to work with gas laws using the absolute temperature scale (the Kelvin scale) instead of the Celsius scale.

CHARLES'S LAW

The volume of a constant mass of gas varies directly with the absolute temperature at constant pressure. Mathematically, Charles's Law is expressed as the following.

$$V = k'T \text{ (}k'\text{ is different from }k\text{ in Boyle's Law.)}$$

or

$$\frac{V}{T} = k' \text{ (constant n, P)}$$

Again, if we wish to consider a gas under two different conditions of volume and temperature (the pressure remaining constant), we can write out the equation as follows.

$$\frac{V_1}{T_1} = \frac{V_2}{T_2} \text{ (P = constant)}$$

This form of Charles's Law is most easily used in calculations involving temperature-volume behavior of gases.

FIGURE 5–11 · *The normal boiling point of a liquid is the temperature at which the pressure exerted by the molecules in the vapor state above the liquid equals the standard pressure of the atmosphere (760 Torr). The freezing point of a liquid is the temperature at which the liquid exists in equilibrium with its solid. The triple point is the temperature at which all three states of matter—solid, liquid, and gas—are in equilibrium.*

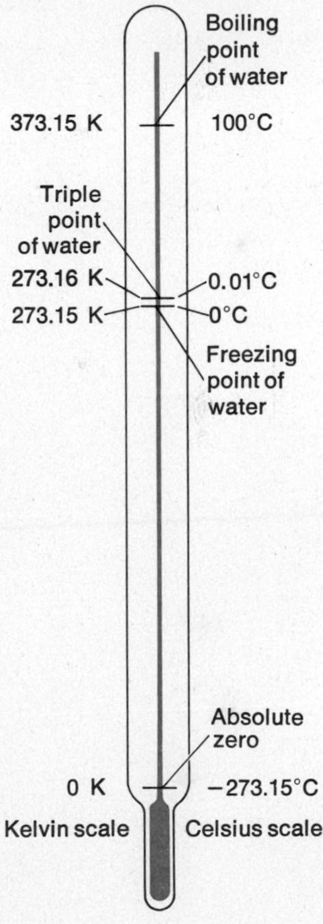

EXAMPLE

A sample of nitrogen gas occupies 20.0 ml at 27.0°C at a pressure of 800 Torr. What volume will the sample occupy at 0°C and 800 Torr?

SOLUTION A

Remember that Charles's Law is based on the Kelvin temperature scale. Therefore, Celsius temperature readings must first be converted to Kelvin temperature readings.

$$T_1 = (27.0°C + 273°) = 300 \text{ K}$$

$$T_2 = (0°C + 273°) = 273 \text{ K}$$

Them, with $V_1 = 20.0$ m, V_2 can be easily determined.

$$\frac{V_1}{T_1} = \frac{V_2}{T_2}$$

$$\frac{20.0 \text{ ml}}{300 \text{ K}} = \frac{V_2}{273 \text{ K}}$$

$$\frac{(273 \text{ K})(20.0 \text{ ml})}{300 \text{ K}} = V_2$$

$$18.2 \text{ ml} = V_2$$

SOLUTION B

Again, approach the problem using common sense and not a formula. Gases expand when heated and contract when cooled. The original volume of 20.0 ml of nitrogen gas will decrease when cooled from 300 K to 273 K. The new volume of nitrogen gas will be less than 20.0 ml. Common sense dictates that you multiply the original volume of 20.0 ml by a factor less than one.

$$V_2 = 20.0 \text{ ml} \left(\frac{273 \text{ K}}{300 \text{ K}}\right)$$

$$V_2 = 18.2 \text{ ml}$$

Our model of particles in the gaseous state (page 89) always predicts an increase in gas volume with a rising temperature at a constant pressure (Figure 5–9). Charles's Law agrees with this prediction.

5–7 · The gas laws may be combined · So far we have examined the behavior of gases in as simple a manner as possible. We have considered how two properties of gases depend on each other when all other properties are held constant. What are the properties of gases with which we have been dealing? We have considered the following.

n, the number of moles of gas molecules
P, the pressure exerted by those molecules
V, the volume occupied by those molecules
T, the absolute temperature of the molecules

We have considered V as a function of P when n and T are held constant (Boyle's Law). However, in practice both the pressure and the temperature of a constant mass of gas would change if the volume were changed. How do we determine the volume dependence under such conditions? An application of Boyle's Law and Charles's Law simultaneously is the answer to the problem. How are the properties of a gas related during a change from one state to a second state?

Look at the diagram. Consider the change of a constant mass of gas from one set of conditions of pressure, absolute temperature, and volume (P_1, T_1, V_1) to a second set of conditions (P_2, T_2, V_2).

State 1 → State 2

$$P_1, T_1, V_1, n \longrightarrow P_2, T_2, V_2, n$$

FIGURE 5–12 · *An explosion involves the rapid heating and simultaneous expansion of gases. What evidence do you see for gas expansion in this photograph?*

Instead of changing the pressure, temperature, and volume from P_1, T_1, and V_1 all at once to P_2, T_2, and V_2, suppose we make the change in two steps. First we change the pressure from P_1 to P_2 but keep the temperature constant, so the volume changes from V_1 to V_i (remember, V_2 is the new volume when both P and T have changed).

1st step:

$$P_1V_1 = P_2V_i$$

$$V_i = \frac{P_1V_1}{P_2}$$

Now we keep the pressure constant and change the temperature from T_1 to T_2. Thus, the volume goes from V_i to V_2.

2nd step:

$$\frac{V_i}{T_1} = \frac{V_2}{T_2}$$

$$V_i = \frac{V_2T_1}{T_2}$$

or

$$V_i = \frac{V_2T_1}{T_2} = \frac{P_1V_2}{P_2}$$

Now we rearrange the last equation.

$$\frac{P_1V_1}{T_1} = \frac{P_2V_2}{T_2}$$

This last relationship is known as the **Combined Gas Law** for an ideal gas.

EXAMPLE

A sample of nitrogen gas occupies 20.0 ml at 27.0°C and 800 Torr. What volume will the sample occupy at 0°C and 760 Torr? (Remember, these are the conditions of STP.)

SOLUTION A

$$P_1 = 800 \text{ Torr}$$
$$V_1 = 20.0 \text{ ml}$$
$$T_1 = (27.0°\text{C} + 273) = 300 \text{ K}$$
$$P_2 = 760 \text{ Torr}$$
$$V_2 = ?$$
$$T_2 = (0°\text{C} + 273) = 273 \text{ K}$$

We use the Combined Gas Law to find V_2.

$$\frac{P_1V_1}{T_1} = \frac{P_2V_2}{T_2}$$

$$\frac{(800 \text{ Torr})\ (20.0 \text{ ml})}{300 \text{ K}} = \frac{(760 \text{ Torr})\ (V_2)}{273 \text{ K}}$$

$$\left(\frac{800 \text{ Torr}}{760 \text{ Torr}}\right)\left(\frac{273 \text{ K}}{300 \text{ K}}\right)(20.0 \text{ ml}) = V_2$$

$$19.2 \text{ ml} = V_2$$

SOLUTION B

Again, it is not necessary to remember a formula if we can approach the problem logically. In going from V_1 to V_2, the original volume will be multiplied by a pressure factor and a temperature factor. Those factors will be fractions less than or greater than one, depending on how the gas volume changes with the indicated pressure and temperature changes. In this case, going from P_1 to P_2 is a pressure decrease (800 Torr to 760 Torr). Gases expand when pressure decreases. Thus, the pressure factor must be a fraction greater than one, or 800 Torr/760 Torr. Going from T_1 to T_2 is a temperature decrease (300 K *to 273 K, and gases contract when cooled. The temperature factor must be less than one, or 273 K/300 K.*

Thus, to find V_2, we must multiply V_1 by the pressure factor and the temperature factor.

$$V_2 = V_1 \text{ (pressure factor) (temperature factor)}$$

$$V_2 = 20.0 \text{ ml} \left(\frac{800 \text{ Torr}}{760 \text{ Torr}}\right)\left(\frac{273 \text{ K}}{300 \text{ K}}\right)$$

(exactly as obtained by using the Combined Gas Law)

$$V_2 = 19.2 \text{ ml}$$

5–8 · Dalton's Law of Partial Pressures · Another check can be made of gas behavior as predicted by our modified Daltonian atomic model of an ideal gas. Suppose we have ten red marbles, representing oxygen molecules, in a box. We must assume that these marbles are in constant, random motion and that they exert pressure by striking the walls of the box. Then suppose we add ten orange marbles, representing molecules of nitrogen gas. The average number of wall collisions per minute will double. In other words, the pressure within the box doubles. If we now add ten white marbles, representing molecules of hydrogen, the total pressure will triple.

How is the analogy related to the behavior of gases? From the facts, we can predict that the total pressure exerted by the mixture of gases is the sum of the individual pressures of each gas. Each gas behaves as if it were the only gas in the container. Each gas exerts its own pressure independently of the other gases present. These individual pressures are called *partial pressures*, and they add up to the total pressure exerted by the gas mixture.

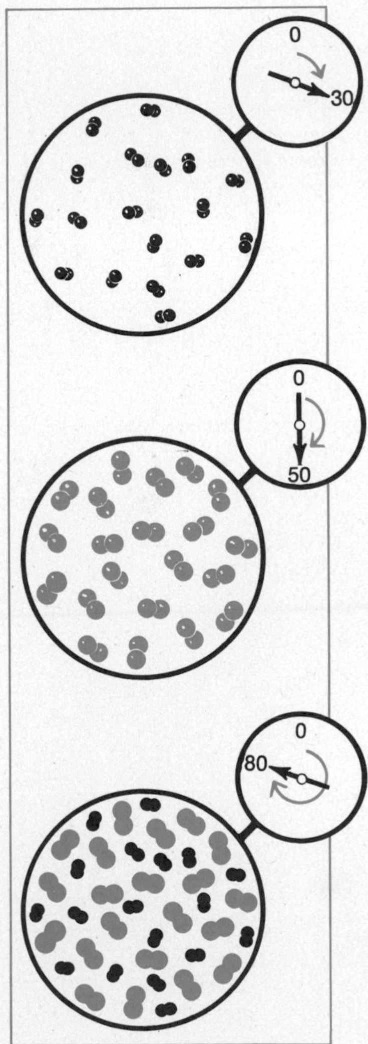

FIGURE 5–13 · *An ideal-gas model that represents Dalton's Law of Partial Pressures.*

DALTON'S LAW OF PARTIAL PRESSURES

The total pressure of a mixture of gases is the sum of the partial pressures. Partial pressures are the individual pressures that each of the gases would exert if it were in the container alone.

For example, suppose 1.00 liter of oxygen in a flask exerts a pressure of 50.0 Torr. Also suppose 1.00 liter of hydrogen in a flask exerts a pressure of 30.0 Torr at the same temperature. If these two gas samples are mixed in one flask with a total volume of 1.00 liter, the total pressure will be 80.0 Torr.

This is shown below.

$$P_{total} = P_{oxygen} + P_{hydrogen} \text{ (in the 1-liter volume)}$$
$$P_{total} = 50.0 \text{ Torr} + 30.0 \text{ Torr}$$
$$P_{total} = 80.0 \text{ Torr}$$

However, if we connect the two 1-liter flasks at the same temperature and allow the gases to mix, the total volume will be 2.00 liters. In effect, this doubles the volume of each gas. Consequently, according to Boyle's Law, the partial pressure of each is halved (Figure 5–14).

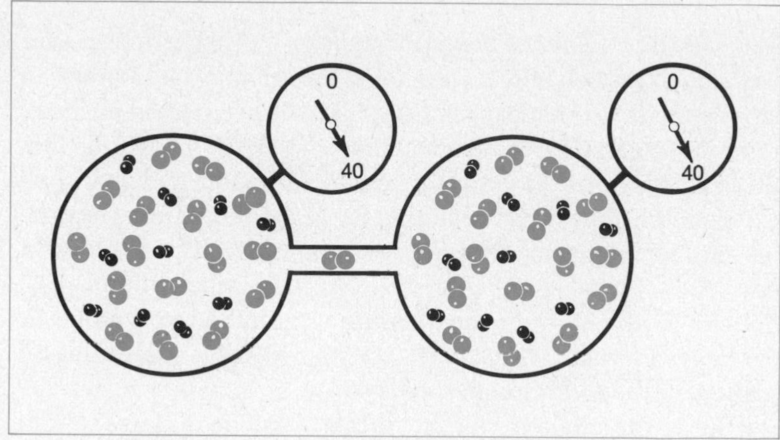

FIGURE 5–14 · *An ideal-gas model representation of two gases conforming to both Dalton's Law of Partial Pressure and Boyle's Law.*

OXYGEN

$$P_1V_1 = P_2V_2$$
$$(50.0 \text{ Torr})\ (1.00 \text{ l}) = (P_2)\ (2.00 \text{ l})$$
$$P_2 = 25.0 \text{ Torr}$$

HYDROGEN

$$P_1V_1 = P_2V_2$$
$$(30.0 \text{ Torr})\ (1.00 \text{ l}) = (P_2)\ (2.00 \text{ l})$$
$$P_2 = 15.0 \text{ Torr}$$

GAS MIXTURE

$$P_{total} = P_{oxygen} + P_{hydrogen} \text{ (in the 2-l volume)}$$
$$P_{total} = 25.0 \text{ Torr} + 15.0 \text{ Torr}$$
$$P_{total} = 40.0 \text{ Torr}$$

Interpret the illustration below in terms of the gas laws.

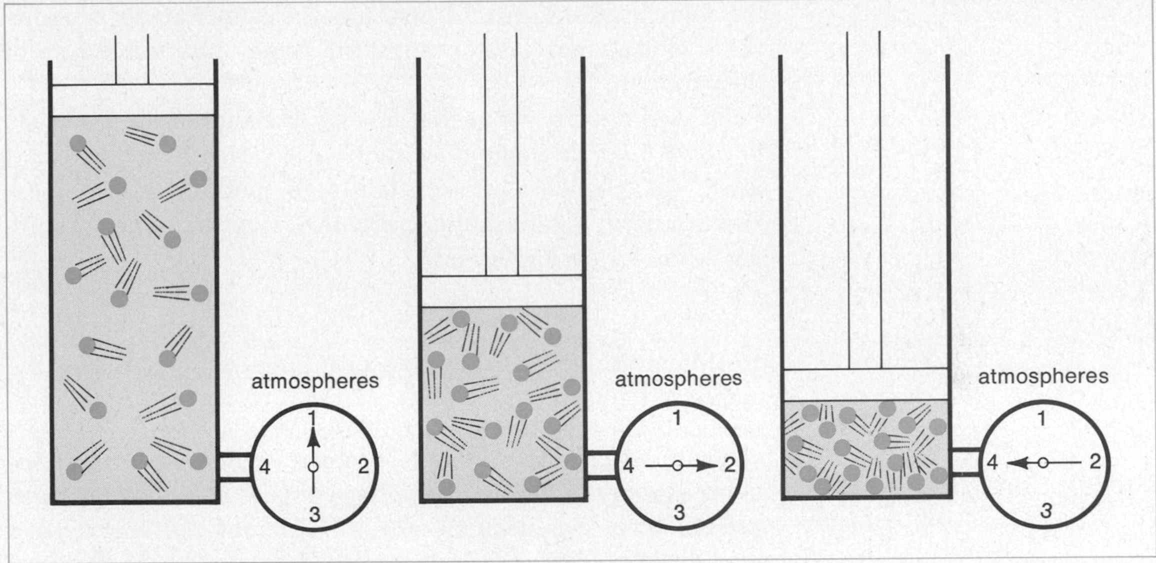

Both the theoretical and the experimental treatments of gases in this chapter have been based on an ideal-gas model. We have assumed throughout that gas particles behave independently of one another. We have assumed that even though the particles collide with one another, interparticle forces of attraction are absent. Also, we have treated gas particles as having no volume of their own. Under laboratory conditions of relatively low pressures and high temperatures, such assumptions are valid. Under such conditions, the gas molecules are moving so rapidly and are on the average so far apart that their behavior is essentially ideal.

REVIEW IT NOW

1. If we double the volume of a gas, what effect will that have on the pressure of the gas?
2. What is meant by the expression $PV = k$.
3. State Boyle's Law.
4. State Charles's Law.
5. Why is Charles's Law based on the Kelvin temperature scale?
6. Explain Dalton's Law of Partial Pressures.

REAL GAS BEHAVIOR

5–9 · The kinetic energy of gases · Avogadro deduced that at the same temperature and pressure, the same number of molecules of different gases occupy the same volume because of their motion.

Perhaps we can verify that. Energy is required for a particle to move, and this energy of motion is called **kinetic energy.** Since gas particles are constantly in motion, they possess kinetic energy. This kinetic energy (KE) may be defined according to the following formula.

$$KE = \frac{1}{2} mv^2$$

(In this formula, m is the mass of the molecule, and v^2 is the square of its velocity.)

Again, let us turn to the laboratory for data to verify Avogadro's theory. Scientists have been able to calculate the average velocity of molecules with considerable accuracy. Let's consider the average velocity of a hydrogen gas molecule and an oxygen gas molecule.

Gas molecule	*Average velocity (meters/sec)*
Hydrogen	1692.0
Oxygen	425.0

(To give you some idea of the average speed of the hydrogen molecule, this is approximately one mile per second!)

With these data, let us inspect our formula for kinetic energy. Suppose we consider the kinetic energy of hydrogen gas.

$$KE_{H_2} = \frac{1}{2} m_{H_2}v^2{}_{H_2}$$

And suppose we consider the kinetic energy of oxygen.

$$KE_{O_2} = \frac{1}{2} m_{O_2}v^2{}_{O_2}$$

If we assume, as Avogadro did, that the kinetic energy of the two gases is the same, *then* the kinetic energy of hydrogen must equal the kinetic energy of oxygen.

$$\frac{1}{2} m_{H_2}v^2{}_{H_2} = \frac{1}{2} m_{O_2}v^2{}_{O_2}$$

or simply

$$m_{H_2}v^2_{H_2} = m_{O_2}v^2_{O_2}$$

From the data on the average velocity of hydrogen and oxygen molecules, we notice that the hydrogen molecule travels approximately 4 times as fast as the oxygen molecule (1692/425.0). Since we are interested only in an approximation, let's substitute the 4:1 ratio into our equations: $m_{H_2}(4)^2 = m_{O_2}(1)^2$. When the velocities are squared, our expression becomes $m_{H_2}(16) = m_{O_2}(1)$.

In order for the kinetic energy of hydrogen and oxygen gas molecules to be the same, it is obvious that the oxygen molecule must be 16 times as heavy as the hydrogen molecule. Again, let us look at some laboratory data.

Gas molecule	*Molecular mass*
Hydrogen	2.016
Oxygen	32.00

The oxygen molecule actually *is* approximately 16 times as heavy as the hydrogen molecule. Therefore, it is logical to assume that as Avogadro proposed, the kinetic energy of the two gases is indeed the same. We can assume that the average kinetic energy of *all* gases is the same. This is true as long as the gases are at the same temperature and pressure.

FIGURE 5–15 · *Any race, such as the motorcycle race below, illustrates velocity distribution.*

5–10 · Temperature and the average velocity of molecules · Qualitatively, we may assume that, on the average, heavy molecules move slowly and light molecules move rapidly at the same temperature. However, it must be emphasized again that chemists do not work with single molecules. The data we have presented were collected for a large number of gas molecules. You will note that we have been very careful to mention the average velocity of molecules. It is extremely important that you do not have the impression that all molecules of the same mass travel at the same speed, even at the same temperature. It would be just as illogical to assume that all racing cars with the same mass would run at the same speed!

Suppose we take this analogy a step further and plot the number of cars at each numbered post (put there for our convenience). Our graph might look something like that shown in Figure 5–16.

FIGURE 5–16 · *Graph of velocity distribution.*

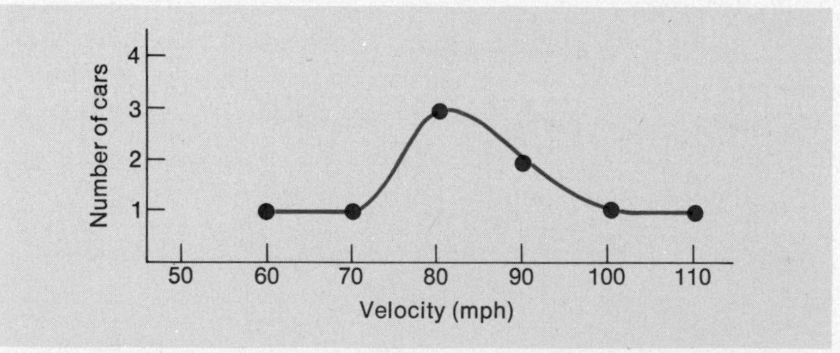

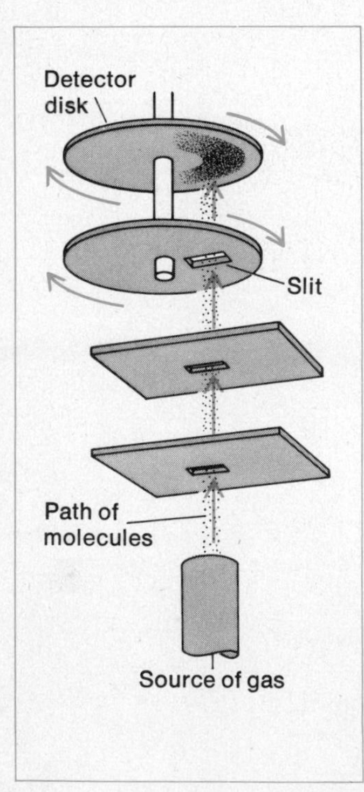

FIGURE 5–17 · *Molecular velocities are calculated from the known distance to the detection disc and the speed of revolution.*

A similar plot would result if we measured the different velocities of molecules of the same kind. This experiment can actually be performed in the laboratory by using a device similar to that shown in Figure 5–17.

Figure 5–18A shows the velocity distribution for molecules of the same mass at the same temperature. You will note that in a large collection of molecules of the same kind, a few molecules move slowly, and a few move quite rapidly. Most of the molecules, however, have a velocity in the narrow middle range of values, just as we saw with the cars.

From the gas laws we can easily derive the relationship between temperature and pressure at a constant volume.

$$\frac{P_1}{T_1} = \frac{P_2}{T_2}$$

If the volume is constant, then the temperature is proportional to the kinetic energy. That relationship can be demonstrated in the following equation.

$$T \propto mv^2$$

An increase in temperature should produce an increase in kinetic energy and change the velocity distribution of gas molecules. Figure 5–18B shows that this is indeed the case. At a higher temperature, there are more molecules with a higher velocity. You will find this relationship to be very important in later chapters that deal with chemical reactions.

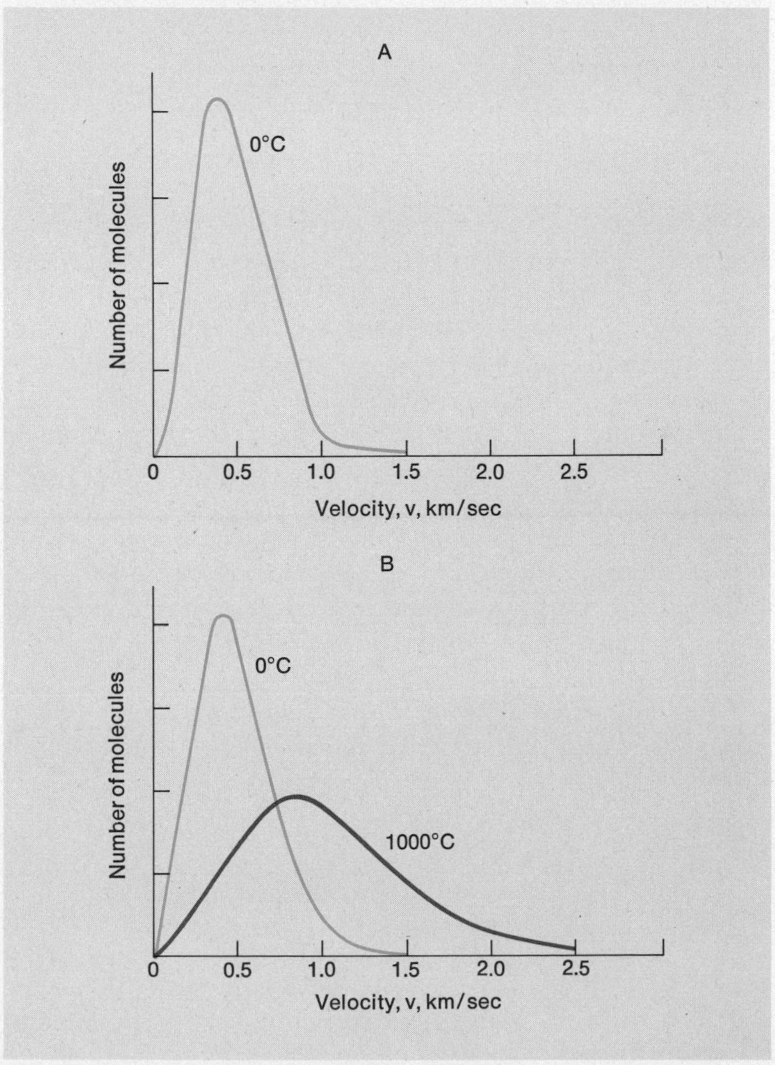

FIGURE 5–18 · *Graph A shows experimentally that all molecules of the same mass, at the same temperature, do not move with the same velocity. Graph B shows that a change in temperature causes a change in the velocity distribution of gas molecules.*

5–11 · Real gas behavior · No real gas behaves ideally under all conditions of pressure and temperature. All gases deviate from ideal behavior, particularly at high pressure and low temperature.

We can get a good idea of just how great the deviation is by considering the data presented in Table 5–2. The PV values for hydrogen and carbon dioxide are compared with the PV values for an ideal gas.

TABLE 5–2 · P × V Values for H_2 and CO_2 Relative to the Constant P × V Value of an Ideal Gas at Different Pressures

PRESSURE (ATM)	$\frac{PV_{H_2}}{PV_{ideal\ gas}}$	$\frac{PV_{CO_2}}{PV_{ideal\ gas}}$
1.0000	1.0000	1.0000
50.000	1.0330	0.7413
100.00	1.0639	0.2695
200.00	1.1336	0.4087
400.00	1.2775	0.7178
800.00	1.5665	1.2990
1000.0	1.7107	1.5525

In our discussion of the behavior of ideal gases, we assumed that gaseous atoms or molecules move about independently of one another. We assumed that one gaseous atom or molecule is not affected by the presence of another gaseous atom or molecule. However, that is not really true.

In real gases, atoms or molecules do not move independently of one another. They do exert an attraction on one another. What is the course of this attraction? Our simple model of atoms cannot account for it. Our marblelike atomic model is incomplete.

Since substances exist in both the liquid state and the solid state, there must be attractive forces between the atoms or molecules that make them "stick together." Since gaseous atoms or molecules deviate from ideal behavior, we must alter our model of atoms to account for that fact. We must assume the existence of attractive forces among the hard, spherical, indivisible atoms.

How might we alter our simple model of atoms to give the marbles the ability to attract each other? Suppose we imagine the marbles with magnets buried within them. The force of attraction between magnets becomes greater as magnets approach one another. Also, as the magnets move farther and farther apart, the force of attraction between them decreases until it finally vanishes. Thus, magnets can attract one another with varying strengths, depending on the distance between them.

We propose that atoms and molecules behave in this manner in the gaseous state. We are not saying, however, that the force is magnetic; we are saying that the force of attraction has properties similar to that of magnetism. Now we are ready to consider why gases deviate from ideal behavior when pressure is increased and temperature is decreased.

5–12 · A model for real-gas behavior · Picture the magnetized marbles rolling along in a random manner in a very large container. The marbles are moving very fast in straight-line paths. Since the marbles are moving very fast, they do not stay near one another for very long. Even if two marbles come close enough to interact with each other, they would soon be out of effective range because of their speed. Under such conditions, the observable effect of the magnetic force on the motion of the marbles would be very small. Now, however, let us either decrease the speed of the marbles, or decrease the size of the container. Either way the marbles will now spend more time near one another, and therefore, the attractive force between marbles will be more pronounced.

The deviation from ideal-gas behavior can be understood in the same manner. Lowering the temperature of a gas leads to a decrease in molecular motion. Increasing the pressure on a gas forces molecules closer to one another. The gas molecules become close enough for attractive forces between them (intermolecular forces) to influence the behavior of neighboring molecules. The deviation by real gases, from ideal-gas behavior, particularly at low temperatures and high pressures, is partly the result of these intermolecular attractive forces.

REVIEW IT NOW

1 What effect does temperature have on the average velocity of molecules?
2 What is the difference between an ideal gas and a real gas?
3 How can we account for the fact that real gases do not behave like ideal gases?
4 Explain a model for the behavior of real gases. Can you think of a better model than is explained in this section?

SUMMARY

Dalton's concept of the atom was extended and applied to the study of the physical properties of gases. An ideal gas model was postulated. That assumed gas particles were small, hard masses moving independently of one another. The model allowed scientists to explain observed behavior of gases in the laboratory. Boyle's Law, Charles's Law, the Combined Gas Law, and Dalton's Law of Partial Pressures are mathematical descriptions of observed gas behavior. These gas laws are valid within the limits of low pressure and high temperature.

An important feature of the ideal-gas model is that at −273°C a gas particle theoretically ceases to move, and the total gas volume theoretically disappears. The absolute, or Kelvin, temperature scale is based on an absolute zero point that corresponds to −273°C. For all calculations of gas behavior when temperature is a variable, temperature must be expressed in absolute units.

REVIEW QUESTIONS

1 What is an ideal gas?

2 At a pressure of 700 Torr, a sample of hydrogen gas has a volume of 500 ml. If the pressure is reduced to 538 Torr, what volume will the gas now occupy?

3 At a temperature of 35.0°C, a sample of oxygen is found to have a volume of 250 ml. What volume change will result if the temperature is decreased to 20.0°C?

4 A sample of carbon dioxide has a temperature of 273 K at 720 Torr. What will happen to the gas if the temperature remains the same, but the pressure is increased to 770 Torr?

5 What will happen to the volume of 800 ml of nitrogen if its temperature is increased from 273 K to 300 K?

6 There are 5.00×10^{23} atoms of a gas held in a volume of 1.00 l by a movable piston located in a 10.0-l container. The external pressure on the piston is kept constant at 1.00 atm.

- **a.** If the absolute temperature of the gas is doubled, how many atoms, on the average, will there be in the *original* 1.00 l of space?
- **b.** State the observation as a law relating gas concentration and absolute temperature.

7
- **a.** An amount of gas occupies 4.00 l at a pressure of 740 Torr. If the temperature remains constant, what volume will the same amount of gas occupy at standard pressure (760 Torr)?
- **b.** When the pressure on a confined amount of a gas was changed from 700 Torr to 800 Torr, the final volume was 4.37 l. What was the initial volume of the confined gas, if the temperature remained constant?
- **c.** A balloon is filled with 10.0 l of helium at 760 Torr and 30.0°C. At what pressure will the volume of helium be increased by 2.00 l at 30.0°C?

8 If 250 ml of nitrogen gas are measured at a temperature of 20.0°C and a pressure of 750 Torr, what volume would this gas occupy at a temperature of 25.0°C and 760 Torr?

9 At 30.0°C and 1.00 atm, a sample of gas has a volume of 435 ml. What will be the effect on the pressure if the volume decreases to 300 ml and the temperature increases to 43.0°C?

10 The pressure of a gas is 760 Torr when its measured volume is 285 ml. What will be the effect on the pressure if the gas is allowed to expand to 350 ml at a constant temperature?

11 An amount of gas at 0°C is confined to a volume of 10.0 ml at a pressure of 1.00 atm. If the volume of the gas doubles while the pressure remains the same, which of the following could be true?

a. The pressure exerted by the gas at this new volume has increased.
b. The temperature of the gas has increased to 273°C.
c. The temperature of the gas remains at 0°C, but a reaction has occurred that has broken each particle of gas into two particles.
d. The temperature of the gas has increased to 273°C, but at this higher temperature, there are only half as many particles as there were initially.

12 A gas occupies a volume of 1000 ml at a temperature of x K and a pressure of p Torr. If the pressure of the gas is decreased to $\frac{1}{2P}$ Torr and the temperature is increased to 2x K, what volume will the gas occupy?

13 Hydrogen gas is collected by displacing water. The total pressure reads 747 Torr. The vapor pressure of water is 23.0 Torr. What is the pressure of dry hydrogen gas?

14 Gases A and B are placed in a container. The pressure reading for both gases is 12.0 Torr. There are twice as many moles of gas A as gas B in the container. What is the partial pressure of each gas?

15 The following chemical equation indicates the initial reactants and final products for the complex photosynthesis reaction.

$$6CO_2(g) + 6H_2O(g) \rightarrow C_6H_{12}O_6(s) + 6O_2(g)$$

The solid product is a sugar for which the simplest formula is given. During the photosynthesis reaction, radiant energy from the sun is converted by the green plant to chemical potential energy. The reverse of this reaction, which occurs in body cells, is a source of animal energy. If you ate a candy bar containing 180 g of the sugar, what volume of oxygen would have to be transported to your cells at body temperature (37.0°C) and pressure (1.00 atm) for the chemical potential energy stored in the sugar to be released?

SUGGESTED READINGS

"Extraordinary Xenon." *Chemistry*, November 1974, p. 27.

"The Helium Problem." *Chemistry*, October 1974, p. 25.

Keller, Eugenia, "Hydrogen—The Simplest." *Chemistry*, November 1969, p. 19.

Waggoner, William H. "Nitrogen by any other Name." *Chemistry*, November 1974, p. 20.

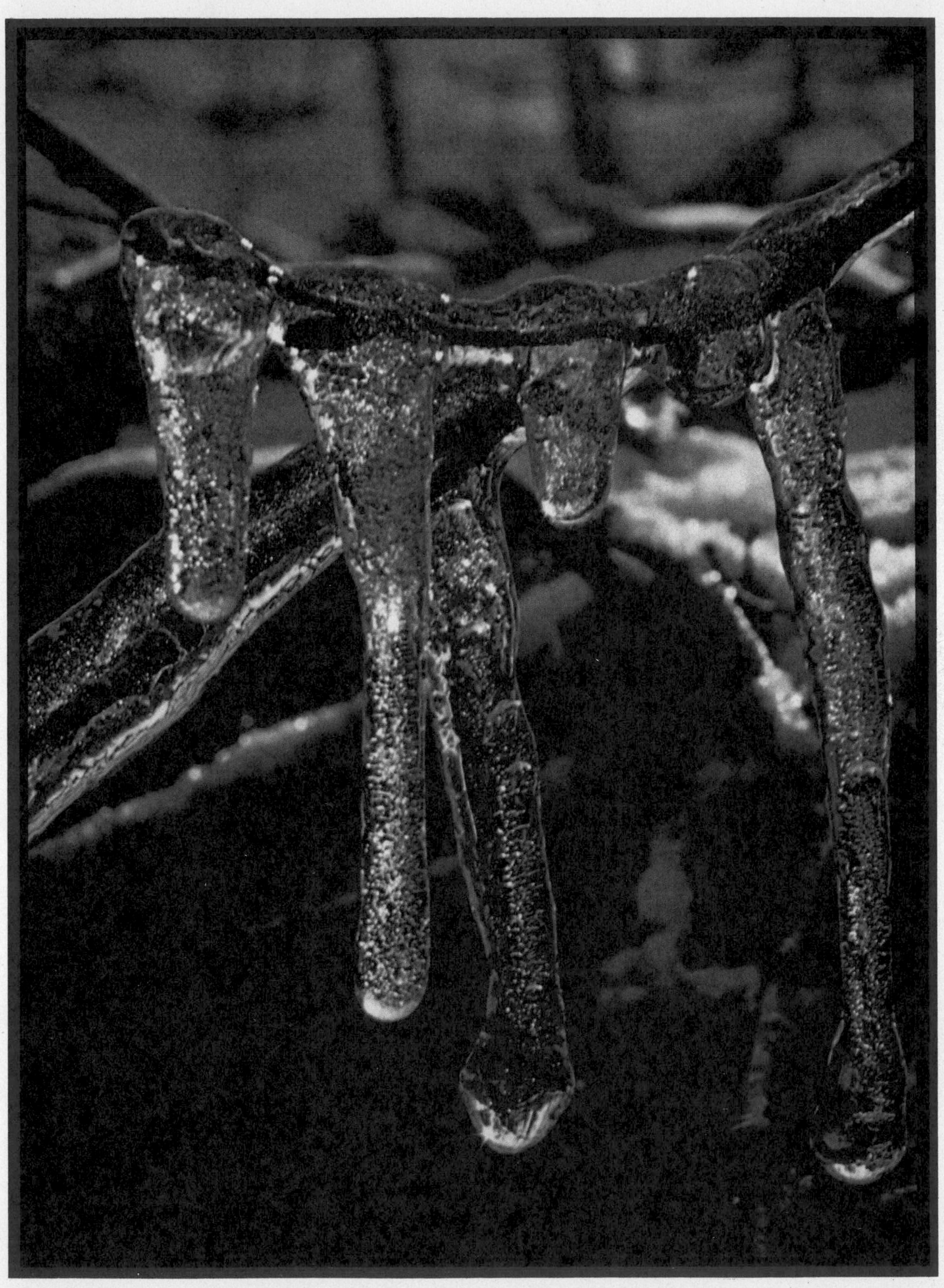

These melting icicles demonstrate the liquid and solid states of matter.

CHAPTER SIX

Liquids and Solids

It is easy to observe the behavior of liquids and gases everywhere around you. You have probably observed some significant differences between gases and liquids. In Chapter 5, you learned several things about gases. For example, when the pressure or temperature of a gas is changed, the volume changes also. In fact, by doubling the pressure, the volume of a gas is halved. You can compare that behavior with the behavior of a liquid such as soup or coffee when it is heated. Liquid undergoes very little change in volume as the temperature is raised. Similarly, the volume of a liquid changes little when the pressure on it is increased. Hydraulic brakes function because of that fact. Applying pressure at one end of a column of liquid results in the same pressure at the other end. That is because the liquid does not reduce in volume to absorb the increase in pressure. The whole column of liquid is pushed, resulting in immediate pressure at the other end.

LIQUIDS

6–1 · The nature of liquids · How can we account for the difference in the compressibility and expansibility of gases and liquids with changes in pressure and temperature? Perhaps it is partly due to the difference in the structure of gases and liquids. The molecules in a gas have very large spaces between them. The actual molecules of a gas occupy only a very small percentage of the total volume. Most of the volume of a gas is made up of empty space. Consequently, as pressure is increased on a gas, it is easy to push the molecules closer together. A liquid does not compress when the pressure on it is increased. Many liquids have been examined by a variety of experimental techniques. We can interpret those observations as follows. The molecules in a liquid are packed so closely together there is little empty space between them.

There is one similarity between the particles in a liquid and the particles in a gas. The particles in a gas are in constant motion. The rate at which the particles move increases as the temperature rises. That is why the pressure increases when the temperature increases. Similarly, the particles in a liquid are moving. Of course, the movement of particles in a liquid is somewhat different from that in gases. Remember, the molecules in a liquid are packed closely together. Many experimental studies have given us a model for liquids in which the molecules are clustered. Molecules continually join and break away from the clusters. Because of that, the clusters keep changing in size. The clusters can vary in size from a few molecules to several hundred molecules at different times. And at any one moment, the liquid often contains many clusters of different sizes. There is usually a definite pattern to the way molecules combine in a cluster. The clusters are not just a random, jumbled bunching of molecules.

There is a pattern for the arrangement of the molecules within each cluster. However, there is no pattern for the arrangement of clusters within the liquid. The clusters are jumbled about randomly. Chemists call the type of molecular arrangement in liquids **short-range order.** Short-range order, as it refers to liquids, means that the molecules are grouped in an orderly fashion within the small clusters. But the pattern does not continue over large numbers of molecules of different clusters. And since the clusters are constantly changing, the short-range order is also constantly changing. There is no order or regularity in the positioning of every molecule throughout the entire liquid. In contrast, the molecules in solids are packed closely and rigidly together. In a solid, the same pattern may exist throughout the entire solid (see Figure 6–1). Scientists refer to that type of arrangement as **long-range order.**

There are two main differences in the three states of matter. First, the distance between the molecules is different in each state. Second, the pattern of arrangement of molecules is different in each state. In a gas, there is no pattern of arrangement at all. The molecules are scattered in a random manner throughout the volume of the gas. The individual gas particles are very far apart. The particles are in constant motion, changing their

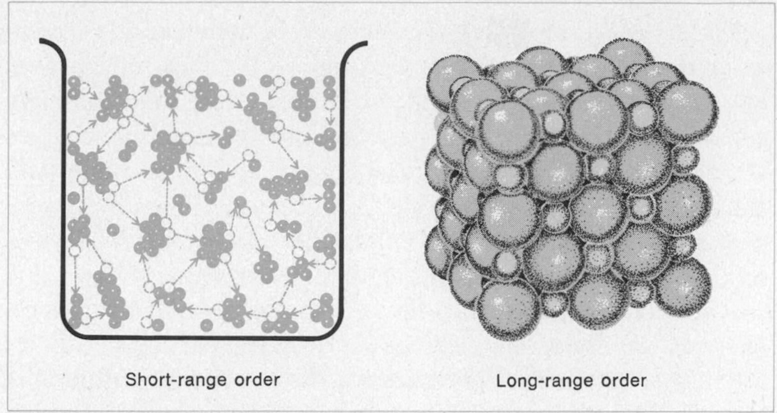

FIGURE 6–1 · *In a liquid, a regular pattern exists for small groups of molecules (short-range order). In a solid, the pattern continues over a very large number of molecules (long-range order).*

positions rapidly. In a solid, the exact opposite is true. The particles of a solid are arranged close together, often in an orderly fashion. There is very little movement of the particles from those positions. The liquid state demonstrates intermediate behavior. Remember, the particles of a liquid are packed closely together like those in a solid. But they resemble those of a gas in two ways. The particles have little regularity in the pattern of arrangement. And the molecules are moving about, constantly changing their arrangement in all parts of the liquid.

6–2 · The attractive forces in liquids and solids · When the molecules in a real gas collide, the attraction between them can cause a deviation from the gas laws. Remember that the gas laws describe the behavior of an ideal gas, in which the particles are not attracted to one another. The attraction between the particles in a gas can help explain the attraction of particles in liquids and solids in which the particles are held closely together. We know of two different forces that explain the attraction. The first is **gravitational force.** Gravitational force is the force of attraction between any two substances that is a result of their mass. A good example of gravitational force is the earth's revolution around the sun. The gravitational attraction between the mass of the earth and the mass of the sun keeps the earth in orbit. Another good example is the gravitational force demonstrated by a falling object. When a stone is thrown into the air, it falls back to the earth. That is because the mass of the earth attracts the mass of the stone. However, the mass of molecules is very small. It is so small that the gravitational force is much too weak to hold the molecules together to form liquids and solids.

The second type of force is electrical in nature and is known as **coulombic force.** Only two kinds of electrical charges are known. They are called *plus* and *minus*. In the laboratory, we can easily show that two particles having opposite charges attract each other. However, two bodies having the same electrical charge repel each other. For example, two positively charged particles repel each other. But a particle with a positive charge attracts a particle with a negative charge. The strength of the coulombic force, like the gravitational force, changes rapidly as the distance between the particles changes. The closer together the particles are, the stronger the coulombic force is. The coulombic force between two molecules is strong enough to explain the attraction of the molecules in liquids and solids. All experimental evidence supports the idea that the particles in liquids and solids are attracted to one another by coulombic force. Remember, the force decreases as the molecules move farther apart. Therefore, we can understand why the particles in a gas have very little attraction for one another. The particles in a gas are great distances apart. Also, gas molecules are very energetic. Because of that, the attractive force between thc particles is not strong enough to hold them together on collision.

6–3 · Condensation of gases · When gases are cooled, the average kinetic energy of the molecules decreases. In other words, the molecules slow down. A decrease in kinetic energy means that the gas molecules are less able to overcome the attractive forces between them. As the temperature drops, the kinetic energy decreases. At some temperature the molecules begin to experience an attraction that is too strong to allow them to separate after a collision. As a result, the molecules tend to stick together when they collide. Additional collisions result in the formation of large collections, or aggregates, of gas molecules. These aggregates can move about as units. Aggregation occurs rapidly once a gas reaches a particular temperature. This temperature varies with the type of gas involved. When the aggregates become so large that they are visible, we see them as mist or fog. Gradually the aggregates become large enough to form droplets. And the droplets collect as a liquid in the bottom of a container. This process, in which a gas is converted to a liquid, is called **condensation.**

All gases will condense if their temperature is lowered and the pressure on them is increased. The temperature and pres-

FIGURE 6–2 · *Condensation results in morning dew on the spider web shown here. Where else have you observed condensation in nature? Where can you observe condensation in your home?*

sure required for condensation vary for each gas. The temperature and pressure depend on the strength of the attractive forces between the molecules in that particular gas. For example, water vapor begins to condense at a pressure of one atmosphere and a temperature of 100°C. Under the same pressure, neon gas must be cooled to −245.8°C before it will condense. At higher temperatures, condensation occurs only at higher pressures.

6–4 · The critical temperature of gases · Can you apply so much pressure to a gas that it will condense regardless of the temperature? The answer is No. For every known gas there is a certain temperature above which the gas cannot be liquefied no matter how much pressure is applied. The highest temperature at which the liquefaction of a gas can occur is known is the **critical temperature** (T_c) of that gas. The **critical pressure** (P_c) of a gas is the minimum pressure needed at its critical temperature for liquefaction to occur. Table 6–1 lists the critical temperatures and pressures of some common gases.

TABLE 6–1 · Critical Constants of Some Common Gases

GAS	T_c (K)	P_c (atm)
Ammonia, NH_3	405.5	111.5
Carbon dioxide, CO_2	304.1	72.9
Chlorine, Cl_2	417.0	76.1
Helium, He	5.10	2.26
Hydrogen, H_2	33.2	12.8
Nitrogen, N_2	126.0	33.5
Oxygen, O_2	154.3	49.7
Sulfur dioxide, SO_2	430.3	77.7
Water, H_2O	647.3	218.2

6–5 · Evaporation of liquids · We have considered in some detail the condensation of gases to the liquid state. Now let us look at the changing of liquids to the vapor state.

Remember, the molecules in a liquid still possess kinetic energy. However, the kinetic energy of a molecule in a liquid is less than that of a molecule in the gaseous state. The molecular kinetic energies within a liquid never become large enough for molecules to move very far apart. The molecules within the body of a liquid are subject to attractive forces in all directions. In contrast, the molecules on the surface of a liquid are not subject to attractive forces in all directions, but only into the liquid. Therefore, it is easier for the surface molecules to gain enough kinetic energy to break away from the surface of the liquid. When they break away, the molecules then enter the gas phase. This process is called **evaporation** (Figure 6–3). Since the kinetic energy increases as the temperature increases, more molecules have sufficient energy to escape, and the rate of evaporation is greater, at higher temperatures.

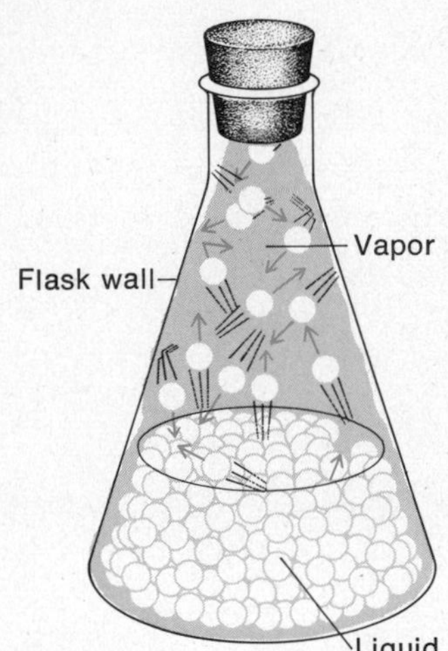

FIGURE 6–3 · *Evaporation leads to the presence of both vapor and liquid in the flask.*

6–6 · Evaporation is a cooling process · When it is very hot, we begin to perspire. This is the body's mechanism for cooling itself in hot weather. You have probably noticed a cooling effect when the moisture on the skin evaporates. In this process, heat energy from the skin is converted into kinetic energy in the water molecules. The kinetic energy enables the water molecules to break away from the liquid and enter the vapor state. Thus, heat energy is lost, and the skin is cooled.

The heat absorption necessary for evaporation is also the key to the refrigeration process. Let's look at the usual refrigeration mechanisms. One step involves the very rapid evaporation of a liquid as the pressure above the liquid is quickly decreased. The heat from the inside of the refrigerator is used for the evaporation of the liquid. Thus, the refrigerator becomes cooler. In a well-insulated refrigerator, low temperatures can be reached and maintained indefinitely. That is accomplished through a cyclic process. During such a process, the coolant gas is condensed and evaporated over and over again in the coolant system.

6–7 · Vapor pressure and how it is measured · When a liquid evaporates, the vapor that is formed exerts a pressure above the liquid. We call this the **vapor pressure.** The experimental determination of the vapor pressure of liquids is shown schematically in Figure 6–4A. The flask represents a closed system at a constant temperature. Suppose we add some liquid to the flask. Initially, evaporation takes place. The molecules escape from the liquid surface into the vapor phase at a constant rate (Figure 6–4B). The mercury level of the manometer slowly rises. The manometer indicates the pressure that is due to the vapor pressure (Figure 6–4C). As the concentration of vapor molecules increases, some of the vapor molecules will strike the liquid surface and recondense. The rate of condensation increases as evaporation continues to increase the vapor pressure. Eventually there will be no further observable change in the mercury level of the manometer (Figure 6–4D). At that point, the rate of condensation has become exactly equal to the

FIGURE 6–4 · *Evaporation causes an increase in vapor pressure until equilibrium is established.*

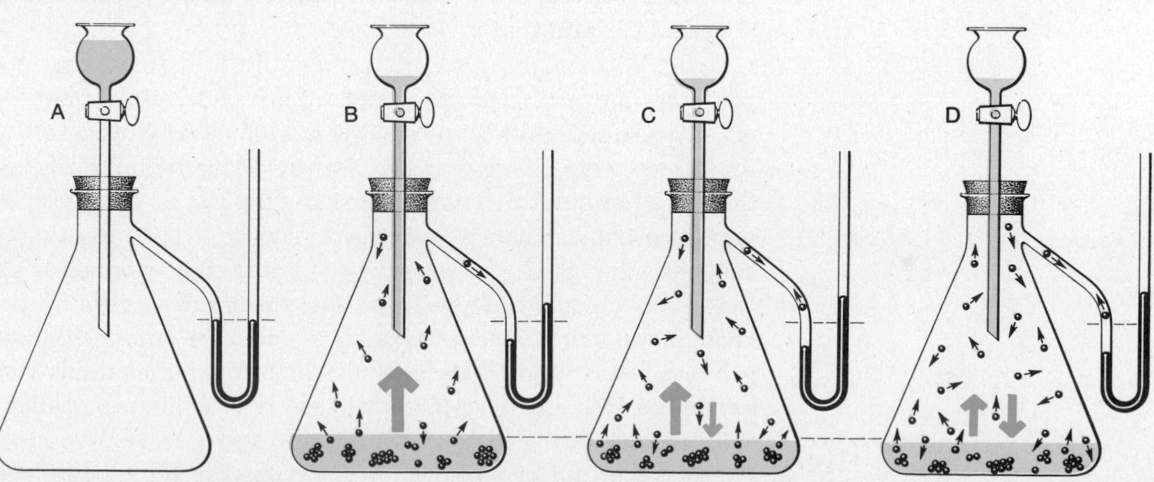

rate of evaporation. The gas volume now holds the maximum amount of vapor it can at the given temperature. It is said to be **saturated.** The pressure exerted by the vapor molecules above the liquid can now be measured.

It is extremely important to understand that the vapor pressure at any given temperature is a property of the liquid that produced the vapor. The presence of air or any other gas in the flask has no influence on the vapor pressure of that liquid (remember Dalton's Law of Partial Pressures mentioned in Chapter 5).

6–8 · Vapor pressure and equilibrium · When the number of molecules leaving the liquid equals the number returning, a **steady state** exists. The steady state attained between a liquid and its vapor is an example of an **equilibrium system.** An equilibrium system is the condition that a system reaches when no further change in measurable properties is apparent. For example, think of a liquid that is in equilibrium with its vapor. At that point, there is no observable change in the liquid level or in the vapor pressure. This definition of equilibrium is based on experimental observations. It is an **operational definition.** An operational definition, then, describes what we can measure on a macroscopic level.

We may consider a second definition of an equilibrium state, based on our interpretation of the experimental observations. A state of equilibrium is defined as the condition of a system that exists when the rates of two opposing processes are equal. What was our interpretation of the steady state between a liquid and its vapor? It was that the rate of evaporation and the rate of condensation were equal.

To emphasize the idea that at equilibrium two opposing processes are taking place (though at the same rate), chemists often speak of equilibrium as being *dynamic* rather than *static.* That infers that changes are constantly occurring on a microscopic (atomic) level. That is true even though no measurable, or macroscopic, change is evident. This is a very important concept. Change can occur between individual molecules or atoms on the microscopic level. But the number of particles changing in one direction is exactly equal to the number changing back to the original state. When we look at large numbers of molecules (the macroscopic level), we observe no net change, as the number of each type of molecule stays the same.

The definition of an equilibrium state that is based on the interpretation of observed facts is a **conceptual definition.** A conceptual definition uses all possible observed facts to infer what is happening on a microscopic level. The relationship between conceptual definitions and operational definitions is the same as that between theory and experiment. A theory must change to fit new experimental facts. In the same way, conceptual definitions will change when new experimental facts are discovered.

The chemist indicates symbolically the state of dynamic equilibrium by means of double arrows, $\rightleftarrows$. The equilibrium state between a liquid and its vapor, like that we have just considered, can therefore be symbolized as liquid $\rightleftarrows$ vapor.

6–9 · Vapor pressure and temperature · The vapor pressure of a liquid depends on the ability of the molecules on its surface to break away. To do that, the molecules must overcome the intermolecular forces of attraction holding them to the surface. Thus, vapor pressure depends on or is a function of the particular compound and always increases with temperature. In Figure 6–5 the vapor pressures of water, acetone, and ethylene glycol are shown. As you can see in Figure 6–5, the vapor pressure of acetone is higher than that of water, at all temperatures. Thus, acetone evaporates more readily than water. Accordingly, we say that acetone is more *volatile* than water. Ethylene glycol, commonly used as radiator antifreeze, is less volatile than water.

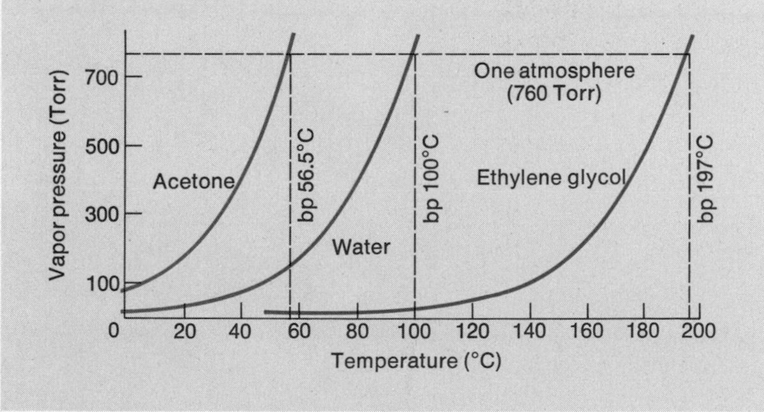

FIGURE 6–5 · *Vapor pressure curves for different liquids. The normal boiling point is indicated.*

6–10 · Boiling · Look at the graph in Figure 6–5. Note that the horizontal broken line is drawn at 760 Torr, one atmosphere pressure. The graph shows the vapor pressures of three liquids at different temperatures. Note, the vapor pressure of acetone is 760 Torr at 56.5°C. Water has a vapor pressure of 760

Torr at 100°C. And ethylene has a vapor pressure of 760 Torr at 197°C. These temperatures are the normal boiling points of the three liquids. The **normal boiling point** of a substance is the temperature at which its vapor pressure equals one atmosphere (760 Torr) of pressure.

Water will boil only when its vapor pressure is equal to the surrounding pressure. Therefore, under certain conditions, water boils at less than one atmosphere (760 Torr). At the top of a high mountain peak, the surrounding pressure is considerably less than one atmosphere. The boiling point of water on such a mountaintop would be less than it is at lower elevations. At an altitude of 1100 meters (1.10 km), water boils at 96.0°C. If the surrounding pressure is greater than 760 Torr (a pressure cooker), the boiling point of water is greater than 100°C.

Unlike simple evaporation, boiling is characterized by the presence of vapor bubbles within the liquid. The vapor pressure within the bubbles exceeds the pressure around them. As the bubbles rise through the liquid, their size increases until they reach the surface. There the bubbles break (Figure 6–6). Unlike evaporation, which is a surface phenomenon, boiling occurs throughout a liquid.

FIGURE 6–6 · *Boiling, unlike evaporation, occurs throughout a liquid.*

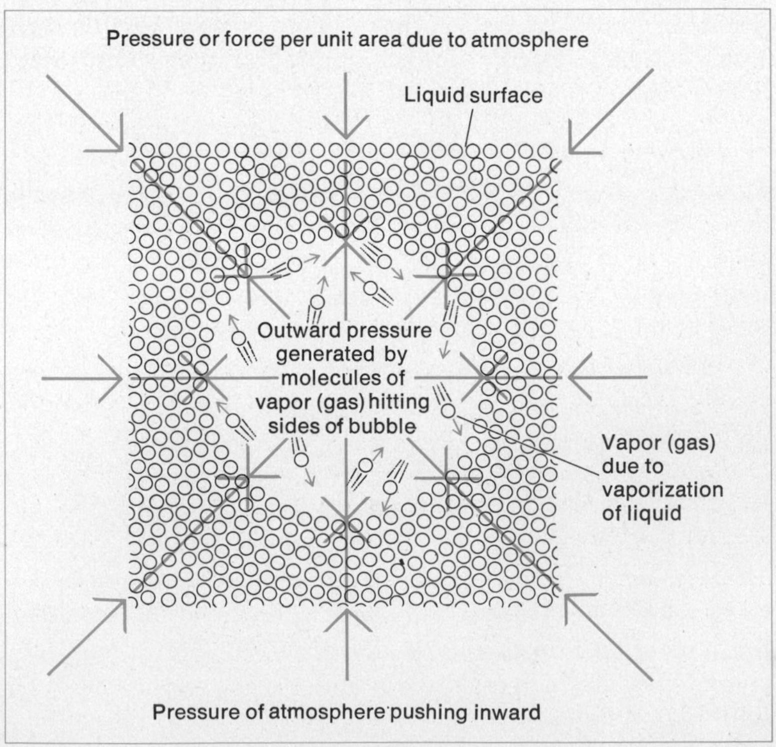

REVIEW IT NOW

1 Explain the difference between short-range order and long-range order.
2 State the two main differences in the three states of matter.
3 Why is there so little attraction between particles in the gas phase?
4 What is condensation? Explain why condensation occurs when a gas is cooled.
5 Why do liquids evaporate?
6 When you apply rubbing alcohol, after-shave lotion, or perfume to the skin, it feels cooler. Why?
7 How does a refrigeration system work?
8 Give an operational definition and a conceptual definition of an equilibrium system.
9 Why would you not want to use acetone as an antifreeze in your automobile radiator?
10 How is boiling point related to vapor pressure? Why do bubbles form when a liquid boils?
11 What is the difference between the microscopic and the macroscopic level of observation?

SOLIDS

6–11 · The solid state · When a liquid freezes, fluidity is lost, and the resulting solid is rigid. The molecules in a solid have very little kinetic energy. Because of that, the attractive forces can hold the molecules tightly in place, as the rigidity of a solid suggests. A wide variety of techniques have been employed in studying the structure of solids. The evidence obtained shows that many solids have an ordered structure that exists throughout the solid.* Thus, we can say that solids have long-range order, as opposed to the short-range order of liquids. As we've learned, liquids are composed of very small clusters packed together. Those clusters are constantly disintegrating and forming. However, a solid is a single, large cluster that does not change with time. Figure 6–7 illustrates the long-range order of molecules in a crystal. Depending on the pressure and the temperature, all substances are capable of assuming a crystalline form, with sharp edges and flat surfaces.

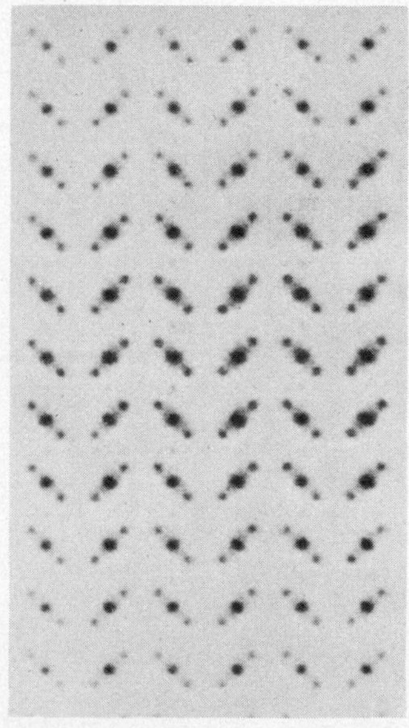

FIGURE 6–7 · *Crystalline solids have long-range order. The long-range order of a pyrite crystal, FeS_2 (44 million diameter magnification), is shown here.*

**Not all solids have the long-range order that is discussed here. Those solids that do have a regular structure are known as crystals. Sugar and salt are crystals, as is sand. Some solids, however, contain no long-range order. They are just like frozen liquids. Window glass is an example of such a solid. Often, these solids behave like very viscous (sticky) liquids.*

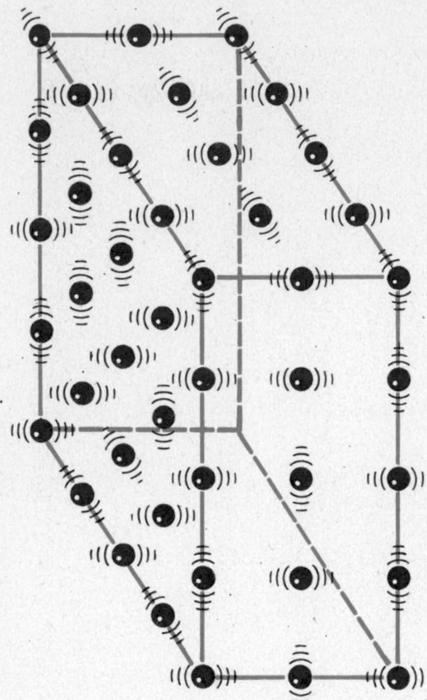

FIGURE 6–8 · *Vibrational motion within a crystal.*

6–12 · Melting solids · As heat energy is added to a solid, the energy is absorbed by the molecules in the framework of the structure. The absorbed energy is stored as molecular kinetic energy. Intermolecular attractive forces are very strong in crystals. Therefore, the motion of molecules within a crystal is restricted to vibrations, **vibrational motion,** rather than movement from once place to another (translational motion). As more energy is added, the molecular vibrations increase. The increase in molecular vibrations results in an increase in the temperature of the solid. The more heat that is added to the solid, the stronger the molecular vibrations become. Eventually the vibrations are strong enough to overcome the forces of attraction holding the framework structure together. When that happens, the solid structure begins to break down. Individual molecules and large aggregates of molecules break apart from one another. The long-range order is lost. Only the short-range order that is characteristic of liquids remains; the solid has melted. In the liquid state, each molecule has more freedom of movement. The increased kinetic energy allows the molecule to rotate about its center of mass. This **rotational motion,** as well as the vibrational movement, of molecules is characteristic of the liquid phase. As more energy is added, the molecules are carried everywhere with the container, showing **translational motion.** Translational motion usually occurs in the gas phase. However, it can be observed in the liquid phase. When this type of movement occurs in the liquid phase, it does so at a much slower rate than in the gas phase.

The temperature at which a solid exists in equilibrium with its *melt* (the liquid form of that solid) is called the **melting**

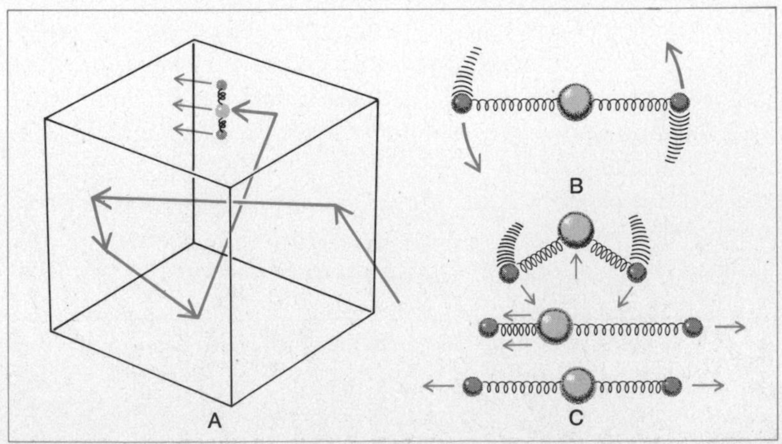

Figure 6–9 · *The three forms of molecular motion are (A) translational, (B) rotational, and (C) vibrational.*

FIGURE 6–10 · *Here copper is being melted and separated to be made into coins. The melting point of copper is 1082°C.*

point (mp). At the melting point, a solid melts at the same rate at which its liquid freezes. Thus,

$$\text{solid} \rightleftarrows \text{liquid}$$

Suppose this dynamic equilibrium system is isolated, so that no heat enters or leaves the system. There would be no apparent change in the amounts of solid and liquid present. On the other hand, suppose some heat energy is added to the system at the melting point. Then more of the solid melts, with no increase in temperature. If heat is removed from the system at its melting point, more liquid freezes, with no decrease in the temperature (Figure 6–11, page 122).

6–13 · Temperature-energy relationship in the melting of solids · Understanding the behavior of a solid when it is heated will help us understand two important facts. *Heat is a form of energy, but temperature is not.* Temperature is the measure of the average kinetic energy of the molecules. The temperature of a material increases as the average kinetic energy of its molecules increases. In order to increase the average kinetic energy of a molecule, it is necessary to add heat energy.

Therefore, a rise in temperature is a measure of the increase in kinetic energy. As energy is added to the sample at a constant rate, the change in temperature is measured (Figure 6–11). Follow the heating curve. The temperature rises as heat energy is added to the cold, solid part of the system (part A–B on the graph). The average kinetic energy increases as heat is added between A and B on the graph. Therefore, we can assume that temperature is a measure of the average kinetic energy in the solid. The particles in the crystal framework are vibrating. With more heat, the vibrations become more intense.

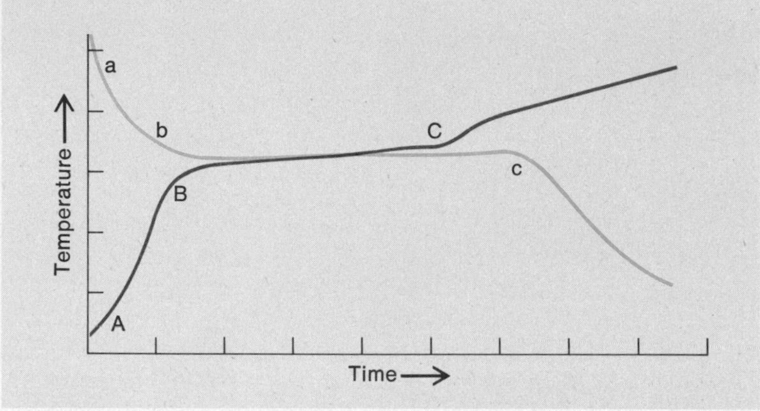

FIGURE 6–11 · *A heating curve and a cooling curve for the same pure substance.*

Now look at part B–C on the graph. The temperature does not increase during this period even though a considerable amount of heat is added. Where does all the heat energy go? The answer clarifies the difference between energy and temperature. On the graph, note that even though energy is being added, the temperature does not increase. This indicates that the average kinetic energy of the particles must not be increasing. The heat energy that is being added must be used by the system for some other purpose. The simplest explanation is that the heat energy is being stored. The stored energy can then be used to overcome the attractive forces between the particles in the solids. As a result, the solid melts. (Remember, energy is required at the melting point to overcome the attractive forces and destroy the long-range order.) The stored energy is called **potential energy.** The potential energy of the system is increased rather than the kinetic energy. When a liquid is frozen, the same amount of energy is released. (Note section a, b, c, of Figure 6–11).

6–14 · Heat energy and the calorie · Temperature, which is measured in degrees, indicates the intensity of energy. But we also need a unit to measure the total energy involved rather than just its intensity. This unit of measurement is the **calorie** (cal). The calorie expresses the amount of energy absorbed or released in a physical or chemical change. The calorie is defined as the amount of energy necessary to increase the temperature of one gram of water by one degree Celsius (1.00°C). In actual measurements, this amount of energy is often in the form of heat.

With that definition, it is possible to calculate the amount of heat energy absorbed, or released, by matter. For example, suppose a sample of 1.00 gram of water increases in temperature by 10.0°C. That sample, by definition, must have absorbed 10.0 calories of heat energy. The following is the formula for determining the amount of heat energy absorbed or released.

$$\text{calories absorbed} = \text{grams} \times \begin{matrix}\text{change in}\\ \text{the number}\\ \text{of degrees}\end{matrix} \times \begin{matrix}\text{calories}\\ \text{per degree}\\ \text{per gram}\end{matrix}$$

When dealing with a large amount of heat energy, chemists prefer to use the **kilocalorie** (kcal). It is equal to 1000 calories. Dietitians and nutritionists call 1000 calories a large Calorie, or Cal. A 900-Calorie diet is therefore a 900-kcal diet, or a 900 000-calorie diet.

6–15 · Heat absorption and heat capacity · Are the heat absorption properties of different substances the same? Suppose you left a wooden baseball bat, an iron garden tool, and a rubber hose in the hot sun all day. Which would you hesitate to pick up? When 10.0 calories of heat energy are absorbed by 1.00 gram of water, the temperature rises 10.0°C. But will the same be true for matter other than water? Will 1.00 gram of copper metal and 1.00 gram of crystalline sugar increase 10.0°C when they absorb 10.0 calories of heat energy? The answer is No. When 1.00 gram of copper absorbs 10.0 calories of heat energy, its temperature rises almost 55.0°C, not 10.0°C. Also, 1.00 gram of sugar (sucrose) increases in temperature nearly 17.0°C when it absorbs 10.0 calories of heat energy. Different substances respond differently to the absorption of the same amount of heat energy.

The heat energy absorbed by matter will be converted into molecular kinetic energy. That is indicated by a rise in the temperature.

The temperature increase is different for water, copper, and sugar when one gram of each substance absorbs 10.0 calories of heat. What can we deduce from that difference in temperature increase? Of the three, copper converts the most heat energy into molecular kinetic energy. Sugar converts less. And water converts the least amount of heat energy into molecular kinetic energy. The following says that more simply.

Copper > Sugar > Water

The conversion of heat energy into potential energy for the 1.00-gram samples is in the following order.

Water > Sugar > Copper

TABLE 6–2 · Molar Heat Capacities of Some Common Substances (Measurements made at 25.0°C unless otherwise noted.)

SOLIDS	$C_p\left(\frac{cal}{mol\text{-}deg}\right)$	LIQUIDS	$C_p\left(\frac{cal}{mol\text{-}deg}\right)$	GASES	$C_p\left(\frac{cal}{mol\text{-}deg}\right)$
Aluminum (Al)	5.82	Acetic acid (CH_3COOH)	28.2	Ammonia (NH_3)	8.523
Carbon as graphite (C)	2.07	Ammonia as a liquid at −77.7°C (NH_3)	19.2	Carbon dioxide (CO_2)	8.874
Copper (Cu)	5.85	Benzene (C_6H_6)	32.0	Hydrogen (H_2)	6.892
Ice at 0°C (H_2O)	8.86	Ethyl alcohol (C_2H_5OH)	26.7	Methane (CH_4)	8.536
Iron (Fe)	6.49	Mercury (Hg)	6.65	Nitrogen (N_2)	6.960
Iron(III) oxide (Fe_2O_3)	25.0	Water (H_2O)	17.996	Oxygen (O_2)	7.017
Lead (Pb)	6.41			Water vapor at 100°C (H_2O)	8.64
Potassium nitrate (KNO_3)	22.2				
Sodium carbonate (Na_2CO_3)	26.41				
Sodium chloride (NaCl)	11.88				
Sucrose ($C_{12}H_{22}O_{11}$)	102.6				
Sulfur (rhombic form) (S_8)	5.40				

Different substances behave differently when they absorb heat. To measure that difference in behavior, chemists have defined the property called the **heat capacity.** The heat capacity of a substance is the amount of energy absorbed per degree rise in temperature. The heat capacity depends on the amount of the substance absorbing the heat energy. A convenient amount of matter for comparison purposes is the mole. The **molar heat capacity** is the amount of heat energy required to increase the temperature of one mole of a substance by 1.00°C.

Remember that one mole of H_2O represents a mass of 18.0 grams. Thus, the molar heat capacity of liquid water (18.0 g/mol) must be 18.0 calories per mole for every 1.00°C rise in temperature. That can be stated more simply as 18.0 calories per mole-degree (cal/mol-deg). Table 6–2 gives the experimental values for the molar heat capacities of some common substances. All the values indicated were experimentally obtained at a constant pressure of one atmosphere. C_p is the symbol for the molar heat capacity measured at constant pressure.

EXAMPLE

How much heat energy would be required to raise the temperature of 1.00 mole of benzene by 10 degrees?

SOLUTION

C_p for benzene = 32.0 cal/mole-degree (read "calories per mole per degree")

Thus, 32.0 cal/mol-deg × 10.0 degrees = 320 calories/mole

EXERCISE

If you added 75.0 calories of heat energy to 1.00 mole of iron (III) oxide (Fe_2O_3), how much would you raise the temperature of the solid?

6–16 · Molar heat of fusion and vaporization · What energy is absorbed when one mole of ice (18.0 g) is heated from −10.0°C to +110°C? Look at Table 6–2. Note that one mole of ice will absorb 8.86 calories for every degree rise in temperature. Thus, heating one mole of ice from −10.0°C to 0°C will involve the following calculation.

$$(1.00\ \cancel{\text{mol}})\left(8.86\ \frac{\text{cal}}{\cancel{\text{mol}}\text{-}\cancel{\text{deg}}}\right)(10.0\ \cancel{\text{deg}}) = 88.6\ \text{cal}$$

As shown earlier, in Figure 6–11, when heat is added continuously to ice at its melting point, the temperature will remain constant until all the ice has melted. Measurement indicates that 1440 cal/m are absorbed during the melting (or fusion) process. There is an energy change associated with the change from solid to liquid even though there is no temperature change. The energy involved in melting one mole of a solid at its melting point is called the **molar heat of fusion.** Therefore, the molar heat of fusion of ice is 1.44 kcal/mol. The heat of fusion is the energy necessary to change from the long-range order in the solid to the short-range order in the liquid.

We have learned that the energy required to change one mole of ice at −10.0°C to a mole of water at 0°C totals 1529 calories (88.6 cal + 1440 cal). The mole of water may now be heated to 100°C. From Table 6–2, we note that one mole of liquid water will absorb 18.0 cal/mol for every degree rise in temperature. Then the additional heat required to raise one mole (18.0 g) of water from 0°C to 100°C can be calculated.

$$(1.00\ \cancel{\text{mol}})\left(18.0\ \frac{\text{cal}}{\cancel{\text{mol-deg}}}\right)(100\ \cancel{\text{deg}}) = 1800\ \text{cal}$$

At 100°C, as water converts from the liquid to the vapor state, we again observe experimentally that energy is added at a constant temperature until the phase change is complete. The potential energy required for the vaporization process is much greater than that required for the melting process. The heat of vaporization represents the amount of kinetic energy needed for molecules in the liquid state to overcome their mutual attraction. It is the energy needed for separation into individual molecules moving away from one another in the characteristic manner of gas molecules. The molar heat of vaporization of water, as it is measured at its normal boiling point, is 9720 cal/mol. Bringing one mole of ice from −10.0°C to the vapor state at 100°C has required 13 049 calories (88.6 cal + 1440 cal + 1800 cal + 9720 cal).

Finally, from Table 6–2 we can calculate the energy needed to heat one mole of water vapor from 100°C to 110°C. The molar heat capacity of water vapor is 8.64 cal/mol-deg. The energy required is shown in the following equation.

$$(1.00\ \cancel{\text{mol}})\left(\frac{8.64\ \text{cal}}{\text{mol-}\cancel{\text{deg}}}\right)(10.0\ \cancel{\text{deg}}) = 86.4\ \text{cal}$$

The overall change can be represented by successive steps in this fashion, where Q represents the energy absorbed.

1. ice (1.00 mol at −10.0°C) ⟶ ice (1.00 mol at 0.0°C) $Q_1 =$ 89 cal
2. ice (1.00 mol at 0.0°C) ⟶ water (1.00 mol at 0.0°C) $Q_2 =$ 1440 cal
3. water (1.00 mol at 0.0°C) ⟶ water (1.00 mol at 100.0°C) $Q_3 =$ 1800 cal
4. water (1.00 mol at 100.0°C) ⟶ water vapor (1.00 mol at 100.0°C) $Q_4 =$ 9270 cal
5. water vapor (1.00 mol at 100.0°C) → water vapor (1.00 mol at 110.0°C) $Q_5 =$ 86 cal

Total $Q =$ 13135 cal

Consequently, the total amount of energy required to change one mole of ice at −10.0°C to one mole of water vapor at 110°C is 13.1 kilocalories.

If the Law of the Conservation of Energy is to hold, the reverse reaction, or the change of one mole of water vapor at 110°C to one mole of ice at −10.0°C, must release exactly the same energy, 13.1 kilocalories. Experiments verify that this, indeed, does occur. Also, the reverse process, in each individual step, releases exactly the same number of calories that the forward process absorbed. Melting a mole of ice requires 1440 calories; when a mole of water freezes, 1440 calories are released. Evaporating a mole of water requires 9720 calories; when a mole of water vapor condenses, 9720 calories are released.

6–17 · Solids may be classified according to structure · Table 6–3 shows that metals, in general, have molar heat capacities (C_p) of approximately six cal/mol-deg. However, solid compounds like iron (III) oxide, potassium nitrate, sodium carbonate, and sodium chloride are different. These solid compounds fall into a group having a higher molar heat capacity. They have C_p values ranging from 11.88 cal/mol-deg to 26.41 cal/mol-deg. It might seem, then, that solids fall into different classes. Indeed, experimental observations prove that there are four classes of crystalline solids. These are known as **metallic** solids, **ionic** solids, **molecular** solids, and **covalent** solids. Table 6–3 gives examples of each of these types.

Later we will discuss structural arrangements in the solid state that cause the four classes of crystalline solids. At this point, however, we will consider only two of the classes.

TABLE 6–3 · Examples of Four Classes of Solids

METALLIC CRYSTALS	IONIC CRYSTALS
Copper, Cu	Barium chloride, $BaCl_2$
Magnesium, Mg	Calcium nitrate, $Ca(NO_3)_2$
Silver, Ag	Potassium nitrate, KNO_3
Tungsten, W	Zinc iodide, ZnI_2
MOLECULAR CRYSTALS	**COVALENT CRYSTALS**
Carbon dioxide, CO_2	Carbon (diamond and graphite), C
Hydrogen chloride, HCl	Phosphorus (red), P
Ice, H_2O	Silicon carbide, SiC
Phosphorus (white), P_4	Silicon dioxide (quartz), SiO_2

6–18 · Ionic and molecular solids · We have chosen to discuss only ionic and molecular solids at this point. They are the two most commonly encountered types of solids. Table 6–4 lists eight compounds of these two classes of solids, with their melting points. Look at the melting points for each group. Notice that the melting points for the ionic solids are higher than the melting points for the molecular solids. Now look back at Table 6–2. The molar heat capacity of potassium nitrate, an ionic solid, is much larger than that of ice, a molecular solid. In fact, ionic solids in general have higher heat capacities than do molecular solids. The attractive forces between particles in ionic solids are greater than those in molecular solids. That is clearly indicated by the data in Table 6–4. Both the heat capacity and the melting point indicate the amount of energy required to overcome the attractive forces between the particles in a solid.

TABLE 6–4 · The Melting Points of Some Ionic and Molecular Solids

IONIC SOLIDS	mp (°C)	MOLECULAR SOLIDS	mp (°C)
$BaCl_2$	962	CO_2	−56.6
$Ca(NO_3)_2$	561	HCl	−112
KNO_3	334	H_2O (ice)	0
ZnI_2	446	P_4	44.1

6–19 · The structure of ionic solids · Why is the attractive force in an ionic solid so much greater than that in a molecular solid? Scientists have done many types of experiments to answer that question. They have learned that ionic solids are composed of oppositely charged particles. And those particles are organized in a rigid and regular structure known as a **crystal lattice.** The charged particles are the atoms of the compounds that form the solid. The metal atoms have positive charges, while the nonmetal atoms have negative charges. Atoms that are either positively or negatively charged are known as ions.

The metal atoms become positive ions. For example, electrically neutral sodium atoms, Na, become positive sodium ions, Na^{+1}. Magnesium atoms, Mg, become magnesium ions bearing a double positive charge, Mg^{+2}. Some other positive ions are Fe^{+2}, Fe^{+3}, K^{+1}, Zn^{+2}, and NH_4^{+1}, (the ammonium ion). The significance of the $^{+1}$, $^{+2}$, and $^{+3}$ charges will be discussed in a later chapter.

The nonmetal atoms become negative ions. For example, chlorine atoms become negative chloride ions, Cl^{-1}. Oxygen atoms, O, become oxygen ions bearing a double negative charge, O^{-2}, called oxide ions. Some other negative ions are N^{-3}, S^{-2}, $(NO_3)^{-1}$, $(SO_4)^{-2}$, and $(PO_4)^{-3}$. There is a strong attraction between the negative charges of the nonmetal ions and the positive charges of the metal ions. That is what causes the strong attractive force in ionic crystals.

Positive ions are called **cations.** Negative ions are called **anions.** Ionic solids consist of crystal lattices in which the cations and anions alternate. Each cation has a number of anions surrounding it. And each anion has a number of cations surrounding it. It is improper to say that any particular anion belongs to or is associated with any particular cation. Therefore, there are no true molecules (associated atoms) in an ionic solid. The ionic crystal lattice is a single giant aggregate of ions. The formula for an ionic solid must be considered only as the simplest formula for the solid and not as an indication of the presence of molecules.

Since a cation and an anion are oppositely charged, they have a strong attraction for each other. It requires a great deal of energy to overcome the attraction. When enough energy is supplied, the crystal lattice falls apart. When that happens, the solid melts, allowing the ions to move about freely in the liquid. Melted ionic solids conduct electricity between two electrodes. That indicates that the ions are still present and are moving about freely in the liquid state. The movement of the ions provides the flow of electric charge for electrical conductivity (See Figure 6–12).

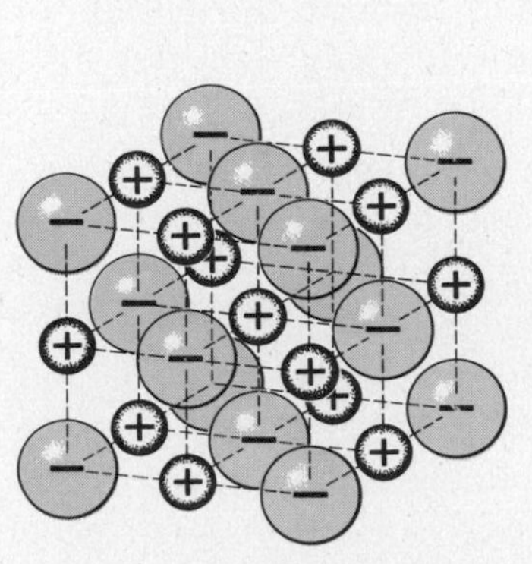

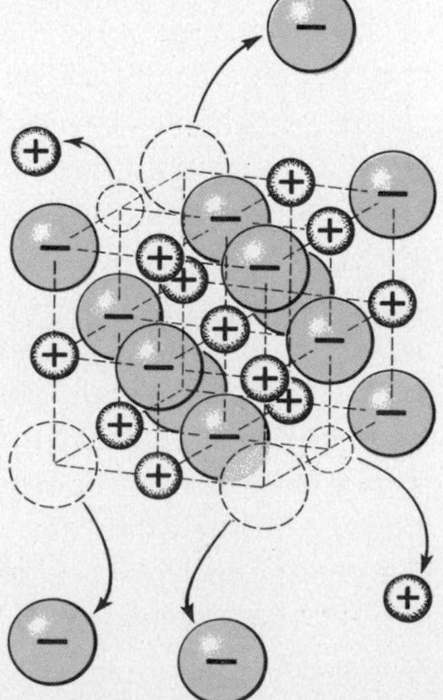

FIGURE 6–12 · *The orderly arrangement of cations and anions in an ionic crystal lattice is shown in the drawing on the left. The drawing on the right shows a partially melted ionic crystal. The ions in the melt are free to move.*

6–20 · The structure of molecular solids · The melts of ionic crystals conduct electricity. But when molecular solids are melted, their liquids do not conduct electricity. That must mean that molecular solids do not contain ions with opposite charges. Such an observation is also consistent with one experimental fact that we have already mentioned. The attractive force between the particles in a molecular solid is weaker than that in an ionic solid. That indicates that the particles in a molecular solid must have a different nature.

In a molecular solid, it would seem reasonable that the force of attraction between particles must still be coulombic. That would require attraction between charged particles. However, the attractive force is much weaker than that between the anions and cations in ionic solids. Therefore, the amount of charge of particles in a molecular solid must be less than that of ions. In electrically neutral molecules, there is often a slightly unequal distribution of positive and negative charge. One part of the molecule has a slight excess of positive charge. Another part of the molecule has a slight excess of negative charge. The amount of excess positive charge is equal to the amount of excess negative charge. Therefore, the molecule as a whole has no net charge. Molecules that are slightly positive at one end and slightly negative at the other end are **dipoles.** That means that within the molecules, there is both a negative and a positive pole (Figure 6–14). Molecular solids consist of an orderly array of molecular dipoles, as shown in Figure 6–14.

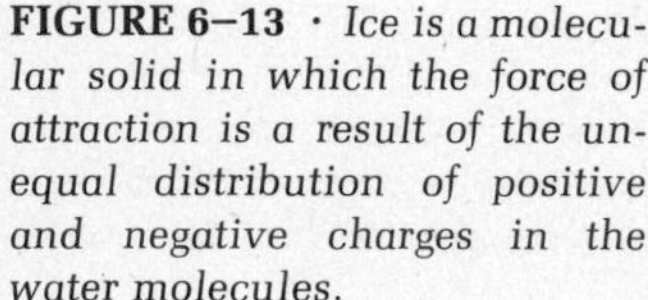

FIGURE 6–13 · *Ice is a molecular solid in which the force of attraction is a result of the unequal distribution of positive and negative charges in the water molecules.*

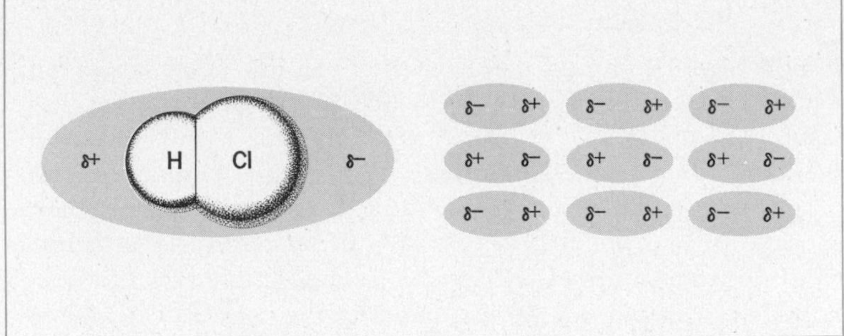

FIGURE 6–14 · *(Left) A dipolar HCl molecule drawn to scale; (Right) An arrangement of molecular dipoles in a solid. How does a molecular solid differ from an ionic solid?*

The force of attraction between particles is rather weak in a molecular solid. Therefore, the charge at the ends of the molecular dipole must be less than that of the cations and anions in ionic solids. In other words, the charge must be less than +1 and −1 in the dipole. We speak of these charges as being "partial charges." And we use the Greek symbol δ (Delta) to indicate this partiality. The symbols δ+ and δ− represent the relative difference in the electrical properties of the different parts of a molecule. The negative end of the molecule is only partially negative. In other words, it is less negative than a unit negative anion such as Cl^{-1}. Similarly the positive end of the molecule is only partially positive. It is less positive than a unit positive cation such as Na^{+1}. Consequently, the coulombic attraction between the opposite ends of dipoles is less than that between anions and cations. Dipole–dipole attractive forces are weaker than ionic forces. Therefore, it takes less heat energy to supply dipoles with sufficient energy to overcome the forces of attraction. As a result, molecular solids have lower melting points and heat capacities than do ionic solids.

EXCURSION TWO

Liquid Crystals

This excursion discusses the properties and behavior of liquid crystals and demonstrates some of their uses.

REVIEW IT NOW

1 Describe three types of molecular motion.
2 Explain the process of melting.
3 Define the *calorie*.
4 Define *molar heat capacity*, *molar heat of fusion*, and *molar heat of vaporization*.
5 What are the four types of crystalline solids?
6 What evidence do we have that the attractive forces in ionic solids are greater than those in molecular solids?
7 Describe the arrangement of particles within an ionic solid and a molecular solid.
8 What is a dipole?

SUMMARY

The existence of the liquid and solid states of matter requires a new model for molecules in the gaseous state—a model in which intermolecular attractive forces are present.

Evaporation occurs when the surface molecules of a liquid gain sufficient kinetic energy to overcome the intermolecular attractive forces. The molecules in the gaseous state above a liquid surface exert a vapor pressure that is dependent only on the temperature of the system. At a given temperature in a closed system, there is a state of equilibrium in which the rates of evaporation and condensation are equal. Boiling occurs at the temperature at which the vapor pressure of the liquid equals the external pressure above the liquid.

Liquids are characterized by short-range order; solids are characterized by long-range order. The temperature at which a solid exists in equilibrium with its melt is called the melting, or the freezing, point of the substance.

When a substance changes its state, large amounts of heat energy are absorbed with *no* increase in the temperature. This energy is present, from the macroscopic point of view, as potential energy.

The arbitrary unit for heat energy is the calorie. To increase the temperature of one gram of water by 1.00°C, one calorie of heat energy is needed. The heat capacity of a substance is a measure of its heat absorption properties. The molar heat capacities of substances have low values when compared with the molar heats of fusion and vaporization.

Coulombic (electrical) forces are the source of the intermolecular attraction. When the coulombic forces in a solid are strong, the solid has a high melting point.

REVIEW QUESTIONS

1 How does a pressure cooker work?

2 Explain, in terms of molecular behavior, how gases condense to form liquids.

3 Explain how evaporation occurs.

4 When an automobile is climbing a high mountain during the summer, its radiator may boil over. Explain this.

5 What is the critical temperature of a gas? How can this be explained in terms of molecular behavior?

6 Why do we refer to equilibrium as a "dynamic" process?

7 Define *equilibrium* in terms of an operational definition and a conceptual definition.

8 What is meant by microscopic and macroscopic changes?

9 Water can be boiled in a paper bag if it is placed on a screen and heated slowly with a burner (try it!). Explain this.

10 How much energy must be absorbed to change 3.00 moles of ice (at 0°C) to 3.00 moles of water vapor (at 100°C)? Express your answer in calories.

11 Define *calorie*. How many calories are required to increase the temperature of 10.0 g of water by 10.0°C? How many kilocalories is this?

12 What properties should a gas have to make it suitable as a refrigerant? Explain.

13 a. Why doesn't ethylene glycol normally boil at 100°C?

b. Under what conditions will ethylene glycol boil at 100°C?

c. Under what conditions will water *not* boil at 100°C?

14 When 5.40 g of aluminum metal at 75.0°C cool to 25.0°C, how much heat is evolved?

15 Suppose a flask contains liquid water and ether vapor. What effect would the ether vapor have on the vapor pressure of the liquid water in the flask?

16 It is an experimental observation that when a gas *in an isolated system* expands to a region of lower pressure, the temperature of the gas is decreased. This called the Joule-Thomson effect conceptually. How would you account for it? (Recall that a decrease in temperature indicates a lower average molecular kinetic energy.)

17 Account for the observation that when a carbon dioxide fire extinguisher is operating, a fine cloud of CO_2 "snow" forms.

18 What is molar heat capacity?

a. How many calories are required to raise the temperature of 780 g of benzene, C_6H_6, by 10.0°C?

b. How many calories are required to raise the temperature of 460 g of ethyl alcohol, C_2H_5OH, from 25.0°C to 35.0°C?

19 Sodium chloride, NaCl, melts at 800°C, while sucrose, $C_{12}H_{22}O_{11}$, melts at 185°C. The melted salt is an electrical conductor; the melted sugar is not. How can you account for these experimental differences?

SUGGESTED READINGS

Alfano, R. R., and S. L. Shapiro. "Ultrafast Phenomena in Liquids and Solids." *Scientific American*, June 1973, p. 43.

Fergason, James L. "Liquid Crystals." *Scientific American*, August 1964, p. 76.

Habashi, Fathi. "Chemistry and Metallurgy." *Chemistry*, October 1972, p. 6.

Wunderlich, Bernard. "The Solid State of Polyethylene." *Scientific American*, November 1964, p. 81.

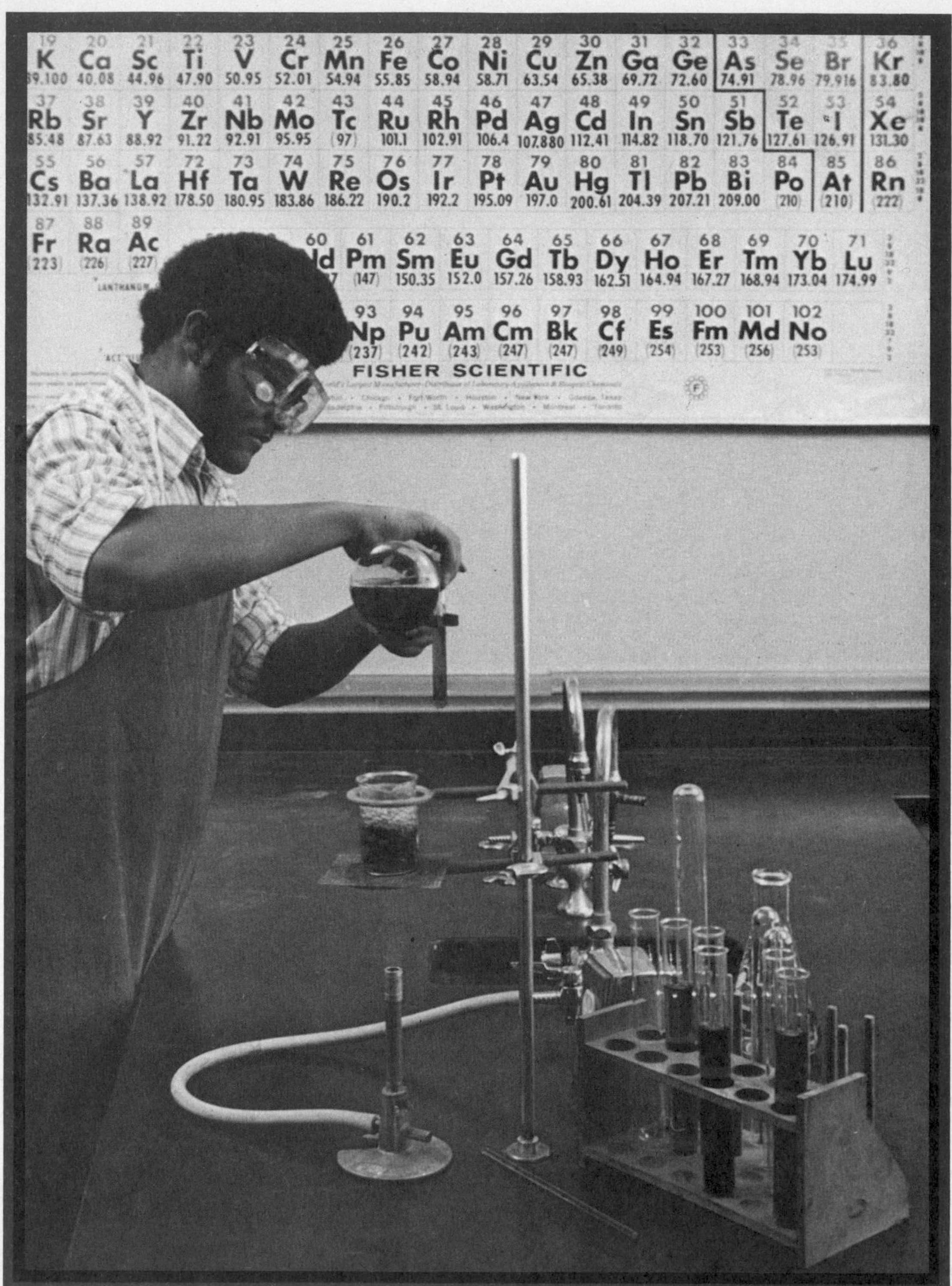

Do you think this periodic table needs to be updated?

CHAPTER SEVEN

Chemical Periodicity

As of now, 108 chemical elements have been isolated and identified. That may seem like a relatively small number of elements. But from that small number of elements, millions of different chemical compounds are formed. Chemistry is the study of those 108 elements and their compounds.

Fortunately there are many patterns or regularities in the behavior of the elements. If that were not true, chemistry would be unbelievably complex. Scientists have already discovered a number of patterns, or regularities. And they have developed theories that explain those regularities. The patterns of behavior and the theories that explain them help us in our understanding of chemistry. From them, we understand the properties of both the elements and the compounds they form.

NOBLE GASES

7–1 · Patterns of behavior of six rare gases · Many of the regularities in behavior and properties of the elements can be easily observed. Let's begin our study of the patterns of behavior by considering the most basic chemical property of the elements. This chemical property is **chemical activity.** Scientists have discovered experimentally that nearly all the elements have the property of chemical activity. Under certain conditions, each of the elements will combine with one or more of the other elements to form a compound. For example, let's consider the elements chlorine, a yellow-green gas, and sodium, a soft, silvery solid. At room temperature, the two elements combine to form the compound sodium chloride, common table salt. However, under other conditions, chlorine combines with hydrogen to form hydrogen chloride gas. Hydrogen chloride gas can dissolve in water to form hydrochloric acid.

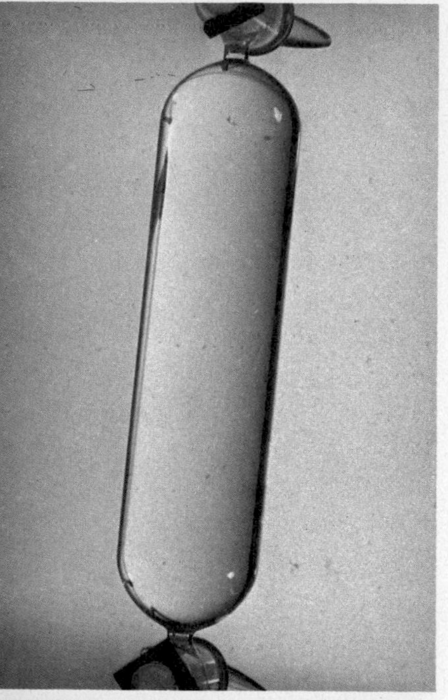

FIGURE 7–1 · *Chlorine gas (top) reacts with sodium metal (center) to form the white, crystalline compound sodium chloride (bottom).*

Only six of the 108 elements do not react with other elements, or react much less readily than all the other elements. Let's study these six elements first.

7–2 · The rare, or noble, gases · As we stated, there are six elements that are not chemically active to any significant degree. These elements are called the **rare,** or noble, **gas elements.** They are helium (He), neon (Ne), argon (Ar), krypton (Kr), xenon (Xe), and radon (Rn). These elements are rare, indeed. They exist only in minute amounts, except for argon (Table 7–1). Argon is third in abundance among all the gases in the atmosphere. These six gases are called noble because of their general chemical inactivity. In fact, for more than seventy years after their discovery, no compounds were known for the six gases. For that reason, they were commonly known as the **inert gases.** Since 1962, a number of stable compounds of some of these elements have been prepared (Table 7–2). However, even today, the total number of noble-gas compounds is very small (about 15). And still, no compounds of helium and neon have been synthesized. The general lack of chemical activity of the noble-gas elements is one of the most easily recognized regularities in nature.

TABLE 7–1 · Composition of Dry Air

SUBSTANCE	PERCENT BY VOLUME
N_2	78
O_2	21
Ar	0.93
CO_2	Varies—average 0.03
H_2	0.01
Ne	0.0018
He	0.0005
Kr	0.0001
Xe	0.00001
Rn	Varies—very low

The chemical inactivity of the noble gases indicates a basic similarity among these six elements. Therefore, it is not surprising that they have a number of other properties in common. For example, at room temperature, all six elements are gases. Also, unlike all other elemental gases, they exist only as monatomic (one atom) species in the gas phase. This is their most distinctive property.

TABLE 7–2 · Some Compounds of the Noble Gases

PROPERTY	KrF_2	XeF_2	XeF_4	XeF_6	XeO_3
Physical form	Colorless crystals	Same	Same	Same	Same
Melting point	Sublimes <0°C	140°C	114°C	48°C	———
Reactivity	Decomposes spontaneously at room temperature.	Reacts with H_2O to form Xe, O_2, and HF.	Stable	Stable	Explosive

7–3 · The discovery of the noble gases · The noble gases are rare, odorless, colorless, and chemically inactive. With such properties, we can see why their presence was difficult to detect. The first clue to their existence was provided by an English scientist, Henry Cavendish (1731–1810), almost two centuries ago.

Cavendish conducted an experiment in which he attempted to change atmospheric nitrogen into nitric acid. He wrote:

Having condensed as much [nitrogen] *as I could, only a small bubble of air remained. So that if there is any part of the nitrogen of our atmosphere which differs from the rest, we may safely conclude that it is not more than 1/120th* [.00833] *part of the whole.*

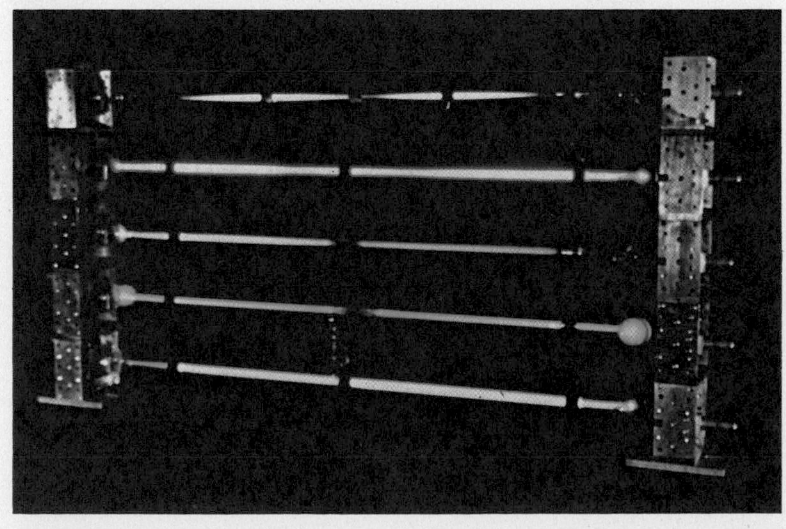

FIGURE 7–2 · *Tubes containing the noble gases emit a characteristic colored light when energy is applied. From top to bottom, the gases are helium, neon, argon, krypton, and xenon.*

In 1894, two other English scientists, John Rayleigh (1842–1919) and William Ramsay (1852–1916), repeated Cavendish's experiment. They isolated a small quantity of the gas that Cavendish had called a "bubble of air." After subjecting it to every known test, they concluded that they had discovered a new element. Unlike any of the known elements, the new element seemed to be chemically inert. They named it argon, from the Greek word meaning "lazy one." Argon exists as 0.00925 part of air, which agrees well with Cavendish's value of 0.00833. Both Ramsay and Rayleigh received a Nobel prize in 1904 for their pioneering work with the inert gases.

Helium, the lightest of the rare gases, was actually discovered some years before argon. Surprisingly, it was first observed around the sun. Its presence was detected by means of an optical instrument called a **spectroscope.** That instrument was invented by Robert Bunsen (1811–1899), who also invented the bunsen burner. The spectroscope is used to separate light rays so that they can be analyzed. When an element is heated to a very high temperature, it radiates light that is characteristic of that element. The light is separated by the spectroscope into its individual colors. Then the pattern of the separated colors can be used to identify the element.

In Chapter 8 we will discuss the spectral patterns of elements and compounds in detail. However, the important point to remember here is that the spectral lines are like fingerprints. In other words, no two elements have been found to have the

FIGURE 7–3 · *The early apparatus developed by Robert Bunsen (left) and Gustav Kirchoff for the analysis of spectral patterns of substances*

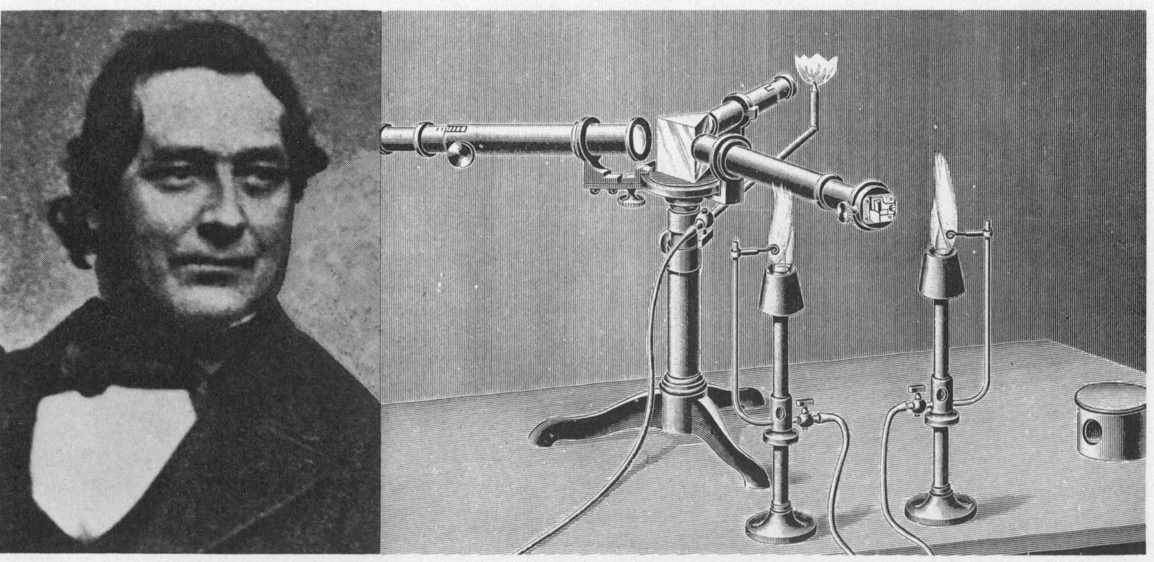

FIGURE 7–4 · *Modern spectropscopic equipment at Argonne National Laboratory. The ruby laser beam can be observed in the center of the photograph.*

same spectral pattern. In 1868, a total solar eclipse was visible in India. At that time Pierre Janssen (1824–1907), a French scientist, used a spectroscope to observe the light streaming from the inner atmosphere of the sun (the chromosphere). He could not relate a yellow line of color that he saw to any of the known elements. Later that year, Joseph Lockyer (1836–1920), an English astronomer, verified Janssen's discovery. He used a specially designed spectroscope for that purpose. Consequently, the discovery of a new chemical element was claimed. The element was named **helium** from the Greek word *helios* meaning "sun." Thirty years later, William Ramsay discovered the new element on the earth.

FIGURE 7–5 · *Helium was discovered by Pierre Janssen through a spectroscopic analysis of the corona of the sun.*

Helium is often formed as a product of the radioactive disintegration of heavy elements. As such, it is found in significant quantities trapped in the earth. Nearly all the helium in the world is recovered from natural gas deposits in the United States. Some of those deposits contain as much as 8 percent helium by volume. Important helium-recovery installations are located in the Texas Panhandle, northwestern New Mexico, Kansas, and Utah. In the United States, the annual production of helium from natural gas deposits is more than 0.50 billion cubic meters.

FIGURE 7–6 · *Helium is obtained by separation from natural gas that is released from the earth by wells like this one in Texas.*

Between 1894 and 1898, Ramsay and his co-workers isolated three other rare gases from samples of liquified air. One was named **neon,** from the Greek word meaning "new." The second was named **krypton,** from the Greek word meaning "hidden." And the third was named **xenon,** from the Greek word meaning "stranger." The last of the rare gases was discovered in 1900. That gas was given off from chemicals containing radium. For this reason, it was given the name **radon.**

7–4 · Properties of the noble gases · Some of the physical properties of the rare gases are listed in Table 7 – 3. Remember, the heat of fusion is the energy required (in kilocalories*) to melt one mole of a solid at its melting point. And the heat of vaporization is the energy (in kilocalories) needed to vaporize one mole of a liquid at its boiling point.

EXERCISE

Study Table 7 – 3. Can you detect some patterns in the properties of the six elements with increasing atomic mass? Do the boiling points increase, or decrease? Do the heats of fusion increase, or decrease? Do the heats of vaporization increase, or decrease?

Suppose scientists discovered another inactive element, with an atomic mass greater than that of radon. What conclusions could you draw about the new element? Do you think it would be a solid, a liquid, or a gas at room temperature? How do you think its boiling point would compare with that of radon? How do you think its other properties would compare with those of radon listed in Table 7 – 3?

7–5 · Attractive forces and the noble gases. · You have learned what factor helps a substance exist in the liquid or solid state. That factor is the strength or weakness of the attractive forces between the atoms or molecules. The heat of fusion and the heat of vaporization of a substance are measures of the strength of those attractive forces. As you can see in Table 7 – 3, the noble-gas elements have low heats of fusion and vaporization. Therefore, little energy is needed to overcome the attractive forces between their atoms in the liquid and solid

---

**1 Kilocalorie = 1000 calories = amount of energy required to raise the temperature of 1000 ml of H_2O from 14.5°C to 15.5°C.*

TABLE 7–3 · Some Physical Properties of the Rare Gases

PROPERTY	He	Ne	Ar	Kr	Xe	Rn
Atomic mass (AMU)	4.00	20.18	39.94	83.80	131.3	222
Melting point (°C)	−270	−249	−189	−157	−112	−71
Boiling point (°C)	−269	−246	−186	−153	−108	−62
Heat of fusion (kcal/mol)	———	0.08	0.27	0.36	0.49	0.8
Heat of vaporization (kcal/mol)	0.02	0.44	1.50	2.31	3.27	3.92

states. We can conclude that the attractive forces are very weak. Look at Table 7–3 again. Which of the noble-gas elements requires the least energy to overcome its attractive forces in the liquid and solid states? Which requires the greatest energy? Is there any relationship between the atomic mass and the strength of the attractive forces within each of the noble-gas elements? The greater the atomic mass of any of these elements, the greater are the attractive forces binding the atoms to one another. For example, the forces that attract helium atoms to one another in the liquid or solid state are very weak. In fact, they are so easily overcome that helium has the lowest boiling point of any known substance. It cannot be solidified at any temperature unless high pressure is applied. Solid helium can be prepared at 1.10 K, at a pressure of 26 atmospheres!

FIGURE 7–7 · *Crystals of xenon tetrafluoride, XeF_4, one of the few compounds of the noble gas elements, are shown here.*

7–6 · Some uses for the noble gases · For many years after their discovery, the noble gases remained chemical curiosities. Helium was the first to be put to use. It was used in place of hydrogen for inflating blimps and weather observation balloons. Now helium is used in many ways. It is mixed with oxygen to form a synthetic air that is used under pressure in caissons. This mixture is supplied to deep-sea divers to prevent the bends. Liquid helium is an important industrial and laboratory coolant, used to obtain very low temperatures. Much of the helium produced today is used in the space program for pressurizing fuel tanks.

But helium is not the only noble gas that can be put to use. For example, metals such as aluminum and magnesium are arc-welded in an atmosphere of argon or helium. That prevents the metals from reacting with the oxygen or nitrogen of the air. Argon is also used as a blanketing gas. As such, it is used during the processing and packaging of certain foods. In its presence, the foods retain their normal color and taste. Electric light bulbs are filled with argon to prevent the burning of the tungsten filament. That allows the lamp to be operated at higher temperatures.

The noble gases are also widely used in the glowing glass tubes in advertising signs. In these lights, an electric current is sent through a tube containing a noble gas. In the case of neon, the gas glows orange-red, the familiar neon light. The gas is at low pressure, about 12 Torr. Neon and krypton lights are also used to mark airplane runways and to signal pilots.

FIGURE 7–8 · *Neon signs do not always contain neon, as the different colors show. What other noble gases might be in the letters of this sign?*

REVIEW IT NOW

1 What noble gas did Henry Cavendish discover?
2 How is a spectroscope useful in identifying an element?
3 Where and how was helium first discovered?
4 List the noble gases.
5 Which of the noble gases is the most abundant in nature?
6 Why were the noble gases considered inert for such a long period of time?
7 What are three distinct features of the noble gases?
8 What is the relationship between an element's atomic mass and the attractive forces between its atoms?
9 Which inert gas do you think has the weakest attractive forces between its atoms? Which do you think has the strongest attractive forces? How can you determine this?
10 How was helium first put to use?
11 What are some other uses of helium?
12 List the uses of some of the other inert gases.

CLASSIFICATION OF THE ELEMENTS

7–7 · Patterns of chemical behavior: a valuable tool of science · You have just studied one specific pattern that exists within a group of elements. There are many other patterns that exist within groups of elements. Those patterns make it possible to predict the properties of different elements within the group. The idea of related groups, or families, of elements developed very slowly during the history of chemistry. The knowledge that elements fall into related groups is one of the most valuable tools of the chemist today.

In addition to the noble gases, several other groups, or families, of elements exist. Two such groups are the **halogens** and the **alkali metals.** Their properties further demonstrate the existence of regularities and similarities among the chemical elements. Other rather easily recognized families of elements include groups such as the **nitrogen group:** N, P, As, Sb, Bi; the **oxygen group:** O, S, Se, Te; the **carbon group:** C, Si, Ge, Sn, Pb; the **alkaline earth family:** Mg, Ca, Sr, Ba, Ra; and the **aluminum group:** Al, Ga, In and Tl. (See Figure 7–9, page 144.)

As early as 1829, the German chemist J. W. Döbereiner (1780–1849) tried to organize the elements according to their atomic masses. However, many elements had not been discovered at that time. Therefore, the atomic-mass scale was still a matter of controversy. Chemistry was not prepared for much progress in that area in 1829.

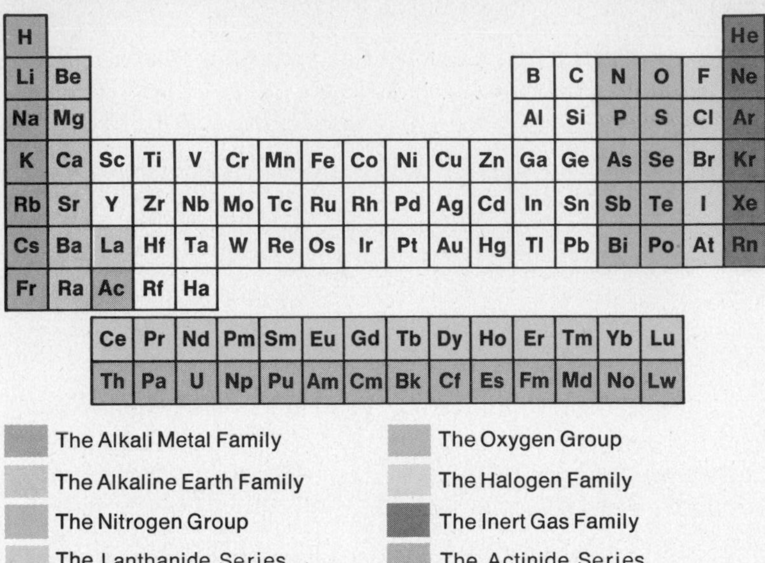

H He
Li Be B C N O F Ne
Na Mg Al Si P S Cl Ar
K Ca Sc Ti V Cr Mn Fe Co Ni Cu Zn Ga Ge As Se Br Kr
Rb Sr Y Zr Nb Mo Tc Ru Rh Pd Ag Cd In Sn Sb Te I Xe
Cs Ba La Hf Ta W Re Os Ir Pt Au Hg Tl Pb Bi Po At Rn
Fr Ra Ac Rf Ha
Ce Pr Nd Pm Sm Eu Gd Tb Dy Ho Er Tm Yb Lu
Th Pa U Np Pu Am Cm Bk Cf Es Fm Md No Lw
The Alkali Metal Family
The Alkaline Earth Family
The Nitrogen Group
The Lanthanide Series
The Oxygen Group
The Halogen Family
The Inert Gas Family
The Actinide Series

FIGURE 7–9 · *A form of the periodic table showing some of the families of elements*

By the 1860's, the list of known elements had greatly increased. Evidence of regularities in the properites of the elemental families was mounting. That additional information led to several attempts to classify all the elements into some regular pattern. In 1863, J. A. R. Newlands (1838–1898) arranged the elements in groups of eight (the law of octaves). His grouping was organized in order of increasing atomic masses. Every eighth element fell in the same chemical family. Newlands' scheme was only partially successful.

In 1869, Dmitri Mendeleev (1834–1907), a Russian, and Lothar Meyer (1830–1895), a German, independently discovered the principle of the periodicity of the elements. On the basis of the systematic study of the properties of the 63 elements known at the time and their compounds, a Periodic Law was stated. *The properties of the elements are periodic functions of their atomic masses*. That great achievement provided a new key to the understanding of the elements.

7–8 · Present basis of the periodic table · Mendeleev's approach was more useful than Meyer's. For that reason, his name is more often associated with the Periodic Table of the Elements. In constructing his table, Mendeleev was guided by the properties of the elements. He used atomic mass as the basis for ordering the elements.

Henry G. J. Moseley (1887–1915) was a brilliant young English scientist who worked with periodicity in 1913. He experimentally demonstrated a more exact basis for the arrangement of elements in the periodic table than the order of atomic masses. He showed that the X-ray emission of the various elements could be arranged in a sequence. Moseley deduced that there is a numerical ordering of the elements. The elements should be arranged according to that numerical ordering rather than according to the atomic-mass ordering of Mendeleev. Moseley gave each element an atomic number that corresponded to the element's position in the sequence.

Difficulties arose from a periodic table based on atomic masses. For example, argon has an atomic mass of 39.9 amu, and the atomic mass of potassium is 39.1 amu. Therefore, argon should follow potassium in a table based on atomic masses. But the properties of argon put it in the family of noble gases in a position that precedes potassium. The periodic table based on Moseley's atomic numbers solved that problem. Moseley's research led to an atomic number of 18 for argon and 19 for potassium. That eliminated the problem of the atomic-mass inversion for the two elements. Similar inversions existed for cobalt and nickel, and for iodine and tellurium. Moseley's table of atomic number ordering eliminated those problems, also (Figure 7–10). As a result of Moseley's work, the Periodic Law had to be restated.

THE PERIODIC LAW

The properties of the elements and their compounds are periodic functions of the atomic numbers of the elements.

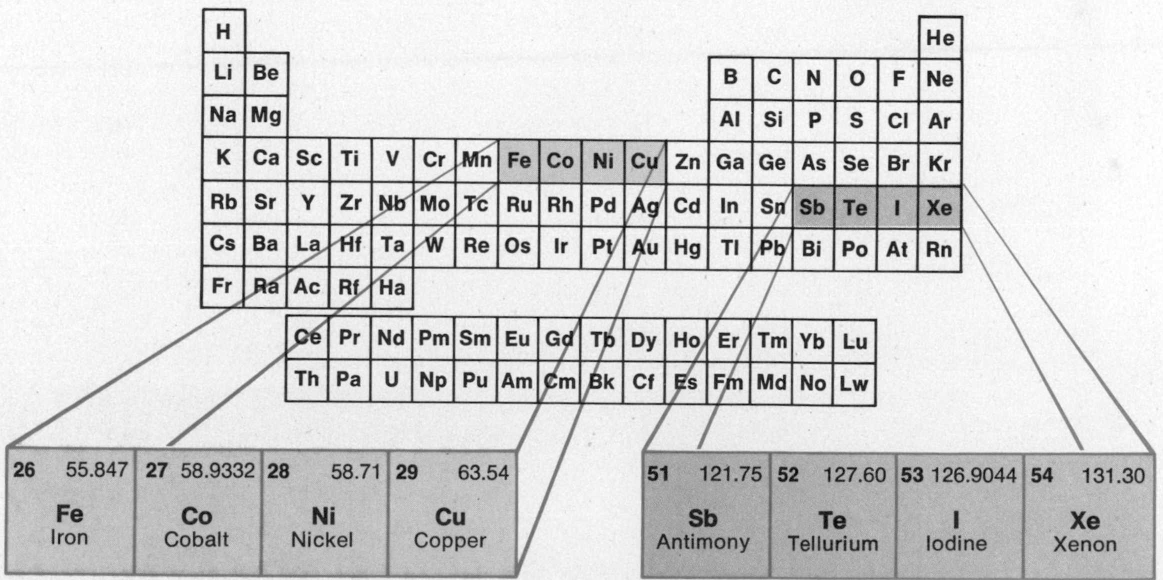

FIGURE 7–10 • *Elements arranged in order of increasing atomic number do not always have increasing atomic masses as in Co and Ni, and Te and I.*

Figure 7–11 is a representation of one of many forms of a modern periodic table. The vertical rows are the **Groups.** He, Ne, Ar, Kr, Xe, and Rn are the Group O elements. Li, Na, K, Rb, Cs, and Fr are in Group I. The horizontal rows are the **Periods.** Li, Be, B, C, N, O, F, and Ne are in Period 2. The reason for the position of hydrogen and many of the other elements will become clear after the next few chapters.

7–9 · Value of the periodic table · Do you know how sodium chloride, NaCl, can be prepared? Combine the water solutions of sodium hydroxide, NaOH, and hydrogen chloride, HCl. The reaction can be represented by the following equation.

$$NaOH(aq) + HCl(aq) \rightarrow NaCl(aq) + H_2O(l)$$

FIGURE 7–11 · *Periodic Table*

PERIODS	GROUPS I	II	TRANSITION ELEMENTS						
1	1 1.00797 **H** Hydrogen								
2	3 6.939 **Li** Lithium	4 9.0122 **Be** Beryllium							
3	11 22.9898 **Na** Sodium	12 24.312 **Mg** Magnesium							
4	19 39.102 **K** Potassium	20 40.08 **Ca** Calcium	21 44.956 **Sc** Scandium	22 47.90 **Ti** Titanium	23 50.942 **V** Vanadium	24 51.996 **Cr** Chromium	25 54.9380 **Mn** Manganese	26 55.847 **Fe** Iron	27 58.9332 **Co** Cobalt
5	37 85.47 **Rb** Rubidium	38 87.62 **Sr** Strontium	39 88.905 **Y** Yttrium	40 91.22 **Zr** Zirconium	41 92.906 **Nb** Niobium	42 95.94 **Mo** Molybdenum	43 (99)* **Tc** Technetium	44 101.07 **Ru** Ruthenium	45 102.905 **Rh** Rhodium
6	55 132.905 **Cs** Cesium	56 137.34 **Ba** Barium	57 138.91 **La** Lanthanum †	72 178.49 **Hf** Hafnium	73 180.948 **Ta** Tantalum	74 183.85 **W** Tungsten	75 186.2 **Re** Rhenium	76 190.2 **Os** Osmium	77 192.2 **Ir** Iridium
7	87 (223)* **Fr** Francium	88 (226)* **Ra** Radium	89 (227)* **Ac** Actinium ‡	104 (259)* **Rf**** Rutherfordium	105 **Ha** Hahnium**	106***	107***	108***	

† LANTHANIDE SERIES	58 140.12 **Ce** Cerium	59 140.907 **Pr** Praseodymium	60 144.24 **Nd** Neodymium	61 (147)* **Pm** Promethium	62 150.35 **Sm** Samarium	63 151.96 **Eu** Europium	64 157.25 **Gd** Gadolinium	65 158.924 **Tb** Terbium
‡ ACTINIDE SERIES	90 232.038 **Th** Thorium	91 (231)* **Pa** Protactinium	92 238.03 **U** Uranium	93 (237)* **Np** Neptunium	94 (242)* **Pu** Plutonium	95 (243)* **Am** Americium	96 (247)* **Cm** Curium	97 (247)* **Bk** Berkelium

*Atomic masses appearing in parentheses are those of the most stable known isotopes.

**Names are unofficial.

Find the Group I elements in the periodic table. Note that the concept of chemical periodicity leads us to predict the following. Water solutions of LiOH, KOH, RbOH, and CsOH should all resemble aqueous NaOH in their chemical behavior. Similarly, aqueous solutions of HF, HBr, and HI should chemically resemble aqueous HCl. Consequently, we can predict the following: The alkali halides can be prepared by the reaction between the aqueous alkali hydroxide and the aqueous hydrogen halide.

$$NaOH(aq) + HBr(aq) \rightarrow NaBr(aq) + H_2O(l)$$
$$KOH(aq) + HI(aq) \rightarrow KI(aq) + H_2O(l)$$
$$RbOH(aq) + HF(aq) \rightarrow RbF(aq) + H_2O(l)$$
$$CsOH(aq) + HCl(aq) \rightarrow CsCl(aq) + H_2O(l), \text{ etc.}$$

			III	IV	V	VI	VII	0
					NONMETALS		1 1.00797 H Hydrogen	2 4.0026 He Helium
			5 10.811 B Boron	6 12.01115 C Carbon	7 14.0067 N Nitrogen	8 15.9994 O Oxygen	9 18.9984 F Fluorine	10 20.183 Ne Neon
			13 26.9815 Al Aluminum	14 28.086 Si Silicon	15 30.9738 P Phosphorus	16 32.064 S Sulfur	17 35.453 Cl Chlorine	18 39.948 Ar Argon
28 58.71 Ni Nickel	29 63.54 Cu Copper	30 65.37 Zn Zinc	31 69.72 Ga Gallium	32 72.59 Ge Germanium	33 74.9216 As Arsenic	34 78.96 Se Selenium	35 79.909 Br Bromine	36 83.80 Kr Krypton
46 106.4 Pd Palladium	47 107.870 Ag Silver	48 112.40 Cd Cadmium	49 114.82 In Indium	50 118.69 Sn Tin	51 121.75 Sb Antimony	52 127.60 Te Tellurium	53 126.9044 I Iodine	54 131.30 Xe Xenon
78 195.09 Pt Platinum	79 196.967 Au Gold	80 200.59 Hg Mercury	81 204.37 Tl Thallium	82 207.19 Pb Lead	83 208.980 Bi Bismuth	84 (210)* Po Polonium	85 (210)* At Astatine	86 (222)* Rn Radon

66 162.50 Dy Dysprosium	67 164.930 Ho Holmium	68 167.26 Er Erbium	69 168.934 Tm Thulium	70 173.04 Yb Ytterbium	71 174.97 Lu Lutetium
98 (251)* Cf Californium	99 (254)* Es Einsteinium	100 (257)* Fm Fermium	101 (258)* Md Mendelevium	102 (255)* No Nobelium	103 (256)* Lw Lawrencium

KEY

Atomic Number → 6 12.01115 ← Atomic Mass
C ← Symbol of Element
Element Name → Carbon

***No names have been given and no mass data are available.

Atomic masses based on C-12 = 12.0000

Thus, because of the periodicty of the elements and from the knowledge of the NaOH(*aq*) + HCl(*aq*) reaction, we know, with a good deal of confidence, twenty reactions. We know the reactions of all five aqueous alkali hydroxides with all four aqueous hydrogen halides. Obviously, such a generalization simplifies chemistry a great deal. If we know the chemistry of sodium, for example, we automatically know a fair amount of the chemistry of Li, K, Rb, and Cs. We should not expect the properties of these elements to be identical, but they are similar.

REVIEW IT NOW

1 How did Mendeleev's arrangement of the elements in the periodic table differ from Döbereiner's and Newlands' arrangements?
2 How did Moseley's arrangement of the elements make the periodic table more meaningful?
3 What does the Periodic Law state?

VALENCES AND FORMULAS

7–10 · Valence and the periodic table · The periodic table allows the chemist to predict the atomic ratios in which elements will combine. That is one of the most useful purposes of the periodic table. So far we have encountered many different compounds with different formulas such as H_2O, HCl, and NaOH. But there are millions of chemical compounds, each with its own formula. It would be quite impossible for even the most brilliant chemist to memorize even a small percentage of those formulas. However, the periodic table makes it unnecessary to attempt such an impossible task. In this and following chapters, you will learn how to use the periodic table. But first, let's define an important term, **valence.** The combining capacity of an element in a compound is called the valence of the element. We must know the valences of the elements to write the correct chemical formulas for the compounds of those elements. The valences of the elements are given numerical values. In a compound of two elements, the total valence value of each element must be equal. Obtaining the total valence value is easy. Simply multiply the valence of the element by the number of atoms of the element in the compound. Let's use the compound Al_2O_3 as an example. The valence of aluminum is 3, and the valence of oxygen is 2. The total valence value of aluminum in Al_2O_3 is the valence, 3, times the number of aluminum atoms, 2. Then the total valence of aluminum in Al_2O_3 is 6 (3 × 2). The total valence of oxygen in that compound is the valence of oxygen, 2, times the number of oxygen atoms, 3. The valence of oxygen is 6 (2 × 3). Since both the aluminum and the oxygen have a total valence of 6, the formula Al_2O_3 must be correct.

Before considering other examples of valences and formulas, let's return to the periodic table. First, we will study the relationship between valence and the families of the elements. Look at the periodic table on pages 146 and 147. The group number of the family is the same as the valence of the elements for Groups I to IV. The elements of Group I, the alkali metals, have a valence of 1. The elements of Group II have a valence of 2. The elements of Group III exhibit a valence of 3. And the elements of Group IV have a valence of 4. Beginning with Group V the valence of the element begins to decrease. The valence of the elements in Groups V through VII is equal to 8 minus the group number. For example, the valence of the elements of Group V is equal to 8 − 5, or 3. The elements of Group VI have a valence of 2. The elements of Group VII have a valence of 1. Following the same rule, we would expect that the noble gases, Group O, should have a valence of 0. Remember, the noble gases are the least likely of all the elements in the periodic table to form chemical compounds. And a valence of 0 is consistent with their chemical inactivity. The following shows the periodic relation for valence.

Group	*I*	*II*	*III*	*IV*	*V*	*VI*	*VII*	*O*
Chief valence	*1*	*2*	*3*	*4*	*3*	*2*	*1*	*0*

Again refer to the periodic table on pages 146 and 147. Note that the transition elements, the lanthanide elements, and the actinide elements do not fall within any of the numbered groups. For the moment, we will not consider those elements.

7-11 · Valences and formula writing · Now we can use the periodic table to determine the valences of a large number of elements. Let's continue by writing the formulas for the compounds formed by the combination of pairs of those elements. In general, certain groups combine more readily with each other. For example, elements of Groups I through IV combine more readily with elements in Groups V through VII. Thus, sodium of Group I will combine readily with sulfur of Group VI or chlorine of Group VII. Sodium has a valence of 1. Chlorine

(Group VII) also has a valence of 1. Therefore, the formula for sodium chloride is NaCl. Actually it is Na_1Cl_1, but the chemist never uses 1 as a subscript. So we simply write NaCl. Sulfur of group VI has a valence of 2. Therefore, the formula for sodium sulfide is Na_2S. Carbon of Group IV will combine with chlorine of Group VII to form the compound CCl_4, carbon tetrachloride. This compound was widely used in dry cleaning.

The compound of aluminum and sulfur must reflect the valence 3 of aluminum and 2 of sulfur. The least common denominator involving 2 and 3 is 6. Therefore, we need 2 atoms of aluminum and 3 atoms of sulfur to achieve a total valence of 6 for each element. That results in the formula Al_2S_3, aluminum sulfide.

FIGURE 7–12 · *Carbon tetrachloride, CCl_4, is a good solvent for many organic compounds. Until recently it was widely used in household and commercial cleaning. Its use is now restricted by the government.*

7–12 · Valence in transition elements · The concept of valence is a very old one. It was used by chemists before the development of the periodic table. Historically the valence of an element is the number of atoms of hydrogen that are equivalent to, or will combine with, one atom of that element. Consider the compounds HCl, H_2O, and Na_2O. Let's demonstrate first with hydrogen chloride, HCl. The definition of valence leads directly to a valence of 1 for chlorine. That is because 1 atom of chlorine is combined with 1 atom of hydrogen. In water, H_2O, the definition yields a valence of 2 for oxygen. That is because 1 atom of oxygen is combined with 2 atoms of hydrogen. Note that these are the same valences obtained by using the group number rule for the periodic table.

The oxygen atom in Na_2O is equivalent to 2 hydrogen atoms. (We know that from the compound H_2O.) Then 2 sodium atoms are indirectly equivalent to 2 hydrogen atoms in the compound Na_2O. That means that 1 sodium atom is equivalent to 1 hydrogen atom. Therefore, the valence of sodium must be 1.

What is the valence of iron in $FeCl_3$? The 3 chlorine atoms are equivalent to 3 hydrogen atoms (from HCl). Then 1 iron atom must be indirectly equivalent to 3 hydrogen atoms. Therefore, the valence of iron in $FeCl_3$ is by definition 3. Using this concept, we can then assign valences to the transition elements. It is not convenient to use the group number of the periodic table with the transition elements.

EXAMPLE

What is the combining capacity, or valence, for Pb in the compound $PbCl_2$?

SOLUTION

Since the valence for hydrogen (H) is 1, then the valence for Cl in HCl must be 1 also. Therefore, since 2 Cl atoms, each with a valence of 1, combine with 1 Pb atom, the valence of the Pb must be 2.

EXERCISE

What is the valence of Zn in ZnO? S in H_2S? Fe in FeS?

7–13 · A brief look at the nature of compounds · We will write more chemical formulas based on the valences of the elements. But first, we must briefly consider some facts about compounds. Most chemical compounds that we have studied and will study are composed of two types of elements or groups of elements. Each of the simplest *binary* compounds (compounds of two elements) consists of a metal atom combined with a nonmetal atom. Examples of binary compounds are FeS, NaCl, Al_2O_3, and Zn_3N_2. Even though hydrogen is a nonmetallic element, it acts like a metal in many compounds.

There are many compounds in which metal atoms are combined with a group of nonmetal atoms. Such compounds are called **salts.** They are produced when oxygen-containing acids and bases react. The group of nonmetal atoms in such a compound comes from the acid. Some acids that produce the nonmetal groups are nitric acid (HNO_3), sulfuric acid (H_2SO_4), and carbonic acid (H_2CO_3). The (NO_3) that comes from HNO_3 very often behaves as a chemical unit. It is called the **nitrate** group. It is found in such salts as $NaNO_3$, $Zn(NO_3)_2$, and $Fe(NO_3)_3$. All those salts are called nitrates. Observe that the (NO_3) group in $H(NO_3)$ is equivalent to 1 hydrogen atom. Hence, its valence is 1. The (SO_4), or **sulfate,** group and the (CO_3), or **carbonate,** group may be considered in a similar way.

Groups of atoms such as (NO_3), (SO_4), (CO_3), and (HCO_3) are often called radicals or **acid radicals.** Their true nature will be considered in later chapters. The acid radicals all behave like nonmetal combinations in chemicals. The one commonly encountered radical that behaves like a metal in compounds is (NH_4). It is called the **ammonium** group.

EXERCISE

What are the valences of the (SO_4) and (CO_3) groups? Carbonic acid, H_2CO_3, is the source of two groups, (CO_3) and (HCO_3).

7–14 · How to write correct chemical formulas · Table 4–1 (page 71) presents a list of the valences of common metals and the valences of common nonmetals and acid radicals. There are 22 metal valences listed, and 28 nonmetal and acid radical valences are listed. In theory, that will allow you to write 22 × 28, or 616, different chemical formulas! However, just because you can write a correct formula for a substance does not necessarily mean that substance actually exists! For example, Hg_2O is a correct formula for the nonexistent compound mercury(I) oxide. Now let's find out how we can write formulas using the following instructions.

1. *Write the symbol for the metal element part of the compound first. Follow it by the symbol for the nonmetal element, or acid radical, part of the compound. Include the valence numbers for each of the species. They are to be written as Roman numerals at the upper right of the symbols. That is, they should be written as superscripts,* $FE^{II}S^{II}$.

2. *If the valences are equal, no subscripts are added. The simplest formula for the compound will then depict a 1:1 atom or radical ratio (*$Fe^{II}S^{II} = FeS$*).*

3. *If the valences are not equal, Arabic numeral subscripts will be necessary to equalize combining capacities. To do that, use the valence of one element in the compound as the subscript in the other. The crossed arrows in any formula, such as that for zinc phosphate on the next page, show the procedure. Again, the subscript 1 is never written in a final formula.*

EXAMPLE

What is the formula for copper(I) chloride?

SOLUTION

1. *Copper has valence of 1, as does chlorine in chlorides. The symbol for copper appears first in the formula, since it is a metal and chlorine is a nonmetal.*

$$Cu^{I}Cl^{I}$$

2. *The valence numbers are equal. No subscripts are written, the subscript for each symbol is understood to be 1.*
3. *Therefore, the simplest formula for copper(I) chloride is CuCl.*

FIGURE 7–13 · *The compound copper (II) chloride ($CuCl_2$)*

EXAMPLE

What is the formula for zinc phosphate?

SOLUTION

1. *Zinc has a valence of 2 and is a metal. The phosphate acid radical has a valence of 3. Zinc appears first in the formula.*

$$Zn^{II}(PO_4)^{III}$$

2. *Since the valences are unequal, subscripts are required.*

$$Zn_3^{II}(PO_4)_2^{III}$$

3. *The formula for zinc phosphate is $Zn_3(PO_4)_2$.*

The table of valences is a summary of the results of many experiments on the percentage composition of compounds. Do you understand the contents and the use of that table? If so, you will be able to begin communicating as a chemist. The use of correct chemical formulas will save you time and effort as you continue in your study of chemistry.

EXERCISE

Let's see how well you can use the table of valences on page 71. Write formulas for the compounds at the top of page 154. Until you are experienced at formula writing, it is strongly suggested that you follow the procedure outlined above.

1. *Sodium fluoride*
2. *Calcium acetate*
3. *Tin(II) carbonate*
4. *Aluminum sulfate*
5. *Potassium dichromate*
6. *Magnesium bromide*
7. *Zinc phosphide*
8. *Barium peroxide*
9. *Silver chromate*
10. *Arsenic(III) sulfide*
11. *Chromium(III) oxide*
12. *Mercury(II) nitrate*
13. *Calcium oxalate*
14. *Copper(II) hydrogen carbonate*
15. *Iron(III) hydroxide*
16. *Barium dihydrogen phosphate*
17. *Magnesium arsenate*

7–15 · Some elements have variable valences · The rich variety of compounds in chemistry is further enhanced by the large number of elements that exhibit variable valences. The table of valences (page 71) indicates the existence of two valence forms of copper, mercury, iron, and oxygen. Note that there are Roman numerals associated with a number of other metal species, such as Sn(II) and Pb(II). That should imply the existence of other valence forms for those metals. Indeed, Sn(IV) and Pb(IV) are well-characterized, though less common, valence forms of tin and lead.

7–16 · The names of chemical compounds of metals with nonmetals · The naming of chemical compounds is called **chemical nomenclature.** The rules of chemical nomenclature follow simple patterns. One general rule that has no exception is as follows: *There can never be more than one compound with the same name*. There can, however, be more than one name for the same compound.

1. **Binary compounds** are compounds that contain only two elements. There are two types of binary compounds. One type is compounds composed of a metal and a nonmetal. The other type is compounds composed of two nonmetals.

Let's consider the metal–nonmetal compounds first. The metallic element is always named and written first. The nonmetallic element is always named and written last. The final letters of the name of the nonmetal are changed to *ide*. For example, NaCl is called sodium chloride, from sodium and chlorine. MgBr is called magnesium bromide, from magnesium and bromine. Al_2S_3 is called aluminum sulfide, from aluminum and sulfur.

Now let's consider the binary compounds composed of two nonmetals. Sulfur and oxygen make two different compounds,

SO_2 and SO_3. According to the general rule of nomenclature mentioned above, sulfur oxide is not an acceptable name for either compound. The accepted names for these compounds are sulfur dioxide and sulfur trioxide respectively. Other examples are CO and CO_2, carbon monoxide and carbon dioxide. P_4O_{10} is named tetraphosphorus decoxide.

Greek prefixes are used to indicate the number of atoms of each nonmetal present in the compound. Those most often used are the following.

mono-	one	tetra-	four	hepta-	seven	deca-	ten
di-	two	penta-	five	octa-	eight		
tri-	three	hexa-	six	ennea-	nine		

2. Another class of compounds is composed of a metal and a radical. The radical is treated as a unit. That simplifies the naming of the compound. For example, in the compound $ZnSO_4$, a zinc atom and a sulfate radical are present. The compound is named zinc sulfate. A compound that seems

FIGURE 7–14 · *A photomicrograph of the structure of magnesium chloride taken under polarized light*

Dmitri Ivanovich Mendeleev *(1834–1907, Russian). Mendeleev was the youngest in a family of 17 children. At 35, he announced his Periodic Law of the Elements, which "gave chemistry that prophetic power long regarded as the peculiar dignity of the sister science, astronomy." Though the Periodic Table of the Elements itself is a lasting memorial to his great insight, Mendeleev is further honored by the name of element 101—mendelevium.*

more complicated is $NaHCO_3$. Sodium is the metal, and hydrogen carbonate is the radical. The compound is named sodium hydrogen carbonate.

3. Suppose the metal part of the specific compound has more than one valence form. The name of the formula must clearly indicate which form is present. The more acceptable way of achieving this is based on a system devised by Alfred Stock, a Polish-born American chemist. The Stock system indicates the valence form of an element by a Roman numeral, which follows the name in parentheses. Examples are FeS, iron(II) sulfide; $CrCl_3$, chromium(III) chloride.

EXERCISE

Give the names of the following compounds.

1. CCl_4 **2.** XeF_6 **3.** PBr_5 **4.** NH_4I_3

An older nomenclature system uses the stem of the name of the metal plus the suffix *ous* or *ic*. The *ous* ending indicates a lower valence form. The *ic* ending indicates a higher one. Examples are Cu_2O, cuprous oxide; CuO, cupric oxide; Hg_2Cl_2, mercurous chloride; $HgCl_2$, mercuric chloride. In the Stock system, the same compounds are named copper(I) oxide, copper(II) oxide, mercury(I) chloride, and mercury(II) chloride.

Note that NaOH is named sodium hydroxide. NaOH is a **ternary compound,** which means it contains three elements. Therefore, that violates the rule that the *ide* ending is used with binary compounds only. However, the hydroxide radical is so common a chemical unit that it has been given a special name. You may be wondering which element in a nonmetal binary compound should be written first. Why, for example, do we write C O instead of OC? These and many other questions raised in Chapter 7 will be answered in following chapters.

7–17 · Mendeleev's predictions · The periodic table is useful in many ways beyond simply providing a convenient means to obtain the valence of an element. Mendeleev himself demonstrated the value of the periodic classification of the elements when he first proposed the periodic table. Mendeleev noted that in order to place the elements in their proper chemical family, it was necessary to leave certain gaps. Before Mendeleev's time, it was not possible to predict how many elements were still to be discovered and what the properties of the unknown elements might be. Mendeleev stated that if a gap had to be left in the periodic table, then an undiscovered element fitted there. Also, the properties of an element could be predicted from its position in the chart. For example, Mendeleev left a gap between the elements silicon and tin. The element arsenic was known and came closest in atomic mass to filling that gap. But its properties resembled those of phosphorus and antimony more than those of silicon and tin. Therefore, it was placed between phosphorus and antimony. A gap still remained between silicon and tin. So Mendeleev predicted the existence of an undiscovered element to fill that gap. He named this missing element eka-silicon, meaning "like silicon." From its position in the chart, he predicted the properties it should have. Table 7–4 lists Mendeleev's predictions for eka-silicon and the experimentally determined data for **germanium.** The element germanium was discovered in 1886 in a silver ore. The concept of periodicity predicted a new element and its properties. Those predictions were verified!

TABLE 7–4 · A Comparison of the Properties of Eka-Silicon (predicted) and Germanium (experimental)

PROPERTY	EKA-SILICON	GERMANIUM
Atomic mass (amu)	72	72.3
Density of element (g/ml)	5.5	5.36
Formula of oxide	MO_2	GeO_2
Density of oxide (g/ml)	4.7	4.70
Formula of chloride	MCl_4	$GeCl_4$
Boiling point of chloride (°C)	<100	83
Density of chloride (g/ml)	1.9	1.88

On the basis of the concept of chemical periodicity, we can now be very confident that there are no undiscovered elements between hydrogen (element 1) and element 107.

REVIEW IT NOW

1 Define the term *valence*.
2 How do you determine the total value of a valence?
3 What is the valence of each element in Group III?
4 What is the valence of each element in Group VI?
5 What are the valences for hydrogen and oxygen in H_2O?
6 What are binary compounds?
7 Of what kinds of elements are salts composed?
8 What are ternary compounds?

SUMMARY

It would be almost impossible to study the chemical and physical properties of the elements without some kind of organization. The recurring, or periodic, properties allow for the grouping of elements into chemical families, or groups.

As a basis for periodicity, we might consider the six members of the noble-gas family—He, Ne, Ar, Kr, Xe, and Rn. They are characterized by their general chemical inactivity. In contrast, four members of the halogen family—the diatomic (two atom) elements F_2, Cl_2, Br_2, and I_2—are the most active nonmetals. A fifth halogen, astatine, At_2, has been synthesized, but little is known about its chemical and physical properties.

These elements react chemically with metals to form salts called halides. The alkali metals—Li, Na, K, Rb, and Cs—are chemically the most active metals. Francium, Fr, a radioactive element, is also a member of this group.

The chemical periodicity of the elements was first thought to be a function of atomic mass. The modern Periodic Law relates chemical periodicity to the atomic number. An understanding of chemical periodicity leads to generalizations regarding the physical properties and the chemical reactivity of any member of a group of elements. Such generalizations may then be used to predict the behavior of new compounds of those elements even before the compounds are synthesized.

The combining capacity of an element is called the valence of the element. Knowledge of the valences of the elements is the key to writing correct formulas. Groups of atoms that usually act together in chemical reactions are called radicals; these groups also have valences. Correct formulas for compounds can be determined by writing the elements of a compound, X and Y, with their respective valences, $X^{III}Y^{IV}$, and then crisscrossing these numbers, as subscripts, to obtain the mole ratio of the elements in the compound, X_4Y_3.

The names of chemical compounds are derived according to certain rules. Binary compounds end in *ide*. Nonmetallic binary compounds use Greek prefixes to indicate the number of atoms. Compounds containing a radical include the name of the radical. When a metal can exist in more than one valence state, a Roman numeral is used to express which valence it has.

REVIEW QUESTIONS

1 Suppose you discovered a new noble gas with an atomic number of 118. What predictions would you make regarding the melting point, boiling point, heat of fusion, and heat of vaporization for the new element?

2 Why is it so difficult to solidify helium?

3 What property of the inert gases accounts for their use as a food preservative? in light bulbs?

4 Devise your own arrangement of the chemical elements showing periodicity of some property. Explain how your table would be helpful to the chemist.

5 It is well known that Mg reacts with oxygen gas in the following manner.

$2Mg + O_2 = 2MgO$

It also reacts with chlorine as follows

$Mg + Cl_2 = MgCl_2$

Considering this, how would

Ca react with O_2?

Ba react with Cl_2?

Sr react with I_2?

Mg react with S?

6 What is meant by the following?

a. Group

b. Radical

c. Salt

7 If an element is said to have a valence of 2, what does this mean?

8 Show, with an equation, the following reactions.

a. Formation of an oxide of potassium

b. Formation of an acid from the acid anhydride SO_3 (What is the name of this acid?)

c. Neutralization reaction between potassium hydroxide and nitric acid

9 Write chemical formulas for the following.

a. Sodium nitrate
b. Zinc acetate
c. Iron(III) sulfate
d. Silver arsenate
e. Tin(II) bromide
f. Mercury(I) chloride
g. Chromium(III) oxide
h. Ferrous phosphate
i. Triphosphorous pentanitride
j. Arsenic(III) sulfide
k. Lithium peroxide
l. Mercuric iodide
m. Disulfur decafluoride
n. Aluminum hydroxide
o. Dinitrogen tetroxide
p. Titanium(III) phosphide
q. Ammonium sulfite
r. Iodine trichloride
s. Calcium chlorate
t. Lead dihydrogen phosphate
u. Ammonium sulfate
v. Potassium permanganate
w. Barium carbonate
x. Sodium chromate
y. Potassium monohydrogen phosphate
z. Tin(IV) chloride

10 Name the following compounds.

a. Na_2SO_3
b. $FeAsO_4$
c. $SnCrO_4$
d. K_2CO_3
e. $Hg_2(NO_3)_2$
f. FeI_2
g. $Li_2Cr_2O_7$
h. K_3N
i. $CuSO_43H_2O$
j. N_2O_4
k. $Fe(CH_3COO)_3$
l. $NaNO_2$
m. $Pb(HCO_3)_2$
n. As_4O_6
o. Ag_2S
p. $Mg(OH)_2$
q. $Hg(CN)_2$
r. $SbCl_3$
s. K_2O_2
t. H_3PO_4
u. $Ca(H_2PO_4)_2$
v. $Al_2(C_2O_4)_3$
w. $Zn(ClO_3)_2$
x. NH_4F
y. $Ca(MnO_4)_2$
z. S_2Cl_2

11 Write chemical equations for each of the following.

a. hydrochloric acid (aq) + aluminum oxide(s) →
aluminum chloride (aq) + water(l)

b. ammonium hydroxide(aq) + nitric acid(aq) →
ammonium nitrate(aq) + water(l)

c. silver nitrate(aq) + hydrogen sulfide(aq) →
silver sulfide(s) + nitric acid(aq)

d. diphosphorus pentasulfide(s) + oxygen(g) →
tetraphosphorus decoxide(s) + sulfur dioxide(g)

e. sodium hydroxide(aq) + phosphoric acid(aq) →
sodium dihydrogen phosphate(aq) + water(l)

f. mercury(I) nitrate(aq) + iron(III) chloride(aq) →
mercury(I) cloride(s) + iron(III) nitrate(aq)

g. sodium hydrogen carbonate(s) →
sodium carbonate(s) + carbon dioxide(g) + water(g)

h. ozone(g) → oxygen(g)

i. sulfur trioxide(g) + water(l) → sulfuric acid(aq)

j. chlorine(aq) + copper(II) bromide(aq) →
copper(II) chloride(aq) + bromine(l)

k. silver nitrate(aq) + sodium hydroxide(aq) →
silver oxide(s) + water(l) + sodium nitrate(aq)

l. iron(s) + sulfuric acid(aq) → hydrogen(g) + iron(III) sulfate(aq)

m. tin(IV) oxide(s) + carbon(s) → tin(s) + carbon monoxide(g)

12 A manufacturer bottles oxygen gas at 0.0°C and 20.0 atm in 22.4 l-cylinders.

a. What mass of $KClO_3$ does the manufacturer need as a source of oxygen for each cylinder?

b. What mass of oxygen does each cylinder contain?

13 The four elements W, X, Y, and Z are found to have the following atomic masses relative to the atomic mass of hydrogen, which is 1.

W = 8 X = 11 Y = 15 Z = 22

Compounds of the four elements show the following mass ratios.

Compound	Mass ratio
1. W with X	6:11
2. W with Y	4:10
3. Z with Y	22:15
4. Z with X	2:1

a. What are the formulas for compounds 1, 2, 3, and 4?

b. What are the valences of W, X, Y, and Z?

SUGGESTED READINGS

Allen, William M. "The Diagonal Periodic Relationship." *Chemistry*, April 1970, p. 22.

Bunting, Roger K. "Periodicity in Chemical Systems." *Chemistry*, April 1972, p. 18.

Goldwater, Leonard J. "Mercury in the Environment." *Scientific American*, May 1971, p. 15.

Keller, O. Lewin, Jr. "Predicted Properties of Elements 113 and 114." *Chemistry*, November 1970, p. 8.

Safrany, David R. "Nitrogen Fixation." *Scientific American*, October 1974, p. 64.

Sanderson, R. T. "How Should Periodic Groups Be Numbered?" *Chemistry*, November 1971, p. 17.

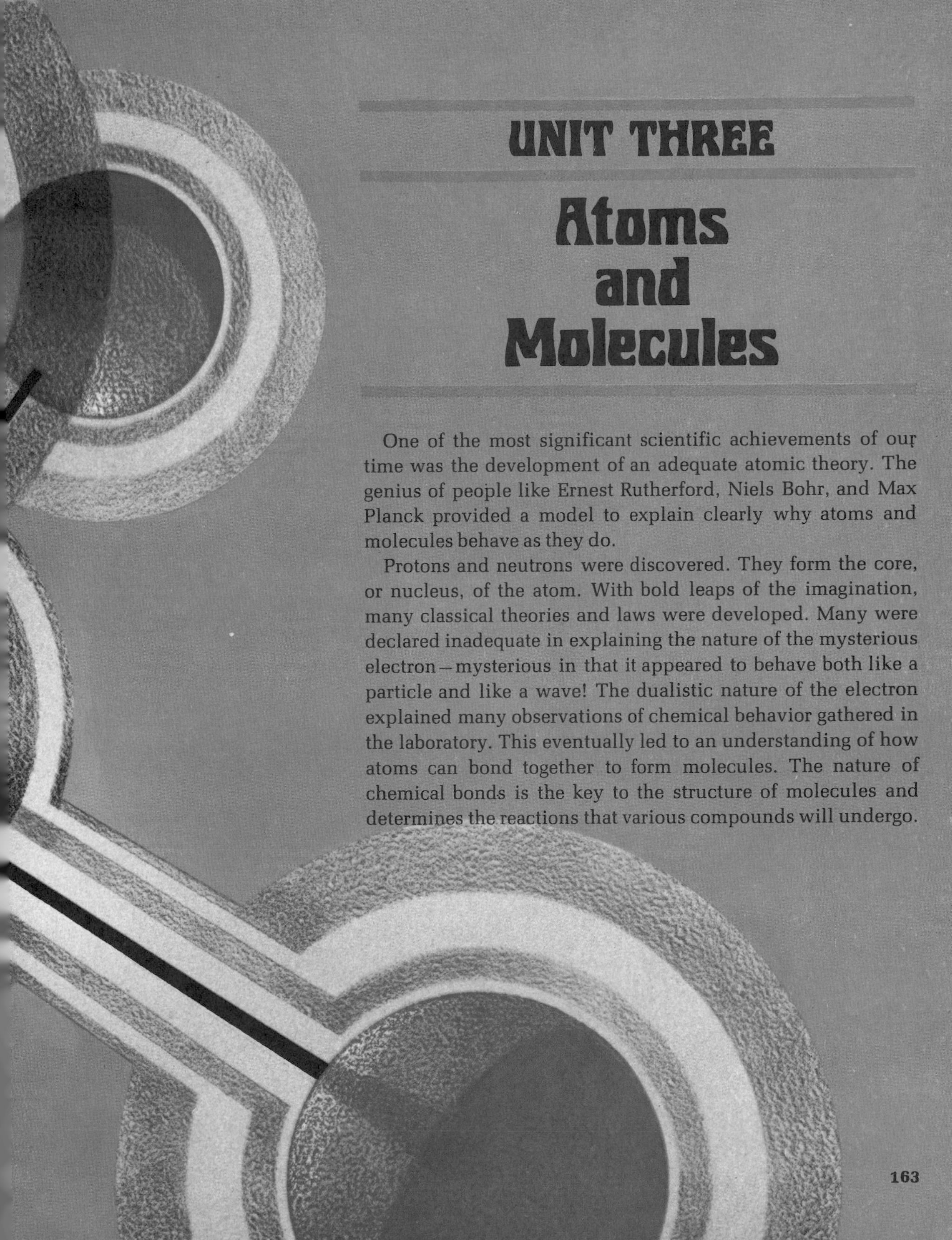

UNIT THREE

Atoms and Molecules

One of the most significant scientific achievements of our time was the development of an adequate atomic theory. The genius of people like Ernest Rutherford, Niels Bohr, and Max Planck provided a model to explain clearly why atoms and molecules behave as they do.

Protons and neutrons were discovered. They form the core, or nucleus, of the atom. With bold leaps of the imagination, many classical theories and laws were developed. Many were declared inadequate in explaining the nature of the mysterious electron—mysterious in that it appeared to behave both like a particle and like a wave! The dualistic nature of the electron explained many observations of chemical behavior gathered in the laboratory. This eventually led to an understanding of how atoms can bond together to form molecules. The nature of chemical bonds is the key to the structure of molecules and determines the reactions that various compounds will undergo.

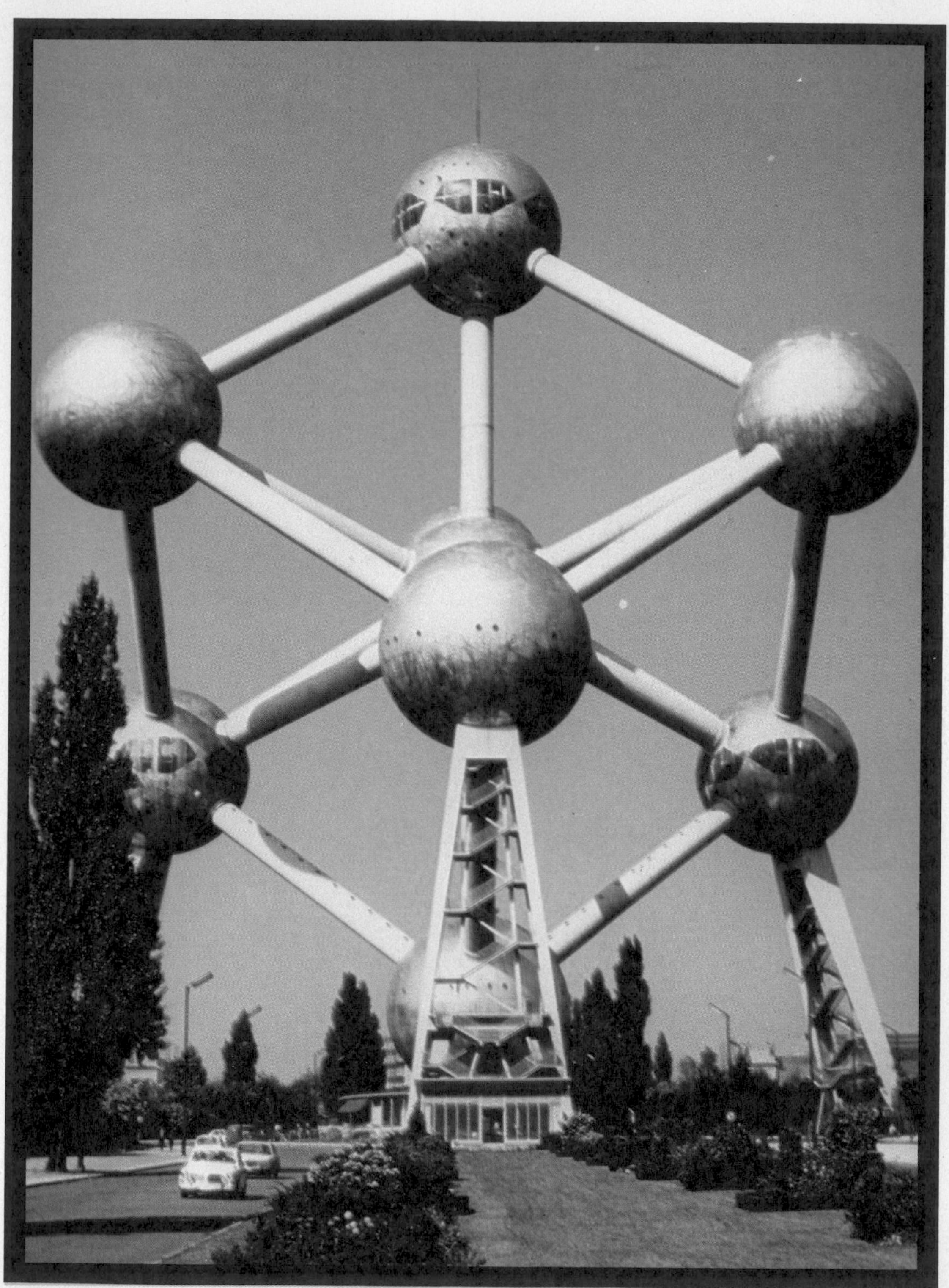

The atomium model designed for the 1958 Brussels World's Fair

CHAPTER EIGHT

The Modern Atom

The idea of the atom is not new. More than 2500 years ago, Greek philosophers speculated on the existence of the atom. For centuries since that time, scientists have investigated whether or not atoms really do exist.

Recall from Chapters 1 and 2 that early scientists were making great strides in chemistry. Some observed regularities in the way elements united to form compounds. Those observations resulted in the Law of Definite Composition and the Law of Multiple Proportions. Other chemists formulated models to help explain the behavior of gases. However, all of those and other great observations could not be completely explained without an atomic model. In Chapter 3, you learned how John Dalton provided that model with his atomic theory. Here, we will see how scientists built on John Dalton's atomic theory.

THE STRUCTURE OF THE ATOM

8–1 · Describing the structure of an atom is not easy · Using Dalton's atomic theory, many scientists could understand their experimental observations. Indeed, the case for the existence of atoms became very strong. However, scientists still knew very little about the actual structure of the atom. It was obvious that atoms did exist. Therefore, they must have some structure. There were two other factors that supported the idea that atoms must have some structure. First, atoms combine chemically to form molecules. Second, matter exists in gaseous, liquid, and solid states. For atoms to be held together in these states of matter, there must be some attractive force between atoms and molecules. The discovery of chemical periodicity indicated that there are certain relationships that exist among the elements. For such relationships to exist, atoms must have some structure.

It's very difficult to describe the structure of an atom. The scientist has a problem similar to that of a police artist. A police artist draws a picture of a suspect, using only a description given by a witness. However, the analogy is not exactly correct. The suspect in a crime is seen by at least one witness. But no one has ever seen an atom! The scientist must formulate an idea of the structure of the atom based solely on the experiences and knowledge obtained through experimentation. But how does the scientist do this? To help you answer this question, we can do the following.

Ask your teacher or a classmate to place a small object (something found in the classroom or laboratory) in a small box or paper bag and to seal it. Now, try to describe the object in the box or bag without opening it. You can do anything you like to the container except open it. When your description is complete, open the container and see how accurate your observations were.

How did you proceed with the little experiment? Was the object large, or small? Was it round, or square? Was it magnetic? Did you obtain the mass of the object? There are many ob-

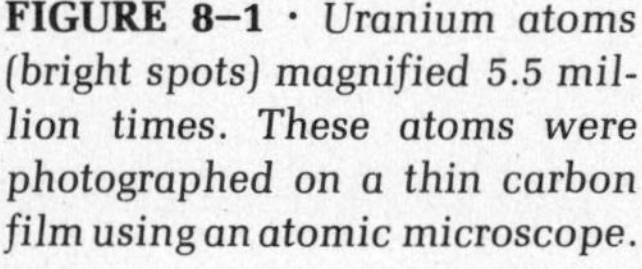

FIGURE 8–1 · *Uranium atoms (bright spots) magnified 5.5 million times. These atoms were photographed on a thin carbon film using an atomic microscope.*

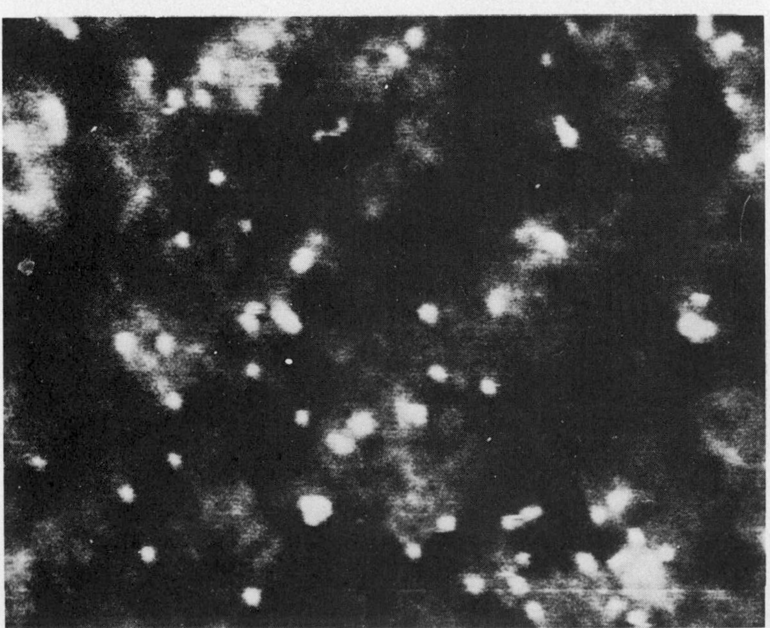

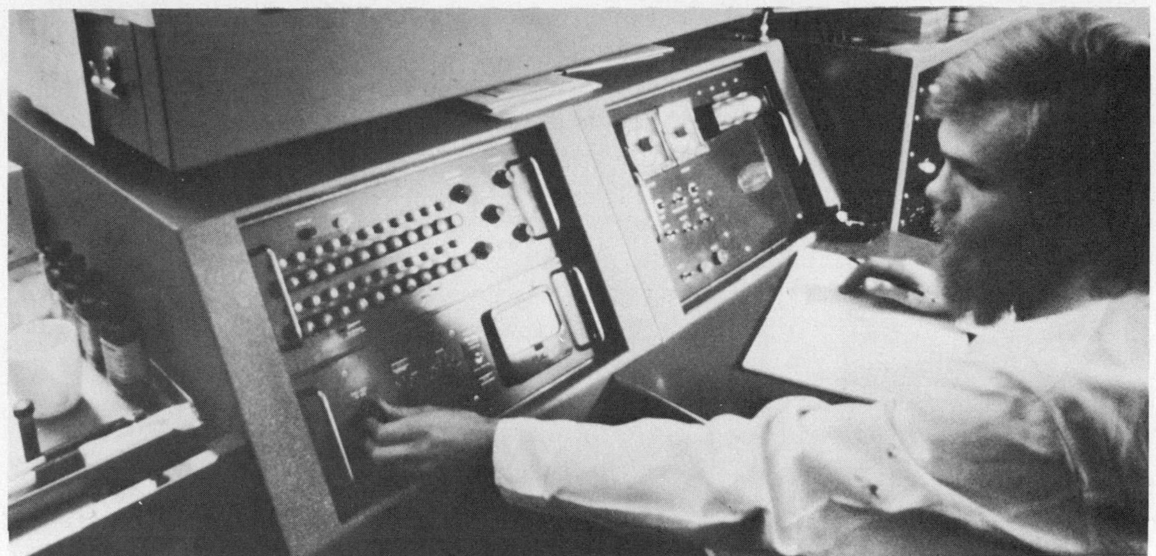

FIGURE 8–2 · *This atomic absorption spectrophotometer is used to analyze metals.*

servations you could have made. And once you analyzed all those observations, you probably attempted to describe the object. Thus, your description was based on *indirect* observations. That is how the scientist learns about something that cannot be seen. Of course, scientists can't open a box containing an atom to see how accurate their observations are. Then how do scientists know that their pictures of the atom are satisfactory? They don't. The scientist can be sure only that the model of the atom satisfactorily interprets the observations and facts known at that time about the behavior of atoms. And as new techniques provide additional information, the scientist may have to revise his or her model to explain those new facts.

8–2 · There have been several models that attempted to explain the atom · In Excursion 3, *What's in an Atom*, you can see how several models to explain the structure of the atom developed. But, let's review some of these models briefly here.

One of the earliest models of the atom assumed that the atom was simply a small, hard sphere. However, as scientists learned more about the electrical nature of matter, they realized that model was not satisfactory for explaining those new studies.

Toward the end of the nineteenth century, J. J. Thomson (1856–1940), an English physicist, discovered **electrons.** He described two characteristics of electrons. First, they carry a

EXCURSION THREE

What's in an Atom?

This excursion lists and discusses some of the models that have been developed to explain the structure of the atom and shows how some of the models were proved to be incorrect.

unit negative charge. And second, electrons are much lighter than atoms. It was also realized that electrons had to be a part of the atom. Therefore, an atom must have some type of internal structure. Since electrons carry a negative charge, the structure of the atom must also involve a positive charge so that the atom has an overall neutral charge. Thomson suggested that the atom might be something like a small piece of gelatin. As such, electrons might be like very tiny grapes in the gelatin. Therefore, the gelatin would represent the rest of the atom that carries a positive charge. Thomson knew the atom must be electrically neutral. Other scientists suggested that the atom might be more like the planet Saturn. In that analogy, there would be a massive positive particle surrounded by the small, light electrons. In that model, the electrons would orbit the heavy positive particle like the rings of Saturn orbit the planet.

Marie Sklodowska Curie *(1867–1934, Polish). Marie Curie and her husband Pierre shared the Nobel Prize in Physics with Becquerel in 1903 for their research in radioactivity. In 1911, five years after her husband's accidental death, she accepted another Nobel prize, this time in chemistry, for their 1902 discovery of radium. Thus, she became the first person ever to win two Nobel prizes.*

8–3 · The discovery of radioactivity helped in the development of a correct model for the atom · For a number of reasons, scientists were unable to accept either of those models of the atom. Radioactivity was discovered by A. H. Becquerel (1852–1908) at the end of the nineteenth century. That discovery made it obvious that the atom must have a more complicated structure. Becquerel and others demonstrated that radioactive atoms emitted three types of radiation. Those were alpha, beta, and gamma rays. The beta rays were identical with the negative electrons discovered by Thomson. The gamma rays were similar to X rays. X rays had been discovered a few years earlier by the German physicist Wilhelm Roentgen (1845–1923). The gamma rays, like X rays, have no mass and are a very high-energy radiation. Alpha rays are heavy, positively charged particles. Alpha rays are identical to helium without its two electrons. Marie Sklodowska Curie and others learned that radioactivity caused one type of atom to be transformed into another type of atom. Those facts indicated that the positive part of the atom was not a single indivisible entity. It could be transformed through emission of alpha and beta rays into different types of atoms.

About the beginning of World War I, a New Zealand physicist, Ernest Rutherford (1871–1937), was living in England. He performed one of the most important experiments in the history of science. Rutherford and his co-workers bombarded different elements with beams of alpha rays. His experiment is described in more detail in Excursion 3. Basically, his scattering experiments showed that the atom consists of electrons that in some fashion circled around an extremely small **nucleus.** The nucleus contains all the positive charge and almost all the mass of the atom. It was a surprise to learn how small the nucleus really is, since it is so massive in comparison with the electron. However, calculations in Rutherford's laboratory soon established that the diameter of the nucleus must be only 10^{-12} cm, whereas the diameter of the atom was known to be about 10^{-8} cm. That means that the diameter of the atom is about ten thousand times greater than the diameter of the nucleus! Let's make an analogy that will help you visualize better the size relationship of an atom. Suppose a nucleus is the size of a dime. Then the atom would be the size of a football field. Also, suppose the dime-sized nucleus weighed a ton. Then the rest of the football field would weigh only one pound. Rutherford's research has led to the model of the atom that we use today. It can be summarized in the following statements.

1. *An atom consists of a dense, central nucleus surrounded by electrons.*
2. *The atom has a diameter of about 10^{-8} cm while the nucleus has a diameter of about 10^{-12} cm.*
3. *The nucleus contains all of the positive charge of the atom and most of its mass.*
4. *In a neutral atom, the number of electrons that surround the nucleus is equal to the number of units of positive charge in the nucleus.*
5. *The negative electrons that surround the nucleus are attracted to the positive nucleus.*

Let's consider the hydrogen atom. It has one electron and an atomic mass of about one amu (atomic mass unit). Recall from earlier chapters that amu is simply a unit term given to express the mass of an atom. The hydrogen atom has a small spherical nucleus that has a charge of +1 and a mass of 1.00 amu. Outside the nucleus there is a single electron that has a −1 charge and a mass of 5.5×10^{-4} amu. The nucleus of the chlorine atom has a charge of +9 and a mass of 19.0 amu. It is surrounded by nine electrons whose total mass is 5×10^{-3} amu.

8–4 · What is the structure of the nucleus? · Extensive research has shown that the nucleus is composed of particles called **neutrons** and **protons.** Protons have a relative mass very close to 1.00 amu and bear the unit charge of +1.

Neutrons also have a relative mass very close to 1.00 amu, but they are electrically neutral. Since neutrons and protons are particles found in the nuclei of atoms, they are called **nucleons.** The number of nucleons in a nucleus is the sum of the number of protons and neutrons. The number for this sum is called the **mass number,** or *A*. The fluorine nucleus consists of nine protons and ten neutrons, or nineteen nucleons. Therefore, the mass number of fluorine is 19. You have probably noticed that the mass number of all the nuclei we have encountered is a whole number. Actually, the mass number of a nucleus must always be a whole number.

Recall from Chapter 7 that Moseley's research demonstrated a specific characteristic of the Periodic Law. That is, the Periodic Law relates the recurring properties of the elements to their atomic numbers. In his research, Moseley developed an arbitrary numerical ordering device, the atomic number, or Z. From further research on the structure of the atom, it was proved that the atomic number is equal to the number of protons in the atomic nucleus.

8-5 · Nuclei have special symbols · Nuclear chemists and physicists have agreed on a special way to represent the nuclei of elements. That representation shows three fundamental facts. From it, one can determine the chemical element that the nucleus forms. Also, the number of protons and neutrons in the nucleus can be determined from the representation. The general symbol for any nucleus is ${}^{A}_{Z}X$. X is the symbol for the element. *Z* is the symbol for the atomic number. And *A* is the mass number. The following examples will indicate how the symbols are used and interpreted.

Atomic mass number, A, equals 1. →
The nucleus is that of a hydrogen atom. → ${}^{1}_{1}H$
Atomic number, Z, equals 1. →

There is one proton in the nucleus of hydrogen. There are 0($A - Z = 1 - 1$) neutrons in the nucleus of hydrogen.

Atomic mass number, *A*, equals 238. →
The nucleus is that of a uranium atom. → ${}^{238}_{92}U$
Atomic number, *Z*, equals 92. →

There are 92 protons in the nucleus of uranium. There are 146($A - Z = 238 - 92$) neutrons in the nucleus of uranium.

8–6 · The discovery of isotopes · Our model of the atom assumes that the nucleus of an atom of any element is composed of only neutrons and protons. And each of those particles has a mass that is very nearly a whole number. Knowing that, it may have occurred to you that the atomic masses of all the elements ought to be whole numbers. However, that is not true. Many atomic masses are not close to whole numbers. For example, chlorine has an atomic mass of 35.457 amu.

In 1913, T. W. Richards (1868–1928) found two different atomic masses for lead obtained from two different sources. In the same year, F. W. Aston (1877–1945) separated neon atoms into two different atomic mass species. There were additional startling discoveries that led to another drastic alteration in the concept of atomic structure.

Those results were interpreted by F. Soddy (1877–1956) in Great Britain. He named those atoms of different atomic masses **isotopes.** Isotopes are atoms of the same element that have the same chemical properties but different mass numbers. The discovery and separation of isotopes of many other elements soon followed. Most of the first eighty-three elements have more than one stable isotopic species. Hydrogen exists as simple hydrogen, $^{1}_{1}H$, with one proton and no neutrons in the nucleus. It also exists in one atom per 6700 atoms of $^{1}_{1}H$ as heavy hydrogen, or **deuterium.** Deuterium, $^{2}_{1}H$(or $^{2}_{1}D$), has one proton and one neutron in the nucleus.

8–7 · How atomic masses may be calculated · Most elements are mixtures of isotopes that have different atomic masses. The atomic mass of each isotope is close to, but not exactly, a whole

FIGURE 8–3 · *Three isotopes of hydrogen: hydrogen, deuterium, and tritium*

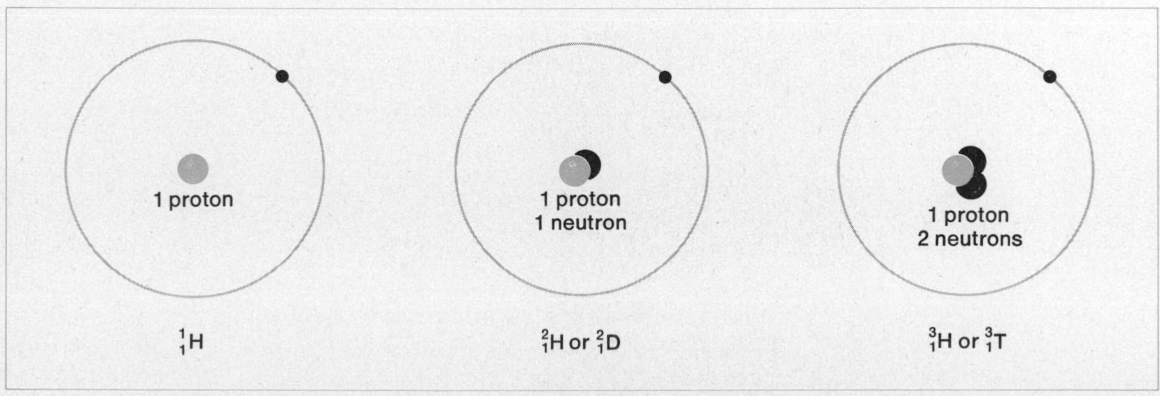

number. For example, chlorine gas is made up of two isotopes. One isotope has a relative atomic mass close to 35.0 amu. The second isotope has a relative atomic mass close to 37.0 amu. The accepted value for the relative atomic mass of chlorine is 35.46 amu. That is the average of the relative atomic masses of its two naturally occurring, stable isotopes.

To illustrate it more directly, let us consider the calculation of the relative atomic mass for chlorine. In an average sample of 10 000 (10^4) atoms of chlorine, we find experimentally that 75.53 percent, or 7553, of those atoms have a mass of 34.98 amu. They contribute this mass.

$$\left(34.98\ \frac{\text{amu}}{\cancel{\text{atom}}}\right)(7553\ \cancel{\text{atoms}}) = 26.42 \times 10^4\ \text{amu}$$

The remaining 24.47 percent, or 2447, of those 10 000 atoms, each having a mass of 36.98 amu, should contribute this mass.

$$\left(36.98\ \frac{\text{amu}}{\cancel{\text{atom}}}\right)(2447\ \cancel{\text{atoms}}) = 9.049 \times 10^4\ \text{amu}$$

Therefore, the total mass of the 10 000-atom sample is this.

$$\begin{array}{r} 26.42\ \ \times 10^4\ \text{amu} \\ +\ 9.049 \times 10^4\ \text{amu} \\ \hline 35.47\ \ \times 10^4\ \text{amu} \end{array}$$

And the average relative atomic mass will be this.

$$\frac{35.47 \times 10^4\ \text{amu}}{10^4\ \text{atom}} = 35.47\ \text{amu/atom}$$

Of course, the calculated value must agree with the experimental value.

8–8 · Elements redefined · Isotopes exist because of the difference in the number of neutrons in the nucleus of each kind of atom. Thus, one isotope of chlorine, ${}^{35}_{17}Cl$, has eighteen neutrons in its nuclei. The other isotope has twenty neutrons in its nuclei. Both isotopes have seventeen protons in their nuclei. If they had different numbers of protons, they would no longer be isotopes of the same element. The isotopes of chlorine behave alike chemically. That is because the chemistry of an element is related to its atomic number, not to its mass number. Therefore, we can redefine an **element** as a substance of which all the atoms have the same atomic number.

8–9 · Radioactive isotopes · There are approximately three hundred nuclei that are stable in the sense that they do not show any radioactive decay. For elements with even atomic numbers, there are usually more than two stable isotopes. For the element tin, atomic number 50, there are ten stable isotopes known. These are ^{112}Sn, ^{114}Sn, ^{115}Sn, ^{116}Sn, ^{117}Sn, ^{118}Sn, ^{119}Sn, ^{120}Sn, ^{122}Sn, and ^{124}Sn. In contrast, the elements with odd atomic numbers only have one, or at most, two stable isotopes each. Element 49, indium, has only one stable isotope, ^{113}In. But element 51, antimony, has two, ^{121}Sb and ^{123}Sb. All the elements with atomic numbers greater than 82 are unstable. And they decay by radioactive emission of alpha particles. Some of these elements are no longer found on the earth. That is because the rate of decay is sufficiently rapid so that all the elements have

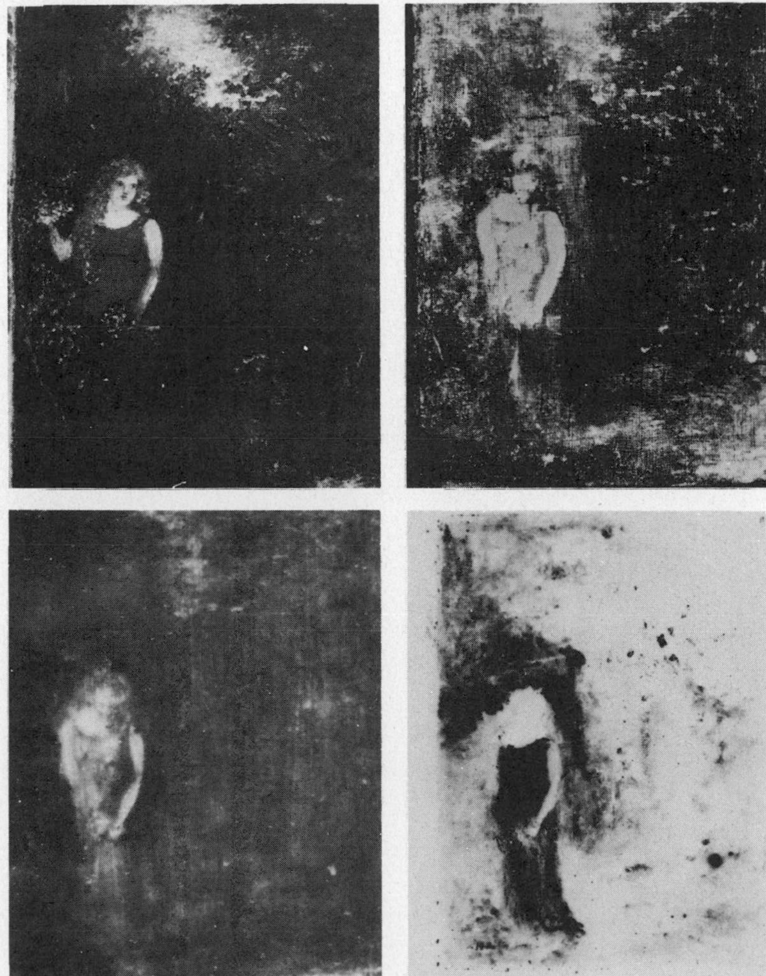

FIGURE 8–4 · *These four pictures illustrate a technique known as neutron activation autoradiography. With this technique, investigators can identify individual characteristics of an artist's style that might go undetected using the conventional method of picture authentication, X-ray radiography. Both methods are used to detect forgeries. Neutron activation autoradiography was used to analyze this painting. Woman in Red, by Marian Blakelock. The original painting is shown in the top left corner. The other three pictures illustrate successive results of exposure to a beam of thermal neutrons for forty-five minutes to two hours. The various elements present in the paint pigments generate radioisotopes that are recorded when a piece of photographic film is placed over the activated painting.*

undergone radioactive decay. Other heavy elements, such as uranium and thorium, can still be found in nature. The rate of decay is small enough so that only a fraction of the earth's supply of those elements has disappeared.

Radioactive decay of the isotopes of an element occurs at a specific rate. The rate depends on the number of protons and neutrons in the element. Therefore, the radioactive isotopes of each element can be characterized by the rate of their radioactive decay. (In the same way, compounds can be identified by their melting points.) You have learned that elements of *even* atomic numbers have more stable isotopes than elements of *odd* atomic numbers. Therefore, we can conclude that there is greater stability when even numbers of protons are present in the nucleus. That conclusion is confirmed by examining two elements found below element 82 that have no stable isotopes. One element is technetium, which has an atomic number of 43. The second is promethium, which has an atomic number of 61.

There are approximately two thousand different radioactive nuclei presently known. Every element, from hydrogen through the heaviest known element, has some radioactive isotopes. Some of those radioactive isotopes are quite important. They have been used in many important ways. For example, some are used to date archaeological objects, treat cancer, improve fertilizers and insecticides, develop new drugs, improve industrial processes, and so on. The use of radioactive isotopes in the last quarter of a century has become tremendously extensive. Many aspects of our modern technological society have been significantly improved through research utilizing radioactive isotopes.

EXCURSION FOUR

The Nucleus: For Better or Worse?

This excursion discusses some investigations leading up to and the discovery of radioactivity. It also discusses some of the benefits and problems of the use of radioactivity.

REVIEW IT NOW

1 How does a scientist formulate a model?
2 Describe Rutherford's classic experiment.
3 List 5 statements regarding the structure of the atom resulting from Rutherford's work.
4 What does the mass number (A) equal?
5 What does the atomic number (Z) equal?
6 What is a nucleon?
7 Why do two isotopes of the same element show the same chemical properties?
8 List three isotopes of hydrogen.
9 How were isotopes first discovered?
10 What are some uses of radioactive isotopes?

QUANTUM MECHANICS AND THE ATOM

8–10 · New observations made it necessary to modify the atomic model · As we stated earlier, sometimes it is necessary to modify scientific models when new information becomes available. But in some cases, it is very difficult to explain everything we observe. In fact, sometimes it even seems impossible. In order to explain experimental facts, it is necessary to contradict the very laws of nature. Let's look at an example of that problem. Ernest Rutherford tried to devise a model of the atom to explain the observed behavior of atoms. He assumed the atom contained a positively charged nucleus, with negatively charged electrons surrounding it. That would explain his experimental observations. However, everyone knew that *positively* charged bodies attracted negatively charged bodies. That was one of the fundamental laws of physics. It could be shown experimentally that it is always true. Now you can see the problem Rutherford faced if the atom was as he predicted. The negative electron would be attracted to the positive nucleus and the atom would simply collapse! Obviously that did not happen, so it was necessary to modify the model of the atom. Perhaps the electron was constantly moving in an orbit around the nucleus. The centrifugal force of its motion would keep it from being attracted to the nucleus. That would be somewhat like the planets revolving around the sun. However, that model also violated a law of physics. It was well known that a moving body would radiate energy. If it gave off energy, it would slow down. And if it slowed down, it could no longer stay in orbit and would collapse into the nucleus. Again, Rutherford faced the seemingly insurmountable task of finding a model to explain his observations that did not conflict with physical laws.

8–11 · Bohr suggested the quantum model of the atom · In 1916, Niels Bohr (1885–1962), a young Danish physicist working in Rutherford's laboratory, proposed a startling theory. He suggested that the laws of physics as known at that time do not apply to atoms. He assumed that there are different laws of physics for atoms. According to Bohr, the relationship of electrons to their nuclei is not like the relationship between magnets or normally charged bodies. There must be a different type of physical law operating in atoms than in other charged bodies.

Niels Bohr
(1885–1962, Danish). Bohr's monumental contribution to the theory of atomic structure earned him a Nobel prize in 1922. He escaped from Nazi-occupied Denmark to England in 1943. After making great contributions to the development of nuclear weapons in the United States, Bohr returned in 1945 to the Institute of Theoretical Physics in Copenhagen, which he had founded in 1920. In his later years, Bohr was a strong advocate of the peaceful use of nuclear energy, and he received the first Atoms for Peace Prize in 1957.

Bohr's theory led to what is known as the **quantum model** of the atom. Although the model has been modified somewhat, his main assumptions are still accepted.

1. *The electrons in atoms exist only in certain definite energy levels. That is something like saying that high school students can only be in certain grades, i.e., 9, 10, 11, or 12. Have you ever heard of a 10.25 grader?*
2. *As long as electrons stay in specific energy levels, they neither gain nor lose energy. These energy levels are called the* **stationary states** *of the atom.*
3. *An electron may change from one energy level of an atom to another energy level in the same atom. For such a transition to occur, a definite amount of energy is involved. The amount of energy required to move an electron to a higher level is equal to the difference in the energies of the two states. Perhaps an analogy will help here. Suppose you pay $4.00 for a ticket to a football game. You would be assigned to a specific seat in a specific row of the stadium. Just as electrons exist only at certain levels, your seat is only in a certain row. It would not be possible for you to sit between two rows. Now suppose your seat is low in the stadium, and the view is not so good. You could invest $2.00 more and get a $6.00 seat in a higher row. The "difference" between the two rows is, in this case, $2.00. Similarly, for an electron to move from a lower to a higher energy level, it must gain energy.*
4. *Electrons can also move from a higher energy state to a lower energy state. Again, a definite amount of energy equal to the difference in energy between the two states is released from the atom. In our analogy, if you decided to return to your original seat in the lower row, you could get $2.00 refunded on your $6.00 ticket.*

It is most important that you realize that energy is associated with each electron level. A definite amount of energy is either absorbed or emitted in each transition of electrons between energy levels.

In the macroscopic world with which we are most familiar, objects can exist in many different energy states. For example, we can lift a weight from the floor to whatever height we please. It can be lifted 1.00 centimeter, 2.00 centimeters, 2.56 centimeters, 3.00 meters, etc. There are no limitations on the exact height to which the weight can be lifted. The only limitation is the height that we can reach. Compare that to our atomic system. There are stationary energy states of definite "heights." An electron can be "lifted" only to those definite heights. The various energy levels make up the quantum system.

Let's use another analogy. Assume that the quantum model of the atom is like a person standing on a stepladder. We can stand on only the rungs of the stepladder. What would happen if you tried to maintain a position halfway between two rungs of the ladder? Right, you'd end up on the ground! For that reason, a ladder is like a quantum system, since only definite levels exist. Also, a specific amount of potential energy exists when you are standing on each rung of the ladder. And a certain amount of energy is required for you to move from one rung to another. Thus, we can say that potential energy is absorbed or emitted as you move from one rung to another rung. That is like the electrons moving from one stationary state to another. And like the ladder analogy, a specific amount of potential energy exists in each stationary state of an atom.

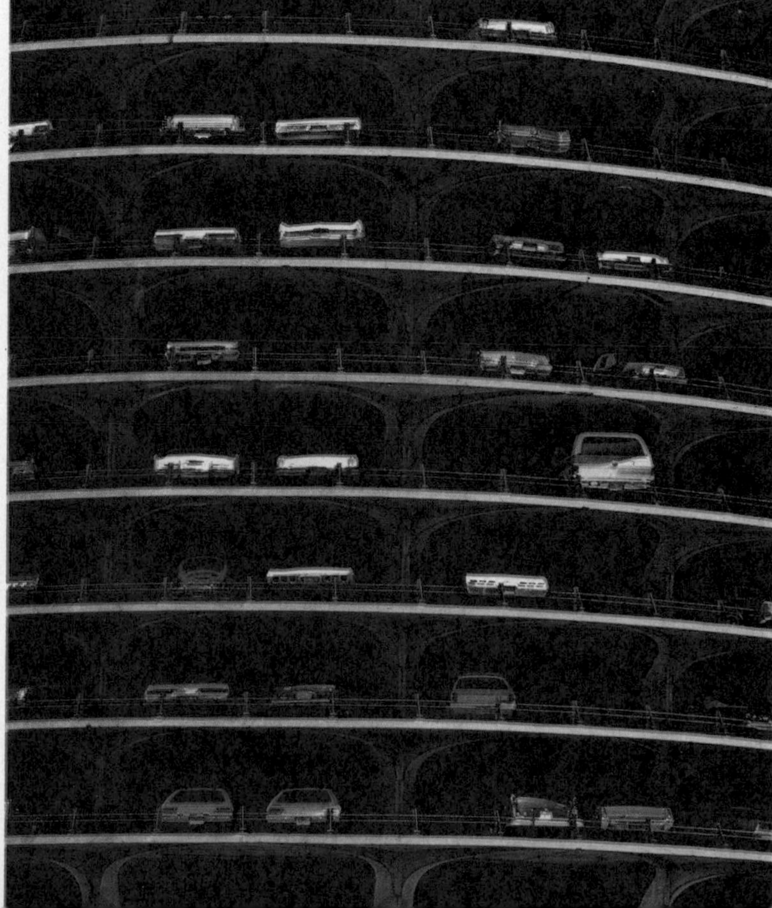

FIGURE 8–5 · *The parking in this garage is quantized. Therefore, cars can be parked only at certain, fixed levels.*

8–12 · Bohr discovered more about energy levels · In our football ticket analogy, remember that we could calculate a specific dollar difference when we went from one row in the stadium to another. Similarly, it would help us understand the atom if we could calculate the amount of energy involved when the electron changes from one energy level to another.

Again, the genius of Niels Bohr provides the solution! Bohr derived an equation to determine the potential energy in each energy state for the hydrogen atom. Remember that this is *potential* energy, due to its position.

Bohr's equation can be expressed simply as follows.

$$E_n = \frac{-313.6}{n^2} \text{ kcal/mole of electrons}$$

By convention, negative values were chosen to represent the energy levels. That will become more meaningful later in the chapter. The value of 313.6 is calculated from several factors. Those factors include the mass of the electron, the mass of the nucleus, and the charge of the electron. Bohr used the small letter n to represent the major energy levels. It has integral values of 1, 2, 3, 4, etc. The letter n is called the **principal quantum number.** Of course, a letter is not a number, but don't let that confuse you. Each value of the principal quantum number corresponds to a different energy level.

For the first, and lowest, energy level, the principal quantum number is 1, and the energy at that level is as follows.

$$E_1 = \frac{-313.6}{1^2} \text{ kcal/mole}$$
$$= -313.6 \text{ kcal/mole}$$

This is the characteristic energy value for the first stationary energy level, $n = 1$.

8–13 · More on energy levels · The lowest ($n = 1$) level is the most negative. Now you can see why Bohr made 313.6 in his calculation negative. Suppose a mole of electrons falls to the lowest energy level of hydrogen. In that case, the Bohr theory predicts that 313.6 kcal of energy will be released. Keep in mind that the value represents the energy involved for a mole of electrons (6.02×10^{23}), not a single electron.

Now let's consider an energy level where the principal quantum number (n) is greater than 1. Calculations for the second ($n = 2$) level give the following value.

$$E_2 = \frac{-313.6}{2^2} \text{ kcal/mole}$$

$$E_2 = \frac{-313.6}{4} = -78.4 \text{ kcal/mole}$$

Less energy is released when a free electron falls into that level. How much energy is *released* when an electron drops from the second level ($n = 2$) to the first energy level ($n = 1$)? Since the energy of the electron at $n = 1$ (−313.6) is 235.2 kcal *less* than the energy of the electron in the second ($n = 2$) level (−78.4), that amount of energy would be released when the electron goes from $n = 2$ to $n = 1$. How much energy must an electron in the first energy level ($n = 1$) *absorb* in order to go to the second energy level ($n = 2$)?

EXERCISE

Calculate the energy values for $n = 3$, $n = 4$, $n = 5$, $n = 6$, $n = 7$, $n = 8$.

When the values you obtained in the exercise above are plotted as an energy-level diagram, Figure 8–6 results. Note that a *set* of energy levels results, not a continuous spread of energies. Thus, Figure 8–6 represents a quantum level diagram for the hydrogen atom.

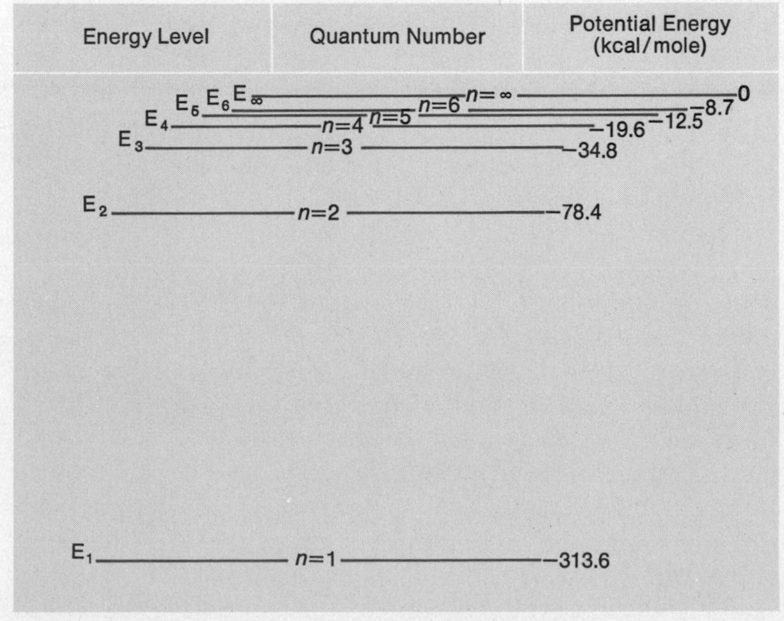

FIGURE 8–6 · *Energy-level diagram calculated for the hydrogen atom.*

The energy levels in Figure 8–6 correspond to the ladder rungs in our analogy. Of course, it is an unusual ladder, with the rungs being closer together near the top. We can see that a great deal of energy is required to raise a mole of electrons from $n = 1$ to $n = 2$. However, it becomes energetically easier to excite the electrons already at higher levels.

EXERCISE

Calculate the energy change for the following transitions.

$E_{2\longrightarrow 3}$; $E_{3\longrightarrow 4}$; $E_{4\longrightarrow 5}$

The level representing the lowest potential energy ($n = 1$) is referred to as the **ground state.** The level to which an electron is elevated is the **excited state.**

REVIEW IT NOW

1 How can we calculate the potential energy at a given stationary energy level in the hydrogen atom?
2 What is meant by the ground state of an atom? What is meant by the excited state?
3 What is the principal quantum number?

8–14 · Bohr and the line spectra problem · Before we can understand just how important Bohr's theory was, we must take a look at a problem that physicists in Bohr's time could not solve.

For centuries, scientists had been puzzled over the formation of colors. Lens makers were at a loss to explain why all their lenses had a colored border, producing a troublesome defect. It was commonly observed that a rainbow consisting of various colors was produced under certain conditions, but no one understood why.

Finally, in 1660, Sir Isaac Newton (1642–1727) proposed a theory to explain that. He constructed a triangular-shaped glass prism. When he passed ordinary light through the prism, the light that came out consisted of six colors, red, orange, yellow, green, blue, and violet. The colors tended to "blend" into one another. Newton called this band of colors a **spectrum.** He proposed that the white light was actually separated into these different colors as it passed through the prism. He further suggested that ordinary light actually was composed of the six different colors. According to Newton, the colors were separated

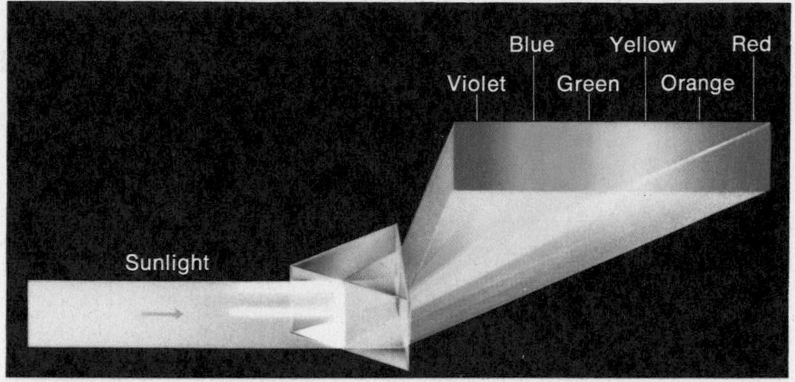

FIGURE 8–7 · *Prismatic refraction and dispersion of white light into a continuous spectrum*

when light passed through the prism because each color light was "bent," or *refracted*, at a different angle.

Two hundred years later, another great discovery was made in the same area. Scientists observed that ordinary light, like sunlight, does indeed produce a continuous spectrum of colors when viewed through a prism. They even devised an instrument to separate the colors, the **spectroscope.** However, if the light emitted from a single element, when it was burned, was observed with a spectroscope, it did not produce a continuous band of colors. Instead, it produced discrete, sharp lines—a **line spectra.** Also, it was found that no two elements had exactly the same line spectra. It was almost like a "fingerprint" for the elements.

In fact, the line spectra were so characteristic that many new elements were discovered with the spectroscope.

Element	Named for
Indium	*Indigo blue*
Cesium	*Latin* caesium, *sky blue*
Thallium	*Latin* thallus, *green twig*
Rubidium	*Latin* rubidus, *darkest red*

Still, scientists were at a loss to explain the origin of the lines in the spectra of individual elements.

Again, Bohr came to the rescue. Bohr's astonishing theory assumed that the characteristic lines in the spectra corresponded *exactly* to the characteristic energies emitted when the electrons at various energy levels were "excited." Let's see how he attempted to prove that.

We are assuming that the energy values calculated by Bohr for the stationary states of the hydrogen atom have meaning.

EMISSION SPECTRA

But to have the same meaning, the energy values must agree with observed experimental facts. As you've learned, transitions from higher to lower energy states should release energy. That energy can be related to the energies that can be experimentally measured when emitted by hydrogen atoms.

In the previous section, you calculated energies absorbed in the transitions $E_{1\longrightarrow 2}$, $E_{2\longrightarrow 3}$, $E_{3\longrightarrow 4}$, and $E_{4\longrightarrow 5}$. The reverse of each of these transitions, $E_{2\longrightarrow 1}$, $E_{3\longrightarrow 2}$, $E_{4\longrightarrow 3}$, and $E_{5\longrightarrow 4}$, must result in the **emission** of quanta, bundles of energy, of exactly the same energies as previously calculated. That can be clearly seen from Figure 8–8. The difference in potential energy for each of those levels determines the amount of absorbed or emitted energy. Thus, just as we calculated the absorbed energy $E_{1\longrightarrow 2}$, so we can calculate the emitted energy $E_{2\longrightarrow 1}$.

$$E_{2\longrightarrow 1} = E_2 - E_1$$

The calculated energy of the emitted quantum is related to frequency ν of radiation by Planck's equation.

$$E_{2\longrightarrow 1} = h\nu_{2\longrightarrow 1} \text{ (}h\text{ is a constant} = 6.624 \times 10^{-27} \text{ erg sec)}$$

And then to a calculated wavelength λ:

$$\lambda_{2\longrightarrow 1} = \frac{c}{\nu_{2\longrightarrow 1}} \text{ (}c\text{ is a constant} = 2.998 \times 10^{10} \text{ cm sec}^{-1}\text{)}$$

By using the Bohr theory, it is possible to calculate the energy and the wavelength of the energy emitted or absorbed by hydrogen. Those energies constitute the energy spectrum of hydrogen. For many of the transitions, the energy falls within the visible region, and our eyes can detect it. However, there are also higher energies that constitute the **ultraviolet spectrum** and lower energies that constitute the **infrared spectrum.** The Bohr theory predicts that the spectrum of an atom should consist of individual energies or lines rather than a continuously varying distribution of energies. Experimentally, that is what is found.

It was clear now that such line spectra meant that the energy changes in atoms had to correspond to definite amounts of energy. The Bohr model required exactly that property of atoms. So the Bohr theory explained why atoms gave line spectra. Every experimental spectral line then known for hydrogen agreed very closely with the value calculated for it by the Bohr theory. Also, many of the lines predicted from the Bohr theory were not known at the time of the original calculation but have since been discovered experimentally.

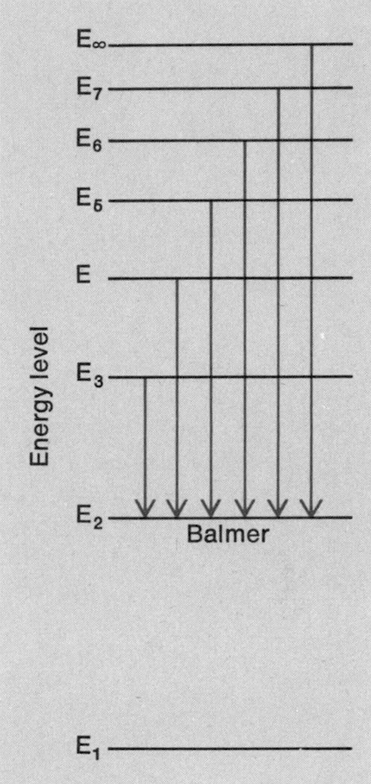

FIGURE 8–8 · *Energy-level diagram showing electron transitions from excited states to lower energy states in the hydrogen atom. How are such transitions related to the hydrogen emission spectrum?*

REVIEW IT NOW

1 How does the Bohr theory explain the existence of line spectra for elements?
2 What is the relationship between line spectra and energy levels in the atom?
3 How is a spectrum explained?

8–15 · The Schrödinger wave equation · For some time, physicists have found it necessary to describe the behavior of light by two types of theories. You've probably observed sunlight passing through prisms or even raindrops. The light can be "refracted" into a spectrum, or a continuous band of colors, to produce rainbows. This familiar type of spectrum is shown in Figure 8–9. The refraction of light can be explained only by using a wave theory. In this theory, it is assumed that light has the properties of waves. Such light waves are bent from their original direction. The degree of bending will be dependent on the distance between peaks of waves. The same refraction phenomenon can be observed by studying the waves on the surface of a pan of water. Suppose you created waves in a pan of water. What would happen if you placed a stick in their path? The waves would be bent by the stick, and they would move out of their original direction.

FIGURE 8–9 · *A rainbow is the result of the refraction of sunlight, as it passes through moisture in the atmosphere.*

Many properties of light can be explained by the use of the wave theory. But not all of them can. For example, we are familiar with photocells. In such cells, the beams of light strike sensitive material and activate electrical circuits. Photocells are used to open doors, in burglar alarms, etc. In order to explain the photoelectric effect, it is necessary to assume that the light consists of small particles of energy known as **photons.** In fact, it was the development of the photon theory of light that led to the original concept of the quantum theory of matter. Only a few years after the original development of the quantum theory of matter, Bohr was able to use those ideas to develop his atomic model.

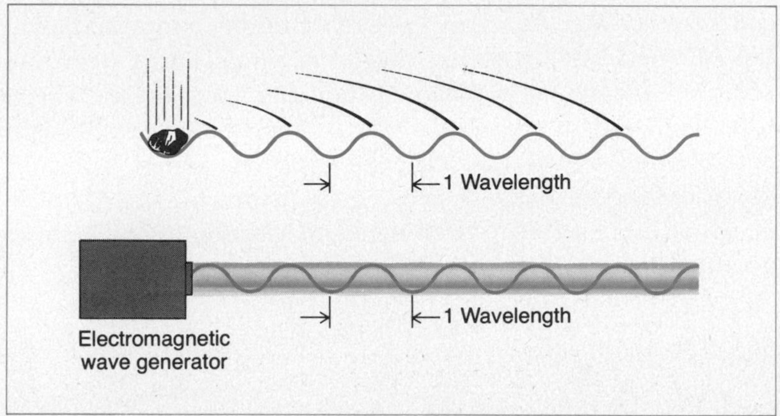

FIGURE 8–10 · *The wave theory of electromagnetic radiation is derived from a consideration of the properties of water waves.*

Louis de Broglie (1892–), a French physicist, reasoned that if it is possible to use both a wave theory and a particle theory to explain light energy, then perhaps one can use both types of theories to explain matter. Prior to de Broglie's proposal, matter had always been explained in terms of a particle theory. The Bohr model of the atom is a particle model. That is because it is assumed that a positive particle, the nucleus, attracts negative particles, the electrons. In 1926, the Austrian physicist Erwin Schrödinger (1887–1961) followed de Broglie's proposal and used a new mathematical equation for calculating the energy states of electrons in atoms. Schrödinger's equation describes the behavior of electron waves. It also allows for the calculation of the energies that such electron waves should have in atoms. Schrödinger learned that solutions to the wave equation were obtained only for certain values of the electron energies. That meant that the Schrödinger wave equation allows only certain energy levels for electrons in

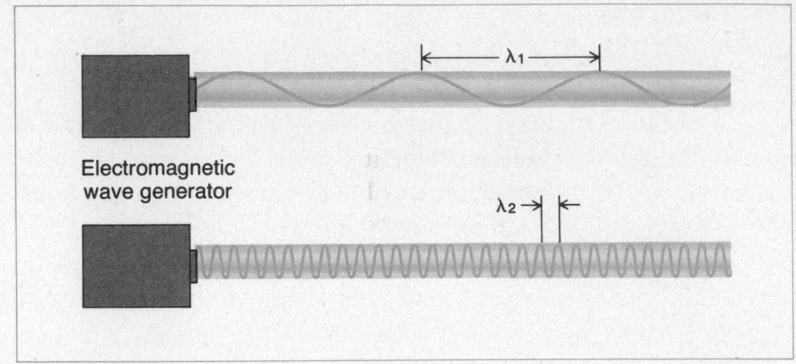

FIGURE 8–11 · *The wavelength of an electromagnetic radiation depends on the electromagnetic system that generates it.*

an atom. That agrees with the stationary energy state concept proposed by Bohr.

When the wave equation was solved for the hydrogen atom, the calculated energy states agreed extremely well with the observed energy levels obtained from the experimental spectrum. Perhaps you can imagine the excitement that gripped scientists when they learned that the electronic energy levels of atoms can be calculated from an equation for waves. In Chapter 9, we will consider in more detail the results of the atomic quantum mechanical wave equation.

REVIEW IT NOW

1 What did de Broglie contribute to understanding the structure of the atom?
2 What did Schrödinger contribute to understanding the structure of the atom?
3 Why is it necessary to have a particle *and* a wave model for light?

SUMMARY

Even though it is obvious that the atom must have some structure, it is difficult to define that structure. Scientists attempt to visualize the atom by fitting indirect evidence into a model to describe the atom. Such a model must be changed when new experimental evidence becomes available. One such model was that proposed by J. J. Thomson. His "grapes in gelatin" model considered the electrons to be like negative grapes, imbedded in a positive gelatin area. The discovery of radioactivity allowed Rutherford to propose a more satisfactory model. His model assumed a small, dense, positive nucleus with the electron a great distance away. The discovery of isotopes did a great deal to help further experimentation on the atomic model.

The current model for the atom is the quantum mechanical model. That model was proposed by Niels Bohr. It considers that the atom consists of electrons arranged in definite energy levels, or quanta. Bohr was able to calculate the energy for each energy level in the hydrogen atom. His calculations were in close agreement with experimentally determined energy values. Bohr also applied his quantum theory to explain the existence of line spectra.

Schrödinger, de Broglie, and others refined Bohr's work to produce a more acceptable model of the atom.

REVIEW QUESTIONS

1 The following scientists received Nobel prizes for their contributions to the understanding of the atom. Go to your school library and find out what each of these Nobel laureates did.

Wilhelm Roentgen	1901 (physics)
Antoine Henri Becquerel	1903 (physics)
Ernest Rutherford	1908 (chemistry)
Marie Curie	1903 (physics with Becquerel)
	1911 (chemistry)
J. J. Thomson	1906 (physics)
Theodore W. Richards	1914 (chemistry)
Frederick Soddy	1921 (chemistry)
Francis W. Aston	1922 (chemistry)
Niels Bohr	1922 (physics)
Louis Victor de Broglie	1929 (physics)
Erwin Schrödinger	1933 (physics)

2 Fill in the blanks for the following table.

Element	Atomic number	Protons	Electrons	Neutrons	Mass number
Gallium (Ga)	31	____	____	____	70
Magnesium (Mg)	____	12	____	____	24
Nitrogen (N)	____	____	7	7	____
Silicon (Si)	____	14	____	14	____
Chlorine (Cl)	____	____	17	____	35
Promethium (Pm)	61	____	____	84	____

3 List the number and kinds of particles found in a sodium atom having a mass number of 23.

4 What information is conveyed by the symbol $^{15}_{7}N$?

5 Briefly describe Rutherford's picture of the atom. What evidence led to this model?

6 Compare alpha, beta, and gamma radiation in terms of mass, charge, origin, and the speed at which they travel.

7 The element copper has two naturally occurring isotopes. From the data below, calculate the atomic mass of the naturally occurring mixture of isotopes of copper. How does your calculated value compare with the value listed in the periodic table?

Atom	Mass number	Atomic mass	Relative abundance (%)
Cu	63	62.949	69.10
Cu	63	64.947	30.90

8 A sample of boron contains atoms with mass numbers of 10 and 11. If the atomic mass of boron is 10.822, calculate the approximate percentage of atoms in the sample that have a mass number of 11.

9 **a.** An isotope of element "X" has 30 protons and 15 neutrons. Write the symbol for its nucleus. What element is it?

b. An isotope of element "Y" has a mass number of 131 and contains 77 neutrons. Write the symbol for its nucleus. What element is it?

c. A neutral isotope of element "Z" has 19 electrons and a mass number of 40. Write the symbol for its nucleus. What element is it?

d. An isotope of silver has a mass number of 107. Write the symbol for its nucleus.

10 **a.** When an atom of $^{238}_{92}U$ undergoes natural radioactive transformation, an alpha particle is ejected from its nucleus. What is the nuclear symbol for the atom that is formed?

b. When an atom of $^{239}_{92}U$ undergoes natural radioactive transformation, a beta particle is ejected from its nucleus. What is the nuclear symbol for the atom that is formed?

11 What is meant by "quantized" energy level? Explain how butter or margarine, as purchased in the supermarket, can be said to be "quantized"?

12 Explain how line spectra give proof that energy radiated by excited atoms is quantized.

13 How did the Bohr theory explain emission and absorption spectra?

14 According to the Bohr theory, how much energy (kcal/mol) must be absorbed for a mole of electrons in hydrogen to go from the ground state to the fifth ($n = 5$) level?

15 How much energy will be released when a mole of electrons drops from the eighth ($n = 8$) level to the second ($n = 2$) level in hydrogen?

16 The energy for the transition of a hydrogen electron is $E_{1 \longrightarrow 2} = +235.2$ kcal/mol and $E_{4 \longrightarrow 5} = +7.1$ kcal/mol. Why does it require more energy to activate an electron from the ground state than from an excited state?

SUGGESTED READINGS

Grotz, L. C., and J. E. Gauerke. "Orbital Energy Memory Devices." *Chemistry*. May 1972, p. 17.

Hochstrasser, Robin. *Behavior of Electrons in Atoms:* Structure, Spectra, and Photochemistry of Atoms. New York: W. A. Benjamin Co., 1964.

Kendall, Henry W., and Wolfgang Panofsky. "The Structure of the Proton and the Neutron." *Scientific American*. June 1971, p. 60.

This spinning ferris wheel gives off the illusion of orbitals.

CHAPTER NINE

Electron Orbitals and Chemical Behavior

In Chapter 8, we learned how various models were proposed to explain the structure of the atom. We also saw the limitations of those models and the need to revise each model in the light of new experimental evidence. We saw how Niels Bohr provided the first sound explanation for experimentally observed spectral lines. Building on Bohr's theory, other scientists devised equations to describe the electron energy states of waves. Now we will examine another problem with Bohr's atomic model.

ELECTRONIC BEHAVIOR AND QUANTUM NUMBERS

9–1 · Energy sublevels · In Chapter 8, we discussed Bohr's calculated wavelengths for electron energy levels. And we learned that those calculations agreed with the wavelengths of experimentally produced spectral lines for hydrogen. However, as instrumentation improved, scientists were able to greatly refine their measurements. As a result, it was soon observed that some spectral lines were not really *single* lines. The observations showed that the spectral lines were really several lines placed very close together. Suppose the larger lines represented major energy levels, which you recall were given the symbol n as the *first quantum number*. Then perhaps the closely spaced lines represented "energy sublevels." Those sublevels were given the symbol l, the *second quantum number*.

It was further determined that even those sublevels consisted not of one level, but of several levels. Their existence became apparent when the electrons in certain energy sublevels (l) were affected by a magnetic field. Thus, a third quantum number was needed. It was referred to as the *magnetic quantum number* and given the symbol *m*. Later, a fourth and final quantum number was assigned to the spin of the electron. The *spin quantum number* is given the symbol *s*. It has been determined that an electron can spin, somewhat like a top. An electron can spin only in one of two directions, either right or left (counterclockwise or clockwise). The *s* quantum number can only be one of two values. We could call these "right" and "left" (or anything else that means opposite directions). For mathematical reasons, chemists give it the value of either $+\frac{1}{2}$ or $-\frac{1}{2}$.

The four quantum numbers, *n*, *l*, *m*, and *s*, describe the total energy of the electron.

9–2 · The location of an electron in an atom · In order to solve the atomic wave equation described in Chapter 8, it is necessary to use the quantum numbers *n*, *l*, and *m*. Each quantum number has a value that depends on the other quantum numbers. The spin quantum number, however, does not depend on the others.

By using the values in the wave equation, we can better understand the nature of the electron in the atom. The values of the quantum numbers also allow the chemist to think of the electron as an **energy wave,** and not necessarily as a *particle*. Sometimes we speak of the electron as being **dualistic.** That means that chemists can think of it both as a particle and as an energy wave.

The most important aspect of the wave equation is that it allows us to give a completely new meaning to the location of the electron in an atom. It allows us to calculate the probability of finding the electron at any location at any one point in time. Perhaps an analogy will help you better understand the concept.

Suppose you have a pet dog Phaedeaux, who is usually in your yard. There will be certain places the dog likes to be more than others. For example, the dog may like to relax in a doghouse, or under a shade tree on hot afternoons. If you are asked at 2:30 P.M. *on July 15 where Phaedeaux is, you could say "In the yard" with confidence. But suppose you are asked to be more specific about Phaedeaux's location. You could only say that Phaedeaux is probably under the tree, or in the doghouse. Perhaps you have watched your dog enough (made enough experiments) to determine the probability of finding Phaedeaux in certain places at certain times. For example, you might know that the chances of Phaedeaux's being under the tree are 4 in 10 (40 percent probability) or 5 in 10 (50 percent probability), or that the chances are only 1 in 10 (10 percent probability) that Phaedeaux is somewhere else in the yard.*

Similarly, the wave equation allows a scientist to predict the probabilities of locating a specific electron at different distances from the nucleus.

9–3 · Values of the quantum numbers · Now that we know how the quantum numbers were assigned, suppose we take a closer look at them. We know that *n* represents the major energy levels. We refer to the major levels as $n = 1, 2, 3, 4$, etc. (At one time, those levels were designated as *k, l, m, n,* etc.) Now let's consider the second quantum number, *l*. Remember that the sublevels indicated by *l* represent different energy sublevels within a major level. In order to show that, we will assign a number to each sublevel. That number will begin with 0. Thus, we can show the sublevels for $n = 4$ as follows.

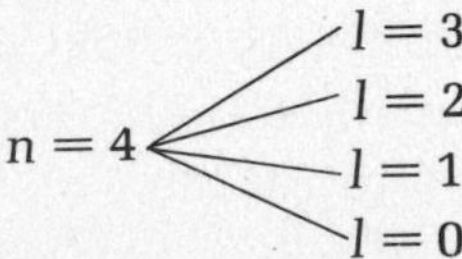

We see that the fourth energy level ($n = 4$) has four values for *l*. That is not a coincidence. It has been experimentally shown that the number of values of *l* is equal to the number of the major energy level. For example, for $n = 1$ there would only be one value of *l*, and that value would be $l = 0$. For $n = 2$ there would be two values of *l*. The values would be 0 and 1. For $n = 3$, there would be three values of *l*, and those would be 0, 1, and 2. $l = 3$ represents a higher energy sublevel than $l = 2$, 1, or 0. $l = 0$ represents the lowest energy sublevel.

9–4 · Orbital types and orbital shapes · An electron energy level is described by a combination of *n* and *l*. This energy level is called an **orbital.** The word *orbital* will be used frequently. Therefore, it is important to understand that orbital refers to energy, and *orbit* to the pattern drawn out by an electron as it moves around the nucleus. An electron in an orbital has a certain amount of energy. The electron is said to occupy a particular energy level. In our example, $n=4$, there are four values of l. Thus, there are four different orbitals. When $l=0$, the orbital is called the *s* orbital. When $l=1$, it is called the *p* orbital. When $l=2$, the orbital is the *d* orbital. Finally, when $l=3$, we say this is the *f* orbital. (Do not be concerned about the origin of the letters *s*, *p*, *d*, and *f*. They were originally used because they described certain spectral lines as being sharp, principle, diffuse, and fundamental.) Other orbitals exist corresponding to $l=4$, 5, 6, etc. However, these orbitals are not important in chemistry.

l value	*orbital type*
0	s
1	p
2	d
3	f

In our understanding of the electron structure of the atom, we will use the orbitals to define the region in space where the electron is most likely found. For the *s* orbital, the electron is most likely found somewhere within a defined spherical area around the nucleus. That is illustrated in Figure 9–1. Our wave equation tells us that an electron with the energy characteristic of the *s* orbital is most probably found within a spherical region that is a short distance from the nucleus. Of course, the electron could be anywhere, but it is most likely to be within the *s*-orbital area.

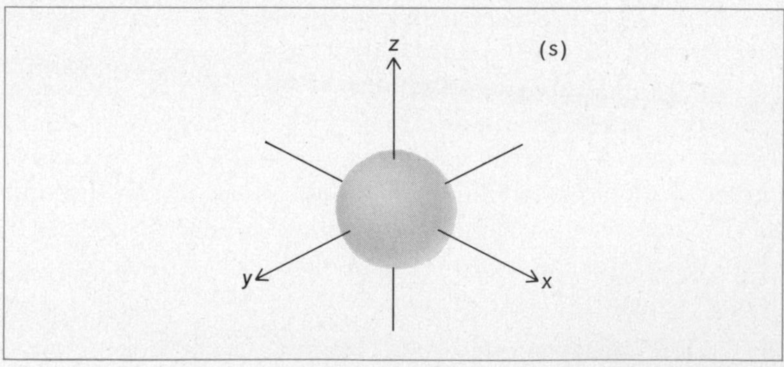

FIGURE 9–1 · *s orbitals are spherical in shape so there is no preferred direction in space.*

What about the *p* orbital? Experimental measurements and calculations tell us that the electron in the *p* orbital is most likely found in an area with a shape similar to that of a dumbbell. That is shown in Figure 9–2. Note that the shape of the *p* orbital is quite different from that of the *s* orbital.

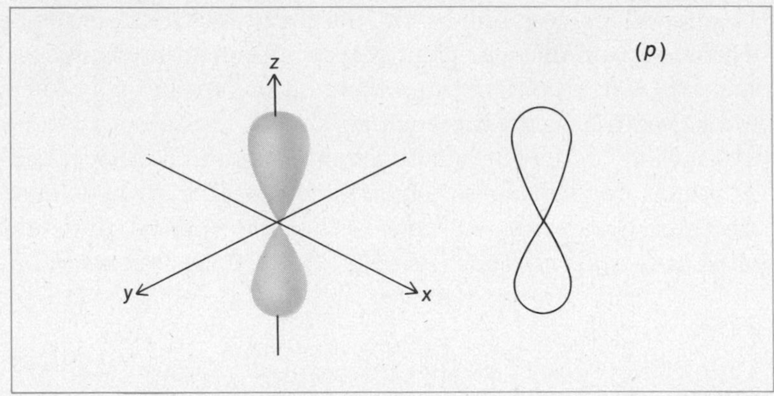

FIGURE 9–2 · p *orbitals are shaped like a dumbbell.*

Expressing the area of probability of the *d* orbital and the *f* orbital as a shape is more complicated. We will discuss those later.

Let's turn our attention to the magnetic quantum number, *m*. That is the number given to the orientation in space that the orbital takes when placed in a magnetic field. Remember, the *s* orbital is described as a sphere. Therefore, its orientation would not be affected by a magnetic field. In other words, no matter which way the spherical shape is oriented, it will still be the same. Thus, for the *s* orbital, which is $l=0$, there is only one value of *m*. That value is 0. So, for $l=0$, $m=0$.

Now let's look at the *p* orbital. Recall that this orbital takes on the shape of a dumbbell, or figure eight. When the *p* orbital is placed in a magnetic field, it can align along any of three axes (*x*, *y*, or *z*), which gives it three possible directions in space. Thus, we can say that the *p* orbital has three values for *m*, −1, 0, and +1. Thus, for the *p* orbital $l=1$, there are three values for *m*. Those are illustrated in Figure 9–3.

FIGURE 9–3 · *A set of* p *orbitals is oriented along the three coordinate axes, x, y, and z.*

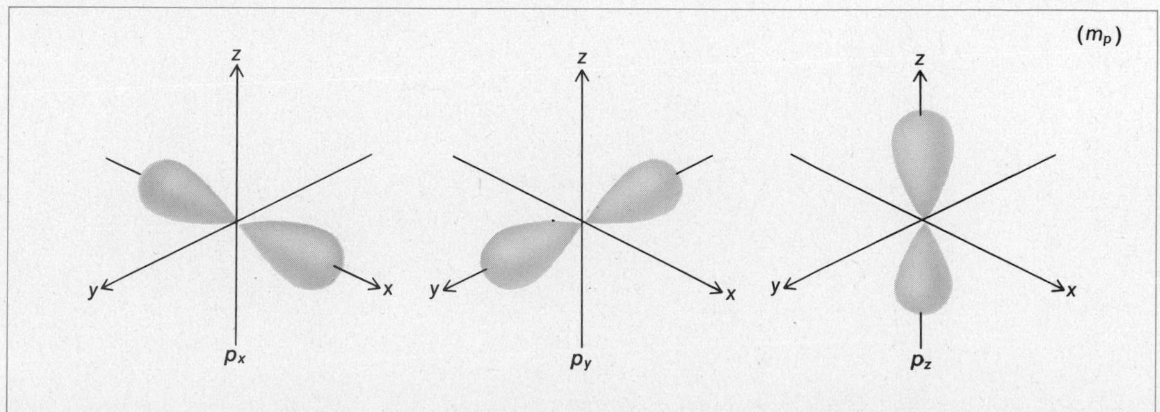

As it was pointed out earlier, the *d* and *f* orbitals are somewhat more complicated. Their shapes are shown in Figures 9–4 and 9–5. It is not important that you understand why the *d* and *f* orbitals have these particular shapes. The important thing is that there are five orientations for the *d* orbital. That means that there are five values of *m* for each *d* orbital. We give those the values −2, −1, 0, +1, and +2. For the *f* orbital, there are seven values for m. *Those are* −3, −2, −1, 0, +1, +2, +3.

EXERCISE

The g *orbitals also exist. How many values of* m *would this orbital have?*

Now, let's put together what we have so far. In the following diagram, we show all the energy levels for $n = 4$:

$$n = 4 \begin{cases} l = 3, \ m = -3, -2, -1, 0, +1, +2, +3 \\ l = 2, \ m = -2, -1, 0, +1, +2 \\ l = 1, \ m = -1, 0, +1 \\ l = 0, \ m = 0 \end{cases}$$

FIGURE 9–4 · *The set of five* d *orbitals has different orientations. Note the unique shape of the* dz_2 *orbital.*

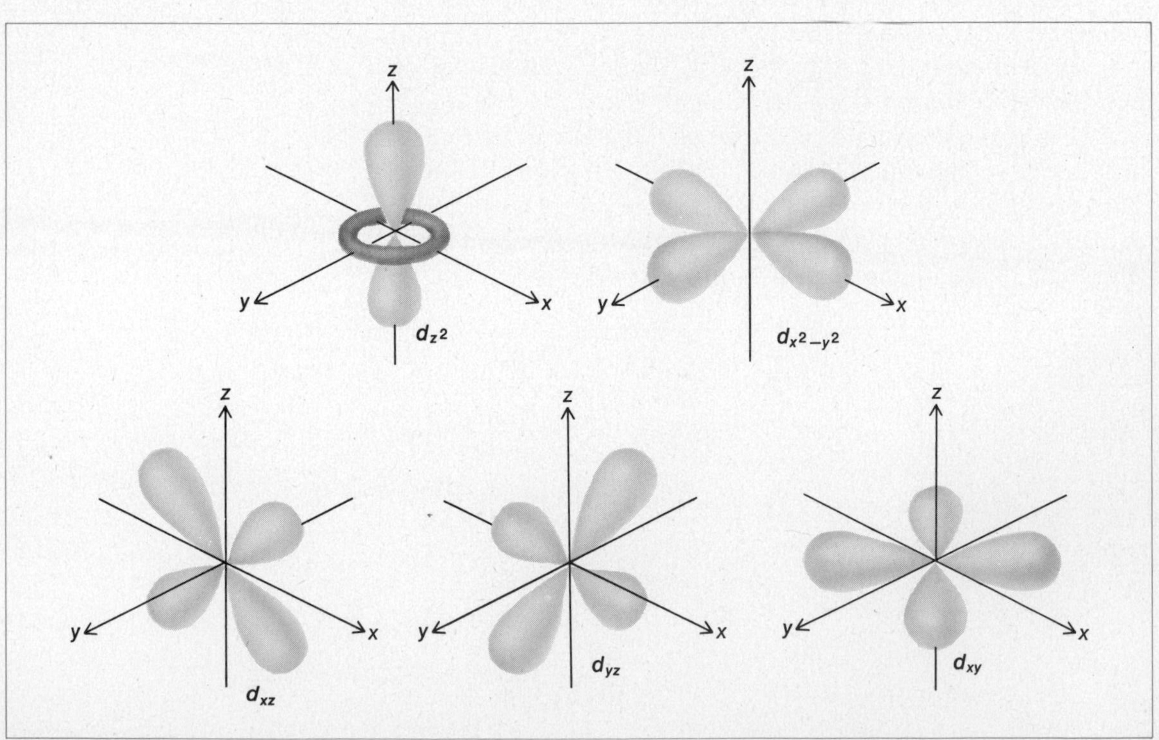

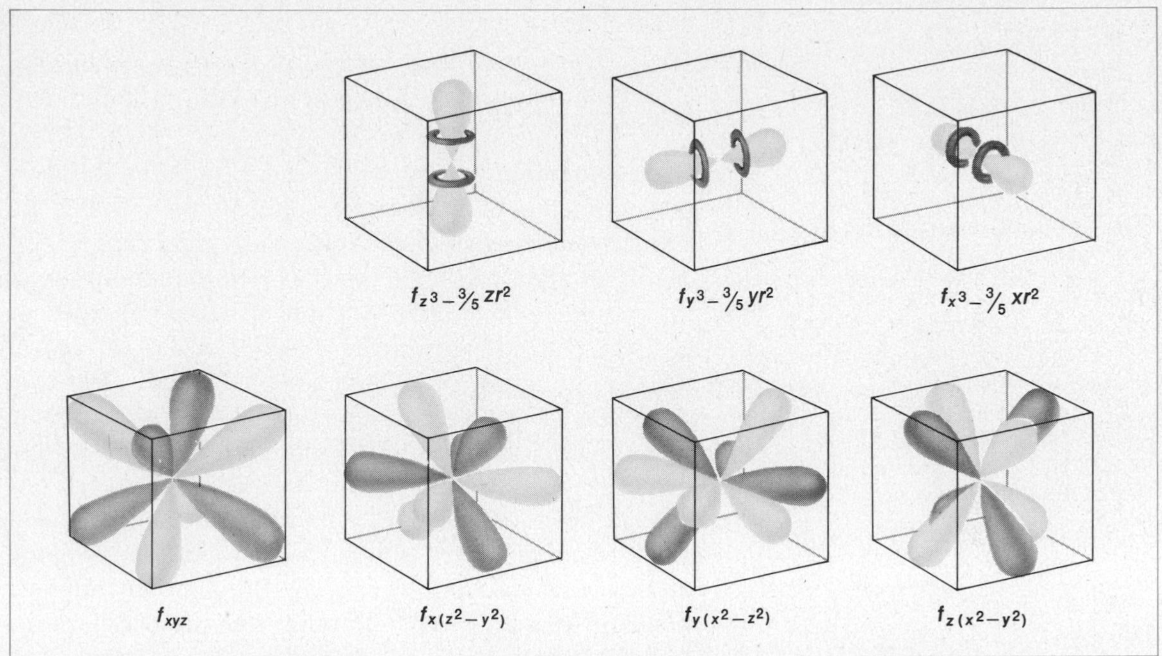

FIGURE 9–5 · *The f orbitals show the increasing complexity of electron distribution shapes of the higher orbitals.*

Recall that the spin quantum number indicated that the electron will spin when it is in a magnetic field. Thus, the electron may have a spin quantum number, s, of either $+\frac{1}{2}$ or $-\frac{1}{2}$. Each orbital can hold only two electrons. One electron will have $s = \frac{1}{2}$ and the other must have $s = -\frac{1}{2}$. We can now diagram the complete picture for the electron. Let's look at the energy diagram for electrons in the first ($n = 1$) and second ($n = 2$) levels.

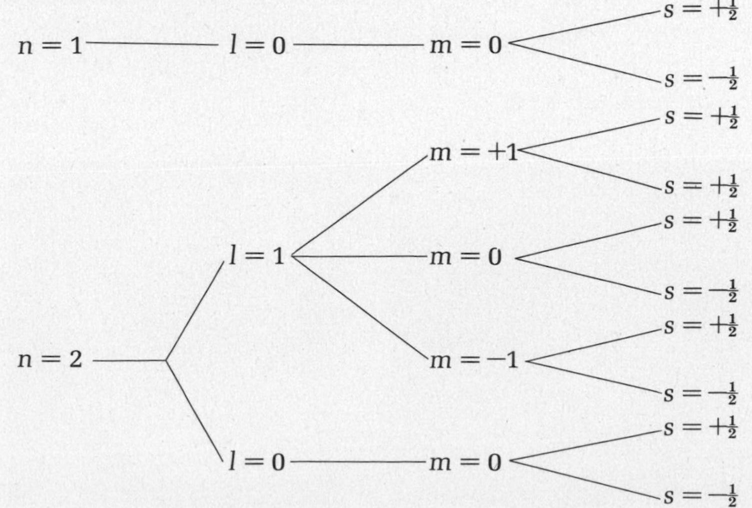

EXERCISE

The previous diagram shows the complete set of quantum number for n = 1 *and* n = 2. *Diagram* n = 3 *and* n = 4.

9–5 · Using quantum numbers · How can quantum numbers help us describe the electrons in an atom? A most valuable aid is the **Pauli Exclusion Principle.** This simply states that no two electrons in an atom can have the same set of quantum numbers. For example, one electron might have a set of numbers as shown in the shaded portion the diagram on the bottom of page 197: $n = 2$, $l = 0$, $m = 0$, and $s = -\frac{1}{2}$. The other electron could have the set of quantum numbers $n = 2$, $l = 0$, $m = 0$, and $s = +\frac{1}{2}$. Although three of the quantum numbers are the same, the fourth is different.

How many electrons can be in the first major energy level ($n = 1$)? There are only two. Another look at the diagram (page 197) will show that one electron can have the quantum numbers $n = 1$, $l = 0$, $m = 0$, and $s = +\frac{1}{2}$. The other electron will have the set of numbers $n = 1$, $l = 0$, $m = 0$, and $s = -\frac{1}{2}$. Only these two electrons can be at this energy level. We know that $l = 0$ represents the spherically shaped *s* orbital. Therefore, the two electrons would most probably be found in a spherical area close to the nucleus. They would have very little energy, since they are in the lowest energy level. What about the third electron? Where would it probably be found? Since the first major energy level ($n = 1$) is "full" the third electron would be found in the second major energy level ($n = 2$). The third electron would also be in an *s* orbital. However, the *s* orbital of the *second* energy level ($n = 2$) would be larger than the *s* orbital of the *first* energy level. In fact, it would encompass the first energy level, as shown in Figure 9–6 (right).

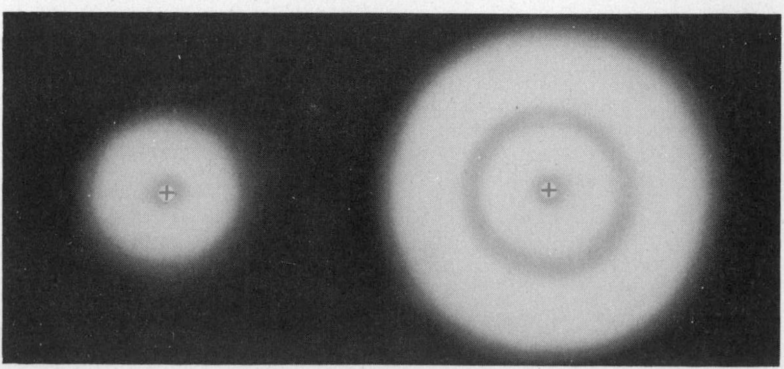

FIGURE 9–6 · *The 1s electron, a model in space, is shown at the left. The 1s and 2s electrons in space are shown at the right.*

The fourth electron would also be in the 2s orbital (Figure 9–6B) since each orbital can accommodate only two electrons. What about the fifth electron? Where is it likely to be found? Since each orbital can accommodate only two electrons, the fifth electron would be in the next orbital. In this case, it would be the *p* orbital of the second energy level. We call this simply the 2*p* orbital. But there are three *p* orbitals in the second level. Which *p* orbital will have the next electron? Since all the *p* orbitals in the second energy level are the same (remember, the three *p* orbitals are identical in shape, but are directed in three different directions in space), it doesn't make any difference. For convenience, we can assume that the fifth electron is found in the *p* orbital directed along the x axis. We can call this the p_x orbital.

Now comes the tricky question: Where will the sixth electron most likely be found? Will it be in the p_x orbital also? Probably not. Although it may seem logical for the sixth electron to go there, remember that electrons are negative. When two electrons are close together, they will repel each other. Their charge will keep them as far apart from each other as possible. Thus, the sixth electron would not be in the p_x orbital; instead, it would be in one of the other *p* orbitals. Again, for convenience, we say that it would be in the p_y orbital. The seventh electron would be in the p_z orbital. Then, if we continue to account for electrons, the eighth electron would have to be in one of the *p* orbitals, paired with an electron already there. Again, for convenience, we assume that the eighth electron would be in the p_x orbital. The ninth electron would be in the p_y orbital. And the tenth electron would be in the p_z orbital. A rule known as **Hund's Rule**, or the **principle of maximum multiplicity**, accounts for this pairing procedure. Hund's Rule states:

The electrons enter each orbital of a given type one at a time and with identical spins before any pairing with electrons of opposite spin occurs within those orbitals.

REVIEW IT NOW

1 What are the four quantum numbers used to describe the energy of an electron?
2 What are the values of the four quantum numbers?
3 What are the orbital types corresponding to *l* values of 0, 1, 2, and 3?
4 What is meant by "shape" of an orbital?
5 What is the "shape" of the *s* orbital?
6 What is the "shape" of the *p* orbital?

9–6 · Orbital patterns for a many-electron atom · Figure 9–7 shows an orbital diagram for atoms with many electrons. As we work our way up the diagram, starting at the 1*s* orbital, we find that the energy of the electron increases. Bohr's quantum theory worked very well with hydrogen. But hydrogen is a very simple atom, with only one electron. Atoms with more than one electron cannot be treated as directly with quantum mechanics as hydrogen can. Therefore, when considering atoms with more than one electron, scientists must use approximations to obtain the orbital patterns from the wave equation. Such an orbital pattern is shown in Figure 9–7. As shown in the diagram, orbitals with the same *n* value, but different *l* values have different energies. For example, the diagram shows that the 3*s* orbital is of lower energy than the 3*p* orbital. And the 3*p* orbital is of lower energy than the 3*d* orbital. The separation of the orbitals of a major energy level is due to the interactions among the many electrons. Note that the separation is severe enough in some cases for orbitals from one major energy level to overlap orbitals in another major energy level (for example, the 4*s* orbital is lower in energy than the 3*d* orbital).

Perhaps a simple analogy will help you understand the overlap in electron energies. Let's look at the sophomores, juniors,

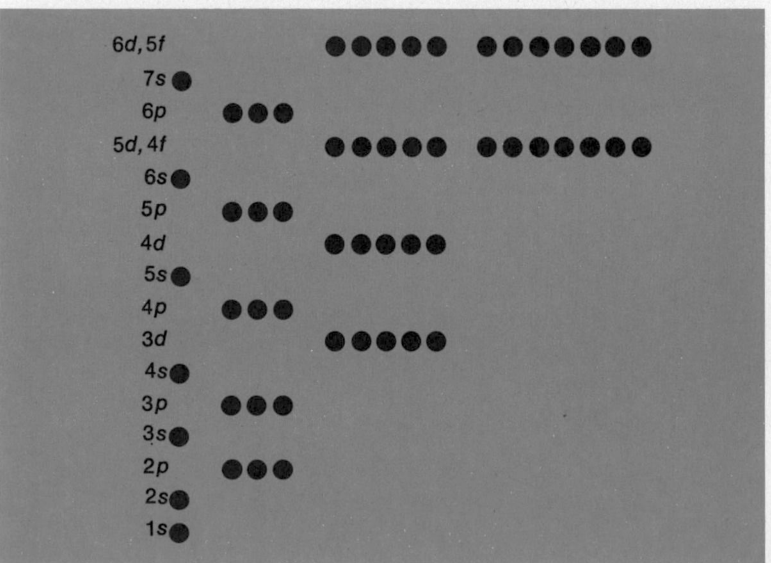

FIGURE 9–7 · *The existence of more than one electron in an atom causes the orbital sequence shown here.*

and seniors in your school. Their grade levels are 10, 11, and 12. Let's assume that this corresponds to the major energy levels, $n=4$, 5, and 6. Even though all the sophomores are in grade 10, it is possible that some of them are really more intelligent (i.e., higher in energy) than some juniors in grade 11. It is also possible that some of the juniors in grade 11 are more intelligent (higher in energy) than some of the seniors. Thus, although the grading scheme used by your school is convenient in grouping large numbers of students together, it does not make allowances for individual students. In a similar manner, some electrons in the third energy level ($n = 3$) may have higher energy than some electrons in the fourth energy level ($n = 4$). That can be seen with 4*s* and 3*d*, for example.

9–7 · Orbital patterns and the structure of atoms · In Figure 9–7, we represented orbitals with an *o* in an energy level diagram. For working purposes, suppose we modify our diagram slightly. That modification is shown in Figure 9–8, page 202. Rather than indicate orbitals with a circle, we will use a line above the orbital. For example,

$\underset{1s}{\_\_}$ indicates the 1*s* orbital

$\underset{2s}{\_\_}$ represents the 2*s* orbital

$\underset{2p_x}{\_\_\_}\ \underset{2p_y}{\_\_\_}\ \underset{2p_z}{\_\_\_}$ represents the $2p_x$, $2p_y$, and $2p_z$ orbitals

and so on.

We will use Figure 9–8 as the basis for describing electrons in the orbitals of an atom. We generally refer to the electron energy states in an atom as the **atomic structure** of an element. In assigning electrons to orbitals in an atom, modern atomic theory takes into account a very old experimental observation. In modern language, the observation is that the most stable systems are those with a minimum of potential energy. In accordance with that, the atomic structures of the elements are built up from the ground floor. That is, all the orbitals of lower potential energy must be occupied before those of higher energy can be filled. A second rule to follow in building up atomic structures is the exclusion principle that was previously mentioned. This principle states that it is not possible for any two electrons in the same atom to have the same set of quantum numbers. At least one quantum number must be different for any two electrons in the same atom.

FIGURE 9–8 · *Electron orbital pattern for a many-electron atom*

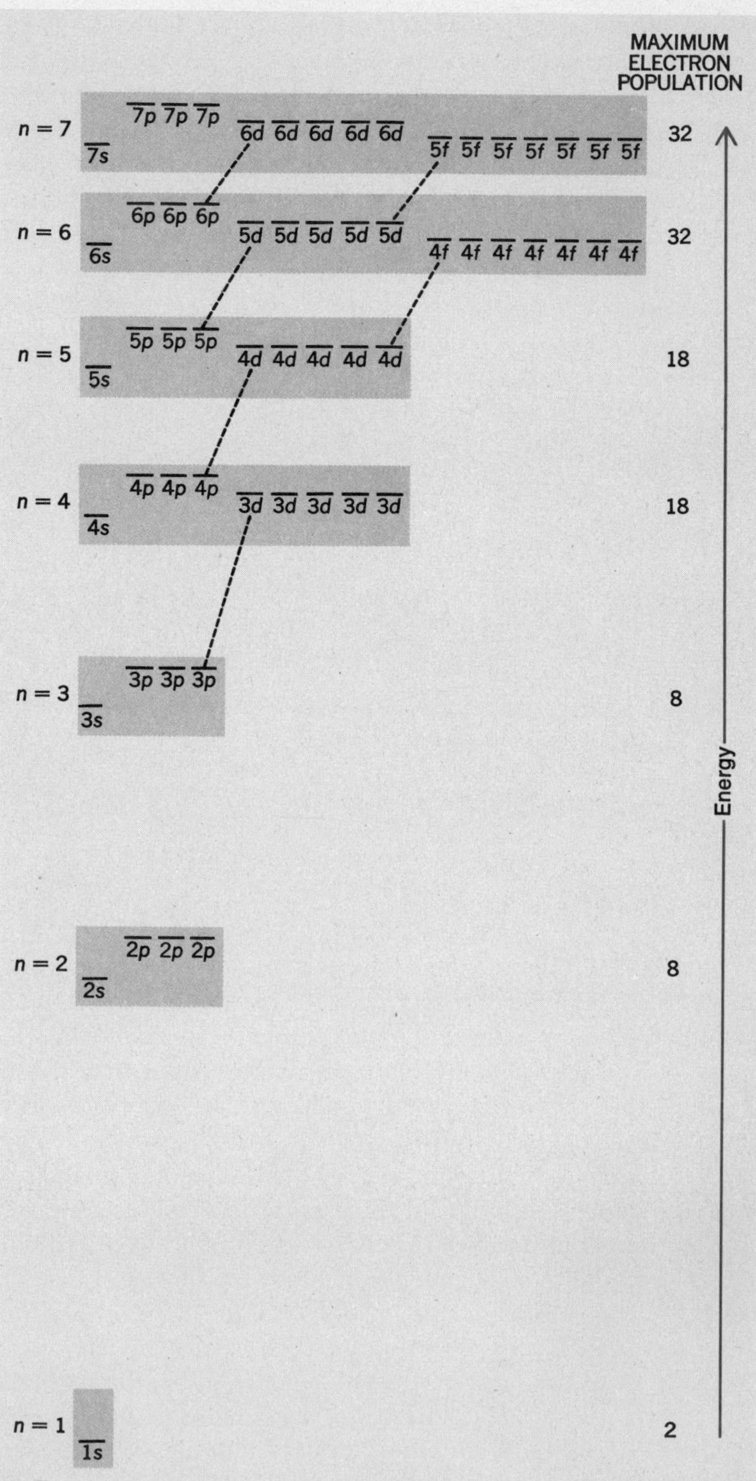

9–8 · Electron configurations for the first ten elements · Hydrogen has only one electron. The electron is in the 1*s* orbital when the atom is in its lowest energy state. Chemists show the atomic structure of hydrogen simply as $1s^1$. That is called the **electron configuration** for hydrogen. Since we will be using electron configurations in later chapters, we will also use a pictorial representation for the electron configuration. For the hydrogen atom, this would be

$$\underset{1s}{\underline{\uparrow}}.$$

The line represents an electron orbital. The 1*s* indicates the orbital. And the upward-pointing arrow is symbolic of one of the two directions of spin for the electron for a single electron in an orbital.

The next element is helium, He, with an atomic number (*Z*) of 2. Helium has two electrons. Both of the electrons would be in the 1*s* orbital. Thus, we would say the electron configuration for He is $1s^2$. We would show that pictorially as

$$\underset{1s}{\underline{\uparrow\downarrow}}.$$

Incidentally, you can follow the series of elements with your periodic table located on the inside cover of your text, or on pages 146–147. Note that the second electron in the 1*s* orbital must have a spin opposite to that of the first electron. Therefore, we represent the second electron with a downward-pointing arrow.

You can see from your periodic chart that the next element is lithium (Li, $Z = 3$). Lithium has three electrons in its atom. Since there is no room for any more electrons in the first energy level, the third electron in Li must be in the 2*s* orbital. Thus, the electron configuration for Li is $1s^2 2s^1$. Pictorially, it is

$$\underset{1s}{\underline{\uparrow\downarrow}}\Big|\underset{2s}{\underline{\uparrow}}.$$

The dividing line between 1*s* and 2*s* indicates that there is a difference in energy between the two orbitals.

Remember that only *two* electrons can be in an orbital. That means that the next atom, beryllium (Be, $Z = 4$) will place its fourth electron in the 2*s* orbital, filling it. Its electron configuration will be $1s^2 2s^2$, and it would be drawn as

$$\underset{1s}{\underline{\uparrow\downarrow}}\Big|\underset{2s}{\underline{\uparrow\downarrow}}.$$

The next element is boron (B, Z = 5). Look again at Figure 9–8. After the 1s and 2s orbitals are filled, where will the next electron go? It will go into the 2p orbital. Remember, all the 2p orbitals are of equal energy, but by convention, we put it into the $2p_x$. Thus boron would have the electron configuration $1s^2 2s^2 2p_x^{\ 1}$, and we would show it this way.

$$\frac{\upharpoonleft\downharpoonright}{1s}\Big|\frac{\upharpoonleft\downharpoonright}{2s}\ \frac{\uparrow}{2p_x}\ \frac{\quad}{2p_y}\ \frac{\quad}{2p_z}$$

The next element is carbon (C, Z = 6), with the electron configuration of $1s^2 2s^2 2p^2$. However, a question arises about the electron configuration of carbon. A given electron orbital can accommodate two electrons of opposite spin. Are the two 2p electrons in the same p orbital, spinning in opposite directions? Or is one electron in each of two p orbitals spinning in the same direction? Let's show these two possible configurations.

$$\frac{\upharpoonleft\downharpoonright}{1s}\Big|\frac{\upharpoonleft\downharpoonright}{2s}\Big|\frac{\upharpoonleft\downharpoonright}{2p_x}\ \frac{\quad}{2p_y}\ \frac{\quad}{2p_z} \quad \text{or} \quad \frac{\upharpoonleft\downharpoonright}{1s}\Big|\frac{\upharpoonleft\downharpoonright}{2s}\Big|\frac{\uparrow}{2p_x}\ \frac{\uparrow}{2p_y}\ \frac{\quad}{2p_z}$$

It is an experimental fact that the second representation is the correct interpretation of the electrons in the carbon atom. Remember Hund's Rule that we discussed earlier? Electrons will fill orbitals of the same energy value one at a time before they pair with electrons in the same orbital.

For the next element, nitrogen (N, Z = 7), we again see Hund's Rule in action. Nitrogen has the configuration $1s^2 2s^2 2p^3$, or

$$\frac{\upharpoonleft\downharpoonright}{1s}\Big|\frac{\upharpoonleft\downharpoonright}{2s}\Big|\frac{\uparrow}{2p_x}\ \frac{\uparrow}{2p_y}\ \frac{\uparrow}{2p_z}.$$

If you are following with your periodic table, you will see that the next element is oxygen (O, Z = 8). Its configuration is $1s^2 2s^2 2p^4$. Again, following our scheme, oxygen is represented as

$$\frac{\upharpoonleft\downharpoonright}{1s}\Big|\frac{\upharpoonleft\downharpoonright}{2s}\Big|\frac{\upharpoonleft\downharpoonright}{2p_x}\ \frac{\uparrow}{2p_y}\ \frac{\uparrow}{2p_z}.$$

The next element is fluorine, F. With 9 electrons, it would have the electron configuration $1s^2 2s^2 2p^5$ and would be drawn thus:

$$\frac{\upharpoonleft\downharpoonright}{1s}\Big|\frac{\upharpoonleft\downharpoonright}{2s}\Big|\frac{\upharpoonleft\downharpoonright}{2p_x}\ \frac{\upharpoonleft\downharpoonright}{2p_y}\ \frac{\uparrow}{2p_z}$$

When we consider the electron configuration of neon (Ne), we see that its 10 electrons completely fill the second energy level.

$$\frac{\uparrow\downarrow}{1s}\Big|\frac{\uparrow\downarrow}{2s}\Big|\frac{\uparrow\downarrow}{2p_x}\ \frac{\uparrow\downarrow}{2p_y}\ \frac{\uparrow\downarrow}{2p_z}$$

Table 9–1 summarizes the electron configuration of the first ten elements. If you will refer to your periodic table, you will see that these ten elements make up Period 1 and Period 2.

You have probably discovered by now that there is a simple check to see if your electron configurations are correct. At least, you can check the number of electrons in a given atom. To do that, add up the superscripts following the orbital symbols. That sum must equal the atomic number for the element. Later we will modify that to work with atoms that are not electrically neutral. But don't worry about that now.

TABLE 9–1 · Electron Configurations for the Elements of Periods 1 and 2

ELEMENT	ELECTRON CONFIGURATION	PICTORIALLY
$_1H$	$1s^1$	$\frac{\uparrow}{1s}$
$_2He$	$1s^2$	$\frac{\uparrow\downarrow}{1s}$
$_3Li$	$1s^22s^1$	$\frac{\uparrow\downarrow}{1s}\Big\vert\frac{\uparrow}{2s}$
$_4Be$	$1s^22s^2$	$\frac{\uparrow\downarrow}{1s}\Big\vert\frac{\uparrow\downarrow}{2s}$
$_5B$	$1s^22s^22p^1$	$\frac{\uparrow\downarrow}{1s}\Big\vert\frac{\uparrow\downarrow}{2s}\Big\vert\frac{\uparrow}{2p}\ \frac{\ }{2p}\ \frac{\ }{2p}$
$_6C$	$1s^22s^22p^2$	$\frac{\uparrow\downarrow}{1s}\Big\vert\frac{\uparrow\downarrow}{2s}\Big\vert\frac{\uparrow}{2p}\ \frac{\uparrow}{2p}\ \frac{\ }{2p}$
$_7N$	$1s^22s^22p^3$	$\frac{\uparrow\downarrow}{1s}\Big\vert\frac{\uparrow\downarrow}{2s}\Big\vert\frac{\uparrow}{2p}\ \frac{\uparrow}{2p}\ \frac{\uparrow}{2p}$
$_8O$	$1s^22s^22p^4$	$\frac{\uparrow\downarrow}{1s}\Big\vert\frac{\uparrow\downarrow}{2s}\Big\vert\frac{\uparrow\downarrow}{2p}\ \frac{\uparrow}{2p}\ \frac{\uparrow}{2p}$
$_9F$	$1s^22s^22p^5$	$\frac{\uparrow\downarrow}{1s}\Big\vert\frac{\uparrow\downarrow}{2s}\Big\vert\frac{\uparrow\downarrow}{2p}\ \frac{\uparrow\downarrow}{2p}\ \frac{\uparrow}{2p}$
$_{10}Ne$	$1s^22s^22p^6$	$\frac{\uparrow\downarrow}{1s}\Big\vert\frac{\uparrow\downarrow}{2s}\Big\vert\frac{\uparrow\downarrow}{2p}\ \frac{\uparrow\downarrow}{2p}\ \frac{\uparrow\downarrow}{2p}$

9–9 · Regularities in the electron configurations of elements · Now let's see if all the discussion of orbitals and electrons has any use. Let's see what it has to do with understanding chemistry. Look again at your periodic table. Find the following elements at the top of the next page that we have discussed in terms of their electron configuration.

hydrogen (H) $1s^1$	*helium (He)* $1s^2$
lithium (Li) $1s^22s^1$	*neon (Ne)* $1s^22s^22p^6$
sodium (Na) $1s^22s^22p^63s^1$	*argon (Ar)* $1s^22s^22p^63s^23p^6$

Can you detect any regularity? What do all the elements in the first column (H, Li, Na) have in common? What do the elements He, Ne, and Ar have in common? Does that give you enough information to make a prediction as to the electron configuration for potassium (K)? for krypton (Kr)?

Perhaps the first observation you made was that H, Li, and Na are all in the same vertical column, column IA. Also, perhaps you noticed that each of these elements is the first element in a horizontal row (Periods 1, 2, and 3). If you predicted that potassium (K) would have the electron configuration $1s^22s^22p^63s^23p^64s^1$, you were correct. In fact, you can easily determine that each element in column IA will have one electron in the *s* orbital. Rb will be $5s^1$, Cs will be $6s^1$, and Fr will be $7s^1$.

The same regularity is true for the elements He, Ne, and Ar. These are inert gases. They all have completely filled outer electron orbitals. Later, we will see that this is what makes them unreactive, or inert.

If you use the examples we have studied so far, the periodic table, and Figure 9–8, you should also be able to make other accurate predictions of electron configurations. You should be able to predict the electron configurations for the elements in columns IIA, IIIA, IVA, VA, VIA, and VIIA of the periodic table.

More interpretation of Figure 9–8 leads us to the following electron configurations for the first two elements of Period 4. All elements past $Z = 18$ have the argon structure as their core.

$${}_{19}\text{K}\;\; 1s^22s^22p^63s^23p^64s^1 \text{ or (Ar)}\left|\underset{4s}{\uparrow}\right.$$

$${}_{20}\text{Ca}\;\; 1s^22s^22p^63s^23p^64s^2 \text{ or (Ar)}\left|\underset{4s}{\uparrow\downarrow}\right.$$

When we reach scandium, Sc($Z = 21$), we place the twenty-first electron in a 3*d* orbital, the next available orbital of higher energy.

$${}_{21}\text{Sc}\;\; 1s^22s^22p^63s^23p^64s^23d^1 \text{ or (Ar)}\left|\underset{4s}{\uparrow\downarrow}\right|\underset{3d}{\downarrow}\;\underset{3d}{\_}\;\underset{3d}{\_}\;\underset{3d}{\_}\;\underset{3d}{\_}$$

Recall that there are five *d* orbitals. Those five *d* orbitals can contain ten electrons. Thus, scandium must be the first in a series of ten elements that are unlike the twenty that precede it.

The first twenty elements involved *s* orbitals and *p* orbitals only. Indeed, the periodic classification of the elements isolates the ten elements in Period 4 between calcium and gallium as **transition elements.** Table 9–2 summarizes the electron configuration of the transition elements in Period 4.

Hund's Rule operates during the occupancy of *d* orbitals. Note that the pictorial representations of the transition elements emphasize that fact. As you recall from Figure 9–8, when the electron configuration of zinc is reached, there are unfilled orbitals of only slightly higher energy, the three 4*p* orbitals.

EXERCISE

Tabulate the electron configurations of the remaining six elements of the fourth period, from gallium, Ga(Z = 31), to krypton, Kr(Z = 36). Using Figure 9–8 as a guide, prepare a table of electron configurations for the eighteen elements of the fifth period, from rubidium, Rb(Z = 37), to xenon, Xe(Z = 54).

TABLE 9–2 · Electron Configurations for the Transition Elements of Period 4

ELEMENT	ELECTRON CONFIGURATION	PICTORIALLY
$_{21}Sc$	$1s^22s^22p^63s^23p^64s^23d^1$	(Ar) 4s: ⇅ | 3d: ↑ _ _ _ _
$_{22}Ti$	$1s^22s^22p^63s^23p^64s^23d^2$	(Ar) 4s: ⇅ | 3d: ↑ ↑ _ _ _
$_{23}V$	$1s^22s^22p^63s^23p^64s^23d^3$	(Ar) 4s: ⇅ | 3d: ↑ ↑ ↑ _ _
$_{24}Cr$	$1s^22s^22p^63s^23p^64s^23d^4$	(Ar) 4s: ⇅ | 3d: ↑ ↑ ↑ ↑ _
$_{25}Mn$	$1s^22s^22p^63s^23p^64s^23d^5$	(Ar) 4s: ⇅ | 3d: ↑ ↑ ↑ ↑ ↑
$_{26}Fe$	$1s^22s^22p^63s^23p^64s^23d^6$	(Ar) 4s: ⇅ | 3d: ⇅ ↑ ↑ ↑ ↑
$_{27}Co$	$1s^22s^22p^63s^23p^64s^23d^7$	(Ar) 4s: ⇅ | 3d: ⇅ ⇅ ↑ ↑ ↑
$_{28}Ni$	$1s^22s^22p^63s^23p^64s^23d^8$	(Ar) 4s: ⇅ | 3d: ⇅ ⇅ ⇅ ↑ ↑
$_{29}Cu$	$1s^22s^22p^63s^23p^64s^23d^9$	(Ar) 4s: ⇅ | 3d: ⇅ ⇅ ⇅ ⇅ ↑
$_{30}Zn$	$1s^22s^22p^63s^23p^64s^23d^{10}$	(Ar) 4s: ⇅ | 3d: ⇅ ⇅ ⇅ ⇅ ⇅

We see how successful the quantum mechanical model of the atom has been in predicting the form of the periodic table. Groups I and II consist of elements in which *s* electron orbitals are being occupied. Groups III to 0 are those for which electrons fill in *p* electron orbitals. The transition elements are called *d* electron orbital elements.

Recall, also, that there are seven *f* orbitals. The lanthanides and the actinides, as you might predict, consist of elements in which the seven *f* electron orbitals are being filled.

9–10 · Electron configurations and chemical families · In Chapter 7, we learned that there are families of elements of similar chemical properties. Let us consider the electron configuration for the members of the three families of elements we studied in Chapter 7—the noble gases, the halogens, and the alkali metals.

EXCURSION FIVE

Where and How Did It all Start?

Having discussed many of the elements that exist around us, you may be interested in finding out where these elements originate. This excursion explains the formation of chemical elements.

As you found earlier, all the noble gases (except helium) have p^6 as their last orbital. All the halogens have p^5, and all the alkali metals have s^1.

Note that Figure 9–8 shows the fundamental relationship between the quantum mechanical model of the atom and the periodic table. *The chemical behavior of the elements is a periodic function of their electron configuration.* Moreover, elements with similar electron configurations have similar chemical properties.

FIGURE 9–9 · *With this chart and Figure 9–8, you should be able to state the electron configuration of almost any element.*

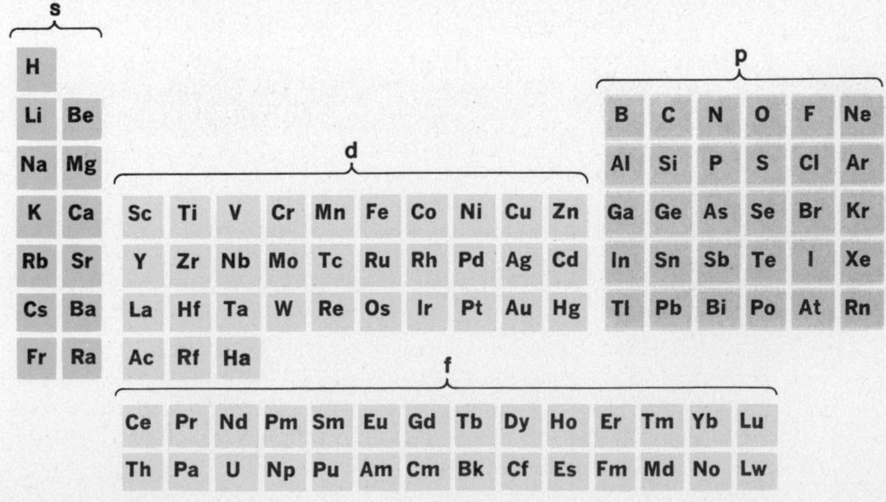

Also, note that Figure 9–8 provide us with a clue to the "why" of chemical reactions. The noble gases, unique among the elements for their chemical stability (their general lack of chemical activity), have unique electron configurations. Only the noble gases among the elements have completely filled orbitals with a great energy difference between the filled orbitals and the next possible orbital. It would be reasonable to conclude that this theoretical fact is connected with the experimental fact of their general chemical inactivity. It might also be reasonable to assume that herein lies a possible theoretical clue to the chemical activity of the other elements. The valence of 1 for the alkali metals would seem to be related to the fact that all the alkali metals have one electron beyond filled quantum levels. Similarly, all the halogens are one electron away from filling all the orbitals in a quantum level. Again that might be related to their common valence of 1.

EXCURSION SIX

The Story of Element 101

This excursion reflects some of the personal excitement experienced by Dr. Choppin as a result of his involvement in the discovery of elements 101, mendelevium.

REVIEW IT NOW

1 State *two* rules to follow when assigning electrons to orbitals.
2 What is meant by the "electron configuration" of an atom?
3 What is the "atomic structure" of an element?
4 What would the electron configuration for the atomic structure of sodium (Na), the eleventh element, be?
5 What is the relationship between the quantum mechanical model of the atom and the periodic table?

SUMMARY

The modern quantum mechanical theory of atomic structure is derived from three fundamental concepts: stationary electron energy states, the description of the behavior of matter by the wave theory, and the inherent uncertainty in measurements involving atomic systems. The complex mathematical theory based on those concepts leads to a description of the electrons in an atom in terms of four quantum numbers: n, l, m, and s.

Each quantum level is characterized by a value of n. For each value of n, there will be a set of energy levels designated by the quantum number l. Also, in a magnetic field, each l level is split into one or more additional energy levels for which m is used as the quantum number. Each set of n, l, and m values is known as an orbital. There can be two electrons of opposite spin, quantum number s, in each orbital.

The potential energy pattern for the orbitals in many-electron atoms is this:
$1s<2s<2p<3s<3p<4s<3d<4p<5s<4d<5p<6s<4f<5d<6p<7s<5f<6d$
The modern theoretical explanation of chemical periodicity is based on a consideration of the quantum mechanical theory of atomic structure, the principle that natural processes occur in a way that minimizes energy, the Pauli Exclusion Principle, and the principle of maximum multiplicity (Hund's Rule). These four principles might also represent a possible reason for chemical reaction.

REVIEW QUESTIONS

1 Briefly outline the three fundamental concepts of the modern atomic theory.

2 For the four quantum numbers studied in this chapter, give the following.
   a. The symbol for each
   b. The values for each
   c. The meaning of each (To what does it relate?)

3 Explain, in your own words, what is meant by the following.
   a. Hund's Rule
   b. Pauli Exclusion Principle

4 **a.** Show the relationship between the n and l quantum numbers by giving all the values of l when n equals 3.
   b. Similarly, give all the values of m when l equals 3.
   c. What are all the values of m when n equals 3?

5 Give the symbol of the orbital type designated by an l value of the following.
   a. 0
   b. 2
   c. 5

6 What n value allows for each of the following?
   a. Only the s orbital type
   b. Only the s, p, and d orbital types
   c. The s, p, d, and f orbital types

7 Describe the following orbitals in terms of their corresponding n and l values.
   a. $3s$
   b. $4d$
   c. $5p$
   d. $6f$
   e. $5g$

8 Referring to the periodic table, write complete electron configurations for the following.
   a. beryllium (Be)
   b. chlorine (Cl)
   c. titanium (Ti)
   d. sodium ion (Na^{+1})
   e. oxide ion (O^{-2})

9 Write the electron configuration for oxygen ($Z = 8$). Show pictorially that this follows the principle of maximum multiplicity.

10 Species that have the same electron configuration are called *isoelectronic*. Which of the following groupings constitute isoelectronic species?
   a. F, Cl, Br
   b. Li, Be, B
   c. N, S, Br
   d. Cl^{-1}, Ar, K^{+1}
   e. Se^{-2}, Br^{-1}, Kr

11 From the following electron configurations, pick the elements that belong to the same chemical family.

a. $1s^22s^22p^63s^23p^6$
b. $1s^22s^22p^4$
c. $1s^22s^1$
d. $1s^22s^22p^63s^23p^4$

12 **a.** Write the electron configuration for the elements with atomic numbers 65 and 83.
b. For each of those elements, indicate the number of energy levels that are completely filled.

13 Name the elements that correspond to each of the following electron configurations.

a. $1s^2$
b. $1s^22s^1$
c. $1s^22s^22p^1$
d. $1s^22s^22p^3$
e. $1s^22s^22p^63s^23p^64s^1$

14 Write pictorially and in shorthand notation the electron configuration for the following elements in the ground state.

a. carbon
b. boron
c. nitrogen

SUGGESTED READINGS

Anderson, Roland G. "Pyramid of Electron Configuration." *Chemistry*, June 1970, p. 27.

Lambert, Frank L. "Atomic Orbitals from Wave Patterns." *Chemistry*, February 1968; March, 1968.

Luder, W. F. "Atomic Structure Without Quantum Theory." *Chemistry*, June 1975, p. 6.

Lynch, P. F. *Orbitals and Chemical Bonding*. Boston, Mass.: Houghton Mifflin Co., 1969.

Patchen, Theodore F. "An Orbital Notation Memory Device." *Chemistry*, September 1974, p. 14.

Sisler, Harry H. *Electronic Structure, Properties, and the Periodic Law* (2nd ed.). New York: Van Nostrand Co., 1973.

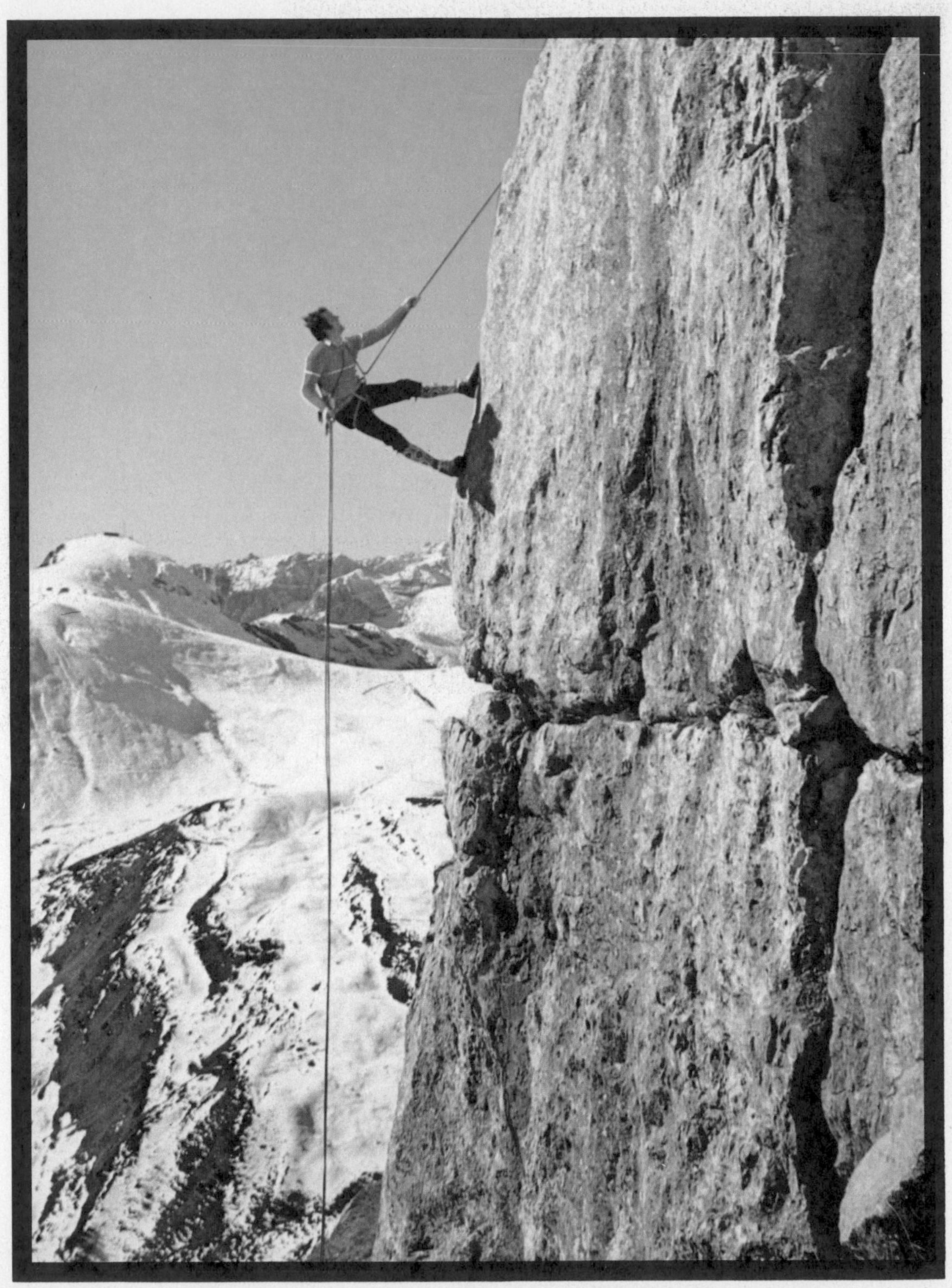

Mountain climbers are bonded together by a safety line.

CHAPTER TEN

Chemical Bonding

A major concern in chemistry is how atoms group together to form molecules and how those molecules react to form different molecules. In preceding chapters, we have seen, that atoms combine in definite fixed ratios to form molecules. Therefore, it is possible to describe a certain substance by its molecular formula. The molecular formulas reflect the valences, or combining power, of atoms. In Chapter 9, you learned that electrons surround the nucleus in an atom. And you learned that the electrons could be described in terms of the orbital model. In Chapter 10, we will relate the types of chemical bonds and the valence of atoms to the electron orbitals of the atoms. In Chapter 6, we discussed the properties of liquids and solids. You learned that there are forces between the molecules that hold them together in those states. But are those forces of attraction influenced by the nature of the chemical bonds between the atoms and the molecules? And if so, what influence do they have? This chapter will help you answer those questions.

IONIC AND MOLECULAR COMPOUNDS

10–1 · There is a difference between ionic and covalent bonds · Solids can be divided into two major groups—ionic solids and molecular solids. Ionic solids are formed by a chemical bond called an **electrovalent,** or **ionic, bond.** Molecular solids are formed by a chemical bond called a **covalent bond.** But how does an ionic bond differ from a covalent bond? In an ionic bond, electrons from the outer orbitals of one atom are transferred to the outer orbitals of a second atom. In the formation of a covalent bond, electrons are shared between the outer orbitals of the atoms that form the bond.

Ionic and covalent bonds represent the extremes in types of bonds for compounds. Not all ionic compounds are purely ionic. That is, electrons are not completely transferred from one atom to another. Nor are all covalent bonds purely covalent. Electrons are not equally shared between the atoms in the bond. In fact, most chemical bonds between different atoms are best described as being *partially ionic* and *partially covalent*. In other words, there is some, but not a complete, transfer of electrons. Therefore, there is also some, but not a complete, sharing of electrons. The differences between the two bond types will become clearer as we begin to study each type of bond in detail.

10–2 · What are ionic compounds? · A very familiar ionic solid is sodium chloride (common table salt). The reaction between sodium metal and chlorine gas to form sodium chloride can be written as follows.

$$2Na(s) + Cl_2(g) \longrightarrow 2NaCl(s)$$

A crystal of sodium chloride contains no molecules of NaCl.

In Chapter 6, we discussed the structure of *ionic solids*. Those solids are composed of negatively charged ions that are called *anions*, and positively charged ions that are called *cations*. An atom becomes an ion by either gaining or losing electrons.

In a crystal of sodium chloride, sodium cations with a +1 charge and chloride anions with a −1 charge are present in alternating layers. That arrangement produces an ionic crystal lattice (Figure 10–1).

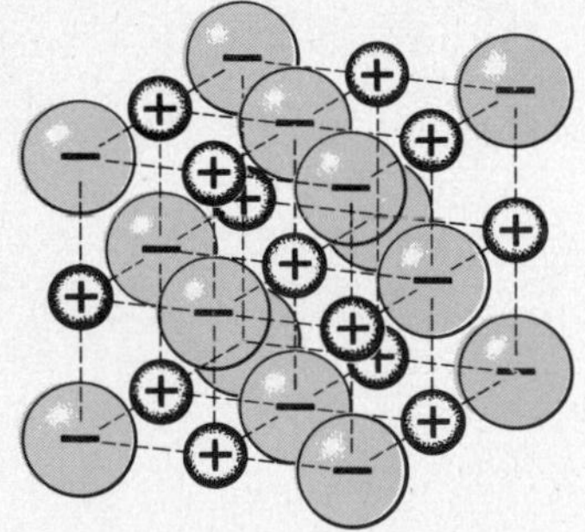

FIGURE 10–1 · *This illustration shows an orderly arrangement of cations and anions in an ionic solid crystal lattice.*

10–3 · The formation of ionic bonds · What holds the anions and cations together in a crystal lattice? The answer is the electrical attraction between the positive and negative charges. The electrical attraction forms a chemical bond between the ions as a result of the electrical attraction between opposite charges. Such chemical bonds are known as electrovalent, or ionic, bonds.

For neutral sodium atoms, Na^0, to form positive sodium ions, Na^+, each sodium atom must *lose* one electron. We can represent the "lost" electron as e^{-1}, since the charge on the electron is −1.

$$Na^0 = Na^{+1} + 1e^{-1}$$

Note that in $Na^0 = Na^{+1} + 1e^{-1}$, the charge on each side of the equation is the same. (See Figure 10–2.)

For neutral chlorine atoms, Cl^0, to form negative chloride ions, Cl^{-1}, each chlorine atom must *gain* one electron.

$$Cl^0 + 1e^{-1} \longrightarrow Cl^{-1}$$

It is logical to assume that in the reaction forming ionic sodium chloride, $Na^{+1}Cl^{-1}$, there is a transfer of electrons. One electron is transferred from the neutral sodium atom to the neutral chlorine atom. Thus, the transfer of electrons from metal atoms to nonmetal atoms during a chemical reaction results in the formation of an ionic bond.

FIGURE 10–2 · *Sodium atoms transfer an electron each to chlorine atoms to form* Na^{+1} *and* Cl^{-1}.

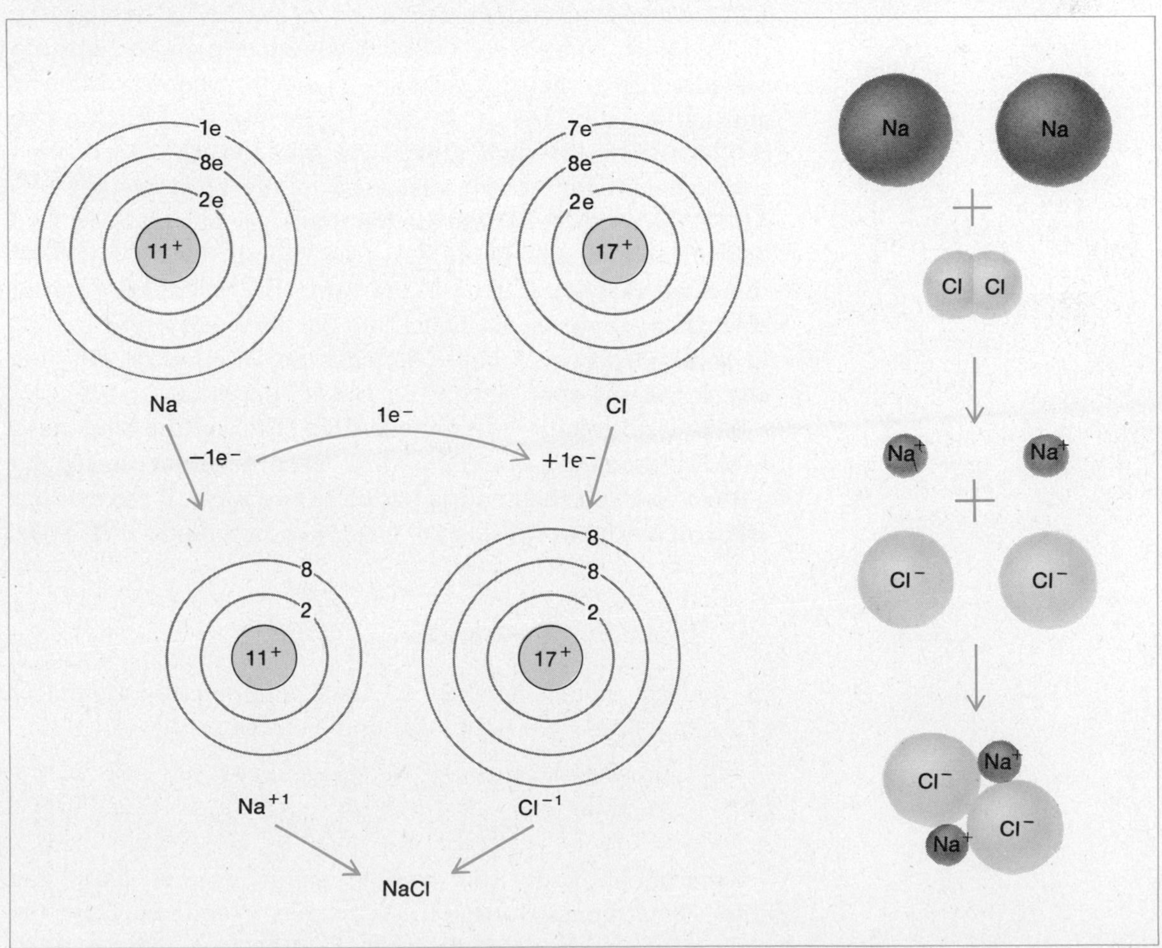

10–4 · Relation of Na^{+1} to the electron orbitals of Na^0 · In the formation of $Na^{+1}Cl^{-1}$, why does sodium form Na^{+1}? That is, what causes a sodium atom to lose an electron to a chlorine atom? And why should sodium (Na^0) lose only one electron (Na^{+1}), not two (Na^{+2}), or three (Na^{+3})? We can answer those questions now that we understand something about the orbitals of an atom. Figure 10–3 indicates the large energy differences between the 1*s* and 2*s* orbitals. There are energy differences between the 2*p* and 3*s*, the 3*p* and 4*s*, the 4*p* and 5*s*, etc. Those energy differences become progressively smaller. The orbitals that are bunched between the energy gaps are commonly called **electron shells.** The first shell has only the 1*s* orbital. The second shell has the 2*s* and 2*p* orbitals. The third shell has the 3*s* and 3*p* orbitals. And the fourth shell consists of the 4*s*, 3*d*, and 4*p* orbitals.

Some electron configurations have all the orbitals in the shells either completely filled or completely empty with no partially filled shells. That kind of electron configuration is unusually stable. Let us consider atoms that have such stable configurations. In such atoms, we find that the filled shell electron configurations correspond to the elements He, Ne, Ar, Kr, Xe, and Rn. These are the noble gas elements. And as you've learned, the noble gases are noted for their lack of chemical reactivity, which indicates the stability of their electron configurations. Therefore, the ability of atoms to lose, or gain, electrons probably depends on whether or not their electron shells are filled.

Now let's consider the sodium atom. The sodium atom has a $1s^22s^22p^63s^1$ electron configuration. A sodium atom can achieve a filled electron shell configuration in two ways. It can lose one electron, going to a $1s^22s^22p^6$ electron configuration (like Ne).

$$Na^0 \longrightarrow Na^{+1} + e^{-1}$$
$$1s^22s^22p^63s^1 \qquad 1s^22s^22p^6$$

Or sodium could achieve 2 filled shell configuration of $1s^22s^22p^63s^23p^6$ (like Ar) by gaining 7 electrons.

$$Na^0 + 7e^{-1} \longrightarrow Na^{-7}$$
$$1s^22s^22p^63s^1 \qquad 1s^22s^22p^63s^23p^6$$

Experiments show that sodium atoms, as well as all the alkali metal atoms, form +1 cations, not −7 anions. Thus, the sodium atom loses the single 3*s* electron to achieve a filled

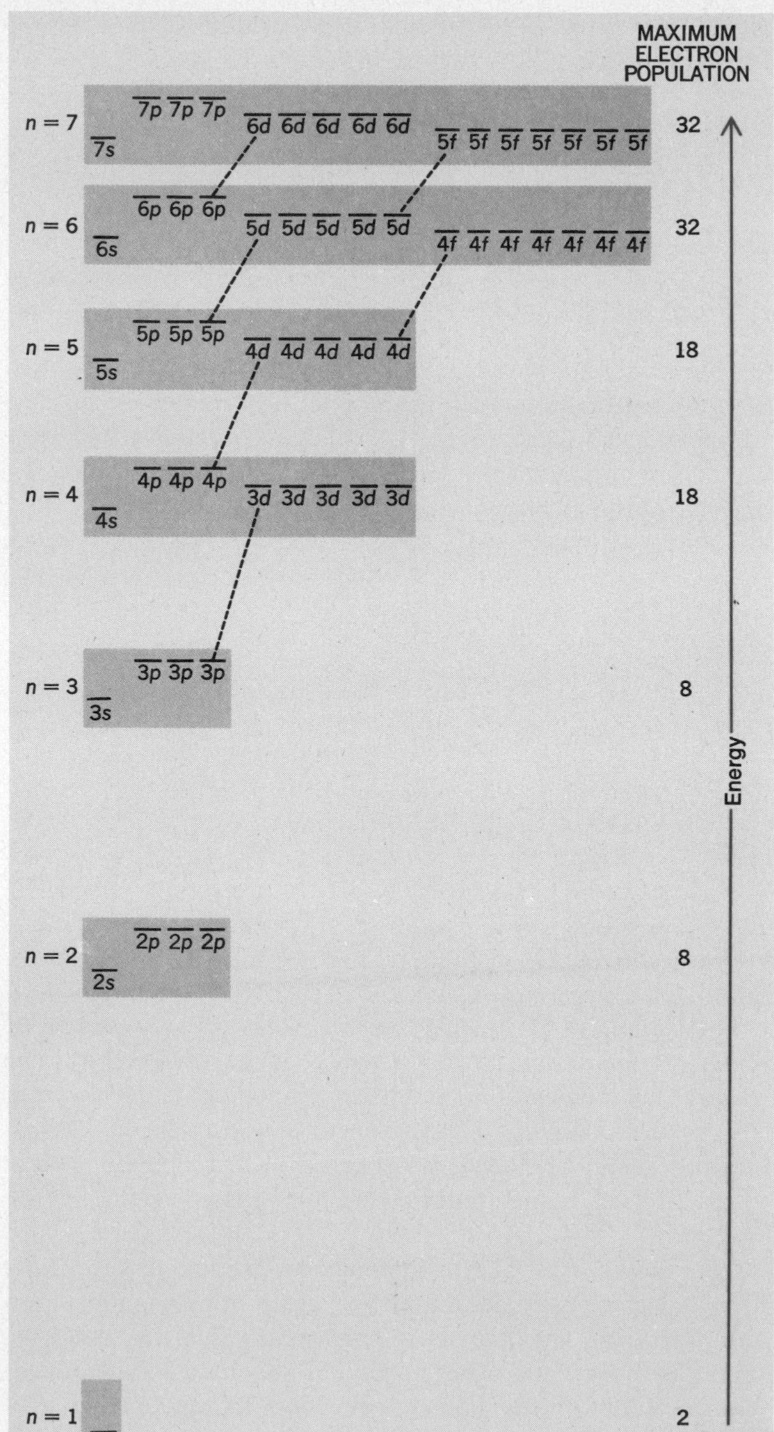

FIGURE 10–3 · *The energy levels of orbits are shown in this chart.*

electron shell configuration. Our model would predict similar behavior for the other alkali metal atoms (Figure 10–4). We can summarize that behavior in the following way.

	Atom		Ion
Li	$1s^2 2s^1$	Li^{+1}	$1s^2$ (like He atom)
Na	$1s^2 2s^2 2p^6 3s^1$	Na^{+1}	$1s^2 2s^2 2p^6$ (like Ne atom)
K	$1s^2 2s^2 2p^6 3s^2 3p^6 4s^1$	K^{+1}	$1s^2 2s^2 2p^6 3s^2 3p^6$ (like Ar atom)
Rb	(Ar) $4s^2 3d^{10} 4p^6 5s^1$	Rb^{+1}	(Ar) $4s^2 3d^{10} 4p^6$ (like Kr atom)
Cs	(Kr) $5s^2 4d^{10} 5p^6 6s^1$	Cs^{+1}	(Kr) $5s^2 4d^{10} 5p^6$ (like Xe atom)

The model in which a filled electron shell is the favored electron configuration is a useful one. That model can be used to explain two things. First, it explains the relative inactivity of the noble gases. And second, it explains the chemical reactivity of the alkali metals to form +1 cations.

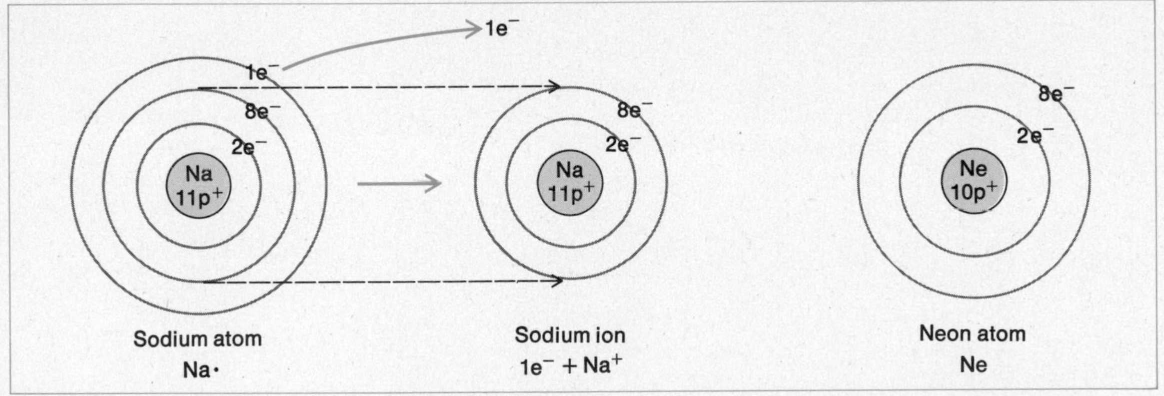

FIGURE 10–4 · *The sodium ion, Na^{+1}, and the neon atom have the same electronic configurations. The ten electrons in Na^{+1} are attracted by a +11 nucleus, so that Na^{+1} is smaller than Ne, where ten electrons are attracted to a +10 nuclear charge.*

The chemistry of the alkali metals is basically a function of the single *s* electron found in the highest energy level of their atoms. That *s* electron is commonly called a **valence electron.** The valence electrons of an element are those in the highest electron energy shell that is occupied in that element. Therefore, that shell is sometimes called the **valence shell.**

10–5 · Relation of Cl^{-1} to the electron orbitals of Cl^0 · Now let us consider the electron change when chlorine atoms form chloride ions. The halogen elements are fluorine, chlorine, bromine, iodine, and astatine. One of the characteristic chemical activities of the halogen elements is the formation of negative ions with a −1 charge. To form such anions, the neutral atom must gain an electron.

The electron configuration of the chlorine atom is $1s^2 2s^2 2p^6 3s^2 3p^5$. To form the chloride ion, Cl^{-1}, the neutral chlorine atom must gain an electron (Figure 10–5). The electron that it gains is the sixth $3p$ electron, which is required for a filled electron shell configuration. Our model would predict a similar behavior for all the halogen atoms.

	Atom		*Ion*
F	$1s^2 2s^2 2p^5$	F^{-1}	$1s^2 2s^2 2p^6$ (like Ne atom)
Cl	$1s^2 2s^2 2p^6 3s^2 3p^5$	Cl^{-1}	$1s^2 2s^2 2p^6 3s^2 3p^6$ (like Ar atom)
Br	(Ar) $4s^2 3d^{10} 4p^5$	Br^{-1}	(Ar) $4s^2 3d^{10} 4p^6$ (like Kr atom)
I	(Kr) $5s^2 4d^{10} 5p^5$	I^{-1}	(Kr) $5s^2 4d^{10} 5p^6$ (like Xe atom)

10–6 · Ionization energies · Filled electron shells are very stable. We can theorize that this is one of the reasons that ions are formed. To test that theory further, we can compare the ionization energies of different elements. The **ionization energy** is the amount of energy necessary to remove the electron in the highest orbital from a gaseous atom or ion in its ground state. Removal of an electron from an atom causes that atom to become a positive ion. Table 10–1 lists some ionization energies.

TABLE 10–1 · Ionization Energies of Some Elements (kcal/mol)

ATOMIC NUMBER	ELEMENT	$(IE)_1$	$(IE)_2$	$(IE)_3$	$(IE)_4$
1	H	313	—	—	—
2	He	567	1254	—	—
3	Li	124	1744	2823	—
4	Be	215	420	3548	5020
5	B	191	580	874	5980
6	C	260	562	1104	1487
7	N	335	683	1094	1786
8	O	314	811	1267	1785
9	F	402	807	1445	2012
10	Ne	497	947	1500	2241
11	Na	118	1091	1652	2280
12	Mg	176	347	1848	2521
13	Al	138	434	656	2766
14	Si	188	377	772	1040
15	P	254	453	695	1184
16	S	239	540	808	1090
17	Cl	300	549	920	1230
18	Ar	363	637	943	1379
19	K	100	734	1100	1405
20	Ca	141	274	1180	1550
35	Br	273	498	828	1154
36	Kr	323	566	851	—

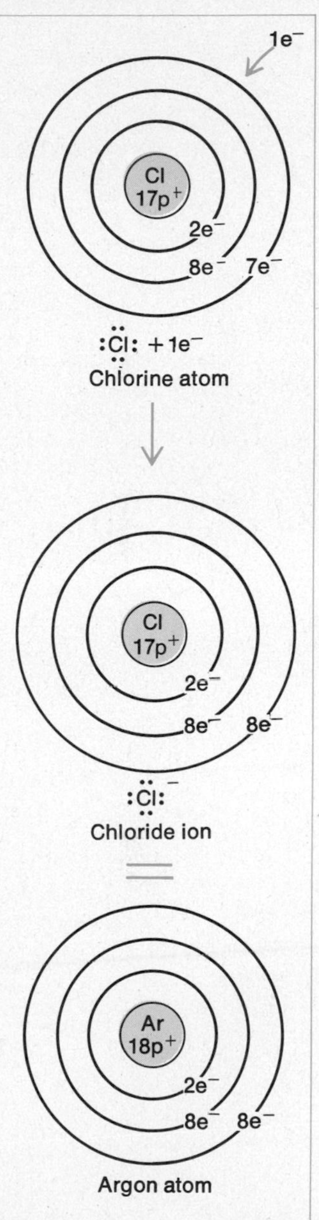

FIGURE 10–5 · *The chloride ion, Cl^{-1}, and the neutral argon atom have the same electronic configurations. Why, do you think, is the Cl^- ion slightly larger than the argon atom?*

The first-ionization energy, $(IE)_1$, is the energy for the following reaction.

gaseous atom + energy ⟶ gaseous unipositive ion + electron

or $$M^0(g) + (IE)_1 \longrightarrow M^{+1}(g) + e^{-1}(g)$$

where $M^0(g)$ stands for an atom of any element in the gaseous state. The second-ionization energy, $(IE)_2$, is the energy required for the following process.

gaseous unipositive ion + energy ⟶ gaseous dipositive ion + electron

or $$M^{+1}(g) + (IE)_2 \longrightarrow M^{+2}(g) + e^{-1}(g)$$

The third-, fourth-, and higher ionization energies can be similarly defined.

10–7 · The ionization energies of lithium · Let us consider the ionization energies of lithium (Z = 3). In Table 10–1, we see that 124 kcal/m are required for the ionization of the first electron in the following reaction.

$$Li^0(g) + (IE)_1 \longrightarrow Li^{+1}(g) + e^{-1}(g)$$
$$1s^2 2s^1 \longrightarrow 1s^2 \text{ (like He atom)}$$

However, ionization of the next electron in the reaction

$$Li^{+1}(g) + (IE)_2 \longrightarrow Li^{+2}(g) + e^{-1}(g)$$
$$1s^2 \longrightarrow 1s^1$$

requires 1744 kcal/m, almost fifteen times as much energy!

TABLE 10–2 · Required Amounts of Energy, kcal/mol

ELEMENT	1st e^-	2nd e^-	3rd e^-	4th e^-	5th e^-
H	314				
He	567	1254			
Li	124	1744	2823		
Be	215	420	3548	5020	
B	191	580	874	5980	7843
C	260	562	1104	1487	9034
Ne	497	947	1500	2241	2913
Na	118	1091	1652	2280	3192

These experimental results are consistent with our theory that filled electron shells are particularly stable. The first ionization resulted in an ion with a filled electron shell. And as such, the ionization requires relatively little energy. But the second ionization requires going from a filled electron shell configuration to an unfilled one. A great deal of energy is required to bring about such a change. Therefore, it is obvious that the change is not a favored one.

10–8 · Why does magnesium form a +2 ion? · Magnesium ($Z = 12$) has a first-ionization energy of 176 kcal/m, a second-ionization energy of 347 kcal/m, and a third-ionization energy of 1848 kcal/m. Therefore, it is not too difficult to remove two electrons from atomic magnesium. But it is very difficult to remove a third electron. According to the electron orbital pattern, magnesium atoms should have a configuration of $1s^22s^22p^63s^2$. The ionization reactions would be the following.

FIRST IONIZATION

$$Mg^0(g) + (IE)_1 \longrightarrow Mg^{+1}(g) + e^{-1}(g)$$
$$1s^22s^22p^63s^2 \longrightarrow 1s^22s^22p^63s^1$$

SECOND IONIZATION

$$Mg^{+1}(g) + (IE)_2 \longrightarrow Mg^{+2}(g) + e^{-1}(g)$$
$$1s^22s^22p^63s^1 \longrightarrow 1s^22s^22p^6 \text{ (like Ne atom)}$$

THIRD IONIZATION

$$Mg^{+2}(g) + (IE)_3 \longrightarrow Mg^{+3}(g) + e^{-1}(g)$$
$$1s^22s^22p^6 \longrightarrow 1s^22s^22p^5$$

Table 10–3 · Ionization Energies of the Alkali Metals

	ELEMENT	ELECTRON CONFIGURATION	IONIZATION REACTION	IONIZATION ENERGY (kcal/mole atoms)	
	H	($1s^1$)	($H_{(g)} \longrightarrow H^+_{(g)} + e^-$)	(313)	
Increasing size of atoms ↓	Li	[He] $2s^1$	$Li_{(g)} \longrightarrow Li^+_{(g)} + e^-$	124	↑ Increasing energy required to detach one electron from outermost shell
	Na	[Ne] $3s^1$	$Na_{(g)} \longrightarrow Na^+_{(g)} + e^-$	118	
	K	[Ar] $4s^1$	$K_{(g)} \longrightarrow K^+_{(g)} + e^-$	100	
	Rb	[Kr] $5s^1$	$Rb_{(g)} \longrightarrow Rb^+_{(g)} + e^-$	96	
	Cs	[Xe] $6s^1$	$Cs_{(g)} \longrightarrow Cs^+_{(g)} + e^-$	90	
	Fr	—	$Fr_{(g)} \longrightarrow Fr^+_{(g)} + e^-$	—	

We see that the loss of the first two electrons results in the formation of an Mg^{+2} ion with filled electron shells. The formation of an Mg^{+3} ion in a third ionization requires going from a filled electron shell configuration to an unfilled one. Such a change requires a tremendous amount of energy, almost two million calories per mole. Thus, it is not a favored change.

Note that the second-ionization energy for magnesium is about twice as high as the first. That is easy to understand. In the first ionization of the neutral atom, one of twelve electrons is removed from around a nucleus with a +12 charge. In the Mg^{+1} ion, the twelve-proton nucleus attracts each of the eleven remaining electrons. It attracts those eleven electrons more than it attracted each of the twelve electrons in the neutral atom. In the formation of the Mg^{+2} ion from the Mg^{+1} ion during the second ionization, there is an increased coulombic attraction. Therefore, additional energy is required for that ionization.

10–9 · Observed trends in ionization energies · In Figure 10–6, the first-ionization energies for the first twenty elements are plotted. As expected, we see that the largest amounts of energy are required to remove an electron from the noble gases He, Ne, and Ar. Note, however, that the ionization energy is less for Ar than for Ne, and less for Ne than for He. In Ar, an electron is removed from a 3*p* orbital, which is higher in energy than a 2*p* orbital. The ionization of Ne removes an electron from the 2*p* orbital. When there is more energy in an electron orbital, less energy is needed for the ionization of an electron from that orbital.

FIGURE 10–6 · *This graph demonstrates the first-ionization energies for the first twenty elements.*

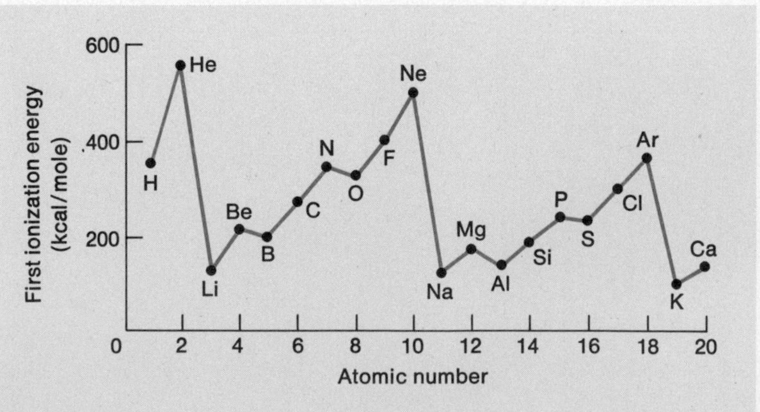

There is another regularity apparent in Figures 10–6 and 10–7. As we go from Li to Ne, we find that the ionization energies generally increase. That can also be observed in going from Na to Ar. Why is that so? Let's consider Li to Ne. In each of those elements, the valence electron is in the second major energy level ($n = 2$). Thus, the electrons in each of those elements have about the same energy. However, the number of protons, and thus the *nuclear charge* of the elements, increases from +3 to +10 as we go from Li to Ne. Similarly, it increases from +11 to +18 in going from Na to Ar. The increasing nuclear charge causes an increase in the coulombic attraction between the electron and the nucleus. Since the electron is pulled more and more by the nucleus as we go from Li to Ne, and Na to Ar, it is reasonable to expect that more energy will be required to remove the electron and form an ion. That trend is seen in Figures 10–6 and 10–7.

FIGURE 10–7 · *This graph demonstrates the first-ionization energies and electron configurations for the elements from hydrogen through magnesium.*

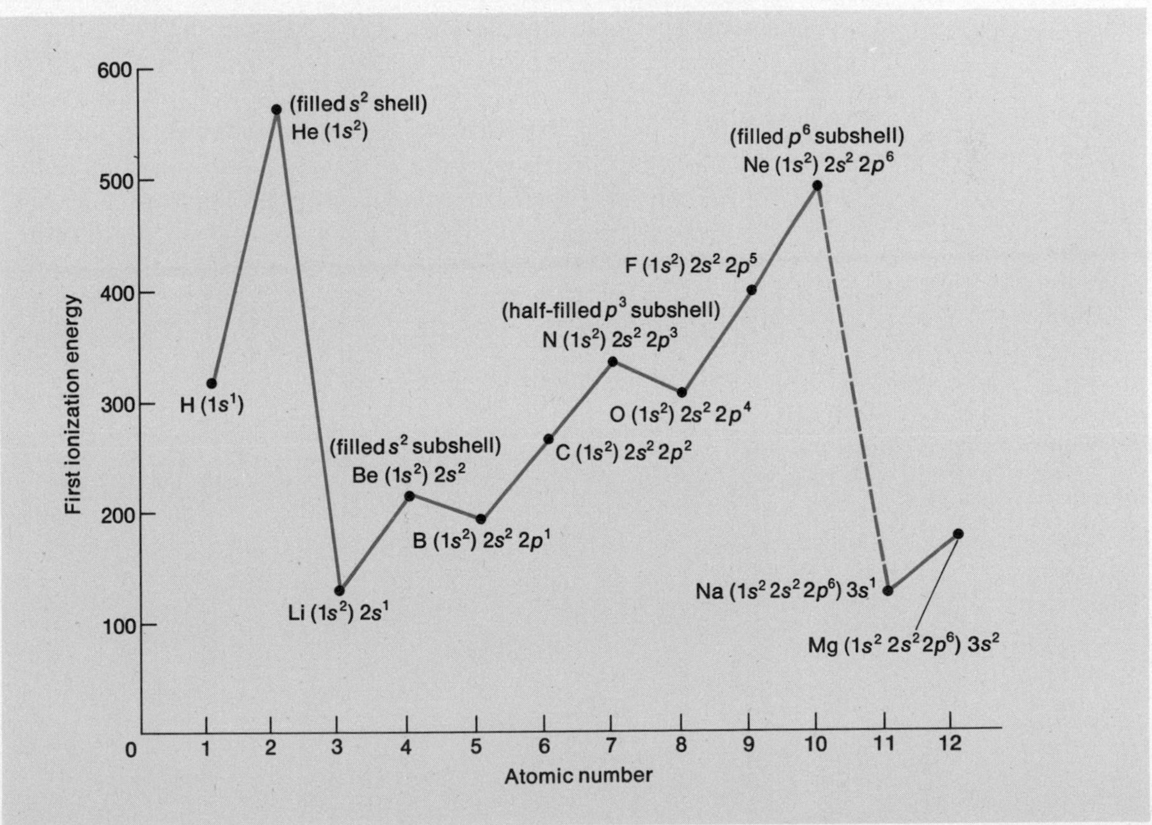

EXERCISE

1. Using Table 10–1, look up the order of ionization energies for the following families of elements.
   a. Li, Na, K
   b. F, Cl, Br, I
   c. Be, Mg, Ca, Sr, Ba
   d. He, Ne, Ar, Kr

   Explain your findings.
2. Can you "predict" the ionization energy for Cesium (Cs)? for Xenon (Xe)?

10–10 · Ionic radii · In a crystal of sodium chloride, each sodium cation is surrounded by six chloride anions. In turn, each chloride anion is surrounded by six sodium cations. In cesium chloride, the cesium cation is surrounded by eight chloride anions. The study of many ionic crystals leads us to the following conclusion. The anions and cations are packed around one another so that they are as close to one another as possible. There are more chloride ions found around cesium ions in CsCl than there are chloride ions around sodium ions in NaCl. That must be related to a larger size of the Cs^{+1} ion.

Soon after the discovery of X rays, two English scientists, William Bragg (1862–1942) and his son Lawrence Bragg (1890–) worked with the measurement of the diffraction of X rays. Their work showed that the measurement of the diffraction of X rays when they passed through crystals could be used to calculate the distance between the ions in the crystal. The X-ray diffraction technique is still a powerful tool of the chemist. It was one of the major factors that led to the discovery of the double helix pattern of DNA, which helps establish our genetic characteristics.

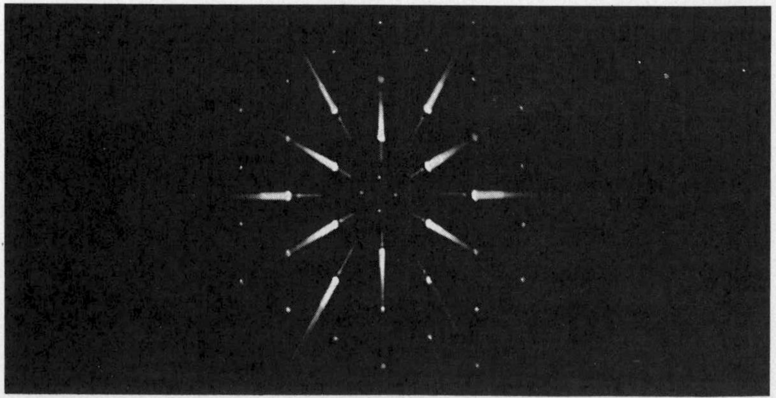

FIGURE 10–8 · *The X-ray diffraction pattern from a single ice crystal is shown here.*

By X-ray diffraction, the distance between sodium and chlorine nuclei in a crystal of sodium chloride is found to be 2.81 A. The problem remains, however, of how much of the 2.81-A distance is taken up by sodium and how much by chlorine. By measuring many compounds of sodium and many compounds of chlorine, it is possible to arrive at values for the radii that are consistent for all the compounds. Table 10–4 lists some of the radii that have been determined for ions.

TABLE 10–4 · Ionic Crystal Radii

ION	RADIUS (A)	ION	RADIUS (A)
Li^{+1}	0.60	Hg^{+2}	1.10
Na^{+1}	0.95	B^{+3}	0.20
K^{+1}	1.33	Al^{+3}	0.50
Rb^{+1}	1.48	Ga^{+3}	0.62
Cs^{+1}	1.69	In^{+3}	0.81
Cu^{+1}	0.96	Tl^{+3}	0.95
Ag^{+1}	1.26	Sc^{+3}	0.81
Au^{+1}	1.37	Y^{+3}	0.93
Be^{+2}	0.31	Ti^{+4}	0.68
Mg^{+2}	0.65	Zr^{+4}	0.80
Ca^{+2}	0.99		
Sr^{+2}	1.13	F^{-1}	1.36
Ba^{+2}	1.35	Cl^{-1}	1.81
Zn^{+2}	0.74	Br^{-1}	1.95
Cd^{+2}	0.97	I^{-1}	2.16

In dealing with wavelengths of radiation, it is convenient to work in angstrom units. One angstrom is 1.00×10^{-8} cm. The angstrom unit (A) has been named in honor of the 19th-century Swedish physicist Ander J. Angström (1814–1874).

Can you observe any trends in those data? The size of the ions increases regularly from Li^{+1} to Cs^{+1}, which is to be expected. The outermost electrons in Li^{+1} ions are in the 1s orbital ($_3Li$ $1s^22s^1$; $_3Li^{+1}$ $1s^2$), whereas those in Cs^{+1} ions are in the 5p orbital. In Chapter 9, we learned that the electrons in orbitals of high *n* values have a greater probability of being found farther from the nucleus.

The trend we just described is observed as one goes vertically down the groups of elements. However, if one goes *horizontally* across the periodic table, another trend is obvious. Figure 10–9 shows the ionic radii of some elements in rows 1, 2, and 3 of the periodic table. Let's look at the elements in row 3. The Na^{+1} ion has eleven protons and 10 electrons. The Mg^{+2} ion has 12 protons, but it also has 10 electrons. Al^{+3} has 10 electrons, as

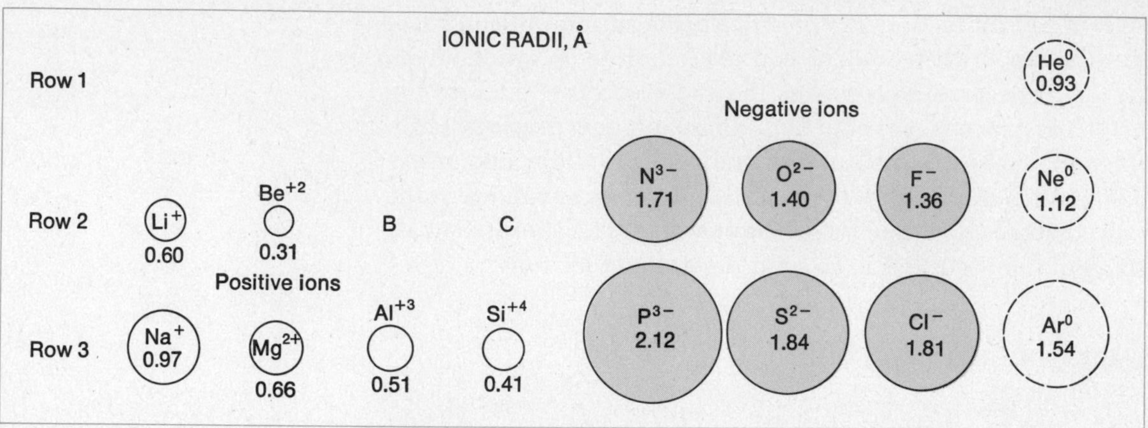

FIGURE 10–9 · *The relative sizes of cations, anions, and noble gas atoms are shown in this illustration.*

does Si^{+4}. The trend we observe is that, even though all the elements in row 3 have the same number of electrons, the size of the ion decreases as we go across the row. The same trend is seen with the elements of rows 1 and 2. That trend is also simple to understand. The ions F^{-1}, Na^{+1}, Mg^{+2}, and Al^{+3} all have the following electron configuration.

$$1s^2 2s^2 2p^6$$

However, the nuclear charge increases from Na^{+1} to Si^{+4}. As we would expect, the electrons are more tightly bound to the nucleus as the number of positive charges increases and, as a result, the radius decreases. In F^{-1}, there is a deficiency of one positive charge (9 protons, 10 electrons). Therefore, the electrons experience the weakest attraction, and the ionic size is the largest.

10–11 · Radius ratios and ionic crystal structure · Using the ionic-radii values in Table 10–4 and assuming spherical shapes for ions, the chemist can calculate how many anions of a certain radius can be packed around a cation of a definite size. This is like calculating how many tennis balls can be packed around a golf ball, with each tennis ball touching the golf ball. Thus, for the Na^{+1} ion of 0.95-A radius, it is possible to calculate that six Cl^{-1} spheres of 1.81-A radius will pack around the Na^{+1} ion symmetrically. That agrees with the structure of NaCl that was determined experimentally.

Using geometry, it is also possible to predict the number of anions that will surround a cation if the value of the ratio between the radii of the two ions is known. The results of these radius-ratio calculations are given in Table 10–5 and are shown in Figure 10–9.

In most cases, the actual packing that was determined by experiment agrees with the predictions. For some crystals, however, there is disagreement. In $Cs^{+1}F^{-1}$, the radius ratio (1.24) predicts eight small F^{-1} ions surrounding each large Cs^{+1} ion. The experimental value, however, is six. In $Li^{+1}I^{-1}$, the radius ratio (0.28) predicts four large I^{-1} ions surrounding each small Li^{+1} ion, whereas six are found experimentally.

It is not surprising to learn that such a simple model, based on the geometric packing of spheres, does not always work. Atoms and ions are not hard spheres. Remember the previous statements about the conflict between definite size and electron probability. In fact, there is evidence that ions change radii slightly depending on what other ions are near. Nevertheless, the simple, sphere-packing model is very useful, because it does predict crystal geometries in many cases.

TABLE 10–5 · Predictions of Packing in Ionic Crystals from Radius Ratio

RADIUS RATIO $\left(\frac{\text{Cation Radius}}{\text{Anion Radius}}\right)$	NUMBER OF NEAREST NEIGHBORS	STRUCTURES
0.16–0.23	3	Triangular
0.23–0.41	4	Tetrahedral
0.41–0.73	6	Octahedral
0.73–1.00	8	Cubic

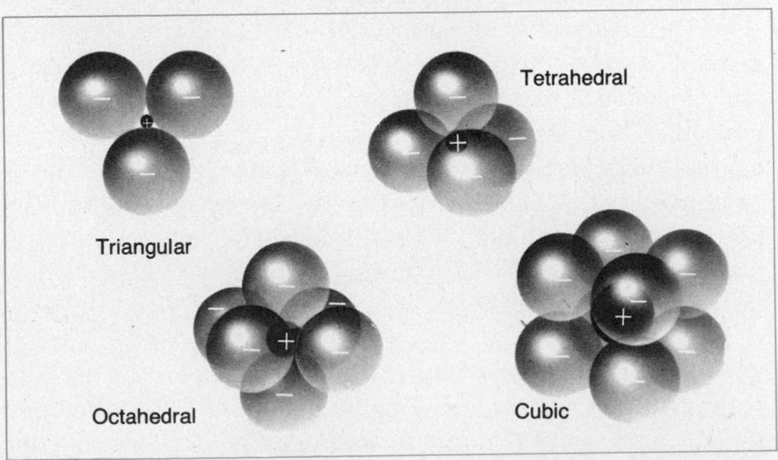

FIGURE 10–10 · *The radius ratio determines the ionic crystal structure.*

REVIEW IT NOW

1. How does the ionic bond differ from the covalent bond?
2. What is a cation? What is an anion?
3. How is an ionic bond formed?
4. Explain the relative inactivity of the inert gases and the chemical reactivity of the alkali metals, using the filled electron shell model.
5. What is a valence electron? How is it related to bonding?
6. How do all the alkali metal atoms become ions?
7. What is a valence shell?
8. Why does chlorine gain an electron to form an ion?
9. How do ionization energies support the theory that filled electron shells are stable?
10. Would you expect Mg to form a Mg^{+3} ion?
11. What trend in ionization energies is observed in a Period of elements?
12. Define the ionic radius of an atom.
13. What trends in ionic radius are evident?
14. Why is the F^{-1} ion larger in radius than the Na^{+1} ion?

THE COVALENT BOND

10–12 · Gilbert Lewis described how covalent bonds form · Sodium ions and chloride ions attract one another to form a crystal of the ionic compound sodium chloride. That is easy to understand, since their opposite ionic charges attract. It is more difficult to understand what holds atoms together in molecular compounds. For example, what is the attractive force that holds the two atoms in the molecular gas hydrogen chloride, HCl, together? There are no ions present in HCl.

In 1916, Gilbert N. Lewis (1875–1946), one of America's greatest chemists, published a famous paper, "The Atom and the Molecule." In that paper, he suggested that nonionic, molecular compounds come from the *sharing* of electrons among atoms. He proposed that a chemical bond in a molecular compound is the result of the sharing of a pair of electrons by two atoms. We call such a bond a covalent bond. A covalent bond forms as a result of the sharing of electrons between atoms during a chemical reaction.

10–13 · Electron pairs and the covalent bond · Let us consider, in detail, a covalent chemical bond. Let's use the bond formed between the atoms of hydrogen and chlorine in the molecular gas hydrogen chloride, HCl. The hydrogen atom has the following electron configuration.

$$_{1}\text{H}\ 1s^1 \text{ or } \frac{\uparrow}{1s}$$

The chlorine atom has the following electron configuration.

$$_{17}\text{Cl}\ 1s^2 2s^2 2p^6 3s^2 3p^5 \text{ or } \frac{\uparrow\downarrow}{1s}\Big|\frac{\uparrow\downarrow}{2s}\Big|\frac{\uparrow\downarrow}{2p}\ \frac{\uparrow\downarrow}{2p}\ \frac{\uparrow\downarrow}{2p}\Big|\frac{\uparrow\downarrow}{3s}\Big|\frac{\uparrow\downarrow}{3p}\ \frac{\uparrow\downarrow}{3p}\ \frac{\uparrow}{3p}$$

We will use symbols, as Lewis did, to represent the situation as follows:

H· and ·C̤̈l:

The H represents the hydrogen nucleus, and the dot (·) represents the one valence electron outside that nucleus. The Cl represents the chlorine nucleus and the filled $1s^2$ and $2s^2 2p^2$ electron shells outside that nucleus. The seven valence electrons in chlorine ($3s^2 3p^5$) are represented by the seven dots. The pairing of six of those electrons in three orbitals (the 3*s* orbital and two of the 3*p* orbitals are filled) is shown by three pairs of dots.

To have a complete valence electron shell, the hydrogen atom requires one more electron. Similarly, one more electron would result in a complete valence electron shell for chlorine. Those requirements are met if hydrogen and chlorine atoms combine to form hydrogen chloride molecules. And in that way, they will mutually share a pair of electrons. We represent that situation symbolically, in terms of a **Lewis electron-dot structure.**

H:C̤̈l:

The (:) represents the **simple covalent bond** formed between hydrogen and chlorine in hydrogen chloride. In HCl, the pair of electrons of the covalent bond is simultaneously a part of the electron configurations of both the hydrogen atom and the chlorine atom. By that sharing of a pair of electrons, the valence electron shells of both hydrogen and chlorine are filled in the covalent molecular compound hydrogen chloride.

The covalent bond structure for HCl represents a satisfactory theoretical interpretation of much experimental data known for this molecular gas. For example, the single covalent bond between these two atoms represents the experimental fact that

Gilbert N. Lewis
(1875–1946, American). Lewis's research on the significance of electron pairs in molecular structure led to modern theories of chemical bonding. He also made valuable contributions to our concepts of acids and bases and to our understanding of fluorescence and phosphorescence. An important part of his career was spent in the study and teaching of thermodynamics—energy relationships in chemical reactions. His textbook on the subject remains a classic in the field.

the valence for each of these elements is 1. Such good correlation between theory and experiment exists for the covalent compounds of a number of nonmetals—H, F, Cl, O, N, S, and P, in particular.

EXERCISE

Write Lewis electron-dot structures for the following compounds.

1. F_2
2. NH_3
3. HF

10–14 · The octet rule · In arriving at a good electron-dot structure, a simple rule can be followed in the majority of cases. This rule is known as the **octet rule.** It states that, for proper electron-dot structures, eight electron dots (four pairs of electrons) must surround each atom. Hydrogen (two dots) and the metallic atoms are notable exceptions. Often the dot structures are simplified by using a dash in place of a dot pair. HCl is represented as H:C̈l: or as H—Cl. Water can be shown as

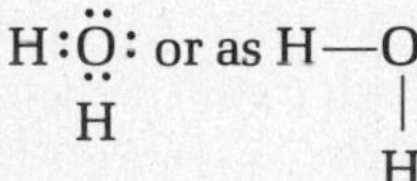

10–15 · Covalent radii · It will come as no surprise to learn that an atom in a predominantly covalent compound has a different radial length than it has in a predominantly ionic compound. Those radii are experimentally determined by measuring the distance between nuclei in gaseous diatomic molecules of identical atoms (e.g., H_2, Cl_2, Na_2). One half the internuclear distance, the covalent bond length, is called the covalent radius of the atom. Figure 10–11 depicts the values of some covalent radii.

Note that the covalent radius for sodium is 1.54 A, compared with the ionic crystal radius of 0.95 A. The covalent radius is based on a sodium atom that has an electron in the 3s orbital. The ionic radius is derived from a sodium atom that has lost the 3s electron and that has the 2p orbitals as the last occupied. As before, the spatial extension of orbitals of different principal quantum numbers predicts the smaller size of the ion.

In the case of chlorine, the ionic radius of 1.81 A is larger than the covalent radius of 0.99 A. We are now dealing with the

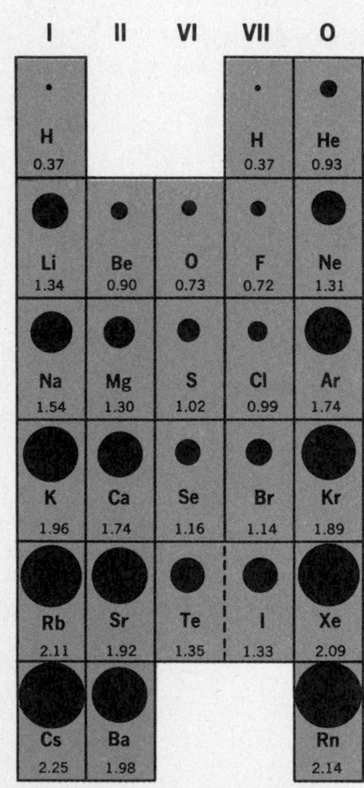

FIGURE 10–11 · *Covalent radii of Group I, II, VI, VII, and 0 elements (Adapted from* Chemical Periodicity *by R. T. Sanderson. New York: Reinhold Publishing Corporation; by permission of the publisher.)*

same electron orbitals for both the ion and the atom in a covalent bond. However, a simple explanation is available to account for the size difference. When the Cl^{-1} ion forms, the incoming extra electron brings about repulsion among the five $3p$ electrons already present. That repulsion leads to an expansion of the $3p$ orbital extension in space and to a large ion size. On the other hand, while the chlorine atom in a covalent bond gains a share in an extra electron, it also loses a share of one of its own $3p$ electrons. In addition, the localization of the bonding-electron pair between the two nuclei of the bonding atoms tends to draw the nuclei closer together. In all, then, the covalent radius of chlorine is smaller when compared with Cl^{-1} ion size. If you would like to look deeper into the nature of covalent bonding, you should explore Excursion 7.

REVIEW IT NOW

1. How do hydrogen and chlorine form a covalent bond?
2. What do the seven dots surrounding the Cl in the Lewis electron-dot structure represent?
3. What does the single dot near the H represent?
4. How is a covalent bond represented in a Lewis electron-dot structure?
5. State the octet rule.
6. Define *covalent radius*.
7. Why is the covalent radius of Na larger than the ionic radius for the Na ion?
8. Why is the covalent radius of Cl smaller than the ionic radius for the Cl ion?

INTERMEDIATE CHEMICAL BONDS

10–16 · Bonds are not always pure covalent bonds or pure ionic bonds · If two atoms are brought close together, and one atom has a much stronger attraction for an electron than the other atom has, we would expect the electron to be transferred. We have seen that sodium atoms do not require much energy to lose the extra valence electron. Chlorine atoms, on the other hand, have a strong attraction for an extra electron. Consequently, sodium and chlorine form ionic bonds. On the other hand, suppose two atoms are brought close together that have exactly equal attraction for electrons. Then it is unlikely that one atom can pull the electrons away from the other one. As a result, the two atoms will share the electrons equally to form a covalent bond.

But those two extremes are not always the case. There are many cases of two atoms in which one atom has more attraction for electrons than does the other atom. But the difference in attraction between the two atoms is not enough to completely transfer the electron. Therefore, electrons are not given up. Due to the inequality in the attraction of the electron when a covalent bond forms, the electron pair will not be equally shared. As a result, the bond formed will not be a pure ionic or pure covalent bond. It is not ionic, because there is not a complete transfer of an electron from one atom to the next. And it is not covalent, because there is not a total equal sharing. Instead, the bonding pair of electrons will be shared, but not equally, between the two atoms. Such a bond is known as a **polar covalent bond.** And it is best understood as being partially ionic and partially covalent in character.

10–17 · Electronegativity and chemical bonds · But how can we tell how much of an attraction there is between one atom and the electrons in another atom? To help us understand that, the American chemist Linus Pauling (1901–   ) calculated and defined an important property of atoms. That calculated property is called the **electronegativity** of an atom. The electronegativity of an atom is a relative measure of the electron-attracting power of an atom when it is in a chemical bond. It has not been possible to measure the electronegativity of atoms

Linus Carl Pauling
(1901–   , American). Pauling was awarded his doctorate from the California Institute of Technology in 1925. He has continued there to investigate the arrangement of atoms in crystals and the interatomic forces that bind these atoms together. This work led to an understanding of the structure of proteins, for which Dr. Pauling was awarded the 1954 Nobel Prize in Chemistry. He has made significant contributions to the quantum mechanical theory of chemical bonding and is particularly renowned for his concept of electronegativity. Dr. Pauling's persistent effort in the movement to ban nuclear weapons and to end the testing of nuclear weapons led to his becoming the first American to win a second Nobel prize—the 1962 Nobel Peace Prize.

directly. But from the measure of various properties of molecules, Pauling derived an equation that allows the calculation of the electronegativity. The results of those calculations are given in Table 10-6. Metals such as sodium and calcium have very low values of electronegativity. However, nonmetals such as oxygen and chlorine have very large values. The electronegativity value of 4.00 for fluorine is the highest for any element. That indicates that fluorine is the strongest electron-attracting atom in compounds. In Table 10-4, the lowest value of electronegativity is assigned to cesium. That means that cesium in a compound has the lowest attraction for electrons.

10–18 · Usefulness for electronegativity · The larger the difference in electronegativity between two atoms, the more likely it is that electrons will be transferred from one to the other to form an ionic bond. From Table 10-6, cesium and fluorine are found to have an electronegativity difference of 4.00 − 0.70, or 3.30. That is the largest difference in electronegativity possible for the elements in Table 10-6. Therefore, we would expect that the compound cesium fluoride, CsF, is the *most* ionic between any pair of atoms in Table 10-6. The difference between sodium and chlorine is 3.00 − 0.90 or 2.10. We know from its properties that sodium chloride is an ionic compound.

TABLE 10–6 · Electronegativities of Some Elements (on the Arbitrary Pauling Scale)

H 2.10						
Li 1.00	**Be** 1.50	**B** 2.00	**C** 2.50	**N** 3.00	**O** 3.50	**F** 4.00
Na 0.90	**Mg** 1.20	**Al** 1.50	**Si** 1.80	**P** 2.10	**S** 2.50	**Cl** 3.00
K 0.80	**Ca** 1.00	**Ga** 1.60	**Ge** 1.70	**As** 2.00	**Se** 2.40	**Br** 2.80
Rb 0.80	**Sr** 1.00					**I** 2.40
Cs 0.70	**Ba** 0.90					

The difference in electronegativity between carbon and hydrogen is only 0.40 units. Thus, the compound methane, CH_4, is a molecular gas exhibiting no ionic characteristics. We can conclude, then, that the small difference in electronegativity is not enough to result in ionic bonding. It has been possible to relate the difference in the electronegativity of compounds to the nature of the chemical bond. That can be done by a comparison of the differences in electronegativity and the properties of the compounds.

If the difference in electronegativity is greater than 2.00, the compound will be strongly ionic. If the difference in electronegativity is less than 1.50, the compound shows mainly covalent character.

Covalent compounds and ionic compounds exhibit quite different characteristics. Therefore, the table of electronegativities is helpful in predicting the properties of compounds.

From the difference in electronegativities between calcium and chlorine (3.00 − 1.00 = 2.00), we expect $CaCl_2$ to be an ionic compound. Ionic compounds have high melting points and high boiling points. They normally dissolve in water, but not in such solvents as benzene or carbon tetrachloride. An electric current easily passes through solutions of ionic compounds. How close is our prediction? The melting point of $CaCl_2$ is 772°C. It dissolves readily in water (about 100 grams in 100 ml of water). The solution conducts an electric current. All those properties agree with the prediction that calcium chloride is an ionic compound.

Carbon and chlorine have an electronegativity difference of only 0.50, so we would expect carbon tetrachloride, CCl_4, to exhibit the properties of a covalent compound. Such compounds have relatively low melting and low boiling points. They are frequently more soluble in benzene or carbon tetrachloride than in water. (Nonaqueous solutions of covalent compounds are not conductors of electricity.) CCl_4 has a low melting point (−22.8°C) and a very low solubility in water (0.08 g per 100 ml water), but it is completely soluble in benzene. And the benzene solution does not conduct an electric current.

10–19 · Intermediate bonds and percent ionic character · Let us now reconsider the compound formed by the union of hydrogen and chlorine, hydrogen chloride. Hydrogen has an electronegativity value of 2.10, and chlorine of 3.00. The difference of 0.90 is much less than the difference (3.00 − 0.90 = 2.10) between sodium and chlorine in an essentially ionic bond. But it is more than the difference (2.10 − 2.10 = 0) between phosphorus and hydrogen in an essentially covalent bond. Therefore, although there is a difference in the relative attraction of electrons between hydrogen and chlorine, the difference is not great enough for chlorine to take the electron completely away from hydrogen. The result might be **intermediate bonding**—a compromise between ionic and covalent bonding. Electrons are still shared between the two atoms, but not equally. The chlorine atom in hydrogen chloride is not a true anion. But it is more negative than the hydrogen because of the unequal sharing. The three cases we have discussed may be represented in this fashion.

EXCURSION SEVEN
What Is a Covalent Bond?

This excursion is a more detailed look into the nature of covalent bonds, in terms of why atoms share electrons.

$$Na^{+1}Cl^{-1} \text{ (Ionic)} \quad \overset{\delta+}{H}—\overset{\delta-}{Cl} \text{ (Intermediate)} \quad H—\underset{}{\overset{\overset{H}{|}}{P}}—H \text{ (Covalent)}$$

The δ^+ indicates that the hydrogen atom in a hydrogen chloride molecule is not a positive ion. But it is less negative (therefore, more positive) than the chlorine atom. The δ^+ is read "partially positive." Similarly, the δ^- indicates that, relatively speaking, the chlorine atom is more negative than the hydrogen atom. The δ^- is read "partially negative."

Unless the atoms in a covalent chemical bond have the same electronegativity value, as in Cl_2 or PH_3, there is an unequal sharing of electrons. And the bond between the atoms cannot be purely covalent. The inequality in the electron sharing increases as the difference in electronegativity increases. Chemists have a special way of indicating the amount of deviation from the equal sharing in a true covalent bond. They refer to that amount of deviation as the percent ionic character of the covalent bond. The percent ionic character of an intermediate bond can be calculated from several types of experimental data such as dipole moments. In Table 10–7, the percent ionic character of the bonds in the hydrogen halides is listed.

TABLE 10–7 · The Percent Ionic Character and Relative Polarity of the Hydrogen Halides

GASEOUS MOLECULE	ELECTRONEGATIVITY DIFFERENCE	PERCENT IONIC CHARACTER	DIPOLE MOMENT
HF	1.9	60	1.91
HCl	0.9	19	1.03
HBr	0.7	11	0.80
HI	0.3	4	0.42

10–20 · The meaning and importance of dipoles · In Chapter 6, it was pointed out that molecules such as water are electrically neutral, but may be dipoles. In other words, the molecules may have an unequal charge distribution within them. Such molecules are said to be polar. The unequal distribution of charge can arise from the unequal sharing of electrons in intermediate bonds. Covalent bonds themselves may be polar. Almost all bonds between unlike atoms are polar. Intermediate bonds are also called polar covalent bonds.

We can measure how unequal the charge is within a molecule. We call the property that measures this charge distribution the **dipole moment** of a molecule. We have explained the origin of the dipole nature of molecules. If our explanation is true, the dipole moments of a related series of diatomic molecules should increase as the difference in electronegativity between the atoms increases. From Table 10–7, we can see that it is indeed the case for the hydrogen halides.

In the case of a polyatomic (many atom) molecule, bond polarity alone may not account qualitatively for the net polarity of the molecule. The orientation in space of the bonds within the molecule must also be considered. CCl_4 has four polar covalent bonds directed toward the apices of a tetrahedron. The polarity of an individual C—Cl bond is offset by the other three bonds. CCl_4 itself is a nonpolar molecule. Finally, the presence and orientation of nonbonded valence electrons will have an effect on the net polar ty of a molecule. For example, though each P—H bond in PH_3 is nonpolar, the presence of one pair of nonbonded valence electrons on the phosphorus atom leads to a small dipole moment for the molecule as a whole (Figure 10–12).

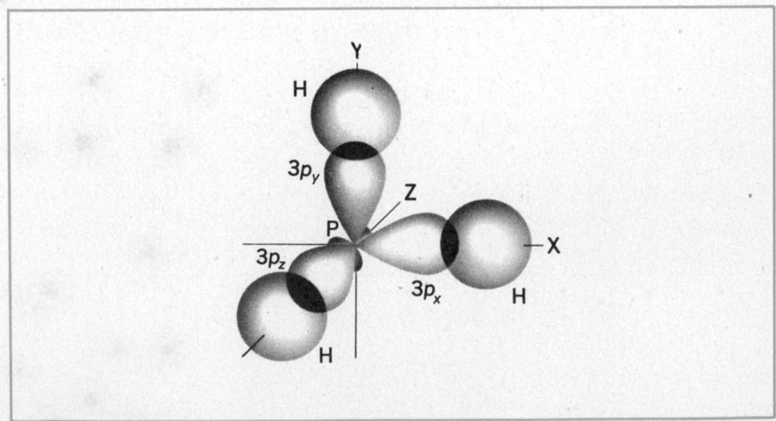

FIGURE 10–12 · *The orbital overlap and the shape of phosphine are shown here.*

You may be wondering why you should be bothered with details such as most chemical compounds having bonds that are neither completely covalent nor completely ionic. The reason is that it is often these "minor and abstract" details that make our physical universe what it is. If chemical bonds were only completely ionic or completely covalent, molecules would not form dipoles. Without this polarity, many compounds could not exist in the liquid and solid states, since it is the attraction between the dipoles that holds the molecules together in the condensed states.

REVIEW IT NOW

1 Define *electronegativity*.
2 Which element has the *greatest* electronegativity?
3 Which element has the *least* electronegativity?
4 How do we use electronegativity values and the electronegativity table?
5 What are some properties of ionic and covalent compounds?
6 Would a compound with a difference in the electronegativities of its atom of 2.50 be more ionic or more covalent?
7 What is a dipole?
8 What is a dipole moment?
9 Why is the compound CCl_4 nonpolar, whereas the compound PH_3 is polar?

SUMMARY

Electrovalent, or ionic, bonds form when a metallic atom loses an electron to a nonmetallic atom. Oppositely charged ions form, and they are held together by electrostatic attraction. The ions usually have filled electron shell configurations. The ionization energies needed for the removal of electrons from gaseous atoms or ions correlate well with the theory that filled electron shell configurations are extremely stable ones. Variations in the ionization energies of the elements in a Period or in a group can be understood in terms of nuclear charge and electron orbital energy variations.

Covalent bonds are formed by the mutual sharing of electron pairs.

The Lewis electron-dot structure is used to represent electrons in the outer orbitals. Atoms sharing electrons are represented with (:), indicating a covalent bond formed between the two atoms.

Both pure ionic and pure covalent bonding are rare. Most chemical bonds have properties lying between those extremes. The concept of electronegativity is useful in understanding intermediate bond types and how they lead to various molecular properties.

REVIEW QUESTIONS

1 For the reaction between lithium metal and fluorine gas,
  a. write the chemical equation.
  b. give the electron configurations of all species.
  c. describe some of the properties of the product, and explain them in terms of the chemical bonds present.

2 **a.** Give electron configurations for each of the following. H^{-1}, Ca^{+2}, N^{-3}, Sc^{+3}, Se^{-2}
  b. What basic difference is there between the electron configurations of the above ions and their corresponding atoms?

3 Represent the electron dot structures for each of the following.
  a. F_2 **c.** PH_3
  b. HCl **d.** CCl_4

4 **a.** Define the *second-ionization energy* for an element.
  b. Using data from Table 10–1, plot the second-ionization energies of the elements Li to Ca as functions of their atomic numbers. Compare with Figures 10–5 and 10–6.

5 **a.** Write the Lewis electron-dot structure for the NH_3 molecule.
  b. Why does this molecule have a high polarity?

6 Draw structural diagrams for the following molecules. Indicate the dipole moment of each polar bond with an arrow pointing toward the *negative* end of the bond. Indicate any nonpolar molecules.
  a. Hydrogen bromide, HBr **d.** Carbon dioxide, CO_2
  b. Water **e.** Ammonia, NH_3
  c. Formaldehyde, H_2CO

7 Using Table 10–6, arrange the following molecules in order of *decreasing* ionic character: PH_3, NH_3, $AlBr_3$, RbCl, CaS, MgO, GaSe, KCl, NaI, ICl.

8 What is each of the following a measure of?
  a. First-ionization energy
  b. Electronegativity
  c. Dipole moment

9 Refer to Table 10–4. Describe and explain the variation in ionic size among these groups.
  a. The alkali metals
  b. The isoelectronic ions F^{-1}, Na^{+1}, Mg^{+2}, and Al^{+3}

10 Write Lewis electron-dot structures for the following compounds.
  a. HI **d.** H_2Se
  b. H_2Se **e.** BrCl
  c. OCl(OH) **f.** $OP(OH)_3$

11 **a.** Using Table 10–1, explain why aluminum forms a +3 ion.
  b. Explain the increases from $(IE)_1$ to $(IE)_2$ to $(IE)_3$ to $(IE)_4$ for aluminum.

12 The covalent radius of chlorine is 0.99 A. The ionic radius of the chloride ion is 1.81 A. Account qualitatively for these values.

SUGGESTED READINGS

Garfield, Eugene, et al. "Fixed Valence and Molecular Formula Verification." *Chemistry*, October 1970, p. 13.

House, J. E., Jr. "Ionic Bonding in Solids." *Chemistry*, February 1970, p. 18.

———. "Weak Intermolecular Interactions." *Chemistry*, April 1972, p. 13.

Jensen, William B. "A Chemist's Annotated Mother Goose of Modern Bonding Theory." *Chemistry*, June 1972, p. 13.

Lynch, P. F. *Orbitals and Chemical Bonding*. Boston: Houghton Mifflin Co., 1969.

Ryschkewitsch, George. *Chemical Bonding and the Geometry of Molecules*. New York: D. Van Nostrand Co., 1963.

Sanderson, R. T. "Ionization Energy and Atomic Structure." *Chemistry*, May 1973, p. 12.

———. "What Is Bond Polarity and What Difference Does It Make?" *Chemistry*, September 1973, p. 12.

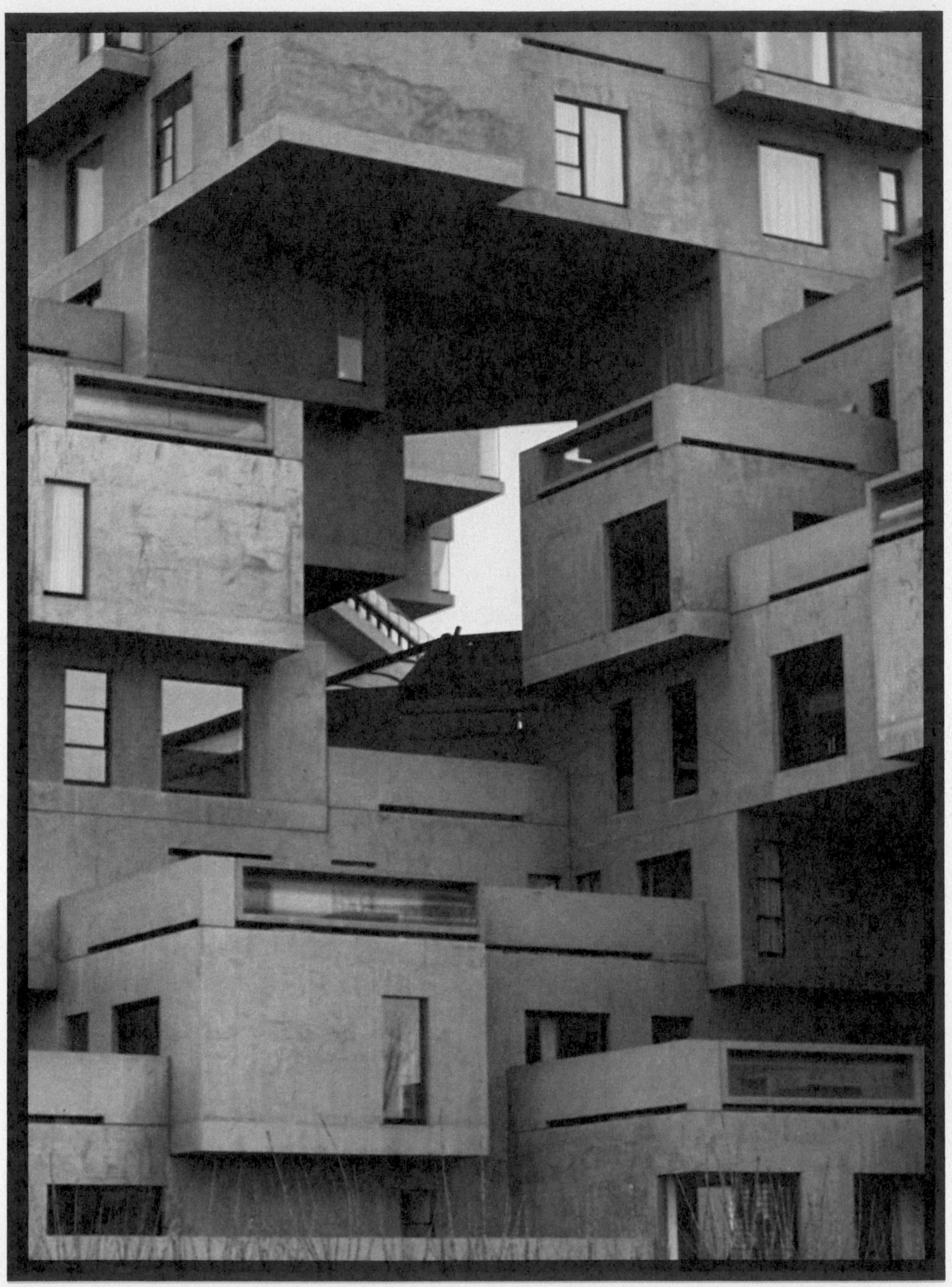

Like atoms in a molecule, these apartments are one modular unit.

CHAPTER ELEVEN

Molecular Structure

In Chapter 10, we learned that when ionic compounds form solids, the anions pack around the cations. Thus, there are as many ions of one charge as possible very close to ions of the opposite charge. For example, six chloride anions are packed around each sodium cation in NaCl. There are also six sodium cations around each chloride anion in NaCl. In other ionic solids, there may be as many as eight anions grouped around each cation, or there may be as few as four. The number of anions surrounding the cation and the number of cations surrounding the anion differ among ionic compounds. The structure of an ionic compound is determined by the size and the charges of the anion and the cation.

The structure of a covalent molecule differs from that of an ionic compound. In a covalent molecule, electrons are shared in a **covalent bond.** The shared electrons come from the valence orbitals of the bonded atoms. We have already learned that electron orbitals have a definite shape and orientation in space. For example, the *s* orbital is spherical in shape, with an equal probability of finding the electron oriented in any direction. In contrast, there are three *p* orbitals. Each of the *p* orbitals has a definite direction in space, and those directions are at right angles to one another. The shape and direction of the orbitals involved in the covalent bond determine the shape of the covalent molecule. The molecular shape may influence, in turn, the shape and nature of material in the macroscopic world.

ORBITALS AND BONDING

11–1 · Orbital overlap and chemical bonding · Let's consider the simplest stable molecule, H_2. When a diatomic hydrogen molecule forms, the pair of bonding electrons is usually found between the nuclei of the two atoms. The probability of finding the electrons in that region is much greater than that of finding them outside of that region. Remember that we can not speak of the precise location of electrons at any moment in time. But we can calculate the probability that an electron is in a particular position.

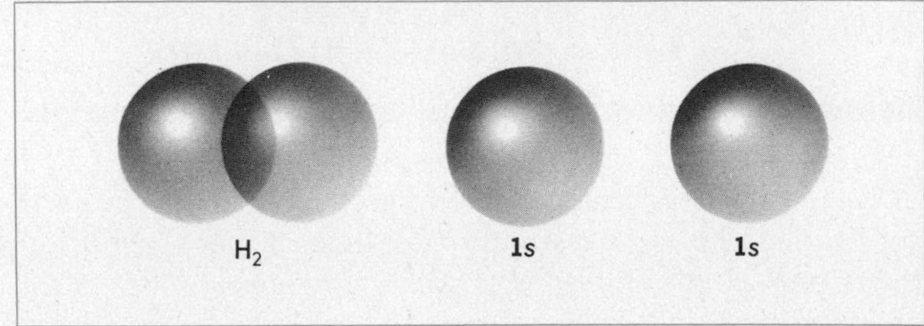

FIGURE 11–1 · *This demonstrates the orbital overlap of 1s orbitals: a model for the hydrogen molecule.*

A hydrogen atom has only an s orbital, which is spherically shaped. Therefore, the electron probability around each hydrogen nucleus in the unbonded hydrogen atom can be described as being spherically symmetrical. When two hydrogen atoms are brought close together, there is an overlapping of their s orbitals. That is illustrated in Figure 11–1. When the two s orbitals overlap, the electron of each hydrogen atom will most often be found in the overlap area. Then the two electrons in the overlap region are shared by the two hydrogen atoms. The sharing of an electron pair in the orbital overlap region forms a chemical bond between the hydrogen atoms (Figure 11–1). This is a covalent bond.

The strength of a covalent bond is directly proportional to the amount of orbital overlap. The closer the two nuclei are to each other, the greater the overlap and the stronger the bond. From Figure 11–1, you can see that the amount of overlap is related to the distance between the two nuclei. If the distance between the two nuclei of hydrogen remains constant, the same degree of overlap will occur regardless of how the atoms are oriented. As we have seen, the orbital overlap makes the atoms attract one another. However, both nuclei have a similar positive charge, and those charges repel each other. As a result, a balance between attraction and repulsion is established. At that point of balance, the two nuclei are close enough together to form the strongest possible bond. But the nuclei are not so close that repulsion between them starts to push the atoms apart.

11–2 · Orbital direction and bond direction · So far we have been discussing only how bonds form between the s orbitals. But how do bonds form between the other orbitals? When an atom uses *p* orbitals to form a bond, not all directions, or orientations, are equally suitable for bond formation. The degree of overlap between the orbitals of the two bonding atoms depends on the direction in which the *p* bonding orbital is pointing.

Figure 11–2 represents a hypothetical case of a covalent bond formed by the overlap of an s and a *p* orbital. Look at the illustration on the left of Figure 11–2. The s orbital of atom a. overlaps the p_y orbital of atom b. along the y-axis. Now examine the illustration on the right in Figure 11–2. The s orbital of atom a. is also overlapping the p_y orbital of atom b. at the same internuclear distance. But it is not overlapping along the preferred *y*-axis orientation of the p_y orbital of atom b. Under those conditions, much less overlap occurs. The larger the degree of overlap, the greater the probability of the bonding pair of electrons being between the two nuclei. When the bonding electrons spend most of their time between the two nuclei, the bond between the nuclei is more stable. Thus, the greater the overlapping of bonding orbitals, the more stable the bond that is formed. As a result, the situation on the left in Figure 11–2 represents a more stable configuration. The bond is formed along the *y*-axis.

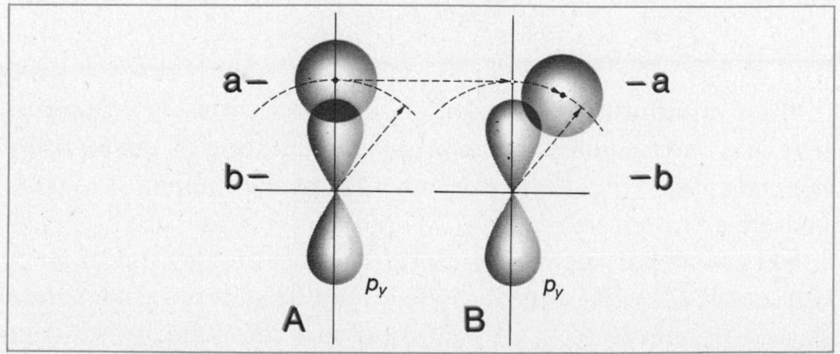

FIGURE 11–2 · *Which model do you think is more stable, A or B?*

REVIEW IT NOW

1 Describe how a covalent bond forms between two hydrogen atoms.
2 How is orbital overlapping related to bond stability?
3 What determines the strength of a covalent bond?
4 When there are 5 *p* electrons, how does one determine which *p* orbital has only 1 electron?

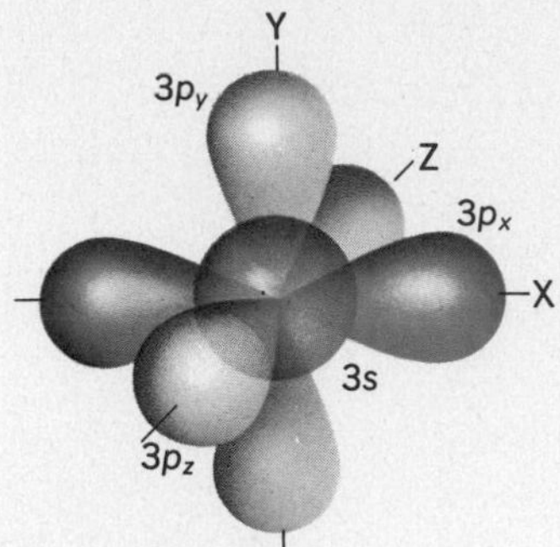

FIGURE 11–3 · *The orbital shapes of sulfur are shown here. (The occupied orbitals are shown in color.)*

11–3 · The structure of H_2S, hydrogen sulfide · Now let's look at the molecular structure of hydrogen sulfide.

The valence electron configuration of sulfur can be shown in the following way.

$$\frac{\uparrow\downarrow}{3s}\Big|\frac{\uparrow\downarrow}{3p_x}\ \frac{\uparrow}{3p_y}\ \frac{\uparrow}{3p_z}\ \text{or}\ \cdot\ddot{\underset{\cdot}{S}}\colon$$

Figure 11–3 shows a second way to demonstrate the valence electron configuration of sulfur, in terms of orbital shapes. The $3p_x$ orbital, which is shown in color, has two electrons and is fully occupied. Several points should be made. First, it is simply arbitrary to label the 3*p* orbital that has two electrons as the $3p_x$ orbital. The important point is that the three 3*p* orbitals are mutually perpendicular regardless of how they are labeled. The two electrons could be in any one of the 3*p* orbitals. We will put them in the $3p_x$ orbital merely for convenience.

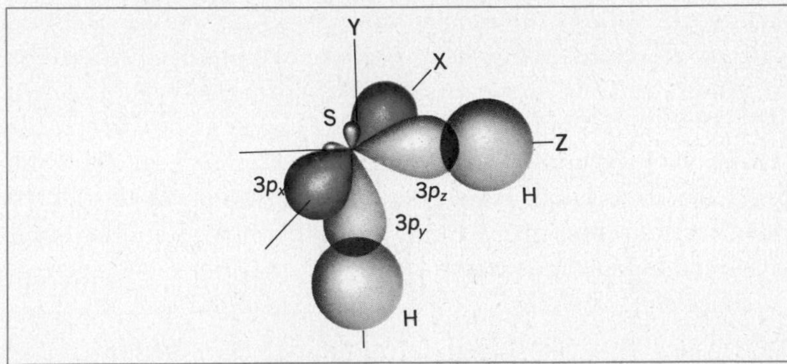

FIGURE 11–4 · *The s-p orbital overlap is shown in this model for hydrogen sulfide.*

Second, since one of the 3*p* orbitals has its maximum electron occupancy, it is unavailable for bonding. If it were to share an additional electron, it would possess three electrons. That is forbidden by the Pauli Exclusion Principle. Thus, in H_2S, the $3p_y$ and $3p_z$ are the only orbitals of sulfur that may be used in bonding. Those orbitals will overlap with the spherical s orbital in the hydrogen atoms (Figure 11–4).

If you have examined Figure 11–4 carefully, you probably noticed a change in the shape of the $3p_y$ and $3p_z$ orbitals after bonding. That change indicates that one bonding electron pair in H_2S is localized between the sulfur nucleus and one of the hydrogen nuclei. The same is true of the other pair of bonding electrons and the other hydrogen atom. The shape of the bonded orbitals is a reflection of the high probability that the electron pair will be found between the sulfur and hydrogen nuclei.

The three 3*p* orbitals are all at right angles to one another. Therefore, the angle between the bonds can be expected to be 90°, or very close to that. That bond angle for the H—S—H bond in H_2S has been experimentally found to be 92°. That is quite close to the expected 90°. Thus, this model allows us to explain the H—S—H bond angle that has been determined experimentally.

11–4 · The structure of PH_3, phosphine · Now that we have discussed a compound formed with *two* hydrogen atoms, let's consider a compound that is formed with *three* hydrogen atoms, such as phosphine, PH_3. Phosphorus has the following electron configuration.

$$_{15}\text{P}\ 1s^2 2s^2 2p^6 3s^2 3p^3$$

or $\frac{\uparrow\downarrow}{1s}\Big|\frac{\uparrow\downarrow}{2s}\Big|\frac{\uparrow\downarrow}{2p_x}\Big|\frac{\uparrow\downarrow}{2p_y}\ \frac{\uparrow\downarrow}{2p_z}\Big|\frac{\uparrow\downarrow}{3s}\Big|\frac{\uparrow}{3p_x}\ \frac{\uparrow}{3p_y}\ \frac{\uparrow}{3p_z}$

or $\cdot\dot{\underset{\cdot}{\text{P}}}\!:$

By concentrating only on the valence electrons, we see that phosphorus may use its three half-filled 3*p* orbitals to form three covalent bonds. The three orbitals are mutually perpendicular. Therefore, we can expect a pyramidal structure for a molecule formed from these three orbitals (Figure 11–5). The experimental bond angles in PH_3 are 93°. That is additional encouraging support for the orbital overlap model for molecular structure.

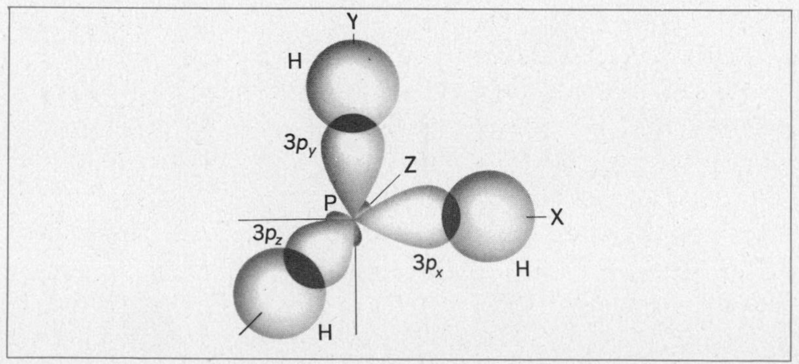

FIGURE 11–5 · *The orbital overlap and shape of phosphine are shown here.*

11–5 · The structure of methane: orbital hybridization · Now let's consider a compound with four hydrogen atoms, methane, CH_4. When we examine methane, we discover a problem that did not arise in the cases of hydrogen sulfide (H_2S) and phosphine (PH_3). From the following electron configuration for carbon, we might conclude that two covalent bonds should form in its compounds.

$$_{6}C\ 1s^22s^22p^2 \qquad \text{or} \qquad \frac{\uparrow\downarrow}{1s}\Big|\frac{\uparrow\downarrow}{2s}\Big|\frac{\uparrow}{2p_x}\ \frac{\uparrow}{2p_y}\ \frac{\quad}{2p_z} \qquad \text{or} \qquad \dot{\underset{\cdot}{C}}\!:$$

Only two of carbon's four valence electrons are available for sharing. But our prediction is a failure. There is no known stable compound of carbon that contains just two covalent bonds.

There are nearly two million molecular carbon compounds known. And the properties of those carbon compounds can be interpreted only if carbon forms *four* covalent bonds. For example, the simplest stable molecular compound of carbon and hydrogen that is known is the gas methane. Methane has the true molecular formula CH_4, not CH_2. Also, all experimental evidence indicates that all carbon-hydrogen bonds in CH_4 are identical. For example, when methane reacts with chlorine,

$$CH_4(g) + Cl_2(g) \longrightarrow CH_3Cl(g) + HCl(g)$$

all the bonds between the four hydrogen atoms and carbon are found to be of the same strength. No one of the four bonds can be more easily substituted for by a chlorine atom than any other. In other words, no one of the four hydrogen atoms in CH_4 is more weakly bonded to carbon than the other three. Further, in molecules such as CH_4 and CH_3Cl, it can be experimentally determined that the bonds are arranged in a *tetrahedral* fashion about the carbon atom (Figure 11–6)

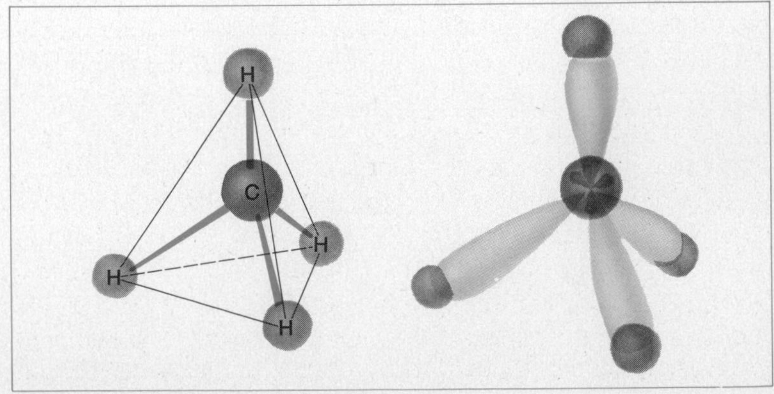

FIGURE 11–6 · *The illustration at left shows the tetrahedral structure of CH_4. The illustration at right shows the orbital overlap of CH_4.*

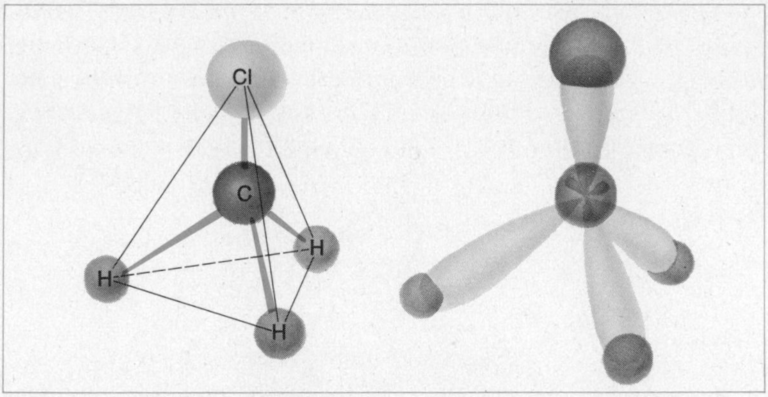

FIGURE 11–7 · *(Left) The tetrahedral structure of CH_3Cl; (right) the orbital overlap of CH_3Cl*

How can we explain such results? In the ground state of carbon, there is a pair of electrons in each of the two *s* orbitals. There is one unpaired electron in the p_x orbital and one in the p_y orbital, but there are no electrons in the p_z orbital. As carbon reacts to form a molecule, its electron structure changes. An electron is moved from the 2*s* orbital to the $2p_z$ orbital. Now each of the orbitals has a single electron, the ground state.

$\uparrow\downarrow$	$\uparrow\downarrow$	$\uparrow$	$\uparrow$	
$1s$	$2s$	$2p_x$	$2p_y$	$2p_z$

The electron structure for carbon in the excited, or bonded, state could be shown as follows.

$\uparrow\downarrow$	$\uparrow$	$\uparrow$	$\uparrow$	$\uparrow$
$1s$	$2s$	$2p_x$	$2p_y$	$2p_z$

If this is correct, carbon in the bonded state would have four half-filled orbitals—one 2*s* orbital and three 2*p* orbitals. Since each of these four orbitals has one electron, they can all be involved in forming bonds. If they do form bonds, one should have the spatial characteristics of an *s* orbital bond (no preferred direction) while three should behave as *p* orbital bonds (directed at 90° from each other). However, experiments show that while carbon does form four bonds, they are all identical, with 109° between them. We explain this by saying that when carbon forms bonds, the orbitals that the electrons occupy no longer have the characteristic shapes of *s* and *p* orbitals. Instead, the bonding orbitals have a shape and direction that make the electron pairs of the bonds all of equal energy and an equal distance from the carbon nucleus and from each other.

The new orbitals are formed from the "mixing" of the original orbitals when the bonds form. To indicate they are formed by mixing normal orbitals, they are called **hybrid orbitals.** The number of hybrid orbitals equals the number of original orbitals (Figure 11–8).

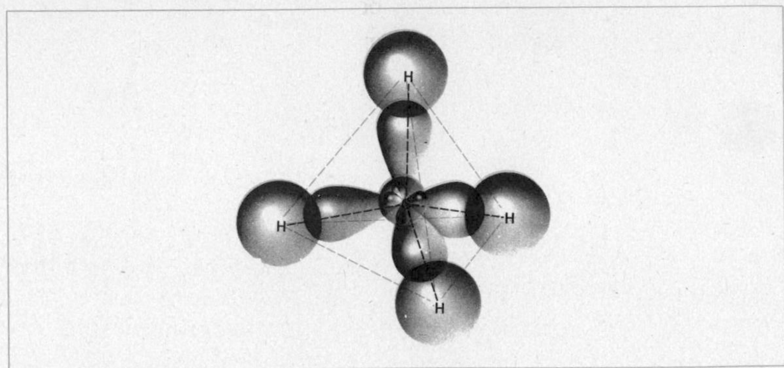

FIGURE 11–8 · *Orbital overlap and orbital hybridization: a model for methane*

11–6 · Hybrid orbitals and molecular shapes · The mixing of the *s* and the three *p* orbitals to form hybrid orbitals gives a tetrahedral set of orbitals around the central atom. Since the hybrid orbitals of carbon in CH_4 are formed by combining one *s* orbital and three *p* orbitals, these orbitals are known as sp^3 hybrids.

In the case of beryllium fluoride, BeF_2, the beryllium atom forms hybrid orbitals from one 2*s* and one 2*p* orbital to form two covalent bonds with fluorine.

$$_4\text{Be}\ \underset{1s}{\underline{\uparrow\downarrow}}\,|\,\underset{2s}{\underline{\uparrow}}\,|\,\underset{2p_x}{\underline{\uparrow}}\ \underset{2p_y}{\underline{\quad}}\ \underset{2p_z}{\underline{\quad}}$$

The hybrid orbitals formed by mixing one *s* and one *p* orbital are known as *sp* orbitals and point in opposite directions. That gives BeF_2 a straight, or linear, structure. The two fluorine atoms are on opposite sides of the beryllium atom in a straight line (Figure 11–9).

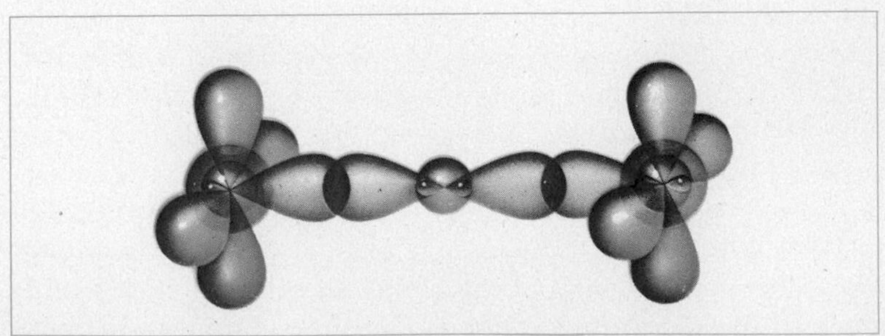

FIGURE 11–9 · *Orbital overlap and orbital hybridization: a model for beryllium bifluoride*

Boron trifluoride, BF_3, contains three covalent bonds. Boron's electron configuration is illustrated here.

$$_{5}B \quad \frac{\uparrow\downarrow}{1s}\Big|\frac{\uparrow\downarrow}{2s}\Big|\frac{\uparrow}{2p_x}\;\frac{}{2p_y}\;\frac{}{2p_z}$$

The *s* and the two *p* orbitals in boron hybridize to form three sp^2 orbitals. Such sp^2 orbitals form a triangular plane structure. In BF_3, the three fluorine atoms lie in a plane that forms a triangular structure around the boron atom (Figure 11–10).

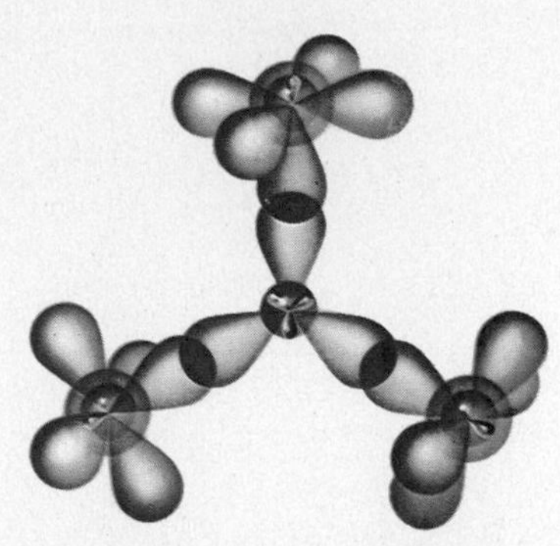

FIGURE 11–10 · *Orbital overlap: a model for boron trifluoride*

11–7 · The shape of the water molecule · One of the most impressive successes of the hybrid orbital model in bonding is the explanation of the structure of the water molecule. The electron structure for oxygen in its ground state is as follows.

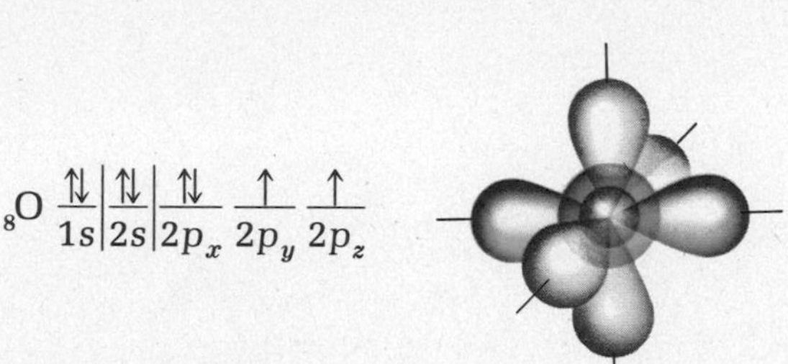

$$_{8}O \quad \frac{\uparrow\downarrow}{1s}\Big|\frac{\uparrow\downarrow}{2s}\Big|\frac{\uparrow\downarrow}{2p_x}\;\frac{\uparrow}{2p_y}\;\frac{\uparrow}{2p_z}$$

That would lead us to expect that the *s* orbitals of the hydrogen atoms would overlap with $2p_y$ and $2p_z$ orbitals of oxygen. The bond angles would then be about 90°. That is the case for H_2S, in which two of the *p* orbitals of the sulfur atom are involved. However, it has been found experimentally that the bond angle in water is 105°. That is much closer to the tetrahedral angle of 109°. How can we account for it? If, when forming water, the oxygen atom hybridizes to

$$\frac{\uparrow\downarrow}{1s}\Big|\frac{\uparrow\downarrow}{2(sp^3)}\;\frac{\uparrow\downarrow}{2(sp^3)}\;\frac{\uparrow}{2(sp^3)}\;\frac{\uparrow}{2(sp^3)},$$

where the *s* and the *p* orbitals have combined to form four hybrid sp^3 orbitals, we can expect an angle of 109°. Two of the sp^3 orbitals already contain a pair of electrons. Therefore, this hybridization still allows only two covalent bonds to be formed by oxygen. The unbonded pairs of electrons in the two sp^3 orbitals are known as *lone pairs*. The lone pairs of electrons actually repulse one another slightly. Because of the repulsion, the hydrogen atoms are pushed closer together. As a result, the angle goes from the tetrahedral angle of 109° to the observed experimental angle of 105°.

11–8 · Molecules having multiple covalent bonds · In many molecular compounds, more than one covalent bond is present between two atoms. Double covalent bonds and triple covalent bonds are important in the chemistry of many molecules.

Let's look at molecular carbon dioxide, CO_2, as our first example. You have already learned the Lewis electron-dot structures of carbon and oxygen.

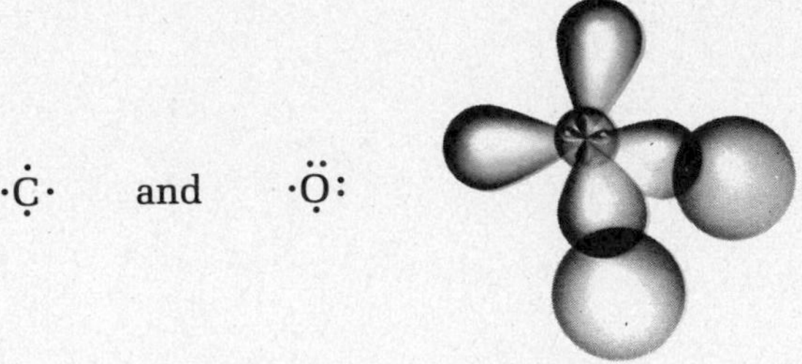

Knowing those structures, you can determine the Lewis electron-dot structure for CO_2.

Remember that the ocetet rule states that eight electron dots must surround each atom. However, note that the octet rule is not satisfied for any of the three atoms in the structure we have just given for CO_2. Each oxygen atom has seven valence electrons; the carbon atom now has six. But the octet rule can be satisfied for all three atoms if an additional electron is shared between each two atoms. That forms a *second* covalent bond between the carbon atom and each oxygen atom.

or

O=C=O

Now each atom in the molecule has eight (four pairs of) valence electrons.

As a second example of multiple covalent bonding, consider the N_2 molecule. You learned the dot structure for the nitrogen atom.

$$\cdot\underset{\cdot}{\ddot{\mathrm{N}}}\cdot$$

Therefore, you can determine the structure for N_2.

$$\cdot\underset{\cdot}{\ddot{\mathrm{N}}}:\underset{\cdot}{\ddot{\mathrm{N}}}\cdot \quad \text{or} \quad \cdot\underset{\cdot}{\ddot{\mathrm{N}}}—\underset{\cdot}{\ddot{\mathrm{N}}}\cdot$$

Note that each atom now has six valence electrons. The formation of a second covalent bond between the two nitrogen atoms leads to seven valence electrons for each.

$$\cdot\ddot{\mathrm{N}}\underset{\cdot\cdot}{-}\ddot{\mathrm{N}}\cdot \quad \text{or} \quad \cdot\ddot{\mathrm{N}}=\ddot{\mathrm{N}}\cdot$$

The octet rule is satisfied only with the formation of a third covalent bond in the molecule.

$$\ddot{\mathrm{N}}\underset{\cdot\cdot}{=}\ddot{\mathrm{N}} \quad \text{or} \quad \cdot\ddot{\mathrm{N}}\equiv\ddot{\mathrm{N}}\cdot$$

$$\text{or}$$

$$\mathrm{N}\equiv\mathrm{N}$$

As an example of a compound in which both single and multiple covalent bonds are present, we will consider ethene (ethylene), C_2H_4.

```
 H H            or         H   H
                           |   |
H:C̈:C̈:H                 H—C—C—H
  .  .                       .   .
```

While each hydrogen atom now has a filled valence electron shell (two electrons), each carbon atom has only seven valence electrons. The octet rule for the carbon atoms is satisfied with the formation of a second covalent bond between the carbon atoms.

```
   H   H                     H   H
   |   |          or         |   |
H—C—C—H                  H—C=C—H
     ..
```

A molecule in which a triple bond is important is acetylene, C_2H_2. If the structure had only single bonds, it would be represented as follows.

$$\mathrm{H}:\underset{\cdot}{\dot{\mathrm{C}}}:\underset{\cdot}{\dot{\mathrm{C}}}:\mathrm{H} \quad \text{or} \quad \mathrm{H}—\underset{\cdot}{\dot{\mathrm{C}}}—\underset{\cdot}{\dot{\mathrm{C}}}—\mathrm{H}$$

As you can see, there are two unpaired electrons on each carbon atom. Thus, the octet rule will be satisfied by the formation of the triple bond between the two carbon atoms.

$$\mathrm{H}—\mathrm{C}\overset{\cdot\cdot}{\underset{\cdot\cdot}{-}}\mathrm{C}—\mathrm{H} \quad \text{or} \quad \mathrm{H}—\mathrm{C}\equiv\mathrm{C}—\mathrm{H}$$

11–9 · The coordinate covalent bond · The following chemical reaction is one that occurs often in chemical laboratories.

$$NH_3(g) + HCl\ (g) \longrightarrow NH_4Cl\ (s)$$

This reaction takes place each time an open bottle of hydrochloric acid is placed near an open bottle of ammonium hydroxide. A solid, white smoke forms in the reaction between the two. Eventually, the solid settles on windows, laboratory bench tops, and so on, as a fine white powder.

The reaction is a very interesting one. Two molecular gases, NH_3 and HCl, in which only covalent bonds are present, combine in the gas phase to form an ionic solid, $(NH_4)^{+1}Cl^{-1}$. The Lewis electron-dot structures for the $(NH_4)^{+1}$ ion and the Cl^{-1} ion are as follows.

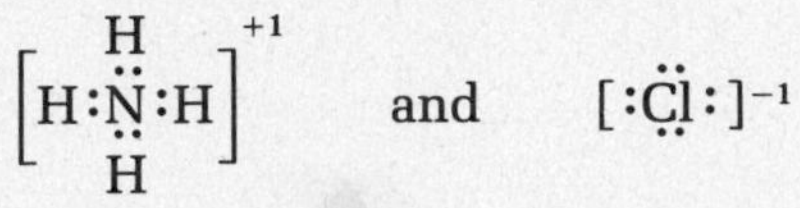

$$\left[\begin{array}{c} H \\ H{:}\ddot{\underset{..}{N}}{:}H \\ H \end{array}\right]^{+1} \quad \text{and} \quad [{:}\ddot{\underset{..}{Cl}}{:}]^{-1}$$

Suppose we examine the electron structure of the tetrahedral $(NH_4)^{+1}$ ion carefully. Let's look at it schematically.

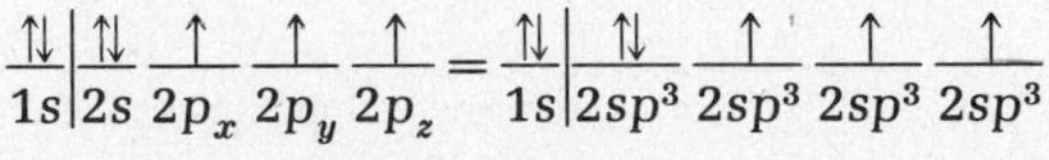

$$\frac{\uparrow\downarrow}{1s}\Big|\frac{\uparrow\downarrow}{2s}\ \frac{\uparrow}{2p_x}\ \frac{\uparrow}{2p_y}\ \frac{\uparrow}{2p_z} = \frac{\uparrow\downarrow}{1s}\Big|\frac{\uparrow\downarrow}{2sp^3}\ \frac{\uparrow}{2sp^3}\ \frac{\uparrow}{2sp^3}\ \frac{\uparrow}{2sp^3}$$

We can also show the electron-dot structure for nitrogen.

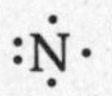

$${:}\dot{\underset{\cdot}{N}}\cdot$$

When the nitrogen atom combines with four hydrogen atoms, the single *s* electron in the hydrogen forms a covalent bond with three of the nitrogen sp^3 orbitals.

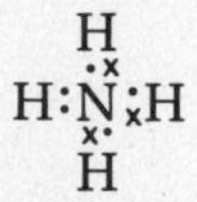

$$\begin{array}{c} H \\ H{:}\overset{\cdot\times}{\underset{\times\cdot}{N}}{\times}H \\ H \end{array}$$

Now the octet rule for nitrogen is satisfied. It is surrounded by eight electrons. Remember that hydrogen does not need to obey the octet rule. However, the octet rule can only be satisfied for nitrogen because the nitrogen atom has contributed *both* electrons from one of the electron pairs. A covalent bond in which one atom contributes both electrons of the bonding pair is called a **coordinate covalent bond.** The coordinate covalent bond is most common in ions containing several atoms, such as the sulfate ion, SO_4^{-2}, the phosphate ion, PO_4^{-3}, and the chlorate ion, ClO_3^-. The method of formation of a coordinate covalent bond is different from that of a simple covalent bond. But the coordinate covalent bond itself cannot be distinguished from the simple covalent bond.

REVIEW IT NOW

1 What is a hybrid orbital?
2 How does the *sp* hybrid orbital form?
3 Explain why BF_3 has a triangular shape.
4 How can we account for the four bonding orbitals that carbon has?
5 Show how a double covalent bond can form.
6 How does formation of a triple covalent bond in acetylene satisfy the octet rule?
7 Show how a compound can have both a single and a double covalent bond.

SUMMARY

When two hydrogen atoms overlap, there is a merging of the *s* orbital of each atom. The area of overlap is the area most likely to contain the electron from each atom. The overlap, with the shared electrons, forms a covalent bond between the two atoms. The strength of the bond is directly proportional to the amount of overlap. Bond overlap can also occur between *p* orbitals.

In order to explain experimentally the measured bond angles in many molecules, the orbital overlap model must be modified. One such modification is to assume that orbitals can hybridize. By moving an electron from the *s* into the *p* orbital, hybrid orbitals are formed. These are designated *sp*, sp^2, and sp^3, depending upon the number of *p* orbitals involved in the hybrid. The *sp* hybrid orbitals can explain the linear nature of compounds such as BeF_2. The sp^2 orbitals can account for triangular planar structures, such as BF_3. The sp^3 hybrids form tetrahedral structures, such as CH_4.

The Lewis electron-dot structure is helpful in understanding the existence of molecules with multiple covalent bonds. These include double covalent bonds, such as O=C=O, and triple covalent bonds, such as N≡N.

Occasionally, both electrons in an electron pair come from a single element. Such a bond is called a coordinate covalent bond.

Orbital overlap, orbital hybridization, and coordinate covalent bonding are models used to describe chemical bonds. These models help the chemist understand chemical bonding and predict reasonably well the geometric and chemical properties of many molecules. The models account for much experimental evidence on the nature of chemical bonds. Just as Dalton was forced to change his ideas and models in light of new evidence regarding atomic structure, the chemist must also change his models as new evidence becomes available.

In the next chapter, you will learn more about bonding by considering the forces that act to hold molecules together.

REVIEW QUESTIONS

1 Explain why H_2O is a "bent" molecule.

2 Describe the bonding of the following compounds. Predict the shape of each molecule.
   a. HCl
   b. $BeCl_2$
   c. H_2S
   d. SiF_4

3 Show the shape of the following molecules.
   a. BF_3
   b. NH_3
   If these are different, explain why.

4 Using the Lewis electron-dot structure, show the bonding for the following molecules.
   a. NaF d. HCl
   b. Cl_2 e. H_2SO_4
   c. O_2 f. S_8
   (Hint: The S_8 molecule has a ring structure.)

5 Draw Lewis electron-dot structures for the following molecules.
   a. CH_3 b. CH_4 c. CF_3 d. CHF_3
   Which of the above molecules would you expect to be extremely reactive?

6 Explain how the orbital model can help account for experimentally measured bond angles in the following compounds.
   a. H_2S
   b. H_2O

7 Explain the difference between the geometric shapes of CH_4 and PH_3.

8 Predict the shape of the compound NH_4.

9 Using the Lewis electron-dot structure, show how a coordinate covalent bond forms in the following molecules.
   a. SO_4^{-2}
   b. PO_4^{-3}
   c. ClO_3^-

SUGGESTED READINGS

Barrow, Gordon. *The Structure of Molecules.* New York: W. A. Benjamin Co., 1965.

Davis, Jeff C., Jr. "Introduction to Spectroscopy." *Chemistry,* October 1974, p. 6; January 1975, p. 11; May 1975, p. 19; July–August 1975, p. 15; December 1975, p. 5.

Dence, Joseph. "Conformational Analysis or How Some Molecules Wiggle." *Chemistry,* June 1970, p. 6.

Kauffman, George B. "Electrostatic Molecular Models." *Chemistry,* October 1975, p. 6.

Stein, Lawrence. "Noble Gas Compounds." *Chemistry,* October 1974, p. 15.

Diamonds are structurally based on carbon.

CHAPTER TWELVE

Carbon-Carbon Bonding

We have seen how carbon can form single covalent bonds with hydrogen. We have also seen how carbon can form double covalent bonds with oxygen, as in CO_2. Carbon atoms can also form bonds with other carbon atoms. We learned that the carbon atom hybridizes to form four sp^3 bonding orbitals. That means that each orbital could form a covalent bond with another carbon atom. Each of those bonded carbon atoms, in turn, could bond with other carbon atoms. Since a carbon atom can form covalent chemical bonds with other carbon atoms, an almost endless variety of chains and rings of carbon molecules can form!

The molecules that are formed when one carbon atom bonds to other carbon atoms are very important. In fact, all living structures, both plant and animal, contain such carbon molecules. In each molecule, there can be as many as a thousand or even a million carbon atoms.

HYDROCARBON BONDS

12–1 · Carbon chains · The type of compound that involves bonding between carbon and hydrogen is known as a **hydrocarbon.** The simplest hydrocarbon is methane, which has the molecular formula CH_4. The next simplest member of the hydrocarbon family, containing two carbon atoms and six hydrogen atoms, C_2H_6, is known as ethane. Other hydrocarbons have a larger number of carbon atoms. Some examples are propane, C_3H_8; butane, C_4H_{10}; pentane, C_5H_{12}; and hexane, C_6H_{14}. (Hydrocarbons will be discussed in more detail in Chapter 19.) The formulas of hydrocarbons follow the rules for the formation of Lewis electron-dot structures. Remember, each carbon atom must be surrounded by eight electrons, and each hydrogen atom must be surrounded by two electrons. For example, let's consider ethane. First, write the two carbon atoms with four dots around each of them and each hydrogen atom with one dot apiece.

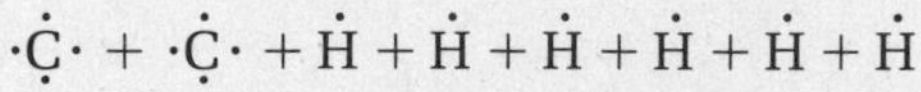

$$\cdot\dot{\underset{\cdot}{C}}\cdot + \cdot\dot{\underset{\cdot}{C}}\cdot + \dot{H} + \dot{H} + \dot{H} + \dot{H} + \dot{H} + \dot{H}$$

Those eight atoms must be combined so that the octet rule holds true for carbon. One possibility is to place a hydrogen atom between each carbon atom. But that won't work. Each carbon–hydrogen bond involves a pair of shared electrons. In order to bond to two carbon atoms, a hydrogen atom would need two unpaired electrons. But each hydrogen atom has only one electron. Then how are the dot structure rules obeyed? Two carbon atoms must share a covalent bond to produce the following structure for ethane.

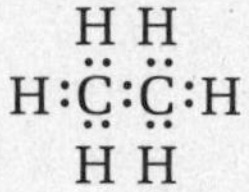

$$\begin{matrix} & H & & H & \\ & \cdot\cdot & & \cdot\cdot & \\ H : & C & : & C & : H \\ & \cdot\cdot & & \cdot\cdot & \\ & H & & H & \end{matrix}$$

12–2 · Experimental data help us understand hydrocarbon bonding · As the molecular masses of the carbon compounds increase, the boiling points also increase. Remember, the boiling point is a measure of the attraction between molecules in the liquid state. Therefore, an *increase* in the boiling point means that the attraction between the molecules must increase as the molecular mass increases. Before we can conclude that that is a valid relationship, we must consider if there are any exceptions to that relationship in experimental data.

Let's consider pentane, C_5H_{12}. One way to draw a satisfactory dot structure is to picture the carbon molecule in a chain.

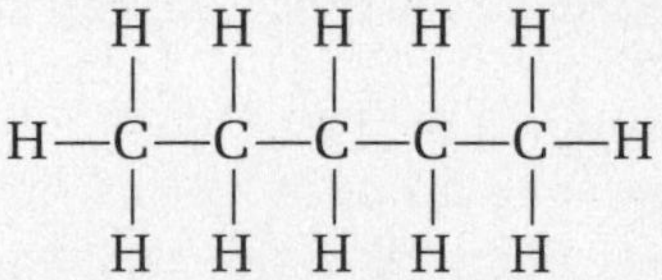

$$\begin{matrix} & H & & H & & H & & H & & H & \\ & | & & | & & | & & | & & | & \\ H- & C & - & C & - & C & - & C & - & C & -H \\ & | & & | & & | & & | & & | & \\ & H & & H & & H & & H & & H & \end{matrix} \quad \text{or}$$

However, pentane can be separated into three different substances with three different boiling points. Each substance has the formula C_5H_{12}, but the boiling point for each is different. In fact, the three different substances each have a complete set of unique chemical properties. Therefore, each substance seems to be a distinct chemical compound. That means that the molecular structure of each substance must be different, even though each one has the same formula. In considering the structure of the pentane molecule, we placed all five atoms in a row. But that is not the only possible way of arranging the atoms. We could show one carbon atom bonded to three other carbon atoms, rather than two as shown in the first structure.

```
            H
            |
          H—C—H
     H      |     H  H
     |      |     |  |
   H—C——————C—————C——C—H
     |      |     |  |
     H      H     H  H
```

In fact, that is the structure of one of the forms of pentane. Its boiling point is 28.0°C, and it is given the name **isopentane.** Another possibility for the molecular structure of pentane is one in which there is a central carbon atom bonded directly to the other four carbon atoms.

```
            H
            |
          H—C—H
     H      |      H
     |      |      |
   H—C——————C——————C—H
     |      |      |
     H      |      H
          H—C—H
            |
            H
```

It has been shown that this structure also corresponds to one of the three forms of pentane. It is known as **neopentane** and has a boiling point of 9.50°C.

Three different forms of pentane with the same molecular mass exist. Each one has a different boiling point. So, we cannot conclude that the attractive forces between the molecules are determined exclusively by the molecular mass. It seems possible that an increase in the boiling point is related more to the length of the molecular chain than it is to the molecular mass. Since isopentane and neopentane have shorter chain lengths than normal pentane, they have lower boiling points. Compounds that have the same molecular formula, but differ in molecular structure, are known as **isomers.**

REVIEW IT NOW

1 What is a hydrocarbon?
2 What is an isomer?
3 Explain why different isomers of a hydrocarbon, such as pentane, have different boiling points.

INTERMOLECULAR FORCES

12–3 · Dispersion forces in molecular structure · In compounds such as pentane, we can account for all the electrons in the carbon and hydrogen atoms. We can show how all those atoms are involved in bonding to form the electrically neutral molecule C_5H_{12}.

Then how does a neutral molecule of C_5H_{12} attract other C_5H_{12} molecules when it is in the liquid, or solid, phase?

Let's explore the problem in a different way. In Chapter 7, it was pointed out that the periodic table is a great help in correlating the properties of different compounds. The properties of a compound should be related in a specific way to the properties of similar compounds that are made up of the other elements in the same chemical group. We expect the properties of oxygen compounds to be related to the properties of similar compounds of sulfur, selenium, and tellurium. If that relationship is not found, it becomes necessary to search for a reason for the discrepancy. Let us consider H_2O, H_2S, H_2Se, and H_2Te to discover any pattern in the properties of those compounds. The boiling points are plotted in Figure 12–1.

The boiling point of the compounds rises steadily from H_2S to H_2Te. That means that the force of attraction that holds the molecules in the liquid state must also increase from H_2S to H_2Te. From the relative electronegativities, H = 2.10, S = 2.50, Se = 2.40, and Te = 2.11, we expect the dipole moments to *decrease* from H_2S to H_2Te. We predict a decrease in the force of attraction between molecules from H_2S to H_2Te. Consequently, the increased force of intermolecular attraction *cannot* be due to the normal dipole character of the molecules. Furthermore, as can be seen in Figure 12–1, an increase in the boiling point with an increase in the molecular mass is a general trend, since that trend can also be found in nonpolar substances, such as the noble gases. We can see that the attractive force must be limited in strength. It must be strong enough to hold molecules together in the liquid state, but too weak to lead to chemical bonding.

Those attractions are called **intermolecular forces.** There are two types of intermolecular forces, which are known as **dispersion forces** and **dipole–dipole forces.** Dispersion forces arise from the interaction of the electrons and the nuclei of

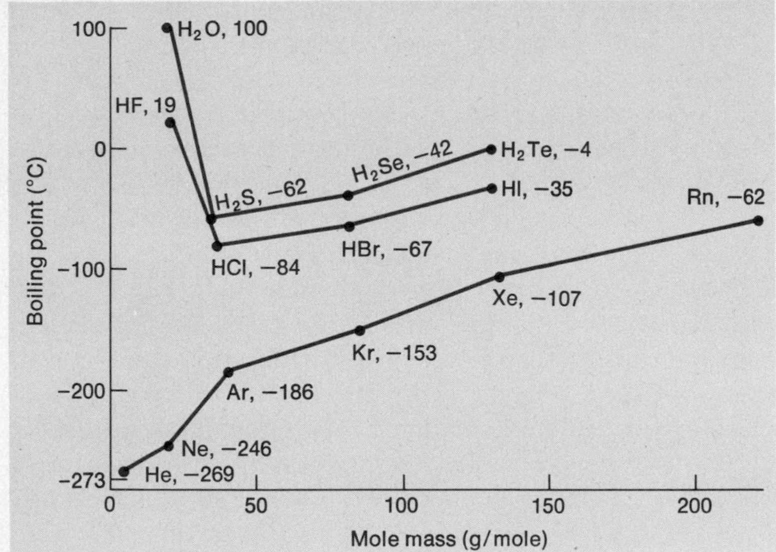

FIGURE 12–1 · *This graph shows the boiling point relationships of various elements.*

atoms or molecules that are extremely close together. The electrons of one molecule or atom are attracted to the nucleus of the adjacent atom and vice versa. In all molecules or atoms the nuclei and the electrons are not at rest, but are in constant motion. At any given moment, the electrons in an atom or molecule may not be evenly spread throughout the structure. There may be more electrons on one side of the atom or molecule than on the other. That produces an electrical imbalance—an instantaneous dipole in the atom or molecule. Two instantaneous dipoles, like any other type of dipole, can attract each other (Figure 12–2A). Also, an instantaneous dipole can induce (cause to appear) a dipole in a nearby atom or molecule (Figure 12–2B).

FIGURE 12–2 · *(A) Instantaneous dipole–instantaneous dipole attraction; (B) Instantaneous dipole–induced dipole attraction*

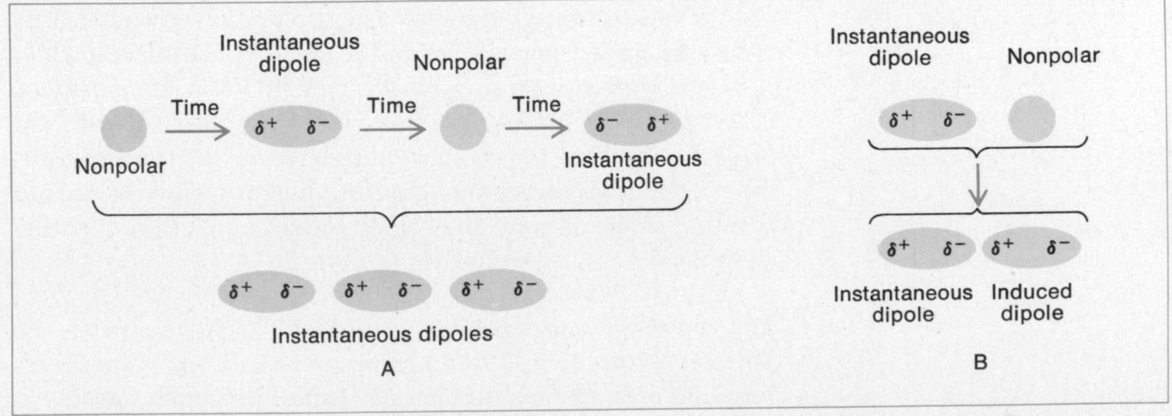

The instantaneous-dipole–instantaneous-dipole attraction and the instantaneous-dipole–induced-dipole attraction form the basis of the dispersion force. If the atoms are close enough to one another, and their kinetic energy is low, they will remain attracted to one another by the repeated interactions of the temporary dipoles.

As the atomic number of the atoms in the molecules increases, there are more electrons present. With an increasing number of electrons, the size of the distortion of the charge balance between the nucleus and the oscillating (movement back and forward between two points) electron can increase. As a result, the strength of the instantaneous dipoles also increases with the atomic number. Therefore, it requires more energy to give heavy molecules the sufficient kinetic energy to break away from one another. In that way, the existence of dispersion forces helps explain the increase in boiling point from H_2S to H_2Te (Figure 12–1).

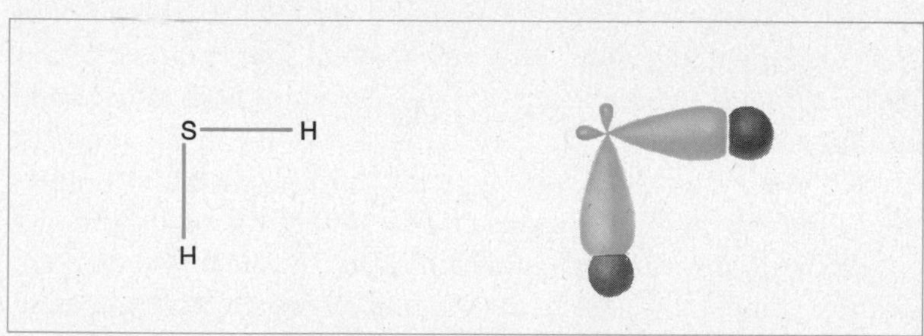

FIGURE 12–3 · *The bond angle of H_2S*

12–4 · Dipole–dipole forces · Some molecules have a permanent dipole. An example is hydrogen sulfide, H_2S, which is a bent molecule. In this molecule, two hydrogen atoms are bonded by the *p* orbitals of the sulfur atom. Since sulfur is higher in electronegativity than hydrogen, the bonding electrons are pulled toward the sulfur end of the molecule. This bent structure results in a permanent dipole in the molecule. The sulfur end of the molecule is slightly negative, and the hydrogen ends of the molecule are slightly positive. In molecules containing permanent dipoles, dispersion forces enhance the permanent dipole–dipole attractive forces that normally exist between such molecules (Figure 12–4).

12–5 · Water and the hydrogen bond · In Figure 12–1, the boiling points of H_2O, H_2S, H_2Se, and H_2Te are plotted as a function of the molecular mass. The boiling points for the hy-

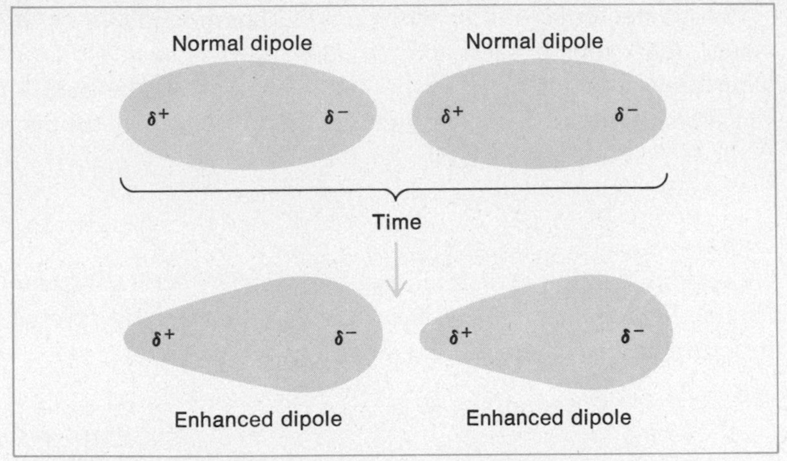

FIGURE 12–4 · *Enhanced dipole–dipole attraction; a model for dispersion forces*

drogen compounds of the halogens and the boiling points of the noble gases are also included. The increase in boiling points for the noble gases is due to an increase in the dispersion forces. In the halides and the Group VI compounds, we can see an increase in the boiling points from HCl to HI and from H S to H_2Te. Those increases in the boiling point are due partially to an increase in the dispersion forces in the molecules.

However, HF and H_2O are abnormal in their behavior. Their boiling points are much higher than would be expected, if only dispersion and dipole–dipole forces were present. If the trends in Figure 12–1 are rigorously followed, we expect that H_2O would have a boiling point of about −79.0°C! That means water would be a gas at a temperature well below the temperature that is possible for life. If water were a gas, and not a liquid, at a temperature capable of maintaining life, life would be very different, if it could exist at all. A different liquid would have to be involved in all the life processes. We often stress the regularities in science and that much of science is a search for those regularities. Yet, sometimes, it is the anomalous (inconsistent) and irregular pattern that helps us understand the physical world. The abnormal boiling point of water is just such an irregularity.

The boiling point of water is abnormal in the sense that it does not follow the relation expected from the periodic table for oxygen. But we can explain the abnormality on the basis of the bonding theory. There must be some new kind of force acting in the molecules of HF and H_2O. That force tends to keep those molecules in a liquid phase.

We see the same kind of force in solid compounds. In solid water, ice, we see each oxygen atom surrounded by four other oxygen atoms in a tetrahedral arrangement. The hydrogen atoms are found on the lines between the oxygen atoms.

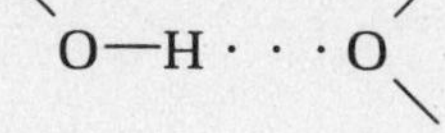

$$\diagdown O—H\cdot\cdot\cdot O \diagup$$

We assume that the attractive force between OH and O must be the bond that joins the water molecules together into the crystal structure of ice. That bond is called a **hydrogen bond.**

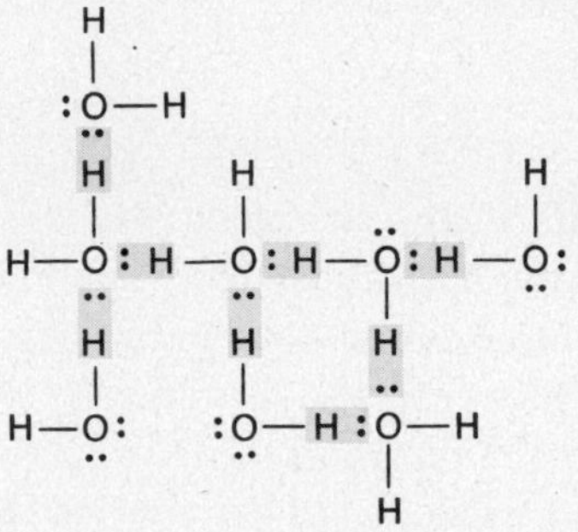

FIGURE 12–5 · *Hydrogen bonding between water molecules*

Hydrogen bonding is exhibited only between hydrogen and the most electronegative atoms—N, O, and F. In compounds with these atoms, the hydrogen atom has a very small share of the electron pair of the covalent bond and resembles a bare proton. It exerts a strong attraction on neighboring electronegative atoms because of the accumulation of negative charge on those atoms. It is important to note that the hydrogen atom is very small. That prohibits crowding more than two atoms around it in any bonding situation.

In water, one oxygen atom is covalently bonded to two hydrogen atoms. The oxygen may have one hydrogen bond, or two, by which it is linked to other water molecules. In liquid HF (hydrogen fluoride), chains of HF molecules exist.

In those chains, the hydrogen atoms link together fluorine atoms (Figure 12–6). In both water and hydrogen fluoride,

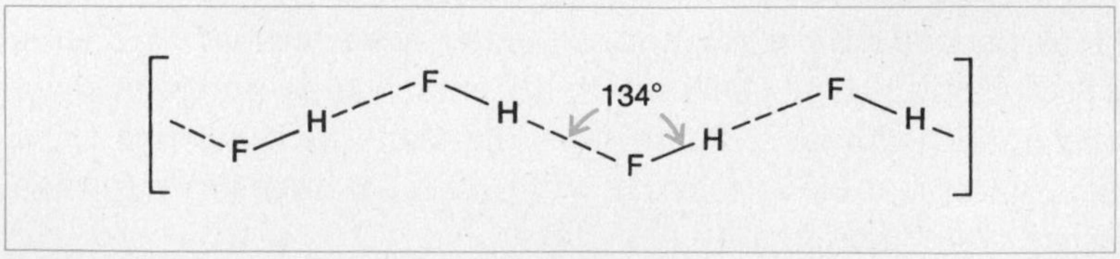

FIGURE 12–6 · *A model of hydrogen bonding in liquid hydrogen fluoride*

molecules may be grouped into clusters of large "supermolecules" by means of hydrogen bonding. That association explains the anomalous boiling points of these compounds. Since fluorine is the most electronegative of the elements, the hydrogen bonding in HF is particularly strong. It is so strong that when liquid HF vaporizes, such species as H_2F_2, H_4F_4, and even H_6F_6 exist in the vapor at moderate temperatures. Water under similar conditions vaporizes as a monomolecular species, H_2O.

REVIEW IT NOW

1 What are dispersion forces?
2 Describe how an instantaneous dipole forms.
3 How do instantaneous-dipole–instantaneous-dipole forces and instantaneous-dipole–induced-dipole forces arise?
4 How do dispersion forces help us explain the increase in boiling point from H_2S to H_2Te?
5 How does the bonding theory explain the fact that H_2O does not fit the pattern of boiling points that can be seen with H_2S, H_2Se, and H_2Te?
6 How is hydrogen bonding related to electronegativity?
7 Why is hydrogen bonding especially strong in HF?

ISOMERISM

12–6 Structural isomerism · As the number of carbon atoms in a hydrocarbon molecule increases, the number of molecular structures that can be formed increases, also. For the molecular formula C_5H_{12}, the octet rule allows only three different molecular structures. In nature, three, and only three, different substances are found with the formula C_5H_{12}. The correspondence between the theoretical prediction and experimental fact indicates the value of our ability to predict molecular structure. As the number of atoms in the molecule increases, the number of possible structures increases rapidly. For example, for the molecular formula C_9H_{20}, there are thirty-five different structures possible. For $C_{10}H_{22}$ there are seventy-five isomers. For $C_{48}H_{82}$ there are 7×10^{13} possible structures! Thus, we can see that two factors lead to the incredibly vast number of organic compounds that exist. First, carbon has the ability to form chains and rings. Second, the same number of atoms can be arranged in a great variety of structural isomers.

Structural isomerism may involve more than just a difference in the arrangement of the carbon atoms. Other atoms may also be involved in providing the variation in molecular structure. One of the most significant experiments in science was conducted in 1828 by Friedrich Wöhler (1800–1882). He formed the organic compound urea, a constituent of urine, by heating the inorganic substance ammonium cyanate. Urea was the first organic compound made outside a living cell. The empirical formula for both urea and ammonium cyanate is N_2CH_4O. Ammonium cyanate has the structure shown in Figure 12–7.

FIGURE 12–7 · *The structure of ammonium cyanate and urea*

$NH_4^+ (N{=}C{=}O)^-$

Ammonium cyanate

$$H_2N-\underset{\underset{O}{\|}}{C}-NH_2$$

Urea

Ammonium cyanate is a typical inorganic substance, with an ammonium cation and a cyanate anion. In contrast, urea, with the molecular structure shown in Figure 12–7, is a typical organic substance produced in living organisms. Prior to Wöhler's experiment, it had been an unchallenged dogma that there were two unrelated types of compounds. Some compounds could be derived from living matter and were known as *organic* substances. That type of compound was considered quite unrelated to and distinct from the chemical substances found in the mineral world—*inorganic substances*. Wöhler's chemical reaction involved rearranging an inorganic substance into a structural isomer that turned out to be an organic substance. That reaction destroyed the notion that there were two unrelated types of chemical substances.

12–7 · Geometric isomerism · A second type of isomerism is known as **geometric isomerism.** Geometric isomers of a substance have the same basic molecular structure, but differ in the distances, or arrangements, of the groups of atoms that make up the substance. For example, platinum compounds involving two ammonia groups and two chlorine atoms can exist in the two geometric structures shown in Figure 12–8. The number of bonds and the arrangement of the bonding in the groups around platinum are the same. Thus, the compounds are not structural isomers. The two isomers shown in

Figure 12–8 are called *cis* and *trans*. *Cis* is derived from Latin and means "on this side." *Trans* is also from Latin and means "across." Thus, in the *cis* isomer the two chlorines are closer together than they are in the *trans* isomer. The same is true for the ammonia groups in the two geometric isomers.

Geometric isomerism in organic compounds is frequently the result of a double bond. Molecules are not rigid structures; they are constantly in motion. The bonds continually lengthen and shorten as the molecule vibrates about 10^{14} to 10^{15} vibrations per second. Groups of atoms can also rotate around bonds. For example, in the molecule $C_2H_4Cl_2$, the two CH_2Cl ends of the molecule will rotate around the covalent bond between the two carbon atoms. As a result, no geometric isomers can exist for $C_2H_4Cl_2$. However, if there is a double bond between the two carbon atoms, the rotation is prevented. For the compound C_2H_4 there are no geometric isomers, even though the double bond prevents rotation. However, the molecule $C_2H_2Cl_2$ has two geometric isomers. In the cis isomer, the two chlorine atoms are close to each other on the *same side* of the bond. In the trans isomer, the two chlorine atoms are on *opposite sides* of the bond and, therefore, farther away from each other. The rotation of the CHCl groups in $C_2H_2Cl_2$ is prevented by the presence of the double bond.

EXCURSION EIGHT

Polymers and Plastics

This excursion discusses the structure and behavior of the giant molecules known as polymers, as well as how they are useful and harmful to us.

The differences in the geometric structure of isomers may result in important differences in their properties. For example, the male gypsy moth is strongly attracted by the cis form of the complex organic molecule gyplure. That molecule is closely related chemically to the female moth's sex attractant. On the other hand, the male moth ignores the trans form of the molecule.

We do not know why the cis form attracts a moth, or how the male moth differentiates between the two isomers so well. Many examples are available of such significant differences in the properties related to the seemingly small structural differences in molecules.

FIGURE 12–8 · *Square planar structures: trans-* $[Pt(NH_3)_2\,Cl_2]$ *(above) and cis-* $[Pt(NH_3)_2\,Cl_2]$ *(below)*

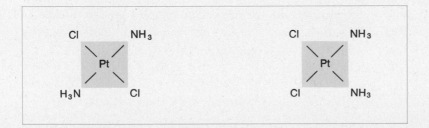

REVIEW IT NOW

1 What is the significance of Wöhler's synthesis of urea?
2 What is a structural isomer?
3 How do the structures of urea and ammonium cyanate differ?
4 What is geometric isomerism?
5 How does a cis isomer differ from a trans isomer?
6 How can a double bond give rise to geometric isomerism?

SUMMARY

The necessity of bonding between molecules is illustrated well with the hydrocarbon compounds. Isomers are two or more compounds that have the same molecular formula, but have differences in properties and molecular structure. Some isomers are different only in structure and are called structural isomers. Others differ in their geometric arrangements and are geometric isomers. The cis isomer and the trans isomer are two types of geometric isomers.

Weak bonding between molecules is the result of dipole–dipole interactions and dispersion forces. Dispersion forces may be instantaneous or induced. Bonding can also occur between the more positive hydrogen atom in a molecule and the more negative part of other molecules. Such hydrogen bonding is very important in many life processes. It also helps us understand the abnormal boiling point of water.

REVIEW QUESTIONS

1 Hexane, C_6H_{14}, is a straight-chain hydrocarbon. Draw a structural formula for this molecule.

2 Draw a structural formula for propylene, C_3H_6. This hydrocarbon has *one* double bond between adjacent carbon atoms. Can you expect more than one isomer for this molecule? Why?

3 The compound C_3H_8O forms more than one isomer. Draw all the possible isomeric forms for this compound.

4 Draw all the possible isomeric structures for the following compounds.
a. $C_2H_3Cl_3$ (trichloroethane)
b. C_4H_9Cl (chlorobutane)
c. C_5H_{12} (pentane)

5 2-butene is a hydrocarbon with a double bond between the two middle carbon atoms.

$$\begin{array}{ccccccc} & & H & & H & & \\ & & | & & | & & \\ H_3C & - & C & = & C & - & CH_3 \end{array}$$

Show the cis and trans isomers for 2-butene. Are the isomers structural, or geometric?

6 Cis dichloro-ethylene has the following structure.

$$\begin{array}{ccc} Cl & & Cl \\ & \diagdown\,\diagup & \\ & C{=}C & \\ & \diagup\,\diagdown & \\ H & & H \end{array}$$

Draw *two* additional isomers for this compound.

7 Acetylene (also called ethyne) has the molecular formula C_2H_2.

a. Draw a structural formula for acetylene.

b. What type of bonding is present?

c. Would you expect acetylene to be a very reactive molecule? Explain.

8 Are the isomers in questions 5 and 6 structural isomers, or geometric isomers?

9 Explain how hydrogen bonding occurs.

10 Describe the difference between dispersion forces and dipole–dipole forces.

SUGGESTED READINGS

Barrow, Gordon. *The Structure of Molecules.* New York: W. A. Benjamin Co., 1965

Dence, Joseph. "Conformational Analysis or How Some Molecules Wiggle." *Chemistry,* June 1970, p. 6.

Hall, Stephen K. "Symmetry." *Chemistry,* March 1973, p. 16.

Lambert, J. R. "The Shapes of Organic Molecules." *Scientific American,* January 1970, p. 58.

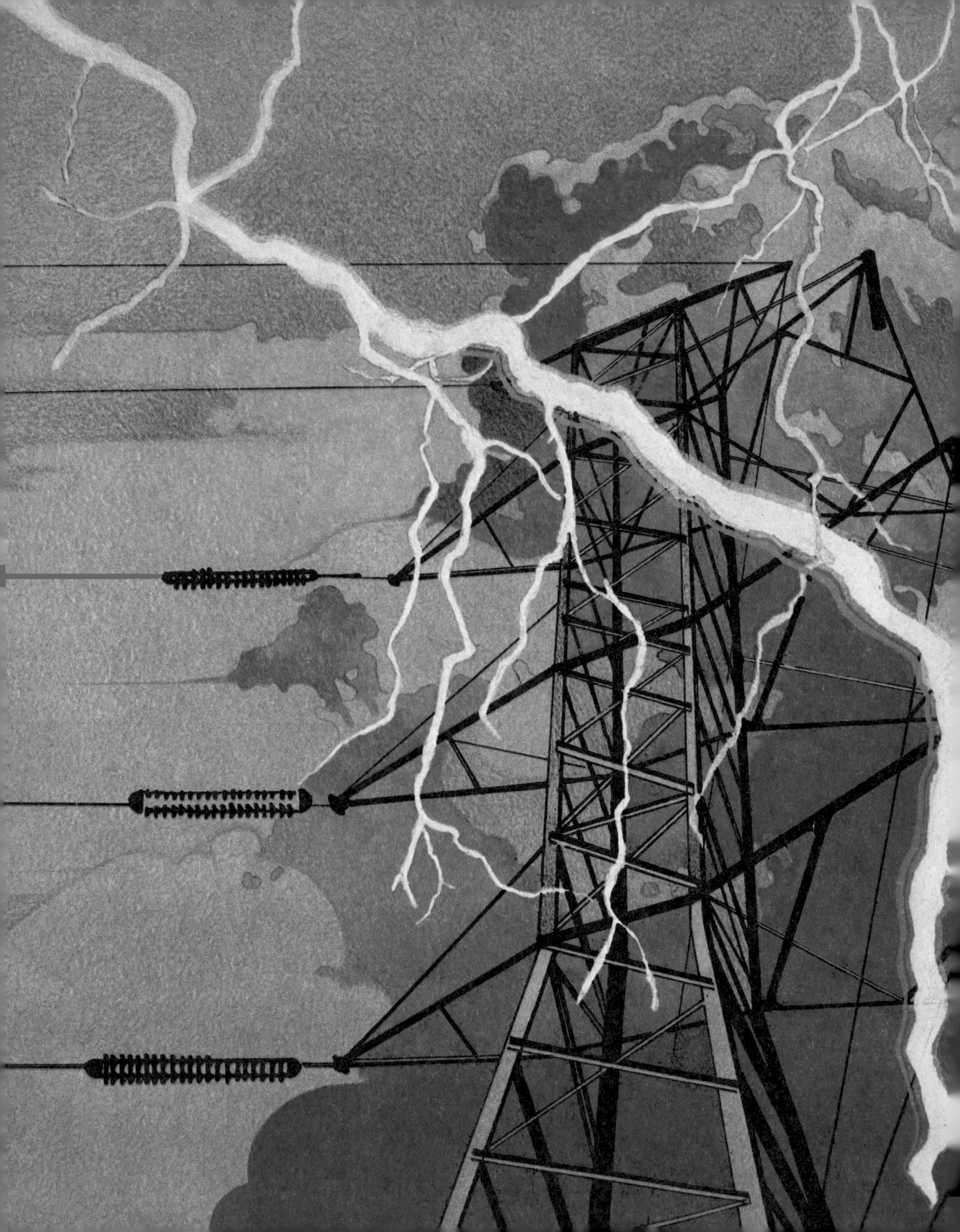

UNIT FOUR

The Behavior of Substances

What makes something chemically active? What makes a reaction go? Why are some reactions very fast, while others are extremely slow? Why must energy be added in some reactions, while it is given off in others? Seeking answers to those questions has provided much of the excitement of chemistry.

This unit will provide you with an opportunity to pull together everything you have learned in previous chapters to help answer questions such as those. We hope you will also see the reactions we study in the laboratory on a very small scale are similar to other reactions that, on a much larger scale, control our environment and shape our lives.

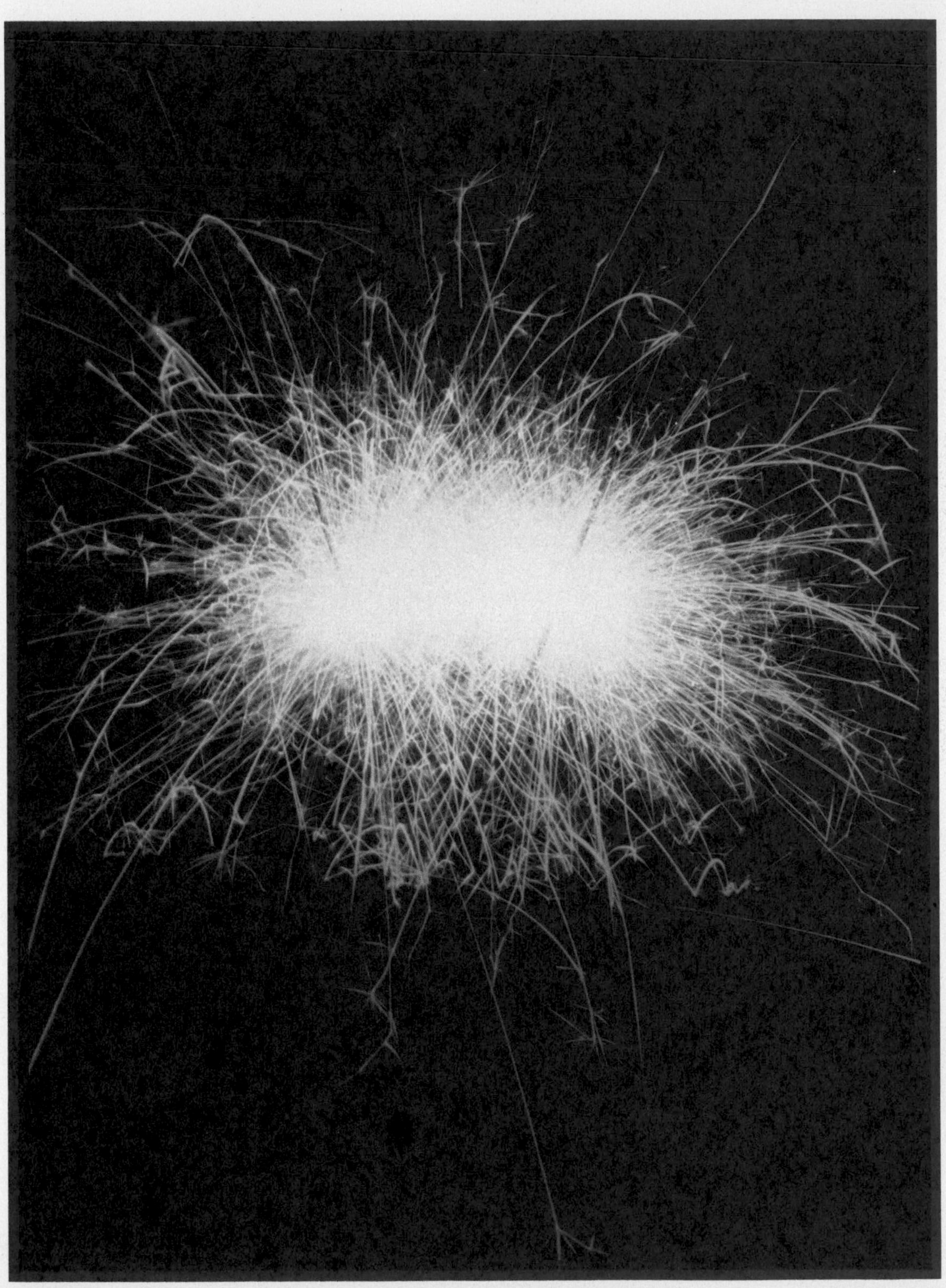

Energy is involved in every reaction, natural or synthetic.

CHAPTER THIRTEEN

Chemical Energy

Since 1800, tremendous changes have occurred in all aspects of life. For example, new modes of transportation have been developed. New medicines have been discovered. Clothing, food, and entertainment are different than they were in 1800. And those are only a very few of the many aspects of our life that have changed as a result of a technological revolution.

The changes were made possible by a fantastic increase in the consumption of energy. Then, in 1974, the energy crisis struck. For years, many knowledgeable individuals have been forecasting the depletion of our petroleum and natural gas resources. What took nature millions of years to make, we are burning away rapidly. Soon there won't be enough petroleum and gas to go around. Fortunately, we still have time to develop new energy sources to take the place of petroleum and gas. But those new sources will probably cost a great deal to develop and use. And the higher cost for the new energy will continue to cause changes in our way of life. To understand our civilization in the technological age, we must understand energy. In Chapter 13 we will study energy, particularly as it is involved in chemical compounds and in chemical reactions.

ENERGY IN GENERAL TERMS

13–1 · Energy: potential or kinetic. Suppose a new second-year student transfers to your school. This particular student not only is likable and bright, but is also big, strong, and still growing! You can imagine the excitement in the coaches' office. They are excited because the student has great *potential* for developing into a fine football player. With proper training, this potential energy can be converted into the *ability* to play football.

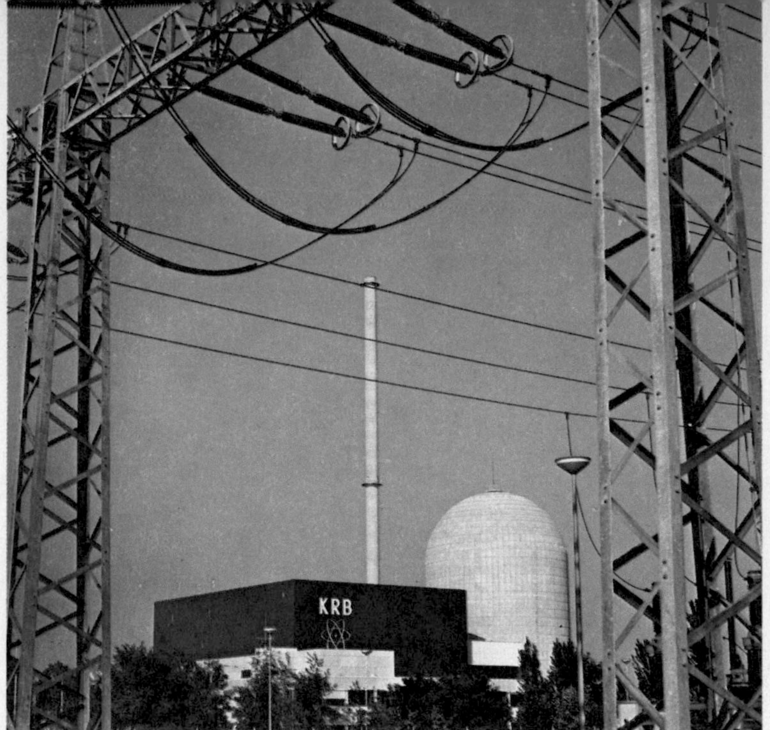

FIGURE 13–1 · *Much research into what types of energy offer a potential relief for the modern energy problem is being done. Nuclear energy is one type of energy being studied. This photograph shows a nuclear energy power plant and research center in West Germany.*

Energy can be described in much the same way. It is the *ability* to do work. One type of energy is **potential energy.** In a similar way as in the example of the football player, potential energy is energy that is *stored* in an object. It is there because of its position in relation to other objects.

But in order to put potential energy to use, we must convert it into useful energy. Let's return to our football player. After a season of training and practice, our student is a first-team linebacker. When crouched in position before the play is called, the athlete represents a considerable amount of potential energy. When the ball is snapped, the athlete goes into *motion* and converts the potential energy into *moving energy*, or **kinetic energy.** This energy is dissipated and absorbed by the opposing players who are unfortunate enough to be in the way and now lie scattered around the field at the end of the play.

Our athlete, or any other moving object, dissipates kinetic energy on impact with another object. Two factors determine the amount of kinetic energy—mass and velocity. The kinetic energy of an object is represented in the following equation.

$$KE = \frac{1}{2} mv^2$$, where m = mass and v = velocity of the moving object

Note that the velocity is *squared.* That explains why an object of relatively small mass moving rapidly (like a bullet) is very energetic. Its great speed gives it high kinetic energy.

Now let's see how energy is involved in chemical reactions. Molecules aren't as massive as the athlete, nor do they always have the speed of a bullet. But molecules do have potential and kinetic energy. And those energies may change in a chemical reaction.

13–2 · Chemical reaction and energy · The burning of gasoline is a good example of the release of energy in a chemical reaction. The equation for the burning of gasoline is shown here.

$$2C_8H_{18} + 25O_2 \longrightarrow 16CO_2 + 18H_2O$$

Thirteen hundred kcal are released for each mole of gasoline that is burned. In the equation, as it is written, two moles of gasoline are burned. Thus, a total of 2600 kcal are released in the reaction. The release of so much energy heats both the surrounding area and the reaction products. That means that the products, CO_2 and H_2O, would be at a higher temperature than the original gasoline and oxygen. Remember, you learned in Chapter 5 that temperature is proportional to kinetic energy. So an increase in temperature means an increase in kinetic energy. Thus, we can conclude that kinetic energy has been formed. In Chapter 1, we learned that energy is conserved, also. In other words, we cannot make new energy; we can merely change the form of energy. The increase in kinetic energy must, then, be accompanied by an equal decrease in the potential energy. Recall that potential energy is opposite to kinetic energy.

FIGURE 13–2 · *At what point do you think the potential energy of the oil being collected in such offshore drilling sites as this one is converted into kinetic energy?*

So, somehow, the 2600 kcal of kinetic energy released when the two moles of gasoline were burned must have been stored in the gasoline and oxygen molecules.

13–3 · Molecules and potential energy · As we have learned, potential energy is stored in molecules. To understand how energy is stored, we can observe a simpler reaction than heating gasoline and oxygen. Let's consider what occurs when the monatomic molecule helium is heated. (Recall from Chapter 5 that helium is a noble gas element, and all noble gases exist as monatomic molecules.) Like all other molecules, helium has a certain amount of stored energy. How can we increase the amount of energy stored in such a molecule? The obvious answer is by adding energy to it. We can heat molecules and then measure the difference between the increase in the kinetic energy and the total energy. That difference is the potential, or stored, energy.

Let's assume that our experiment is conducted under conditions of constant pressure. (Refer back to Chapter 6 if you need to refresh your memory on heat capacity.) In the laboratory, we find that if a mole of He gas absorbs 50.0 calories of energy, the temperature of the gas increases by 10.0°C. We would say that the *heat capacity* of helium is 5.00 calories per mole per degree, or 5.00 cal/mol-deg.

What happens to that energy? Since helium is monatomic, there are only two things that might happen. One possibility is that the absorption of 5.00 cal/mol-deg of energy excites the He electrons. But experiments prove that it requires 450 kilocalories (kcal) to move the 1*s* electron to the 2*s* energy level in a mole of helium atoms. Obviously, absorption of only 50.0 calories/mole cannot lead to the excitation of electrons.

The only other way He can use the additional energy is to increase its motion, or to increase its kinetic energy. Thus, we can assume that the heat capacity for He reflects an increase in kinetic energy, and *not* stored, or potential, energy.

What heat capacity would you expect for other monatomic gases—such as neon, argon, krypton, and xenon? Experiments show that the heat capacity of *all* monatomic gases is the same as that for helium—5.00 cal/mol-deg. That is in agreement with what we learned about kinetic energy in Chapter 5. Kinetic energy is proportional to temperature. So, for the monatomic gases, adding 5.00 cal of energy will increase the temperature of one mole of that gas by 1.00°C.

But what about molecules that have two or more atoms? Table 13–1 lists several gases and their molar heat capacities (C_p), given in calories per mole per degree. Generally, the molar heat capacity increases as the number of atoms increases. Suppose we assume that 5.00 cal/mol-deg is the amount involved in the increase of kinetic energy for all the molecules. Then the difference between the molar heat capacity and the heat capacity involved in the increase of kinetic energy ($C_p - 5.00$) is a measure of the potential energy that the molecules store as the temperature increases 1.00°C. That difference in value is also listed in Table 13–1. Data such as C_p values are important to the chemist. For example, Table 13–1 shows us that one mole of NH_3 molecules ($C_p - 5.00 = 3.48$) would store more than *twice* as much energy as one mole of oxygen molecules ($C_p - 5.00 = 1.57$). That will become more meaningful later in this chapter.

Why do molecules with more than one atom absorb *more* energy than monatomic species? For one thing, molecules with two or more atoms can do some things that simple monatomic molecules cannot. Of course, like monatomic molecules, they can move around with translational kinetic energy. But they can also move in other ways. They can rotate, and they can vibrate. First, let's look at rotation. A simple, diatomic molecule is shaped like a dumbbell. Such a molecule can turn end over end, as shown in Figure 13–3. Also, the molecule can *vibrate*. When the molecule vibrates, the distance between the nuclei of the two atoms increases and decreases, as shown in Figure 13–3. If you hold a rubber band between the thumb and index finger of both hands, you can stretch and relax the

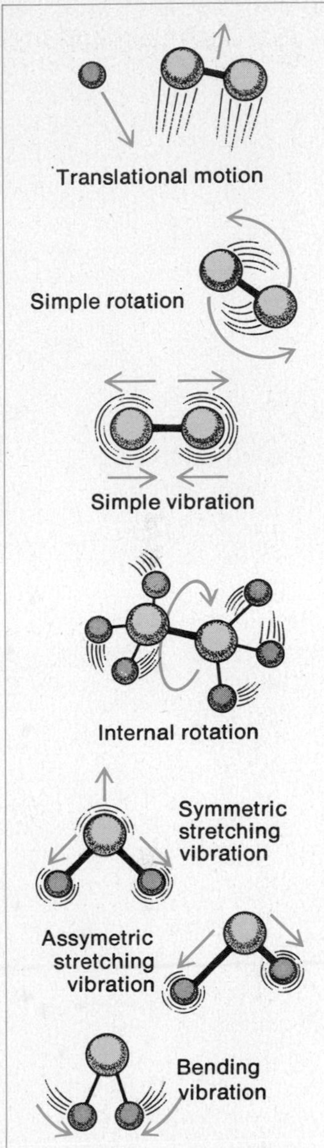

FIGURE 13–3 · *This diagram illustrates the various types of motions of atoms in molecules.*

TABLE 13–1 · Molar Heat Capacities of Some Gases

GAS	$C_p\left(\frac{cal}{mol\text{-}deg}\right)$	$C_p - 5.0$
He	5.0	0
H_2	7.03	2.03
N_2	6.82	1.82
O_2	6.57	1.57
F_2	7.49	2.49
Cl_2	7.57	2.57
Br_2	8.62	3.62
H_2O	8.03	3.03
NH_3	8.48	3.48
CH_4	8.54	3.54
CO	6.96	1.96
CO_2	8.88	3.33

band by moving your hands. That is similar to the vibrational motion that the diatomic molecule can have.

We said earlier that the amount of energy the molecule can store increases as the number of atoms in the molecule increases. If you look again at Table 13-1, you can see that the energy of rotation and vibration is also related to the *mass* of the atoms. Compare the data for H_2, F_2, and Br_2. Those data show that the heavier the mass, the more energy stored in molecules by vibrational and rotational motions. N_2 and O_2 have low values, but they are not comparable to H_2, F_2, and Br_2, which have a single bond between the atoms. Both O_2 and N_2 are multiply bonded. Carbon monoxide, CO, is a double-bonded molecule. It also has lower C_p values than the singly bonded diatomic molecules. We can guess that double and triple bonding shortens the distance between nuclei and, therefore, decreases the rotational energies.

If the molecule has many atoms (polyatomic), it can rotate and vibrate in a variety of ways. Some complex molecules have internal rotations, like those shown in Figure 13-3, in addition to the end-over-end rotations.

The vibrational motions also become more complex, as is shown by H_2O in Figure 13-3. By comparing the data for H_2O, NH_3, and CH_4 in Table 13-1, we see that the ($C_p - 5.00$) values increase as the number of atoms increases. That is a result of the increase in the number of rotational and vibrational motions for more complicated molecules.

Thus, there appear to be several factors that cause polyatomic molecules to absorb more energy than single atom species, such as the noble gases. Those factors are mass, type of bonding, and types of motion that the absorbed energy produces.

Why is that important? It is important simply because the manner in which a molecule reacts in a chemical reaction depends largely on the energy that the molecule possesses.

REVIEW IT NOW

1 Define *molar heat capacity* (C_p). Define $C_p - 5.00$.
2 What type(s) of motion is(are) characteristic of monatomic molecules? of diatomic molecules? of polyatomic molecules?
3 Describe three types of molecular motion.
4 What is the relationship between the mass of a molecule and the energy stored in it?

BOND ENERGIES AND REACTIONS

13–4 · Bond energies · To continue our study of chemical energy, let us consider a reaction much simpler than the burning of gasoline shown earlier.

$$2H_2(g) + O_2(g) = 2H_2O(g) + 115.6 \text{ kcal}$$

When two moles of $H_2O(g)$ are formed, 115.6 kcal of energy are released. Note that we have added that to our reaction, since it is a product. Now let's look at Table 13–1 again. Estimate how much potential energy stored as rotational and vibrational motions can be released in the following reaction.

$$\begin{aligned} 1 \text{ mole } O_2 &= 1.57 \text{ cal} = 1.57 \text{ cal} \\ 2 \text{ moles } H_2 &= 2 \times 2.03 \text{ cal} = 4.06 \text{ cal} \\ \text{Energy freed when } O_2 \text{ combines with } 2H_2 &= 5.63 \text{ cal} \\ \text{Energy tied up by } H_2O \text{ formed} &= 2 \times 3.03 = 6.06 \text{ cal} \\ \text{Potential energy released} &= -0.43 \text{ cal} \end{aligned}$$

The calculation shows that more energy (−0.43 cal) is *stored* by the rotational and vibrational motions in the two moles of H_2O formed than is *released* by the H_2 and O_2 when water is formed.

Obviously, the potential energy stored as rotational and vibrational motions is not all or even most of the potential energy in molecules. How is the rest stored? The answer to that question must be "in the chemical bonds." The total energy stored in the hydrogen–oxygen bonds of two moles of H_2O must be 115.6 + 0.40, or 116.0, kcal less than that stored in the two moles of hydrogen–hydrogen bonds and the one mole of oxygen–oxygen bonds of O_2.

Let's look at another reaction in which hydrogen gas (H_2) and chlorine gas (Cl_2) react to form hydrogen chloride gas (HCl).

$$H_2(g) + Cl_2(g) = 2HCl(g) + 44.0 \text{ kcal}$$

In the reaction, the energy released is 22.0 kcal per one mole of HCl(g). Note that we have added that to our reaction. Again, there is less potential energy in two hydrogen–chlorine bonds than in a hydrogen–hydrogen plus a chlorine–chlorine bond.

EXERCISE

Calculate the difference in energy stored in the hydrogen–chlorine bonds when HCl is formed from H_2 and Cl_2. (C_p – 5.0 for HCl is 1.70.)

13–5 · Exothermic and endothermic reactions · The examples of reactions that we have studied all *release* energy on reaction. However, reactions often absorb rather than release energy. In those reactions, the bonds of the *products* store more potential energy than the bonds of the *reactants*. Reactions that release energy are called **exothermic,** or **exoergic,** reactions. **Endothermic,** or **endoergic,** reactions absorb heat. The symbol H is used to indicate the energy content of a molecule. ΔH (delta H) is the symbol for the change in energy. Recall that Δ generally means "difference," or a change in something. For example, ΔT means a change in temperature from an initial to a final state. ΔH is the energy released, or absorbed, in a chemical reaction. We call that energy the **enthalpy,** H. The change in enthalpy, then, we represent as ΔH.

To make the point quite clear, we can use a bank account as a simple analogy.

Define BA = Bank Account.

If a person has \$100.00 in a bank account and cashes a check for \$10.00,we might show the transaction as follows.

$$\underset{(\$100.00)}{\text{BA}} \xrightarrow{\$10.00 \text{ check cashed}} \underset{(\$90.00)}{\text{BA}} + \$10.00$$

After cashing the check, the person has \$10.00 in tangible, countable (measurable) money. Accordingly, the bank account is decreased by \$10.00.

$$\Delta \text{BA} = -\$10.00$$

We might say that when money is removed from a bank account, the account goes down and the ΔBA is negative.

$$\textit{exo}\text{money} = -\Delta \text{BA}$$

In a similar manner, we can say that if \$10.00 is deposited, the bank account goes up, and the ΔBA is positive.

$$\textit{endo}\text{money} = +\Delta \text{BA}$$

This transaction may be represented as follows.

$$\underset{(\$100.00)}{\text{BA} + \$10.00} \longrightarrow \underset{(\$110.00)}{\text{BA}}$$

The money put into a bank account is *absorbed* into the account. The tangible, countable (measureable) money that was deposited loses its identity. (We might even say the deposit is now used to help operate the bank!)

Now suppose the $10.00 that is deposited is similar to the heat put into a reaction. Likewise, that heat is *absorbed*—into the product.

We can now apply our analogy to a chemical reaction.

$$H_2(g) + 0.50\ O_2(g) = H_2O(g)$$

In this reaction, $\Delta H = -57.8$ kcal. Since ΔH is negative (bank account decreases), heat must have been released during the reaction. We took 57.8 kcal out of our bank account. Thus, the heat content of the product water is 57.8 kcal *less* than the heat content of the reactants. This is an exothermic reaction. The 57.8 kcal of energy is *released* as heat that we can measure with a thermometer.

Let's look at an endothermic reaction.

$$0.50\ I_2(g) + 0.50\ H_2(g) = HI(g)$$

In this reaction, $\Delta H = +6.20$ kcal. Since ΔH is positive, we have *more* heat in our product than we had in our reactants. Where did the energy come from? It came from the heat that we had to *add* to the reaction to make it "go."

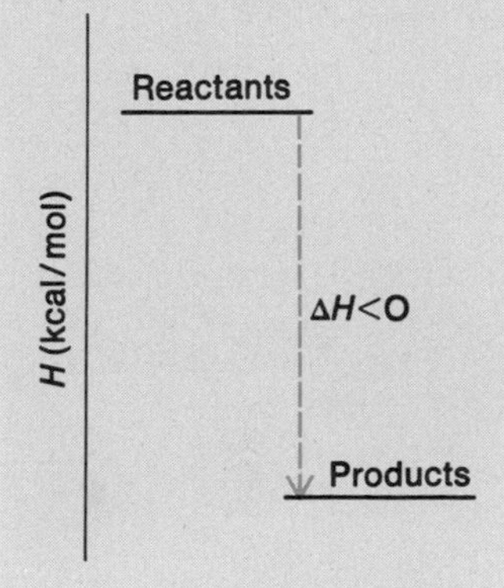

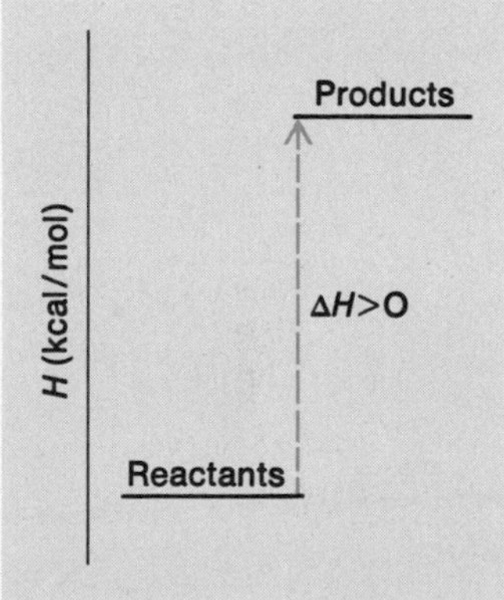

FIGURE 13–4. *(Top) Enthalpy relationship for an exothermic reaction system. (Bottom) Enthalpy relationship for an endothermic reaction system*

EXERCISE

1. Are the following reactions *exothermic*, or *endothermic*?
   a. $0.50\ N_2(g) + 0.50\ O_2(g) = NO(g);\ \Delta H = +21.6$ kcal
   b. $Na(g) + Cl(g) = NaCl(g);\ \Delta H = -98.23$ kcal
   c. $0.50\ H_2(g) + 0.50\ Cl(g) = HCl(g) + 22.06$ kcal
   d. 8.09 kcal $+ 0.50\ N_2(g) + O_2(g) = NO_2(g)$
2. *What is ΔH for* **c** *and* **d** *above?*

The relationships of $H_{reactants}$ and $H_{products}$ are shown schematically for exothermic and endothermic reactions in Figure 13–4.

REVIEW IT NOW

1. Define an *exothermic reaction.*
2. Define an *endothermic reaction.*
3. Define *enthalpy.*
4. What does it mean when ΔH for a reaction is negative? when it is positive?

MEASUREMENT OF ENERGY

13–6 · Measurement of energy change in a calorimeter · We can measure the energy absorbed or given off in a reaction. The energy change in a chemical reaction is measured using an instrument called a *calorimeter*. There are many different kinds of calorimeters, but all operate on the same principle. A change in the temperature of the calorimeter is used to calculate the number of calories released or absorbed in the chemical reaction. Figure 13–5 shows a type of calorimeter used to measure the energy change when compounds are burned in oxygen. This energy change is known as the **heat of combustion** of the compound.

FIGURE 13–5 · Calorimeters such as this one are used to determine the heats of reactions. The sample being measured and a pressurized gas, usually oxygen, are placed in the inner chamber.

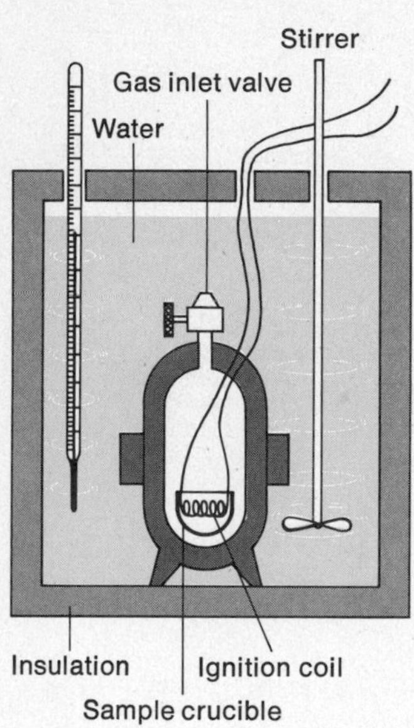

The calorimeter is a container that is insulated from its surroundings by an outer layer of a liquid, solid, or vacuum. A first experiment is run to determine the heat necessary to cause a rise in temperature of 1.00°C for the calorimeter itself. The heat energy needed for that rise in temperature is called the **calorimeter constant.** Then a known amount of reactants, usually 0.01 to 0.10 mole, is placed in the calorimeter. The reaction chamber is filled with oxygen gas. The combustion of the reactants is initiated by electrically heating the sample, or by using a spark. The reaction releases heat energy, which after a short time is evenly distributed throughout the calorimeter. That causes the temperature of the water surrounding the combustion chamber to increase. Knowing the temperature rise in the calorimeter and the calorimeter constant, it is possible to calculate the number of calories released in the reaction. From the known mass of the reactant, the energy released per mole of that reactant, or per mole of the product formed, can be calculated.

13–7 · Enthalpies of formation · The enthalpy of a reaction in which a compound is formed from its elements is called the **enthalpy of formation,** or the **heat of formation.** Among the reactions already discussed in Chapter 13, the following enthalpies of formation have been reported: H_2O, −57.8 kcal/mol; HCl, −22.0 kcal/mol; HI, +6.2 kcal/mol. As we shall see later in the chapter, knowledge of the enthalpy of formation of compounds is very useful to the chemist. Study Table 13–2. Notice that in Table 13–2 there is a list of the values for some of the more important compounds.

TABLE 13–2 · Enthalpies of Formation (25.0°C; 2.00 atm)

COMPOUND	ΔH_f(kcal/mol)	COMPOUND	ΔH_f(kcal/mol)
$H_2O(g)$	−57.8	$CO_2(g)$	−94.0
$H_2O(l)$	−68.3	$CH_4(g)$	−19.8
$H_2O_2(l)$	−44.5	$CH_3OH(l)$	−57.0
$HF(g)$	−64.2	$NaF(s)$	−136.0
$HCl(g)$	−22.1	$NaCl(s)$	−98.2
$HBr(g)$	−8.6	$NaBr(s)$	−86.0
$HI(g)$	+6.2	$NaI(s)$	−68.8
$SO_2(g)$	−71.0	$MgCl_2(s)$	−153.4
$SO_3(g)$	−94.4	$CaCl_2(s)$	−190.0
$NO(g)$	+21.6	$SrCl_2(s)$	−198.0
$NO_2(g)$	+8.1	$BaCl_2(s)$	−205.6
$NH_3(g)$	−11.0	$CuO(s)$	−37.1
$CO(g)$	−26.4	$Cu_2O(s)$	−39.8

13–8 · Hess's law of constant heat summation · In Chapter 6, we calculated the energy absorbed when one mole of H_2O is heated from −10.0°C (as ice) to +110.0°C (as water vapor) by adding the energy absorbed in a series of steps. That is a result of the first law of thermodynamics—the Law of the Conservation of Energy. Let us see how that applied to chemical reactions. As an example, consider the combustion of methane, CH_4, the natural gas used in many homes. The reaction follows.

$$CH_4(g) + 2O_2(g) \longrightarrow CO_2(g) + 2H_2O(l) \ \Delta H = -210.8 \text{ kcal/mol}$$

Let us calculate the enthalpy of formation of CH_4, and compare it with the value given in Table 13–2.

It takes experience to know which step reactions we should use.

First, we will give the reactions leading to the compounds found in the product. These are CO_2 and H_2O.

STEP 1

$$C(s) + O_2(g) = CO_2(g);\ \Delta H = -94.0 \text{ kcal/mol}$$

STEP 2

$$2H_2(g) + O_2(g) = 2H_2O(l);\ \Delta H = -136.6 \text{ kcal}/2 \text{ moles } H_2O$$

(Note that we *doubled* the ΔH_f value for H_2O, since we have two moles in our reaction above and also that we must use ΔH_f for $H_2O(l)$.) Now let's include the reaction for the formation of CH_4. Since we are trying to determine ΔH_f for CH_4, we do not know that value.

STEP 3

$$C(s) + 2H_2(g) = CH_4(g);\ \Delta H_f = ?$$

Suppose we add Steps 1 and 2 showing ΔH_f for the products, and subtract the total combustion reaction. This is shown in the following calculations.

$$[C(s) + 2H_2(g) + 20_2(g) = CO_2(g) + 2H_2O(l)]; \{\Delta H' = 230.6\}$$
$$-[CH_4(g) + 20_2(g) = CO_2(g) + 2H_2O(l)]; -\{\Delta H'' = -210.8\}$$

$$C(s) + 2H_2(g) + 20_2(g) = CH_4(g) - 20_2(g) = CO_2(g) + 2H_2O(l) - CO_2(g) - 2H_2O(l)$$

$$\Delta H' - \Delta H'' = -230.6 - (-210.8)$$

NET REACTION

$$C(s) + 2H_2(g) = CH_4(g); \Delta H = -19.8 \text{ kcal/mol}$$

The value of ΔH calculated by the step reactions is the same as ΔH_f in Table 13–0. It must be, since energy is constant if the sum of the reactions is the same. That result of the Law of the Conservation of Energy was discovered in 1840 by G. H. Hess, a Russian chemist.

HESS'S LAW OF CONSTANT HEAT SUMMATION
The heat evolved or absorbed in any chemical reaction is constant and is independent of whether the reaction takes place in one step or in many steps.

13–9 · Calculation of enthalpies of reaction · Hess's law allows us to calculate the enthalpies of reaction from the enthalpies of formation of compounds. Methanol, CH_3OH, has been suggested as an alternative liquid fuel to replace gasoline for automobiles. Let us use Hess's law to calculate the energy released when methanol burns.

The reaction follows.

$$2CH_3OH(l) + 30_2(g) = 2CO_2(g) + 4H_2O(l); \Delta H = ?$$

The following step reactions can be used to add to the above reaction.

1. $C(s) + O_2(g) = CO_2(g); \Delta H_1 = -94.0$ kcal/mol

2. $H_2(g) + 0.50\ O_2(g) = H_2O(g); \Delta H_2 = -68.3$ kcal/mol

3. $C(s) + 2H_2(g) + 0.50\ O_2(g) = CH_3OH(l); \Delta H_3 = 57.0$ kcal/mol

To get a net equation identical to the combustion reaction of CH_3OH, we need to add [2 × equation 1] + [4 × equation 2] − [2 × equation 3].

$$
\begin{aligned}
2C(s) + 2O_2(g) &= 2CO_2(g) \\
4H_2(g) + 2O_2(g) &= 4H_2O(l) \\
2\,CH_3OH(l) &= 2C(s) + 4H_2(g) + O_2(g) \\
\hline
2\,CH_3OH(l) + 3O_2(g) &= 2CO_2(g) + 4H_2O(g)
\end{aligned}
$$

$$
\begin{aligned}
\text{Similarly, } \Delta H &= 2 \times \Delta H_1 + 4 \times \Delta H_2 - 2\Delta H_3 \\
&= -\ 188.0 - 273.2 - (-114.0) \\
&= -\ 347.2 \text{ kcal/2 moles of } CH_3OH \\
&= -\ 174 \text{ kcal/mol}
\end{aligned}
$$

That can be compared with the value of −1300 kcal/mol for gasoline, which we discussed earlier. Perhaps a better comparison is one based on mass.

Gasoline

$$\frac{-1300 \text{ kcal/mol}}{114.2 \text{ g/mol}} = 11.4 \text{ kcal/g}$$

Methanol

$$\frac{-174 \text{ kcal/mol}}{32 \text{ g/mol}} = 5.4 \text{ kcal/g}$$

To use Table 13−1 in the predictive manner that was just illustrated, it is necessary that the enthalpy of formation for every compound in the reaction that is being studied be listed. It is important to realize that the step reaction sequence used in such calculations is merely a matter of convenience. Chemists usually do not know in what steps, or even in how many steps, a reaction actually takes place. Only the *total enthalpy change* between the initial reactants and the final products is known. The power of Hess's Law of Constant Heat Summation is precisely that the total enthalpy change is completely independent of the kind and number of steps between the initial reactants and the final products. Therefore, we are free to use any sequence of reactions that will result algebraically in the net reaction under study.

13–10 · What is the significance of chemical energy? · Chemical reactions are occurring all around us. Studies of chemical energies not only allow the chemist to predict if a reaction will need an input of energy to occur, but also allow the chemist to predict exactly how much energy is required. Similarly, if a reaction produces energy, we can determine how much.

Let's look at two common examples. As you know, green plants produce carbohydrates, such as sugar, by the reaction known as photosynthesis. We can show that reaction in the following way.

$$6CO_2(g) + 6H_2O(l) \longrightarrow C_6H_{12}O_6(s) + 6O_2(g);\ \Delta H + 673\ \text{kcal}$$

Since photosynthesis is an endothermic reaction, the equation tells us how much energy would be needed to make a *mole* of sugar. Can you calculate how much energy would be required to produce a kilogram of sugar? Can you think of other endothermic reactions? We are probably more interested in reactions that *produce* energy. Let's take another look at the reaction that makes our automobiles run. We can represent the exothermic reaction when gasoline burns in our automobile engines in the following equation.

$$C_8H_{18}(l) + \frac{25}{2}O_2(g) \longrightarrow 8CO_2(g) + 9H_2O(l)$$

$$\Delta H = -1.30 \times 10^3\ \text{kcal}$$

There is a large amount of heat produced in our automobile engines! In fact, without an efficient automobile cooling system, that amount of heat would soon overheat an engine.

FIGURE 13–6 · *Like nuclear energy mentioned in Figure 13–1, solar energy is one of the energy sources that could be useful in the future. Home heating is one example of the benefit of solar energy. This experimental solar home is totally run on the energy generated in the boxlike solar units shown.*

FIGURE 13–7 · *A tremendous amount of energy is released as heat when rockets such as this one are launched.*

The chemist can search for fuels that release less heat, and the engineer can search for better ways to remove the heat that is released.

In some cases, it is very desirable that the reaction release a large amount of energy. For example, the following reaction occurs when dynamite containing one mole of nitroglycerine is exploded.

$$C_3H_5(NO_3)_3(l) \longrightarrow 1.50\ N_2(g) + 0.25\ O_2(g) + 3CO_2(g) + 2.50\ H_2O(l) \quad \Delta H = -370\ \text{kcal}$$

EXERCISE

1 Which releases more energy *per mole*: octane or nitroglycerine?
2 Which releases more energy *per kilogram*: octane or nitroglycerine?

A knowledge of energy effects in chemical reactions is important if we are to understand the reactions that occur all around us.

REVIEW IT NOW

1 Describe how a calorimeter works.
2 What is a calorimeter constant? Why do we need it?
3 Define *enthalpy of formation* (heat of formation).

SUMMARY

In Chapter 13, we learn that energy is stored in molecules. Some of that energy of the molecule is in the form of kinetic energy, or energy of motion. Molecules may undergo several types of motion. Simple monatomic molecules undergo only translational motion. Molecules with two or more atoms can also undergo rotational and vibrational motions. If we look at the total heat involved when reactants combine to form products, we can estimate the molar heat capacities of many elements and molecules. However, not all the energy of molecules can be accounted for by their motion. Some energy is stored in the chemical bonds that hold atoms together in molecules.

By causing a reaction of molecules in a calorimeter, we can determine the energy change, or the heat of combustion. Some reactions are endothermic, or absorb heat. Others are exothermic, or release heat. Calorimetry allows us to determine the heat of formation, or the enthalpy, of a substance. Sometimes that cannot be done directly. In such cases, we can look at ΔH_f values for every component of the reaction in a step fashion. That allows us to indirectly arrive at a ΔH_f value for a reactant or product. The indirect process is called Hess's Law of Constant Heat Summation.

REVIEW QUESTIONS

1. What does it mean if the enthalpy of a reaction is negative?
2. Express in your own words the meaning of Hess's Law of Constant Heat Summation.
3. How do we use Hess's law?
4. When 1.00 g carbon burns in air to form carbon dioxide, 7.87 kcal are liberated. Express that as heat liberated per mole of carbon.
5. Name all the forms of energy you think might possibly be associated with chemical action.
6. What is the relationship between the thermal stability of a compound and its heat of formation?
7. The calorimeter constant for a particular experimental setup is 1.69 kcal/°C. When 2.00 g calcium are reacted with chlorine gas in a calorimeter, the observed temperature rise is 5.60°C. What is the molar enthalpy of formation of calcium chloride?
8. If 0.450 g ethane is ignited in an atmosphere of excess oxygen, using the equipment described in question 7, and the observed temperature rise is 4.84°C, what is the molar enthalpy of combustion for ethane?
9. Using data from Table 13–1, calculate the heat of reaction per mole of the first reactant given in each of the following equations.
   a. $SO_2(g) + 0.50\ O_2(g) = SO_3(g)$
   b. $4NH_3(g) + 50_2(g) = 4NO(g) + 6H_2O(g)$
   c. $2CO(g) + O_2(g) = 2CO_2(g)$

10 The enthalpy of formation for $CO_2(g)$ listed in Table 13–0 was determined for the following reaction.

$$C(graphite) + O_2(g) = CO_2(g)$$

The combustion of the second allotropic form of carbon may be written as follows.

$$C(diamond) + O_2(g) = CO_2(g) + 94.5 \text{ kcal/mol}$$

What is ΔH for the following reaction?

$$C(graphite) = C(diamond)$$

11 Using data from Table 13–1, calculate the molar enthalpy of vaporization of water. Compare your answer with the 9.720 kcal/mol given as the accepted value. Explain the difference in terms of structure.

SUGGESTED READINGS

Hildebrand, J. *An Introduction to Molecular Kinetic Theory*. New York: D. Van Nostrand Co., 1963.

Kokes, Richard. "Elements of Chemical Thermodynamics." *The Science Teacher*, November 1966, p. 72.

Mahan, Bruce. *Elementary Chemical Thermodynamics*. New York: W. A. Benjamin Co., 1965.

Porter, George. "The Laws of Disorder." *Chemistry*, May 1968–February 1969.

Spence, J. N., *et al.* "Entropy and Chemical Reactions." *Chemistry*, December 1974, pp. 12–15.

Strong, L. E., and W. J. Stratton. *Chemical Energy*. New York: D. Van Nostrand Co., 1963.

Thompson, J. J. *An Introduction to Chemical Energetics*. Boston: Houghton Mifflin Co., 1966.

Reactions in nature tend to release energy.

CHAPTER FOURTEEN

Entropy and Equilibrium

As a stone rolls downhill, it loses potential energy. A clock runs down as its spring unwinds. A flashlight dims as its battery dies. Paper burns to an ash. Once any action starts, it will continue until the potential energy is lost, unless the action is interfered with in some way. In isolated systems (those in which there is no outside interference), the tendency in nature is to act in a manner that releases energy. There is a natural tendency to go to a state of lower energy.

However, we must not jump to the conclusion that every system does in fact always act to release energy. Nor should we conclude that every system acts to release all its potential energy. We saw in Chapter 13 that it may not be so. For example, suppose we dissolve table salt (NaCl) in water in a calorimeter. We will find that 1.20 kcal of heat are released when a mole of salt dissolves in one liter of water. Only five moles of salt can dissolve in one liter of water. No more salt dissolves even though energy would be released if it continued to dissolve. Often the reaction seems to stop after a certain amount of reaction has taken place. That is true for both energy-releasing (exothermic) and energy-absorbing (endothermic) reactions.

CHEMICAL EQUILIBRIUM

14–1 · What is chemical equilibrium? · Let us consider a rather simple chemical reaction—the exothermic decomposition of HI (hydrogen iodide) into H_2 and I_2. The equation follows.

$$2HI(g) = H_2(g) + I_2(g)$$

In order to keep iodine in the vapor state, the reaction is carried out above room temperature. At 445°C, the reaction releases 8.30 kcal per mole of HI that decomposes.

Both H_2 and HI are colorless gases. I_2 vapor, however, has a purple color. That difference in color makes this particular reaction easy to study. As HI decomposes into H_2 and I_2, a purple color appears in the reaction vessel. As the concentration of I_2 increases, the color also increases (Figure 14 – 2).

Suppose we add 2.00 moles of HI gas to a one-liter glass flask at a temperature of 445°C. Soon a faint purple color begins to appear. Then the purple deepens in intensity. But after a while, there is no further change in the intensity of the purple color. What does that mean? It must mean that the reaction has produced all the I_2 that it can under the present conditions of temperature and gas concentration. If we now measure the amount of I_2 present in the reaction vessel, we will find 0.20 mole of I_2.

We know from the reaction that the same number of moles of I_2 and H_2 are produced when a given amount of HI decomposes. Thus, we would also expect to find that 0.20 mole of H_2 has been produced. Our equation for the reaction also tells us that two moles of HI are required to produce one mole of H_2. Thus, we can see that only 0.40 mole of HI reacted. The remaining 1.60 moles remain unchanged. The reaction seems to have stopped after only 20 percent of HI has decomposed.

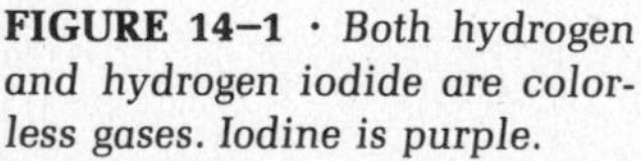

FIGURE 14–1 · *Both hydrogen and hydrogen iodide are colorless gases. Iodine is purple.*

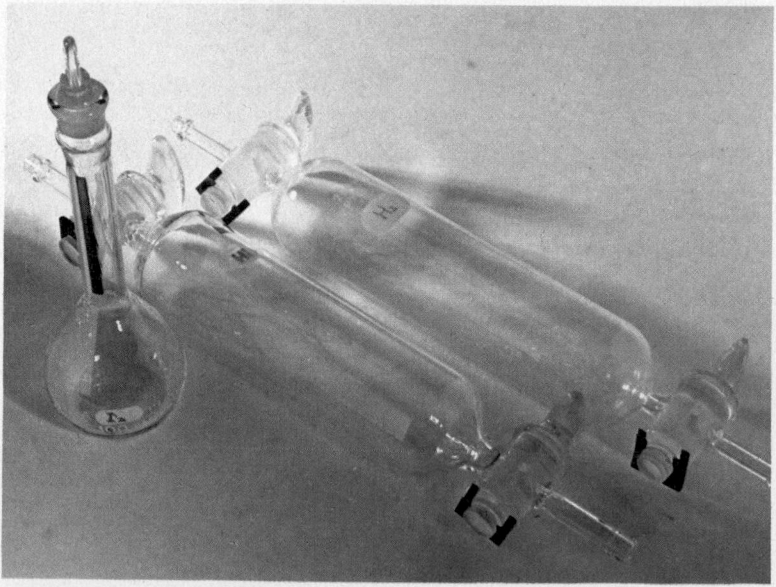

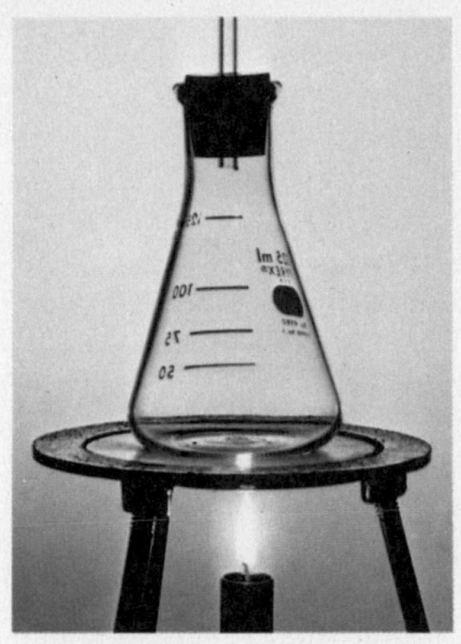

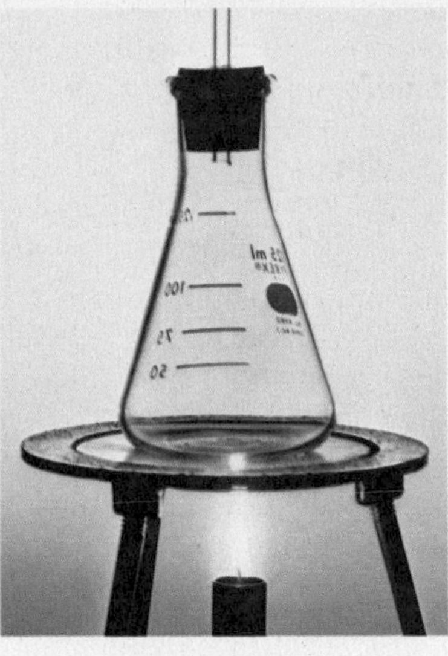

FIGURE 14–2 · *As HI decomposes into H_2 and I_2, a purple color appears and deepens in intensity.*

Now suppose we perform another experiment. This time we will simply reverse the reaction we carried out earlier. We will start with 1.00 mole of H_2 and 1.00 mole of I_2 in the one-liter flask at 445°C. This time the purple color of iodine begins to fade. It indicates that the I_2 is disappearing, or being used up by the reaction.

$$H_2(g) + I_2(g) = 2HI(g)$$

When no further color intensity change can be observed, the contents of the flask can be analyzed. The flask is found to contain 1.60 moles of HI, 0.20 mole of H_2, and 0.20 mole of I_2. That is just what we saw in the first experiment.

Both the experiments demonstrate chemical equilibrium. Chemical equilibrium exists when both the reactants and the products are present, but no further change in their concentration occurs. Our two experiments show another property of chemical equilibrium. At equilibrium, the ratio of the concentrations of the reactants and products is the same no matter from which side of the reaction we start. In one case, we began with $H_2 + I_2$, while in the second experiment, we began with HI. But in both experiments, the ratio at equilibrium of HI/I_2 and HI/H_2 was 1.60/0.20, or 8 to 1.

Before continuing, let us reconsider the experiments. We have learned that an exothermic reaction may reach a state of equilibrium rather than go to completion. We have also seen that an *endothermic* reaction occurs spontaneously until the same equilibrium is reached. So we have two new questions about chemical reactions to answer. Why doesn't an exothermic reaction go to completion? And why does an endothermic reaction occur at all? Before trying to answer those questions, let's study equilibrium in more detail.

14–2 · Equilibrium is dynamic · Earlier we discussed equilibrium in relation to a liquid and its vapor. When the vapor could not escape, equilibrium was established between the liquid and the vapor. And it seemed that further change did not occur. In that state of equilibrium, the liquid continued to evaporate, and the vapor continued to condense. The amount of evaporation was identical to the amount of condensation during any set period of time. Therefore, in the equilibrium process, there is no net change, even though both evaporation and condensation continue. Thus, equilibrium is a **dynamic state.** In other words, change is occurring in both directions, but at an equal rate.

Let's illustrate equilibrium with a simple analogy. Suppose your chemistry classroom is connected to the school library by a revolving door. Also, assume that your chemistry classroom can contain only sixty students. As students pass through the revolving door to enter the library, the number of students in the chemistry classroom decreases. Likewise, the number of students in the library increases. Let's further assume that the library will accommodate only twenty students. What happens when twenty students have passed through the revolving door into the library? More students can enter the library *only* if students leave the library and reenter the classroom through the revolving door at the same time. Thus, a situation exists in which the same number of students are entering the library as are leaving the library. But the total number of students in the two rooms remains unchanged. Like the reaction for HI, that would be a dynamic state of equilibrium. Change occurs in *both* directions, at an equal rate.

We can conduct an experiment with the $HI-H_2-I_2$ system to see if reaction is still going on when the system is at equilibrium. As before, suppose we add two moles of HI to a one-liter flask and allow the reaction to reach equilibrium at 445°C. Now suppose we add a very small amount of radioactive iodine as I_2 to the mixture. The amount added is too small to cause any detectable change in the equilibrium mixture. And the purple iodine color does not change. But when we measure the radioactivity, we find that the radioactive iodine, which was originally only in I_2, is soon found in the HI. Also, the amount of the radioactive iodine in HI gradually increases. After a while, no further change is noted in the distribution of the radioactivity between I_2 and HI. At that time, we find that 80 percent of the original radioactive iodine is now in HI, while 20 percent remains in I_2. That is the same ratio of concentration at equilibrium as the nonradioactive iodine. The overall reaction remained at equilibrium the whole time. But the radioactive iodine reacted to form HI until it reached the equilibrium ratio of concentration.

Suppose we repeat the experiment but add the radioactive iodine as HI. Again we observe no overall change. But the radioactivity distributes itself again into 80 percent in HI and 20 percent in I_2 by reacting to form I_2. We must conclude that at equilibrium both the forward reaction and the reverse reaction still occur.

Forward reaction

$$2HI(g) \longrightarrow H_2(g) + I_2(g)$$

Reverse reaction

$$H_2(g) + I_2(g) \longrightarrow 2HI(g)$$

Chemical equilibrium is a dynamic process. To reflect that, we write reactions that go to equilibrium with a double arrow.

$$2HI(g) \leftrightarrows H_2(g) + I_2(g)$$

14–3 · The equilibrium constant · In our test system, it does not matter whether we started with HI or with $H_2 + I_2$, since we had the same ratio of concentrations at equilibrium. Suppose we continue to study the reaction at 445°C, but with different initial amounts of HI or $H_2 + I_2$. We would find that at equilibrium, the product of the concentrations of H_2 and I_2 divided by the square of the concentration of HI is *always* equal to 0.0156.

$$\frac{[H_2][I_2]}{[HI]^2} = 0.0156$$

Let's use our earlier results.

$$\frac{[0.20][0.20]}{[1.60]^2} = \frac{0.04}{2.56} = 0.0156$$

This constant is known as the **equilibrium constant** and has the symbol *K*. We can write the equilibrium constant for the general reaction at the top of page 296.

$$aA + bB \leftrightarrows cC + dD$$

$$K = \frac{[C]^c[D]^d}{[A]^a[B]^b}$$

Our general reaction shows *a* moles of A, *b* moles of B, etc. When we write an equilibrium constant, we express the concentration by a bracket. Thus, the concentration of reactant A is shown as [A], that for product C is [C], etc. Also, we raise the concentration to a power equal to the number of moles. For example, if one reaction shows two moles of reactant A, we would show that as $[A]^2$. The reactants appear in the denominator. The products appear in the numerator.

If you study the expressions shown in Table 14–1, the procedure will become clear. It is important to remember that the concentration terms in those expressions always relate to the actual concentrations present when the state of equilibrium exists. Observe that when a pure solid or pure liquid appears as a reactant or a product in an equilibrium system, *it does not appear in the equilibrium-law expression.* However, the concentrations of dissolved substances do appear in the expression. The concentration of a substance in a condensed state is constant. Consider pure water, for example. In one liter of pure water, there are 55.6 moles of water. The concentration is 55.6 mol/l. If only 0.10 liter is present, there are 5.56 moles, and the concentration is still 55.6 mol/l. No matter what amount is present, the concentration of pure water is always 55.6 mol/l. Likewise, if you break a solid in half, you

TABLE 14–1 · Equilibrium-Law Expressions

SYSTEM	K
$2NO_2(g) \rightleftharpoons N_2O_4(g)$	$\frac{[N_2O_4]}{[NO_2]^2}$
$N_2(g) + 3H_2(g) \rightleftharpoons 2NH_3(g)$	$\frac{[NH_3]^2}{[N_2][H_2]^3}$
$C(s) + H_2O(g) \rightleftharpoons CO(g) + H_2(g)$	$\frac{[CO][H_2]}{[H_2O]}$
$H_2(g) + S(l) \rightleftharpoons H_2S(g)$	$\frac{[H_2S]}{[H_2]}$
$Fe_3O_4(s) + 4H_2(g) \rightleftharpoons 4H_2O(g) + 3Fe(s)$	$\frac{[H_2O]^4}{[H_2]^4}$
$NaF(aq) + H_2O(l) \rightleftharpoons HF(aq) + NaOH(aq)$	$\frac{[HF][NaOH]}{[NaF]}$

haven't changed the concentration, or the amount of a substance per volume of the solid. You may think of the constant concentration of a pure solid or a pure liquid as being incorporated in the final equilibrium constant, K.

14–4 · Equilibrium constant and temperature · The equilibrium constant is dependent on the temperature. For the $HI-H_2-I_2$ reaction, the equilibrium constant has a value of 0.0156 only at 445°C. At 25.0°C, the value of the equilibrium constant of the same reaction is 1.70. A small value of K means a larger concentration of reactants than of products. A larger value of K means a larger concentration of products than of reactants. At 445°C, K is small, so $[HI] > [H_2], [I_2]$. At 25.0°C, K is greater than one, so $[H_2], [I_2] > [HI]$.

14–5 · Calculations involving K · An equilibrium constant is calculated from the concentrations of reactants and products at equilibrium. For example, at 200°C, a one-liter flask contains 0.10 mole N_2, 0.30 mole H_2, and 1.30 moles NH_3 at equilibrium. Look at the following reaction.

$$3H_2 + N_2 \rightleftharpoons 2NH_3$$

For the reaction, the equilibrium constant follows.

$$K = \frac{[NH_3]^2}{[H_2]^3[N_2]} = \frac{[1.30]^2}{[0.30]^3[0.10]} = \frac{1.69}{(0.027)(0.10)} = 625.9 \text{ (or 626)}$$

By convention, chemists do not include units for K values in tabulations or calculations. In calculating equilibrium concentrations, however, a concentration unit must be added to the answer. We may use the value of K at a particular temperature to determine the equilibrium concentrations.

EXAMPLE 1

At 445°C, an equilibrium mixture contains 0.80 mol/l HI and 0.40 mol/l I_2. What is the equilibrium concentration of H_2? (Remember, K at 445°C is 0.0156.)

SOLUTION

$$2HI(g) \rightleftharpoons H_2(g) + I_2(g)$$

At equilibrium: $0.80 \text{ mol/l} = x(0.40 \text{ mol/l})$

$$K = \frac{[H_2][I_2]}{[HI]^2}$$

$$\text{At } 445°\text{C} = \qquad K = 0.0156 = \frac{[H_2][0.40]}{[0.80]^2}$$

$$[H_2] = \frac{(0.80)^2(0.0156)}{(0.40)}$$

$$[H_2] = 2.5 \times 10^{-2} \text{ mol/l}$$

EXAMPLE 2

If at 25.0°C the equilibrium mixture contains 0.080 mol/l HI and 0.040 mol/l I_2, what is the equilibrium concentration of H_2?

SOLUTION

At 25.0°C, K=1.70

$$K = 1.70 = \frac{[H_2][I_2]}{[HI]^2} = \frac{[H_2](0.040)}{(0.080)^2}$$

$$[H_2] = \frac{(0.080)^2(1.70)}{(0.040)}$$

$$[H_2] = 0.272 \text{ mol/l}$$

Note that at 445°C, K is small, and the equilibrium concentration of HI is much greater than that of H_2. At 25.0°C, K is larger, and the equilibrium concentration of H_2 is much greater than that of HI. Let's look at another reaction.

$$N_2(g) + O_2(g) \rightleftharpoons 2NO(g)$$

At 25.0°C, the value of K is extremely small, 10^{-30}. Only a few molecules of NO form. However at 2500°C, K is equal to 10^{-2}, and much more NO forms. That is about the temperature of an automobile engine cylinder in which NO is formed from the air present to burn the gasoline. The K is large enough at 2500°C so that NO can be a serious pollutant of the atmosphere when automobile traffic is heavy.

REVIEW IT NOW

1 Give examples to show that there is a natural tendency for energy to decrease.
2 How is the concept of equilibrium demonstrated experimentally?
3 What do we mean when we say that equilibrium is "dynamic"?
4 How is an equilibrium state expressed in an equation showing the reaction?
5 Write the equilibrium constant for a general reaction.
6 Calculate the equilibrium concentration of a reactant, given the equilibrium concentration of products and the equilibrium constant in Example 1.

LE CHÂTELIER'S PRINCIPLE

14–6 · Certain factors affect chemical equilibrium · Three factors have a significant effect on chemical equilibrium. Those factors are change in pressure, change in concentration, and change in temperature. Let's look at the effect of each of the factors in detail.

PRESSURE CHANGES · If we keep constant the temperature of a system at equilibrium, the value of the equilibrium constant does not change. However, the lack of change doesn't mean that the equilibrium concentrations remain the same. Consider this gas phase equilibrium system at constant temperature.

$$2NO_2(g) \rightleftharpoons N_2O_4(g)$$

If we increase the pressure on the system, the brownish color, which is due to the presence of NO_2, diminishes in intensity until a new constant intensity is observed. Why might that be true?

An increase in the pressure on this equilibrium system at constant temperature causes a decrease in the volume. In the smaller volume, the total number of moles per unit volume becomes greater than it was under the original conditions. This increase in concentration caused by the pressure change could be reduced if a decrease in the total number of moles of gas could occur. When NO_2 combines to form N_2O_4, such a reduction occurs. The concentrations of NO_2 and N_2O_4 change to new values, which still give the same *K* value. However, the decrease in brownish color indicates that the ratio between $[N_2O_4]$ and $[NO_2]$ is greater at the higher pressure than it is at

$$\frac{[N_2O_4]}{[NO_2]^2 \text{ (at } P_1)} < \frac{[N_2O_4]}{[NO_2]^2 \text{ (at } P_2)}$$

$$\frac{[N_2O_4]}{[NO_2]^2 \text{ (at } P_1)} = \frac{[N_2O_4]}{[NO_2]^2 \text{ (at } P_2)} = K$$

the lower pressure. When a pressure increase is imposed on the H_2–I_2–HI equilibrium system at a constant temperature, no change in the equilibrium concentrations is observed. Inspection of the equation for that equilibrium reaction shows that a chemical change in either direction does not change the number of moles of gas.

$$H_2(g) + I_2(g) \rightleftharpoons 2HI(g)$$

In the reaction, there is no response to a pressure change, and no change occurs.

REACTANT CONCENTRATION CHANGES · If sulfuric acid is added to the equilibrium system, the equilibrium is momentarily unbalanced.

$$2K_2CrO_4(aq) + H_2SO_4(aq) \rightleftharpoons K_2Cr_2O_7(aq) + K_2SO_4(aq) + H_2O(l)$$

When equilibrium is restored at the same temperature, the increased intensity of orange color indicates that yellow K_2CrO_4 has been converted to orange $K_2Cr_2O_7$. Before and after the addition of the H_2SO_4, the law of chemical equilibrium for the system has to be satisfied.

$$K = \frac{[K_2Cr_2O_7][K_2SO_4]}{[K_2CrO_4]^2[H_2SO_4]}$$

If no chemical changes take place when H_2SO_4 is added, the concentration of the H_2SO_4 will increase, and K will decrease. So when H_2SO_4 is added, some reaction must occur until a new equilibrium is reached. The new equilibrium concentrations must yield the same K value. In other words, K is constant.

The nineteenth-century French chemist Henry Le Châtelier (1850–1936) summarized observations concerning the effect of external conditions on chemical equilibriums.

LE CHÂTELIER'S PRINCIPLE

When a system at equilibrium is subjected to a stress by some imposed change in conditions, the equilibrium concentrations will attempt to change in such a way as to reduce the stress.

That principle is also useful in considering a physical equilibrium. When pressure is applied to the equilibrium system of ice $\rightleftharpoons$ water, Le Châtelier's principle allows us to predict that there will be a shift to a smaller volume to counteract the increased pressure. Since ice has a greater volume than water, we predict that ice will melt when pressure is applied to it. That prediction is verified by the experiment shown in Figure 14–3.

TEMPERATURE CHANGES · Le Châtelier's principle is useful in predicting how an equilibrium will change with temperature. Consider the following endothermic reaction.

$$0.50\ H_2(g) + 0.50\ I_2(g) \rightleftharpoons HI(g);\ \Delta H = +6.20\ \text{kcal/mol}$$

We may rewrite this reaction with the enthalpy change as a reactant.

$$6.20\ \text{kcal} + 0.50\ H_2(g) + 0.50\ I_2(g) \rightleftharpoons HI(g)$$

Le Châtelier's principle allows us to predict the effect of increasing the temperature. In effect, an increase in temperature increases the concentration of a "reactant," the enthalpy. The equilibrium state, then, should shift to favor the products. Thus, we predict that the K values for an endothermic reaction will increase with temperature. Experimentally, that can be proven to be true.

Conversely, for the exothermic reaction we predict that at higher temperatures, the equilibrium concentrations should shift in favor of the reactants.

$$0.50\ H_2(g) + 0.50\ Br_2(g) \rightleftharpoons HBr(g);\ \Delta H = -8.65\ \text{kcal/mol}$$

In such exothermic reactions, the enthalpy change can be considered a product. Higher temperatures now increase the concentration of the enthalpy "product," so that the equilibrium shifts to favor the reactants. Experiment bears out our prediction and leads to the general conclusion that K values for an exothermic reaction decrease with increasing temperature.

We can summarize the effects of changes in reaction conditions on equilibrium.

1. An increase in pressure shifts the equilibrium to the side of a lower total number of moles of gas.

$$2H_2(g) + O_2(g) \rightleftharpoons 2H_2O(g)$$

An increase in pressure decreases H_2 and O_2 and increases $H_2O(g)$.

2. An increase in the concentration of a reactant increases the concentration of the products, and decreases the concentrations of other reactants. An increase in the concentrations of a product does the reverse.

$$H_2CO_3(aq) \rightleftharpoons H^+(aq) + HCO_3^-(aq)$$

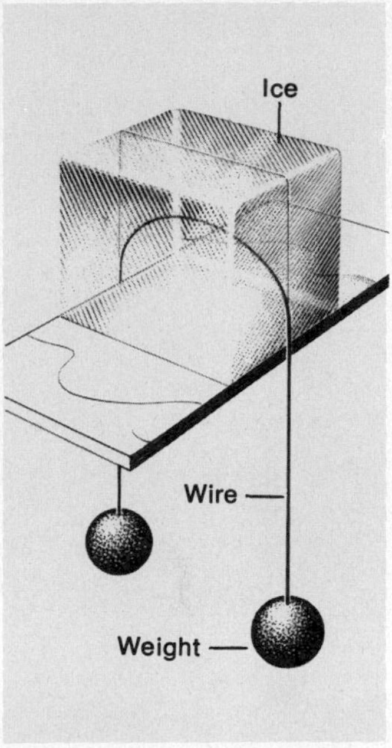

FIGURE 14–3 · *The wire cuts through the ice, but the cut refreezes. Why? (Consider Le Chatelier's principle in answering.)*

An increase in [$H^+(aq)$] will decrease [$HCO_3^-(aq)$] and increase [$H_2CO_3(aq)$]; an increase in [$H_2CO_3(aq)$] will increase both [$H^+(aq)$] and [$HCO_3^-(aq)$].

3. For an exothermic reaction, an increase in temperature decreases K and, so, decreases the concentration of the products. For an endothermic reaction, an increase in temperature increases K and, so, increases the concentration of the products.

REVIEW IT NOW

1. Why is the concentration of a pure liquid or pure solid *not* included in the equilibrium constant expression?
2. What effect does temperature have on the equilibrium constant?
3. State Le Châtelier's principle.
4. Explain how changes in pressure and concentration affect equilibrium.

ENTROPY

14–7 · Entropy: an important property of matter · Let's return to our earlier questions. Why do many reactions go to equilibrium rather than to completion? Why do endothermic reactions occur spontaneously at all? Those are very important questions. Let's see if we can find answers for them now.

Perhaps the most directly observable spontaneous endothermic processes are melting and boiling. To melt one gram of ica at 0.00°C requires the absorption of 79.0 calories. Although the change is endothermic, the ice completely melts to liquid at 0.00°C. To evaporate one gram of water to steam at 100°C requires 540 calories. And we know that water boils at that temperature. Obviously, the question of whether a change, physical or chemical, will occur spontaneously is more complex than simply deciding if there is a decrease in potential energy as measured by the endothermic nature of the change. The other factor involved in the spontaneity or nonspontaneity of change is called **entropy.**

To understand entropy, let's study what happens during melting and during boiling. A solid is a highly ordered arrangement of ions, or molecules (Figure 14–4). When a solid melts, the ordered arrangement becomes jumbled. When a liquid boils, all order is lost, and a random system of fast-moving, widely separated molecules is present in the gas. So, as energy

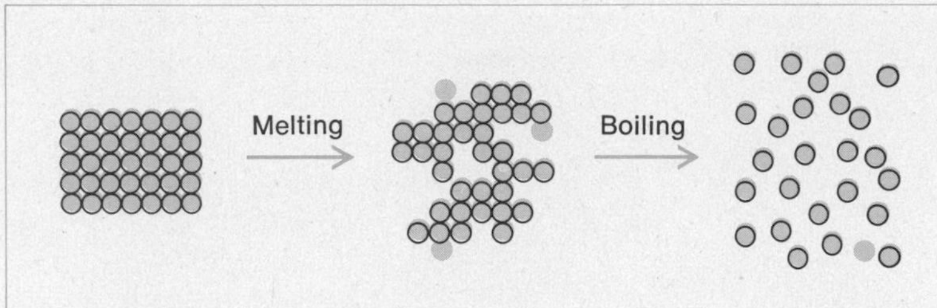

FIGURE 14–4 · *This illustration demonstrates the changes that occur in particle arrangement as a substance melts and boils.*

is added, the system becomes more disordered. Since the energy change is endothermic, it seems that the spontaneity of change must arise from the decrease in order.

Let's consider another process that occurs spontaneously without any change in energy content (Figure 14–5).

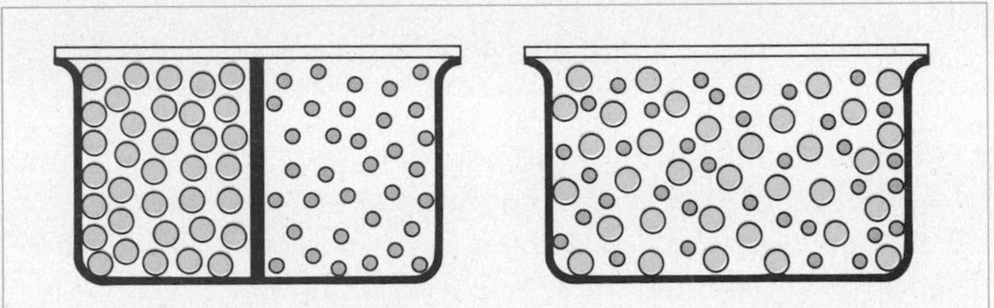

FIGURE 14–5 · *When helium and neon mix, there is no measurable energy change. Would an input of energy be required to restore the gases to their original distribution?*

Suppose helium and neon gases are in two separate containers separated by a barrier. Each compartment contains only one type of molecule—either helium or neon—so there is a certain degree of order. When the separating barrier is removed, the two gases mix spontaneously and randomly in both containers, with no observed release or absorption of enthalpy. After the barrier has been removed, such a random mixture is a much more probable state than a state in which the two gases remain unmixed.

Entropy is the measure of the randomness of a system. The symbol S represents entropy and the symbol ΔS represents a change in entropy.

14–8 · Entropy tends to increase · The universal tendency of every system is to increase its entropy—to become more disordered. Much of our technology expends energy to overcome entropy. That is, we make complex, organized machines, buildings, etc., from the disorganized raw materials of nature. But eventually buildings crumble and are destroyed. Machines wear out and rust away. The natural processes gradually diminish the order. Perhaps the simplest view of entropy is that

FIGURE 14–6 · *All substances, natural or synthetic, have a tendency to wear out or decay.*

it is the measure of the spontaneous tendency of all substances to wear out, or to decay. The recognition of that tendency is as old as humanity. The authors of Genesis recognized it when they wrote "dust thou art, and to dust thou must return." Dust is a more random state than is a living organism.

We can write some fundamental rules. Chemical reactions *tend* to occur spontaneously in the direction leading to a potential energy decrease ($\Delta H < 0$). Also, chemical reactions tend to occur spontaneously in the direction leading to an entropy increase ($\Delta S > 0$). Only through experimental knowledge of both the enthalpy change and the entropy change can the spontaneity or lack of spontaneity for a chemical reaction be predicted. But now we can answer our two questions. Many exothermic reactions go to an equilibrium state rather than to completion because the entropy change balances the enthalpy change. For example, to have iodine in both I_2 and HI is more random than having it only in either HI or I_2 in the following reaction.

$$2HI(g) \rightleftarrows H_2(g) + I_2(g)$$

So an equilibrium state with both HI and I_2 present occurs. Conversely, the endothermic reaction occurs in order to obtain the same increased randomness of having both HI and I_2 present.

$$H_2(g) + I_2(g) \rightleftarrows 2HI(g)$$

14–9 · Entropy and K · Both ΔH and ΔS influence the amount of reactant and product that is formed at equilibrium. Thus, the magnitude of the equilibrium constant K depends on both ΔH and ΔS. For the $HI-H_2-I_2$ system, $\Delta H = -8.3$ kcal/mol and K is 0.0156. For the following reaction, $\Delta H = -57.8$ kcal/mol.

$$2H_2(g) + O_2(g) \rightleftarrows 2H_2O(g)$$

Again we can expect a favorable entropy in forming H_2O, as now the H and O molecules are mixed in different molecules (H_2 and H_2O), (O_2 and H_2O). However, only two molecules of water form when three molecules (two hydrogen molecules and one oxygen molecule) react. Such a decrease in the number of molecules is a decrease in randomness. That change would represent an unfavorable entropy change. So the overall ΔS should be small, and since ΔH is so large and exothermic, K is very large.

As the temperature increases, the entropy factor increases. At very high temperatures, the entropy change is much larger than even very exothermic enthalpy changes. And reactions always tend to go in the direction of increased randomness since that represents the lower energy state.

As the temperature increases, K decreases, if ΔS favors the reactants. In fact, at ultrahigh temperatures ΔS opposes any molecules, so that above 10^5°C, only individual atoms exist.

IN SUMMARY

1. Any reaction that is exothermic and results in the formation of simpler molecules has a relatively large value of K.
2. Any reaction that is endothermic and forms more ordered molecules has a small value of K.
3. As the temperature increases, K increases for **A** but decreases for **B.**
4. The prediction of K is more difficult for endothermic reactions that form simpler molecules or exothermic reactions that form more complicated molecules.

EXCURSION NINE
Thermodynamics, Progress, and Pollution

The science of energy, Thermodynamics, and its importance in our lives and in our physical world is discussed in this excursion.

REVIEW IT NOW

1 Define *entropy*.
2 What symbol represents entropy?
3 What is the difference between *entropy* and *enthalpy*?
4 How is entropy related to *K*?

SUMMARY

The tendency in nature is to decrease energy. However, many reactions reach a state of equilibrium after a certain amount of reaction has taken place. Not all reactions go to completion. A situation often results in which both reactants and products are present, but no further change is evident. That is known as chemical equilibrium. Equilibrium is dynamic; that is, even though the total amount of reactants or products remains unchanged at equilibrium, change is occurring in both directions at an equal rate. We can write this equilibrium constant expression for a general reaction $aA + bB = cC + dD$:

$$K = \frac{C^cD^d}{A^aB^b}$$

Solids and liquids are not included in the expression for an equilibrium constant, since their concentrations do not change. The equilibrium constant varies with temperature. Le Châtelier's principle is useful in considering equilibrium. It helps us understand the effect temperature, pressure, and concentration have on the position of equilibrium. One factor that is important in determining the spontaneity of reactions is *entropy*. Entropy, S, is a measure of the randomness, or disorder, in a system. The more randomness, the higher the entropy. In the universe, entropy tends to increase. In considering reactions, one must consider the balance between entropy change and enthalpy change. Entropy also influences the magnitude of K. As the temperature increases, S increases.

REVIEW QUESTIONS

1 Write the equilibrium constant expression for the following general reaction.

$wW + xX \rightleftharpoons yY + zZ$

2 Write the equilibrium constant expression for each of the following reactions.

a. $H_2(g) + S(l) \rightleftharpoons H_2S(g)$

b. $H_2O(g) + CO(g) \rightleftharpoons H_2(g) + CO_2(g)$

c. $CaCO_3(s) \rightleftharpoons CaO(s) + CO_2(g)$

d. $COCl_2(g) \rightleftharpoons CO(g) + Cl_2(g)$

e. $4NH_3(g) + 5O_2(g) \rightleftharpoons 4NO(g) + 6H_2O(g)$

3 Consider the following reaction.

$H_2(g) + Br_2(g) \rightleftharpoons 2HBr(g)$

The K for this reaction at a particular temperature is 1.00 mol/l. The equilibrium concentration of HBr is 0.50 mol/l. Calculate the equilibrium concentration of $H_2(g)$, assuming H_2 and Br_2 are present in equal amounts.

4 Write an equilibrium constant expression to show the formation of ammonia (liquid) from nitrogen gas and hydrogen gas.

5 How does application of Le Châtelier's principle aid in the production of ammonia from its elements?

6 At 1000°C, a 1.00-l container has an equilibrium mixture consisting of 0.102 mol of ammonia, 1.03 mol of nitrogen, and 1.62 mol of hydrogen. Calculate K for the equilibrium system $N_2(g) + 3H_2(g) = 2NH_3(g)$.

7 Colorless dinitrogen tetroxide gas decomposes endothermically to form brown nitrogen dioxide gas. At 55.0°C, a 1.00-l vessel is found to contain 1.15 mol N_2O_4 gas in equilibrium with 2.00 mol NO_2 gas. Calculate the value of the equilibrium constant for the decomposition of N_2O_4 at 55.0°C.

8 How will the equilibrium concentration of N_2O_4 in question **7** be affected by the following?

a. An increase in pressure

b. An increase in temperature

c. The addition of a catalyst

SUGGESTED READINGS

Bent, Henry A. "Haste Makes Waste—Pollution and Entropy." *Chemistry*, October 1971, p. 6.

Blackburn, Thomas. *Equilibrium: A Chemistry of Solutions*. New York: Holt, Rinehart and Winston, Inc., 1969.

Morris, Daniel L. *Principles of Chemical Equilibrium*. New York: D. Van Nostrand Co., 1963.

———. "The Carbonates: An Entertainment in Equilibrium." *Chemistry*, July–August 1974, p. 6.

Fischer, Robert B., and Dennis Peters. *Chemical Equilibrium*. Philadelphia: W. B. Saunders Co., 1970.

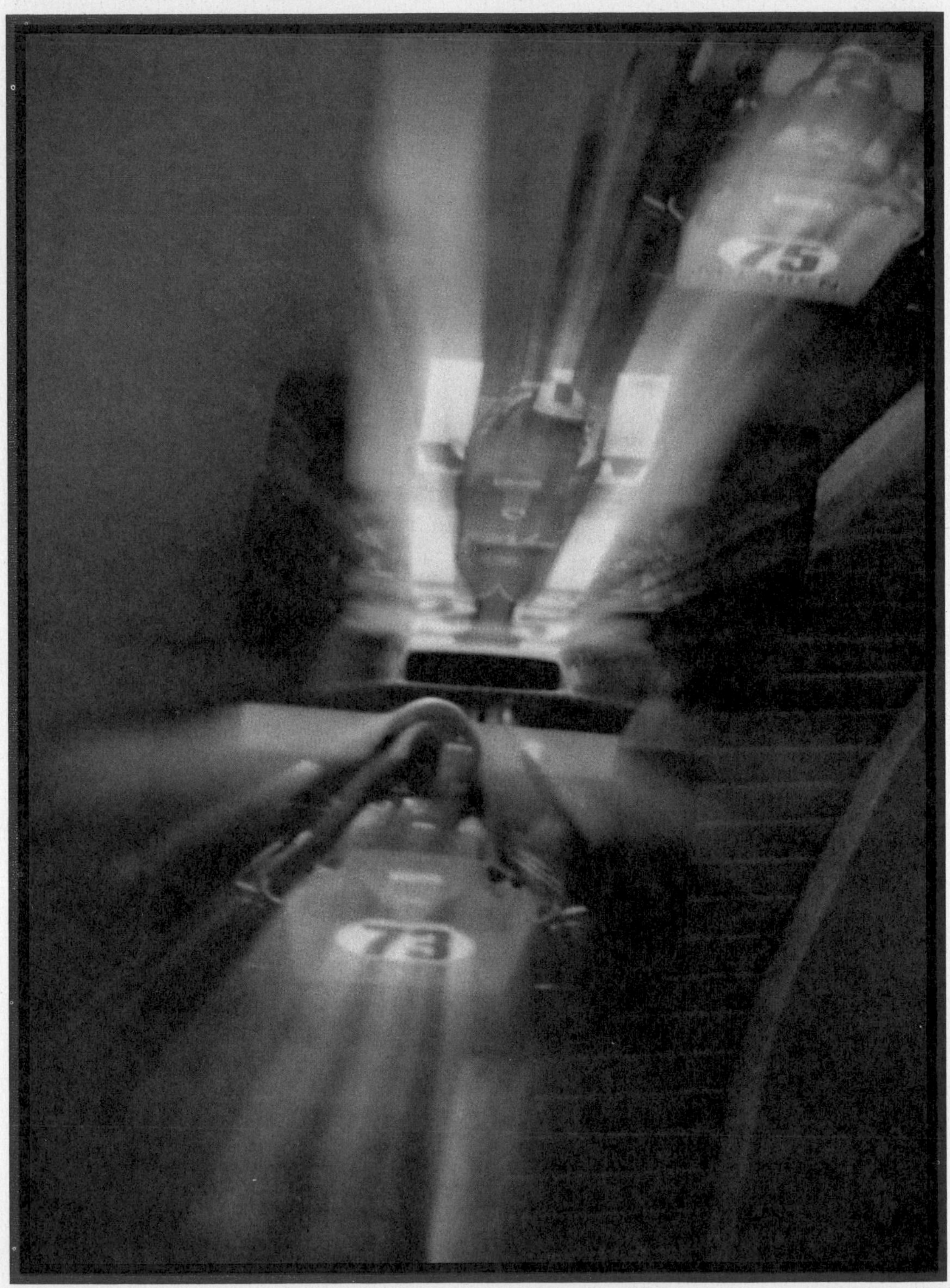

Reaction rates are important to the variety of reactions occurring around us.

CHAPTER FIFTEEN

Chemical Kinetics

In Chapters 13 and 14, we discussed the factors that are involved in determining whether or not a chemical reaction can occur spontaneously. We also learned that when a reaction occurs spontaneously, it may go to a state of equilibrium rather than to completion. Perhaps you noticed that the phrase "tends to occur spontaneously" was often used in Chapters 13 and 14. We carefully avoided using the phrase "does occur spontaneously." In fact, many reactions that we would predict should occur spontaneously actually need help to start. A very good example is the following reaction.

$$2H_2(g) + O_2(g) = 2H_2O(g);\ \Delta H = -57.8 \text{ kcal/mol}$$

The simple mixing of H_2 and O_2 does not produce a detectable amount of H_2O. But if we set off an electric spark in the gas mixture, the reaction occurs so rapidly that it actually explodes. Obviously, knowing the energy change (ΔH) alone is not enough information to predict whether or not a reaction will take place.

In Chapter 14, we learned that one aspect of chemical equilibrium is its dynamic nature. At equilibrium, both forward and reverse reactions take place simultaneously at equal rates. Therefore, there is no net change. During any period of time, the amount of forward reaction that changes reactants into products must be exactly equal to the amount of reverse reaction that changes the products back into the reactants. In other words, at equilibrium, the rate of the forward reaction must be exactly equal to the rate of the reverse reaction. By the same reasoning, before reaching equilibrium in a reaction, the rate of the forward reaction must be greater than the rate of the reverse reaction. That follows from the fact that the concentration of the products increases with time.

Reaction rates are very important in nature. To illustrate that, let's study the problem of atmospheric pollution. Much of our atmospheric pollution is caused by the nitric oxide (NO) in automobile exhausts.

$$N_2(g) + O_2(g) \rightleftharpoons 2NO(g) \qquad K = 10^{-2} \text{ at } 2500°C$$

Since the temperature in the automobile engine is around 2500°C, we expect a large amount of NO as a product. The gas cools on emission, and since the K at ordinary temperature is so small, most of the NO dissociates to N_2 and O_2. Unfortunately, the dissociation rate is very slow.

The study of the way in which a reaction actually takes place and the factors that affect the rate of reaction is known as **chemical kinetics.** In Chapter 15, we will discuss some of the things chemists have learned about the kinetics of reactions. Kinetics is one of the least studied and least understood areas of chemistry. Therefore, it represents a challenging frontier in which a great deal of research is needed.

RATES OF REACTIONS

15–1 · Some reactions are very fast · A reaction between ionic compounds dissolved in water is usually very rapid. For example, if hydrochloric acid is added to lead nitrate in solution, a white precipitate forms immediately. That is due to the following rapid reaction.

$$Pb^{+2}(aq) + 2Cl^-(aq) = PbCl_2(s)$$

Similarly, $Al(OH)_3$ is precipitated instantaneously by the reaction of Al in water.

$$Al^{+3}(aq) + 3OH^-(aq) = Al(OH)_3(s)$$

The formation of the complex anion hexafluoroaluminate, AlF_6^{-3}, is very rapid when sodium fluoride acid is added to a solution of aluminum nitrate.

$$Al^{+3}(aq) + 6F^-(aq) = AlF_6^{-3}(aq)$$

$PbCl_2$, $Al(OH)_3$, and AlF_6^{-3} are all ionic compounds, as are the $Pb(NO_3)_2$, $Al(NO_3)_3$, and NaF from which they are made. In an aqueous solution, the ionic compounds rapidly dissociate into hydrated cations and anions. The reactions are simple combinations of cations and anions usually occurring in a fraction of a second.

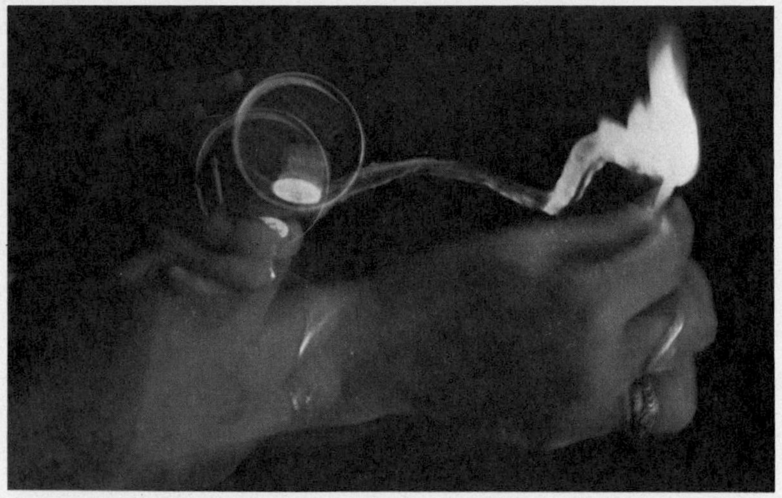

FIGURE 15–1 · *Do you think striking a match is a reaction? If so, what do you think are the products? Is the reaction fast, or slow?*

The kinetics of reactions are often poorly understood. One reason is that the techniques for studying very fast reactions are difficult and require very sophisticated equipment. Chemists have learned that reactions usually occur in a stepwise manner. The separate steps that make up an overall reaction are referred to as a **reaction mechanism.**

For example, most ionic reactions, such as the reaction that forms AlF_6^{+2}, have the following mechanism, or steps.

1. The hydrated Al^{+3} and F^- ions from their respective solutions collide with one or more H_2O molecules between them.

$$Al^{+}(H_2O)^{+3} + F(H_2O)_y^{-1} \longrightarrow [(H_2O)_z\ Al(H_2O)\ F(H_2O)_w{}^{+2}]$$

2. As the water molecules between the Al and F are eliminated, the Al and F come in direct contact. That is a slow step in the reaction mechanism relative to the first step, but still only takes a fraction of a second.

$$[H_2O]_z[Al(H_2O)\ F(H_2O)_w]^{+2} \longrightarrow AlF^{+2}(aq)$$

3. The same slow process continues as more fluorides are added. Finally, $AlF_6^{-3}(aq)$ is formed.

15–2 · Slow reactions · Reactions are not all very rapid. Some take minutes or hours to occur. Others take days or even years to reach completion. Some reactions occur so slowly that they don't seem to take place at all. The reaction of $Al^{+3}(aq) + F^-(aq)$ is very rapid even though the reaction mechanism involves two steps. The first step is a very rapid collision followed by a slower, (~ 10^{-6}s) elimination step that removes water so that the Al^{+3} and F^- ions come into direct contact.

Let's look at another reaction. This reaction involves a trivalent cation and fluoride anions.

$$Cr^{+3}(aq) + 6F^-(aq) \rightleftharpoons CrF_6^{-3}(aq)$$

The mechanism of the reaction is described by the same two-step process describing the Al^{+3}–F^- reaction. However, the reaction of $Cr^{+3} + F^-$ is much slower. It takes many hours to occur, as compared to the microseconds of the Al^{+3}–F^- reaction. Why are the rates of the two reactions so different?

One likely reason for such a difference in the behavior of Al^{+3} and Cr^{+3} is found in the bonds they form. Al^{+3} forms ionic bonds. Therefore, the second step requires breaking $Al-OH_2$ ionic bonds and forming $Al-F$ ionic bonds. The bonds formed by Cr^{+3} are much more covalent. Therefore, in that reaction, the $Cr-OH_2$ bonds that must be broken and the $Cr-F$ bonds that are formed have a high degree of covalency. Recall that ionic bonds are generally weaker than covalent bonds. Thus, it may take longer to break or form a covalent bond than an ionic bond.

Organic molecules and biological molecules are made up almost exclusively of covalent bonds. As you might guess, the reaction rates of those molecules are rarely very fast. Wine

FIGURE 15–2 · *Tarnishing and polishing silver are two types of reactions. Which of these reactions do you think is fast and which is slow? Tarnishing is an oxidation reaction. Does the word oxidation tell you anything about any element involved in this reaction? (Oxidation and reduction will be discussed in Chapter 18.)*

sours because the oxygen in the air oxidizes the ethyl alcohol in the wine to acetic acid. But wine does not sour during a meal. It sours slowly over several days, or longer, after the wine is exposed to air. Similarly, milk sours, foods cook, we sunburn (all chemical reactions of covalently bonded molecules) at measurably slow rates. From a large amount of such evidence, we can reach a very important principle of kinetics.

When reactions involve the breaking and forming of ionic bonds, the rates are often very rapid. When reactions involve the breaking and forming of covalent bonds, the rates are usually slow.

REVIEW IT NOW

1 Define *chemical kinetics.*
2 Generally, what is the relationship between bond type and the rate of a chemical reaction?

DIFFERENT FACTORS AFFECT REACTION RATE

15–3 · Increasing temperature increases reaction rate · One of the earliest chemical observations any of us can make is that reactions occur faster at higher temperatures. The higher the temperature, the faster foods cook, the faster water comes to a boil, and the faster salt and sugar dissolve. Conversely, the lower the temperature, the slower the reaction. For example, by placing food in a refrigerator, we slow down the rate at which it spoils. If we measure the rate of a chemical reaction carefully, we discover a second important principle of kinetics:

The rate of a chemical reaction approximately doubles for every 10.0°C increase in temperature. If a reaction requires 10 minutes at 35.0°C to reach equilibrium, it requires only 5 minutes at 45.0°C, or 20 minutes at 25.0°C.

Remember that the kinetic energy of molecules is directly proportional to the temperature. Increasing the temperature increases the kinetic energy. That means the molecules move about faster. If the molecules move about faster, they must collide more often. That leads to the following model for chemical reactions. A reaction occurs when molecules or ions collide. The greater the number of collisions per unit of time, the faster the reaction rate.

15–4 · The energy barrier to reaction · If we mix one mole of $H_2(g)$ and one mole of $Cl_2(g)$ molecules in a flask at 1.00 atm and 25.0°C, we will have an Avogadro number (6.02×10^{23}) of molecules of each gas per liter. That would be around 10^{20} molecules of each gas per milliliter of volume.

The chemist can calculate that within the one-milliliter volume, H_2 and Cl_2 molecules would collide 10^{28} times per second. That means that all the molecules would collide in less than 10^{-8} seconds! If all those collisions lead to reaction, it would be a very fast reaction indeed.

However, it is really a very slow reaction. Obviously, each collision does not result in a reaction. If each collision did, the reaction would be complete in much less than a microsecond.

We must reconsider the fundmental concept in our collision model for reactions. Not every collision causes a reaction. In fact, only a very small percentage of the total number of collisions leads to a reaction. In most of the collisions, the two molecules bump each other and bounce apart without a chemical reaction taking place.

Our collision model of reaction must be modified to take into account the energy of collision. For a reaction to occur, it is not enough for the molecules to merely collide. The molecules must collide with sufficient energy to break the chemical bonds. The minimum amount of energy required to break the bonds and initiate a chemical reaction is called the **activation energy.**

15–5 · The collision energy must equal or exceed the activation energy to cause reaction · Recalling our discussion of average molecular kinetic energies as a function of temperature, we can explain why relatively few molecular collisions lead to reaction. Suppose one of the molecules in a bimolecular collision has zero kinetic energy. The total collision energy in such a case is provided by the kinetic energy of the second molecule. The average kinetic energy of gas molecules increases with temperature. At any single temperature, some molecules will have a kinetic energy less than the average, while others will have a kinetic energy greater than the average. Therefore, there is a distribution of kinetic energies around an average value found for each temperature (Figure 15–3A). In our simplified case, reaction can occur in the bimolecular collision when the kinetic energy of the second molecule is equal to, or greater than, the activation energy. If the activation

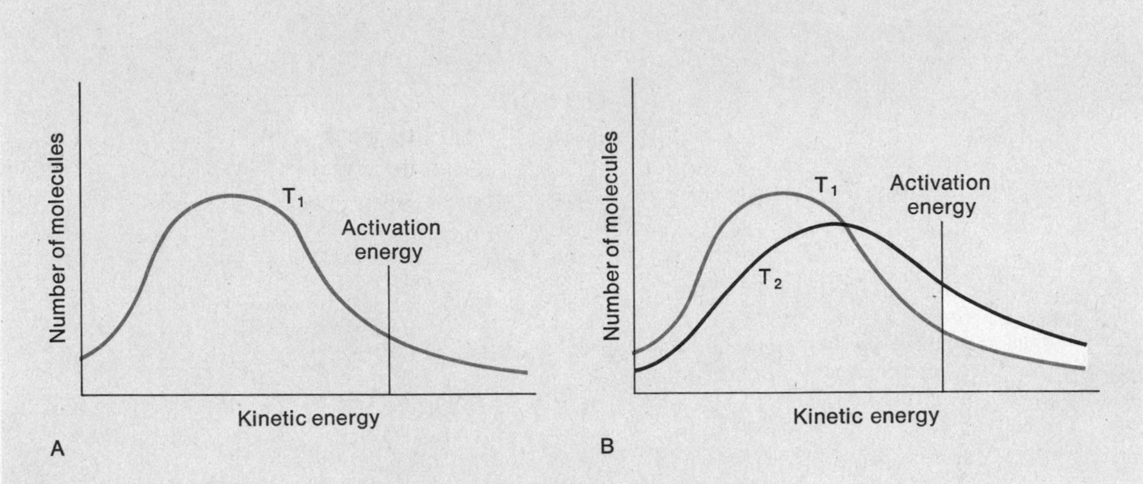

FIGURE 15–3 · *(A) Experimentally, all molecules of the same mass, at the same temperature, do not have the minimum energy required for reaction. (B) An increase in temperature results in more molecules having the minimum energy required for reaction.*

energy is high, very few molecules will have sufficient energy to bring about reaction (Figure 15–3A), and the reaction will be slow.

This model requires the collision energy to equal or exceed the activation energy for a collision to cause reaction. At a higher temperature, there are more molecules having the minimum collision energy required for reaction (Figure 15–3B). We can see this from the change in the energy-distribution curve, which has more high-energy molecules at the higher temperature. So we expect the reaction rate to increase with an increase in temperature—and that is exactly what experiment shows to be true.

15–6 · The activation energy must be overcome · The activation energy can be viewed as an energy barrier that must be overcome (Figure 15–4). That explains why many exothermic reactions do not occur spontaneously, but must be started with some initial energy. We add a spark of electricity to $H_2 + O_2$, and they react explosively. The explosion occurs because the spark pushes some molecules of H_2 and O_2 over the energy barrier, and they react. When the first molecules react, enough energy is released to cause more reaction until the reaction is complete. The reactants have an energy, H_1, and the products have an energy, H_2. The activation energy is ΔH_a. The reaction energy is ΔH_r.

We can better illustrate the energy involved in a reaction by using a graph. In our graph, we can also illustrate the

FIGURE 15–4 · *This graph is an enthalpy diagram of a chemical reaction showing the activation energy, ΔH_a, as a barrier. ΔH_r is the enthalpy of reaction.*

activation energy. The graph in Figure 15–5 shows an *exothermic* reaction. An exothermic reaction is a reaction that produces heat.

Note that a certain amount of energy, ΔH_a, must be put into the reaction before it will "go." When the reaction occurs, the same amount of energy is released together with additional energy, ΔH_r. The energy ΔH_r is the heat, or enthalpy, actually produced by the reaction. Note that the products, C and D, have a much lower energy than the reactants, A and B.

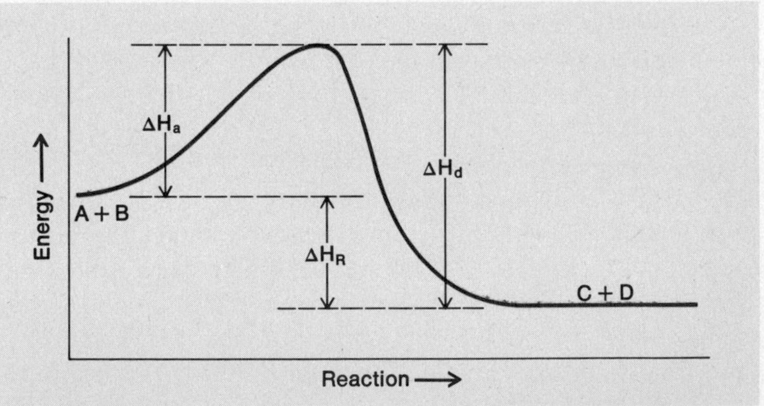

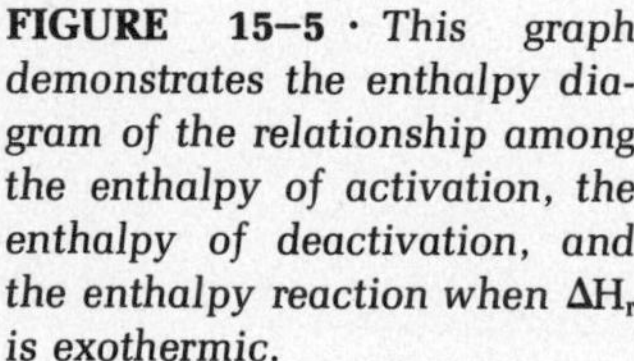

FIGURE 15–5 · *This graph demonstrates the enthalpy diagram of the relationship among the enthalpy of activation, the enthalpy of deactivation, and the enthalpy reaction when ΔH_r is exothermic.*

Now let's look at a graph showing an endothermic reaction. We know that an endothermic reaction requires an input of heat. Thus, the products can be expected to be at a higher energy level than the reactants. That is obvious from the graph.

Also, we see from the graph that we must subtract the energy lost as the activation complex decomposes (ΔH_d) in order to obtain the net energy gain in the endothermic reaction.

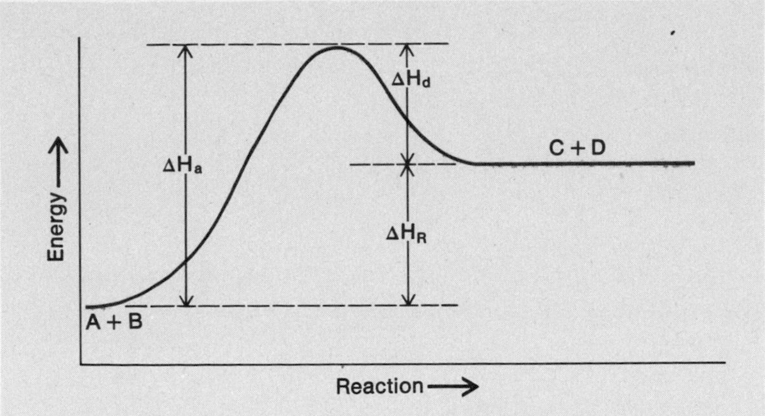

FIGURE 15–6 · *This graph demonstrates the enthalpy diagram of the relationship among the enthalpy of activation, the enthalpy of deactivation, and the enthalpy reaction when ΔH_r is endothermic.*

15–7 · Effect of concentration on reaction rate: rate laws · We have learned that molecules must collide with an energy equal to, or greater than, the activation energy. We have also learned that the kind of chemical bonds that are broken in a reaction affect the overall reaction rate. Another factor that can affect reaction rates is the concentration of the reactants.

In 1867, Cato Guldberg (1836–1902) and Peter Waage (1833–1900), professors at the University of Oslo in Norway, demonstrated that the rate of a chemical reaction is proportional to the product of the concentrations of the reactants. If the concentration of either or both reactants increases, the rate of the reaction will increase. Thus, combustion that occurs slowly in air (21 percent O_2) will occur much more rapidly in pure oxygen. That may be tested easily by observing a glowing splint when it is moved from air into a sample of pure oxygen.

We may consider the quantitative dependence of reaction rates by returning to the reaction between H_2 and Cl_2 in the gas phase. Experimentally, it is found that a mixture of H_2 and Cl_2, each at a partial pressure of 0.50 atm, reacts at a certain rate. If, in another mixture of H_2 and Cl_2, the H_2 is at a partial pressure of 1.00 atm while the Cl_2 remains at 0.50 atm, the measured reaction rate will be twice as fast as that of the first mixture. Remember that the partial pressure of a gas is, in effect, a measure of its concentration. Doubling the partial pressure, or the concentration, of H_2 has doubled the reaction rate. So the rate is proportional to the concentration of H_2.

$$\text{Rate} \propto [H_2]$$

The square bracket is used to symbolize the concentration of a substance expressed in moles per liter (mol/l).

If you study a third mixture, in which the partial pressure of H_2 is held at 0.50 atm but the partial pressure of Cl_2 is 1.00 atm, the rate is again found to be double that of the first mixture.

$$\text{Rate} \propto [Cl_2]$$

By combining results, we determine that the rate of the reaction between H_2 and Cl_2 in the gas phase is proportional to the product of the concentrations of both gases.

$$\text{Rate} \propto [H_2][Cl_2]$$

or

$$\text{Rate} = k[H_2][Cl_2]$$

The proportionality constant, *K*, is known as the **reaction-rate constant.** The entire expression is known as the **reaction-rate law.** It is an experimentally derived expression.

When the H_2-Br_2 gas phase reaction is studied, a free-radical chain-reaction mechanism similar to that of the H_2-Cl_2 reaction is deduced. Yet for the simple stoichiometry

$$H_2(g) + Br_2(g) \longrightarrow 2HBr(g)$$

the experimental rate law is found to be the following.

$$\text{Rate} = \frac{k[H_2][Br_2]0.50}{k' + \dfrac{[HBr]}{[Br_2]}}$$

Note the important point that it is not possible to deduce the rate law from the stoichiometric equation. The kinetic properties of a reaction system cannot be predicted from the overall equation. They must be experimentally determined. Moreover, reactions with similar net equations can have very different mechanisms.

The dependence of the reaction rate on the reactant concentration is easily understood by knowing that molecules must collide to react. Increasing the number of molecules in a certain volume increases the frequency of collision and, thus, increases the rate of reaction.

15–8 · Determination of the mechanism of a reaction · At the beginning of Chapter 15, we stated that the sequence of steps involved in the overall reaction is known as the *reaction* *mechanism*. Frequently, it is extremely difficult to determine the correct reaction mechanism. From a measurement of the change that occurs in the reaction rate as changes occur in the concentration of the various reactants, it may be possible to deduce the slow, rate-determining step. If only a few steps are involved in the total reaction mechanism, the knowledge of the slow step may allow the chemist to suggest the other steps.

The determination of a reaction mechanism still requires careful, imaginative experimentation. One of the challenging facets of the study of reaction mechanisms is our present inability to accurately predict the mechanism from the net reaction equation. As an example of a mechanism, let us return to a familiar reaction.

$$H_2(g) + I_2(g) \longrightarrow 2HI(g)$$

For the last fifty years, most chemistry texts have stated that this reaction has a simple, one-step mechanism involving bimolecular collisions between hydrogen and iodine molecules. However, new research results show that the mechanism is actually quite different and much more complex. This reaction probably has a mechanism that is similar to the reaction between hydrogen and chlorine gas.

$$H_2(g) + Cl_2(g) \longrightarrow 2HCl(g)$$

This reaction involves a **chain mechanism** in which a sequence of reactions occur like links in a chain. The initial reaction, the **chain-initiating step,** involves the dissociation of chlorine molecules into chlorine atoms when the radiant energy is absorbed.

$$Cl_2 + h\nu \longrightarrow 2Cl$$

$Cl_2 + h\nu \longrightarrow 2Cl$ occurs whenever $Cl_2(g)$ is exposed to light of sufficient energy. The energetic chlorine atoms are very reactive **free radicals.** They have an unpaired electron, but no net charge. The chlorine atoms become involved in **chain-propagating steps** when they collide with hydrogen molecules.

$$Cl + H_2 \longrightarrow HCl + H$$
$$H + Cl_2 \longrightarrow HCl + Cl$$

In these chain-propagating steps the generation of free radicals continues.

As long as there are chlorine and hydrogen free radicals present, the chain reaction proceeds, and hydrogen chloride molecules are continually formed. However, there are some chain-breaking reactions that fail to produce new free radicals to keep the chain going. Such **chain-breaking steps** follow.

$$Cl + Cl \longrightarrow Cl_2$$
$$H + H \longrightarrow H_2$$
$$H + Cl \longrightarrow HCl$$

In summary, we may hypothesize the following complex, four-step chain-reaction mechanism for the formation of HCl from H_2 and Cl_2 in the gas state.

$$\begin{array}{l} 1.\ Cl_2 + h\nu \longrightarrow 2Cl \\ 2.\ Cl + H_2 \longrightarrow HCl + H \\ 3.\ H + Cl_2 \longrightarrow HCl + Cl \\ 4.\ Cl + Cl \longrightarrow Cl_2 \\ \hline \text{Net: } Cl_2 + H_2 \xrightarrow{h\nu} 2HCl \end{array}$$

This reaction again illustrates how unlikely it is that the reaction mechanism can be deduced from the net chemical change.

15–9 · Reaction rates have very practical applications · It has been suggested that certain hydrocarbons called *freons* that are released into the atmosphere from aerosols were reacting with the ozone (O_3) layer in the upper atmosphere. That has serious implications, since the O_3 layer is primarily responsible for protecting us from the sun's damaging ultraviolet radiation. One type of freon is called fluorocarbon-11. It is used as a propellant in aerosol sprays such as paint, deodorant, and hair spray. Many environmentalists and chemists feared that this would have disastrous effects. Some states even banned the use of the aerosol sprays that used freons.

It was necessary for chemists to determine the mechanism of the reaction for freon and ozone so that the problem could be understood. One suggested mechanism was that the fluorocarbon released into the atmosphere is decomposed by sunlight into a simpler fluorocarbon and two chlorine atoms.

$$\begin{array}{c} F \\ | \\ Cl{-}C{-}Cl \\ | \\ Cl \end{array} \xrightarrow{\text{sunlight}} CFCl + 2Cl$$

The Cl atom, which is very reactive, reacts with ozone to form oxygen gas and another compound, ClO.

$$Cl + O_3 \longrightarrow ClO + O_2$$

Note, however, that this reaction occurs twice for each molecule of freon, since the first reaction produced two moles of Cl.

The ClO, also very reactive, reacts with atomic oxygen, O, to produce oxygen gas and another reactive Cl atom.

$$ClO + O \longrightarrow Cl + O_2$$

This Cl reacts with another O_3, as shown in the second reaction, and the process continues. Perhaps you can see how that mechanism does indeed suggest that O_3 would soon be depleted. Fortunately, ozone is replenished by the action of sunlight on oxygen molecules, producing oxygen atoms that in turn combine with molecular oxygen.

$$O_2 \xrightarrow{\text{sunlight}} O + O$$

$$O + O_2 \longrightarrow O_3$$

Chemists are still trying to solve the freon–ozone problem in order to determine the danger of freon to the ozone layer. Their research involves much of what you are studying here.

15–10 · Summary of kinetics · Let's summarize what has been discussed about the kinetics of reactions with the six points that follow.

1. The rate of reaction is dependent on the concentration of reactants.

2. The rate of reaction increases with temperature.

3. There is an energy barrier to reaction.

The three observations are consistent with a reaction model in which the reaction rate increases as the number of collisions increases. The energy involved in the collisions must exceed the activation-energy barrier.

4. In a reaction that has several steps in its mechanism, the rate is determined by the rate of the slowest step. That is common experience. In any sequence of events, the whole process can only be as fast as the slowest step.

5. It is unlikely that the mechanism can be deduced simply from the net chemical reaction.

15–11 · Heterogeneous and homogeneous catalysis · Solid manganese dioxide increases the rate of the decomposition of aqueous hydrogen peroxide.

$$H_2O_2(aq) \xrightarrow{MnO_2(s)} H_2O(l) + 0.50\ O_2(g)$$

The rate of many gas phase reactions is increased by certain solids. Materials that increase the rate of chemical reactions but are not involved with the net chemical equation are known as catalysts. One industrial method for manufacturing sulfuric acid involves oxidizing sulfur dioxide to sulfur trioxide. Solid vanadium pentoxide is used as a catalyst.

$$2SO_2(g) + O_2(g) \xrightarrow{V_2O_5(s)} 2SO_3(g)$$

A **heterogeneous catalyst** is one that is not in the same physical state as the reactants. Presumably with a heterogeneous catalyst, a reactant forms weak chemical bonds with the surface of the catalyst. This process is known as **chemisorption.** Chemisorption is the process that allows the reactants to react with a lower activation energy. As a result, the reaction rate is increased as more collisions have an energy greater than the activation energy.

If the catalyst is in the same physical form as the reactants, it is termed a **homogeneous catalyst.** In the lead chamber process, a second industrial method for manufacturing sulfuric acid, the oxidation of SO_2 gas to SO_3 is catalyzed by nitrogen dioxide gas, NO_2.

$$2SO_2(g) + O_2(g) \xrightarrow{NO_2(g)} 2SO_3(g)$$

The reaction between solutions of thallium(I) chloride and cerium(IV) chloride is catalyzed by a small amount of aqueous manganese(II) chloride.

$$TlCl(aq) + 2CeCl_4(aq) \xrightarrow{MnCl_2(aq)} TlCl_3(aq) + 2CeCl_3(aq)$$

In both of the homogeneously catalyzed reactions, it is probable that the catalyst becomes chemically involved in a sequence of steps involving bimolecular collisions only. The uncatalyzed reactions might involve termolecular steps in their reaction mechanisms. Since termolecular collisions occur much less frequently than bimolecular ones, the catalyst results in a faster reaction rate.

EXCURSION TEN
How Do Reactions Go?

This excursion discusses reaction rates in greater detail.

Catalysts are used extensively in industrial processes. To a large extent, the selection of a catalyst appropriate to a given reaction involves guesswork. Unraveling catalytic mechanisms is important not merely in industry but in life itself. It is now realized that almost all reactions that occur within living cells are catalyzed by substances known as **enzymes.** There is still much to be learned about catalytic mechanisms.

REVIEW IT NOW

1. What effect on the rate of a reaction is produced by increasing the temperature of the reaction by 10.0°C?
2. Explain the collision model for chemical kinetics.
3. What is the activation energy?
4. Why must we consider the *average* kinetic energy of molecules in using the collision model?
5. What effect does a change in concentration have on the reaction rate?
6. Is it possible to predict the reaction mechanism from a chemical equation?
7. How are the kinetic properties of a reaction determined?
8. Which step in a reaction is the rate-determining step?
9. What effect does a catalyst have on the reaction rate?
10. What is a heterogeneous catalyst? a homogeneous catalyst?
11. Define *chemisorption.*

SUMMARY

From a knowledge of thermodynamic properties we can predict whether a certain reaction should occur. But, we cannot predict the rate of the reaction. Reaction rates range from essentially instantaneous to extremely slow. Reaction rates depend on the nature of the reacting substances, the temperature, and the concentration of reactants, and sometimes of products.

Measurement of the reaction rate leads to a reaction-rate law showing the dependency of the rate on the concentration of substances in the reaction system. This rate law may allow the deduction of the reaction mechanism. The reaction-rate laws and reaction mechanisms cannot be predicted from reaction stoichiometries.

A theory of reaction rates has been developed which assumes bimolecular collisions of reacting species. In such collisions, energies equal to or in excess of the activation energy of the reaction occur. An energy state exists that corresponds to a transition state between reactants and products. It may not be possible to determine the nature of the activated complex that exists only in this transition state. The concentration and temperature dependencies of reaction rates, as well as the phenomenon of catalysis is explained by this theory of reaction rates.

REVIEW QUESTIONS

1 How is collision frequency related to each of the following?

a. Temperature

b. Pressure

c. Concentration of reactant

2 Find at least one example of a process occurring around your school that involves several steps. Determine which of the steps is the rate-determining step.

(Example: The lunchroom might be an example. What (or who) is the rate-determining step in this case?)

3 A certain reaction is complete in 12 minutes when carried out at 50°C.

a. If you wished to do the same experiment in 6 minutes, at what temperature should the reaction be carried out?

b. How long would it take the same reaction to occur at a temperature of 30.0°C?

4 You can cause many powders, such as coal dust, to explode in air. Yet a large lump of coal burns slowly. Explain this.

5 In many places in the text, you have seen the following equation for the formation of water.

$$2H_2 + O_2 = 2H_2O$$

Explain why it is not likely that the reaction occurs in a single step.

6 Consider the following reactions as they occur at room temperature.

$Ag^+(aq) + Cl^-(aq) \rightleftharpoons AgCl(s)$

$2H_2(g) + O_2(g) \rightleftharpoons 2H_2O(g)$

$C_{12}H_{22}O_{11}(s) + 12O_2(s) \rightleftharpoons 12CO_2(s) + 11H_2O(g)$

a. Which of the above reactions are likely to be slow?

b. Which of the above reactions would be extremely fast?

7 The following diagram shows the potential energy for a hypothetical reaction. $Br + H_2 \rightleftharpoons HBr + H$

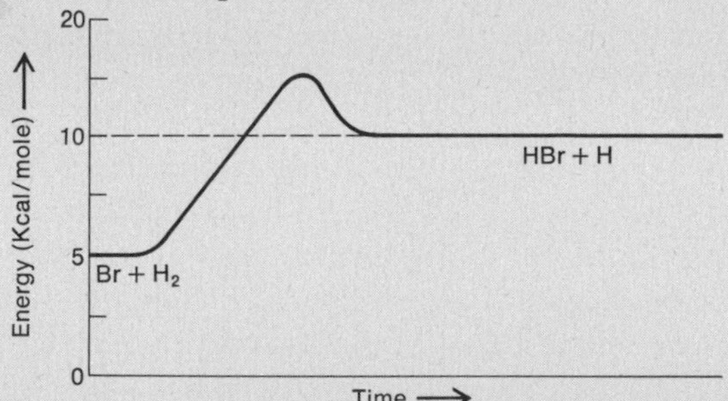

a. What is the enthalpy of reaction, ΔH, for the formation of the products?

b. What is the energy of activation for the forward reaction?

c. What is the energy of activation for the reverse reaction?

d. Is the reaction as shown endothermic, or exothermic?

e. How would the graph look if a catalyst were added?

f. Which part of the graph represents the activated complex?

8 Some automobiles have catalytic converters in the exhaust system. They were added because unburned gasoline and carbon monoxide were leaving exhaust and polluting the atmosphere. How would such catalytic converters work?

9 A certain nuclear power plant uses water from a local river as a coolant. It releases the water back into the river unchanged, except that the discharged water is 5.00°C warmer. Explain, in terms of chemical kinetics, what effect this might have.

SUGGESTED READINGS

Campbell, J. Arthur. *Why Do Chemical Reactions Occur?* Englewood Cliffs, N.J.: Prentice-Hall Inc., 1965.

Edwards, John O. *Inorganic Reaction Mechanisms*. New York: W. A. Benjamin Co., 1964.

Eyring and Eyring. *Modern Chemical Kinetics*. New York: D. Van Nostrand Co., 1963.

King, E. L. *How Chemical Reactions Occur*. New York: W. A. Benjamin Co., 1965.

Yohe, G. R. "The Catalyst." *Chemistry*, September 1973, p. 8.

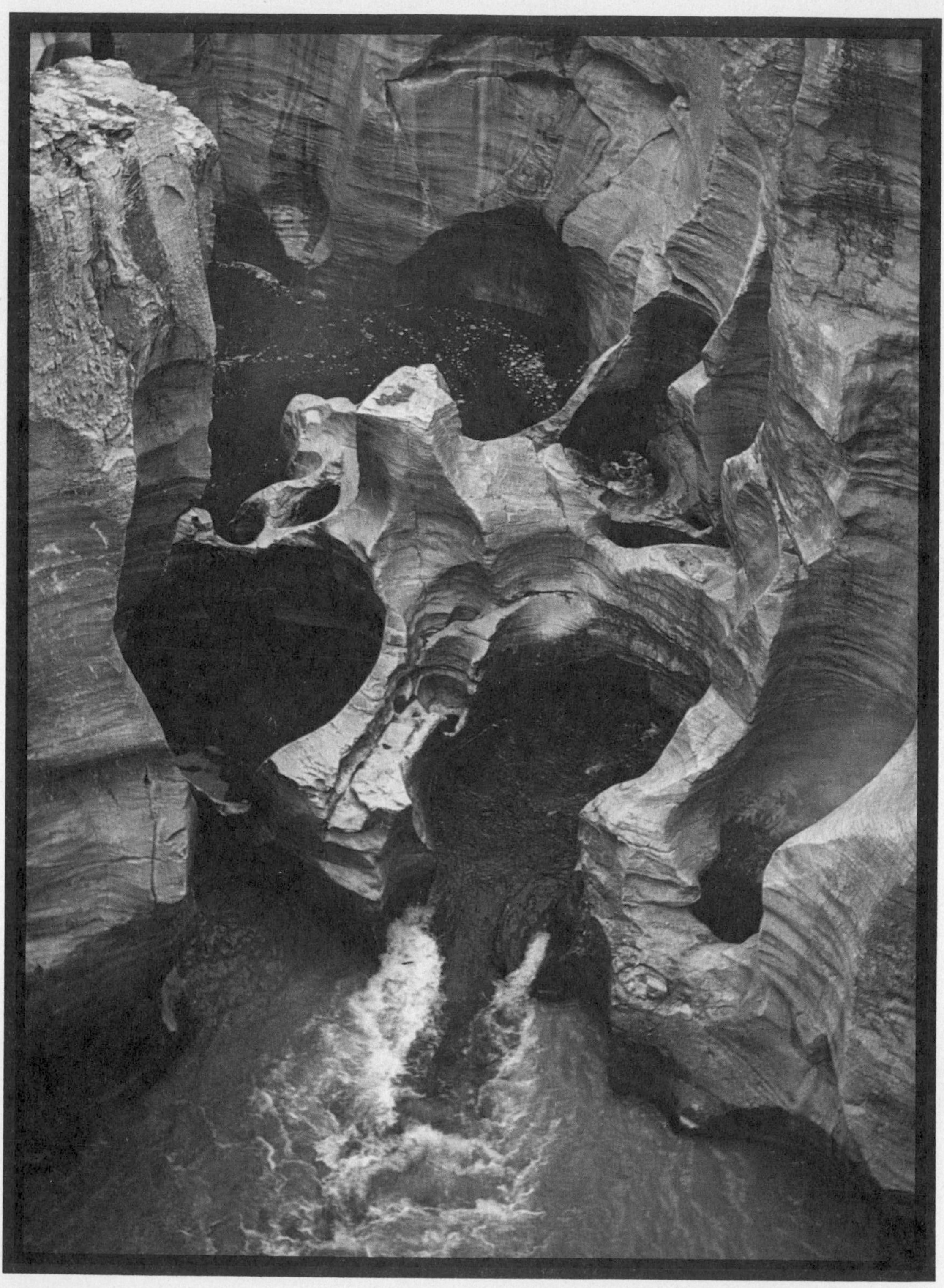

The power of water is illustrated in this eroded rock formation.

CHAPTER SIXTEEN

Water and Ionic Solutions

To Apollo astronauts returning from the moon, the earth seemed a small oasis in a bleak, hostile universe. The earth is neither a hot, baked desert nor a cold, barren wasteland. Instead, it is a world of unique beauty, moderately comfortable climates, and a fantastic variety of life. If you were asked which compound, more than any other, makes our world the small oasis the Apollo astronauts described, your answer should be water. Water covers almost three fourths of the earth's surface. It determines our climate, shapes our geology, and sustains our life. In Chapter 16, we will study water and see how one compound is capable of determining what our world is like.

SOME PHYSICAL PROPERTIES OF WATER

16–1 · Density · One of the most fascinating aspects of the very common substance water is its uncommon properties. Earlier, you learned that water should really be a gas and not a liquid at our normal temperatures on the earth. However, because of the weak hydrogen bonds between water molecules, water remains a liquid until the temperature reaches 100° C.

The high boiling point of water is only one of its surprising, but very important, properties. Most solids are heavier than their liquid form. Water is different. Its solid form, ice, has a *lower* density than the liquid. Imagine how different the world would be if water behaved normally, and ice sank rather than floated in water. If ice had sunk as it formed on the oceans during the past history of the earth, the water of the oceans would have insulated the ice from warming conditions. Eventually,

FIGURE 16–1 · *What does the fact that this iceberg is floating tell you about the densities of liquid and solid water?*

there would have been a gradual decrease in the temperature of the oceans, and part of the world might be frozen over today. Also, the lower density of ice means that water expands in volume as it freezes. That is why you must be careful not to let the water in your automobile cooling system freeze. If it does, the pressure of expansion can cause the engine block to crack. The same pressure of expansion causes rocks in the mountains to fracture when water freezes in small cracks. Most of the weathering of mountains, which gives form to our physical world, is caused by the freezing and expanding of water. Another example of the effect of freezing water is the breaking up of sidewalks. That is caused by water freezing and expanding in cracks in the cement.

16–2 · Specific heat of water · Another unusual property of water is the high value of its **specific heat.** The specific heat of a substance is the amount of energy required to raise the temperature of 1.00 gram of that substance 1.00°C. Water is used to define the calorie. Then by definition, the specific heat of water is 1.00 calorie/gram-degree (cal/g-deg) at 15.0°C. In contrast, at the same temperature, the specific heat of mercury is only 0.033 cal/g-deg, and that of benzene is only 0.41 cal/g-deg.

On a gram-for-gram basis, water absorbs more heat energy per degree than most other substances. That has led to its extensive use as the coolant in automobile engines. For the same reason, it is widely used in home heating systems. Most important, however, is the moderating effect of the unusually high specific heat of water on our climate. In a desert area, there is usually a great difference in temperature between nighttime and daytime. But where there is water—a coastal land or an area near a lake—the difference between nighttime and daytime temperatures is much less. The daytime temperature does not rise as high because the high specific heat of water causes a smaller increase in temperature for the absorption of the same amount of heat. Then at night, the stored energy in water is released with a smaller decrease in temperature.

16–3 · A model for liquid water · Let's consider some of the things that scientists have learned about water. Then we can see how they have used those facts to develop a model for water.

The structure of ice can be determined by studying how X rays are deflected as they pass through ice crystals. In each H_2O molecule in ice, the two hydrogen atoms are attracted by the oxygen that is bonded to the hydrogen atoms of two other H_2O molecules. Also, the oxygen atom of H_2O attracts one hydrogen atom from each of two other H_2O molecules. So each H_2O molecule has four other H_2O molecules held to it by hydrogen bonds. Those four H_2O molecules are grouped around the central H_2O molecule in a tetrahedral arrangement, as shown in Figure 16–2. Ice consists of a three-dimensional network of H_2O molecules, each molecule bonded by hydrogen bonds to four other H_2O molecules.

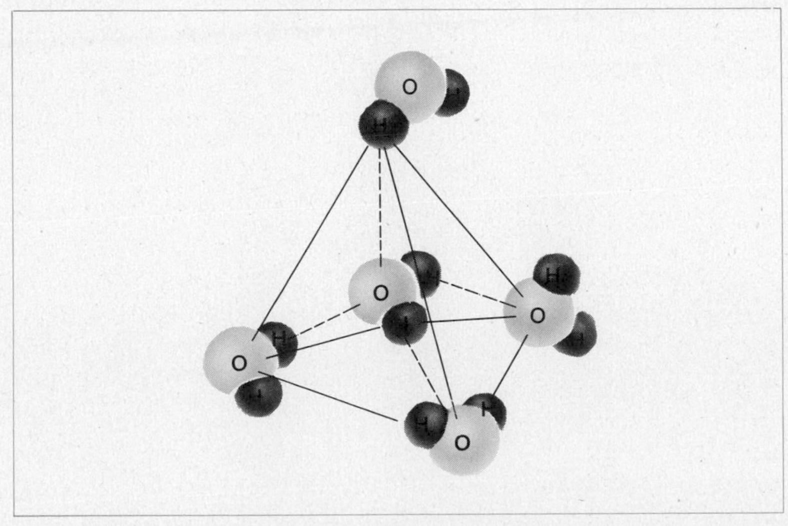

FIGURE 16–2 · *This illustrates the tetrahedral arrangement of water molecules. The central H_2O molecule has four other H_2O molecules held to it by hydrogen bonds. The hydrogen bonds are shown by dashed lines.*

Ice is less dense than liquid water. Suppose enough energy is added to break the hydrogen bonds in the ice network. Then the whole network can be compressed, since the H_2O molecules next to one another can be pushed closer together. If that happens, there are more H_2O molecules in one cm^3 of the broken structure than there are in ice. In that situation, the density of the broken structure is greater than the density of ice.

The following is a model of liquid water. When ice melts, some hydrogen bonds break. The H_2O molecules, now with less than four hydrogen bonds, are closer together. While ice is essentially one giant hydrogen-bonded structure, liquid water is formed of groups of hydrogen-bonded molecules. Those groups vary from very large groups with hundreds of H_2O molecules, to much smaller groups of just two or three H_2O molecules. Thus, the true formula for water would be $(H_2O)_x$, where x can be any integral number. But for the purpose of simplicity, the formula for water is usually expressed as H_2O.

Another interesting property of liquid water is that its density increases from 0°C to 4.00°C, then begins to decrease at 4.00°C. It continues to decrease as the temperature increases (Figure 16 – 3). That can easily be explained by our model of liquid water. As the temperature increases, more hydrogen bonds break, and the icelike groups of molecules in the liquid break down into even smaller units. At the same time, the groups of molecules and the single molecules gain kinetic energy. The increased molecular motion causes the liquid to expand as the molecules push one another away. From 0°C to 4.00°C, the collapsing of the rigid ice structure is the important effect, and the density of water increases between those temperatures. Above 4.00°C, the increased molecular-motion effect dominates, and

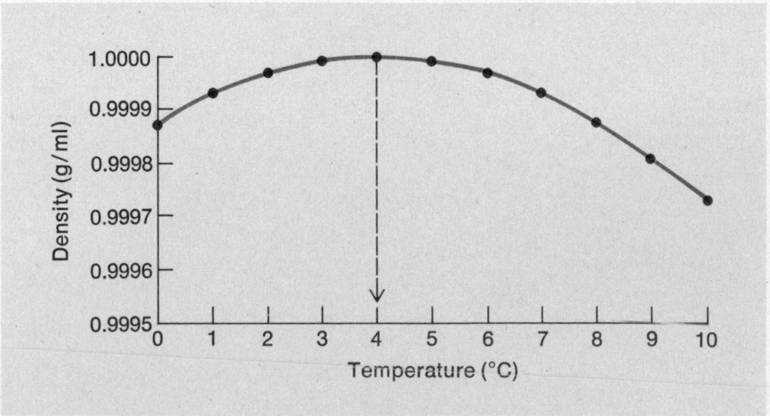

FIGURE 16–3 · *The density of water between 0°C and 10°C*

the liquid expands in volume, thereby decreasing in density. At 4.00°C, when the two opposing effects balance each other, water exhibits its maximum density of 1.00 gram/milliliter.

REVIEW IT NOW

1 Give three properties of water that make it an atypical liquid.
2 Define *specific heat.*
3 What effect does the high specific heat of water have on climate?
4 Describe models for water in the liquid and solid state.
5 What is the significance of 4.00°C in Figure 16–3?
6 How can we explain the unusual density characteristics of liquid water?

SOME CHEMICAL PROPERTIES OF WATER

16–4 · Water is a stable compound · Water cannot be decomposed easily because the covalent O–H bonds are high-energy bonds. Water does not even begin to decompose thermally into hydrogen and oxygen until a temperature of 1000°C is reached. Even at 2500°C, only 2 percent of water is decomposed.

At ordinary temperatures, water reacts violently with the chemically *active metals,* such as sodium and potassium, to liberate hydrogen gas.

$$Na(s) + H_2O(l) = NaOH(aq) + 0.50H_2(g)$$

At higher temperatures, less active metals, such as zinc, will react with steam to liberate H_2 gas. In such cases, the oxide of the metal is formed.

$$Zn(s) + H_2O(g) = ZnO(s) + H_2(g)$$

The oxygen of water may be chemically liberated by a reaction with very active nonmetals. Fluorine gas will react violently with water to liberate O_2 gas.

$$F_2(g) + H_2O(l) = 2HF(aq) + O_2(g)$$

16–5 · Heavy water · Recall that a small amount of hydrogen exists as "heavy hydrogen" (^2H, or deuterium). Water that is formed from oxygen and deuterium is known as "heavy water." Deuterium oxide is present in ordinary water to the extent of about one part in 6000. It can be separated from ordinary water

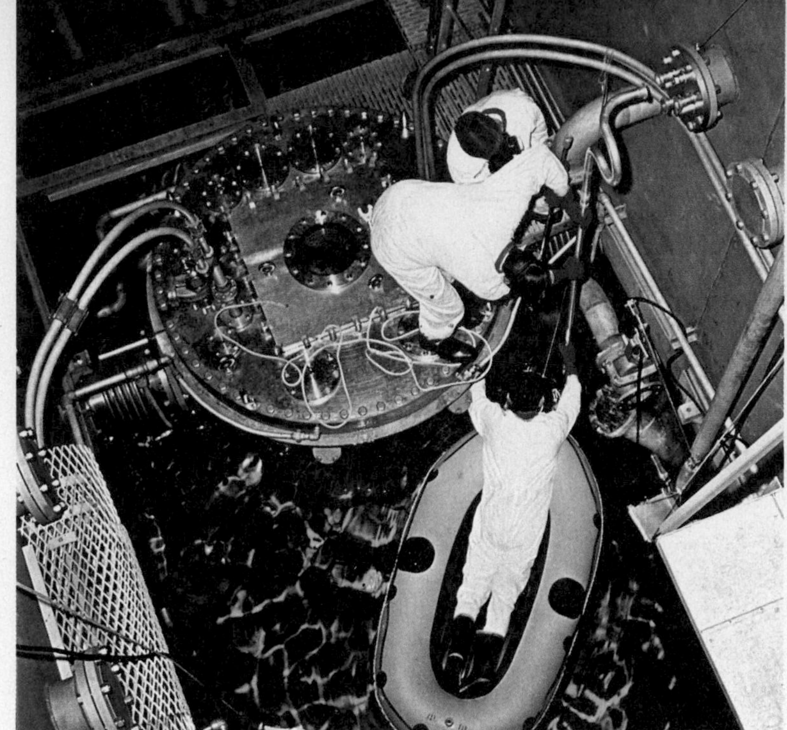

FIGURE 16–4 · *The water in the swimming-pool type of nuclear reactor is heavy water, D_2O.*

by electrolysis or distillation. D_2O has a slightly higher melting and boiling point, as well as a higher density, than H_2O. The maximum density of liquid D_2O occurs at 11.6°C rather than at 4.00°C, where it occurs for liquid H_2O. That is because of the greater molecular mass of D_2O.

Heavy water is used mainly as a neutron moderator in swimming-pool-type nuclear reactors and in modern scientific research. That will be discussed in more detail in Chapter 17. D_2O is very similar in chemical properties to H_2O. However, it has some different physiological effects and is toxic to many organisms.

FIGURE 16–5 · *A model of a hydrogen peroxide molecule*

16–6 · Hydrogen peroxide · The chemical stability of H_2O has a direct influence on the chemical behavior of the related compound hydrogen peroxide, H_2O_2. H_2O_2 is a polar molecule with the two oxygens bonded together and a hydrogen bonded to each oxygen (Figure 16–5). Hydrogen peroxide is useful because it decomposes readily into water and oxygen.

$$H_2O_2(l) \rightarrow H_2O(l) + 0.50O_2(g)$$

The rate of this reaction is increased greatly by heat, light, or a catalyst such as charcoal.

Some colored compounds lose their color when they are oxidized. Fibers containing compounds that give them their color can be bleached by exposure to atomic oxygen. Hydrogen peroxide is used as an oxidizing agent to bleach, or decolorize, cotton goods, wool, wood pulp, and some wood used for furniture, as well as silk, hair, feathers, glue, and other animal substances.

Many bacteria are killed when exposed to oxygen. Therefore, hydrogen peroxide is used as a household antiseptic. The household product is mostly water with a small amount (usually 3 percent) of hydrogen peroxide dissolved in it. It also contains an inhibitor, which retards the decomposition of the hydrogen peroxide.

FIGURE 16–6 · *Hydrogen peroxide is used in the fabric industry for bleaching raw materials.*

REVIEW IT NOW

1 Under what conditions will water produce hydrogen gas? oxygen gas?
2 What are some of the properties of heavy water?
3 How do we account for the physical properties of deuterium oxide?
4 Describe several uses for H_2O_2.

SOLUTIONS, SOLUTES, AND SOLVENTS

16–7 · Water, the universal solvent · Perhaps the property of water that sets it apart from other liquids is its ability to dissolve so many other substances. In Chapter 1, we learned that a solution is a homogeneous mixture. In such a mixture, the substance that is present in greater amounts is called the **solvent.** We can define the solvent as the substance in which a second substance dissolves. The second substance, which is dissolved in the solvent, is termed the **solute.**

Gases can dissolve in other gases (air is considered a solution of the solute O_2, 21 percent, in the solvent N_2, 79 percent). Gases can also dissolve in liquids (soft drinks have the solute CO_2 dissolved in the solvent water) or even in solids (H_2 dissolves in palladium metal). You can certainly name many common examples of liquids dissolved in liquids and of solids dissolved in liquids. Metal alloys such as steel, bronze, and brass are examples of solids dissolved in solids.

Because of its polar structure, water can attract and hold other polar molecules in solution. Sugar, alcohol, and ammonia are only three examples of the polar solids, liquids, and gases that can dissolve in water (Figure 16–7). The negative (oxygen)

FIGURE 16–7 · *Three different types of solutions. What gas do you think is present in the carbonated beverage? The teapot demonstrates solids dissolved in solids: brass and pewter. A solid bouillon cube is dissolving in water in the teacup.*

end of the dipolar water molecule interacts with the positive end of the dipolar solute molecule. The positive (hydrogen) end of the H_2O molecule interacts with the negative end of the solute. In ionic solids such as sodium chloride, cations and anions are already present in the solid. The attraction of the solvent water molecules to the solute is called **hydration.** Hydration results in a layer of water molecules around the cation, and another layer around the anion. The hydration layers insulate the cations and anions from one another, and they move apart independently into the solution (Figure 16–8).

FIGURE 16–8 · *An ionic compound can dissolve in water because of the energy released by the hydration of the ions.*

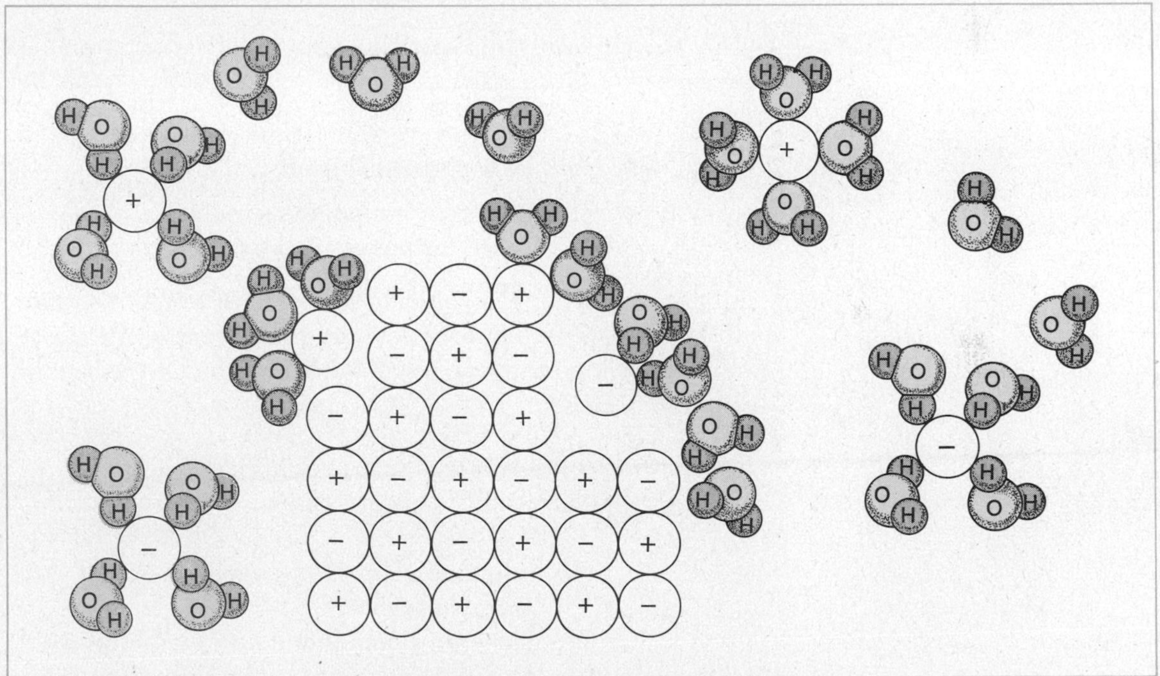

Water also dissolves many substances by causing them to separate into ions, or **ionize.** For example, hydrogen chloride gas is composed of polar molecules. Those molecules, according to Table 10–5 in Chapter 10, have 19 percent ionic character. So the bonding is not fully covalent. As the HCl molecules enter liquid water, water dipoles orient around the H atom and the Cl atom. The hydration interaction is strong enough to break the H–Cl bond, and hydrated hydrogen cations and chloride anions form.

16–8 · Why like dissolves like · An old phrase in chemistry is that "like dissolves like." In other words, polar solutes dissolve in polar solvents, and nonpolar solutes dissolve in nonpolar solvents. We can understand why such a rule should be valid by considering the energy change involved in the solution process. First, when a solute is dissolved, the interaction between the molecules or ions in the solute must be broken. That requires energy.

Solute aggregates
(solid or liquid) → Separated solute species
(molecules or ions)

Energy A required: *Usually* small *for nonpolar solutes*
Usually large *for polar solutes*

The solvent must also have its intermolecular attraction overcome for those solvent molecules to interact with the solute.

Solvent → Separated solvent molecules

Energy B required: Small *for nonpolar solvents*
Large *for polar solvents*

Finally, the separated solvent molecules interact, or solvate, with the separated solute species to release energy. If that is enough to overcome the energy required for the first two steps, a solution occurs.

Solute + Solvent → Solution

Energy C released: Small *for polar solute and nonpolar solvent*
Intermediate *for nonpolar solute and nonpolar solvent*
Large *for polar solute and polar solvent*
Small *for nonpolar solute and polar solvent*

From this, we see that nonpolar substances, such as waxes and oils, do not dissolve in water because the interaction Energy **C** is too small to overcome **A + B.** But nonpolar substances dissolve in nonpolar solvents, partially because **C** is larger, and partially because **B** is smaller. Some ionic substances, such as $BaSO_4$, are insoluble in water because the hydration energy, **C,** is not enough to overcome the large values of **A** in those compounds.

In those comparisons, we have been considering the enthalpy changes. The formation of a solution almost always has a positive entropy change, since a very organized solid is broken down to a very random state in the solution. Occasionally, there is an appreciable solubility, even though the net enthalpy is endothermic [**C** < **A** + **B**]. That is because the entropy term is large enough to overcome the enthalpy [$\Delta S_{Sol.} > \Delta H_{Sol.}$]

16–9 · Solubility limits · Suppose we took a sample of air from your classroom and analyzed it. The typical gases—nitrogen, oxygen, carbon dioxide, and perhaps a little carbon monoxide—would be found. Also, suppose we analyzed a sample of air from a busy downtown intersection. The same gases found in the air of your classroom would be present in that sample, but in different proportions. The amount of carbon dioxide and carbon monoxide might be much higher in the air of a busy intersection. It is a characteristic property of gases that when they mix with other gases to form solutions, they mix in any proportion. Two substances, such as the gases oxygen and carbon dioxide, that mix in any proportion are said to be **miscible.** However, if we try to mix water and mercury, we find that they will not mix. The two liquids, water and mercury, are **immiscible.**

These two examples show extremes of solubility. But between those two limits, there are many examples of substances that mix only up to a certain maximum proportion of solute to solvent. In the case of water solutions, the solubility in water is expressed as the number of grams of solute that will dissolve in either 100 grams or 0.10 liter of water at a given temperature. Perhaps you have observed people adding sugar to ice tea. Some prefer a little sugar, and some will add a great deal. You can in fact, dissolve over 300 grams of sugar in a glass of tea! The solubility of sugar is 1311 grams per liter at room temperature. If you wished to dissolve NaCl in water you would find that only 311 grams would dissolve in one liter of water at room temperature. Perhaps you have also noticed that sugar will often "settle out" when a glass of ice tea becomes very cold.

Since the mechanism of forming solutions involves the motion of molecules, we would expect both temperature and pressure to have an effect on solubility. Solids dissolve in water in certain amounts that are dependent upon temperature. Although there are exceptions, most solids are more soluble near the boiling point of water than near the freezing point. Anyone who cooks is certainly aware of that. Pressure normally has very little effect on the solubility of a solid.

Unlike solids, gases are generally more soluble in cold water. A gas tends to leave the solution as bubbles when the water gets warmer. You can easily see that if you warm a beaker of water. The maximum solubility of most gases in water is near the freezing point of water.

Also, unlike solids, the solubility of gases is very much affected by pressure. The "pop" of a champagne bottle illustrates that. The solubility of gas in water is directly proportional to the pressure of the gas above the water for a given temperature.

There are many liquids that are completely miscible with water. Slightly soluble, or partly immiscible, liquids have a solubility pattern similar to that of solids. Their solubility tends to increase with an increasing temperature.

When the limit of solubility is reached at a particular temperature, and some undissolved solute remains, a **saturated** solution has been formed. In that state, we have established a dynamic equilibrium between dissolved and undissolved solute molecules. The solution process never stops. The rate at which solute particles go into solution is equaled by the rate at which they crystallize out. We may represent the equilibrium state for a saturated solution of glucose, a simple sugar.

$$\text{glucose}(s) \rightleftharpoons \text{glucose}(aq)$$

The forward reaction for glucose is **endothermic.** This is also true of many of the soluble solids. Thus, with glucose and other soluble solids, there is an increase in the solubility as the temperature increases. (Remember Le Châtelier's principle.) Solutes for which the ΔH of solution is positive show an increase in solubility with increased temperature.

It may be possible to heat a solution of glucose and get more solute to dissolve. Suppose all the solute dissolves and the solution is allowed to cool. Recrystallization may not occur, leaving the excess solute in solution. Thus, a **supersaturated** solution has been formed. In other words, more solute remains in solution than would dissolve under normal conditions at that temperature. Supersaturated solutions are not in equilibrium. Agitation or the addition of solute crystals to the solution will immediately cause the solution to go toward equilibrium again. Recrystallization will take place almost instantaneously. And the solution remains saturated.

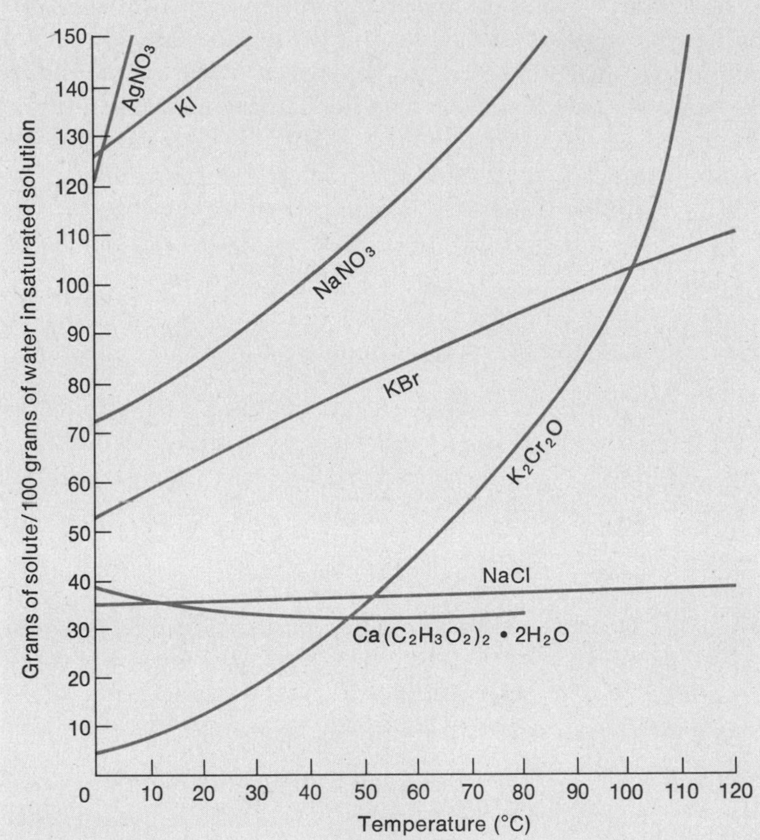

FIGURE 16–9 · *The solubilities of ionic compounds in water with respect to temperature are plotted in this graph.*

16–10 · Concentration terms · The solution concentration is called **solubility** at the saturation point. It is expressed as the mass of the solute per mass of the solvent. For solutions in which water is the solvent, solubility is usually expressed as the mass (in grams) of the solute per 100 grams of water for a given temperature.

It is more convenient to use concentration terms that express mole quantities of reagents. This is especially true in laboratory work. **Molarity** is one common concentration label. Molarity *(M)* is defined as the number of moles of solute dissolved in each liter of solution. The advantage of the molar solution is that it can be used as a sort of liquid form of the solute. It is easily measured in milliliter quantities, each milliliter having a known amount of reagent as the solute. From the definition of molarity, we know that one liter of a 1-molar solution of NaOH contains 40.0 grams of NaOH. One milliliter of the solution, therefore, contains 10^{-3} moles, or 0.04 grams, of NaOH.

A second concentration term used often in chemistry is **molality.** The molality of a solution is the number of moles of solute in a kilogram of solvent. If we dissolve 58.5 g NaCl in 1.00 kg of water, the solution is 1.00 molal, or 1.00*m*. A solution of 14.5 g of acetone (Mass = 58.0 g/mol) in 500 g of ethanol is 0.50*m*. Note that *molarity* is moles of solute in a *volume* of solution. *Molality* is moles of solute in a *mass* of *solvent*.

EXERCISE

How would you prepare a 1.00 M (molar) solution of KCl?

SOLUTION

One mole of KCl has a mass of 39.1 g (K) + 35.5 g (Cl) = 74.6 g. Add 74.6 g KCl to a one-liter container, and fill the container to the one-liter mark with water.

EXERCISE

How would you prepare a 1.00 molal (m) solution of the same substance?

SOLUTION

1.00 ml of water has a mass of 1.00 g, under ordinary conditions. Add 74.6 g KCl to 1000 ml (1.00 liter), or 1000 g water.

16–11 · Colligative properties · When solutes are present, some properties of the solvent are affected. The amount of change in the properties is directly dependent on the concentration of solute. The properties of a solution that are determined by the number of particles of solute present are called the **colligative properties.** Those properties include freezing point, boiling point, vapor pressure, and osmotic pressure.

Let's look first at the effect of concentration on freezing point. We have seen in an earlier chapter how water freezes. The individual water molecules get close enough to form clusters. When the molecules lose enough energy, the clusters form the rigid framework that we see as ice. Under ordinary conditions, water freezes at 0°C. However, if some material is dissolved in the water, that solute gets in the way of the water molecules as they attempt to form clusters. The water molecules have to lose even more energy to overcome the hindering effect of the dissolved particles in the water. That would result in a lower freezing point for an aqueous solution.

Observations made on many substances show that the freezing point of water is lowered by 1.86°C for each mole of solute species present per kilogram of water. There are two important aspects of this definition that must be understood. First, we are considering the *molality* of the solution. Second, this definition applies only to water. Of course, we can have a solution in liquids other than water. Such nonaqueous solutions, however, would have a freezing-point depression different from the 1.86°C that we see in the water solutions.

Thus, a 0.10 molal solution of glucose has the following freezing-point depression.

$$(0.10) \times (1.86°C) = 0.19°C$$

Since water freezes at 0°C, the freezing point of such a glucose solution would be −0.19°C.

What would be the freezing point of a 0.10 molal solution of NaCl? The 0.10 molal solution of NaCl releases 0.10 mole of Na^+ ions and 0.10 mole of Cl^- ions. Thus, there are 0.20 mole of dissolved "species" per kilogram. Look again at the definition given above. Remember, the number of moles of solute "species" is important. Therefore, in this example, the freezing point would be depressed by this amount.

$$(2 \times 0.10) \times (1.86) = 0.37°C$$

The freezing point of the solution would be −0.37°C.

EXERCISE

A solution of glucose has a freezing point of −0.93°C. What is the concentration of the solution (molality)?

SOLUTION

A 1.00 m solution will have a freezing point of −1.86°C. Thus, using dimensional analysis, we find the molality.

$$.93°\not{C} \times \frac{1 \text{ m}}{1.86°\not{C}} = 0.5 \text{ m}$$

EXERCISE

1. *A solution of glucose is 2.50* m. *What is the freezing point?*
2. *What is the freezing point of 0.25* m *solution of KCl?*

Now let's look at the effect a solute has on the boiling point of a solution. Recall that molecules escape from the surface of a liquid during the process of boiling. Again, we may assume that solute particles in solution get in the way of solvent molecules as they attempt to break away from the surface. We know that the boiling point for pure water is 100°C at 760 Torr. Laboratory observations show that the boiling point is increased by 0.51°C for each mole of solute species in solution. Thus, a 1.00 molal solution of glucose boils at 100.51°C.

Since boiling occurs only when the vapor pressure of a liquid equals the atmospheric pressure, we also expect the vapor pressure of a solvent to be decreased in solution. Thus, an aqueous solution has a vapor pressure of 760 Torr at a higher temperature than that for pure water.

EXERCISE

1. *What is the boiling point of a 0.15 m solution of glucose?*
2. *At what temperature will a 0.50 m solution of KBr boil?*

REVIEW IT NOW

1 Define *solution*, *solvent*, and *solute*.
2 Describe two ways in which water can hold a substance in solution.
3 Explain the process *hydration*.
4 Define *solubility* and *miscible*.
5 Upon what factors does the solubility of gas in water depend?
6 How is a saturated solution formed?
7 How does a supersaturated solution form?
8 Distinguish between molarity and molality.
9 What are colligative properties? List some.
10 What effect does a solute have on the freezing point of water as a solvent?
11 What effect does a solute have on the boiling point of water as a solvent?

IONIZATION AND ELECTROLYTES

16–12 · Electrolytes are conductors · In the early part of the nineteenth century, an English scientist named Michael Faraday (1791–1867) defined those substances that allowed the passage of electricity in aqueous solutions as **electrolytes.** The ability to pass electricity through a solution is called **conductance.** A substance in a solution that does not exhibit electrical conductance is called a **nonelectrolyte.** Pure water is a nonconductor (nonelectrolyte). In 1887, Svante Arrhenius (1859–1927), a Swedish scientist, proposed that the conductance of electrolytes is due to the existence of electrolytes as ions in the solution. The movement of the charged cations and anions between the electrodes results in the flow of electrical current through the solution. At the time of Arrhenius's proposal, little was known of the electrical nature of substances, and his proposal was a bold and brilliant one. Arrhenius exhibited similar intellectual boldness throughout his life. For example, he proposed that life on the earth may have come from other planets. He worked for the acceptance of a common language for all people on the earth. He also developed a theory of the origin of the universe. But the enduring monument to Arrhenius's brilliance is his theory of electrolyte solutions.

Arrhenius assumed that solid electrolytes were formed of molecules that dissociated into ions when they were in solution. In some cases, that is a valid model (Figure 16–8, page 335). But we now know that many of those substances are already ionic in the solid state. In solution, the cations and anions are separated by hydration (Figure 16–10). The polar compounds that dissolve in water to form electrolyte solutions may not dissociate completely into ions. Some hydrated molecules may exist in equilibrium with the hydrated cations and anions.

$$M{-}X_{(s)} \xrightarrow{\text{(Solution)}} M{-}X(aq) + M^{+}(aq) + X^{-}(aq)$$

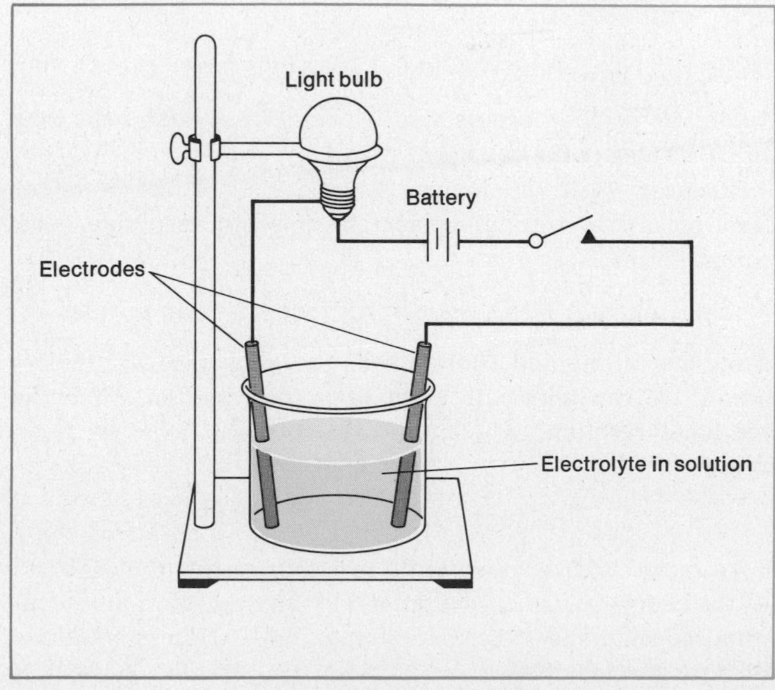

FIGURE 16–10 · *An electrolyte conducts an electric current in solution.*

Svante Arrhenius *(1859–1927, Swedish). Although an accomplished chemist, he also delved into other fields. He developed a theory of the origin of the solar system, suggested that life on the earth may have come from some other planet, and dreamed of a universal language.*

The polar covalent compounds that are ionized in water show a wide range of ionization—for example, nearly 100 percent for HCl in water, but a very small amount for acetic acid. From measurement of the colligative properties, we can determine the apparent degree of ionization, since that measurement tells us the number of dissolved species. The complete ionization of a molecule such as HCl results in twice the effect expected from the molality value of the solution.

Often we find that the colligative properties of a solution of ionic solids have values indicating less than 100-percent ionization. That effect becomes more pronounced as the concentration increases. It is not because of incomplete dissociation as it is with the polar compounds. When the concentration of cations and anions becomes large, they can interfere with one another. Then the cations are less free to move about, because of the interaction with anions nearby in the solution and vice versa.

16–13 · Net ionic reactions · Suppose we add a certain amount of a solution of sodium chloride to one of potassium nitrate. Both sodium chloride and potassium nitrate are strong electrolytes. If other strong electrolytes, like potassium chloride and sodium nitrate, form, everything in the solution is ionized.

$$Na^+(aq) + Cl^-(aq) + K^+(aq) + NO_3^-(aq) \rightleftharpoons Na^+(aq) + NO_3^-(aq) + K^+(aq) + Cl^-(aq)$$

In fact, no reaction occurs, and we can cancel out all the ions on both sides of the equation.

However, what will happen if we use silver nitrate, rather than potassium nitrate? Silver chloride, an insoluble compound, forms.

$$Na^+(aq) + Cl^-(aq) + Ag^+(aq) + NO_3^-(aq) \rightleftharpoons Na^+(aq) + NO_3^-(aq) + AgCl(s)$$

Since the nitrate and sodium ions are unchanged by the reaction, we can eliminate them from the equation. Then the net ionic reaction, which indicates the only change, is as follows.

$$Ag^+(aq) + Cl^-(aq) \rightleftharpoons AgCl(s)$$

It is correct to write *net* ionic reactions so that they express all the change. That can be proved by mixing solutions of calcium chloride and silver perchlorate. Both of these solutions are strong electrolytes.

$$Ca^{2+}(aq) + 2Cl^{-}(aq) + 2Ag^{+}(aq) + 2ClO_4^{-}(aq) \rightleftharpoons Ca^{+2} + 2ClO_4^{-}(aq) + 2AgCl(s)$$

The net ionic reaction follows.

$$\not{2}Ag^{+}(aq) + \not{2}Cl^{-}(aq) \rightleftharpoons \not{2}AgCl(s)$$

As the net ionic reaction indicates, it doesn't matter which cation was originally associated with chloride as long as the compound of that cation and anion is a strong electrolyte. So it does not matter which anion was associated with silver, since AgCl is a strong electrolyte.

16–14 · Solubility and K_{sp} · Let's consider a saturated solution of AgCl. This solid is relatively insoluble; 1.30×10^{-5} moles of AgCl dissolve per liter of solution at 25.0°C. In writing the equation for the equilibrium reaction, however, we must not forget that the small amount of AgCl that does dissolve will dissociate completely. Thus, the equilibrium reaction is written as follows.

$$AgCl(s) \rightleftharpoons Ag^{+1}(aq) + Cl^{-1}(aq)$$

This is the equilibrium-law expression for the system.

$$K = [Ag^{+1}]\,[Cl^{-1}]$$

Recall that the concentration of a pure solid does not appear in the equilibrium-law expression and that the symbol $[Ag^{+1}]$ means the molar concentration of Ag^{+1} ions at equilibrium. The constant, K for a solubility equilibrium is called the solubility product constant and is given the special symbol K_{sp}. Table 16 – 1 lists the K_{sp} values of some commonly encountered, insoluble ionic solids. For solids that are not very insoluble, the K_{sp} values are usually calculated from measured solubilities.

TABLE 16–1 · Solubility Product Constants (25.0°C)

FORMULA	K_{sp}	FORMULA	K_{sp}
$BaCO_3$	4.9×10^{-9}	PbS	7×10^{-28}
$BaSO_4$	1.5×10^{-9}	$MgCO_3$	1×10^{-5}
$CdCO_3$	2.5×10^{-14}	MnS	1.4×10^{-15}
CdS	1×10^{-28}	AgBr	7.7×10^{-13}
$CaCO_3$	4.8×10^{-9}	AgCl	1.7×10^{-10}
$CaSO_4$	6.1×10^{-5}	AgCN	2×10^{-12}
$PbCO_3$	1.6×10^{-13}	AgI	8.3×10^{-17}
$PbCrO_4$	1.8×10^{-14}	$SrSO_4$	2.8×10^{-7}
$PbSO_4$	1.9×10^{-8}	ZnS	4.5×10^{-24}

Conversely, it is possible to calculate the solubility of an ionic solid if its K_{sp} value is known. As we saw with other equilibrium expressions, the K_{sp} is dependent on the temperature. For convenience, the K_{sp} is generally measured at 25.0°C.

Let's see how we can determine the K_{sp} from solubility data. Suppose we wish to find the K_{sp} for a solution of $PbCrO_4$. Measurements tell us that the solubility of this compound is 1.34×10^{-7} mole/liter.

We can show the ionization reaction of $PbCrO_4$.

$$PbCrO_4(s) \rightleftharpoons Pb^{+2}(aq) + CrO_4^{-2}(aq)$$

The expression for the K_{sp} of the solution is written below.

$$K_{sp} = [Pb^{+2}]\,[CrO_4^{-2}]$$

Remember, a solid, like $PbCrO_4$, is not included in the equilibrium expression, since its concentration does not change.

We know that the solubility is 1.34×10^{-7} mole/liter. That means at equilibrium, we would find 1.34×10^{-7} mole of Pb^{+2} and 1.34×10^{-7} mole of CrO_4^{-2} in solution. We can substitute those into our K_{sp} expression as follows. (Remember, when multiplying exponents, add the superscripts.) That agrees with the valuc given in Table 16–1.

$$K_{sp} = [Pb^{+2}][CrO_4^{-2}]$$
$$K_{sp} = [1.34 \times 10^{-7}][1.34 \times 10^{-7}]$$
$$K_{sp} = 1.8 \times 10^{-14}$$

Can we reverse the process and determine the solubility from a known K_{sp}? Let's see. Table 16–1 gives 1.7×10^{-10} as the K_{sp} for AgCl. What is the solubility of AgCl? Our reaction for the ionization of AgCl shows the same number of moles of Ag^+ and Cl^- ions produced when AgCl ionizes.

$$AgCl(s) = Ag^+(aq) + Cl^-(aq)$$

Since Ag^+ and Cl^- exist in equal amounts, and we wish to determine this, let's symbolize this concentration as "x." (Remember, to divide exponents, subtract the superscripts.)

$$K_{sp} = [Ag^+][Cl^-]$$
$$1.70 \times 10^{-10} = [x][x]$$
$$1.70 \times 10^{-10} = x^2$$
$$x = \sqrt{1.7 \times 10^{-10}}$$
$$x = 1.30 \times 10^{-5}$$

EXERCISE

1. *From the data in Table 16–1, determine the solubility of $CdCO_3$, $BaCO_3$, and $MgCO_3$.*

2. *The solubility of AgI is 9.10×10^{-9} mol/l. Determine the K_{sp} for AgI.*

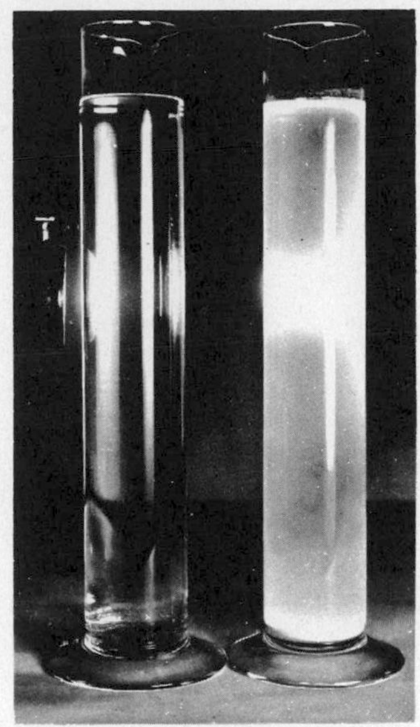

FIGURE 16–11 · *Particles in colloidal suspensions are large enough to scatter light. Particles in true solutions are not. The optical phenomenon of light-scattering by colloidal particles is known as the Tyndall effect. Where have you encountered this effect?*

16–15 · Colloids · Certain combinations of solvent and solute make what appear to be solutions. But in fact they are not true molecular dispersions. The size of the particles in the system is really quite large. Such systems, **colloidal suspensions,** are actually not homogeneous. They have a set of properties that are very different from those of true solutions. Those differences are due to particle size. The resulting observable characteristics of colloidal suspensions are very interesting.

A colloid is composed of a solvent with solute particles that are large enough to scatter visible light. Therefore, it is possible to distinguish a suspension from a true solution by shining a beam of light through the liquid. Like a pure liquid, a solution diffracts a light beam. A colloid will scatter the light so that, from the side of the beam, you see a bright path of light. The scattering effect is called the **Tyndall effect** (Figure 16–11), after John Tyndall (1820–1893) who noted it first in 1869.

Because the suspended particles of a colloid are so large, we might wonder why they don't precipitate immediately from the solution. If we study the movement of an individual particle, we find that it moves in a zigzag, random path that suggests bombardment by solvent molecules. The colloidal particles are kept in suspension by those movements. The motion of suspended particles is known as **Brownian movement.** Robert Brown (1773–1858), an English botanist, reported that type of motion in his study of pollen grains suspended in water.

The kinetic theory tells us that the random motion of gases should cause a similar bombardment of particles in a gas. Therefore, we expect Brownian movement in air suspensions. If you observe smoke or dust particles in a bright shaft of sunlight, you can observe the effect quite clearly.

In water suspensions, the attractive forces between colloid particles sometimes become very great, and the particles form aggregates. If the system becomes semisolid and Brownian movement is nearly stopped, the suspension is called a **gel.** As long as the system is free-flowing, it is called a **sol.**

Colloids are of practical importance to us in our everyday lives. Many foods that we eat are colloidal in nature. The living cell is dependent on colloidal particles in the protoplasm for the chemical functions of growth and metabolism. One of the functions of the cell is to separate suspensions by a process called **dialysis.** We can demonstrate dialysis very easily by using cellophane or filter paper treated with a colloidal substance. The cellophane, or other membrane, is called a **dialyzing membrane.** The principle is very simple. If the membrane has holes, or spaces, that are the proper size, molecular particles pass through, and colloidal particles do not. For example, if we put gelatin and sugar in a cellophane bag and allow the bag to hang in pure water for a time, the sugar will pass through the cellophane, but the gelatin will remain inside. Dialysis is useful in separating many suspended materials. With membranes of the proper type, we can separate two suspended materials from each other by using the difference in particle size.

TABLE 16–2 · Some Common Colloidal Systems

TYPE	EXAMPLES
Solid-in-liquid	Gelatin
Liquid-in-liquid (emulsion)	Milk
Gas-in-liquid (foam)	Whipped cream
Solid-in-solid	Black diamond
Gas-in-solid	Marshmallow
Solid-in-gas	Smoke
Liquid-in-gas (aerosol)	Fog

The holes in the dialyzing membrane must be the proper size to exclude the one substance but allow the other to pass.

Colloidal suspensions are most important in biology. All biological systems are colloidal in some way. Protoplasm is a colloidal suspension, as is blood and other body fluids. Colloids are also important in industry. Practically every industry in some way involves colloids. The behavior of plastics is a colloidal effect. The same is true for rubber, paints, cement, ceramics, and detergents. Even in the purification of water and the treatment of sewage, we find colloidal systems playing a major role. Space-age research has given the scientist a much better insight into the nature of colloidal systems. Much research is going on in order to better understand these complex and important systems.

REVIEW IT NOW

1 What did Faraday and Arrhenius contribute to our understanding of ionization?
2 How does the modern theory of electrolyte solution differ from that proposed by Arrhenius?
3 How can the apparent degree of ionization be determined?
4 What is a net ionic reaction?
5 What does it mean to say the K_{sp} of CdS is 1.00×10^{-28} at 25.0°C?
6 Which compound in Table 16-1 is least soluble?
7 How can a suspension be distinguished from a true solution?
8 Explain Brownian movement.
9 List several types of colloidal systems, and give examples of each.
10 Explain the process of dialysis.

SUMMARY

Water is unique in many ways. Because of the weak hydrogen bonds between water molecules, water has a boiling point higher than one would expect. It is also unusual in that the solid form of water, ice, has a lower density than the liquid. Water also has a high specific heat—the amount of energy required to raise the temperature of 1.00 gram of water by 1.00°C. Water is especially important in moderating our climate.

X-ray studies have led us to formulate models for the structure of water and ice. Those models allow us to account for the strange properties of water. Water reacts chemically with active metals, such as sodium, to form hydrogen gas. In the form of steam, it also reacts with less active metals to release hydrogen gas. Water reacts violently with fluorine to produce oxygen gas.

A rare form of water, deuterium oxide, D_2O, exists in about 1 part in 6000. It has slightly different physical properties, but its chemical properties are similar to those of ordinary water. D_2O is used as a neutron moderator in some types of nuclear reactors.

Hydrogen peroxide, H_2O_2, is a compound related to H_2O. Hydrogen peroxide is used as an oxidizing agent, since it readily decomposes to release oxygen.

Water is a most important universal solvent. It dissolves other polar molecules, as well as ions. We can explain the solution process by considering the energy effect involved. However, there are often limits to solubility. We express solubility in molarity (moles per liter of solution) and molality (moles per 1000 grams of solvent). Some properties of a solution are determined by the concentration of the solute present. Those properties are colligative properties. They include freezing point, boiling point, vapor pressure, and osmotic pressure.

Faraday and Arrhenius gave us models to explain the process of ionization in water. In writing a *net* ionic reaction, we show only those substances actually reacting with one another. Certain combinations of solute and solvent result in colloidal suspensions, rather than true solutions. Such colloidal suspensions include gels, emulsions, foams, and aerosols. Colloids are important in biological processes.

REVIEW QUESTIONS

1. What factors can affect solubility, other than the ionic dissociation, or ionization, of the solute?
2. At any given temperature, why will rock salt dissolve more slowly than salt from a salt shaker?
3. Discuss the difference in the energy involved in dissolving a gas and dissolving a crystalline solid in water.
4. What effects will you observe if you add a sugar crystal to each of the following?
   a. A beaker of water
   b. A beaker containing a saturated sugar solution
   c. A beaker containing a supersaturated sugar solution
5. Describe the steps involved in making up 2.00 liters of 0.10 *M* sodium chloride.
6. Calculate the number of grams of sucrose present in 1.00 liter of 0.25 *M* solution.
7. Describe the steps necessary to make up 5.00 liters of 0.2 *m* KOH.
8. What final volume will be required for a sample of 7.40 g $Ca(OH)_2$ dissolved in water to be placed in a reagent bottle labeled 0.50 *M*?
9. Write the net ionic equation for each of the following reactions.
   a. Dissolving HCl gas in water
   b. Dissolving KNO_3 in water
   c. Reaction between $KOH(aq)$ and $H_2SO_4(aq)$
   d. Reaction between $H_2S(aq)$ and $Cd(NO_3)_2(aq)$
   e. Reaction between NH_3 and HCl in water solution
10. Ideally, what is the freezing point of a 0.1 *m* solution of $Al_2(SO_4)_3$?
11. Calculate the molecular mass of a substance for which 3.00 g dissolved in 200 g of water lowers the freezing point to −0.93°C.
12. Given 2.00×10^{-3} *M* solutions of $Pb(NO_3)_2$ and Na_2SO_4, determine the following.
    a. What ions will be present in each of the solutions? In what concentrations will they be present?
    b. Write an equilibrium equation for the most probable reaction when equal volumes of the two solutions are mixed together.
13. Why does the solid species *not* appear in K_{sp} for dissolving the solid?
14. Using Table 16–1, calculate the molar solubility at 25.0°C of each of the following.
    a. Calcium carbonate
    b. Lead(II) sulfate
    c. Cadmium sulfide
    d. Silver iodide
15. Calculate the solubility product constant at 25.0°C for each of the following solids (the solubility of each at 25.0°C is given).
    a. Barium chromate (1.4×10^{-2} mol/l)
    b. Copper(II) oxalate (1.69×10^{-4} mol/l)

c. Thallium(I) bromide (0.57 g/l)
d. Radium sulfate (2.0×10^{-3} g/l)

16 Why are yellow headlights more effective in a fog than white lights?

17 Write the solubility product expression for the dissolution of each of the following solids.
a. PdS
b. Ag_3PO_4
c. Chromic carbonate
d. Gallium hydroxide

18 The compound HCN gives CN^- (cyanide ion) when it is dissolved in water. Given the clue that CN^- behaves somewhat like a halide ion, write formulas for the following compounds, and indicate those you expect to have low solubility in water.
a. Ammonium cyanide
b. Barium cyanide
c. Silver cyanide

SUGGESTED READINGS

Boyd, T. A. "The Wonder of Water." *Chemistry*, June 1974, p. 6.

Hall, Christopher. "Water." *Chemistry*, September 1971, p. 6.

"Ice—A Common Mystery." *Chemistry*, January 1974, p. 20.

Keller, Eugenia. "What Is Happening to Our Drinking Water?" *Chemistry*, February 1975, p. 16.

Knight, Charles and Mary. "Snow Crystals." *Scientific American*, January 1973, p. 100.

Marshall, William. "Water and Its Solutions at High Temperatures and Pressures." *Chemistry*, February 1975, p. 6.

"Model for H_2O Properties." *Science News*, January 15, 1972, p. 37.

Othmer, Donald F. "Water and Life." *Chemistry*, November 1970, p. 12.

Raw, Isaias, and Gerald Holleman. "Water—Energy for Life." *Chemistry*, May 1973, p. 6.

Slabaugh, Wendell H. "Clay Colloids." *Chemistry*, April 1970, p. 8.

"Structure for Water." *Science News*, October 14, 1972, p. 246.

Vold and Vold. *Colloid Chemistry*. New York: D. Van Nostrand Co., 1963.

Acidic pollution has eroded this stone face in Venice.

CHAPTER SEVENTEEN

Acids and Bases

In Chapter 17, we will study two of the major classes of chemical compounds—acids and bases. These two classifications of substances are among the oldest in science. Moreoever, for centuries the relationship between acids and bases has been known and put to use. For example, land formerly covered by forests is often too "sour" (too acid) for the best agricultural use. To remedy that situation, a basic substance, such as lime, is added. Alternatively, desert soils are usually too basic and can be improved by acidification. Industrial processes such as brewing, paper manufacturing, sugar refining, and food production require careful control of acidity or basicity. Also, many biological processes are quite sensitive to acidity. For example, who has not experienced the acid indigestion that we treat with antacids?

EXPLAINING ACIDS AND BASES

17–1 · Operational definitions · Substances have been classified as acidic or basic for centuries. That classification was based on **operational definitions.** Such definitions state that if a substance has certain observable qualities, it is an acid, or it is a base. Those definitions do not specify anything about molecular structure, nor do they explain why acids have such properties. **Conceptual definitions** attempt to explain the molecular basis of the operational definitions.

Acids may be operationally defined as substances that

1. liberate H_2 gas when they react with certain metals;
2. neutralize the actions of basic solutions;

3. cause the blue form of litmus to convert to its red form;
4. taste sour, like vinegar or lemon.

Bases may be operationally defined as substances that

1. react with the solutions of salts of heavy metals to form insoluble hydroxides (in some cases, insoluble oxides form);
2. neutralize the actions of acid solutions;
3. cause the red form of litmus to convert to its blue form;
4. taste bitter, like soap;
5. feel slippery to the touch.

Those characteristics are convenient for classifying a substance as an acid or a base. But a definition that attempts to explain why acids and bases act as they do is even more useful to the chemist. Let's turn our attention now to conceptual models of acids and bases.

17–2 · Arrhenius's model · As we saw in Chapter 16, Svante Arrhenius developed a conceptual model for electrolytes in aqueous solution. He extended his studies to acidic and basic solutions. Arrhenius proposed that when acid solutions form, the hydrogen ion, H^+, is set free in solution. We can represent any acid as HA, and we show a general reaction as follows.

$$HA(aq) \rightarrow H^+(aq) + A^-(aq)$$

Then according to that theory, the common properties of all acid solutions are due to the existence of the H^+ ion. The reaction of zinc metal with hydrochloric acid is one example.

$$Zn(s) + 2HCl(aq) = ZnCl_2(aq) + H_2(g)$$

The reaction can be more simply expressed showing only the hydrogen ion. We call that the net ionic equation.

$$Zn(s) + 2H^+(aq) \rightarrow Zn^{+2}(aq) + H_2(g)$$

Arrhenius also proposed that when basic solutions form, the hydroxyl ion, OH^-, is set free in solution.

$$MOH(aq) \rightarrow M^+(aq) + OH^-(aq)$$

The common properties of all basic solutions would then be due to the existence of the OH^- ion. The reaction between iron(III) chloride and sodium hydroxide solutions follows.

$$FeCl_3(aq) + 3NaOH(aq) = Fe(OH)_3(s) + 3NaCl(aq)$$

FIGURE 17–1 · *Most common fruits we eat are acidic. What acid do you think is present in the fruits shown here?*

The reaction can be more simply expressed as a net ionic equation.

$$Fe^{+3}(aq) + 3OH^-(aq) = Fe(OH)_3(s)$$

What happens in a solution when an electric current passes through it? When Svante Arrhenius chose that problem for his doctoral thesis at the University of Uppsala in Sweden, his professors thought the problem was too difficult and tried to discourage him. Not easily dissuaded, Arrhenius proceeded to study a great number of solutions in order to determine the effects of temperature and concentration on the ability of a solution to conduct electricity.

There was nothing particularly spectacular about Arrhenius's experiments. He used simple equipment, made accurate measurements, and recorded his results carefully. His genius was reflected in the way he planned his experiments, interpreted his data, and related his work to that of other scientists.

He knew that the heat of neutralization of strong acids with strong bases is almost the same for all acids and bases in equivalent quantities. His measurements showed that acids and bases were good conductors of electricity when they dissolved in water. Arrhenius also discovered that acids and bases that were poor conductors of electricity in concentrated aqueous solutions became better conductors when diluted.

As a result of his experiments, Arrhenius proposed that solute molecules dissociate into tiny particles, called ions, that carry electric current through solutions. He interpreted the similarity of the heats of neutralization of acids and bases as an indication that all acids must form hydrogen ions, and that all bases must form hydroxide ions. He predicted that the chemical activity of aqueous solutions of acids and bases should be proportional to their conductivity.

Arrhenius's conclusions were so radical that his professors accepted his thesis with great reluctance. During the next few years, he conducted many experiments to verify his theories, but doubt persisted. Eventually, his experiments and conclusions were confirmed by other noted scientists, and he was awarded the Nobel Prize for Chemistry in 1903.

17–3 · The hydronium ion, H_3O^+ · When substances are dissolved in water, their ions are hydrated. That is, they attract water molecules to themselves. We also know that water molecules interact with one another by hydrogen bonding. A hydrogen ion, H^+, is hydrated by forming a hydrogen bond with a water molecule. We saw in Chapter 16 how water forms clusters of hydrogen-bonded H_2O molecules. Thus, we could expect the H^+ ion to simply attach itself to one of those clusters. Then we write the hydrated hydrogen ion as $H(H_2O)_x^+$, where the values of x would cover a wide range. Since we do not know the values of x (and, in fact, they should change with concentration, temperature, etc.), we use a simpler formula. The hydrated hydrogen ion is written as $H_3O^+(aq)$ and called the **hydronium ion.**

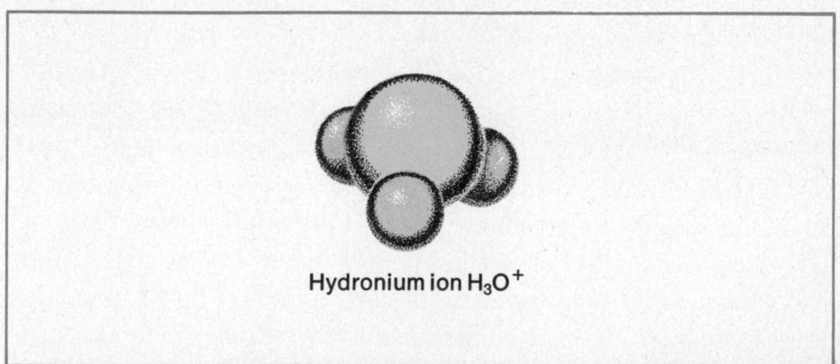

FIGURE 17–2 · *The hydronium ion*

17–4 · Acids are proton donors · With the hydronium ion, it is possible to include water as a reactant in the ionization of acids in water.

$$HBr(aq) + H_2O(l) = H_3O^+(aq) + Br^-(aq)$$

In this case, the water accepts the hydrogen ion from the acid, HBr, forming the hydronium ion.

We can extend that idea to bases. The action of water on metal hydroxides solvates the cations and hydroxide ions. That provides enough energy to cause the crystal lattice of the metal hydroxide to break down and the base to dissolve. That can be shown with NaOH.

$$NaOH(s) \xrightarrow{H_2O} Na^+(aq) + OH^-(aq)$$

In some cases, however, the base that accepts the H^+ ion does not contain an OH^- group. For a base such as aqueous ammonia, we can show a more direct effect of water in the ionization.

$$NH_3(aq) + H_2O(l) \rightarrow NH_4^+(aq) + OH^-(aq)$$

Here we see aqueous ammonia acting as a base and accepting an H^+ from H_2O.

From the evidence of the action of water in the ionization of HBr and NH_3, we can make a general statement about acids and bases that is useful in defining their chemical activity. Acids, such as HBr, donate a proton to the water. Bases, such as aqueous ammonia, accept a proton from the water. That mechanism leads us to a more general definition of acids as **proton donors** and of bases as **proton acceptors.**

FIGURE 17–3 · *Two models for the hydronium ion*

17–5 · Conjugate acid-base pairs · About fifty years ago, Arrhenius's definition of acids and bases was replaced by a newer conceptual definition. The newer definition states that acids are substances that donate protons, and bases are substances that accept protons. That definition has a very practical and valuable application in interpreting experimental facts. If we write balanced equations representing reactions between common mineral acids and bases, we obtain these ionic equations.

$$H_3O^+(aq) + Cl^-(aq) + Na^+(aq) + OH^-(aq) \rightarrow 2H_2O(l) + Na^+(aq) + Cl^-(aq)$$

$$H_3O^+(aq) + NO_3^-(aq) + K^+(aq) + OH^-(aq) \rightarrow 2H_2O(l) + K^+(aq) + NO_3^-(aq)$$

If we eliminate the unchanged ions from the reactions, we get a net ionic equation.

$$H_3O^+(aq) + OH^-(aq) \rightarrow 2H_2O(l)$$

That general reaction is the net ionic equation for any neutralization reaction. The new model for an acid-base reaction involves proton transfer. That model can be extended also to the explanation of the reverse of an ionization reaction. The reverse of an ionization reaction is a reaction forming an acid molecule and water.

$$H_3O^{+1}(aq) + CH_3COO^{-1}(aq) \rightarrow CH_3COOH(aq) + H_2O(l)$$

The proton-transfer theory says that when the acid donates a proton, the negative ion produced by the reaction is a base.

$$\begin{array}{c} HA(aq) + H_2O(l) \rightarrow H_3O^{+1}(aq) + A^{-1}(aq) \\ \text{acid}_1 \xrightarrow{\qquad\qquad\qquad\qquad} \text{base}_1 \end{array}$$

When that base accepts a proton, it becomes the original acid. The arrow shows where the proton is transferred.

$$\begin{array}{c} H_3O^{+1}(aq) + A^{-1}(aq) \rightarrow HA(aq) + H_2O(l) \\ \text{base}_1 \longrightarrow \text{acid}_1 \end{array}$$

The acid-base pair is called a **conjugate acid-base pair.** In any neutralization reaction, two such conjugate acid-base pairs are involved.

$$\begin{array}{cccc} HA(aq) + & B^{-1}(aq) \rightleftharpoons & HB(aq) + & A^{-1}(aq) \\ \text{acid}_1 & \text{base}_2 & \text{acid}_2 & \text{base}_1 \end{array}$$

Table 17−1 lists some common conjugate acid-base pairs.

TABLE 17–1 · Common Conjugate Acid-Base Pairs

ACID	BASE	ACID	BASE
$HClO_4$	ClO_4^{-1}	H_3PO_4	$H_2PO_4^{-1}$
HCl	Cl^{-1}	CH_3COOH	CH_3COO^{-1}
HNO_3	NO_3^{-1}	H_2CO_3	HCO_3^{-1}
H_2SO_4	HSO_4^{-1}	H_2S	HS^{-1}
HOOCCOOH	$HOOCCOO^{-1}$	NH_4^{+1}	NH_3
H_2SO_3	HSO_3^{-1}	HCO_3^{-1}	CO_3^{-2}
HSO_4^{-1}	SO_4^{-2}	H_2O	OH^{-1}

EXAMPLE

Write an equation showing a reaction between conjugate acid-base pairs, using the acid $HClO_4$ and the base OH^{-1}.

SOLUTION

From Table 17−1, we see that the conjugate base for $HClO_4$ is ClO_4^{-1}. Also, the conjugate acid for the base OH^{-1} is H_2O.

We can put the two pairs together as follows.

$$HClO_4(aq) + OH^-(aq) \rightarrow H_2O(l) + ClO_4^-(aq)$$

Finally, we use two brackets to show the acid-base conjugate pairs.

$$\underset{\text{acid}_1}{HClO_4(aq)} + \underset{\text{base}_2}{OH^-(aq)} \rightarrow \underset{\text{acid}_2}{H_2O(l)} + \underset{\text{base}_1}{ClO_4^-(aq)}$$

EXERCISE

Using the preceding reaction as an example, show the reaction between the following acids and bases.

a. *HCl and* OH^-
b. HNO_3 *and* CO_3^{-2}
c. *HOOCCOOH and* NH_3

We can summarize what we have learned thus far and state the theory of acids and bases.

1. An acid is a substance that donates a proton in a chemical reaction.
2. A base is a substance that accepts a proton from an acid.
3. Every acid, when it donates a proton, becomes a base.
4. Every base, when it accepts a proton, becomes an acid.

17–6 · Strength of acids and bases · Not all acids release an H^+ with the same ease. Some acids release very little hydrogen ion in solution. Other acids release almost all their hydrogen as H^+. We call the acids that release very little H^+ **weak acids.** Those acids that release most of their H^+ are called **strong acids.** We can illustrate a strong acid, using hydrogen chloride. If we prepare a 1.00 molar solution of hydrogen chloride in water, we can show experimentally that the HCl releases almost 100 percent of its protons to the water. Thus, HCl is a very strong acid.

$$HCl(aq) + H_2O(l) \rightleftarrows H_3O^+(aq) + Cl^-(aq)$$

The large arrow indicates that most of the H^+ from HCl appears in the product H_3O^+. At equilibrium, the reverse reaction is very slight, as indicated by the small arrow.

FIGURE 17–4 · *Which of these common household substances do you think are basic, and which do you think are acidic?*

However, in a 1.00 molar solution of acetic acid, experiments show that less than 1 percent ionization occurs.

$$HC_2H_3O_2(aq) + H_2O(l) \rightleftarrows H_3O^+(aq) + C_2H_3O_2^-(aq)$$

Acetic acid is a very weak acid.

Now let's consider the strength of the conjugate bases. If sodium chloride is dissolved in an acid solution, the amount of $HCl(aq)$ formed is slight, as we expect from the equilibrium reaction below. (Note that it is just the reverse of the reaction shown earlier.)

$$Cl^-(aq) + H_3O^+(aq) \leftrightarrows HCl(aq) + H_2O(l)$$

So $Cl^-(aq)$ does not accept protons very readily. By definition, then, it is a very weak base. If sodium acetate is added to an acidic solution, the equilibrium favors the formation of $HC_2H_3O_2(aq)$. Therefore, acetate is a strong base. The strong acid, HCl, has a weak conjugate base, Cl^-. The weak acid, $HC_2H_3O_2$, has a strong conjugate base. If you think about that for a while, you will realize that it is a necessary relationship. HCl is a strong acid, because it readily releases protons to H_2O. That must be because of the stronger affinity of H_2O for H^+ than of Cl^- for H^+. So Cl^- must have a weak attraction for H^+. That makes it a weak base.

Since acids and bases vary greatly in their ability to give up and accept protons, it is only logical that we find that some way to express that in a more systematic manner.

The strength of an acid can be expressed quantitatively by using the equilibrium constant for the ionization reaction.

$$HA(aq) + H_2O(l) = H_3O^+(aq) + A^-(aq)$$

In Chapter 15, we learned to express the equilibrium constant for a reaction. Since acids and bases exist in an equilibrium state, it is logical that we use the same equilibrium expression for them. (Remember, we do not include $H_2O(l)$ in the equilibrium constant equation, because its concentration remains constant.) The acid equilibrium constant is designated as K_A. $[H_3O^+]$ and $[A^-]$ are the equilibrium concentrations of the aqueous ions in the product, and [HA] is the equilibrium concentration of un-ionized reacting acid.

$$K_A = \frac{[H_3O^+][A^-]}{[HA]}$$

Table 17–2 lists K_A values for some acids and compares the acidic and basic strengths of the conjugate acid-base pairs.

With Table 17–2, we can predict acid-base reactions. Suppose we add a solution of NaF to a solution of $HClO_4$. From

TABLE 17–2 · K_A Values for Conjugate Acid-Base Pairs

ACID	BASE	K_A	ACID STRENGTH	BASE STRENGTH
$HClO_4$	ClO_4^{-1}	Large	Very strong	Very weak
HI	I^{-1}	Large	Very strong	Very weak
HBr	Br^{-1}	Large	Very strong	Very weak
HCl	Cl^{-1}	Large	Very strong	Very weak
HNO_3	NO_3^{-1}	Large	Very strong	Very weak
H_2SO_4	HSO_4^{-1}	Large	Very strong	Very weak
H_3O^{+1}	H_2O	1.0	Strong	Weak
HOOCCOOH	$HOOCCOO^{-1}$	5.4×10^{-2}	Moderately weak	Moderately strong
H_2SO_3	HSO_3^{-1}	1.7×10^{-2}	Moderately weak	Moderately strong
HSO_4^{-1}	SO_4^{-2}	1.3×10^{-2}	Moderately weak	Moderately strong
H_3PO_4	$H_2PO_4^{-1}$	7.1×10^{-3}	Moderately weak	Moderately strong
HF	F^{-1}	6.7×10^{-4}	Weak	Strong
HNO_2	NO_2^{-1}	5.1×10^{-4}	Weak	Strong
CH_3COOH	CH_3COO^{-1}	1.8×10^{-5}	Weak	Strong
H_2CO_3	HCO_3^{-1}	4.4×10^{-7}	Very weak	Very strong
H_2S	HS^{-1}	1.0×10^{-7}	Very weak	Very strong
$H_2PO_4^{-1}$	HPO_4^{-2}	6.3×10^{-8}	Very weak	Very strong
HSO_3^{-1}	SO_3^{-2}	6.2×10^{-8}	Very weak	Very strong
NH_4^{+1}	NH_3	5.7×10^{-10}	Very weak	Very strong
HCO_3^{-1}	CO_3^{-2}	4.7×10^{-11}	Very weak	Very strong
HPO_4^{-2}	PO_4^{-3}	4.4×10^{-13}	Very weak	Very strong
HS^{-1}	S^{-2}	1.3×10^{-13}	Very weak	Very strong
H_2O	OH^{-1}	1.0×10^{-14}	Very weak	Very strong

Table 17–2, we see that perchloric acid $HClO_4$, is a very strong acid. Its solution consists of H_3O^+ and ClO_4^- ions. The addition of the NaF solution adds Na^+ and F^- ions. However, as Table 17–2 indicates, F^- is a strong base. Thus, we would expect the F^- to accept a proton to form HF.

$$H_3O^+(aq) + ClO_4^-(aq) + Na^+(aq) + F^-(aq) \rightleftharpoons HF(aq) + H_2O(l) + Na^+(aq) + ClO_4^-(aq)$$

The net ionic reaction follows.

$$H_3O^+(aq) + F^-(aq) \rightleftharpoons HF(aq) + H_2O(l)$$

17–7 · Amphoteric substances · Let us consider further the consequences of the acid-base conjugate-pair concept. If the acid is strong, its conjugate base is weak. Conversely, a weak acid has a strong conjugate base. By now you may have realized that the reaction determines whether a substance is an acid or a base. Note the role of water in the following reactions.

$$HCl + H_2O \rightleftharpoons H_3O^+ + Cl^-$$

acid base acid base

$$NH_3 + H_2O \rightleftharpoons NH_4^+ + OH^-$$

base acid acid base

We see that H_2O is a base to the strong acid HCl. Yet it is an acid to the strong base NH_3. Substances that can act either as an acid or a base are called **amphoteric.** The hydroxides of some metals of Groups III, IV, and V are amphoteric. Aluminum hydroxide dissolves and reacts with either acid or base.

$$Al(OH)_3 + 3HCl = AlCl_3 + 3H_2O$$
$$Al(OH)_3 + NaOH = NaAlO_2 + 2H_2O$$

Perhaps the acid nature of $Al(OH)_3$ will be clearer if we express it as H_3AlO_3 or $HAlO_2 \cdot H_2O$.

17–8 · Lewis acid-base theory · In 1916, G. N. Lewis (1875–1946) suggested the electron-pair concept of acids and bases. That more general theory of acids and bases classifies an acid as an electron-pair acceptor and a base as an electron-pair donor. Lewis's theory is useful in explaining some reactions that are difficult to classify, such as the reaction between the seemingly stable compounds BF_3 and NH_3.

$$BF_3 + NH_3 \rightarrow BF_3NH_3$$

In this reaction, ammonia is a Lewis base, or donor of an electron pair. BF_3 is a Lewis acid, or acceptor of an electron pair.

$$\begin{array}{c} \text{F} \\ \text{F}:\ddot{\underset{\cdot\cdot}{\text{B}}} \\ \text{F} \end{array} + \begin{array}{c} \text{H} \\ :\ddot{\underset{\cdot\cdot}{\text{N}}}:\text{H} \\ \text{H} \end{array} \rightarrow \begin{array}{c} \text{F}\ \text{H} \\ \text{F}:\ddot{\underset{\cdot\cdot}{\text{B}}}:\ddot{\underset{\cdot\cdot}{\text{N}}}:\text{H} \\ \text{F}\ \text{H} \end{array}$$

According to the theory, not only proton-donating compounds are classified as acids. Any compound capable of accepting a pair of electrons to form a new compound is an acid.

REVIEW IT NOW

1 How do we operationally define acids and bases?
2 Describe the Arrhenius model for acids and bases.
3 What is the hydronium ion?
4 How does the hydronium ion concept allow us to describe acids and bases as proton donors and proton acceptors?
5 Define a *conjugate acid-base pair.*
6 What determines the "strength" of an acid?
7 Write an expression for the equilibrium constant for an acid.
8 How is Table 17–2 used to predict acid-base reactions?

REACTIONS OF ACIDS AND BASES

17–9 · Hydrolysis · When a water solution of NH_4Cl is tested with a strip of litmus paper, the paper turns red. But a solution of sodium acetate will cause litmus to turn blue. The acid-base conjugate-pair theory provides an explanation of why ammonium chloride is an acidic salt and why sodium acetate is a basic salt. To understand the behavior of salts, we must include water as a reactant. Such reactions are called **hydrolysis reactions.** The salt produces positive and negative ions in solution. From Table 17–2, we see that acetate is a stronger base than H_2O. So it can take hydrogen from H_2O.

$$C_2H_3O_2^-(aq) + H_2O(l) \rightleftarrows HC_2H_3O_2(aq) + OH^-(aq)$$

The formation of the $OH^-(aq)$ results in a basic solution. When the NH_4Cl is dissolved in water to form NH_4^+ and Cl^- ions, NH_4^+ is a stronger acid than H_2O.

$$NH_4^+(aq) + 2H_2O(l) = NH_4OH(aq) + H_3O^+(aq)$$

The relative acid or base strength in comparison with H_2O as an acid or a base allows us to predict the nature of the hydrolysis of salts. The general rule is that when salts from a strong acid are neutralized by a weak base, they hydrolyze to form an acid solution. When salts from a weak acid are neutralized by a strong base, they hydrolyze to form an alkaline solution. If the conjugate base (the anion supplied by the salt) is from a strong acid electrolyte, it will not hydrolyze to the molecular form of the acid. If the conjugate acid (the cation supplied by the salt) is from a strong base, it will not hydrolyze. Only the ions from weak electrolytes are hydrolyzed to any great extent. **Hydrolysis,** then, is the reaction between water and an acid or a base to form the conjugate base or acid.

17–10 · Neutralization reactions · When an acid reacts with a base to form a salt and H_2O, the process is called a **neutralization reaction.** It is found experimentally that 13.7 kcal heat per mole of water formed is released whenever any strong acid neutralizes any strong base. That is not surprising, since the net ionic equation for all such reactions is the same.

$$H_3O^+(aq) + OH^-(aq) \rightarrow 2H_2O(l);$$
$$\Delta H = -13.7 \text{ kcal/mol}$$

The enthalpy change is for the same reaction—transferring a mole of protons from a mole of hydronium ions to a mole of hydroxyl ions.

When weak acids are neutralized by strong bases, ΔH is less than 13.7 kcal/mol. For example, the results of the neutralization of acetic acid, CH_3COOH, and of hydrocyanic acid, HCN, by any strong base are as follows.

$$CH_3COOH(aq) + OH^-(aq) \rightleftharpoons CH_3COO^-(aq) + H_2O(l);$$
$$\Delta H = -13.3 \text{ kcal/mol}$$
$$HCN(aq) + OH^-(aq) \rightleftharpoons CN^-(aq) + H_2O(l);$$
$$\Delta H = -2.9 \text{ kcal/mol}$$

Why are those enthalpies of neutralization smaller? Since the acids are weak, they release very little H^+. The difference between 13.7 kcal and the energy that is actually released by neutralization is that energy required to ionize the acids. HCN ($K_A = 4.0 \times 10^{-10}$) is a far weaker acid than CH_3COOH ($K_A = 1.8 \times 10^{-5}$). Thus, more energy should be required to ionize HCN than CH_3COOH.

There is another way to show that HCN is a far weaker acid than CH_3COOH.

If we consider a two-step mechanism for the neutralization of a weak acid with a strong base, we can calculate the energy of ionization of the acid. For CH_3COOH, we postulate the following.

$$CH_3COOH(aq) + H_2O(l) \rightleftharpoons H_3O^+(aq) + CH_3COO^-(aq) \qquad \Delta H_1$$
$$H_3O^+(aq) + OH^-(aq) \rightleftharpoons 2H_2O(l) \qquad \Delta H_2$$
$$\overline{CH_3COOH(aq) + OH^{-1}(aq) \rightleftharpoons CH_3COO^{-1}(aq) + H_2O(l) \quad \Delta H_{neut}}$$

Recall that in Chapter 14 we learned that Hess's law allowed us to determine the energy involved in a reaction by considering the steps in the reaction. We can also apply Hess's law here.

$$\Delta H_{neut} = \Delta H_1 + \Delta H_2$$

We can solve for ΔH_1, the energy of ionization.

$$\Delta H_1 = \Delta H_{neut} - \Delta H_2$$

Using our previous experimental data, we solve for ΔH_1.

$$\Delta H_2 = -13.7 \text{ kcal/mol}$$
$$\Delta H_{neut} = -13.3 \text{ kcal/mol}$$
$$\text{Therefore: } \Delta H_1 = +0.4 \text{ kcal/mol}$$

Ionizing a mole of aqueous CH_3COOH molecules requires 400 calories. A similar calculation for the case of HCN shows that 10 800 calories are required for the ionization of one mole of HCN molecules. Those results are experimental verification that aqueous HCN is a weaker acid than aqueous CH_3COOH.

In many of the reactions we have studied thus far, we include the ionization of water. Since that is an important part of acid-base equilibrium, we will now turn our attention to the reaction of water.

17–11 · Ionization of water · The following is the ionization reaction of water.

$$H_2O(l) + H_2O(l) \rightleftharpoons H_3O^+(aq) + OH^-(aq)$$

The ionization constant for the ionization of water, K_w, is the product of the molar concentrations of the hydronium and hydroxide ions at equilibrium.

$$K_w = [H_3O^+][OH^-]$$

At 25.0°C, the value of K_w is 1×10^{-14}. Thus, water ionizes only to a very slight extent. Water is the weakest of all the acids listcd in Table 17–2. (HS^- is the next-to-last). Since water forms very few charged ions at equilibrium, we would not expect H_2O to be a good conductor of electricity. In fact, it is a very poor conductor.

According to the reaction, an equal number of H_3O^+ and OH^- ions are formed by the ionization. Therefore, we find the concentration of the hydronium and hydroxide ions thus.

$$[H_3O^+] = [OH^-]$$
$$K_w = [H_3O^+][OH^-] = 1 \times 10^{-14}$$
$$[H_3O^+] = 1 \times 10^{-7}\ mol/l$$
$$[OH^-] = 1 \times 10^{-7}\ \text{mol/l}$$

In pure water at 25.0°C, the concentration of H_3O^+ is the same as that of OH^-, 1.0×10^{-7} mol/l. Because there are equal amounts of the acid, H_3O^+, and the base, OH^-, pure water is neutral.

It is important to realize that in all aqueous solutions, the equilibrium law for the H_3O^+–OH^- system must be satisfied. Thus, at the instant than an acid is added to water, thereby increasing the H_3O^+ ion concentration, the H_3O^+–OH^- system must adjust for the change by decreasing the OH^- concentration. For example, let us calculate the OH^- concentration in a 0.01 *M* solution of HCl at 25.0°C. The $H_3O^+(l)$ ion concentration at equilibrium is equal to the sum of the concentrations of H_3O^+ contributed by the two acids in solution.

$$[H_3O^+]_{\text{equilibrium}} = [H_3O^+]_{\text{HCl}} + [H_3O^+]_{H_2O}$$
$$[H_3O^+]_{\text{equilibrium}} = 1.0 \times 10^{-2}\ \text{mol/l} + 1.0 \times 10^{-7}\ \text{mol/l}$$

We can mathematically ignore the contribution that water makes to the H_3O^+ ion concentration, since 10^{-7} is very small, as compared with 10^{-2}.

$$[H_3O^+]_{\text{equilibrium}} = 1.0 \times 10^{-2}\ \text{mol/l}$$

Since $K_w = 1.0 \times 10^{-14} = [H_3O^+][OH^-]$

$$[OH^-] = \frac{K_w}{[H_3O^+]}$$
$$[OH^-] = \frac{1.0 \times 10^{-14}}{1.0 \times 10^{-2}}$$
$$[OH^-] = 1.0 \times 10^{-12}\ \text{mol/l}$$

Thus, we see that an increase in the H_3O^+ ion concentration by 100 000, or a factor of 10^5 ($10^{-7} \times 10^5 = 10^{-2}$), brings about a decrease ($10^{-7} \times 10^{-5} = 10^{-12}$) in the OH^{-1} ion concentration by a factor of 10^5.

Any change in the H_3O^+ or OH^- ion concentrations from the value of 10^{-7} mol/l upsets the acid-base neutrality of pure water. When $[H_3O^+] > 1.0 \times 10^{-7}$ mol/l, the solution is acidic. When $[OH^-] > 1.0 \times 10^{-7}$ mol/l, the solution is basic.

REVIEW IT NOW

1. What do we mean when we say that water is "amphoteric"?
2. Define *hydrolysis.*
3. Give a general rule regarding hydrolysis.
4. What is a neutralization reaction? Write one.
5. When the hydronium ion concentration, $[H_3O^+]$, is greater than 1.0×10^{-7} mol/l, is the solution acidic, or basic?

EXPRESSING THE CONCENTRATION OF ACIDS AND BASES

17–12 · Hydrogen ion concentration and pH · The hydrogen ion concentration of an aqueous solution plays an important role in many geological, chemical, and biological systems. The industrial pollution of the air over the Italian city of Venice causes the rain to be acidic. That acid, in turn, is causing a severe erosion of the marble facades and monuments.

FIGURE 17–5 · *This student is using a pH meter to determine the pH of vinegar. From the reading on the meter, is vinegar basic, or acidic?*

Also, some tropical fish, such as mollies, thrive best in water that is slightly basic ($[H_3O^+] < 10^{-7}$ mol/l); other fish prefer slightly acidic ($[H_3O^+] \approx 3 \times 10^{-7}$ mol/l) conditions. Indigestion results in "acid stomach" for which we take antacid tablets. Since the hydrogen ion concentration is of such common interest, the description of $[H_3O^+]$ has been simplified by use of the expression **pH.** The pH of a solution is defined as the log of the reciprocal of the hydrogen ion concentration, or the negative log of the hydrogen ion concentration.

$$pH = \log \frac{1}{[H_3O^+]} = {}^{-}\log [H_3O^+]$$

For example, the logarithm of 10^{-1} is 1.00. Thus, a solution with a H_3O^+ concentration of 10^{-1} would have a pH of 1.00. Table 17–3 shows the relationship between pH, $[H_3O]^+$, pOH, and $[OH]^-$.

TABLE 17–3 · The Scale of pH

$[H_3O^+]$	pH	$[OH^-]$	pOH	
10^0	0	10^{-14}	14	
10^{-1}	1	10^{-13}	13	
10^{-2}	2	10^{-12}	12	
10^{-3}	3	10^{-11}	11	Acid solution
10^{-4}	4	10^{-10}	10	
10^{-5}	5	10^{-9}	9	
10^{-6}	6	10^{-8}	8	
10^{-7}	7	10^{-7}	7	Neutral solution
10^{-8}	8	10^{-6}	6	
10^{-9}	9	10^{-5}	5	
10^{-10}	10	10^{-4}	4	
10^{-11}	11	10^{-3}	3	Basic solution
10^{-12}	12	10^{-2}	2	
10^{-13}	13	10^{-1}	1	
10^{-14}	14	10^0	0	

EXERCISE

1. *What is the pH of a solution with $[H_3O^+]$ of 10^{-12}? Is the solution acidic, or basic?*
2. *What is the pH of a 0.001 M solution of HCl?*

Since $[H_3O^+]$ values are usually less than one, the log of $[H_3O^+]$ would be negative. For example, a solution of 0.01 *M* HCl in which $[H_3O^+] = 0.01$ will have a $[H_3O^+]$ of 10^{-2}. Therefore, log $[H^+]$ is equal to −2. To avoid negative values, log $\frac{1}{[H_3O^+]}$ is used. Thus, the pH of the 0.01 *M* HCl solution is 2.00.

In pure water at 25.0°C, $[H_3O^+] = 1.00 \times 10^{-7}$ M. Therefore, we can find the pH of pure water by the following.

$$\log 1/[H_3O^+] = \log \frac{1}{1.0 \times 10^{-7}}$$

$$= \log 10^{+7} = 7$$

$$\text{pH} = 7 \text{ for pure water}$$

We can also define pOH values as the following.

$$\text{pOH} = \log \frac{1}{[OH^-]}$$

In pure water $[OH^-] = 10^{-7}$ M, so pOH = 7.
Consequently, for pure water at 25.0°C, we discover the following.

$$\text{pH} + \text{pOH} = 14$$

As we have previously noted, many chemical and biological processes depend on the careful control of acidity. Body fluids vary in pH from a value of about 7.40 (slightly basic) for blood to 1–2 (quite acid) for gastric juices. In digestion, the enzyme pepsin is an important factor. That enzyme has been shown to be inactive except in an acid solution. It is the pH rather than any particular acid that activates pepsin.

Saliva has a pH that varies considerably, although it is usually about 6.80. But it increases as high as 7.80 when a person is eating. In saliva, the enzyme ptyalin is active in the digestion of starches. It is also interesting that the calcium phosphate in teeth would normally dissolve somewhat at the normal pH of saliva. However, saliva also contains calcium ions and phosphate ions that suppress the solubility according to the solubility product equilibrium. Table 17–4 lists the pH values of some commonly encountered solutions.

TABLE 17–4 · pH Values of Some Solutions

Solution	pH	Solution	pH
Limes	1.8–2.0	0.1N HCl	1.0
Lemon juice	2.3	0.1N H_2SO_4	1.2
Apples	3.0	0.1N $HC_2H_3O_2$ (vinegar)	2.9
Orange juice	3.3	0.1N H_3BO_3	5.1
Tomatoes	4.2	0.1N $NaHCO_3$	8.4
Carrots	5.0	0.1N $Na_2B_4O_7$	9.2
Cabbage	5.3	0.1N NH_4OH	11.1
Cow's milk	6.6	0.1N Na_2CO_3	11.3
Milk of magnesia	10.5	0.1N NaOH	13.0

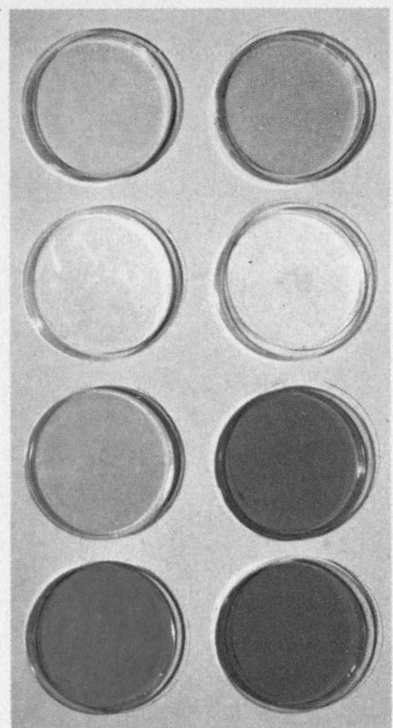

FIGURE 17–6 · *Bromthymol blue was added to the substances in each of the four petri dishes on the left. Which of the substances are basic, and which are acidic? Phenol red was the indicator used in the four petri dishes on the right. Which of these substances are basic, and which are acidic?*

17–13 · Indicators · A number of compounds are known that change color when the pH of a solution changes. Such compounds can be used as **indicators** of a pH change. The indicators are usually very weak organic acids that have different colors for the acid and the base forms. Using the formula HIn for the indicator acid, we can write a general equation.

$$\underset{\text{Color A}}{HIn(aq)} + H_2O(l) = H_3O^+(aq) + \underset{\text{Color B}}{In^-(aq)}$$

In a solution of an acid stronger than HIn, color A would be present. But in a solution of a weaker acid (or of a stronger base than In^-), color B is present. Table 17–5 lists some common indicators and the pH range in which they change color. By testing a solution with several of the indicators, it is possible to estimate the pH of a solution rather well. Often the indicator is available in test paper form. The pH can be determined to within a few tenths of a unit from this pH paper.

TABLE 17–5 · Some Acid-Base Indicators

INDICATOR	COLOR CHANGE WITH INCREASING pH	pH RANGE
Thymol blue	Red to yellow	1.2–2.8
Bromphenol blue	Yellow to blue	3.0–4.6
Methyl orange	Red to yellow	3.1–4.4
Bromcresol green	Yellow to blue	3.8–5.4
Methyl red	Red to yellow	4.2–6.2
Litmus	Red to blue	4.5–8.3
Bromthymol blue	Yellow to blue	6.0–7.6
Phenol red	Yellow to red	6.8–8.4
Phenolphthalein	Colorless to red	8.3–10.0
Alizarin yellow	Yellow to violet	10.1–12.0
1,3,5-trinitrobenzene	Colorless to yellow	12.0–14.0

A more accurate way to obtain the pH quickly and accurately is to use an electronic pH meter. This device will measure one of the electrical properties of the solution that is a function of the H_3O^+ concentration. The meter is usually calibrated to read pH directly.

17–14 · Buffer solutions · Sometimes it is desirable to maintain a constant pH, even when small amounts of H_3O^+ or OH^- are to be added. A solution that has the ability to maintain a constant pH is called a **buffer solution.** A typical buffer solution contains a weak acid and a salt of that acid, or a weak base

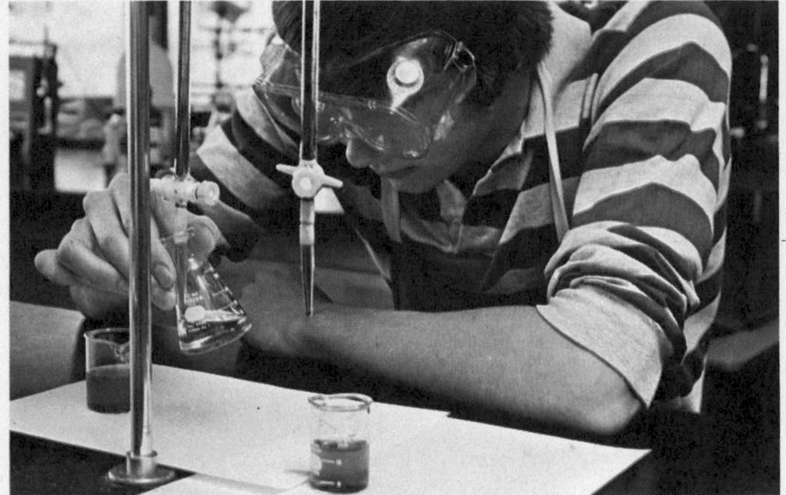

FIGURE 17–7 · *The classic chemical method of determining pH is to use acid-base titration. Glass tubes called burettes are used to deliver carefully measured amounts of a standard base and the unknown acid into a flask containing an indicator. When complete neutralization has occurred at the end point of the titration, a sharp color change is observed in the acid-base indicator.*

and a salt of that base. An example is NH_4OH and NH_4Cl in the same water solution. Because NH_4OH is slightly ionized, there is a reserve of OH^- ready to replace those ions that are removed by adding H_3O^+. If a strong base is added, NH_4^+ ions join the OH^- ions to form NH_4OH. In this reaction, excess hydroxide ions are removed.

An acid-base-salt combination that is often used is either acetic acid and sodium acetate, or phosphoric acid and various phosphates. Table 17–6 lists some buffer combinations and their pH. Buffer action is important in the chemistry of most fluids within a living organism, where the correct biological activity occurs if the pH remains within fairly narrow limits.

TABLE 17–6 · Approximate pH Values of Some Buffer Solutions

BUFFER PAIR	APPROXIMATE pH
Potassium acid phthalate – hydrochloric acid	1.8 – 3.8
Sodium acetate – acetic acid	3.6 – 5.6
Potassium acid phthalate – sodium hydroxide	4.0 – 6.0
Potassium acid phosphate – sodium hydroxide	5.8 – 7.8
Boric acid – sodium borate	7.5 – 9.5
Boric acid – sodium hydroxide	8.2 – 10.2
Disodium phosphate – sodium hydroxide	10.5 – 12.0

REVIEW IT NOW

1 What are indicators? How do they work?
2 Describe several ways to determine pH.
3 Why are buffers important? How do they work?

SUMMARY

Two of the major classes of chemical compounds are acids and bases. There are certain characteristics of those substances that we call acids and bases. Arrhenius proposed to explain those characteristics by showing that all acids release H^+ in solution, and all bases release OH^-. Modern acid-base theory, however, suggests that all acids release a proton, or are proton donors. All bases are proton acceptors. The proton released by an acid is hydrated in water solution and forms a hydronium ion, H_3O^+. Thus, an acid can become a base by releasing a proton. The acid-base pair is called a conjugate acid-base pair. Acids differ in their tendency to release a proton. The amount of H_3O^+ in solution at equilibrium determines if the acid is strong or weak. An equilibrium expression can be written for an acid-base reaction, giving K_A, the acid equilibrium constant. Acids and bases undergo characteristic reactions. Two such reactions are hydrolysis and neutralization. The negative log of the hydrogen ion concentration at equilibrium is called the pH of the solution. A pH of less than 7 is acidic; a pH that is greater than 7 is basic. The pOH of a solution can be defined similarly. Many biological and chemical reactions operate within a very narrow pH range. Indicators are weak acids that are helpful in determining the pH of a solution.

REVIEW QUESTIONS

1 As a chemist, you have come across a substance that you suspect is an acid. It has a sour taste. What other tests can you make to help determine if the substance is, in fact, an acid?

2 Explain fully the differences between the following acid-base theories.
   a. Arrhenius's theory
   b. Proton donor theory

3 Using the conjugate acid-base concept, show the reaction between the following acids and bases.
   a. $HClO_4$ and OH^-
   b. HCl and F^-
   c. $NH_4{}^+$ and $CO_3{}^{-2}$

4 K_A values for some acids are given below. Which is the *strongest* acid? Which is the *weakest*?
   a. Phosphoric acid, H_3PO_4; $K_{H_3PO_4} = 7.0 \times 10^{-3}$
   b. Acetic acid, CH_3COOH; $K_{CH_3COOH} = 1.8 \times 10^{-5}$
   c. Hydronium ion, H_3O^+; $K_{H_3O^+} = 1.0$
   d. Sulfurous acid, H_2SO_3; $K_{H_2SO_3} = 1.7 \times 10^{-2}$
   e. Nitrous acid, HNO_2; $K_{HNO_2} = 5.1 \times 10^{-4}$

5 Give the conjugate base for each acid listed in question **4**.

6 A solution has $[H_3O^+] = 1.0 \times 10^{-3}$mol/l. What is the concentration of OH^-?

7 Is nitric acid a strong, or a weak, acid? What is the $[H^+]$ in a 0.050 *M* HNO_3 solution?

8 A solution has a pH = 10.

a. Is it acidic, or basic?

b. What is the $[H^+]$?

c. What is the pOH?

d. What is the $[OH^-]$?

9 Consider a solution that has a $[H^+] = 10^{-5}$.

a. Is it acidic, or basic?

b. What is the pH?

c. What is the pOH?

10 Suppose you have a 0.01 *M* NaOH solution.

a. Calculate the hydrogen ion concentration.

b. What is the pH?

c. What is the pOH?

11 HF is a weak acid, with $K_A = 6.7 \times 10^{-4}$. We can represent the ionization of HF as follows. $HF(aq) \rightleftharpoons H^+(aq) + F^-(aq)$

a. Suppose you have a 0.10 *M* solution of HF; what is the concentration of $F^-(aq)$?

b. At equilibrium, the concentration of H^+ is found to be 8.2×10^{-3} mol/l. Write an acid equilibrium constant expression for the reaction.

12 The reaction for the ionization of acetic acid is as follows.

$$CH_3COOH(aq) \rightleftharpoons H^+(aq) + CH_3COO^-(aq)$$

Suppose you now add sodium acetate, $NaCH_3COO$, to the reaction mixture.

a. What will happen to $[H^+]$?

b. What will happen to $[CH_3COO^-]$?

c. State the principle that predicts **a** and **b.**

SUGGESTED READINGS

House, J. E., Jr. "Negative Hydrogen." *Chemistry,* March 1971, p. 8.

Jensen, William. "Lewis Acid–Base Theory." *Chemistry,* March 1974, p. 11.

Klein, Aaron E. "Acid Rain in the United States." *The Science Teacher,* May 1974, p. 36.

Morris, Daniel L. "Stress, Collisions, and Constants. Part I: Solutions." *Chemistry,* April 1971, p. 10.

——— "Brönsted-Lowry Acid-Base Theory—A Brief Survey." *Chemistry,* March 1970, p. 18.

Schofield, Maurice. "Early Days of Sulfuric Acid." *Chemistry,* October 1972, p. 11.

Van Der Werf, Calvin. *Acids, Bases and Chemistry of the Covalent Bond.* New York: D. Van Nostrand Co., 1961.

A familiar example of oxidation is the slow formation of rust.

CHAPTER EIGHTEEN

Oxidation and Reduction

The chemical battery is an achievement of chemistry on which we all depend. In a chemical battery, chemical energy is converted to electrical energy. That electrical energy is used to start our cars, run our transistor radios, and power spacecraft in flight. In Chapter 13, we learned that chemical energy is produced by a chemical reaction. It follows, therefore, that the electrical energy of a chemical battery is produced by a chemical reaction. The type of chemical reaction involved in a battery is classified as a **reduction-oxidation,** or a **redox,** reaction. We have already studied one major type of chemical reaction—those involving acids and bases. In Chapter 18, we will study redox reactions—a second major type of chemical change.

THE PROCESS OF GAINING AND LOSING ELECTRONS

18–1 · Oxidation and oxygen · Fire and burning fascinated people long before the development of modern science. Antoine Lavoisier studied combustion in a careful, logical fashion in 1774. He placed metallic mercury in a sealed glass vessel and heated it for twelve days, until most of the mercury had been converted to a red powder. Then he opened the vessel and observed that air was sucked into it. That convinced Lavoisier that part of the air originally in the vessel had combined with the mercury to form the red powder. We now know that the red powder is mercuric oxide. Scientists soon learned that burning is a rapid combination of substances with oxygen and causes the release of a great amount of energy in the form of heat.

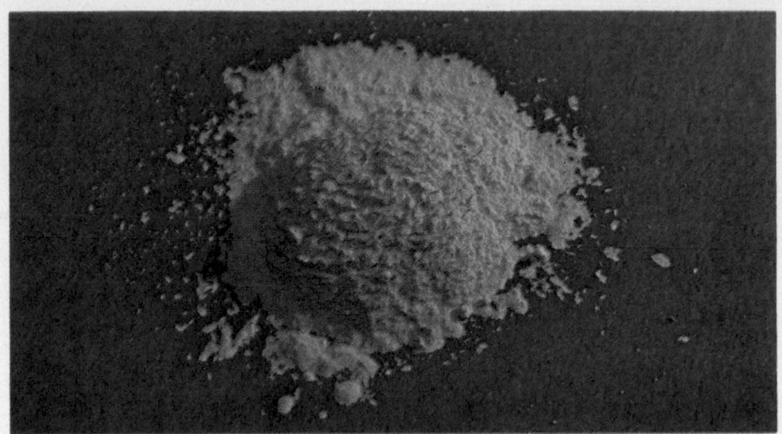

FIGURE 18–1 · *The production of red mercuric oxide is an example of oxidation.*

Many substances burn rapidly in air. Coal is one example.

$$C(s) + O_2(g) \rightarrow CO_2(g)$$

Other substances react more slowly with oxygen. We see that in the corrosion of metals. The rusting of iron is a slow reaction.

$$4Fe(s) + 3O_2(g) \rightarrow 2Fe_2O_3(s)$$

The rotting of dead organic material is another slow reaction with oxygen.

$$C_xH_yO_z + qO_2 \rightarrow xCO_2(g) + 0.5y\ H_2O(g)$$

Reaction with oxygen is very common and very important. Such reactions have been given the name **oxidation.** The reverse process in which oxides (compounds of oxygen) are converted to elements or compounds with a lower oxygen content is called **reduction.**

18–2 · A new definition of oxidation and reduction · Let's study a simple oxidation reaction more closely. Calcium metal reacts with oxygen to form calcium oxide.

$$Ca(s) + 0.50\ O_2(g) \rightarrow CaO(s)$$

You have learned that chemical bonding is related to electron configuration. Let's look at the electron configurations involved in this oxidation reaction. Calcium changes from neutral calcium atoms to *dipositive* calcium cations. Thus, each calcium must lose two electrons.

$$Ca^\circ \longrightarrow Ca^{+2} + 2e$$

$$(1s^2 2s^2 2p^6 3s^2 3p^6 4s^2) \rightarrow (1s^2 2s^2 2p^6 3s^2 3p^6)$$

The oxygen must acquire these two electrons, as it becomes a *dinegative* anion.

$$0.50\ O_2 + 2e \rightarrow O^{-2}$$
$$(1s^22s^22p^4) \rightarrow (1s^22s^22p^6)$$

Since the reaction occurs with oxygen, it is an oxidation reaction. Now compare the oxidation reaction with the reaction of calcium and chlorine gas.

$$Ca(s) + Cl_2(g) \rightarrow CaCl_2(s)$$

Again calcium atoms lose two electrons to form the Ca^{+2} cations.

$$Ca \longrightarrow Ca^{+2} + 2e$$
$$(1s^22s^22p^63s^23p^64s^2) \rightarrow (1s^22s^22p^63s^23p^6)$$

Recall the evolution of the definition of acids and bases. Beginning with the operational definition, chemists found a conceptual definition based on the common mechanism of proton donation (acids) and proton acceptance (bases). A similar evolution has occurred with the definition of oxidation reactions. First, it was understood that the reaction of elements to form oxides always involves a loss of electrons by the element. It seemed logical to make that loss of electrons the basis of defining a reaction as oxidation. Therefore, oxidation involves the loss of electrons. Just as bases were defined as the opposite of acids, so reduction has been defined as the opposite of oxidation. Consequently, reduction involves the gain of electrons.

18–3 · No oxidation without reduction · There is one more similarity of oxidation and reduction reactions to acid-base reactions. Recall that acid-base reactions always involve conjugate pairs. Moreover, for a substance to act as an acid (proton donor), a base (proton acceptor) had to be present. (It's impossible to give something away unless something else accepts it.) Recall our two oxidation reactions—$Ca + O_2$ and $Ca + Cl_2$. We have already learned that oxygen accepted electrons. Chlorine must accept electrons in the second example, since neutral Cl_2 becomes Cl^- anions. According to the definition, the oxygen in the first example and the chlorine in the second are reduced.

We can now make a general statement. In any reaction in which one substance is oxidized (loses electrons), another substance must be reduced (gains electrons). So reactions simultaneously involve reduction and oxidation. To reflect that, such reactions are called redox reactions. Redox reactions are a second major class of chemical reactions. In the first major type, acid-base reactions, electron pairs are shared (the Lewis theory). In the second type, redox reactions, electrons are lost and gained. Since calcium in our example loses electrons, we say it has been oxidized.

The oxygen, which accepts the electrons, causes the calcium to be oxidized. So oxygen is called the **oxidizing agent.** Conversely, the calcium causes reduction, so it is the **reducing agent.** Note that the oxidizing agent is reduced while the reducing agent is oxidized!

EXERCISE

Metallic sodium reacts with fluorine gas according to the following reaction.

$$Na(s) + 0.50\ F_2(g) = NaF(s)$$

In this reaction, Na loses an electron.

$$Na(s) = Na^+ + 1e$$

The fluorine gains an electron.

$$0.50\ F_2 + 1e = F^-$$

1. *Which substance is oxidized?*
2. *Which substance is reduced?*
3. *Which is the reducing agent?*
4. *Which is the oxidizing agent?*

18–4 · Oxidation numbers · For reactions in which ionic compounds such as CaO and $CaCl_2$ are formed, it is easy to discuss the loss of electrons by calcium and the gain of electrons by oxygen and chlorine. However, consider another reaction in which a covalent compound is formed.

$$H_2(g) + 0.50\ O_2(g) = H_2O(l)$$

This is obviously a redox reaction, since it is a combination with oxygen, which is the old definition of oxidation-reduction. And the new definition of redox reactions (loss and gain of electrons) must include all reactions covered by the older definition. Since H_2O is covalent, we cannot speak of H or O gaining or losing electrons, since they are sharing electrons.

That dilemma is solved by the use of a fictional property of atoms known as the **oxidation number.** The oxidation number is obtained by assigning the shared electrons of a covalent bond to the more electronegative atom of the bonded pair. Therefore, the oxidation number of each atom is the formal charge on it. Since oxygen is more electronegative than hydrogen, the electron pairs are assigned to it.

$$\begin{array}{c} \mathrm{H}:\ddot{\underset{\cdot\cdot}{\mathrm{O}}}: \\ \quad\mathrm{H} \end{array}$$

This arbitrary assignment gives oxygen eight electrons in the outer orbitals ($2s^2 2p^6$). Since this is two more electrons than in the normal configuration of $2s^2 2p^4$, or six electrons, we say that oxygen has an oxidation number of −2. By the same arbitrary assignment, hydrogen has no electrons, since we assigned them all to oxygen. So the oxidation number for hydrogen is +1. The oxidation number essentially corresponds to the ionic charge that an atom would have if the bond was ionic rather than covalent. A monatomic ion also has an oxidation number that corresponds to its ionic charge. For example, the oxidation number of oxygen in calcium oxide is −2 and that of calcium is +2.

The following simple rules can be followed to obtain oxidation numbers.

1. Atoms present in their elemental state are assigned oxidation numbers of zero. Some examples are Ca(*s*), O_2, Hg(*l*), and all elements in the 0 oxidation state.
2. If an atom exists as a monatomic ion, the oxidation number is the same as the ionic charge. For example, the oxidation number of Na^+ is +1; of Al^{+3}, +3; of S^{-2}; −2; of I^-, −1.
3. For neutral molecules the sum of all the oxidation numbers must be zero. For example, in Al_2S_3 the total for Al is 2 x (+3) = +6, while for S it is 3 x (−2) = −6.
4. For complex ions and molecules,
   a. the oxidation number of hydrogen is defined as +1, except in hydrides, such as NaH, when it is −1;
   b. the oxidation number of oxygen is defined as −2, except in peroxides, when it is −1;
   c. the oxidation number of any other element is such that the sum of the oxidation numbers of the elements in a complex ion equals the charge of that ion. In a molecular compound, that sum equals zero.

Table 18-1 indicates how these rules are applied in some familiar complex ions and covalent molecules. A useful definition of oxidation and reduction, based on the oxidation-number concept, is that oxidation is the process by which the oxidation number of an element is increased. Reduction is the process by which the oxidation number of an element is decreased, or reduced in value.

TABLE 18-1 · Oxidation Numbers

COMPLEX ION OR COVALENT MOLECULE	OXIDATION NUMBERS	CONSERVATION OF CHARGE
H_2O	$\overset{+1}{H_2}\overset{-2}{O}$	$2(+1) + (-2) = 0$
H_3O^{+1}	$(\overset{+1}{H_3}\overset{-2}{O})^{+1}$	$3(+1) + (-2) = +1$
NH_3	$\overset{-3}{N}\overset{+1}{H_3}$	$(-3) + 3(+1) = 0$
NH_4^{+1}	$(\overset{-3}{N}\overset{+1}{H_4})^{+1}$	$(-3) + 4(+1) = +1$
CH_3COOH	$\overset{0}{C}\overset{+1}{H_3}\overset{0}{C}\overset{-2}{O}\overset{-2}{O}\overset{+1}{H}$	$4(+1) + 2(-2) + 2(0) = 0$
CH_3COO^{-1}	$(\overset{0}{C}\overset{+1}{H_3}\overset{0}{C}\overset{-2}{O}\overset{-2}{O})^{-1}$	$3(+1) + 2(-2) + 2(0) = -1$

EXERCISE

Write the oxidation number for each element in the following chemical species.

1. Na^{+1} 3. $MgCl_2$ 5. $(MnO_4)^{-1}$
2. $PbSO_4$ 4. HNO_3 6. $Al(H_2O)_4(OH)_2^{+1}$

18-5 · Balancing redox equations · Many redox equations can be balanced simply by counting atoms. An example is the oxidation of phosphorus.

$$P_4(s) + 5O_2(g) \rightleftharpoons 2P_2O_5(s)$$

Since we can easily account for four phosphorus atoms and ten oxygen atoms on each side of the equation, the reaction is balanced. Often, however, redox reactions are rather complicated, and balancing them is not so simple. An example is the reaction of copper metal with nitric acid.

$$Cu + HNO_3 \rightleftharpoons Cu(NO_3)_2 + NO_2 + H_2O$$

It is possible to balance this equation by using algebra. However, a simpler method has been developed involving the changes in oxidation numbers. Before we balance the $Cu + HNO_3$ equation, let us work on a somewhat simpler example to illustrate the method. Zinc reacts with HCl in the following equation.

$$Zn(s) + HCl(aq) = ZnCl_2(aq) + H_2(g)$$

The first step in the procedure is to decide on the oxidation number of all species.

$$Zn^{\circ} + H^{+1}Cl^{-1} = Zn^{+2}Cl_2^{-1} + H_2$$

Obviously, zinc is oxidized and hydrogen reduced, while the oxidation state of chlorine is unchanged. The second step is to write the part of the reaction that involves oxidation and, separately, the part that involves reduction. Since each reaction accounts for half of the total reaction, we call them **half-reactions.** We must also include electrons in the half-reaction equations in order to balance the charges. Each half-reaction is balanced for atoms and for charge, also.

Oxidation half-reaction.

$$Zn \rightarrow Zn^{+2} + 2e^{-1}$$

Reduction half-reaction

$$2H^{+} + 2e^{-1} \rightarrow H_2$$

Next the number of electrons lost in the oxidation and the number gained in the reduction are made equal. In our example, they are already equal (2). Now the two half-reactions are simply added together to obtain a net equation.

$$\begin{array}{l} \textit{Oxidation } Zn^{\circ} \rightarrow Zn^{+2} + 2e^{-1} \\ \textit{Reduction } 2H^{+} + 2e^{-1} = H_2 \\ \hline \textit{Net } Zn + 2H^{+} = Zn^{+2} + H_2 \end{array}$$

The full equation follows.

$$Zn(s) + 2HCl(aq) = ZnCl_2(aq) + H_2(g)$$

EXAMPLE

For an example of balancing a redox equation, let's use the reaction mentioned earlier between Cu and HNO_3.

1. *Write the skeleton equation.*

$$Cu + HNO_3 = Cu(NO_3)_2 + NO_2 + H_2O$$

2. *Assign oxidation numbers.*

$$Cu^{\circ} + H^{+1}N^{+5}O_3^{-2} = Cu^{+2}(N^{+5}O_3^{-2})_2 + N^{+4}O_2^{-2} + H_2^{+1}O^{-2}$$

3. *Write and balance each half-reaction.*

$$\text{Oxidation } Cu^\circ \rightarrow Cu^{+2} + 2e$$

$$\text{Reduction } 2H^+ + NO_3^- + e^- = NO_2 + H_2O$$

4. *Balance the electron change in the two half-reactions.*

$$\text{Oxidation } Cu \rightarrow Cu^{+2} + 2e$$

$$\text{Reduction } 4H^+ + 2NO_3^- + 2e^{-1} = 2NO_2 + 2H_2O$$

5. *Write the net reaction, checking to be sure that the charges and the number of atoms are balanced.*

$$\text{Net } Cu + 4H^+ + 2NO_3^- = Cu^{+2} + 2NO_2 + 2H_2O$$

We then have a total, balanced equation.

$$Cu(s) + 4HNO_3(aq) = Cu(NO_3)_2(aq) + 2NO_2(g) + 2H_2O(l)$$

Note that of the four NO_3^- in $4HNO_3$, two are reduced, while two are unchanged, appearing in $Cu(NO_3)_2$.

REVIEW IT NOW

1 Give a *conceptual* definition of oxidation.
2 Give an *operational* definition of oxidation.
3 Give an *operational* definition of reduction.
4 Give a *conceptual* definition of reduction.
5 What is an oxidation number?
6 How are oxidation numbers assigned?
7 State the rules to be followed in obtaining oxidation numbers.
8 What is a half-reaction?
9 What is the significance of half-reactions in balancing redox reactions?
10 Go through the steps necessary to balance a redox reaction.

OXIDATION-REDUCTION POTENTIALS

18–6 · Redox and electrochemical cells · When a strip of zinc metal is placed into a solution of copper (II) sulfate, some copper metal is deposited on the zinc surface. An analysis of the solution shows that some zinc has dissolved. The following is the net reaction (Figure 18–2).

$$Zn^\circ(s) + Cu^{+2}(aq) = Zn^{+2}(aq) + Cu^\circ(s)$$

We determine the oxidation half-reaction.

$$Zn^\circ(s) = Zn^{+2}(aq) + 2e^{-1}$$

And we determine the reduction half-reaction.

$$Cu^{+2}(aq) + 2e^{-1} = Cu^{\circ}(s)$$

Now we can ask an interesting question. Does separating the reaction into two half-reactions have any meaning? Is it only a pen-and-paper trick? To answer those questions, we must think of an experiment from which the results can be readily interpreted in terms of half-reactions. Consider the two half-reactions of the redox equation shown above. In the oxidation half-reaction, a zinc metal atom releases two electrons and goes into solution as Zn^{+2}. In the reduction half-reaction, as a Cu^{+2} ion leaves the solution and becomes a copper metal atom, it gains two electrons. In our first experiment of dipping zinc in $Cu(NO_3)_2$ solution, the electrons gained by the Cu^{+2} transferred directly from the zinc metal to the copper as it contacted the zinc strip.

Recall that electricity is a flow of electrons. If electrons are really lost and gained, suppose we do the following. Let's place the zinc strip in a solution of $Zn(NO_3)_2$. Place a copper metal strip in a solution of $Cu(NO_3)_2$. Then we connect the two metal strips by a wire. If electrons are really lost by zinc ions and gained by copper ions, the electrons can move through the wire from the zinc to the copper. To complete the circuit, we must arrange the experiment as shown in Figure 18–3. In the arrangement, the two solutions are in contact but not mixed. This system is known as a **Daniell cell.**

In the Daniell cell, we find that electrons do move from the zinc to the copper. We know that because a light bulb in the circuit glows, which indicates that the current is passing through the system. An ammeter, which measures the flow of electric current, can be placed in the circuit to measure the electron movement. Moreover, as the electricity continues to move from the zinc to the copper, we find that the zinc is dissolving (oxidizing) as Zn^{+2}, and the Cu^{+2} is being deposited (reduced) as copper metal. So we have shown that half-reactions can be real and can occur separately, but simultaneously. If we separate two half-reactions physically, the electrons must travel through an external system of conductors to complete the reaction. The electrical energy of the reaction is then available for use. A physical separation of the two half-reactions produces an electrochemical cell, or battery. The Daniell cell formed by the Zn–Cu redox reaction has a voltage of about one volt.

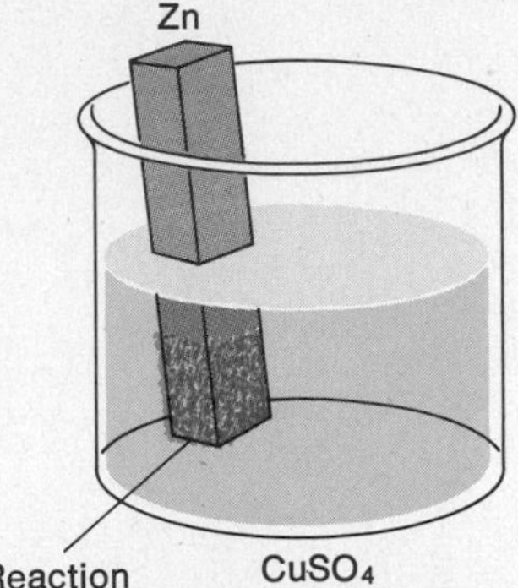

FIGURE 18–2 · *In this net reaction, some copper metal is deposited on the zinc surface.*

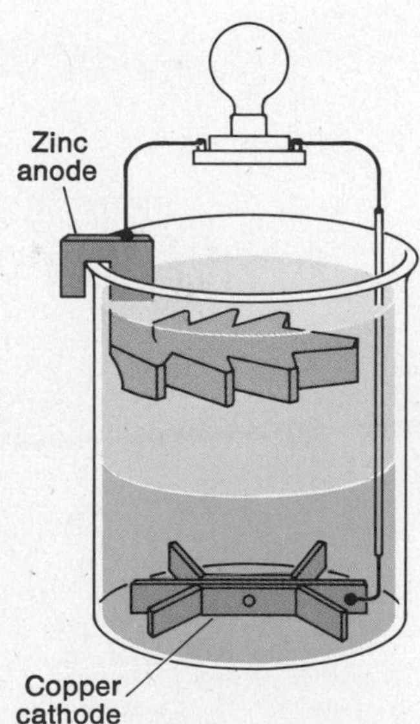

FIGURE 18–3 · *In the Daniell cell, a copper cathode is immersed in a copper sulfate solution. A zinc anode is immersed in a zinc sulfate solution, which floats on the denser copper sulfate solution. What serves as a barrier to the bulk diffusion of ions?*

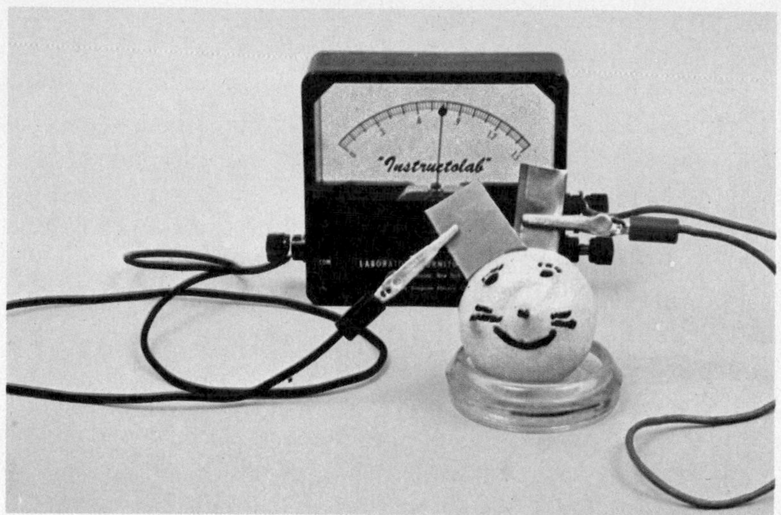

FIGURE 18–4 · *An electrochemical cell like this one, using a lemon and strips of zinc and copper, is easily made.*

The lead storage battery used in automobiles produces about two volts per redox cell. Usually three or six cells are used in the battery, in order to obtain six or twelve volts. In the cells, the half-reactions occur on the surfaces of plates made of porous lead and lead(IV) oxide. The following represents the redox reaction in the sulfuric acid electrolyte solution found in the storage battery of an automobile.

$$Pb(s) + PbO_2(s) + 4H_3O^{+1}(aq) + 2SO_4^{-2}(aq) \rightarrow 2PbSO_4(s) + 6H_2O(l)$$

Oxidation half-reaction

$$Pb(s) + SO_4^{-2}(aq) \rightarrow PbSO_4(s) + 2e^{-1}$$

Reduction half-reaction

$$PbO_2(s) + SO_4^{-2}(aq) + 4H_3O^{+1}(aq) + 2e^{-1} \rightarrow PbSO_4(s) + 6H_2O(l)$$

Insoluble $PbSO_4$ is a product of both half-reactions.

Many new combinations of half-reactions have been used to make the electrochemical cells that are commonly used in battery-operated appliances and in the NASA space program. As new methods of the physical separation of energetic half-cell reactions are developed, we can expect an even greater use of battery-powered devices.

18–7 · Measuring redox potentials · Suppose we make a Daniell cell as shown in Figure 18–5. The zinc and copper metal strips are called **electrodes.** When the circuit is closed and electric current flows, the voltmeter shown in Figure 18–5 will read +1.10 volts. That indicates an electron flow from the zinc to the copper electrode. The surface on which oxidation occurs is called the **anode.** The surface on which reduction occurs is the **cathode**—in this case, the copper electrode. That is important to remember. The anode is where oxidation occurs; the cathode is where reduction occurs.

We use the symbol V for voltage or, perhaps a better expression, for the **electromotive force** (EMF). The voltage is also known as the **potential** *(E)*. Since we can break the redox reactions into half-reactions, it is reasonable to consider that the cell potential is the sum of the potential of the oxidation half-reaction and the potential of the reduction half-reaction.

$$E_{cell} = E_{oxid} + E_{red} = 1.10 \text{ V}$$

We abbreviate the half-cell potentials as $E_{Zn/Zn^{+2}}$ and $E_{Cu^{+2}/Cu}$. Suppose the oxidation half-reaction of Zn/Zn^{+2} has a potential of −0.76 volt. Then when the same "couple," Zn and Zn^{+2}, is a *reduction* half-reaction, we see the reverse of the reaction, or the gaining of two electrons. Thus, the potential would be just the reverse, or +0.76 volt. That is shown below.

Oxidation

$$Zn^{\circ} \rightarrow Zn^{+2} + 2e^{-1};\ E_{anode} = -0.76 \text{ V}$$

Reduction

$$Zn^{+2} + 2e^{-1} \rightleftharpoons Zn^{\circ};\ E_{cathode} = +0.76 \text{ V}$$

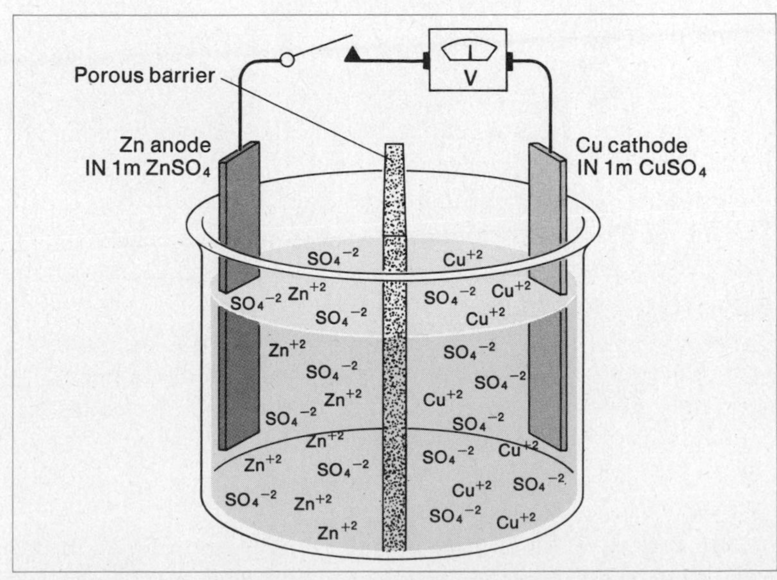

FIGURE 18–5 · *When the switch is closed in this system at 25.0°C, an electrochemical cell is operating under standard conditions.*

Let's take a closer look at half-reactions. First, consider the following reaction of copper. In the reaction, a Cu^{+2} ion is formed, and two electrons are produced.

$$Cu(s) \rightleftharpoons Cu^{+2}(aq) + 2e^-$$

We can perform the reaction experimentally by placing a metal copper electrode in a solution of $CuSO_4$. However, as indicated earlier, we can never observe only one half-reaction. Another reaction must occur at the same time to accept the electrons. The following experiment will illustrate this.

Suppose we set up a cell with a porous barrier separating two compartments, like that shown in Figure 18–5. On one side of the barrier, we will place a copper electrode in a solution of $CuSO_4$. On the other side, we will place a silver metal electrode in a solution of $AgNO_3$. After an hour or so, the following observations can be made.

1. The solution in which the silver electrode is placed has turned blue, characteristic of the copper ion in solution.
2. A silvery deposit has coated the copper electrode.

The silvery deposit is metallic silver. It was produced by the Ag^+ ions in the $AgNO_3$ solution. Those ions picked up the electrons released by the copper metal, forming metallic Ag.

$$2Ag^{+2}(aq) + 2e^- \rightleftharpoons 2Ag(s)$$

Now we can show both half-reactions as a total oxidation-reduction reaction.

$$Cu(s) + 2Ag^+(aq) \rightleftharpoons 2Ag(s) + Cu^{+2}(aq)$$

The important thing to realize here is that copper metal *gave up* electrons to the silver ion.

Now let's perform another experiment. We will use a cell like the one in our previous experiment. However, this time we will place a zinc metal electrode and a solution of zinc sulfate in the cell instead of silver and silver nitrate.

This time our results are quite different. The Cu^{+2} ions *accept* electrons from the Zn(s) and form solid copper. The copper is deposited on the surface of the zinc electrode. We can show the total reaction as follows.

$$Zn(s) + Cu^{+2}(aq) \rightleftharpoons Zn^{+2}(aq) + Cu(s)$$

In one situation, Cu(s) gave up electrons to form Cu^{+2}. In the other case, the Cu^{+2} accepted electrons to form Cu(s).

Why does copper give up electrons in one cell, but accept them in another? We can explain this if we assume that all metals have a tendency to give up electrons. Some, however, have a greater tendency than others.

EXERCISE

From what we have learned so far, arrange the following half-cell reactions in the order of decreasing *tendency of the metal to give up electrons.*

1. $Cu(s) \rightleftharpoons Cu^{+2}(aq) + 2e^-$

2. $Zn(s) \rightleftharpoons Zn^{+2}(aq) + 2e^-$

3. $2Ag(s) \rightleftharpoons 2Ag^+(aq) + 2e^-$

Our two experiments would lead us to believe zinc gives up electrons to copper, and copper gives up electrons to silver. Thus, the order of half-cells would be Zn:Cu:Ag. If our assumption is correct, what do you expect to happen if a zinc half-cell is placed in a silver half-cell?

If you predicted that Ag^+ will still accept electrons from Zn(s) to form metallic Ag, you are correct. Experimentally, that is just what happens.

It now seems logical to compare many half-cells with one another. We can then determine an *order* of half-cells and, list them according to their tendency to gain or lose electrons.

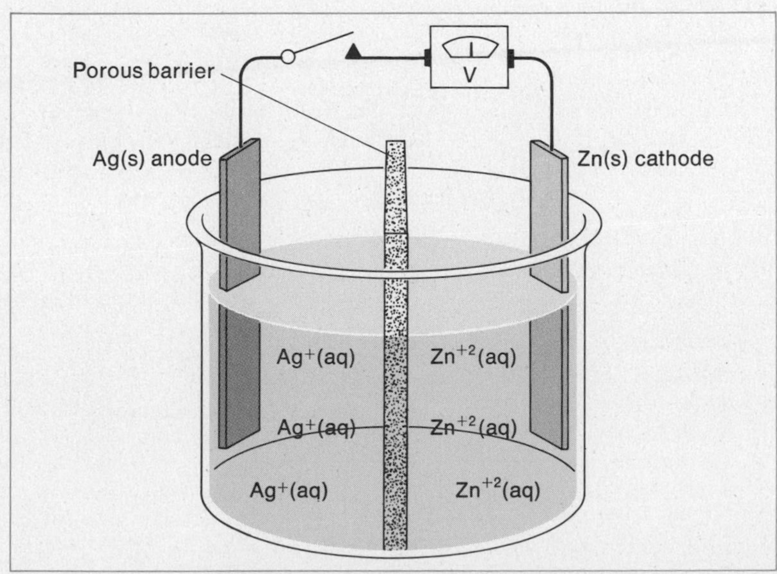

FIGURE 18–6 · *Ag and Zn half-reactions*

That allows us to make predictions, somewhat like predictions made during football season. If team A beats team B by scoring more points (gaining electrons), and team B beats team C, perhaps we can predict that team A will also beat team C. Fortunately for the football fan, the regularities observed in chemistry are not always seen in other situations!

Based on many experimental observations with half-cell reactions in various combinations, we can list the half-cell reactions according to their tendency to give up electrons. That list is shown in Table 18–2. Recall that we developed a similar list in Chapter 17, showing the tendency for acids and bases to give up or accept a proton.

Let's return to our football analogy. When team A plays team B, both are attempting to score points. That is analogous to the tendency of an element to give up electrons. Suppose team A scores twelve points, and team B scores seven points. Team

TABLE 18–2 · Standard Reduction Potentials

HALF-REACTION			E* VOLTS
$Li^{+1}(aq) + e^{-1}$	$\longrightarrow$	$Li(s)$	−3.05
$K^{+1}(aq) + e^{-1}$	$\longrightarrow$	$K(s)$	−2.93
$Rb^{+1}(aq) + e^{-1}$	$\longrightarrow$	$Rb(s)$	−2.93
$Cs^{+1}(aq) + e^{-1}$	$\longrightarrow$	$Cs(s)$	−2.92
$Ba^{+2}(aq) + 2e^{-1}$	$\longrightarrow$	$Ba(s)$	−2.90
$Sr^{+2}(aq) + 2e^{-1}$	$\longrightarrow$	$Sr(s)$	−2.89
$Ca^{+2}(aq) + 2e^{-1}$	$\longrightarrow$	$Ca(s)$	−2.87
$Na^{+1}(aq) + e^{-1}$	$\longrightarrow$	$Na(s)$	−2.71
$Mg^{+2}(aq) + 2e^{-1}$	$\longrightarrow$	$Mg(s)$	−2.37
$Al^{+3}(aq) + 3e^{-1}$	$\longrightarrow$	$Al(s)$	−1.66
$Mn^{+2}(aq) + 2e^{-1}$	$\longrightarrow$	$Mn(s)$	−1.18
$2H_2O(l) + 2e^{-1}$	$\longrightarrow$	$H_2(g) + 2OH^{-1}(aq)$	−0.83
$Zn^{+2}(aq) + 2e^{-1}$	$\longrightarrow$	$Zn(s)$	−0.76
$Cr^{+3}(aq) + 3e^{-1}$	$\longrightarrow$	$Cr(s)$	−0.74
$S(s) + 2e^{-1}$	$\longrightarrow$	$S^{-2}(aq)$	−0.48
$Fe^{+2}(aq) + 2e^{-1}$	$\longrightarrow$	$Fe(s)$	−0.44
$2H_3O^{+1}(1.0 \times 10^{-7}\ M) + 2e^{-1}$	$\longrightarrow$	$H_2(g) + 2H_2O(l)$	−0.41
$PbSO_4(s) + 2e^{-1}$	$\longrightarrow$	$Pb(s) + SO_4^{-2}(aq)$	−0.36
$Ni^{+2}(aq) + 2e^{-1}$	$\longrightarrow$	$Ni(s)$	−0.25
$Sn^{+2}(aq) + 2e^{-1}$	$\longrightarrow$	$Sn(s)$	−0.14
$Pb^{+2}(aq) + 2e^{-1}$	$\longrightarrow$	$Pb(s)$	−0.13
$2H_3O^{+1}(1.0\ M) + 2e^{-1}$	$\longrightarrow$	$H_2(g) + 2H_2O(l)$	0.00
$S(s) + 2H_3O^{+1}(aq) + 2e^{-1}$	$\longrightarrow$	$H_2S(g) + 2H_2O(l)$	+0.14
$Sn^{+4}(aq) + 2e^{-1}$	$\longrightarrow$	$Sn^{+2}(aq)$	+0.15
$Cu^{+2}(aq) + e^{-1}$	$\longrightarrow$	$Cu^{+1}(aq)$	+0.15
$SO_4^{-2}(aq) + 4H_3O^{+1}(aq) + 2e^{-1}$	$\longrightarrow$	$SO_2(g) + 6H_2O(l)$	+0.17
$AgCl(s) + e^{-1}$	$\longrightarrow$	$Ag(s) + Cl^{-1}(aq)$	+0.22
$Cu^{+2}(aq) + 2e^{-1}$	$\longrightarrow$	$Cu(s)$	+0.34

A would *win* by five points. We can get a similar quantitative measure of the difference between two half-cells of their potential to give up electrons when they are together in an oxidation-reduction reaction. Let's see how that is done experimentally.

18–8 · Standard reduction potentials · Let's examine another system in order to more fully understand half-reaction potentials. The reaction between zinc and strong acids that produces diatomic hydrogen gas can serve our purpose.

$$Zn(s) + 2H_3O^{+1}(aq) \rightarrow Zn^{+2}(aq) + H_2(g) + 2H_2O(l)$$

That may be broken down into two half-reactions.

Oxidation

$$Zn(s) \rightarrow Zn^{+2}(aq) + 2e^{-1}$$

Reduction

$$2H_3O^{+1}(aq) + 2e^{-1} \rightarrow H_2(g) + 2H_2O(l)$$

HALF-REACTION			E* VOLTS
$Cu^{+1}(aq) + e^{-1}$	$\rightarrow$	$Cu(s)$	+0.52
$I_2(s) + 2e^{-1}$	$\rightarrow$	$2I^{-1}(aq)$	+0.54
$MnO_4^{-1}(aq) + 2H_2O(l) + 3e^{-1}$	$\rightarrow$	$MnO_2(s) + 4OH^{-1}(aq)$	+0.60
$O_2(g) + 2H_3O^{+1}(aq) + 2e^{-1}$	$\rightarrow$	$H_2O_2(aq) + 2H_2O(l)$	+0.68
$Fe^{+3}(aq) + e^{-1}$	$\rightarrow$	$Fe^{+2}(aq)$	+0.77
$NO_3^{-1}(aq) + 2H_3O^{+1}(aq) + e^{-1}$	$\rightarrow$	$NO_2(g) + 3H_2O(l)$	+0.78
$Hg_2^{+2}(aq) + 2e^{-1}$	$\rightarrow$	$2Hg(l)$	+0.79
$Ag^{+1}(aq) + e^{-1}$	$\rightarrow$	$Ag(s)$	+0.80
$O_2(g) + 4H_3O^{+1}(1.0 \times 10^{-7}\ M) + 4e^{-1}$	$\rightarrow$	$6H_2O(l)$	+0.82
$Hg^{+2}(aq) + 2e^{-1}$	$\rightarrow$	$Hg(l)$	+0.85
$OCl^{-1}(aq) + H_2O(l) + 2e^{-1}$	$\rightarrow$	$Cl^{-1}(aq) + 2OH^{-1}(aq)$	+0.89
$2Hg^{+2}(aq) + 2e^{-1}$	$\rightarrow$	$Hg_2^{+2}(aq)$	+0.92
$NO_3^{-1}(aq) + 4H_3O^{+1}(aq) + 3e^{-1}$	$\rightarrow$	$NO(g) + 6H_2O(l)$	+0.96
$Br_2(l) + 2e^{-1}$	$\rightarrow$	$2Br^{-1}(aq)$	+1.07
$O_2(g) + 4H_3O^{+1}(1.0\ M) + 4e^{-1}$	$\rightarrow$	$6H_2O(l)$	+1.23
$Cr_2O_7^{-2}(aq) + 14H_3O^{+1}(aq) + 6e^{-1}$	$\rightarrow$	$2Cr^{+3}(aq) + 21H_2O(l)$	+1.33
$Cl_2(aq) + 2e^{-1}$	$\rightarrow$	$2Cl^{-1}(aq)$	+1.36
$2ClO_3^{-1}(aq) + 12H_3O^{+1}(aq) + 10e^{-1}$	$\rightarrow$	$Cl_2(g) + 18H_2O(l)$	+1.47
$HOCl(aq) + H_3O^{+1}(aq) + 2e^{-1}$	$\rightarrow$	$Cl^{-1}(aq) + 2H_2O(l)$	+1.49
$Au^{+3}(aq) + 3e^{-1}$	$\rightarrow$	$Au(s)$	+1.50
$MnO_4^{-1}(aq) + 8H_3O^{+1}(aq) + 5e^{-1}$	$\rightarrow$	$Mn^{+2}(aq) + 12H_2O(l)$	+1.51
$PbO_2(s) + 4H_3O^{+1}(aq) + SO_4^{-2}(aq) + 2e^{-1}$	$\rightarrow$	$PbSO_4(s) + 6H_2O(l)$	+1.69
$H_2O_2(aq) + 2H_3O^{+1}(aq) + 2e^{-1}$	$\rightarrow$	$4H_2O(l)$	+1.77
$O_3(g) + 2H_3O^{+1}(aq) + 2e^{-1}$	$\rightarrow$	$O_2(g) + 3H_2O(l)$	+2.07
$F_2(g) + 2e^{-1}$	$\rightarrow$	$2F^{-1}(aq)$	+2.87
$F_2(g) + 2H_3O^{+1}(aq) + 2e^{-1}$	$\rightarrow$	$2HF(aq) + 2H_2O(l)$	+3.06

*Standard conditions are temperature, 25.0°C; gases at a partial pressure of 1.00 atm; and aqueous ions at 1.00 *M* concentration, unless otherwise specified.

Under conditions such as those shown in Figure 18–7, we can measure the potential difference between the Zn/Zn^{+2} couple and the H_3O^+/H_2 couple. The chemical result of the operation of this cell is the same as when zinc metal and hydrochloric acid are used to produce elementary hydrogen in the laboratory. (Recall that acids react with most metals to liberate hydrogen gas.) The technique of separating the oxidation and reduction steps into two separate half-cell reactions enables us to measure the difference in redox potentials for our system, E_{cell}, for this reaction. When the circuit is closed, the voltmeter reads +0.76 volt.

$$E_{cell} = E_{cathode} + E_{anode}$$

For convenience, chemists always use the reduction half-reaction potential.

$$E_{cathode} = E_{H_3O^+/H_2};\ E_{anode} = -E_{Zn^{+2}/Zn}$$

Remember, $E_{M^{+x}/M}$ is a *reduction* half-reaction potential, so, if that reaction is really the oxidation half-reaction, reverse the sign. For our cell, we determine the following.

$$E_{cell} = E_{H_3O^+/H_2} - E_{Zn^{+2}/Zn} = 0.76\ \mathrm{V}$$

Unfortunately, we cannot measure any half-reaction potential by itself. Remember, redox reactions must include both oxidation and reduction half-reactions. So only the sum of the

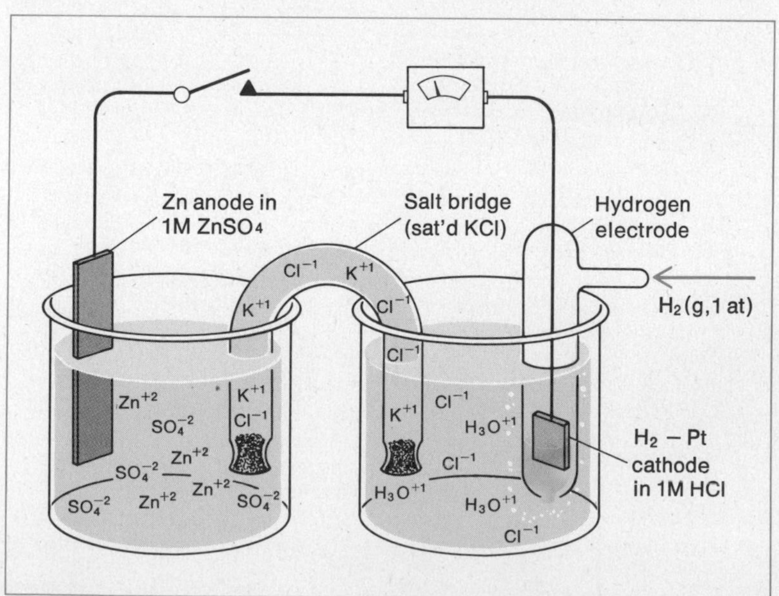

Figure 18–7 · *When the switch is closed in this system at 25.0°C, an electrochemical cell is operating under standard conditions.*

potentials of the two half-reactions can be measured. However, chemists have established a relative scale of half-reaction potentials. They have agreed to set $E_{H_3O^+/H_2}$ as zero. Then all other half-reaction potentials can be measured against the H_3O^+/O_2 couple.

By that scale, the potential of the reduction half-reaction potential of the Zn^{+2}/Zn° couple in the cell in Figure 18 – 7 is as follows.

$$+0.76 = E_{H_3O^+/H_2} - E_{Zn^{2+}/Zn}$$

$$E_{Zn^{+2}/Zn} = -0.76 \text{ V}$$

The Daniell cell in Figure 18 – 5 had a potential of +1.10 volts. Therefore, we can determine the half-reaction potential of the $Cu^{+2} = Cu^\circ$ couple.

$$E_{cell} = E_{Cu^{+2}/Cu} - E_{Zn^{+2}/Zn} = 1.10 \text{ V}$$

$$E_{Cu^{+2}/Cu} = 1.10 \text{ V} + E_{Zn^{+2}/Zn} = 1.10 \text{ volts} - 0.76 \text{ volt} = +0.34 \text{ V}$$

If half-reaction potentials can be added and subtracted to obtain cell voltages, then the cell for the following redox reaction can be determined.

$$Cu^{+2}(aq) + H_2(g) + 2H_2O(l) = Cu(s) + 2H_3O^+$$

Oxidation

$$H_2 + 2H_2O \rightarrow 2H_3O^+ + 2e^{-1}$$

Reduction

$$Cu^{+2} + 2e^{-1} \rightarrow Cu$$

$$E_{cell} = E_{Cu^{+2}/Cu} - E_{H_3O^+/H_2} = +0.34 \text{ V} - 0.0 \text{ V} = +0.34 \text{ V}$$

And, experimentally, this cell gives 0.34 volt.

These potentials are for cells in which the concentration of all ionic species is 1.00 *M*, and all gases are at 1.00 atm pressure. The half-reaction potentials for these conditions are known as **standard reduction potentials** and are designated by E°. Table 18 – 2 is a list of standard reduction potentials.

Table 18 – 2 can be used to predict whether or not a redox reaction will occur. If E_{cell} is positive, then in principle, the reaction will occur spontaneously. If E_{cell} is negative, the reaction will go in the reverse direction. Let us consider an example of this use of Table 18 – 2. We wish to dissolve a piece of copper, but are not sure which acid can be used. Will copper dissolve in hydrochloric acid? The reaction would be the following.

$$Cu(s) + H^+(aq) = Cu^{+2}(aq) + H_2°(g)$$

It is not necessary to balance the equation, as we are interested only in the half-reaction potentials.

Oxidation

$$Cu° \rightarrow Cu^{+2} + 2e$$

Reduction

$$2H^+ + 2e^- \rightarrow H_2$$

$$\begin{aligned} E_{cell} &= E_{anode} + E_{cathode} \\ &= -E_{Cu^{+2}/Cu} + E_{H^+/H_2} \\ &= -0.34 \text{ V} + 0.0 \text{ V} = -0.34 \text{ V} \end{aligned}$$

Since the potential is negative, the reaction will not occur spontaneously. Copper metal does not dissolve in acids in which the reduction half-reaction involves the formation of hydrogen gas from hydrogen ions.

Would copper metal dissolve in nitric acid? The reaction would involve the following half-reactions.

Oxidation

$$Cu° \rightarrow Cu^{+2} + 2e$$

Reduction

$$2(NO_3^- + 2H_3O^+ + e \rightarrow NO_2 + 3H_2O)$$

Net reaction

$$Cu + 2NO_3^- + 4H_3O^+ = Cu^{+2} + 2NO_2 + 6H_2O$$

$$\begin{aligned} E_{cell} &= E_{anode} + E_{cathode} \\ &= -E_{cu^{+2}/Cu} + E_{H^+/H_2O} \\ &= -0.34 \text{ V} + 0.78 \text{ V} = +0.44 \text{ V} \end{aligned}$$

Since the voltage is positive, the reaction can occur spontaneously. We can conclude that copper metal will dissolve in nitric acid.

18–9 · Redox potentials and nonstandard conditions · $E°$ is defined as the potential under standard conditions—1.00 *M* for solutions and 1.00 atm for gases. At concentrations and pressures greater or less than the standard values, we find that the half-reaction potentials vary from the $E°$ value.

Le Châtelier's principle can be used to predict the effect of changes in concentration or pressure on the potential values.

Consider the oxidation half-reaction of copper.

$$Cu^{\circ}(s) \rightarrow Cu^{+2}(aq) + 2e$$

If $[Cu^{+2}] = 2.00\ M$, Le Châtelier's principle predicts a shift to Cu, that is, a lower tendency to oxidize Cu° to Cu^{+2}. The oxidation potential is −0.34 volt, so we predict that as $[Cu^{+2}]$ exceeds 1.00 *M*, the *E*(oxidation) becomes more negative than −0.34 volt. Conversely, at $[Cu^{+2}] < 1.00\ M$, Le Châtelier's principle predicts a shift favoring Cu^{+2}, so oxidation is more favored. Therefore, for $[Cu^{+2}] < 1.00\ M$, the potential for the oxidation half-reaction should be more positive. In other words, it would not be as negative as −0.34 volt.

REVIEW IT NOW

1 How can we show that electrons really are lost and gained during a redox reaction?
2 Describe how a Daniell cell operates.
3 Show the reactions involved in the operation of a lead storage battery.
4 What is a standard reduction potential?
5 What half-cell is set as zero?
6 How are standard reduction potentials used?
7 Why is it sometimes necessary to reverse the sign of a reduction potential?

OXIDATION-REDUCTION: SOME APPLICATIONS

18–10 · Recharging batteries · Anyone who drives a car is familiar with the problem of a dead battery. The redox reaction in the automobile battery has been discussed previously in section 18–6. After a period of operation, the battery will "die" because all available chemical energy has been utilized as electrical energy. However, dead batteries can be recharged by attaching them to an external voltage source. The external voltage reverses the reaction and converts electrical energy into chemical energy. In recharging the battery, the reaction is:

$$2PbSO_4(s) + 6H_2O(l) \rightarrow Pb(s) + PbO_2(s) + 4H_3O^+(aq) + 2SO_4^{-2}(aq)$$

That is not the spontaneous direction for the reaction. Consequently, energy must be used to force the reaction to go. That energy can be released by the recharged battery when it operates spontaneously.

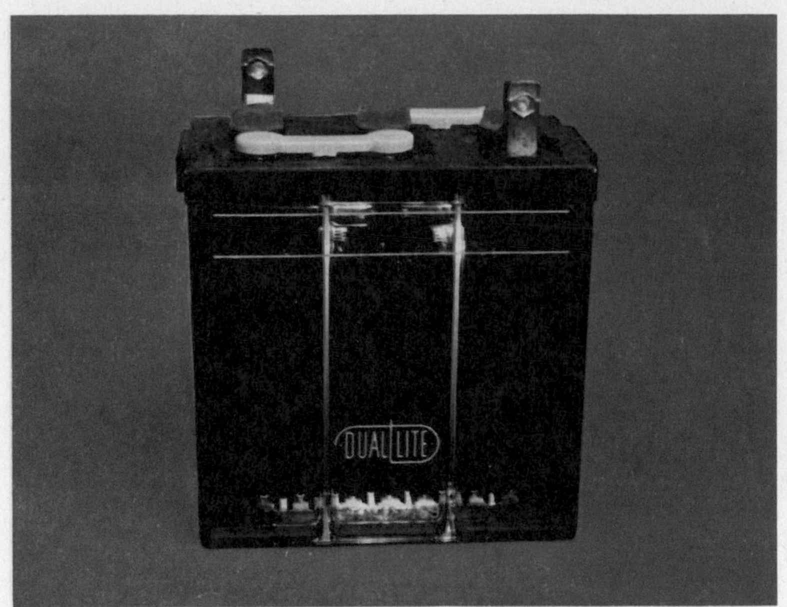

FIGURE 18–8 · *A battery is two or more electrochemical cells placed in series. The flashlight battery is really a single cell.*

18–11 · Electrolysis · The process of using an external voltage to cause a redox reaction to occur in the nonspontaneous direction is known as **electrolysis.** Electrolysis is important to technology, since it is used in the production of many elements such as aluminum, magnesium, copper, phosphorus, and silicon, and many gases such as H_2, O_2, and Cl_2. It is also the basis of the electroplating of metals.

Let us consider the electrolysis of water. The wire connecting the external circuitry to the electrodes provides a path for electric current flow. It is also necessary, whether in a battery or in an electrolytic cell, to have current flow between the electrodes in the cell. That is accomplished by the movement of cations to the cathode and anions to the anode. Since pure water has so few ions (1.0×10^{-7} *M*), the electrolytic current flow is extremely small, and pure water acts as an insulator. However, when a small amount of an electrolyte, such as sodium sulfate, is added, current can flow. If water is to be electrolyzed to H_2 and O_2, hydrogen ions must be reduced at the cathode and hydroxide ions oxidized at the anode.

Cathode

$$2H^+(aq) + 2e \rightarrow H_2(g); \qquad E^\circ = -0.41 \text{ V}$$

Anode

$$4OH^-(aq) \rightarrow O_2 + 2H_2O(l) + 4e; \; E^\circ = -0.82 \text{ V}$$

The E values are for $H^+(aq)$ and $OH^-(aq)$ concentrations of 1×10^{-7} M.

The minimum voltage required to electrolyze water is 1.23 volts. But in practice, a somewhat higher voltage is needed, because of the phenomenon of **overvoltage.** Overvoltage is a complex effect, but is related to the absorption of gases on the electrode surfaces. Overvoltage varies for different electrodes and different gases. Overvoltage is used industrially to produce Cl_2 at the anode in the electrolysis of brine (concentrated NaCl solution) rather than O_2. That occurs even though thermodynamics predicts that O_2 should be formed at a lower voltage than Cl_2.

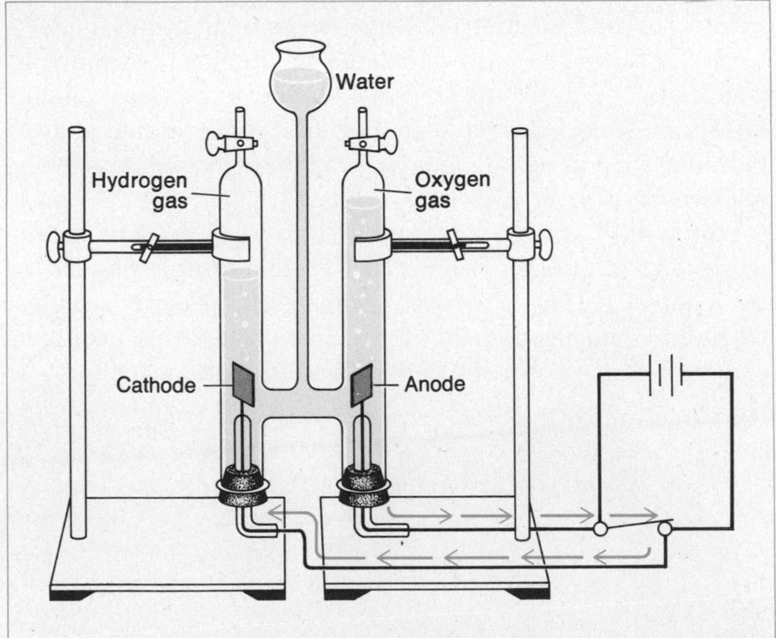

FIGURE 18–9 · *Electrolysis*

18–12 · Electrochemical equivalent weights · The voltage determines the reaction that occurs in a cell, but the amount of current flow determines how much reaction occurs. Michael Faraday (1791–1867), an English scientist, showed that the extent of reaction was directly related to the total current passed through a cell. When 96 500 coulombs (one faraday) pass through molten sodium chloride, exactly one mole of sodium metal and a half mole of chlorine gas are produced. In the electrolysis of water, one faraday (F) of current produces a half mole of hydrogen gas and a fourth of a mole of oxygen.

The reactions are as follows.

Electrolysis of NaCl

$$Na^{+}(q) + 1e \rightarrow Na^{\circ}(s)$$

$$Cl^{-}(aq) \rightarrow 0.50\ Cl_2(g) + 1e$$

Electrolysis of H_2O

$$H^{+}(aq) + 1e \rightarrow 0.50\ H_2(g)$$

$$OH^{-} \rightarrow 0.25\ O_2 + 0.50\ H_2O + 1e$$

Faraday recognized the equivalence of one mole of sodium, 0.50 mole of Cl_2, 0.50 mole of H_2, and 0.25 mole of O_2. For example, from those two reactions, we can correctly predict that the electrolysis of hydrochloric acid would lead to 0.50 mole H_2 and 0.50 mole Cl_2 for each faraday of electricity. Extending beyond electrochemistry, the equivalence of the electrochemical masses also allows us to predict the following. One mole of zinc would dissolve in acid to release one mole of H_2 gas, since both the oxidation of a mole of zinc and the reduction of a mole of hydrogen are half-cell reactions involving *two* faradays of electrons.

Following Faraday's ideas, the equivalent mass of an element, or ion, can be defined as its atomic mass divided by the change in the oxidation number in the redox reaction. Obviously, equal numbers of equivalent masses of oxidizing and reducing agents must be involved in redox reactions.

Michael Faraday
(1791–1867, English). Faraday began his career as a bookbinder's apprentice, later was an assistant to Humphry Davy, and finally became the foremost scientist of his day. Although his discoveries in chemistry were minor, his contributions in the fields of electricity and magnetism were great. The faraday, a unit of amount of electricity, and the farad, a unit of electrical capacity, are named in honor of his achievements.

REVIEW IT NOW

1 How do we apply Le Châtelier's principle in oxidation-reduction reactions?
2 Show the reaction that occurs when a battery is recharged.
3 Define *electrolysis*. Why is electrolysis important?

SUMMARY

The model for all redox reactions involves the transfer of electrons from a donor (reducing agent) to an acceptor (oxidizing agent). The quantitative study of a redox process is possible only by breaking it down into its two half-reactions. The physical separation of oxidation and reduction half-cells that are connected by an external circuit is also the basis for the production of useful electrical energy from redox reactions. Relative oxidation potentials can be experimentally obtained by opposing oxidation half-cells. By defining the oxidation potential of the H_3O^-(1.00 *M*)/H_2(1.00 atm) half-cell as exactly zero volts at 25.0°C, a table of standard oxidation potentials, $E°$, can be established. Important predictive use is made of such a table.

Chemists use fictitious oxidation numbers as an electron bookkeeping device. Those numbers are valuable in writing net ionic equations for oxidation half-cell reactions. In those reactions, the role of H_3O^+ or OH^- ions can often have an important effect on the oxidation potential.

Electrolysis is the process in which an input of electrical energy into a chemical system causes a chemical change to occur. Knowledge of oxidation potentials for the components of the system permits the prediction of electrode reactions.

REVIEW QUESTIONS

1 Why is it not possible to measure a single half-cell reaction potential?
2 Assign an oxidation number for each element that appears in the following formulas.
a. $HOCl$ **d.** H_2SO_3
b. $HOClO_2$ **e.** H_2SO_4
c. SO_3 **f.** $KMnO_4$
3 Suppose you wanted to replate a silver spoon. Do you make the spoon the anode or the cathode for a plating reaction?
4 **a.** As a chemist, you wish to stir a $Fe(NO_3)_2$ solution. You have an aluminum spoon and an iron spoon. Which spoon would you use? Why? Show the reaction to justify your answer.
b. Which spoon would you use to stir an $AlCl_3$ solution? Why? Show the reactions.

REVIEW QUESTIONS

5 Can you store a $Fe_2(SO_4)_3$ solution in a container made of nickel metal? Explain your answer.

6 For the reactions given below, write the half-reaction, and determine the net reaction.

a. $Cu(s) + Cl_2 \rightarrow$
b. $Mg(s) + Sn^{+2}(aq) \rightarrow$
c. $Zn(s) + Fe^{+2}(aq) \rightarrow$
d. $Mn(s) + Cs^{+}(aq) \rightarrow$
e. $Fe(s) + Fe^{+3}(aq) \rightarrow$

7 Using oxidation numbers, show that the following are oxidation-reduction reactions.

a. $Mg(s) + Cl_2(g) \rightarrow MgCl_2(g)$
b. $CH_4(g) + 2O_2(g) \rightarrow CO_2(g) + 2H_2O(g)$
c. $Zn(s) + 2HCl(aq) \rightarrow ZnCl_2(aq) + H_2(g)$
d. $C_2H_4(g) + Cl_2(g) \rightarrow C_2H_4Cl_2(g)$

8 Write net ionic equations for the half-reaction of each of the couples given below.

a. $Ca(s)/Ca(OH)_2(s)$
b. $S^{-2}(aq)/SO_2(aq)$
c. $Cr(OH)_3(s)/CrO_4^{-2}(aq)$
d. $NH_3(g)/NO_3^{-1}(aq)$
e. $O_2(g)/O_3(g)$ (basic system)

9 Using Table 18–2, predict whether or not a reaction will occur when the following reactants are brought together under standard conditions.

a. $Mg(s)$ and $Ag^{+1}(aq)$
b. $Fe^{+3}(aq)$ and $NO_3^{-1}(aq)$
c. $Cr(s)$ and $Zn^{+2}(aq)$
d. $H_2S(g)$ and $NO_3^{-1}(aq)$
e. $SO_2(g)$ and $Hg_2^{+2}(aq)$

10 Which is the better oxidizing agent, concentrated sulfuric acid or concentrated nitric acid?

11 The four hypothetical elements *A*, *B*, *C*, and *D* form the aqueous ions A^{+2}, B^{+2}, C^{+2}, and D^{+2}. The following statements indicate some reactions some reactions that can, or cannot, occur. Use these data to arrange the metal-ion couples into a short oxidation-reduction potential series, putting at the top the oxidation half-reaction that has the greatest tendency to release electrons.

$B^{+2} + D \rightarrow D^{+2} + B$ (reacts appreciably)
$B^{+2} + A$ (will not react appreciably)
$D^{+2} + C \rightarrow C^{+2} + D$ (reacts appreciably)

SUGGESTED READINGS

Bishop, John A. "Redox Reactions and the Acid-Base Properties of Solvents." *Chemistry*, January 1970, p. 18.

Miller, Jack R. "The Direct Reduction of Iron Ore." *Scientific American*, July 1976, p. 68.

Oesper, Ralph. "Michael Faraday: An Informal Sketch." *Chemistry*, March 1970, p. 16.

Smith, Wayne L. "Corrosion." *Chemistry*, January–February 1976, p. 16; June 1976, p. 7.

Weissman, Eugene Y. "Batteries: The Workhorses of Chemical Energy Conversion." *Chemistry*, December 1972, p. 6.

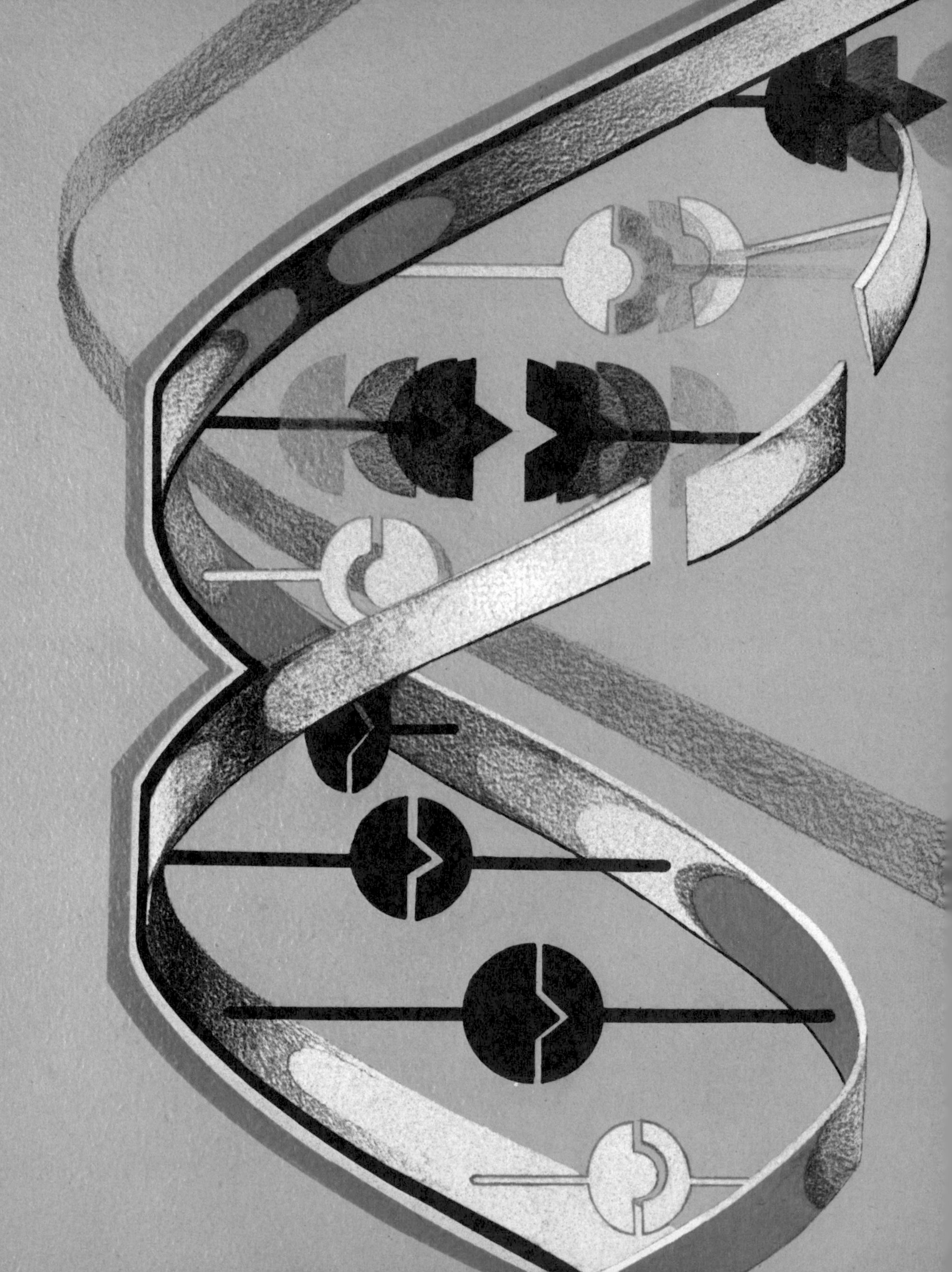

UNIT FIVE

The Basis of Life Processes

Did you ever stop to think that the chemical elements making up the natural world also make up the living things that inhabit it? The chemistry of life is basically the chemistry of the element carbon. The ability of carbon to form complex chains and rings allows it to be the basis for the complex structures and activities of life. In this unit you will be introduced to organic chemistry and a study of the compounds, such as proteins, that are necessary for life.

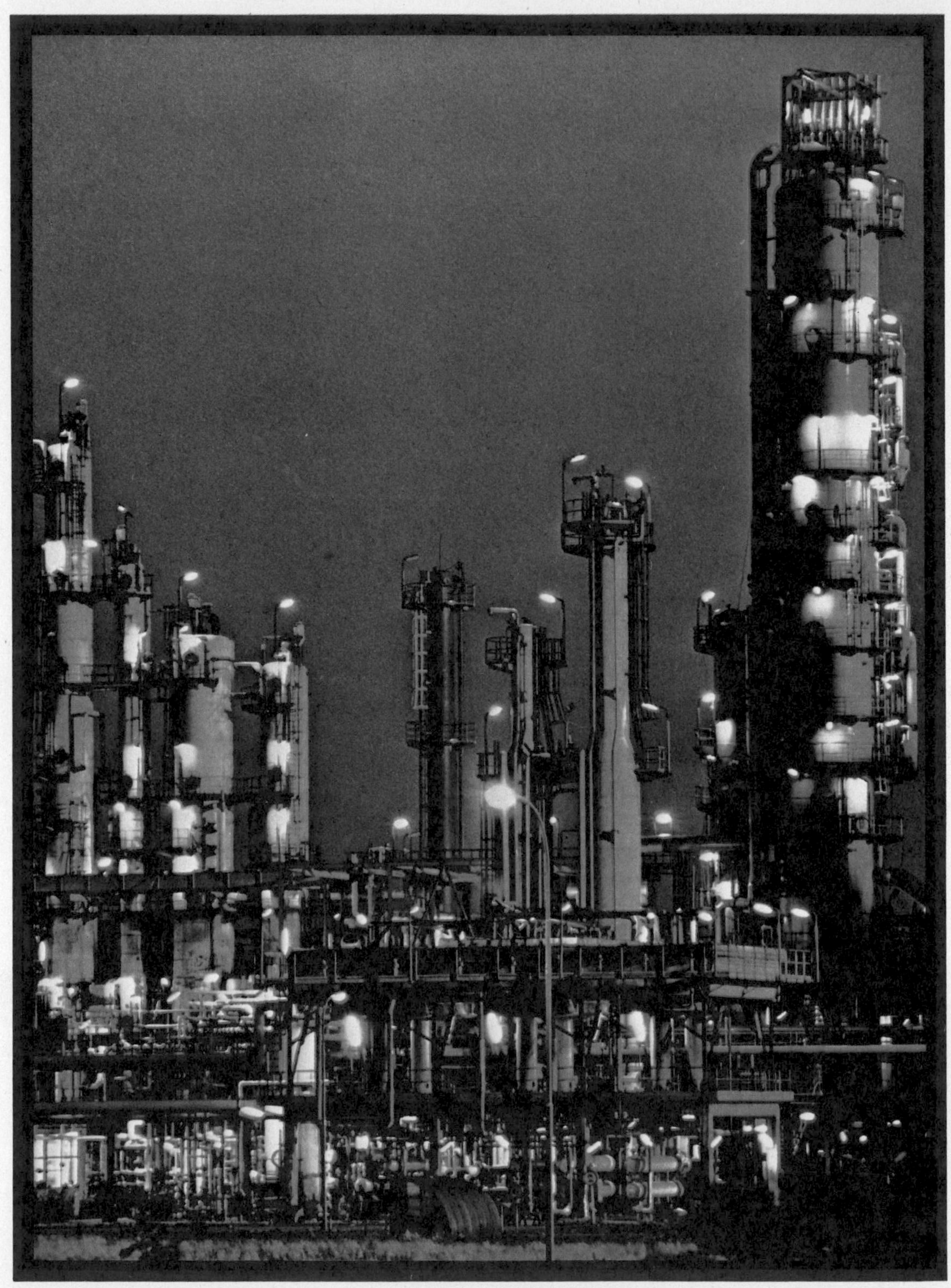

One of the most essential mixtures of organic compounds today is crude oil.

CHAPTER NINETEEN

Organic Chemistry

Early in the history of chemistry, it seemed that an important difference existed between the compounds obtained from animal or vegetable material and those from the mineral, nonliving world. For one thing, those derived from animal or vegetable material were usually either liquids or noncrystalline solids. The study of the compounds derived from vegetable or animal substances was the object of **organic chemistry. Inorganic chemistry** became the study of the compounds from nonliving substances.

ORGANIC VERSUS INORGANIC

19–1 · Friedrich Wöhler synthesized organic compounds · It was believed organic compounds could be made only in living substances. However, in 1828, a German chemist, Friedrich Wöhler (1800–1882), showed that it was not so. He heated an **inorganic** compound, ammonium cyanate. From this procedure, he found that the **organic** compound urea was formed.

$$\underset{\text{ammonium cyanate}}{NH_4NCO} \xrightarrow{\Delta} \underset{\text{urea}}{(NH_2)_2CO}$$

That was one of the most important experiments in chemical history. It showed that organic compounds could be synthesized in the laboratory and were not just made in living substances. It created an area of chemical research that has changed the world. Most of our clothes, medicines, construction materials—in fact, almost everything with which we come in contact daily—have resulted from research in organic chemistry. The amazing thing is that all the fantastic variety is due to the unique properties of a single element—**carbon.**

19–2 · Carbon–chains and rings · What is the unique property of carbon that makes it possible? Carbon atoms can form bonds to other carbon atoms to produce long chains and rings of carbon atoms. Many elements we have studied form small aggregates, such as S_8. But carbon can form molecules with chains of *thousands* of carbon atoms. That makes the formation of very large, complex molecules possible. Such molecules form the material of life itself. They provide the energy of life, and they give us the ability to transmit genetic information, to see, to think, and to perform every other function of life. Our bodies are made of organic chemicals and, in truth, are factories constantly making new organic molecules to replace those we use up daily.

How can we explain the unique bonding character of carbon? Recall that carbon atoms can form four chemical bonds. That can be illustrated by using a "ball and stick" model in which atoms are represented by balls attached by sticks. The number of sticks equals the number of bonds. Each carbon atom has four sticks. In the shortest chain of two carbon atoms, one bond unites the two atoms. Therefore, each carbon has three bonds available for other atoms.

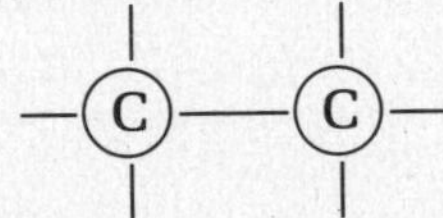

Carbon forms bonds with almost every other type of atom in the periodic table. However, the most common elements in organic compounds are H, N, and O. The C–H compound of the simple two-carbon chain is C_2H_6.

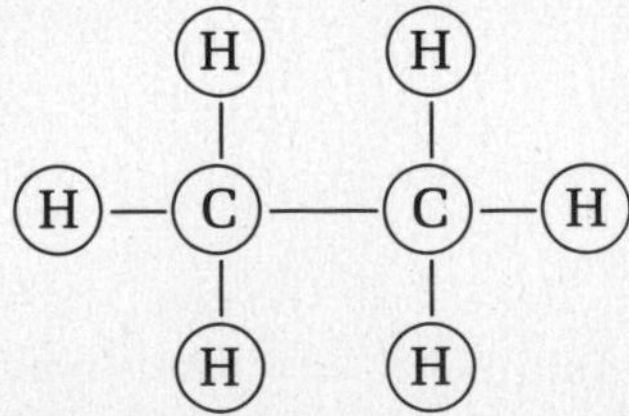

This compound is called ethane. In addition to the single bond in ethane between the carbon atoms, carbon can form double and even triple bonds.

H H
H–C=C–H

C_2H_4, ethene (also called ethylene)

and

$H{-}C{\equiv}C{-}H$ C_2H_2, ethyne (also called acetylene)

In a ring of carbon atoms, the same possibilities occur.

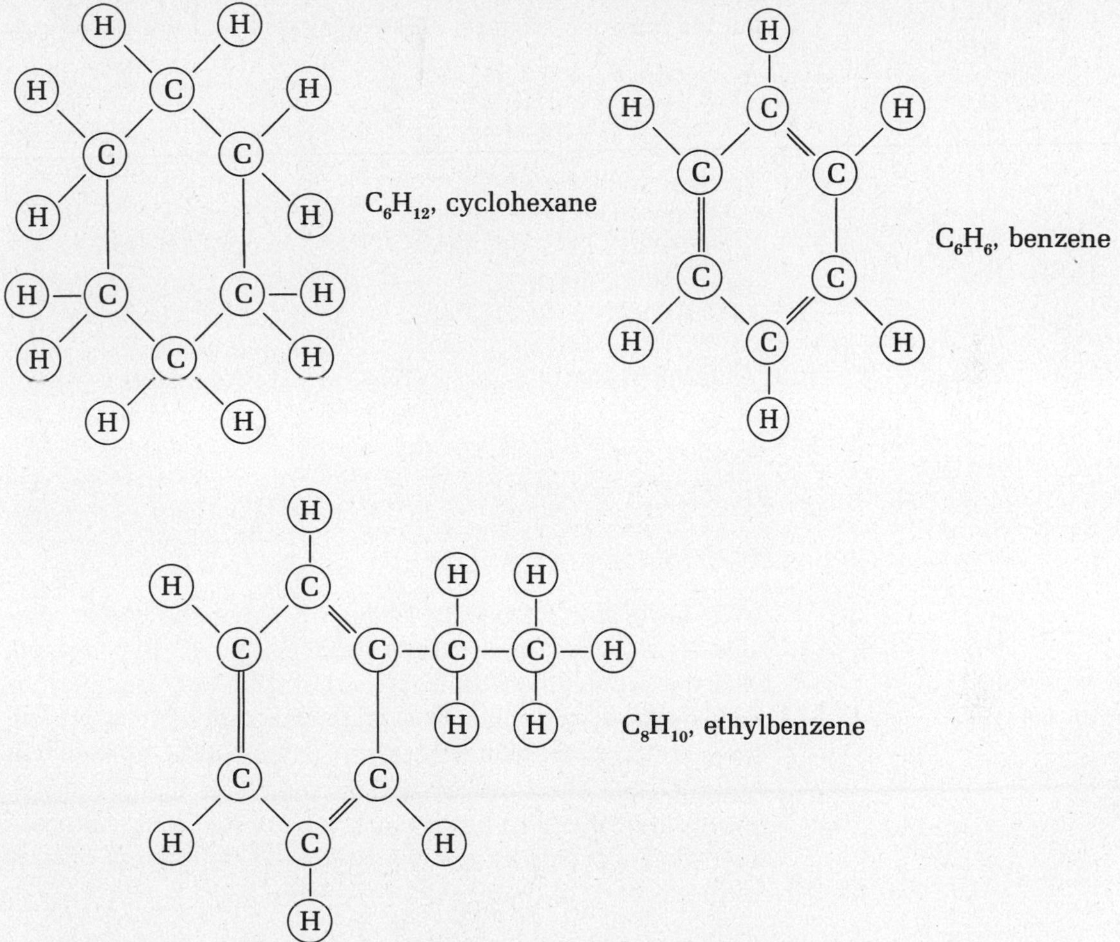

C_6H_{12}, cyclohexane

C_6H_6, benzene

C_8H_{10}, ethylbenzene

With all the variations, it is easy to see that the number of possible organic compounds must be tremendously large. Over two million combinations are known, compared with about a quarter of a million inorganic compounds.

The C–H chain compounds are called **aliphatic** hydrocarbons. C–H ring compounds with alternating double and single bonds, as in benzene, are called **aromatic** hydrocarbons. Cyclohexane does not have alternating double and single bonds. Thus, it is not an aromatic hydrocarbon. Cyclohexane is an **alicyclic** (ring) hydrocarbon.

```
H      H  H  H     H
 \     |  |  |    /
H—C—C—C—C—C—H
 /     |  |  |    \
H      H  H  H     H
```

Normal or n-Pentane
(bp 36° C)

```
H     H  H     H
 \    |  |    /
H—C—C—C—C—H
 /    |  |    \
H     C  H     H
     /|\
    H H H
```

Isopentane
(bp 28° C)

```
    H  H  H
     \ | /
H      C      H
 \     |     /
H—C—C—C—H
 /     |     \
H      C      H
      /|\
     H H H
```

Neopentane
(bp 9.5°C)

FIGURE 19–1 · *The isomers of pentane*

19–3 · The alkanes · In Chapter 12, you learned a little about the hydrocarbons. The simplest C–H molecule is CH_4, named methane. The next is C_2H_6, ethane, then C_3H_8, propane, and so on. For this series in which only single bonds are present, the general formula for the hydrocarbon is C_nH_{2n+2}. These compounds form the **alkanes.** A few are listed in Table 19–1.

TABLE 19–1. · The Alkanes

COMPOUND	MOLECULAR FORMULA	BOILING POINT (°C)	USE
Methane	CH_4	−161.4	Natural gas (C_1–C_4)
Ethane	C_2H_6	−88.6	
Propane	C_3H_8	−41.1	High-grade fuel
Butane	C_4H_{10}	−0.5	Naphtha (C_4–C_6)
Pentane	C_5H_{12}	36.0	
Hexane	C_6H_{14}	68.7	
Heptane	C_7H_{16}	98.4	Gasoline (C_8–C_{10})
Octane	C_8H_{18}	125.7	
Nonane	C_9H_{20}	151	
Decane	$C_{10}H_{22}$	174	
Dodecane	$C_{12}H_{26}$	214	Kerosene (C_{12}–C_{15})
Octadecane	$C_{18}H_{38}$	Melts at 28°C	Lubricant (C_{16}–C_{25})
Triacontane	$C_{30}H_{62}$	Melts at 66.1°C	Paraffin (C_{20}–C_{30})

We have also learned in Chapter 12 that the chain compounds can exist as **structural isomers.** Recall that isomers have the same molecular formula, but different structural arrangements. Each isomer has somewhat different properties. There are three possible isomers of C_5H_{12}, pentane, as shown in Figure 19–1. There are thirty-five isomers of C_9H_{20}, nonane, seventy-five of $C_{10}H_{22}$, decane, and 7×10^{13} of $C_{40}H_{82}$, tetracontane. That accounts for the many millions of different organic compounds.

19–4 · The nomenclature of the aliphatic hydrocarbons · With so many organic compounds, it is absolutely essential that scientists have a logical, relatively simple system of naming them. From the name, we must be able to draw the molecular structure. The chemist has drawn up rules that can be followed in naming organic compounds. For naming the **alkanes,** the following rules apply.

1. For branched-chain hydrocarbons and hydrocarbon derivatives, the longest chain of the molecule is used as the basis for the name. The following are examples.

```
 |   |   |   |            |   |   |   |   |
—C—C—C—C—                 —C—C—C—C—C
 |   |   |   |            |   |   |   |   |
  —C—                               —C—
    |                                 |
                                    —C—
                                      |
```

a *butane* derivative

a *hexane* derivative,
(not a pentane derivative)

2. Each carbon of the straight chain is given a number to establish its position along that chain. The carbons are numbered so that those positions at which branching, or substitution for hydrogen atoms, takes place have the lowest possible numbers.

```
 |    |    |    |                    |    |    |    |
—C¹—C②—C³—C⁴—      and not      —C⁴—C③—C²—C¹—
 |    |    |    |                    |    |    |    |
    —C—                                 —C—
      |                                   |

 |    |    |    |    |    |                 |    |    |    |    |    |
—C⁶—C⁵—C⁴—C③—C²—C¹— and not —C¹—C²—C³—C④—C⁵—C⁶═
 |    |    |    |    |    |                 |    |    |    |    |    |
             —C—                                         —C—
               |                                           |
             —C—                                         —C—
               |                                           |
```

3. The hydrocarbon groups that branch off a given carbon atom along the chain are named as derivatives of the alkanes and end in *yl*. They are known as **alkyl groups,** or **radicals.**

```
   H               H                 H     H   H     H
   |               |                  \    |   |    /
H—C:H  →  H—C·     as in    H—C—C—C—C—H
   |               |                  /    |   |    \
   H               H                 H     C   H     H
                                          /|\
                                         H H H
methane    methyl                      2-methylbutane
```

```
H       H   H       H               H    H  H  H  H    H
 \     /     \     /                 \   |  |  |  |   /
H—C—C:H → H—C—C·        as in   H—C—C—C—C—C—C—H
 /     \     /     \                 /   |  |  |  |   \
H       H   H       H               H    H  C  H  H    H
                                           /|\
   ethane        ethyl                    H C H
                                           /|\
                                          H H H
                                                    3-ethylhexane
```

Lucy W. Pickett
(American) Lucy Pickett is an authority on organic compound identification and structure. She was awarded the Garvan Medal for her work in using far ultraviolet spectroscopy to determine molecular structures. At present, she is pioneering in the field of vacuum ultraviolet, which promises to become an important analytical tool.

4. Halogen and other nonalkyl derivatives of the alkanes are also named from their position along the carbon chain.

```
H     H  H     H        H     H  H  H  H     H
 \    |  |    /          \    |  |  |  |    /
H—C—C—C—C—Cl            H—C—C—C—C—C—C—H
 /    |  |    \          /    |  |  |  |    \
H     C  H     H        H     H  H  C  H     H
     /|\                           /|\
    H H H                         H C H
                                   /|\
                                  H H Cl
```

1-chloro-3-methylbutane (better than 2-methyl-4-chlorobutane)

1-chloro-3-ethylhexane (better than 4-ethyl-6-chlorohexane)

EXERCISES

1. *Propose a name for the following compounds.*

```
   H     H  H  H  H  H     H
    \    |  |  |  |  |    /
a. H—C—C—C—C—C—C—C—H
    /    |  |  |  |  |    \
   H     H  Cl C  H  H     H
              /|\
             H H H

   H     H  Cl H  H  H     H
    \    |  |  |  |  |    /
b. H—C—C—C—C—C—C—C—H
    /    |  |  |  |  |    \
   H     H  Cl C  H  H     H
              /|\
             H H H
```

(Hint: *Di* is used when two atoms of the same elément are attached to a carbon atom)

2. *Show the structure of the following compounds.*

a. *2-methylhexane*

b. *1-bromo-2,2-dimethylbutane*

c. $CH_3(CH_2)_5CH_3$

d. $CH_3C(CH_3)_2CH_2CH_2Cl$

The alicyclic hydrocarbons have a closed chain of singly bonded carbon atoms. Those ring compounds are named by adding the prefix *cyclo* to the name of the corresponding open-chain hydrocarbon.

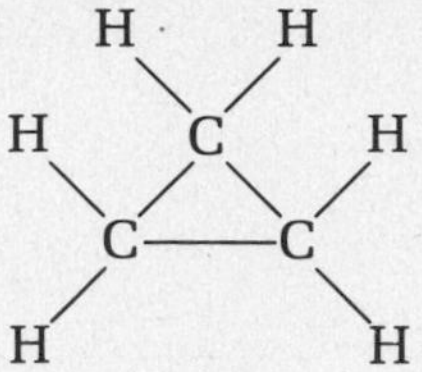

cyclopropane

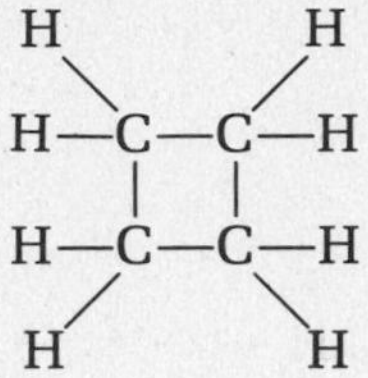

cyclobutane

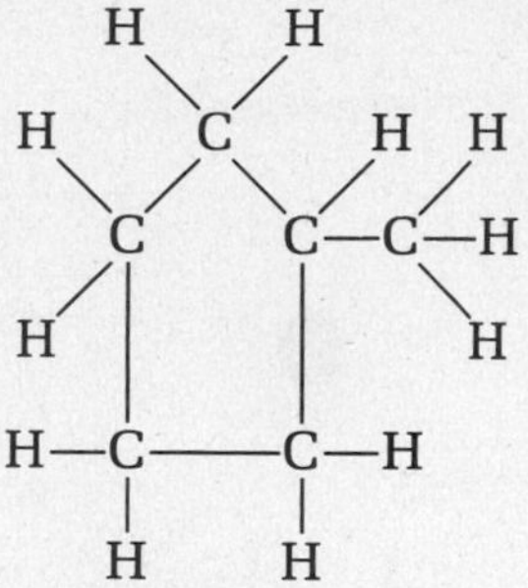

methylcyclopentane

All the compounds we have considered thus far have only single bonds. However, many organic compounds contain double bonds between the carbon atoms. The aliphatic hydrocarbons with double bonds in the chain are called **alkenes.** Of course, the double bonding between carbons in alkenes reduces the number of hydrogen atoms compared with the corresponding alkane. Since alkenes contain fewer hydrogens than the alkanes, they are known as **unsaturated hydrocarbons.** Alkanes are **saturated hydrocarbons.** An alkene is named by adding *ene* to the appropriate prefix. The position of the double bond, is indicated by the number for its position in the chain.

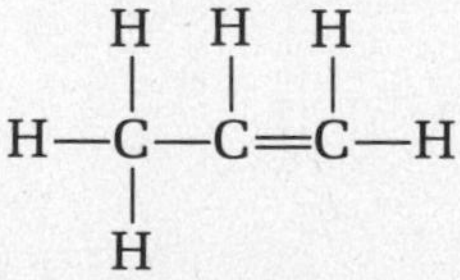

propene

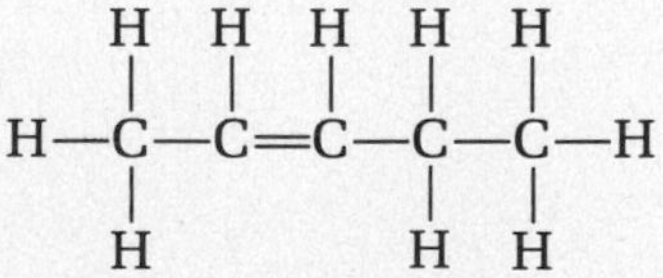

2-pentene

(Why don't we write 1-propene?)

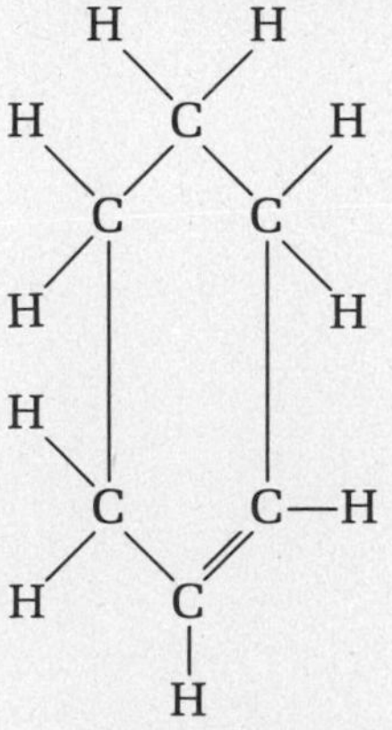

cyclohexene

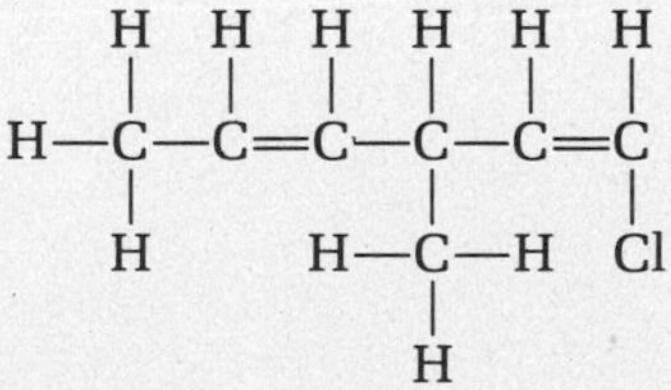

1-chloro-3-methyl-1,4-hexene

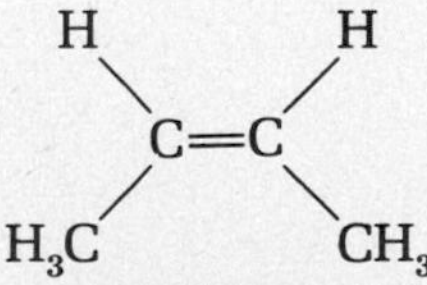

cis-2-butene

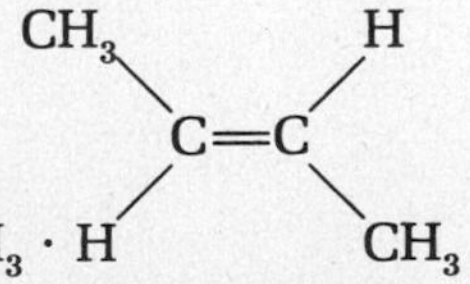

trans-2-butene

(Recall isomers in Ch. 12.)

EXERCISES

1. Name the following alkenes.

```
      H  CH3  H
      |   |   |
a. H—C——C===C
      |       |
      H       H
```

```
       H  CH3
       |   |
b. Cl—C——C=C—H
       |     |
       H     H
```

2. *Draw structural formulas for the following alkenes.*

a. *Chloroethene*

b. *4,4-dimethyl-2-pentene*

c. *$CH_2 = CHC(CH_3)_3$*

It is also possible to have a **triple** bond in the chain. These compounds are called **alkynes.** The alkynes are named by adding *yne* to the appropriate prefix.

```
                         H          CH3    H
                         |           |    /
H—C≡C—H              H—C—C≡C—C—C
                         |           |   |\
                         H           H   H H
```

ethyne
(also acetylene)

2 methyl-3-pentyne

19–5 · The aromatics · Unsaturated rings with alternate double and single bonding are the basis of a group of organic compounds known as the aromatics. The following are examples of those rings.

```
       H
       |
 H     C     H
  \  //  \  /
   C       C
   |       ||
   C       C—H
  /  \\   /
 H     C
       |
       H
```

benzene, C_6H_6

```
        H      H
        |      |
 H      C      C      H
  \  //  \  /   \\  /
   C       C       C
   |       ||      |
   C       C       C
  /  \\  /   \  //  \
 H      C      C      H
        |      |
        H      H
```

naphthalene, $C_{10}H_8$

```
        H      H      H
        |      |      |
 H      C      C      C      H
  \  //  \  /   \\  /   \\  /
   C       C       C       C
   |       ||      |       |
   C       C       C       C
  /  \\  /   \\  /   \\  /  \
 H      C      C      C      H
        |      |      |
        H      H      H
```

anthracene, $C_{14}H_{10}$

Note that since the aromatics have alternate double and single bonds, we can show benzene in two ways.

```
         H                          H
         |                          |
   H     C     H              H     C     H
    \  //  \  /                \  /  \\  /
     C      C                   C      C
     |      ||        or        ||     |
     C      C                   C      C
    /  \\  /  \                /  \  //  \
   H     C     H              H     C     H
         |                          |
         H                          H
```

Of course, the two structures represent the same compound. The possible difference in such structures is more obvious for a compound like dibromobenzene, $C_6H_4Br_2$. Two structural isomers that differ only in the positions of the double bonds can be expected to exist.

```
         H                          H
         |                          |
   H     C     Br             H     C     Br
    \  //  \  /                \  /  \\  /
     C      C                   C      C
     |      ||        and       ||     |
     C      C                   C      C
    /  \\  /  \                /  \  //  \
   H     C     Br             H     C     Br
         |                          |
         H                          H
```

However, only one compound of $C_6H_4Br_2$, with the two bromine atoms on adjacent carbons, has ever been isolated. Furthermore, bond measurements on alkanes and alkenes have shown that the normal C–C single-bond distance is 1.54 A, while the normal C–C double-bond distance is 1.34 A. For benzene, each of the six carbon atoms is at a distance of 1.39 A from each of its two neighbors. The constant distance could not exist if the molecule had a structure in which single and double bonds alternated. Moreover, the constant length is "in between" a double and a single bond length. Other clues to the true nature of the structure of benzene are that all the angles between the C–C bonds are 120° (compared with the 109° for tetrahedral structure) and that benzene is a planar molecule. All those data are consistent with a single structure for benzene with the same bonding between all carbon atoms. Those bonds are stronger than single but weaker than double. A structure to reflect this situation follows.

or

We can rewrite naphthalene and anthracene in the following way. The *C*'s and *H*'s are omitted for simplicity.

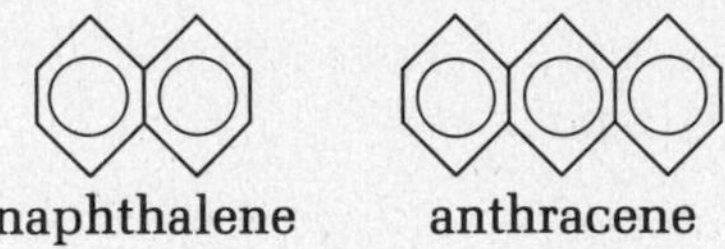

naphthalene anthracene

19–6 · Nomenclature of benzene compounds · To name derivatives of benzene, the ring carbons are numbered. Often the portion is designated as the "phenyl" group. Study the following examples, and the nomenclature system should be obvious.

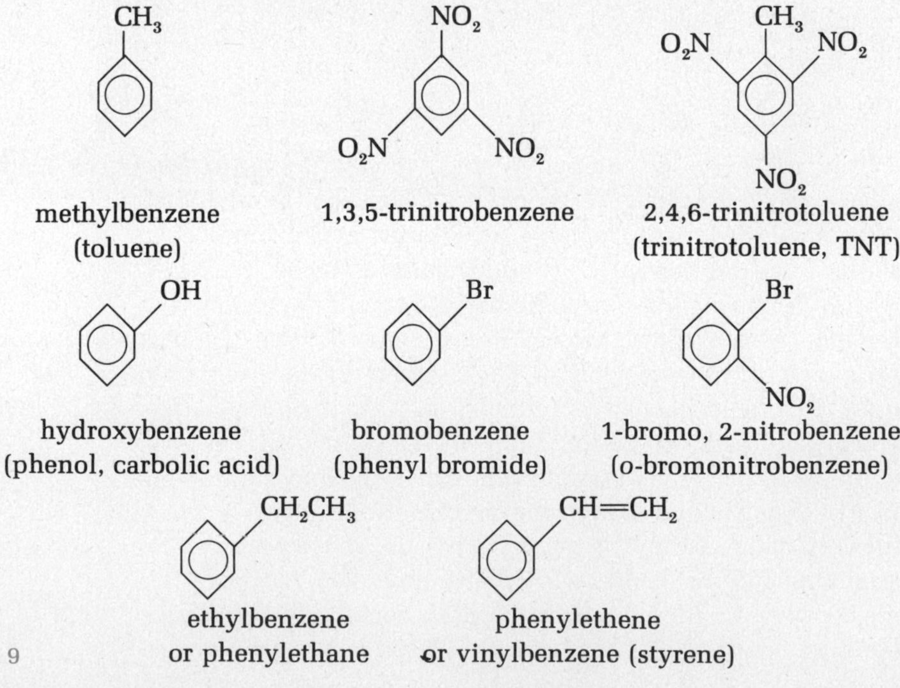

methylbenzene (toluene)

1,3,5-trinitrobenzene

2,4,6-trinitrotoluene (trinitrotoluene, TNT)

hydroxybenzene (phenol, carbolic acid)

bromobenzene (phenyl bromide)

1-bromo, 2-nitrobenzene (*o*-bromonitrobenzene)

ethylbenzene or phenylethane

phenylethene or vinylbenzene (styrene)

REVIEW IT NOW

1 Define *organic chemistry*. What did Wöhler contribute to organic chemistry?
2 What is an aliphatic hydrocarbon?
3 Describe the system used to name aliphatic hydrocarbons.
4 Define *alkenes*, *alkynes*, and *alicyclic compounds*.
5 Show the structure of an aromatic compound.
6 What is the nature of the bonding in an aromatic compound?

SOME REACTIONS OF HYDROCARBONS

19–7 · Addition reactions · Double and triple bonds in an unsaturated hydrocarbon are positions of special chemical reactivity. One reaction characteristic of alkenes and alkynes is **addition.** In an addition reaction, an atom is added to each carbon where the double bond is located.

$$H_3C{-}\overset{\displaystyle H}{\overset{|}{C}}{=}CH_2 + HCl \rightarrow H_3C{-}\underset{\underset{\displaystyle Cl}{|}}{\overset{\displaystyle H}{\overset{|}{C}}}{-}CH_3$$

$$CH_2{=}CH_2 + Cl_2 \rightarrow CH_2ClCH_2Cl$$

$$CH_3CH{=}CH_2 + H_2 \rightarrow CH_3CH_2CH_3$$

In the last reaction shown above, hydrogen is added. This is known as **hydrogenation.** Perhaps you have heard liquid vegetable oils advertised as being "unsaturated." This means that they have many double bonds in their long chains. When saturated with hydrogen, the oils become solid fats like those used in cooking.

Another alkane reaction is called **dehydrogenation,** which, as the name implies, is the removal of hydrogen from an alkane. It is usually brought about catalytically in the absence of oxygen. It leads to the formation of the more reactive *unsaturated* hydrocarbons.

$$\mathrm{H_3C{-}CH_3} \xrightarrow[\text{catalyst}]{\text{high temperature}} \mathrm{H_2C{=}CH_2} + H_2$$

ethane ⟶ ethylene + hydrogen

A very important reaction involving hydrocarbons is known as **cracking.** Cracking involves the breaking of a hydrocarbon chain. It occurs at high temperatures in the absence of oxygen.

$$\underset{\text{propane}}{H_3C-\overset{\displaystyle H}{\overset{|}{\underset{\displaystyle H}{\underset{|}{C}}}}-CH_3} \xrightarrow[\text{catalyst}]{400°-600°C} \underset{\text{ethene}}{\overset{\displaystyle H\ \ H}{\overset{|\ \ \ |}{\underset{\displaystyle H\ \ H}{\underset{|\ \ \ |}{C=C}}}}} + \underset{\text{methane}}{\overset{\displaystyle H}{\overset{|}{\underset{\displaystyle H}{\underset{|}{HCH}}}}}$$

Cracking is a very important process in the petroleum industry. Large alkane molecules are cracked in large "cat" towers. Those fractions of the large chains that contain smaller carbon chains are purified for various uses, such as kerosene, gasoline, or naptha. Figure 19–2 illustrates the many products that result from the refining and cracking of petroleum.

FIGURE 19–2 · *More than 650 000 compounds can be produced from petrochemicals. Some of those products are shown in this chart.*

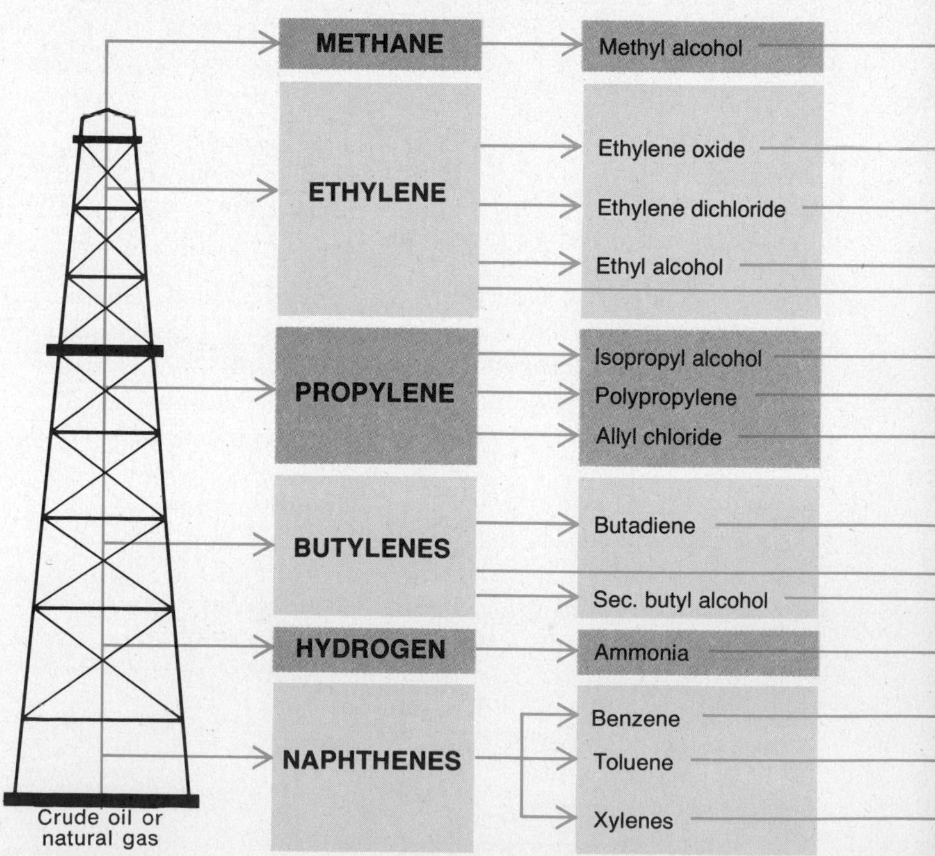

19–8 · Octane rating of gasoline · "Knocking" in automobile engines is the result of an uneven burning of the fuel. If the gasoline ignites prematurely, the piston is not in the proper position, and the engine knocks. It has been learned that branched-chain molecules with about eight carbon atoms cause less knocking than straight-chain hydrocarbons. Petroleum refineries convert small molecules into larger branched ones, crack large molecules into smaller ones, and convert straight-chain molecules into branched-chain molecules, so that the yield of low-knock hydrocarbons is increased.

The antiknock quality of a gasoline is described by a scale of octane rating. Iso-octane is shown below.

$$\begin{array}{ccccccccc} H & & CH_3 & & H & & CH_3 & & H \\ | & & | & & | & & | & & | \\ HC & — & C & — & C & — & C & — & CH \\ | & & | & & | & & | & & | \\ H & & CH_3 & & H & & H & & H \end{array}$$

iso-octane

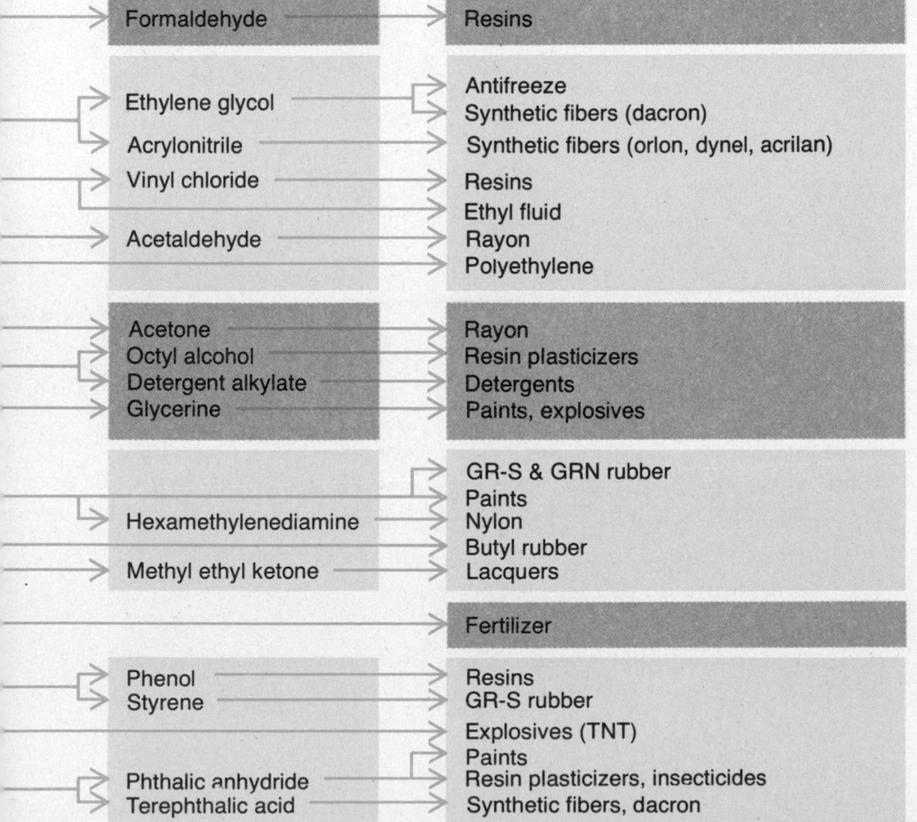

Iso-octane is assigned a rating of one hundred octane. N-heptane is assigned a rating of zero octane. Thus, a gasoline of ninety-five octane is a mixture of hydrocarbons that has the same antiknock performance as a mixture of 95.0 percent iso-octane and 5.00 percent n-heptane.

```
H   H   H   H   H   H   H
|   |   |   |   |   |   |
HC—C—C—C—C—C—CH
|   |   |   |   |   |   |
H   H   H   H   H   H   H
```

n-heptane

19–9 · Substitution reactions · Another type of reaction of the alkanes is known as **substitution.** In a substitution reaction, a hydrogen atom is replaced by another type of atom. If methane gas is mixed with chlorine gas at a high temperature, a substitution reaction occurs.

$$CH_4(g) + Cl_2(g) \rightarrow CH_3Cl(g) + HCl(g)$$

If the amount of Cl_2 is large compared with the amount of CH_4, substitution reactions may occur in the following sequence.

$$CH_4 \xrightarrow{Cl_2} CH_3Cl \xrightarrow{Cl_2} CH_2Cl_2 \xrightarrow{Cl_2} CHCl_3 \xrightarrow{Cl_2} CCl_4$$

CH_4	CH_3Cl	CH_2Cl_2	$CHCl_3$	CCl_4
methane	chloromethane	dichloromethane	trichlormethane	tetrachloro-methane
bp = −161°C	(methylchloride)	(methylenechloride)	(chloroform)	(carbon tetra-chloride)
	bp = −24.0°C	bp = 40.0°C	bp = 61.0°C	bp = 77.0°C.

Reactions such as those that involve the making and breaking of covalent bonds occur more slowly than those that involve ionic bonds. The extent of covalency of the bonds between carbon and the halides are in the order C–I most covalent, C–Br less, C–Cl still less, and C–F least. We are not surprised, therefore, to learn that the substitution reaction of $CH_4 + F_2$ is the fastest. In fact, only CF_4 forms. The reaction of $CH_4 + Br_2$ is slower than that of $CH_4 + Cl_2$. I_2 does not have a substitution reaction with CH_4.

Although we have described substitution reactions of methane, all alkanes react in the same way. The general reaction follows.

$$RCH_3 + X_2 \rightarrow RCH_2X + HX$$

R represents an alkyl group, C_nH_{2n+1}.

19–10 · Oxidation reactions · Since we live in an atmosphere of oxygen, the reactions of hydrocarbons with oxygen are most important. These are called **oxidation** reactions. When hydrocarbons are oxidized, different products are obtained depending on the conditions. The complete oxidation of all hydrocarbons produces carbon dioxide and water.

$$C_8H_{18} + 12.5O_2 \rightarrow 8CO_2 + 9H_2O$$

Complete oxidation can occur immediately, as in combustion, or it may occur as the final step in a sequence of partial oxidation reactions. Let us consider the possible sequence of oxidation steps for ethane.

$$
\begin{array}{ccccccccc}
\text{H}\ \ \text{H} & & \text{H}\ \ \text{H} & & \text{H}\qquad\text{O} & & \text{H}\qquad\text{O} & & \\
\text{H—C—C—H} & \xrightarrow{[O]} & \text{H—C—C—O—H} & \xrightarrow{[O]} & \text{H—C—C} & \xrightarrow{[O]} & \text{H—C—C} & \xrightarrow{[O]} & CO_2 + H_2O \\
\text{H}\ \ \text{H} & & \text{H}\ \ \text{H} & & \text{H}\qquad\text{H} & & \text{H}\qquad\text{OH} & &
\end{array}
$$

ethane — ethanol (ethyl alcohol) — ethanal (acetaldehyde) — ethanoic acid (acetic acid)

Part of this particular sequence of oxidation has played an important role in the culture of almost all peoples. The fermentation of starches and sugars forms ethyl alcohol. That fermentation was used in beers and wines from earliest recorded history. Later, ancient peoples learned to distill the alcohol to obtain liquors of higher alcohol content, such as whiskeys and brandies. If the wine is not protected from the air, it "sours" because of the oxidation of the ethyl alcohol to acetic acid (remember, a characteristic of acids is a sour taste). Household vinegar is a weak solution of acetic acid. The aging of milk results in souring because of the formation of lactic acid.

REVIEW IT NOW

1 Give an example of an addition reaction.
2 What is "cracking"? What is its importance?
3 How is octane rating of a gasoline determined?
4 Show how an alkane can undergo a substitution reaction.
5 Define an *oxidation reaction*. What are some practical applications of oxidation reactions?
6 What happens when wine sours?
7 What happens when milk sours?

FUNCTIONAL GROUPS IN ORGANIC MOLECULES

19–11 · Three types of organic compounds · Let's look at the three types of organic compounds shown below. These compounds are alcohols, aldehydes, and acids. Consider their structures.

$H_3C-\overset{\displaystyle H}{\underset{\displaystyle H}{C}}-OH$	$H_3C-C\begin{smallmatrix}{}^{\nearrow O}\\ {}_{\searrow H}\end{smallmatrix}$	$H_3C-C\begin{smallmatrix}{}^{\nearrow O}\\ {}_{\searrow OH}\end{smallmatrix}$
ethyl alcohol	acetaldehyde	acetic acid

It is also useful to consider some other compounds.

$H-\overset{\displaystyle H}{\underset{\displaystyle H}{C}}-OH$	$H-C\begin{smallmatrix}{}^{\nearrow O}\\ {}_{\searrow H}\end{smallmatrix}$	$H-C\begin{smallmatrix}{}^{\nearrow O}\\ {}_{\searrow OH}\end{smallmatrix}$
methyl alcohol	formaldehyde	formic acid
$(H_5C_2)\overset{\displaystyle H}{\underset{\displaystyle H}{C}}-OH$	$(H_5C_2)C\begin{smallmatrix}{}^{\nearrow O}\\ {}_{\searrow H}\end{smallmatrix}$	$(H_5C_2)C\begin{smallmatrix}{}^{\nearrow O}\\ {}_{\searrow OH}\end{smallmatrix}$
propyl alcohol	propyl aldehyde	propionic acid
$(H_7C_3)-\overset{\displaystyle H}{\underset{\displaystyle H}{C}}-OH$	$(H_7C_3)C\begin{smallmatrix}{}^{\nearrow O}\\ {}_{\searrow H}\end{smallmatrix}$	$(H_7C_3)C\begin{smallmatrix}{}^{\nearrow O}\\ {}_{\searrow OH}\end{smallmatrix}$
butyl alcohol	butyl aldehyde	butyric acid

The **alcohols** are all characterized by a hydrocarbon group plus a CH_2OH group. All **aldehydes** have a hydrocarbon group plus a CHO group. The **acids** have a hydrocarbon group plus a COOH group. These characteristic groups attached to the hydrocarbons are called **functional groups.**

Organic chemistry is simplified by the functional-group principle. The chemical reactions of organic compounds can be interpreted in terms of the functional (reactive) groups of the molecules. All alcohols have similar behavior, since it is the CH_2OH group that imparts the reactivity and not the hydrocarbon group. Consequently, C_2H_5OH and CH_3OH react in the same way. Likewise, CH_3COOH and $C_5H_{11}COOH$ have similar acidic reactivity due to the attached COOH group. The COOH is called a **carboxylate** group. Some functional groups are listed in Table 19–2.

Organic molecules may have more than one functional group. Oxalic acid, used in removing rust stains, has two carboxylate groups.

$$\begin{array}{ccc} O & & O \\ & \diagdown\!\!\diagdown \quad /\!\!/ & \\ & C{-}C & \\ & / \quad \diagdown & \\ HO & & OH \end{array}$$

TABLE 19–2 · Organic Functional Groups and Compound Types

FUNCTIONAL GROUP	COMPOUND TYPE	COMPOUND FORMULA
Halogen, —X	Halide	RX
Hydroxyl, —OH	Alcohol	ROH
Oxy, —O—R′	Ether	ROR′
Carbonyl, —C(=O)—	Aldehyde, —C(=O)—H	RCHO
	Ketone, —C(=O)—R′	R(CO)R′
Carboxyl, —C(=O)—O—	Acid, —C(=O)—OH	RCOOH
	Ester, —C(=O)—O—R′	RCOOR′
Amino, —N(H)—H	Amine	RNH_2
Nitro, —N(=O)—O	Nitro	RNO_2
		R and R′ may be the same.

Lactic acid has a hydroxyl and a carboxylate group.

$$
\begin{array}{ccccc}
 & & OH & & O \\
 & & | & & /\!/ \\
H & - & C & - & C \\
 & & | & & \backslash \\
 & & H & & OH
\end{array}
$$

Glycine, the simplest amino acid, has the following structure.

$$
\begin{array}{ccccc}
 & & NH_2 & & O \\
 & & | & & /\!/ \\
H & - & C & - & C \\
 & & | & & \backslash \\
 & & H & & OH
\end{array}
$$

Glucose (also called dextrose, a simple sugar used in candy and baking) has alcohol and aldehyde groups.

$$
\begin{array}{ccccccccccccc}
 & & H & & H & & H & & OH & & H & & O \\
 & & | & & | & & | & & | & & | & & /\!/ \\
HO & - & C & - & C & - & C & - & C & - & C & - & C \\
 & & | & & | & & | & & | & & | & & \backslash \\
 & & H & & OH & & OH & & H & & OH & & H
\end{array}
$$

FIGURE 19–3 · *These substances are composed of organic compounds. Try to determine what functional groups would be found in each product.*

Vitamin C, or ascorbic acid, is another example of a polyfunctional compound.

```
           OH
           |
   HO      C       O
     \   //  \   //
      C         C
      |         |
    H—C—————————O
       \
        C—H
       / \
      H   OH
```

The structure of another polyfunctional compound, vitamin B_1, or thiamine, is as follows.

```
              NH2
             /          CH3
            /            |
       N—C       H       C
     //    \\    |     /   \\
H3C—C        C—C—N            C—CH2CH2—OH
     \      /    |     \     /
       N=C       H      C—S
          \            /  \
           H          H    H
```

REVIEW IT NOW	**1** Draw the structures for typical alcohol, aldehyde, and organic acids. **2** Define a *functional group*. **3** What is the significance of the functional group? **4** Show the structure for the carboxylate group.
SUMMARY	Because of the great number of possible arrangements of carbon atoms within a carbon chain and the specificity of the functional groups, you can easily see how so many different organic compounds can exist. However, regardless of how large or how complicated the organic molecule, it is still defined by the rules you have learned. And it is generally characterized by the functional groups you have studied. If you would like to study more about organic chemicals and their uses, you should study Excursions 8 and 12.

REVIEW QUESTIONS

1 Discuss the importance of Wöhler's synthesis of urea.

2 What is meant by "cracking"? How is it important as an industrial process?

3 Design a chart, showing the relationships of the various types of hydrocarbons.

4 Define *structural isomerism*. A certain compound has the formula C_6H_{14}.

a. Name the compound.
b. What type hydrocarbon is this?
c. Give extended structural formulas for all the structural isomers of this compound.

5 A certain organic compound has the formula $C_2H_3Cl_3$. Draw all the possible structural formulas for this compound.

6 Name each of the following.

a. $(CH_3)_2CHC(CH_3)(C_2H_5)_2$
b. $(CH_3)_3CCH_2CH(CH_3)_2$
c. CCl_4
d. $CH_2=CHCH_2Cl$
e. $CH_3C(CH_3)_2CH=C(CH_3)_2$

7 Give extended structural formulas for the following.

a. 2, 2, 4-trimethylpentane
b. 2, 4, 6-trimethyl-3, 5-dichloroheptane
c. Methyl-cyclohexane
d. Cyclobutane
e. 1, 3-dimethylcyclopentane
f. Acetylene

8 Give extended structural formulas for the following.

a. 1-butene
b. 1, 2-butadiene
c. 3-heptyne
d. 3-methyl-1-hexyne

9 The boiling point of cis-dichloroethene is 60.1°C, that of trans-dichloroethene is 48.4°C. Explain.

10 Write equations for the following reactions.

a. Bromine addition to 1-butene
b. Addition of HCl to propene
c. Hydrogenation of 2-pentene

11 Show complete combustion for the following.

a. $CH_3(CH_2)_5CH_3$
b. $(CH_3)_2CHC(CH_3)(C_2H_5)_2$
c. $CH_3CH(CH_2CH_2CH_3)_2$

12 Give the structural formula and name for an alcohol derived from each of the following.

a. Methane
b. Ethane
c. Butane

13 Give the structural formula for an acid derived from each of the following.
- **a.** Propane
- **b.** Butane
- **c.** Octane

14 Give extended structural formulas for the following.
- **a.** Butyl alcohol
- **b.** 2-butanol (2-hydroxy butane)
- **c.** 2, 2, diethyl propanol
- **d.** 1, 2 benzene dicarboxylic acid (phthalic acid)

SUGGESTED READINGS

Blumer, Max. "Polycyclic Aromatic Compounds in Nature." *Scientific American*, March 1976, p. 34.

Eliel, Ernest L. "Stereo Chemistry Since LeBel and van't Hoff." *Chemistry*, Part I: January–February 1976, p. 6; Part II: April 1976, p. 8.

Evans, Gary. "A Proposed Structural Shorthand for Organic Chemistry." *Chemistry*, May 1970, p. 18.

Geoghegan, J. T. and W. E. Bambrick. "Turpentine and Its Derivatives." *Chemistry*, March 1972, p. 6.

Herz, Werner. *The Shape of Organic Compounds*. New York: W. A. Benjamin Co., 1965.

Lambert, J. B. "The Shape of Organic Molecules." *Scientific American*, January 1970, p. 58.

Mills, G. Alex. "Ubiquitous Hydrocarbons." *Chemistry*, February 1971, p. 8; March 1971, p. 12.

Rochow. *Organometallic Chemistry*. New York: D. Van Nostrand Co., 1963.

Rouvray, Dennis H. "The Mathematical Theory of Isomerism." *Chemistry*, February 1972, p. 6.

Szabadvary, Ferenc. "Great Moments in Chemistry: Birth of Organic Chemistry." *Chemistry*, December 1973, p. 12.

Whitfield, R. C. *A Guide to Understanding Basic Organic Reactions*. Boston: Houghton Mifflin Co., 1966.

Zuffanti, Saverio. "Electron Repulsion Theory: Application to Aliphatic and Aromatic Hydrocarbons." *Chemistry*, May 1970, p. 8.

Our bodies can be likened to a chemical plant.

CHAPTER TWENTY

Biochemistry: The Chemistry of Life

Biochemistry is the branch of science that bridges the gap between the study of chemistry and the study of biology. It is not a new science. Even the earliest humans wondered about the functioning of their bodies and tried to explain why certain organs function as they do. Many of those explanations took the form of superstitions. For example, around A.D. 600, Isadore of Seville wrote a compendium of all knowledge, titled *Etymologia*. In his book, he described the heart as the organ that pumped air throughout the body. The liver was the seat of all emotions and, also, contained a great deal of heat that converted food directly into blood. The spleen was responsible for laughter and the bile for anger. All understanding centered in the heart. The liver was responsible for love. Many of those ideas have persisted. Even in Shakespeare's writing, you may recall that a cowardly person is referred to as being "lily-livered" and "lacking gall."

EXCURSION TWELVE
Using Organic Chemicals

In Chapter 19 we discussed organic chemistry. At this point you might want to read Excursion 12. This excursion covers the properties and the uses of some organic compounds.

The attempt to apply chemistry to understand how the body functions is a recent development. Only during the twentieth century were physiological chemists able to draw together many of the seemingly unrelated facts that had been accumulated before their time. Biochemistry became a unified science. The role of carbohydrates, fats, and proteins in metabolic processes, the role of vitamins and enzymes, and the development of metabolic pathways became clear. The importance of chemical principles such as oxidation-reduction, acid-base balance, solubility, and chemical bonding became obvious. Then in 1954, Watson and Crick proposed their famous double helix theory that gave clear evidence that genetic inheritance was due to a biochemical mechanism. Recent research in biochemistry suggests that our emotions are possibly controlled

James Watson
United States geneticist James Watson and British biophysicist Francis Crick were co-winners of the 1962 Nobel Prize for Medicine. Their discoveries concerned the complex structure of the DNA molecule and its ability to transmit genetic messages.

by chemical mechanisms. And scientists are learning more about the processes involved in memory.

The study of biochemistry is an ever-expanding field. It has become one of the major branches of chemistry. In Chapter 20, we will study some biochemical processes. But it is impossible in such limited space to survey even briefly the field of biochemistry. Therefore, we will concentrate on the chemical processes that produce energy and those that involve some of the metals and other inorganic substances that we have studied in previous chapters. We will begin with a discussion of carbohydrates, fats, proteins, and nucleic acids—the basic raw materials for many biochemical processes.

CARBOHYDRATES

20–1 · The structure of carbohydrates · Carbohydrates contain the elements carbon, hydrogen, and oxygen. Carbohydrates have the general formula CH_2O. The simplest carbohydrates are the **monosaccharides.** The most important monosaccharides in biochemistry are **glucose** and **galactose.** Glucose is also called **dextrose.** All **simple sugars** have the formula $C_6H_{12}O_6$. However, their structural formulas differ, as shown below.

```
         CH2OH
          |
          C---------O
 H       /|          \        H
 |      / H           \      /
 C                      C
 |  \   OH      H     /   \
 HO  \   |      |    /     O—H
      C---------C
      |         |
      H         OH

              CH2OH
               |
               C---------O
  OH          /|          \         H
  |          / H           \       /
  C                          C
  |  \     OH      H       /   \
  H   \    |       |      /     OH
       C-----------C
       |           |
       H           OH
```

Carbohydrates that can be broken down into two monosaccharides are called **disaccharides. Sucrose,** ordinary table sugar, is a disaccharide. The third type of carbohydrate consists of starches and cellulose. This type of carbohydrate is made up of large, complex chains that yield many monosaccharides. These are called **polysaccharides.** Polysaccharides and disaccharides are broken down to monosaccharides by the process of hydrolysis. That involves the removal of a water molecule.

Carbohydrates are produced by photosynthesis in green plants. Photosynthesis can be represented as the following general reaction.

$$CO_2 + H_2O + \text{Solar energy} \rightarrow (CH_2O) + O_2$$

The (CH_2O) is the basic unit in carbohydrates. In the reaction above, we see that solar energy is a reactant in the photosynthesis of carbohydrates. We know from our previous studies that this energy must be accounted for on the product side of the equation. Some of the energy is lost, but much of it is stored in the carbohydrate molecule. Recall that glucose is the simplest form of carbohydrate. During the photochemical process, 686 kcal of energy are stored in each mole of glucose produced.

Glucose is a most important food source because of the energy in its molecule. When glucose is ingested, or produced in the body by the hydrolysis of disaccharides and polysaccharides, it combines with oxygen to produce water and carbon dioxide, and to release its stored energy. That is essentially the reverse of the photosynthesis reaction shown above. However, so that the energy may be used most efficiently, it is released slowly over a period of time, rather than all at once, as happens during open burning.

Francis Crick

20–2 · Where is energy needed in the body? · Suppose we look at the simple procedure of raising your arm. The brain sends out the message, which is transmitted by a series of chemical reactions, that the arm is to be raised. Energy is required to produce the chemical compounds involved in those reactions. Next a message is sent along the nerves to the muscles in the arm. That requires electrical energy. The message reaches the muscles, and the muscles contract—requiring more chemical energy. The muscles pull on the bones of the arm, and the arm is raised—requiring mechanical energy.

Clearly, the body needs energy in many forms, and not just the heat that is produced during ordinary combustion. Some of the energy available from glucose must be channeled into other forms of energy without ever appearing as heat. How does that interconversion take place? How is energy stored in the body? Providing answers to such questions has been one of chemistry's greatest scientific achievements. Energy is stored in the form of a high-energy molecule produced during the oxidation process. This high-energy molecule is **adenosine triphosphate,** or **ATP.** ATP acts as the body's store-house for energy. It stores energy and distributes it where and when it is needed.

20–3 · ATP—a closer look · The structure of ATP is shown in Figure 20–1. We will show an abbreviated form, because we are mainly concerned with the phosphate groups on the molecule.

FIGURE 20–1 · *Adenosine triphosphate, ATP*

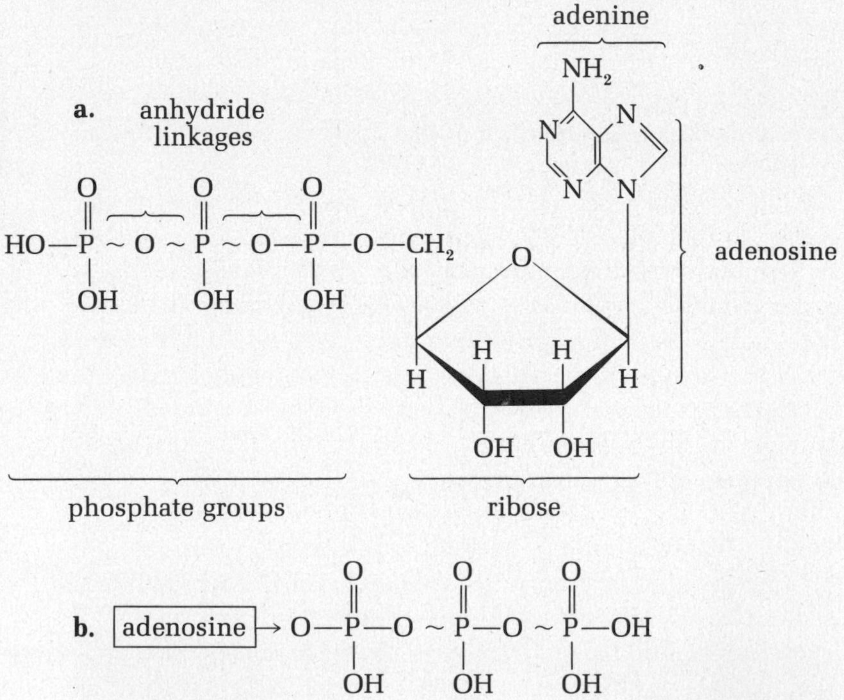

a. anhydride linkages

$$\mathrm{HO{-}\overset{\displaystyle O}{\overset{\|}{\underset{\underset{\displaystyle OH}{|}}{P}}}{\sim}O{\sim}\overset{\displaystyle O}{\overset{\|}{\underset{\underset{\displaystyle OH}{|}}{P}}}{\sim}O{-}\overset{\displaystyle O}{\overset{\|}{\underset{\underset{\displaystyle OH}{|}}{P}}}{-}O{-}CH_2}$$

adenine (NH_2, N, N, N, N) — ribose (O, H, H, H, H, OH, OH)

adenosine

phosphate groups

ribose

b.

$$\boxed{\text{adenosine}}\rightarrow \mathrm{O{-}\overset{\displaystyle O}{\overset{\|}{\underset{\underset{\displaystyle OH}{|}}{P}}}{-}O{\sim}\overset{\displaystyle O}{\overset{\|}{\underset{\underset{\displaystyle OH}{|}}{P}}}{-}O{\sim}\overset{\displaystyle O}{\overset{\|}{\underset{\underset{\displaystyle OH}{|}}{P}}}{-}OH}$$

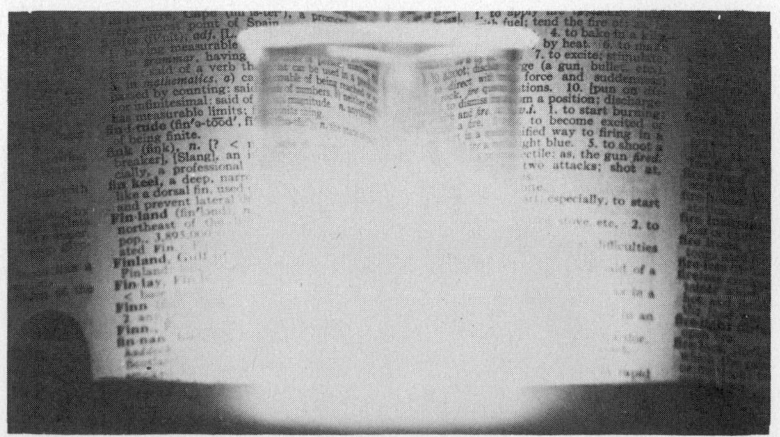

FIGURE 20–2 · *An illuminating experiment: 2 grams of ATP added to 5 grams of dehydrated firefly tails*

ATP is a high-energy molecule because some of the bonds between phosphorus and oxygen are high-energy bonds. The high-energy bonds are shown with wavy lines. They are called high-energy bonds because in a chemical reaction that releases energy, they are the bonds usually broken. When the high-energy bonds are broken, energy is released and low-energy **adenosine diphosphate,** or **ADP,** is formed.

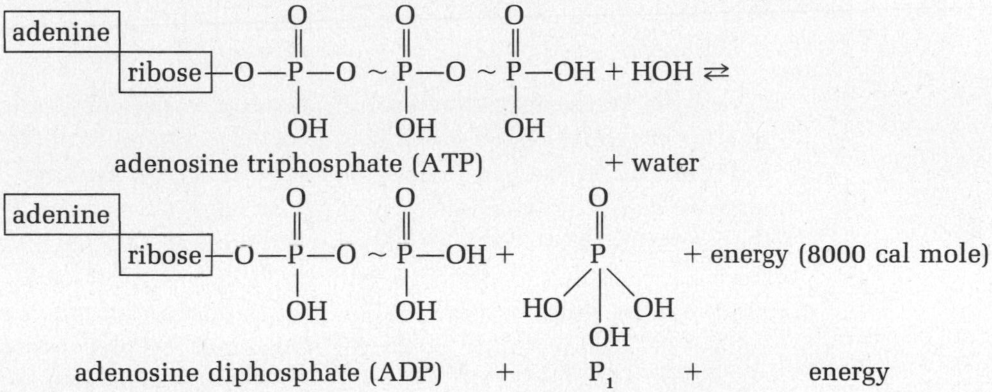

$$\boxed{\text{adenine}}\,\boxed{\text{ribose}}\!-\!O\!-\!\underset{\substack{|\\OH}}{\overset{\substack{O\\\|}}{P}}\!-\!O\sim\underset{\substack{|\\OH}}{\overset{\substack{O\\\|}}{P}}\!-\!O\sim\underset{\substack{|\\OH}}{\overset{\substack{O\\\|}}{P}}\!-\!OH + HOH \rightleftarrows$$

adenosine triphosphate (ATP) + water

$$\boxed{\text{adenine}}\,\boxed{\text{ribose}}\!-\!O\!-\!\underset{\substack{|\\OH}}{\overset{\substack{O\\\|}}{P}}\!-\!O\sim\underset{\substack{|\\OH}}{\overset{\substack{O\\\|}}{P}}\!-\!OH + HO\!-\!\underset{\substack{|\\OH}}{\overset{\substack{O\\\|}}{P}}\!-\!OH + \text{energy (8000 cal mole)}$$

adenosine diphosphate (ADP) + P_1 + energy

The energy released in the formation of ADP can be used to help contract a muscle or provide the energy needed for a chemical reaction to occur in some other metabolic pathway. ATP is somewhat like a loaded mousetrap, ready to snap with the slightest touch. After it snaps, the mousetrap now represents ADP. When glucose is oxidized in the body, ATP is produced in the process. The complete oxidation of *one* molecule of glucose will generate a net of thirty-six molecules of ATP. The reactions that provide the driving force for the production of ATP occur within the cells. Since those reactions must use the oxygen you breathe, the term **cellular respiration** is used to describe the metabolic reactions in the cell. In cellular respiration, a chain of chemical reactions eventually leads to the reduction of oxygen to water in the cells. Although the actual step-by-step process in cellular respiration has been carefully worked out in great detail by biochemists, we will not concern ourselves with the details. If you wish to look at the process of cellular respiration in depth, you can consult any general biochemistry textbook. We can merely state here that the process allows the transfer of energy from the food we eat and the oxygen we breathe to ATP without that energy being lost as unwanted heat.

20–4 · Glycolysis · We have seen how glucose is used in cellular respiration to produce ATP. Glucose can also undergo another series of reactions in the absence of oxygen. Such a process is called **glycolysis.** In this series of twelve reactions, a small amount of ATP is formed along with **lactic acid,** the end product of glycolysis.

$$\underset{\text{glucose}}{C_6H_{12}O_6} + 2ADP + 2P_1 \rightarrow \underset{\text{lactic acid}}{2CH_3\text{—}\underset{\displaystyle OH}{\underset{|}{CH}}\text{—}CO_2H} + 2ATP$$

Glycolysis produces only two ATP molecules per molecule of glucose, so it is not a major source of ATP. However, there are times when the body needs this extra ATP. During strenuous exercise—long-distance running, for example—the body may demand more ATP than the cells can provide. Oxygen just can't be delivered to the cells rapidly enough to produce all the ATP the muscles need. When that happens, the muscle cells will produce additional ATP molecules by glycolysis. However, with this ATP formation, the muscle cells also receive a large amount of lactic acid. The accumulation of lactic acid in the cells causes soreness in the muscles. Typically, after physical exertion, such as running, the runner will breathe heavily (hyperventilate) to meet the oxygen demand of the body and to break down the lactic acid.

20–5 · Glycogen · For storage, many plants convert their glucose and other sugars to starch. We see that in many vegetables, such as potatoes. Animals, however, do not store starch. The reserve carbohydrate in animals is called **glycogen.** Any of the sugars, including starches, can be easily converted in the body to glycogen. When the supply of glucose runs low, animals draw on their stored glycogen for glucose. Glycogen is a large molecule with many repeating glucose units.

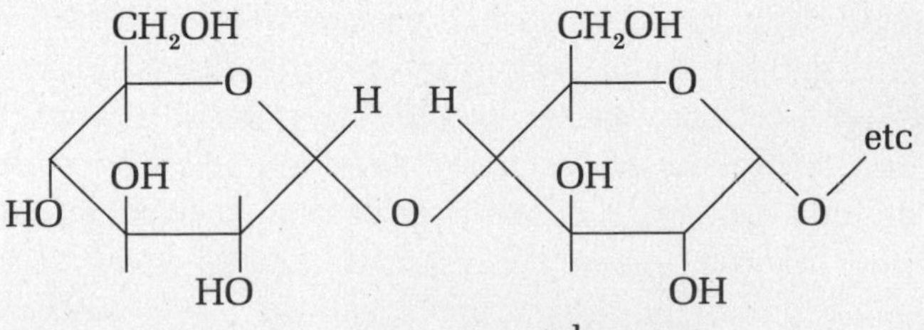

glycogen

Glycogen is usually stored in the liver, the kidneys, and the muscles. Not only can glucose and other sugars be converted to glycogen, but lactic acid can also be changed into glycogen. Recall that lactic acid builds up in muscle cells during exertion. The muscle cells are not capable of converting lactic acid into glycogen. That is done in the liver and kidneys. The lactic acid must somehow leave the muscle cells and be carried to the liver and kidneys for the conversion to occur. The actual mechanism for this process was discovered by Drs. Carl and Gerty Cori and is called the *Cori Cycle*. The Coris were awarded a Nobel prize in 1947 for their work.

Drs. Gerty and Carl Cori · *As a team, Drs. Gerty and Carl Cori shared the Nobel Prize for Medicine in 1947. Their work concerned the enzymatic synthesis of glycogen, or animal starch. Through this process, the body stores sugar in the liver as glycogen. Later, this glycogen is reconverted to sugar as it is needed.*

REVIEW IT NOW

1 Give the general formula for a carbohydrate.
2 List three types of carbohydrates, and give examples of each.
3 What is the function of ATP?
4 What is a high-energy bond?
5 Discuss the production of lactic acid by glycolysis.
6 What is the function of glycogen?

FAT AND FAT METABOLISM

20–6 · The structure of fats · If we eat more than we need to, we get fat. Some prefer to sày we "gain weight," but the result is the same. The body is capable of converting excess food and nutrients into fat. This fat is stored in **adipose** tissue that is found distributed throughout the body. Fat can be made from excess carbohydrate and fat in the diet, but only to a small extent from protein. This process is called **lipigenesis.**

There are several types of fats, or lipids. These are generally placed into one of two classes, depending on whether or not they can be saponified. The saponification reaction is shown in Figure 20–3. Generally, **saponification** means that fat will react with NaOH to form glycerol and the sodium salt of the fatty acid. The sodium salt is called **soap.** That is the way the soaps we use for cleaning purposes are prepared. The class of lipids that can be saponified includes most of the important lipids.

FIGURE 20–3 · *Saponification reaction*

$$\begin{array}{lcll}
R-\overset{O}{\overset{\|}{C}}-O-CH_2 & & R-\overset{O}{\overset{\|}{C}}-O\ Na^+ & HO-CH_2 \\
R'-\overset{O}{\overset{\|}{C}}-O-CH + 3NaOH & \xrightarrow[\Delta]{} & R'-\overset{O}{\overset{\|}{C}}-O\ Na^+ + & HO-CH \\
R''-\overset{O}{\overset{\|}{C}}-O-CH_2 & & R''-\overset{O}{\overset{\|}{C}}-O\ Na^+ & HO-CH_2 \\
 & & \text{three soaps} & \text{glycerol}
\end{array}$$

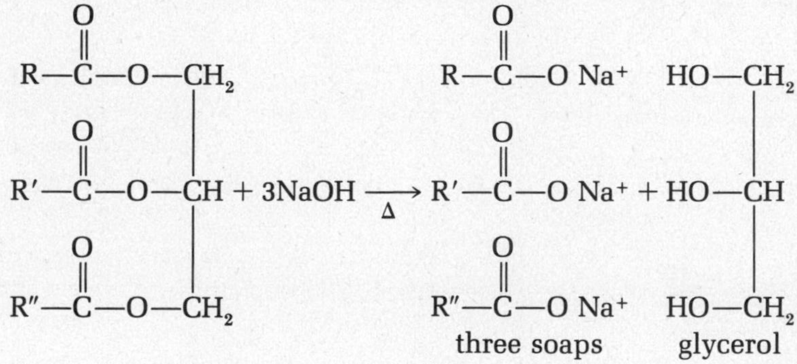

R, R′, and R″ represent long-chain hydrocarbons.

Those lipids include the waxes, the glycerides, the lecithins (found in nerve tissue), and the sphingomyelins and cerebrosides (both found in brain tissue). From a nutritional standpoint, the glycerides are the most important lipids in the group. The principle nonsaponifiable lipids are the **steroids.** They will be discussed later.

20–7 · Glycerides · This group of lipids consists of long-chain carboxylic acids. For that reason, they are often called **fatty acids.** Some of the fatty acids have only single bonds between the carbon atoms. Those are called **saturated fatty acids.** The four saturated fatty acids that are important in biochemistry are shown in Figure 20–4.

FIGURE 20–4 · *Important saturated fatty acids*

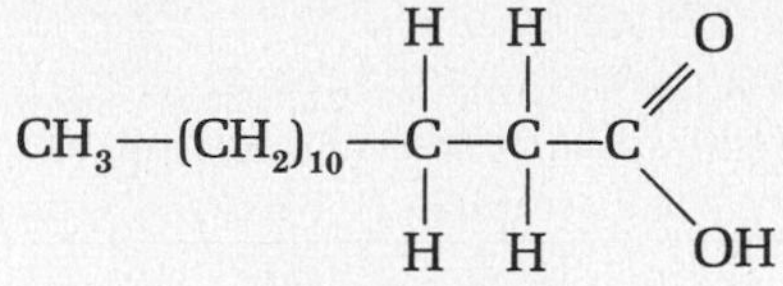

$$CH_3{-}(CH_2)_{10}{-}\overset{H}{\underset{H}{C}}{-}\overset{H}{\underset{H}{C}}{-}C\begin{array}{l} /\!\!/ O \\ \backslash OH \end{array}$$

myristic acid
(mp = 58°C)

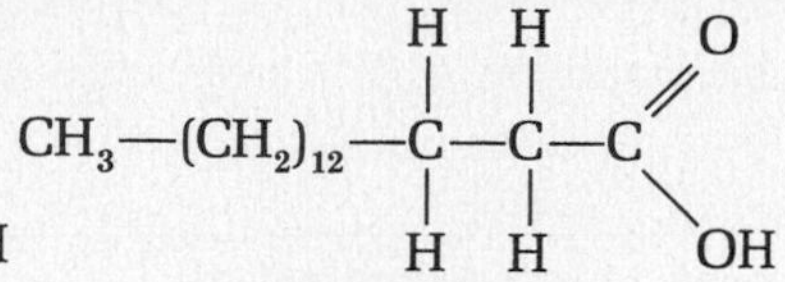

$$CH_3{-}(CH_2)_{12}{-}\overset{H}{\underset{H}{C}}{-}\overset{H}{\underset{H}{C}}{-}C\begin{array}{l} /\!\!/ O \\ \backslash OH \end{array}$$

palmitic acid
(mp = 63°C)

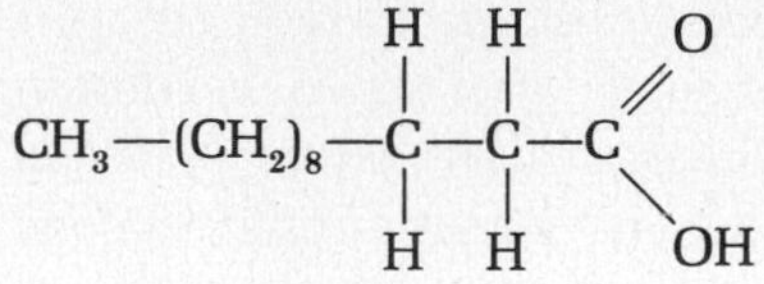

$$CH_3{-}(CH_2)_{8}{-}\overset{H}{\underset{H}{C}}{-}\overset{H}{\underset{H}{C}}{-}C\begin{array}{l} /\!\!/ O \\ \backslash OH \end{array}$$

lauric acid
(mp = 44°C)

$$CH_3{-}(CH_2)_{14}{-}\overset{H}{\underset{H}{C}}{-}\overset{H}{\underset{H}{C}}{-}C\begin{array}{l} /\!\!/ O \\ \backslash OH \end{array}$$

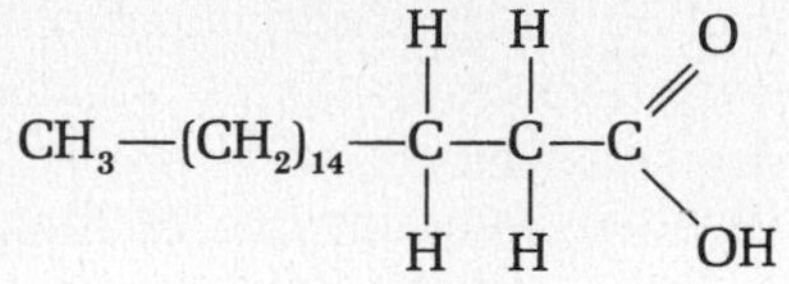

stearic acid
(mp = 70°C)

A fatty acid with double bonds between the carbon atoms is said to be unsaturated. There are also four important **unsaturated fatty acids.** These are shown in Table 20–1.

Note that linoleic acid has two double bonds. Because of the double bonds, linolenic acid and arachidonic acid are said to be **polyunsaturated.** This is a term you have no doubt heard on television commercials advertising cooking oils.

TABLE 20–1 · **Important Unsaturated Fatty Acids**

ACID NAME	NUMBER OF DOUBLE BONDS	NUMBER OF CARBONS	STRUCTURE AND MELTING POINT
Oleic	One	18	$CH_3(CH_2)_4CH{=}CH(CH_2)_7\overset{O}{\overset{\|}{C}}{-}OH$ **(4°C)**
Linoleic	Two	18	$CH_3(CH_2)_4CH{=}CHCH_2CH{=}CH(CH_2)_7\overset{O}{\overset{\|}{C}}{-}OH$ **(–5°C)**
Linolenic	Three	18	$CH_3CH_2CH{=}CHCH_2CH{=}CHCH_2CH{=}CH(CH_2)_2\overset{O}{\overset{\|}{C}}{-}OH$ **(–11°C)**
Arachidonic	Four	20	$CH_4(CH_2)_4CH{=}CHCH_2CH{=}CHCH_2CH{=}CHCH_2CH{=}CH(CH_2)_4\overset{O}{\overset{\|}{C}}{-}OH$ **(–49.5°C)**

Note the melting points given in Figure 20–4 and Table 20–1 for the saturated and unsaturated fatty acids, respectively. In saturated fatty acids, the melting point increases as the carbon chain increases. Also, in unsaturated fatty acids, the greater the degree of unsaturation, the lower the melting points. That explains why animal fats (saturated) are solid at room temperature, while vegetable oils (unsaturated) are generally liquids at room temperature. Animal fats include butter and lard. Vegetable oils include olive, peanut, corn, linseed, soybean, and cottonseed oil.

20–8 · The importance of fatty acids · Fatty acids are important in biochemistry for two main reasons. First, they are a very important source of energy. It was stated earlier in this chapter that one molecule of glucose produces a net of thirty-six molecules of ATP. Even more impressively, one molecule of a typical fatty acid, such as palmitic acid, will produce 130 molecules of ATP! One gram of carbohydrate will produce four kcal of energy; one gram of fat will produce nine kcal. The large fatty acids undergo reactions in the body to allow them to provide intermediate products necessary for ATP production. Since the fatty acid molecule is so large, it goes through a series of reactions that "knock off" two carbons at a time. By repeating the process over and over, the large molecule is eventually used up.

A second reason why fatty acids are important is that fat can serve as an energy reserve. At least 10 percent of a typical person's body weight is fat. That amount of fat is adequate to fulfill the energy requirement for that individual for over a month. The body's supply of glucose, on the other hand, will last only for about twenty-four hours. Remember, protein is not generally coverted to fat, but carbohydrates are. That is the basis for the popular high protein diet. The dieter eats only protein, forcing the body to draw upon the supply of fat deposited in adipose tissue for ATP production. This procedure can result in dramatic fat loss in a very short period of time. However, a high protein diet can also be harmful to the body because of the lack of many important nutrients.

20–9 · Steroids · The steroids comprise the major portion of the nonsaponifiable fats. Steroids are characterized by a polycyclic carbon skeleton, as shown in Figure 20–5. They typically include an alcohol group and a double bond. Even though the structure of many steroids is similar, their function is extremely varied. The steroids range from the vitamins to sex hormones. A few steroids are shown in Figure 20–5.

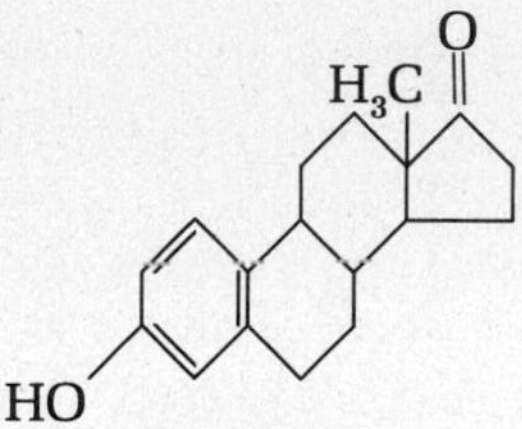

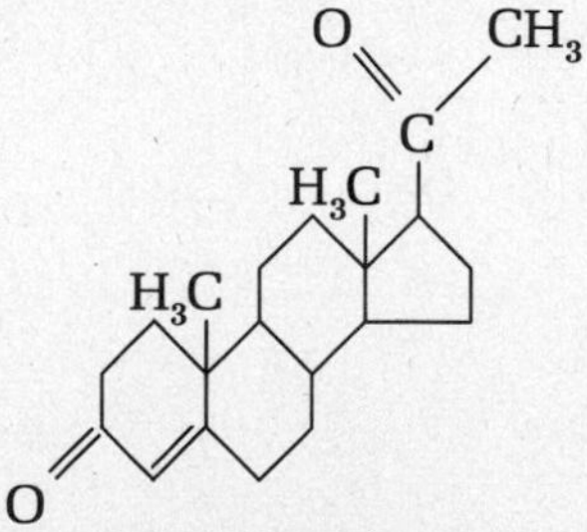

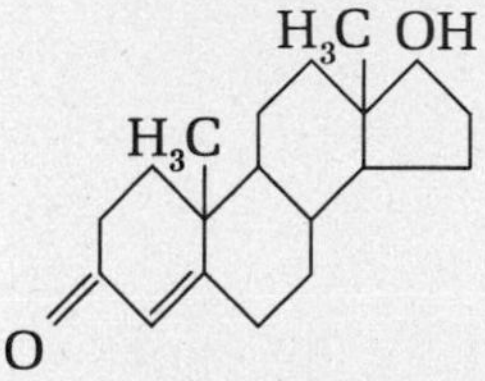

FIGURE 20–5 · *Some typical steroids*

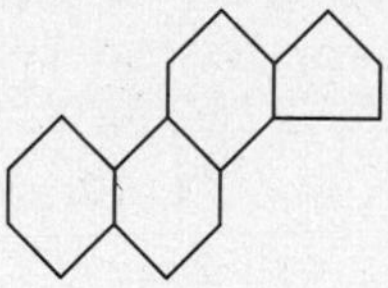

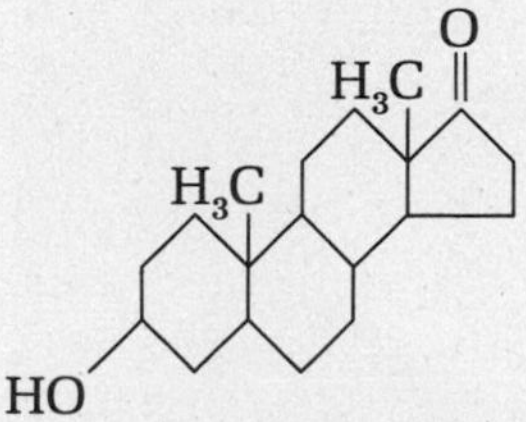

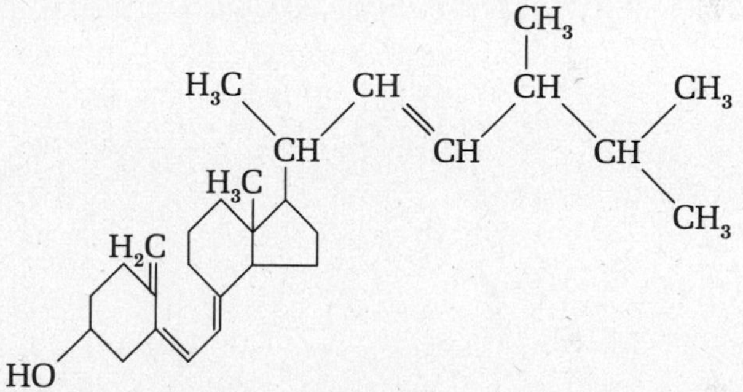

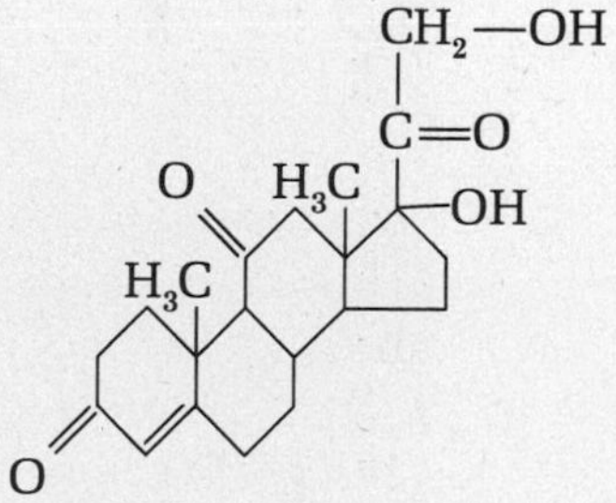

One of the most controversial steroids is **cholesterol.** The structure of cholesterol is shown in Figure 20–6. Cholesterol is found in almost every tissue of the body. It is concentrated particularly in the brain and the spinal cord. Gallstones consist mainly of cholesterol. The function of cholesterol is not completely understood. It is assumed that it is needed for the synthesis of other steroids. Cholesterol can be synthesized easily in the body. Recent research indicates that it requires only a few seconds for the body to make cholesterol from simple raw materials, although the process requires thirty-six separate chemical reactions. About one gram of cholesterol is synthesized in the body per day, whereas only about 0.30 gram per day is provided by the average diet. Cholesterol is found in foods of animal origin, such as liver or brain. Eggs are particularly rich in cholesterol.

FIGURE 26–6 · *Cholesterol (Greek: Chole, bile; stereos, solid; plus "-ol," alcohol)*

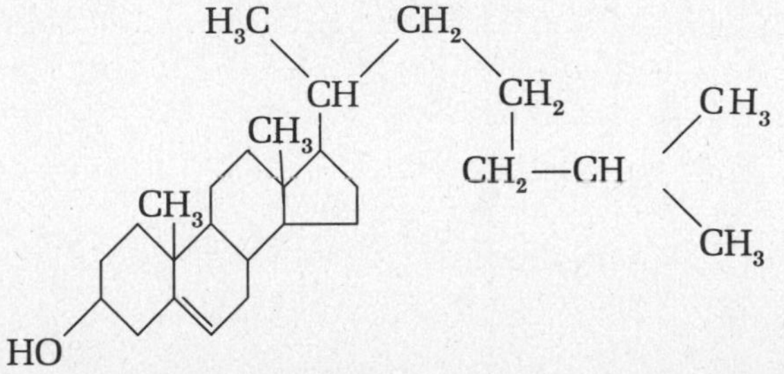

H_3C CH_2 CH CH_2 CH_3 CH_3 CH_2—CH CH_3 CH_3 HO

FIGURE 20–7 · *This photograph shows cholesterol plaque build-up on an artery. Cholesterol has been implicated as one of the causes of arteriosclerosis.*

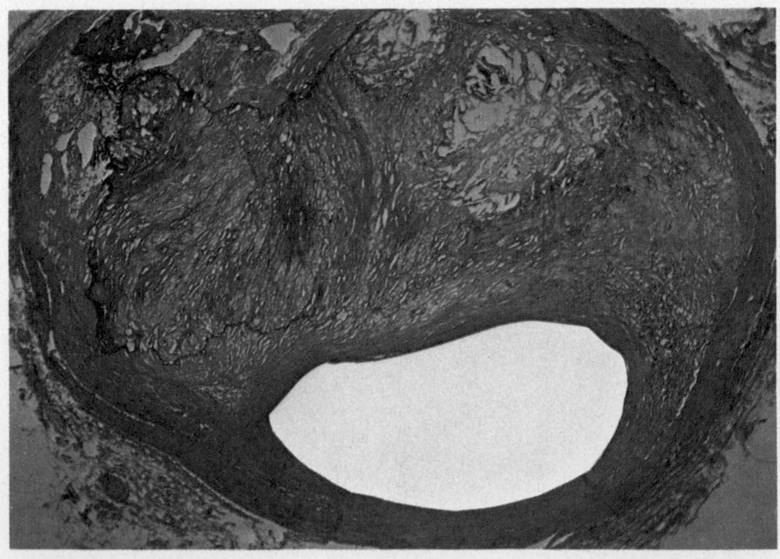

Cholesterol is of particular concern because of the high correlation between cholesterol levels in the blood and the incidence of heart disease. Avoiding cholesterol-laden products, such as eggs, has little effect on decreasing blood cholesterol, since most cholesterol is produced in the body. However, there is evidence to suggest that polyunsaturated fatty acids, such as peanut oil, cottonseed oil, corn oil, and soybean oil, are effective in lowering blood cholesterol. On the other hand, butterfat and coconut oil will cause an increase in the cholosterol level. For that reason, older people, especially those prone to coronary diseases, usually include only polyunsaturated oils in their diet. The fatty acid analysis of some animal and vegetable fats is given in Table 20–2.

TABLE 20–2 · Typical Fatty Acid Analyses

	SATURATED			UNSATURATED		
	PALMITIC	STEARIC	OTHER	OLEIC	LINOLEIC	OTHER
ANIMAL FATS						
Lard	29.8	12.7	1.0	47.8	3.1	5.6
Chicken	25.6	7.0	0.3	39.4	21.8	5.9
Butterfat	25.2	9.2	25.6	29.5	3.6	7.2
Beef fat	29.2	21.0	3.4	41.1	1.8	3.5
VEGETABLE OILS						
Corn	8.1	2.5	0.1	30.1	56.3	2.9
Peanuts	6.3	4.9	5.9	61.1	21.8	. . .
Cottonseed	23.4	1.1	2.7	22.9	47.8	2.1
Soybean	9.8	2.4	1.2	28.9	50.7	7.0†
Olive	10.0	3.3	0.6	77.5	8.6	. . .
Coconut	10.5	2.3	78.4	7.5	trace	1.3

*Reproduced from NRC Publication No. 575: *The Role of Dietary Fat in Human Health. A Report.* Food and Nutrition Board, National Academy of Sciences.
†Mostly linolenic acid.

REVIEW IT NOW

1 Define a *saturated fatty acid* and an *unsaturated fatty acid*.
2 What is the relationship between the melting point and the degree of unsaturation of a fatty acid?
3 Discuss the significance of fatty acids.
4 Draw the polycyclic carbon skeleton for a steroid.
5 Name some typical steroids.
6 What is the significance of cholesterol in the diet?

PROTEINS

20–10 · The importance of proteins · We have discussed the importance of carbohydrates and fats as a source of energy for body functions. Although energy production is not a chief function of protein, it is the most important class of biochemical compounds. In fact, the word "protein" is derived from the Greek word *proteios* which means "first." Protein is of first importance in life processes. Protein is found in cells from every part of the body. Muscles, tendons, skin, hair, nerves, and the blood are composed chiefly of protein. Unlike carbohydrate and fat, protein has a structural function in the body. It is a building material. In addition, many of the hormones and enzymes that regulate the metabolism of carbohydrate and fat are protein.

20–11 · The structure of protein · The molecules of protein are built up from smaller molecules of **amino acids.** Amino acids have the following general structure.

$$H_2N{-}\underset{\displaystyle R}{\overset{\displaystyle H}{C}}{-}COOH$$

The H_2N is the **amine group,** and the COOH is the **carboxyl group.** R can be any one of about twenty different groups of atoms. The following are examples.

$$H_2N{-}\underset{\displaystyle H}{\overset{\displaystyle H}{C}}{-}\overset{\displaystyle O}{\overset{\|}{C}}{-}OH$$

glycine

$$H_2N{-}\underset{\displaystyle CH_3}{\overset{\displaystyle H}{C}}{-}\overset{\displaystyle O}{\overset{\|}{C}}{-}OH$$

alanine

$$H_2N{-}\underset{\displaystyle CH_2}{\overset{\displaystyle H}{C}}{-}\overset{\displaystyle O}{\overset{\|}{C}}{-}OH$$

(CH₂ attached to imidazole ring with NH and N)

histidine

There are about twenty amino acids generally found in protein. Very few proteins contain more than seventeen different amino acids. Only eight amino acids cannot be synthesized in the body and, therefore, must be included in a person's diet. Those amino acids that cannot be synthesized are indicated with an asterisk in Table 20–3.

TABLE 20–3 · Amino Acids Found in Proteins

NAME	ABBREVIATION	NAME	ABBREVIATION
alanine	Ala	isoleucine*	Ileu
arginine	Arg	leucine*	Leu
asparagine	Asp-NH_2	lysine*	Lys
aspartic acid	Asp	methionine*	Met
cysteine	CySH	phenylalanine*	Phe
cystine	CyS-SCy	proline	Pro
glutamic acid	Glu	serine	Ser
glutamine	Glu-NH_2	threonine*	Thr
glycine	Gly	tryptophan*	Try
histidine	His	tyrosine	Tyr
hydroxylysine	Hylys	valine*	Val
hydroxyproline	Hypro		

*Essential in the diet. The body is unable to synthesize them.

A protein is characterized by the sequence of its various amino acids. Each organ in the body has its own type of protein. The proteins are also different in each animal. It has been estimated that there are over 100 000 different kinds of protein molecules in a human being. And humans are only one of thousands of animal organisms. That means that there must be an almost infinite variety of protein molecules. How can there be so many different proteins when they are all composed of only twenty or so different amino acids?

To understand that, let's see how amino acids combine to form protein molecules. Amino acids link together by reacting the **amine group** of one amino acid with the **carboxyl group** of another amino acid. That produces water and a basic protein structure. Let's look at such a reaction between the amino acids glycine and alanine.

$$\underset{\substack{\text{glycine}\\\text{(acid)}}}{NH_2CH_2\overset{\overset{\displaystyle O}{\|}}{C}-OH} + \underset{\substack{\text{alanine}\\\text{(amine)}}}{H-NH\underset{\underset{\displaystyle CH_3}{|}}{C}H\overset{\overset{\displaystyle O}{\|}}{C}-OH} \rightarrow \underset{\substack{\text{glycylalanine, Gly·Ala}\\\text{(a dipeptide)}}}{NH_2CH_2\overset{\overset{\displaystyle O}{\|}}{C}-NH\underset{\underset{\displaystyle CH_3}{|}}{C}H\overset{\overset{\displaystyle O}{\|}}{C}-OH} + H_2O$$

Since the resulting molecule is very large, we will simply abbreviate it Gly·Ala. Of course, the carboxyl group of Ala could have reacted with the amine group of Gly.

$$\underset{\substack{\text{alanine}\\ \text{(acid)}}}{NH_2CH(CH_3)C(=O)\text{—}OH} + \underset{\substack{\text{glycine}\\ \text{(amine)}}}{H\text{—}NHCH_2C(=O)\text{—}OH} \rightarrow \underset{\substack{\text{alanylglycine, Ala·Gly}\\ \text{(a dipeptide)}}}{NH_2CH(CH_3)C(=O)\text{—}NHCH_2C(=O)\text{—}OH}$$

In this case, we would have Ala·Gly, which is a completely different molecule from Gly·Ala. Since each amino acid contains both an amine group and a carboxyl group, many amino acids can link together like beads on a string.

$$\underset{\text{glycine}}{H_2N\text{—}CH_2\text{—}C(=O)\text{—}OH} + \underset{\text{alanine}}{H\text{—}NH\text{—}CH(CH_3)\text{—}C(=O)\text{—}OH} + \underset{\text{alanine}}{H\text{—}NH\text{—}CH(CH_3)\text{—}C(=O)\text{—}OH} + \underset{\text{histidine}}{H\text{—}NH\text{—}CH(CH_2\text{—}C_3H_3N_2)\text{—}C(=O)\text{—}OH} \rightarrow$$

$$H_2N\text{—}CH_2\text{—}C(=O)\text{—}NH\text{—}CH(CH_3)\text{—}C(=O)\text{—}NH\text{—}CH(CH_3)\text{—}C(=O)\text{—}NH\text{—}CH(CH_2\text{—}C_3H_3N_2)\text{—}C(=O)\text{—}OH + 3H_2O$$

In order for the resulting molecule to be called a protein, it must have at least fifty amino acids in its chain. If there are fewer than fifty, the molecule is called a **peptide.** The type of linkage between an amine group and a carboxyl group is called a **peptide bond.**

Peptide Bond

$$\underset{\substack{\text{alanine}\\ \text{(acid)}}}{NH_2CH(CH_3)C(=O)\text{—}OH} + \underset{\substack{\text{glycine}\\ \text{(amine)}}}{H\text{—}NHCH_2C(=O)\text{—}OH} \rightarrow \underset{\substack{\text{alanylglycine, Ala·Gly}\\ \text{(a dipeptide)}}}{NH_2CH(CH_3)C(=O)\overset{\downarrow}{\text{—}}NHCH_2C(=O)\text{—}OH}$$

The peptide bond permits literally thousands of different combinations of amino acids to form proteins. We can illustrate that with the three amino acids glycine, cysteine, and alanine. These can react to produce a tripeptide, Gly·Ala·Cys, as shown below.

$$\underset{\substack{\text{glycylalanine}\\ \text{Gly·Ala}}}{NH_2CH_2\overset{\overset{\displaystyle O}{\|}}{C}-NH\underset{\underset{\displaystyle CH_3}{|}}{C}H\overset{\overset{\displaystyle O}{\|}}{C}-OH} + \underset{\substack{\text{cysteine}\\ \text{Cys}}}{H-NH\underset{\underset{\displaystyle CH_2SH}{|}}{C}H\overset{\overset{\displaystyle O}{\|}}{C}-OH} \rightarrow \underset{\text{a tripeptide: Gly·Ala·Cys}}{NH_2CH_2\overset{\overset{\displaystyle O}{\|}}{C}-NH\underset{\underset{\displaystyle CH_3}{|}}{C}H\overset{\overset{\displaystyle O}{\|}}{C}-NH\underset{\underset{\displaystyle CH_2SH}{|}}{C}H\overset{\overset{\displaystyle O}{\|}}{C}-OH} + H_2O$$

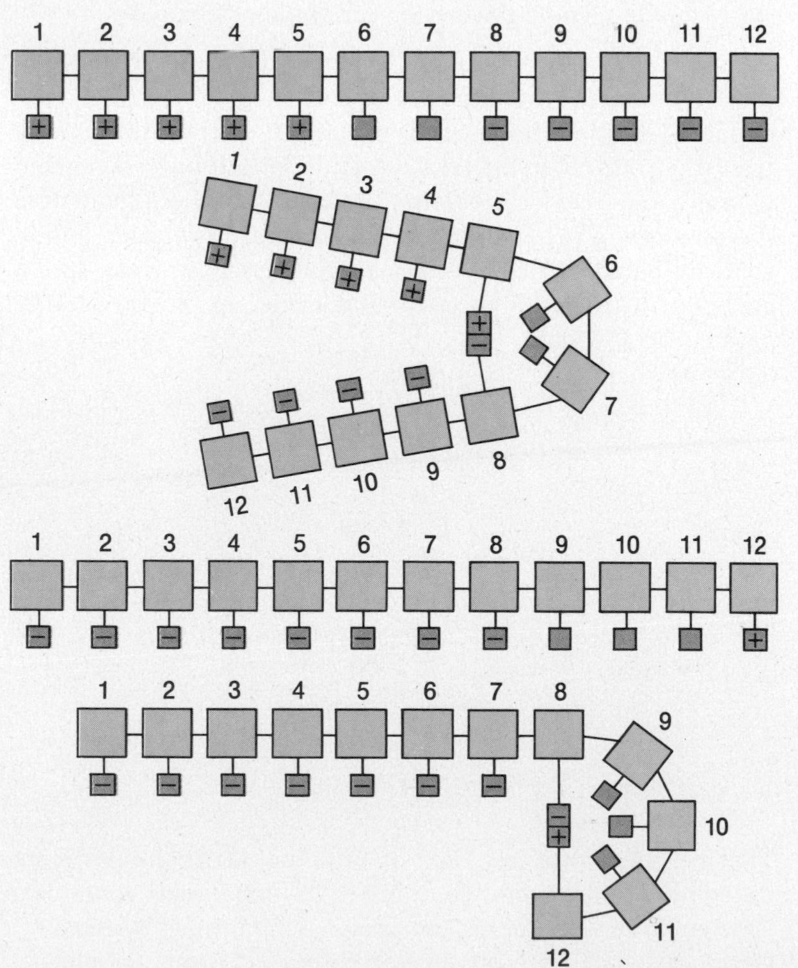

FIGURE 20–8 · *Once a protein, a chain of amino acids is formed, it can twist and bend in a variety of ways. This occurs because certain amino acids bond with each other. In the top illustration, amino acids 5 and 8 bond with each other, producing a protein chain that is bent in half. In the bottom illustration, amino acids 8 and 12 bond with each other. Therefore, the shape of this protein is very different from the shape of the protein in the top illustration. (The pluses and minuses indicate that only certain amino acids can bond with each other.)*

Or the same three amino acids can react in a different order to produce Ala·Gly·Cys.

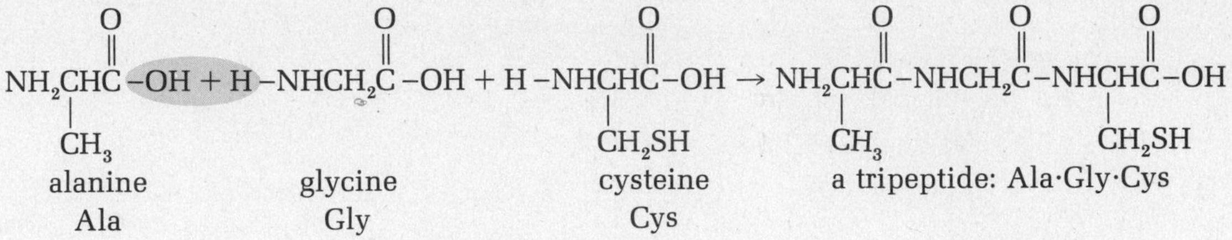

$$\underset{\substack{\text{alanine}\\ \text{Ala}}}{NH_2\underset{\substack{|\\ CH_3}}{CH}\overset{\substack{O\\ \|}}{C}-OH} + \underset{\substack{\text{glycine}\\ \text{Gly}}}{H-NHCH_2\overset{\substack{O\\ \|}}{C}-OH} + \underset{\substack{\text{cysteine}\\ \text{Cys}}}{H-NH\underset{\substack{|\\ CH_2SH}}{CH}\overset{\substack{O\\ \|}}{C}-OH} \rightarrow \underset{\text{a tripeptide: Ala·Gly·Cys}}{NH_2\underset{\substack{|\\ CH_3}}{CH}\overset{\substack{O\\ \|}}{C}-NHCH_2\overset{\substack{O\\ \|}}{C}-NH\underset{\substack{|\\ CH_2SH}}{CH}\overset{\substack{O\\ \|}}{C}-OH}$$

If we continue to play at rearranging just these three amino acids, we can come up with a total of six different combinations.

Glycine-cysteine-alanine	*Cysteine-glycine-alanine*
Glycine-alanine-cysteine	*Cysteine-alanine-glycine*
Alanine-glycine-cysteine	*Alanine-cysteine-glycine*

Each of these are completely different molecules with completely different properties. Obviously, the more different amino acids used, the more peptides and **polypeptides** (more than three amino acids) will result. In fact, if only seventeen different amino acids are used, 3.56×10^{14} different sequences are possible! That is possible only because the same amino acid can be used several times, and also because some amino acids, such as cysteine, are really made up of two smaller amino acids.

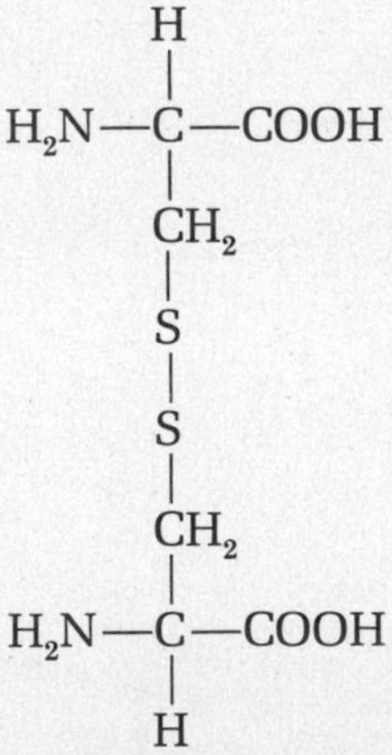

$$\begin{array}{c} H \\ | \\ H_2N-C-COOH \\ | \\ CH_2 \\ | \\ S \\ | \\ S \\ | \\ CH_2 \\ | \\ H_2N-C-COOH \\ | \\ H \end{array}$$

cysteine, Cys—Cys

That permits "crosslinking," or bridging, to form even more different combinations. The protein in human hair contains a large amount of cysteine. The crosslinking formed by the S–S group gives hair its shape and strength. When people get permanents, a treatment first breaks the S–S bonds. Then the hair is reset in a different style. After drying or heating, fresh crosslinks occur to hold the hair in its new shape.

The importance of crosslinking can be seen in the structure of sheep insulin (see Figure 20–9). Even though this molecule seems large to you, chemists regard this as a very small protein molecule. The formula masses of proteins can range from 10 000 to well over a million. The sequence of amino acids in sheep insulin was determined in 1955 by F. Sanger. He was given a Nobel prize for his discovery.

FIGURE 20–9 · *The structure of sheep insulin*

Phe		Gly
Val		Leu
Asp—NH_2		Val
Glu—NH_2		Glu
His		Glu—NH_2
Leu		Cy (—S—, to Cy below)
Cy	—S—S—	Cy
Gly		Ala (S)
Ser		Gly
His		Val
Leu		Cy (—S—, to Cy above)
Val		Ser
Glu		Leu
Ala		Tyr
Leu		Glu—NH_2
Tyr		Leu
Leu		Glu
Val		Asp—NH_2
Cy	—S—S—	Tyr
Gly		Cy
Glu		Asp—NH_2
Arg		
Gly		
Phe		
Phe		
Tyr		
Thr		
Pro		
Lys		
Ala		

20–12 · The sequence of amino acids in proteins · Not only is the size of the protein important, but the exact sequence of amino acids in the protein molecule is also important. In fact, many diseases and malfunctions of various body processes can result when amino acids are not in the proper sequence. The disease sickle-cell anemia, for example, results when a glutamic acid R group is replaced by a valine R group in a certain place on the giant hemoglobin molecule (Figure 20–10).

FIGURE 20–10 · *The picture on the left shows two normal red blood cells. The two red blood cells on the right are sickle cells. Sickle-cell anemia is a good example of how important the amino acid sequence is in a protein. It is a genetic disease (a disease one generation inherits from another). People suffering from this disease have red blood cells that are abnormal in both shape and function. Some of their red blood cells are "caved-in," having a sickle shape.*

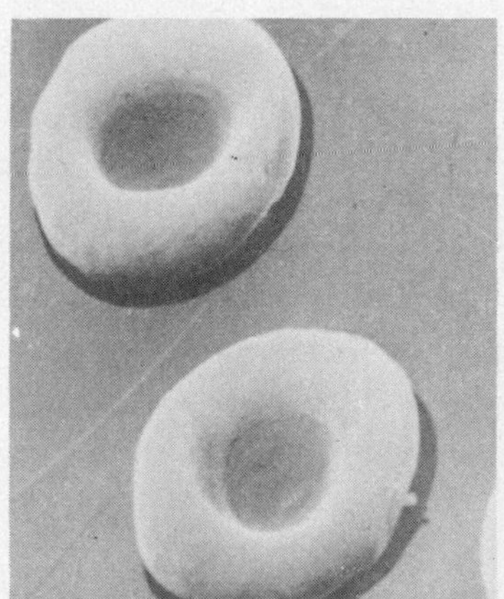

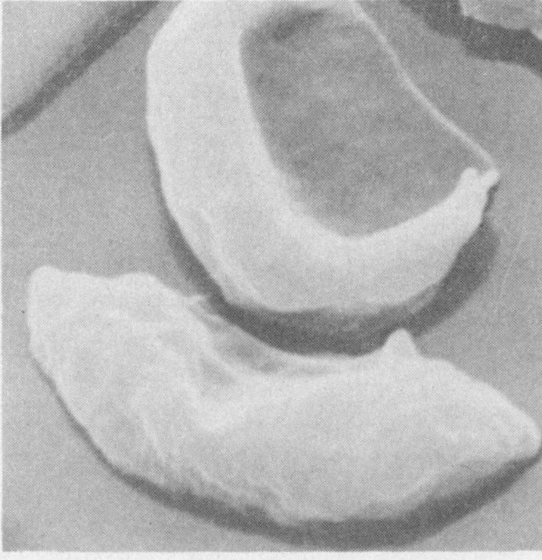

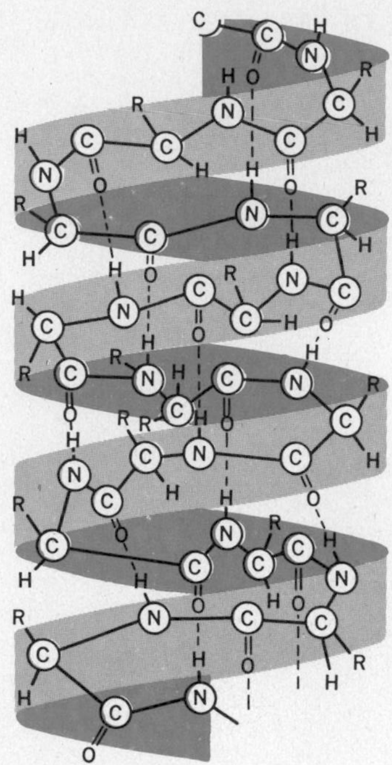

FIGURE 20–11 · *The alpha helix protein structure proposed by Pauling and others is shown here.*

There are three related aspects of structure in protein chemistry: the **primary, secondary,** and **tertiary** structures.

The primary structure of a protein refers to the sequence of amino acid residues in the polypeptide. Any variation in the sequence leads to a different protein with a different biochemical significance. Painstaking biochemical research is making slow but steady progress in determining the primary structure of proteins.

In 1951, Linus Pauling and his co-workers at the California Institute of Technology were able to show that some proteins have a secondary structure. Their work was based on complex X-ray diffraction patterns yielded by crystalline proteins. The secondary structure is a helical shape made possible by intramolecular hydrogen bonding (Figure 20–11). The linearity implied by such a model correlates well with the properties of the fibrous proteins. Long, threadlike polypeptides arrange themselves in hydrogen-bonded layers to form water-insoluble fibers. Examples of fibrous proteins are keratin, found in skin, hair, nails, wool, horn, and feathers; collagen, found in tendons; myosin, the contractile protein of muscles; and fibroin, the structural basis of silk.

More detailed structural studies of proteins indicate the existence of some very complicated tertiary structures, in which the polypeptide chain wraps around itself. As a result, one particular site along the chain is especially exposed. It is believed the biochemical function of a protein takes place at this site. Figure 20–12 shows a model for the tertiary structure of hemoglobin deduced by Professors Kendrew and Perutz, of Cambridge University in England. Apparently the very complicated tertiary structure of the polypeptide chain is necessary to provide a site for the iron atom in hemoglobin. At this site an oxygen molecule is bound for its transport to body cells. The tertiary structure imparts a spheroidal shape to some proteins. The class of globular proteins includes the vital hormones insulin, thyroglobin, and ACTH, as well as albumin, gamma globulin, and fibrinogen, three major constituents of blood. It seems likely that the mechanisms of the specific biochemical activities of these globular proteins are related to their tertiary structures. For example, it seems that the uncoiling of the fibrinogen tertiary structure to form the fibrous protein fibrin is responsible for blood clotting.

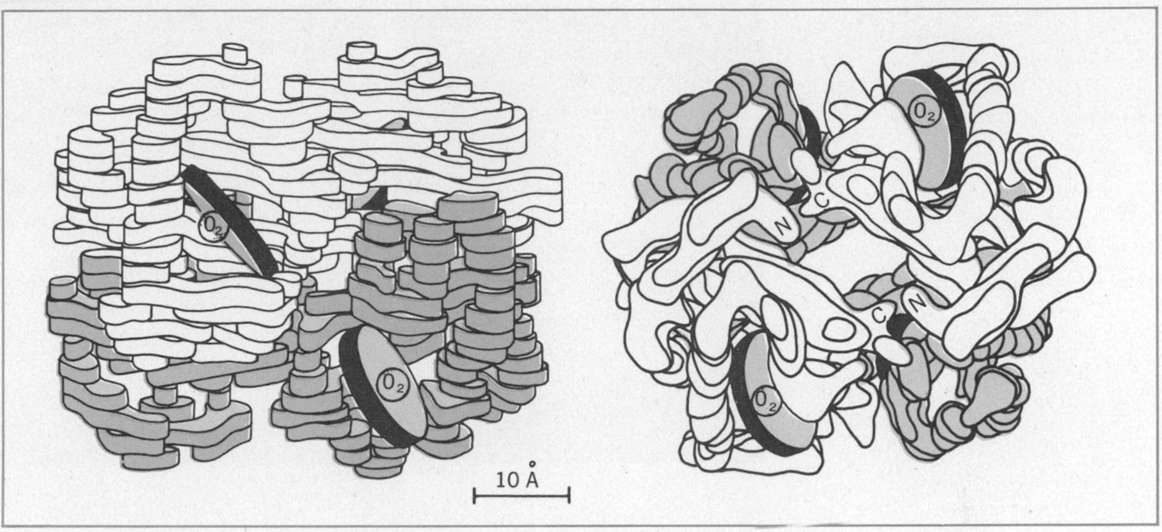

FIGURE 20–12 · *This illustration shows the top (left) and the side (right) views of the model of the tertiary structure of hemoglobin that was suggested by Professors Kendrew and Perutz. Note the oxygen (O_2) molecules. These molecules are bound to the iron atom in the hemoglobin for transport to the body cells.*

Since the pioneering work of Kendrew and Perutz, the techniques of X-ray crystallography have yielded the three-dimensional structure of several proteins. Undoubtedly, more will be realized soon. These techniques are very tedious and involved, but in several cases they have produced such detailed pictures that it is possible to visualize the individual amino acid residue in a protein molecule. From such studies, we can begin to understand the forces holding globular proteins in their particular shape. It is apparent that spatial orientation is vital to the biochemical function of a protein. That orientation is brought about by intramolecular hydrogen bonding. Knowing that the hydrogen bond is relatively weak, we are not surprised to learn that proteins are very sensitive to heat. Heating, or changing the chemical environment that supports the formations of hydrogen bonds, causes the hydrogen bonds in proteins to break. The secondary and tertiary structures of the protein become undone, and its biological activity is lost. This generally irreversible process is known as **protein denaturation.** It is most familiarly observed in the cooking of an egg. A raw egg is water soluble. The cooked egg in which protein denaturation has occurred is insoluble (Figure 20–13).

FIGURE 20–13 · *Protein denaturation occurs as this egg is cooked. Denaturation causes the egg to turn from a clear liquid to an opaque solid.*

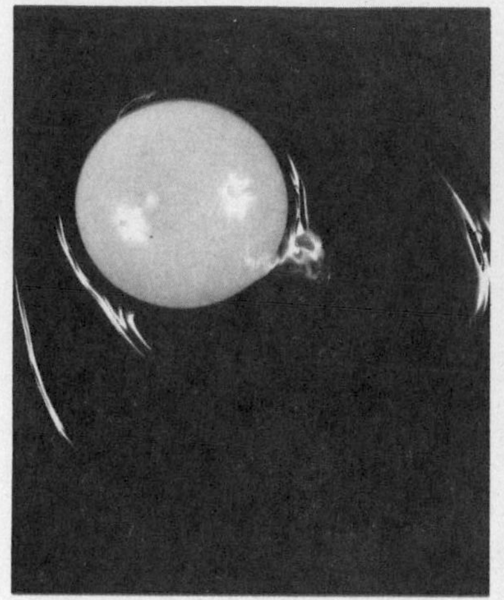

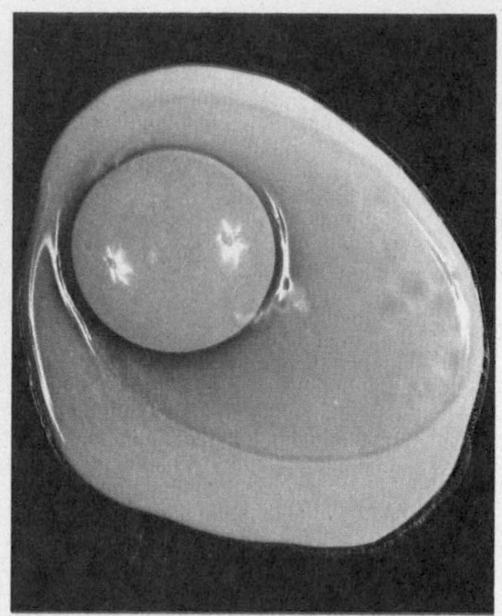

20–13 · Enzymes and metabolism · All of biochemistry is involved in the study of **metabolism**—the chemical fate of all substances used by living matter. The metabolic reactions of many substances have been determined in exact detail by experimentation. An important property of these metabolic processes is that they occur within a narrow and relatively low range of temperatures. Scientists have learned that at biological temperatures, the reactant molecules in a biological reaction do not have enough energy to overcome the energy of activation. Since these reactions do occur, biochemical catalysts must exist. These biochemical catalysts are called **enzymes.** So far, all known enzymes are protein molecules.

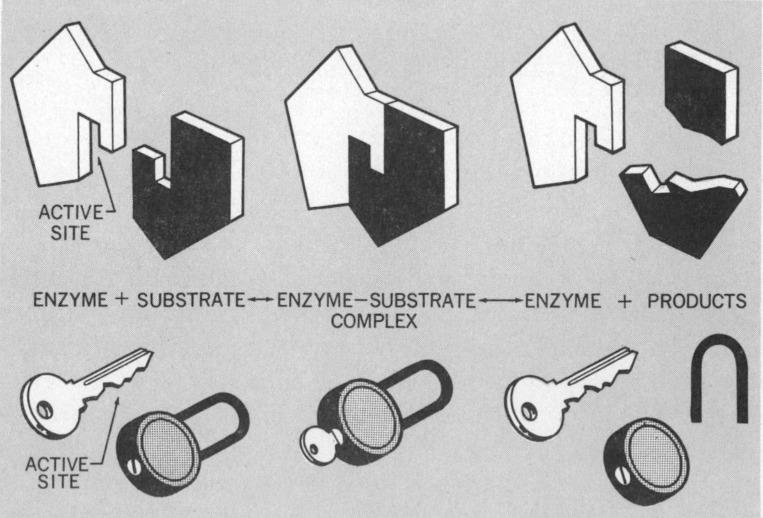

FIGURE 20–14 · *This illustration demonstrates the "lock-and-key" model for enzyme specificity.*

The number and kinds of reactions that take place in a cell depend on the particular enzymes that the cell contains. Each biochemical reaction is catalyzed by a specific enzyme. This enzyme specificity has led to a "lock-and-key" model for enzyme catalysis (Figure 20 – 14).

According to the lock-and-key hypothesis, the three-dimensional shape of the enzyme protein produces a particular region on its surface called the active site. It is the active site that is capable of reacting with the **substrate** (the substance acted upon) molecule.

Experiments indicate that the amino acid sequence (the primary structure) is the principal factor involved in determining how the protein chain will fold up into its characteristic (tertiary) shape. The tertiary shape determines the specificity in biochemical reactions. Thus, the structural and metabolic characteristics of a living organism depend primarily on the amino acid sequence in the protein catalysts contained in the cells of that organism.

20–14 · The nucleic acids · Comparable to the proteins in biochemical significance are the giant molecules known as the **nucleic acids.** On the basis of recent research, it appears that nucleic acids possess the ultimate in biological activity. These acids control the biochemical synthesis of proteins. They are also responsible for the genetic transfer of characteristics during cell reproduction.

Unlike the proteins, which are polypeptides, the nucleic acids are **polyesters.** The acid involved in the esterification (the formation of an ester by reacting an acid with an alcohol) is phosphoric acid. The hydroxyl compound is not an alcohol, but is a derivative of one of two sugars, ribose or 2-deoxyribose (Figure 20 – 15).

ribose

deoxyribose

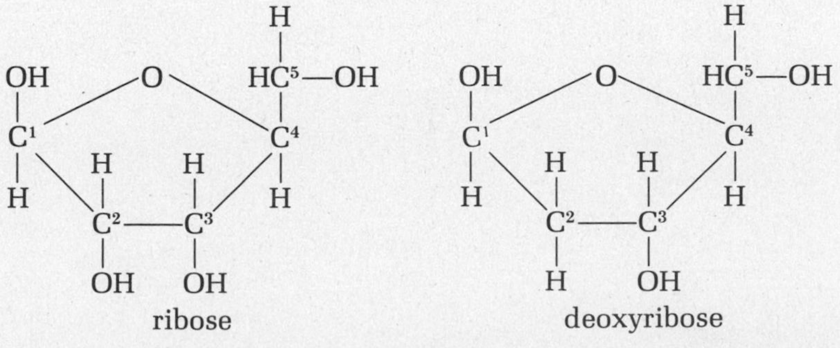

FIGURE 20–15 · *The formulas for the two sugars, ribose and 2-deoxyribose*

The sugar derivatives arise from the substitution of one of five organic bases on the carbon atom in the number one position in the sugar ring (Figure 20–16). Esterification with phosphoric acid occurs at the number five carbon.

FIGURE 20–16 · *The structural formulas of the nitrogen bases occurring in nucleic acids are shown below. Thymine is found only in DNA, while uracil is found only in RNA. On the opposite page are ball-and-stick models of cytosine (top), thymine (left), and uracil (right). Red represents oxygen, white represents hydrogen, black represents carbon, and yellow represents nitrogen.*

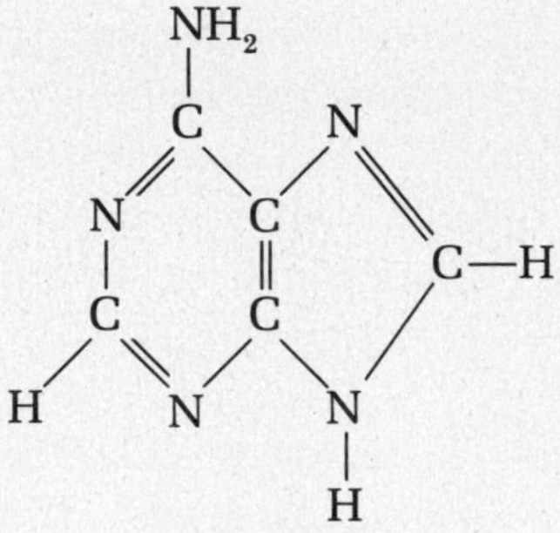

adenine

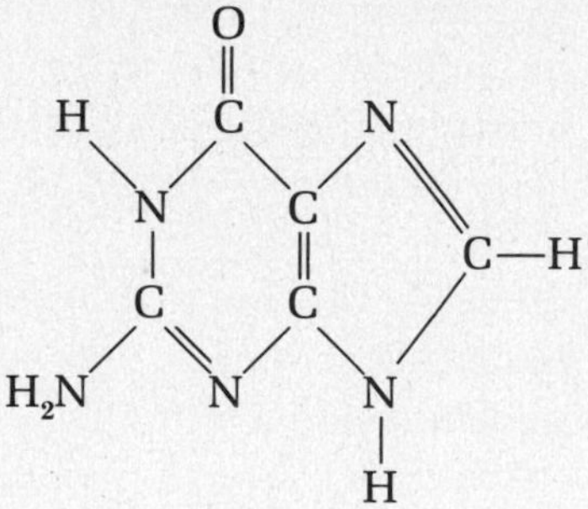

guanine

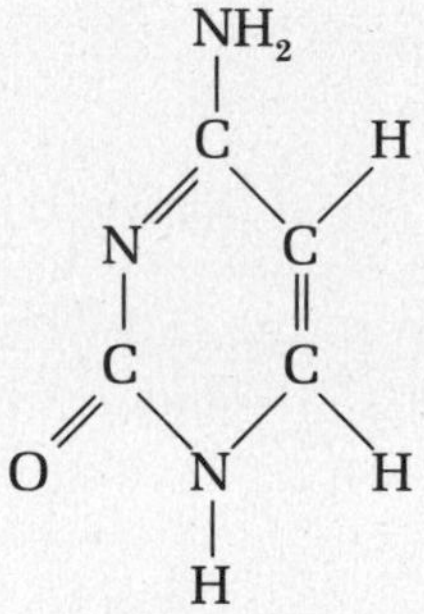

cytosine

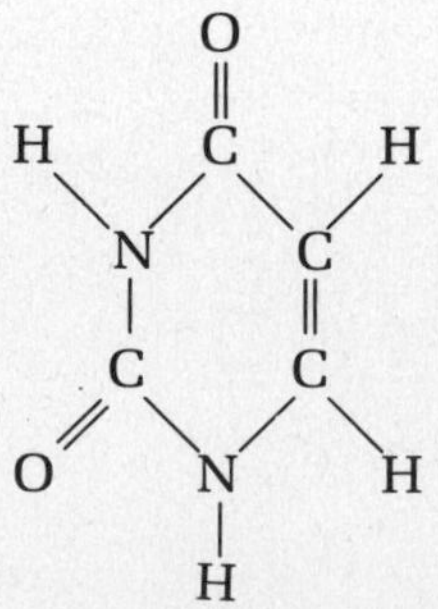

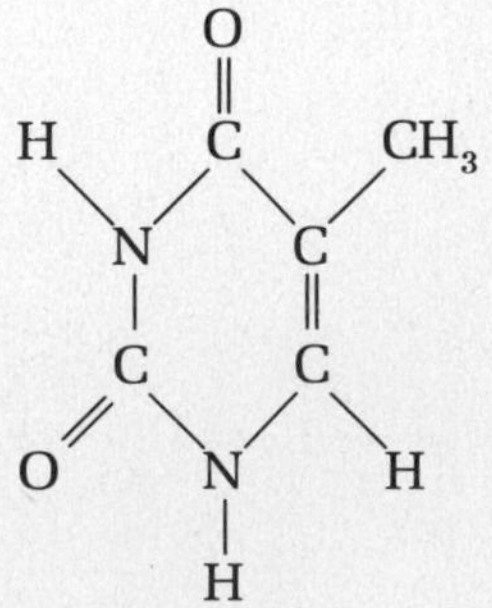

thymine

uracil

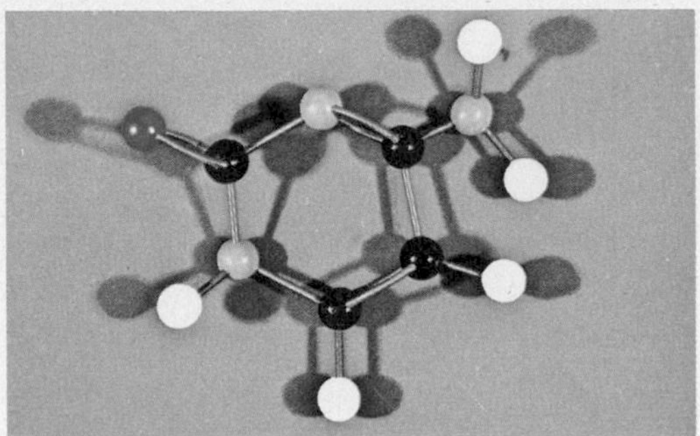

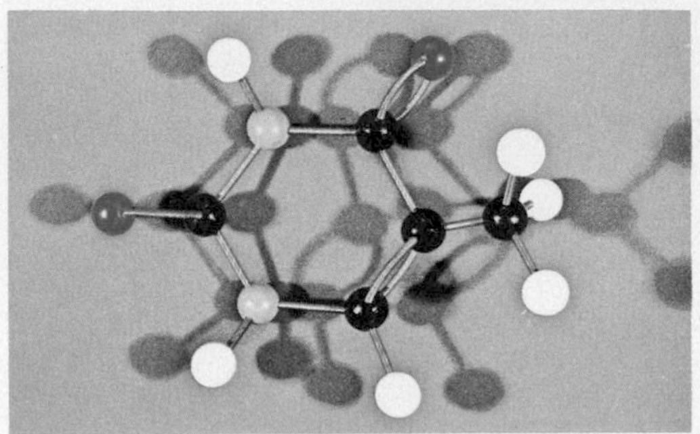

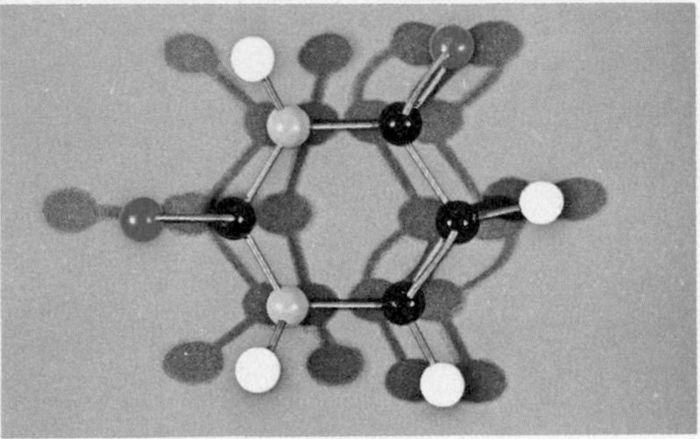

The monomeric species, consisting of acid, sugar, and base, are called **nucleotides** (see below). It is important to note that upon polymerization (the formation of large molecules) of the nucleotides, two families of nucleic acids exist. **Deoxyribonucleic acids (DNA)** consist of nucleotides containing the bases adenine (A), thymine (T), guanine (G), and cytosine (C). In **ribonucleic acids (RNA),** uracil (U), replaces thymine in one of the nucleotides. The symbols A, T, G, C, and U are conveniently used to represent a whole nucleotide unit.

```
         O                                       H       O
         ‖                                       |       ‖
   H     C        N                          H—C—O—P—OH
     \  / \      / \\                            |       |
      N     C        \\                          |       OH
      |     ‖          C—H                       |
      C     C         /                          |
     / \\  / \      /          O                 |
 H2N     N     N                /   \              |
               L__________ C   H    H    C
                           |    |    |    |
                           H    C——C    H
                                |    |
                               OH   OH
```

base   sugar   acid

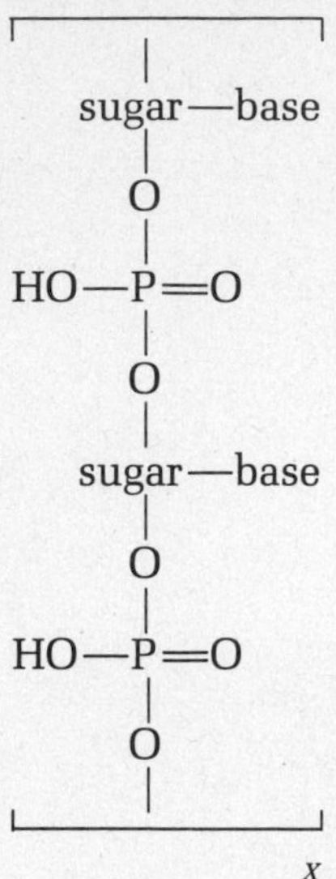

FIGURE 20–17 · *Nucleotide sequence of phosphate groups and sugars*

The polymerization of the nucleotides occurs with the hydroxyl group on the carbon atom at position three and the phosphate group of another nucleotide. Giant polynucleotides result (from such polymerization). It should be apparent that DNA and RNA are truly families of compounds. The number of times that a given base appears in a chain and the sequence of bases along that chain differ from one nucleic acid to another. Consider a pentanucleotide made up of one or more of the four different nucleotides, A, T, C, and G. There are 4^4, or 256, possible sequences for these four nucleotides. When it is realized that thousands of nucleotides are present in DNA and RNA molecules, the number of possible sequences is staggering. We now believe it is the sequence of nucleotides in the DNA molecules of the chromosomes of cells that carries genetic information.

20–15 · DNA and the genetic code · If a DNA molecule is responsible for the storage of genetic information, it must be a self-replicating molecule. When a cell divides, it forms two identical daughter cells. The DNA molecules present in the mother cell must likewise divide and form two identical DNA molecules that will be present in the daughter cells.

Analysis of the X-ray diffraction patterns of crystalline DNA led Dr. James Watson and Dr. Francis Crick in 1953 to deduce a three-dimensional structure for DNA. They concluded that DNA exists as a double helix. The double helix of the Watson-Crick model is the result of intermolecular hydrogen bonding between pairs of complementary bases. An A on one helix is always hydrogen-bonded to a T on the second. A C is always hydrogen-bonded to a G. It is this specific reaction of complementary bases that is responsible for the self-replication of DNA. The Nobel Prize for Medicine was awarded to these scientists in 1962.

Another Nobel prize winner, Dr. Arthur Kornberg, and his co-workers have succeeded in isolating enzymes that can catalyze the complete synthesis of a particular DNA isolated from a bacterial virus. This synthesized DNA has all the biological properties of the original virus DNA. However, confirmation of the Watson-Crick model is found in the fact that the synthetic process requires a copy of the virus DNA to act as a template.

If DNA stores the information necessary to assemble all the cell's proteins, that information must tell how to arrange the

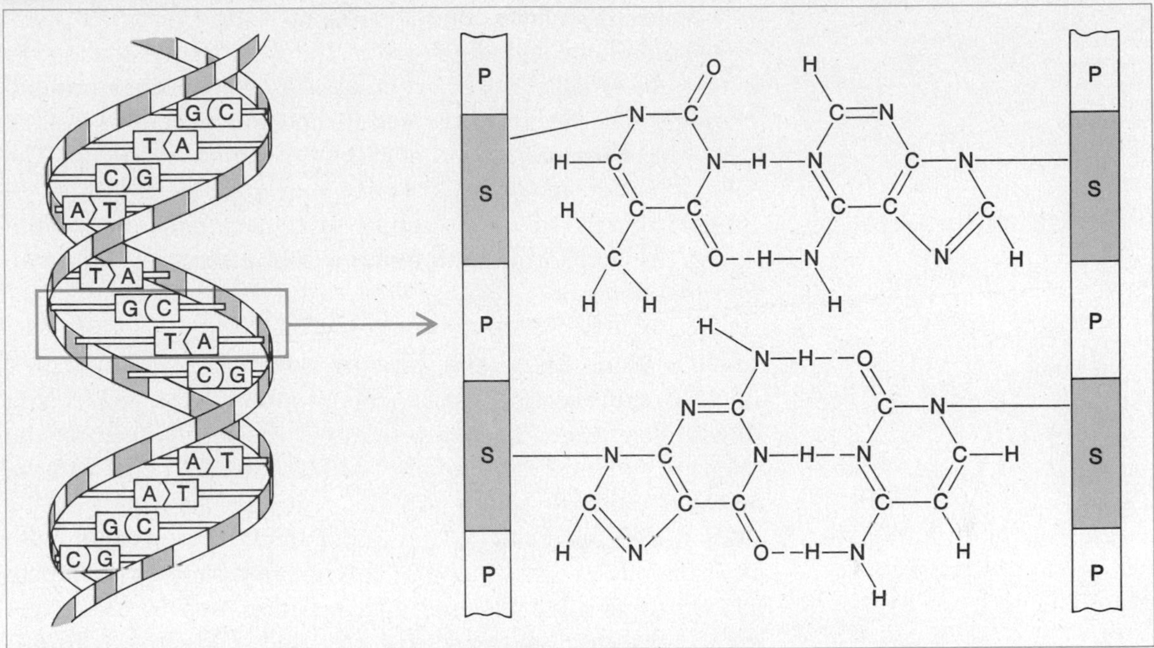

FIGURE 20–18 · *The Watson-Crick model of DNA*

amino acids in proper sequence. The sequence information must be stored in the sequence of nucleotides in the DNA molecule. The relationship between the nucleotide sequence of DNA and the corresponding amino acid sequences of protein is known as the **genetic code.** This is the critical information contained in the gene.

The next matter that concerns DNA in its role as bearer of the genetic code involves the number of letters in such a code. The ultimate transcription of the genetic code is in the synthesis of proteins from the twenty amino acids present in cell fluids. Thus, the code must be able to account for specific amino acids to be bound in a specific sequence. How many of the four nucleotides A, T, G, and C are required for encoding the amino acids? There cannot be a one-to-one correspondence between a letter and an acid, since that would lead to the utilization of only four amino acids. If a combination of two letters is used to correspond to a given amino acid, only 4^2, or 16, acids can be accounted for. Since the use of all four letters would encode 4^4, or 256, acids, molecular biologists feel that a three-letter code with a possibility of 4^3, or 64, combinations, is the simplest to work with. There is significant experimental evidence to support the idea of a three-letter code.

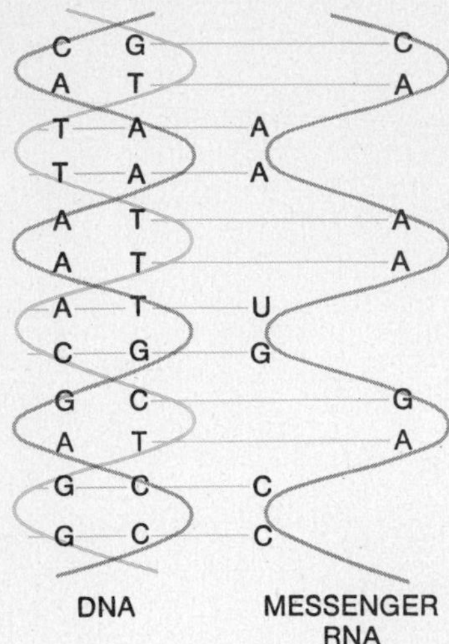

FIGURE 20–19 · *A model for genetic code transcription and transfer*

The linear sequence of nucleotides in a DNA molecule, then, must contain enough three-letter code words for the amino acids to be arranged in a particular sequence within a protein. Those proteins become involved in metabolic reactions in such a way that a particular kind of cell, or organism, develops. The cellular difference between mice and people, therefore, is related directly to the structure of their nucleic acids. But how is the coded information of the DNA molecules translated into proteins?

20–16 · DNA, RNA, and protein synthesis · The complex story of the genetic ordering of protein synthesis is being slowly discovered. The story involves the mechanism for the transcription and the transfer of the genetic code and its ultimate translation into protein synthesis. One part of the story already seems to be well understood. In accordance with experimental evidence, one of the features of the mechanism appears to involve the intermediate formation of **messenger RNA** molecules that transcribe the genetic code from the DNA molecule (Figure 20–19). The transcribed code is transferred out of the cell nucleus by the messenger RNA molecules into the ribosomes. In the ribosomes, amino-acid-bearing **transfer RNA** molecules "read" and translate the transcribed code in some unknown manner, and protein synthesis results. Evidence indicates that enzymes are involved in each step of the total mechanism, though not all the details are known. Indeed, there are many unknown factors about the role of DNA and RNA in the synthesis of proteins. That is as it must be in an area of concern at the very frontier of scientific research.

Because proteins are involved in so many biochemical reactions, their metabolism is very complex. One important metabolic pathway taken by proteins results in the production of ammonium ions and pyruvic acid. Ammonia is excreted in the urine as the compound urea. Pyruvic acid is important, because it is used in the production of a compound called **acetyl coenzyme A.** In fact, carbohydrates, fats (triglycerides) and proteins can all produce acetyl coenzyme A. The overall view of the process is shown in Figure 20–20.

Like ATP mentioned earlier, acetyl coenzyme A contains a high-energy bond. Some of the B vitamins are involved in the production of acetyl coenzyme A also. The energy contained in the high-energy acetyl coenzyme A is released in the cell by a very complicated process that ultimately produces carbon

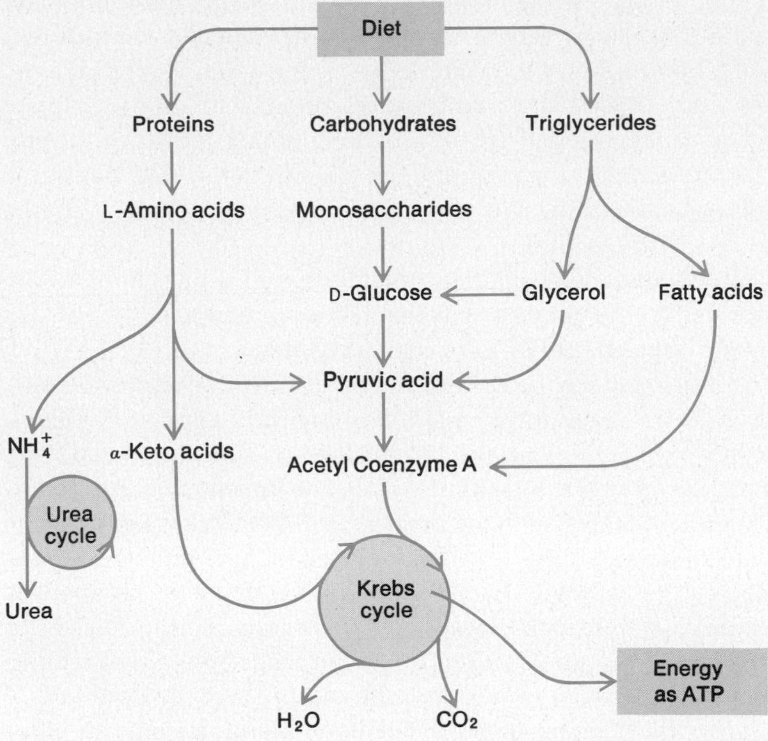

FIGURE 20–20 · *The Krebs cycle is very important in the production of energy within the body.*

dioxide and water as well. The sequence of reactions involved in the process was worked out in England by the chemist Sir Hans Krebs. He was awarded a Nobel prize for his work. In his honor, this chain of reactions is called the *Krebs cycle.* If you wish to learn more about the Krebs cycle, you can consult any biochemistry textbook.

20–17 · The elements and life · We have seen that most compounds of biochemical importance contain the basic elements carbon, hydrogen, oxygen, and nitrogen. The amino acids cysteine and methionine also contain sulfur. These elements are important, but there are other elements with biological significance.

Many enzymes that have been discussed depend on certain metal ions. Those enzymes generally fall into two groups—**metal-activated enzymes** and **metallo-enzymes.**

Metal-activated enzymes are enzymes that in a sense are "turned on and off" by certain metal ions. Such metal ions act as modifiers by decreasing, or speeding up, the activity of certain enzymes. Metal ions with this property include K^+, Cu^+, Fe^{++}, Mg^{++}, Ca^{++}, Zn^{++}, Cu^{++}, Mo^{++}, Fe^{+++}, and Mo^{++++}. Fe, Mo, and Cu are primarily responsible for the activity of many enzymes that involve oxidation and reduction within the cells. Mg^{++} is required in all reactions that transfer a phosphate group. We see the importance of Mg^{++} in the ATP – ADP reaction.

In the metal-activated enzyme, the metal is only temporarily bonded to the enzyme. In some cases, an enzyme can use any one of several metals to become activated.

Metallo-enzymes, on the other hand, are much more specific. In metallo-enzymes, the metal ion is firmly bonded to the enzyme and cannot be substituted for another metal ion. The enzyme minus its metal ion is called an **apoenzyme.** An apoenzyme is inactive without the specific metal that is part of its molecular structure. Metallo-enzymes include large molecules such as heme, which has a central Fe ion. Heme is a component of hemoglobin and is responsible for transporting oxygen to the cells. Oxygen is picked up in the lungs by the hemoglobin molecule. The oxygen is then bound to the iron atom and is transported by the blood to the cells. Here, the oxygen is released, thus forming reduced hemoglobin. That is illustrated in Figure 20 – 21.

FIGURE 20–21 · *Reduced hemoglobin*

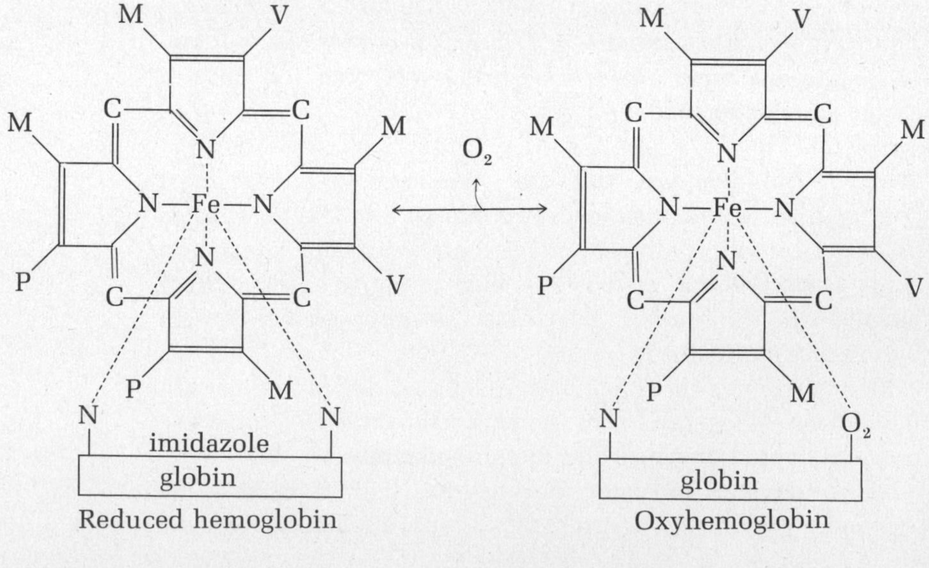

In addition to hemoglobin in the blood, iron is also present in myoglobin in muscle, cytochrome in all cells, and a number of other enzymes.

Cobalomine (Vitamin B_{12}) is also a metallo-enzyme. It contains the cobalt ion. In 1964, Dr. Dorothy Hodgkin received a Nobel prize for her work in determining the structure for Vitamin B_{12}. That structure is shown in Figure 20–22.

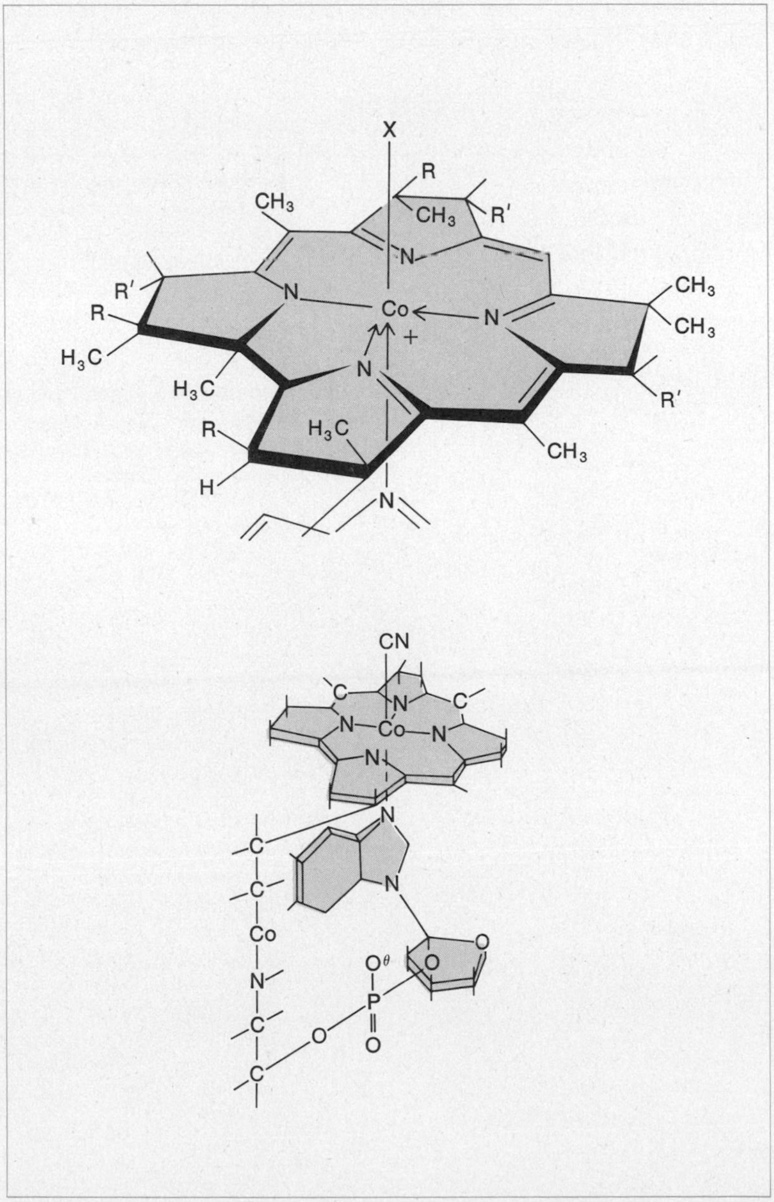

FIGURE 20–22 · *The structure of Vitamin B_{12}*

Dorothy Crowfoot Hodgkin *(American) Dr. Hodgkin received the Nobel prize in 1964 for her work in X-ray studies of compounds such as vitamin B_{12} and penicillin.*

In order for iron to be absorbed, a small amount of copper must be present. Copper is also found in some enzymes, especially in tyrosinase. Tyrosinase was one of the first oxidative enzymes discovered. It is responsible for the production of the black pigment melanin, which controlls the pigmentation of human's skin. Tyrosinase is also responsible for the darkening of ripe bananas and bruised potatoes, apples, and other fruit. Erythrocuprein is a protein containing copper in our red cells. Its

TABLE 20–4 · Biological Significance of Some Chemical Elements

ELEMENT	SYMBOL	ATOMIC NUMBER	COMMENTS
Hydrogen	H	1	Universally required for organic compounds and water
Helium	He	2	Inert and unused
Lithium	Li	3	Probably unimportant
Beryllium	Be	4	Probably unimportant; toxic
Boron	B	5	An essential constituent of some plants; function not known
Carbon	C	6	Universally required for organic compounds
Nitrogen	N	7	Universally required for many organic compounds
Oxygen	O	8	Universally required for organic compounds and water
Fluorine	F	9	Possible minor constituent of some bony structures, such as teeth
Neon	Ne	10	Inert and unused
Sodium	Na	11	Principal extracellular cation
Magnesium	Mg	12	Essential divalent cation required for the activity of many enzymes; present in chlorophyll and involved in photosynthesis
Aluminum	Al	13	Importance not known
Silicon	Si	14	Possible structural unit of diatoms and of possible importance to some plants
Phosphorus	P	15	Indispensable for biochemical synthesis and energy transfer as well as a structural component of many macromolecules
Sulfur	S	16	Constituent of proteins and many other important biological compounds
Chlorine	Cl	17	Principal intracellular and extracellular anion

function is not known.

It is interesting that oxygen is carried in the human blood by becoming attached to an iron atom. However, in some animals, such as the squid, a hemocyanin is present rather than a hemoglobin. In hemocyanin, there are up to twenty atoms of copper in the molecule that serve to transport oxygen.

The biological significance of some other chemical elements is given in Table 20–4.

EXCURSION THIRTEEN
Careers in Chemical Sciences

This excursion lists some of the careers available in chemistry.

ELEMENT	SYMBOL	ATOMIC NUMBER	COMMENTS
Argon	A	18	Inert and unused
Potassium	K	19	Principal intracellular cation
Calcium	Ca	20	Major structural component of bone; required for the activity of some enzymes
Scandium	Sc	21	Probably unused
Titanium	Ti	22	Probably unused
Vanadium	V	23	Essential in lower plants, tunicates, and rats
Chromium	Cr	24	Essential to higher animals
Manganese	Mn	25	Trace element required for the activity of several enzymes
Iron	Fe	26	Most important transition metal ion; used in hemoglobin for oxygen transport and as an active site for many metalloenzymes in higher animals
Cobalt	Co	27	Structural component of vitamin B_{12}; required as trace element for the activity of several enzymes
Nickel	Ni	28	Importance unknown
Copper	Cu	29	Comparable to iron as an essential constituent of vital oxidative enzymes and oxygen transport proteins (hemocyanin)
Zinc	Zn	30	Trace element required for the activity of numerous enzymes
Molybdenum	Mo	42	Trace element required for several enzymes
Tin	Sn	50	Required in the rat; role unknown
Iodine	I	53	Required as an essential constituent of the thyroid hormone found in most higher animals

REVIEW IT NOW

1 Draw the structure of a typical amino acid.
2 Show how a peptide bond is formed.
3 Explain how literally thousands of different proteins can be formed from only twenty-three different amino acids.
4 How do enzymes function?
5 What is the role of DNA and RNA?

SUMMARY

The chemistry of living organisms is of tremendous complexity. Yet only a relatively few elements constitute most of the compounds of biological significance.

Though the cell, with its proteins, nucleic acids, polysaccharides, carbohydrates, fats, lipids, salts, and water, may be microscopic in size, it would take an entire industrial complex to synthesize cellular products.

Modern biochemical research has shown clearly that the structure of molecules has a profound effect on their biochemical activity. That is especially true of proteins, the underlying structure of all living organisms, and of nucleic acids, the bearers, transmitters, and executors of the genetic code.

The metabolic rate of all substances used by living matter depends upon the enzymatic control of the biochemical reactions involving those substances. In addition, most metabolic reactions depend upon adenosine triphosphate, ATP, the biochemical energy currency.

REVIEW QUESTIONS

1 What important contribution did each of the following Nobel prize winners make to biochemistry?
  a. Linus Pauling
  b. James Watson and Francis Crick
  c. Arthur Kornberg
  d. Carl and Gerty Cori
  e. John Kendrew and Max Perutz
  f. Dorothy C. Hodgkin
  g. Sir Hans Krebs
2 Explain how ATP acts as an energy "carrier."
3 What is the difference between a saturated fatty acid and an unsaturated fatty acid? What is the importance of this difference from a nutritional standpoint?
4 Defend the following statement: "The amino acids are the building blocks of animate nature."
5 **a.** Give the extended formula for the amino acid valine (2-amino-3-methylbutanoic acid, or 2-amino-3-methylbutyric acid).
  b. Give a structural equation showing the formation of the dipeptide from two valine molecules.

6 Briefly discuss the primary, secondary, and tertiary structure of proteins in relation to protein function.
7 Defend the following statement: "DNA is the molecule of life."
8 Briefly describe the lock-and-key mechanism for enzymatic catalysis.
9 **a.** What are the components of a nucleotide?
b. In what ways can nucleotides differ from each other?
10 Diagrammatically describe a model for the role of the nucleic acids in protein synthesis.
11 What similar structural property of the compounds adenine, thymine, guanine, and cytosine causes them to behave alike chemically?
12 Distinguish between metal-activated enzymes and metallo-enzymes. Give an example of each type.

SUGGESTED READINGS

Cohen, Carolyn. "The Protein Switch of Muscle Contraction." *Scientific American*, November 1975, p. 36.

Cheldelin, V. H., and R. W. Newburgh. *The Chemistry of Some Life Processes*. New York: D. Van Nostrand Co., 1964.

"Developments in Human Genetics." *The Science Teacher*, November 1973.

Evans, Gary W. "Biological Function of Copper." *Chemistry*, June 1971, p. 10.

Ferguson, Harold, and Wolfgang Vogel, "Is there a Chemical Basis for Learning?" *The Science Teacher*, March 1974, p. 16.

Fox, J. Lawrence. "Chemical Origins of Life." *The Science Teacher*, January 1974, p. 29.

Hoare, James P., and Mitchell LaBoda. "Electrochemical Machining." *Scientific American*, January 1974, p. 30.

Lykken, Louis. "Chemical Control of Pests." *Chemistry*, July–August 1971, p. 18.

Nyberg, Sister Helen. "Schizophrenia—The Body's Chemical Mistake." *Chemistry*, May 1970, p. 14.

Petty, A. Wayne. "Trace Elements and Health." *The Science Teacher*, May 1972, p. 37.

Sharon, Nathan. "Glycoproteins." *Scientific American*, May 1974, p. 78.

EXCURSIONS

Exploring and Applying

In the series of Excursions that follow, we will discuss some of the concepts and areas of chemistry not previously covered. These Excursions are not written in the same style as the basic chapters. It is our hope that you will read them to understand chemistry better and to learn how important, interesting, and exciting chemistry can be.

EXCURSION ONE

A Look at the Elements

As you study chemistry, you will become familiar with the chemical elements. You will learn how the elements are related to one another and how they react to form chemical compounds. That is the basis for the study of chemistry. In this excursion, however, we will look at the elements in a somewhat lighter manner. Let's see how some of the elements were discovered and how they were named. As you study this excursion, locate the elements in the periodic table. Note the symbol assigned to each of the elements. At first glance, the table of elements may appear to be difficult and confusing. But as you progress through your study of chemistry, most of the elements will become familiar to you.

NAMING NEW ELEMENTS

It has always been a great honor to discover a chemical element. Usually, the discoverers have exercised the right to name their element. Sometimes, "false" discoveries have been made by well-meaning scientists. Later when the actual discovery was made, the name given to an element by the previous scientist was changed. Thus, as chemistry progressed, several names appeared for certain elements. For example, columbium became niobium; alabamine became astatine; virginium became francium; and glucinium became beryllium. You will find only the new names in your periodic table. But if you had studied chemistry in the early 1900's, you might have found some of the names first given to the elements.

In some cases, the same element has been discovered simultaneously in different parts of the world. That has led to some confusion, since each chemist gave a different name to the element. In some cases, both names have been retained in some way. For example, tungsten has the chemical symbol W. That may seem strange to you. Actually tungsten was discovered in Sweden, in a heavy, yellow mineral. It was named tungsten from the Swedish words *tung* ("heavy") and *sten* ("stone"). At about the same time, two Spanish scientists isolated the same element from a heavy mineral called wolframite. So they claimed discovery and named their element wolfram. Today, most of the world calls the element wolfram. In the United States, we call it tungsten, but still use the symbol W. More recently, the synthesis of several elements has led to great controversy. For example, both Russian and American scientists have claimed the discovery of elements 104, 105, 107, and 108. If you look in your periodic table, you will see that we have listed element 104 as Rf, rutherfordium. The Russians proposed the name kurchatovium (Ku), for one of their great scientists. Also, you will see that we list element 105 as hahnium (Ha). The Russians claim the same discovery and have named the element nielsbohrium, for Niels Bohr. With the advanced technology of both countries, it is quite likely that more elements will be synthesized. Therefore, both countries have agreed to allow the International Union of Pure and Applied Chemistry (IUPAC) to settle disputes over naming elements. Even though elements 106, 107, and 108 have been synthesized, it may be a while before they are given names and entered in the periodic table.

Clemens Alexander Winkler (German, 1838–1904) Clemens Winkler discovered the element Germanium in 1886. With this discovery, he confirmed Mendeleev's prediction of an element below silicon. Winkler also investigated the properties of the little known element indium and its compounds.

It is curious just how names are given to elements. Surprisingly, no scientist has ever named an element for himself or herself. Usually, names are given to honor other famous scientists, the country where the discoverer lived or worked, the name of a mythical god or goddess that seems to characterize the element, or a name for a color that is characteristic of the element.

Some elements have names that describe their properties. For example, both bromine (Br) and osmium (Os) are noted for their very strong odor. Their names come from the Greek word *bromos*, which means "to stink." Since argon (Ar) is a very unreactive element, it takes its name from the Greek word meaning "lazy one." Krypton (Kr) exists in only one part per million parts of air. Thus, the Greek word *krypton*, meaning "the hidden one," seemed appropriate. Astatine, a synthetic element that decays in less than a day, was named from the Greek word meaning "unstable."

TABLE E1–1 · Elements Named for Mythical Gods and Goddesses

ELEMENT	SYMBOL	ATOMIC NUMBER	NAMED FOR	DISCOVERED BY	DATE
Titanium	Ti	22	Titans, Greek first Sons of Earth	Martin Klaproth	1795
Vanadium	V	23	Vanadis, Scandinavian goddess of beauty	Manuel del Rio	1801
Nickel	Ni	28	Nick, German "devil"	A. F. Cronstedt	1751
Selenium	Se	34	Selene, Greek moon goddess	Jöns Berzelius	1818
Niobium	Nb	41	Niobe, Greek goddess (daughter of Tantalus)	Heinrich Rose	1844
Promethium	Pm	61	Prometheus, Greek bearer of fire	J. A. Marinsky (and colleagues)	1945
Tantalum	Ta	73	Tantalus, Greek god of frustration	Anders Ekeberg	1802
Mercury	Hg	80	Mercury, Roman messenger of the gods	?	?
Thorium	Th	90	Thor, Scandinavian god of war	Jöns Berzelius	1828

Many elements have symbols derived from very old Latin names for the elements. In some cases, the elements are so ancient we don't really know who discovered them or how they were named. Those include the Latin *aurium* from which we get Au as the symbol for gold, *argentum* ("the shiny metal") that gives silver the symbol Ag, and *plumbum* that gives lead the symbol Pb. A person who worked with lead pipes in Roman times was called a "plumber," a name we use even today.

Copper, with the symbol Cu, was mined during the Roman Empire on the island of Cyprus. Thus, it is believed the metal

FIGURE E1–1 · *Pure copper is produced by froth flotation. The pure copper is separated from copper ore.*

was originally called cyprium, which over the years became *cuprium*, the Latin word for "copper."

There is a fascinating story behind the discovery of each of the elements. In Excursion 6, the story of the discovery of mendelevium, element 101, is described by one of the members of the discovery team, Dr. Gregory Choppin. We would like to single out a few of the other elements and tell you how their discovery came about.

Let's begin with Sir Humphry Davy (1778–1829), a young English scientist, who discovered a very important element in 1807. By the end of the eighteenth century, great advances had been made in studying electricity. Volta (1745–1827), the great Italian scientist, had developed the battery. For the first time, scientists were able to produce large amounts of electrical energy. Davy built a powerful battery and used that to study the effects of electricity on many substances. One substance he studied was potash. That is the ash that remains after wood has been burned in a pot. Davy passed an electric current through a solution of potash. To his surprise, small, silvery, metallic beads were formed. Many of them burst into flame when they were exposed to air. Upon analysis, Davy realized that he had discovered a new element. He named it **potassium,** since it was produced from potash. The next day, he repeated his experiment with soda ash, the product that remains when marsh grass has been burned. Again, he was able to produce a metal, similar to potassium, when he passed an electric current through the soda ash solution. He named that new element **sodium.** Two new elements had been discovered in two days! Davy didn't stop there. During the next year, he used his battery to isolate and name the elements barium (Ba), strontium (Sr), calcium (Ca), and magnesium (Mg). Davy's fame spread through England and all of Europe. Later, he also discovered the elements chlorine (Cl) and boron (B). Scientists throughout the world spoke of Davy's achievements. But there was one particular person who was most envious of Davy's achievements. That was the French emperor, Napoleon. France was at war with England at the time, and Napoleon could not bear to see England claim the honor of discovering six elements, while his own French chemists had discovered none. Although some of the best chemists in the world at that time were French, and although Napoleon supplied them with huge batteries—much larger than Davy's—they were still unable to identify additional elements. Oddly enough, to show his respect for Davy and

FIGURE E1–2 · *Gold, the coinage metal*

TABLE E1–2 · Elements Named for States and Cities

ELEMENT	SYMBOL	ATOMIC NUMBER	NAMED FOR	DISCOVERED BY	DATE
Magnesium	Mg	12	Magnesia, city in ancient Greece	Sir Humphry Davy	1808
Strontium	Sr	38	Strontia, Scotland	Sir Humphry Davy	1808
Yttrium	Y	39	Ytterby, Sweden	Carl G. Mosander	1843
Holmium	Ho	67	Stock*holm*, Sweden	P. T. Cleve	1879
Erbium	Er	68	Ytt*erby*, Sweden	Carl G. Mosander	1843
Terbium	Tb	65	Yt*terby*, Sweden	Carl G. Mosander	1843
Ytterbium	Yb	70	Ytterby, Sweden	Georges Urbain	1907
Lutetium	Lu	71	Paris (*Lutetia*, Latin for Paris)	Georges Urbain	1907
Hafnium	Hf	72	Hafnia, ancient name for Copenhagen, Denmark	D. Coster	1923
Berkelium	Bk	97	Berkeley, Calif. (U. of Calif.)	Glenn Seaborg (and colleagues)	1950
Californium	Cf	98	California (U. of Calif., at Berkeley)	Glenn Seaborg (and colleagues)	1950

his disdain for his own chemists, Napoleon brought Davy to France and awarded him the highest honor that could be bestowed on a French scientist, the Annual Scientific Prize of France.

A STUDENT PRODUCES ALUMINUM

Davy also tried to extract a metal from the mineral alum. Davy suspected that the new element was there and even named it aluminum. But his batteries were not strong enough to isolate the element. Chemists around the world began a frantic search for that element. Those chemists included the famous Danish scientist Hans Oersted (1777–1851), the German chemist Frederick Wöhler (1800–1882), and the French chemist Henri Deville (1818–1881). After years of work, Deville finally extracted enough aluminum to produce a small bar of the metal. The new, unique metal was considered so valuable that it was exhibited along with the crown jewels at the Paris Exposition. The wealthier families of France had knives, forks, and spoons made of aluminum, which they proudly displayed for their most important dinner guests. Visitors of less importance were given utensils made of gold or silver! Napoleon III saw the great potential of the unusual metal. Aluminum is lightweight, easy to shape, durable, and does not rust or corrode. Therefore, it was an ideal metal for armor with which to outfit his army! So, he strongly supported the efforts of his chemists to find a way to produce aluminum economically on a large scale. Unfortunately for Napoleon, France was again denied a scientific victory. The race to produce aluminum easily and economically was won by a young American student, Charles Martin Hall (1863 – 1914). Charles Hall was a student at Oberlin College, in Oberlin, Ohio. His professor had been a student of Wöhler's in Germany and told his young student of the efforts to produce aluminum. Charles Hall became obsessed with the possibility of discovering a process to produce aluminum. He built a crude laboratory in his father's woodshed and went to work. After two years of work, Hall decided to try a new approach to the problem. Other chemists had tried to extract aluminum by the direct electrolysis of aluminum ore. Hall tried something different. He heated aluminum ore (bauxite) and a material called iceland spar (cryolite) together. Much to his surprise, the two melted together when they were heated, just as sugar dissolves in water. Then when he passed an electric current through the solution, the shiny, metallic element aluminum was produced. At the age of twenty-one, Charles Martin Hall had discovered an inexpensive, efficient way to produce aluminum. He rushed into his professor's office and handed him a handful of aluminum buttons that he had produced. The next year, young Hall started a company now known as the Aluminum Company of America (ALCOA). A chest containing the original buttons of aluminum that Hall made is proudly displayed by ALCOA, and affectionately referred to as the "Crown Jewels." To show the pride that our country felt in Hall's achievement, it was decided to place a small sample of his aluminum in a high place where it would always remain to remind the world of his accomplishment. The Washington Monument was selected as the site, and to this day, a small piece of Hall's aluminum is on the very top! An aluminum statue of Hall stands at Oberlin College in Ohio.

FIGURE E1–3 · *This aluminum statue of Charles Martin Hall at Oberlin College is a fitting tribute to a brilliant alumnus.*

UNFORTUNATE GUINEA PIGS

Find the element antimony in your periodic table. Note that this element has the symbol Sb, for stibnite, the ore from which the element was discovered. Stibnite, or stibium, has been in existence for centuries. In the Bible, we find that Jezebel "painted her face with stibic stone" (II Kings 9:30). Stibium

FIGURE E1–4 · *This chalk statuette of Queen Nefertiti (first half of the fourteenth century B.C.) shows how some Egyptians used stibnite as makeup.*

was used to darken the eyes. That is why many pictures of the ancient Egyptians show them with large, dark eyes. No one knows for sure how stibium was discovered, or by whom. However, there is an interesting account of the origin of the name antimony, as stibium is now called.

Our story begins in a Benedictine monastery in France, with a monk named Basilius Valentinus. Let's call him Basil Valentine. Basil Valentine had been experimenting with stibium ore and accidently threw the results of his old experiments into the slop that was used to feed the pigs in the monastery. After a few days, Basil noticed that the pigs became sick and lost weight. However, they soon got better, developed a tremendous appetite, and grew into large, fat hogs. Noticing that many of the monks in the monastery were a little on the slim side, Basil Valentine decided that a little stibium in their food might produce the same effect, allowing them to put on a little weight. Following through with his plan, he carefully observed the monks. Just as had happened with the pigs, the monks became sick and began to lose weight. But unlike the pigs, the monks all died! Obviously, Basil Valentine felt badly that his experiment had failed. So he set out on a campaign to let all France know the result of his ill-fated experiment. He traveled

TABLE E1–3 · **Elements Named for Color**

ELEMENT	SYMBOL	ATOMIC NUMBER	NAMED FOR	DISCOVERED BY	DATE
Chromium	Cr	24	*Chroma*, Greek, "color"	L. N. Vauquelin	1797
Rubidium	Rb	37	*Rubidus*, Latin, "dark red"	Robert Bunsen, Gustav Kirchoff	1861
Zirconium	Zr	40	*Zargun* (zircon), Arabic, "golden fire"	Martin Klaproth	1789
Rhodium	Rh	45	*Rhodon*, Greek, "rose"	W. H. Wollaston	1804
Indium	In	49	*Indigo* (intense blue)	Ferninand Reich, Theodor Richter	1863
Iodine	I	53	*Iodes*, Greek, "violet"	Bernard Courtois	1811
Cesium	Cs	55	*Caesius*, Latin, "light blue"	Robert Bunsen, Gustav Kirchoff	1860
Praseodymium	Pr	59	*Prasios*, Greek, "leek green"	Carl Auer von Welsbach	1885
Iridium	Ir	77	*Iris*, Greek, "rainbow"	Smithson Tennant	1804
Thallium	Tl	81	*Thallus*, Latin, "green twig"	Sir William Crookes	1861

throughout France declaring that stibium was not good for monks, or *anti* ("not good for") *moine* ("monks). Hence, we get our word *antimony*.

TABLE E1–4 · Elements Named for Famous People

ELEMENT	SYMBOL	ATOMIC NUMBER	NAMED FOR	DISCOVERED BY	DATE
Samarium	Sm	62	Colonel Samarski, Russian mining engineer	Lecoq de Boisbaudran	1879
Gadolinium	Gd	64	Johann Gadolin, Finnish chemist	J. C. G. de Marignac	1880
Curium	Cm	96	Marie and Pierre Curie, chemists who discovered radium and radioactivity	Glenn Seaborg (and colleagues)	1944
Einsteinium	Es	99	Albert Einstein, physicist	Albert Ghiorso (and colleagues)	1952
Fermium	Fm	100	Enrico Fermi, nuclear physicist	Albert Ghiorso (and colleagues)	1952
*Mendelevium	Md	101	Dmitri Mendeleev, Russian scientist who developed the periodic table	Albert Ghiorso, Gregory Choppin (and colleagues)	1955
Nobelium	No	102	Alfred Nobel, Swedish inventor of dynamite	Albert Ghiorso (and colleagues)	1958
Lawrencium	Lw	103	Ernest O. Lawrence, scientist who invented the cyclotron	Albert Ghiorso (and colleagues)	1961
Rutherfordium**	Rf	104	Ernest Rutherford, English physicist	Albert Ghiorso (and colleagues)	1964
Hahnium**	Ha	105	Otto Hahn, German scientist	Albert Ghiorso (and colleagues)	1970

*See Excursion 6 (Choppin's)

**Unofficial: Russians, kurchatovium and nielsbohrium; Americans, rutherfordium and hahnium.

ELEMENTS FROM ORE

Many elements were discovered as a result of a study of their ores. Some were named directly for the ore from which they were extracted. For example, beryllium is from the mineral beryl; zirconium is from the gemstone zircon; molybdenum from the mineral molybdenite; and calcium from the Latin word *calx*, meaning "lime." Let's turn our attention to two interesting metals that were discovered in the Middle Ages by German copper miners. Occasionally while mining red copper ore, German miners would run across a blue ore. That particular ore was nothing but a nuisance to the miners, who had to stop their work to remove it from the red copper ore. Being a

TABLE E1–5 · Elements Named for Planets and Other Celestial Bodies

ELEMENT	SYMBOL	ATOMIC NUMBER	NAMED FOR	DISCOVERED BY	DATE
Helium	He	2	*Helios* (Greek for sun)	Pierre Janssen	1868
Tellurium	Te	52	*Tellus* (Latin for Earth)	Franz Joseph Muller	1782
Cerium	Ce	58	Ceres (asteroid)	Jöns Berzelius and Martin Klaproth (independently)	1803
Uranium	U	92	Uranus	Martin Klaproth	1789
Neptunium	Np	93	Neptune	Edwin McMillan	1940
Plutonium	Pu	94	Pluto	Glenn Seaborg (and colleagues)	1940
Palladium	Pd	46	Pallas (asteroid)	William Wollaston	1803

superstitious group, the German miners assumed that during the night, goblins placed the blue ore in their paths to torment them. Thus, the miners called the blue ore *Kobald*, the German word for "gremlin." Later, it was discovered that the ore contained a new element, which the Swedish chemist Georg Brandt called kobalt. Today, we call the element cobalt (Co).

Another story also centers around the German copper miners. Around 1600, German miners observed a red ore that was very similar to copper ore. It was so similar that it was almost impossible to separate it from the red copper ore. However, when the strange ore was heated, it produced dense, choking fumes. Also, slivers of the ore would often get into the miner's skin, producing sores that were slow to heal. The German miners (remember their superstitions) assumed that the ore was

FIGURE E1–5 · *A representation of the German devil for which nickel was named.*

made by the devil! So they called the red ore the "devil's copper," or in German, *Kupfer-Nickel*. (Perhaps you have heard the devil referred to as "Old Nick.") Later, as we saw with cobalt, an analysis of kupfer-nickel showed the presence of a new element. Since it was really a new element, not at all like copper, its Swedish discoverer, Axel Cronstedt (1722–1765), simply called it nickel.

These are only a few of the interesting stories regarding the discovery of the chemical elements. Perhaps this will help you see that the elements are not merely a group of mysterious and threatening symbols for you to learn. The elements were all identified by people, although often under most unusual circumstances.

If you are interested in learning more about the elements, you will find any of the college chemistry texts helpful. The *Journal of Chemical Education* and the journal *Chemistry* often publish articles about the elements. Ask your school librarian for assistance in locating these journals.

TABLE E1–6 · Elements Named for Countries and Continents

ELEMENT	SYMBOL	ATOMIC NUMBER	NAMED FOR	DISCOVERED BY	DATE
Scandium	Sc	21	Scandinavia	Lars Nilson	1879
Gallium	Ga	31	*Gallia*, Latin for France	Lecoq de Boisbaudran	1875
Germanium	Ge	32	Germany	Clemens Winkler	1886
Ruthenium	Ru	44	Ruthenia, Russia	Karl K. Klaus	1844
Europium	Eu	63	Europe	Eugène DeMarcay	1896
Thulium	Tm	69	Thule, ancient name for far north	P. T. Cleve	1879
Polonium	Po	84	Poland	Marie and Pierre Curie	1898
Francium	Fr	87	France	Marguerite Perey	1939
Americium	Am	95	America	Albert Ghiorso (and colleagues)	1944

REVIEW QUESTIONS

1 Marie Sklodowska Curie and her husband Pierre made significant contributions to chemistry. Using your school library, find out which chemical elements they discovered.

2 Why was element 43 named technetium?

3 Find out the origin of the names of the following elements.
a. Lithium (Li); At. No 3 **c.** Carbon (C); At. No. 6
b. Hydrogen (H); At. No. 1

4 Suppose you discovered a new element. Propose three different names for your element.

EXCURSION TWO

Liquid Crystals

In our discussion of liquids and solids in Chapter 6, you may have been left with the impression that condensed states of matter are *either* liquids *or* solids. But this may not necessarily be so. For over a hundred years, a class of compounds that have the properties of both liquids and solids has been studied. Such substances are called **liquid crystals.** They are liquid, in that they have fluid properties. But, at the same time, their molecules are highly ordered, like those in a solid. This phase of matter—somewhere between that of a liquid and a solid—has been called the metaphase.

THE PROPERTIES OF LIQUID CRYSTALS

One of the most important characteristics of liquid crystals is their spectacular ability to reflect, refract, or scatter light when they are spread in a thin film. One example of this reflective characteristic of liquid crystals that you may have observed is the "rainbow" produced when sunlight is scattered by a soap bubble. The soap bubble, as well as many other organic compounds, is a liquid crystal. In fact, it has been estimated that about one out of every two hundred organic compounds can form liquid crystals. Recent evidence suggests that many compounds, such as those associated with nerve fibers and the retina of the eye, are really liquid crystals.

Liquid crystals are not new. They were discovered many years ago when it was observed that some crystalline substances behave in a peculiar manner when heated. Some have more than one melting point! In fact, some crystalline substances have as many as three melting points. The first melting point produces a thick, turbid fluid. If more heat is added to the compound, another melting point is reached, producing a turbid liquid. At an even higher temperature, the third melting point is reached. When the third melting point is reached, the clear liquid that we ordinarily think of as characterizing the liquid phase is produced.

Scientists were fascinated with the ability of liquid crystals to respond to almost any type of stimulus by changing their color. Heat, light, ultraviolet radiation, sound, electricity, and even pressure can cause these strange compounds to turn from one color to another.

We see liquid crystals in use every day, perhaps without ever realizing what they are. Many small calculators, for example, use liquid crystals to display the digits. Watches and clocks of the digital variety use liquid crystals to display the time, the day, and/or the month. Perhaps you had a "mood" ring when they were popular several years ago. These rings were made of liquid crystals that responded to even the slightest change in the body temperature, thus reflecting the wearer's "mood" by their color. There are several toys and office decorations available that use liquid crystals. Such decorations and toys create fascinating arrays of color with the slightest change in pressure or temperature.

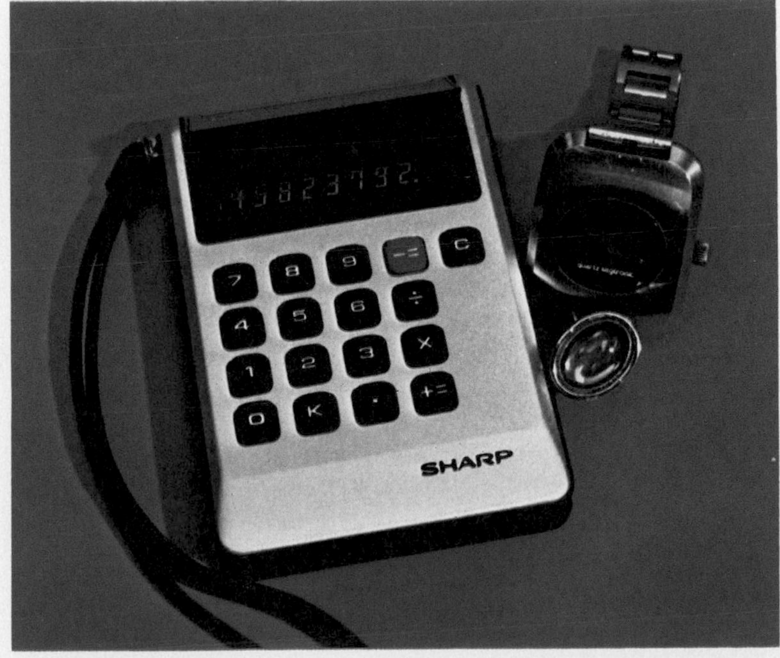

FIGURE E2–1 · *Liquid crystals are used in the calculator, mood ring, and quartz watch shown here.*

TYPES OF LIQUID CRYSTALS

Let's see how liquid crystals work. The strange effect produced by liquid crystals is due to their molecular patterns or, more properly, the way their molecules are arranged. There are basically three types of liquid crystals, each with a somewhat different type of molecular arrangement.

The first type is shown in Figure E2–2. It has the most rigid arrangement of molecules. All the molecules are arranged in neat, orderly rows—somewhat like the seats in an auditorium. This type of liquid crystal is called **smectic.** The molecules are parallel to each other. They are also aligned in layers that are usually only one molecule thick. The layers can slide over each other, which gives this type of liquid crystal a thick, cloudy appearance.

FIGURE E2–2 · *Smectic-type liquid crystal behavior*

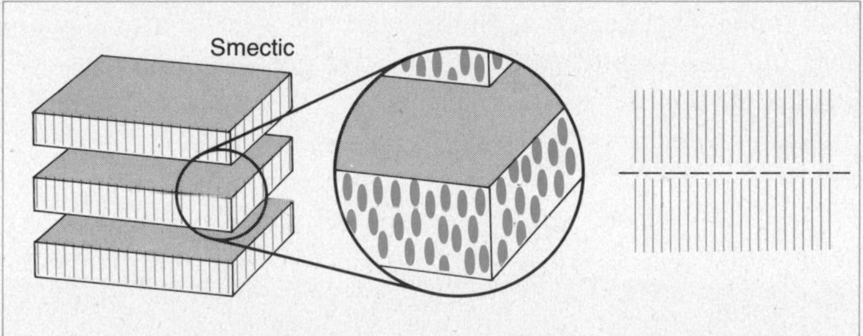

The second type of liquid crystal is shown in Figure E2–3. The molecules in this type are more random in their arrangement, allowing much more slippage of one molecule over another. This produces a more fluid effect. These liquid crystals are called **nematic.** This type is perhaps the most important, because it responds to a slight electronic stimulus by rearranging its molecules.

FIGURE E2–3 · *Nematic-type liquid crystal behavior*

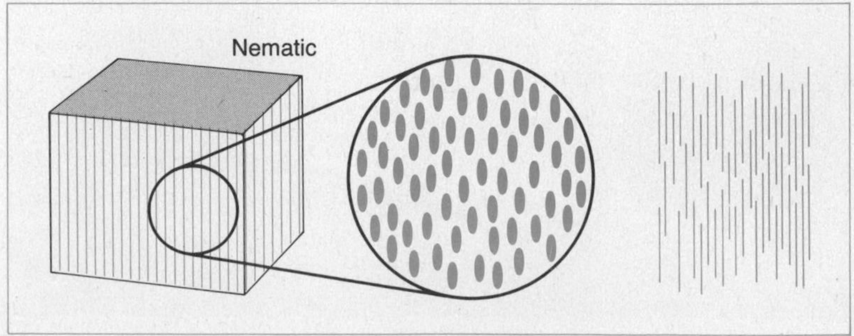

The third type is characterized by the biochemical cholesterol, found in the bloodstream. These are called **cholesteric** and have the structure shown in Figure E2–4. Cholesteric liquid crystals, when spread in a thin film, will turn blue over warm areas and red over cooler ones.

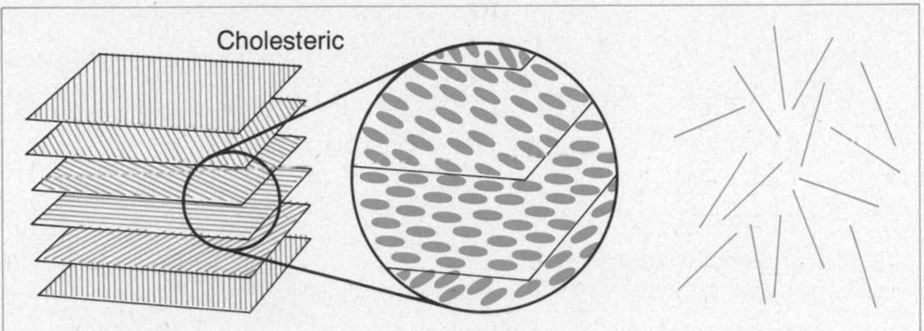

FIGURE E2–4 · *Cholesteric-type liquid crystal behavior*

THE BEHAVIOR OF LIQUID CRYSTALS

How do liquid crystals display the time on a watch or the answer on a calculator? When the nematic type of crystal is used in optical displays such as watches, calculators, thermometers, and automobile speedometers, a very small layer of liquid crystal is sealed between two pieces of glass. Since the liquid crystal has the spreading properties of a liquid, a very small amount is needed. One piece of glass is transparent, or may act as a mirror. The other piece of glass may be coated with a conducting substance such as tin oxide, which acts as an electrode. The electrode is shaped according to what is to be displayed, such as a number.

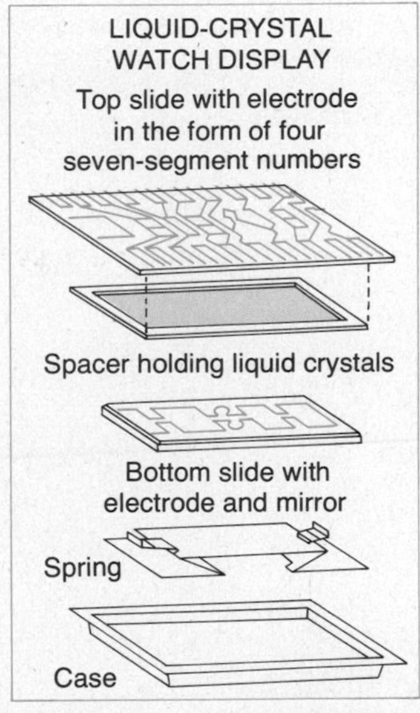

FIGURE E2–5 · *This illustration demonstrates the process involved in the digital display of numbers in a liquid crystal watch.*

Remember that all the molecules are arranged in some pattern within liquid crystals. Light passing through the molecules would simply hit the other side and be reflected. However, when the electrode side is charged—perhaps with a small battery—the molecules beneath the electrode are disrupted and lose their orderly arrangement. This is shown in Figure E2–6.

Light passing through this disorderly group of molecules is not simply reflected. It is scattered by the scrambled molecules and reflected in a random fashion. This causes the liquid crystal area directly beneath the electrode (remember, the electrode is shaped like a number) to appear opaque, or "milky," while the area surrounding the electrode is clear and transparent. Thus, the number on the watch or calculator "stands out." When the electrical stimulus ceases, the molecules in liquid crystals realign themselves until the next stimulus. This accounts for the digital display effect, producing milky letters on a clear background.

A similar effect can produce a dark number on a clear background or a clear number on a dark background. This is how we commonly see liquid crystals used in wristwatches. To produce this effect, polarizing film is used. As the molecules are scrambled by the electronic stimulus, they realign and polarize the light coming through. By using additional polarizing effects, dark or light numbers can be produced.

FIGURE E2–6 · *Molecules of liquid crystals scramble and realign by electronic stimulus on polarizing film.*

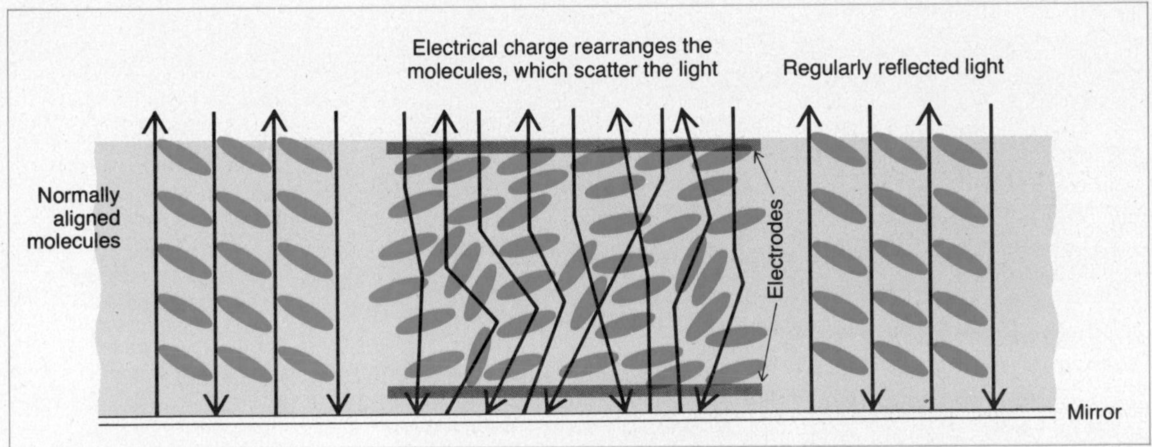

Perhaps you can imagine the tremendous number of ways liquid crystals could be used. They are commonly used to detect very small changes in almost any environmental condition. Most hospitals use digital thermometers that register the slightest change in body temperature. Industries use liquid crystals to detect very slight defects in manufactured instruments.

The future looks very bright for liquid crystals. Some can be used to store information, both electronically and optically. Think of the tremendous application this will have for every form of communication!

REFERENCES

Castellano, J. A., and G. H. Brown. "Thermotropic Liquid Crystals, Part I: The Underlying Science". *Chemical Technology*, March 1973.

__________________ and G. H. Brown. "Thermotropic Liquid Crystals, Part II: Current Uses and Future Ones." *Chemical Technology*, March 1973.

"Liquid Crystals Get Improved Properties." *Chemical and Engineering News*, September 27, 1971.

EXCURSION THREE

What's in an Atom?

The history of the evolution of the atomic theory is fascinating. It illustrates how science progresses. The scientists of many nations have built upon the work of one another over a period of decades. Such collective work helped formulate a model for the atom. That model satisfactorily explains experimental observations as diverse as the spectrum of stars, the toughness of plastics, the transfer of genetic traits, the atomic bomb, semiconductors, the laser, and so forth. Intelligence, hard work, perseverance, imagination, and luck have all played an important role in the development of the atomic theory. The story of the evolution of the atomic theory is one of the great adventures and highest achievements of the human race.

THE EARLY ATOMIC MODELS

To the Greek philosophers, the atom was the ultimate, indivisible bit of matter. However, their speculative approach to the study of the atom was faulty. The Greeks did not experiment in order to learn more about the nature of the atom. The recognition of the difference between an element and a compound and the discovery of the quantitative laws of compound formation (the Laws of the Conservation of Matter, of Definite Composition, and of Multiple Proportions) provided the atomists with a useful atomic theory around 1800. Dalton's theory suggested many new experiments that might help scientists learn more about elements and compounds. However, Dalton's theory did not explain or describe the internal structure of the atom.

In the first seventy years of the nineteenth century, there was little interest in determining atomic structure. But, many scientists were conducting experiments that later helped describe atomic structure. Faraday studied ions in solution. Kekulé learned that carbon atoms joined together in long chains in organic compounds. Mendeleev organized the elements into a periodic table. Such observations showed that atoms are more complex structures than very small marblelike particles of different mass and size. In the last decades of the nineteenth century, the study of the structure of the atom began with the discovery of the electron.

THE ELECTRON

Between 1850 and 1900, many physicists were studying the effects of an electric discharge through a gas at a very low pressure. The glass tubes in which such experiments were carried out were the primitive ancestors of our present-day vacuum tube and television picture tube. The phenomenon that interested those physicists may be observed if you look at the vacuum tube in either a radio or a television set. Note the glow between the metal electrodes in the tube when the set is turned on. Physicists came to the conclusion that such a glow is caused by rays originating at the negative electrode (the cathode). Those rays were named **cathode rays.**

FIGURE E3–1 · *Two electrons collide, producing new elementary particles.*

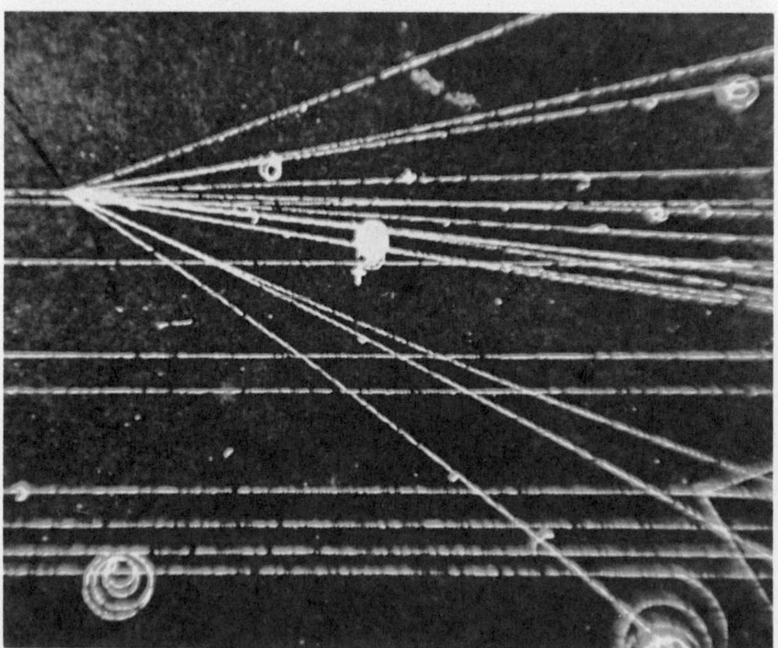

THE DISCOVERY OF THE ELECTRON

J. J. Thomson (1856–1940), a famous English physicist, investigated the strange behavior of cathode rays. In 1897, after twenty years of brilliant research, he announced his results. Thomson showed that cathode rays were bent from their paths by both electric and magnetic fields (Figure E3–2). Unless those rays are actually streams of charged particles, they would not have been bent. It was known that moving positive particles are bent in the opposite direction from moving negative particles. Therefore, Thomson could prove, from the direction of bending, that the cathode rays were negative particles. Those negative particles were named **electrons.**

FIGURE E3–2 · *Cathode rays, which ordinarily move in straight lines (center), are deflected from their paths in a magnetic field (left) and in an electric field (right).*

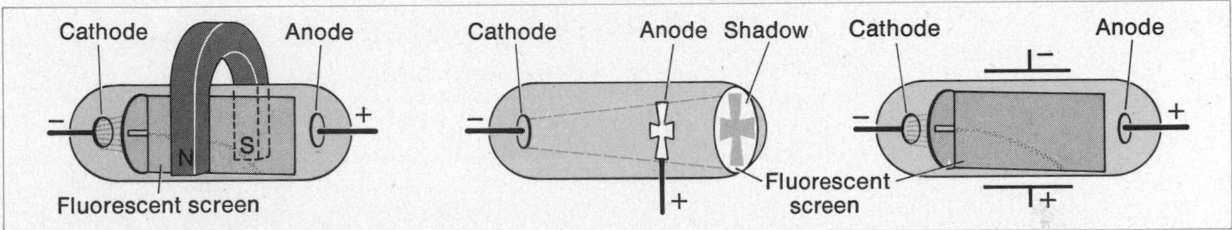

In order to understand Thomson's experiment, consider how a modern picture tube works. When the electrons in a tube are emitted from the cathode, they pass through the tube and strike a fluorescent coating on the screen. That causes the coating to glow, and a spot of light appears. When the set is first turned on, and when it has just been turned off, a single bright spot appears, as all the electrons strike the same place. However, when the set has warmed up, the whole screen glows, as a result of electrons striking the whole surface. The electron beam is being moved rapidly back and forth, up and down, and across the entire surface of the screen.

The movement is so rapid that we see only the total glow, as though all parts of the surface are being struck simultaneously. The movement of the electron beam occurs because moving electrons can be deflected from their straight-line paths by both electric and magnetic fields. When all the electrons in a beam are deflected in that way, the beam itself appears to curve, or bend. That can be observed in a black and white television set. Here small electromagnets deflect an electronic beam over the picture tube. Those areas of the screen that the deflected beam hits appear light. Where the beam does not hit, it appears dark. The light and dark pattern formed by the constant bombardment and deflection of electron beams produces the picture on your television set.

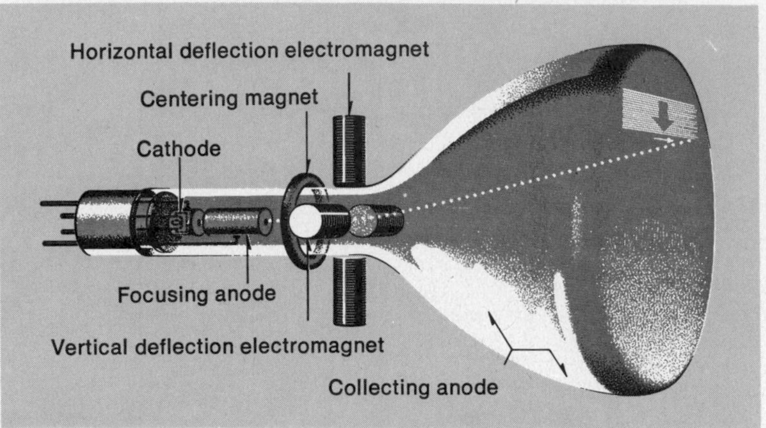

FIGURE E3–3 · *Television picture tube. The electron beam is deflected by both electric and magnetic fields so that it sweeps across and down. The electrons activate the atoms in the fluorescent screen.*

THE CHARGE AND MASS OF THE ELECTRON

The electric charge carried by the electron is given the arbitrary, relative value of −1. This is referred to as a unit-negative charge.

An **ion** is a charged particle (see Chapter 6 for a more detailed discussion of ions). Certain elements known as the halide ions – chlorine, bromine, and fluorine, for example – become ions by becoming negatively charged. Therefore, the negative chloride ion is represented as Cl^{-1}. The alkali metals, such as sodium, lithium, and potassium, have the same amount of charge, but that charge is positive. Therefore, the positive sodium ion is represented as Na^{+1}. The charge of an ion is always an integral multiple, either positive or negative, of the value of the charge of the electron.

The extent to which a charged particle is deflected by a magnetic field is dependent on the ratio between its charge, e, and its mass, m, or the e/m ratio. Since it is possible to measure quantitatively the bending of a cathode-ray beam in a magnetic field, the e/m ratio can be determined quantitatively. Thomson was the first to measure and determine the e/m ratio quantitatively.

THE PHOTOELECTRIC EFFECT

Just before the end of the nineteenth century, Thomson began to study another interesting phenomenon. When a light of high energy strikes certain metals, such as zinc, negatively charged particles are emitted by the metallic surface. That is known as the **photoelectric effect** (Figure E3-4). Thomson proved that those negative particles are identical to the electrons of the cathode rays.

The fact that electrons can be obtained from matter in different ways was strong evidence that the electron is a fundamental constituent, or part, of an atom. Therefore, Dalton's indivisible atom was no longer a useful model.

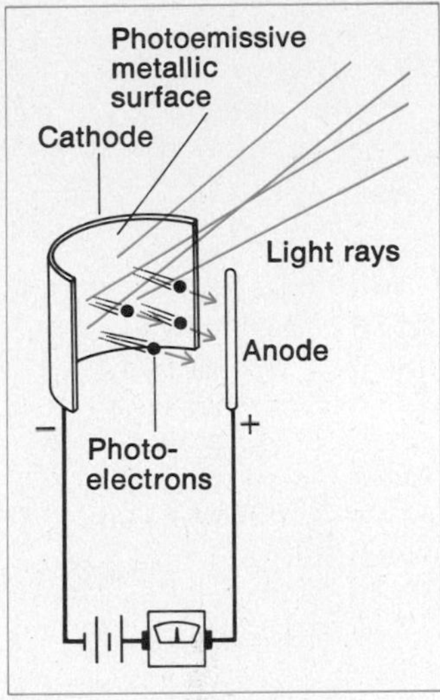

FIGURE E3-4 · *In this photoelectric cell, light energy is converted into electrical energy via the photoelectric effect.*

THE THOMSON MODEL OF THE ATOM

Thomson suggested a new model of the atom that took into account the existence of the electron.

We suppose that the atom consists of a number of [electrons] *moving about in a sphere of uniform positive electrification. . . . The* [electrons] *will arrange themselves in a series . . . of concentric shells. The gradual change in the properties of the elements which takes place as we travel along the horizontal rows in* [the periodic] *arrangement of the elements is also illustrated by the properties possessed by these groups of* [electrons].

Thomson's picture might be called the "grapes-in-Jello" model of the atom (Figure E3-5). In his model, the electrons correspond to the grapes, while the sphere of positive electricity corresponds to the Jello in which the grapes are embedded.

Thomson, however, realized the inadequacy of such a model. The assumption of a vague and undefined sphere of positive electricity was unsatisfying. Yet positive electricity had to be present to neutralize the electrons' negative charges.

The Thomson model of the atom was useful, because it was the first attempt to explain the relationship between the electron and atomic structure. Also, Thomson clearly suggested that the periodic relation of elemental properties depends on the electron groups in the atom. That last suggestion is retained in our modern model of the atom.

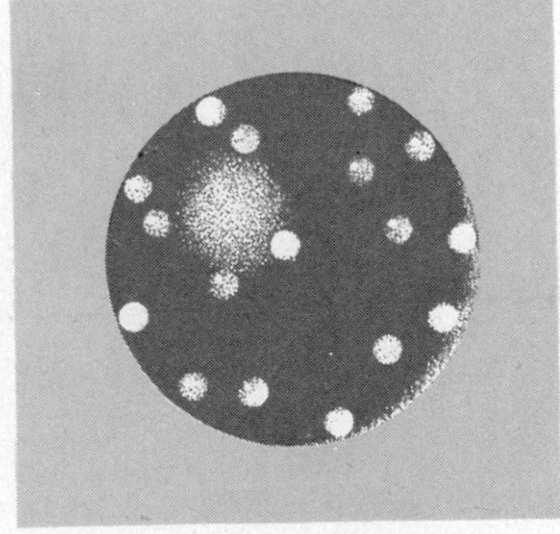

FIGURE E3-5 · *Thomson model of the atom*

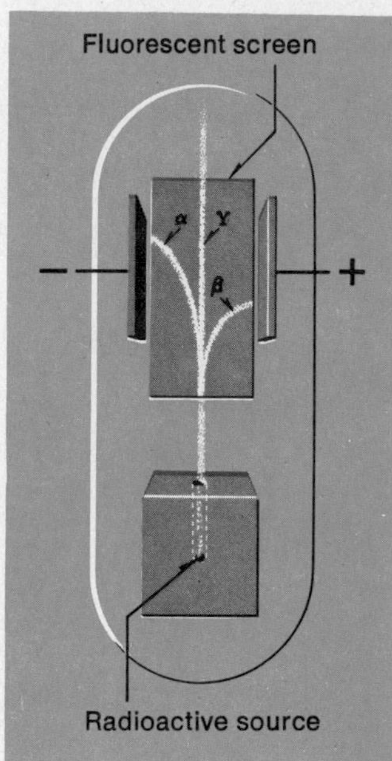

FIGURE E3–6 · *Behavior of alpha, beta, and gamma radiation in an electric field*

ALPHA, BETA, AND GAMMA RAYS

While Thomson was unraveling the mystery of cathode rays, other scientists who studied radioactive substances, such as Henri Becquerel (1852–1908), discovered three other types of "rays." One ray was deflected slightly to one side in an electrical field. It was named an alpha (α) ray. Another was deflected more strongly, but to the opposite side. It was termed a beta (β) ray. The third, not deflected at all in an electrical field, was called a gamma (γ) ray (Figure E3–6).

Becquerel proved that beta rays consist of negative particles identical in charge and mass to the electron. Ernest Rutherford (1871–1937), a New Zealand-born physicist, demonstrated that alpha rays are positively charged particles, with a mass greater than that of the hydrogen atom. Since it was found that helium gas is present in mineral deposits of radioactive substances, Rutherford believed alpha rays were composed of doubly charged helium ions, He^{+2}. Gamma rays were found to have neither mass nor charge. They are similar to light rays and X rays, but are of higher energy.

In 1909, Rutherford's assumption that alpha particles are He^{+2} ions was proved correct. Rutherford and his associate, Royds, placed an alpha-emitting substance in an evacuated tube. After a few days, they passed an electric discharge through the tube. From this experiment, Rutherford and Royds were able to observe the characteristic emission spectrum of helium.

A THEORY OF RADIOACTIVE DISINTEGRATION

Rutherford and a co-worker, Frederick Soddy, began a detailed study of the phenomenon of radioactivity of uranium ores. They considered the nature of the rays emitted by those ores and the existence of new elements in them. Such considerations led them to propose a theory of radioactivity in 1902. Their theory directly contradicted Dalton's notion of a solid, indivisible atom. The Rutherford-Soddy theory stated the following. When a radioactive substance emits an alpha or a beta particle, that substance is transformed into a different element with different chemical and physical properties. In other words, when the original radioactive atom disintegrates, a charged particle is ejected from it. And an atom of a different element is formed.

The existence of the electron and the discovery of radioactivity demanded a new model of the atom—a model that showed there were subatomic particles, as well as positive and negative electrical charges, contained in an atom. We have seen how Thomson attempted to account for that in his atomic model. Rutherford interpreted the results of an experiment that ruled out Thomson's model. He then proposed a better one.

THE NUCLEUS OF THE ATOM IS DISCOVERED

In 1909, two of Rutherford's students, Hans Geiger and Ernest Marsden, carefully investigated the passage of a beam of alpha particles through very thin gold foil (Figure E3–7). The vast majority of the alpha particles passed straight through the foil, as expected. However, a small number were scattered in large angles from the beam direction. About one in every 8000 alpha particles was deflected by 90°.

When Rutherford was told about it, he was astonished. His reaction to the news was, "It was quite the most incredible event that has ever happened to me in my life. It was almost as incredible as if you fired a fifteen-inch shell at a piece of tissue paper, and it came back and hit you."

FIGURE E3–7 · *This illustration shows the alpha-particle-scattering technique. This is the classic experiment that led to the Rutherford model of the atom.*

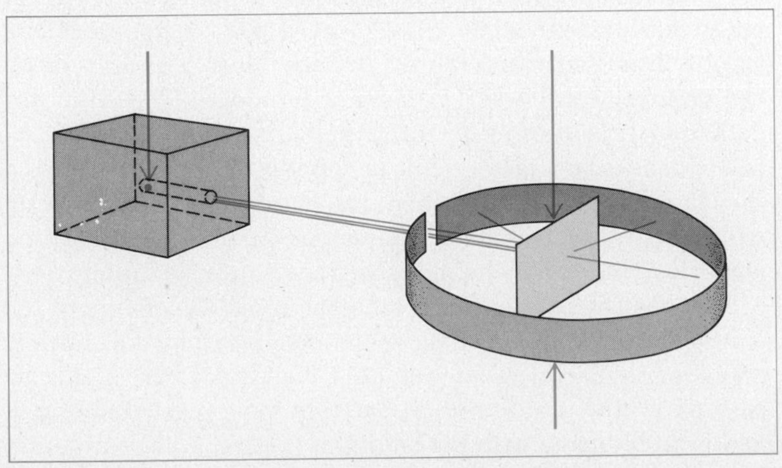

Since most of the alpha particles passed straight through the gold foil, there had to be a very large amount of empty space in the atoms of gold. If the atoms were solid particles, as Dalton had suggested, all the alpha particles would have been deflected. Rutherford then suggested that since only a few alpha particles were deflected very strongly, only a very tiny part of the gold atom was involved. That tiny piece of the atom has to be very dense and electrically charged, in order to account for the deflection of positively charged alpha particles. The very light and singly charged electrons cannot cause such large deflections.

Within two years of the alpha-particle-scattering experiments, Rutherford postulated the following explanation. The atom must have a very small central core in which all the positive charge and most of the mass of the atom are concentrated. That small, positively charged, heavy center later became known as the **atomic nucleus.** Rutherford published his momentous theory in the *Journal of the Literary and Philosophical Society of Manchester*, in which, a little more than a century before, Dalton had announced his concept of the atom.

RADIOACTIVITY: A KEY TO ATOMIC STRUCTURE

You have learned how Rutherford defined the structure of the nucleus. Now let's go back to the discoveries about radioactivity that allowed Rutherford to carry out his experiments.

Henri Becquerel was interested in studying fluorescence. In 1895, Becquerel was studying the fluorescence of uranium compounds. In one of his experiments, he placed crystals of potassium uranyl sulfate ($K_2SO_4 \cdot (UO_2)SO_4 \cdot 2H_2$) on photographic film that was wrapped in dark paper. The crystals on the wrapped film were exposed to sunlight. The film was darkened directly beneath the crystal sample. Becquerel interpreted that to be a result of the penetration of the dark paper by the fluorescence of the uranium compound. In a control experiment, sunlight itself caused no darkening of the film, since it could not penetrate the dark paper wrapping. That proved that there was a difference between the energy of the sunlight and the energy of the radiation emitted by the uranium compound. Becquerel concluded that since the radiation emitted by the uranium did penetrate the paper wrapping, it had greater energy than the sunlight.

THE WORLD OF RADIOACTIVITY IS UNCOVERED

Becquerel was convinced that the darkening of the film was the result of fluorescence. During February of 1896, he began another, similar experiment. For several days, the cloudy winter weather in northern France prevented the sun from shining through, so the experiment could not be completed. On March 1, Becquerel decided to use new sets of uranium compounds and photographic film. Fortunately, he developed the earlier films, which had been kept with the crystal samples in a drawer. Becquerel expected that there might be a faint darkening under the crystals, since exposure to room light did

FIGURE E3–8 · *This radiograph of a key, taken with carnotite ore, shows approximately what Henri Becquerel saw in his laboratory.*

produce some fluorescence. To his amazement, the spots were as dark as if sunlight had been striking the uranium. Becquerel correctly interpreted that to mean that the uranium was spontaneously emitting rays without the stimulation of external light. It was that emission that had caused the darkening of the photographic plate.

He repeated the experiment with other substances that contained uranium, such as pitchblende, a mineral ore that contains oxides of uranium. Pitchblende affected a photographic plate even more than other uranium-containing substances did. Becquerel suspected some unknown element in the ore to be the cause. He asked Marie Sklodowska Curie (1867–1934), a science teacher and research assistant in Paris, to undertake the isolation of the unknown element.

With her husband, Pierre, Marie Curie began the search for the unknown element—an element that, like uranium, exhibited the phenomenon of spontaneous emission of high-energy radiation. She named that phenomenon **radioactivity.**

THE DISCOVERY OF POLONIUM AND RADIUM

The Curies hypothesized that the greater radioactivity of some uranium minerals indicated the existence of a substance in those minerals that is more radioactive than uranium. They began an intense chemical separation and analysis of the minerals. The story of the Curies' search is one of the most interesting and inspiring in the history of science. Perseverance, dedication, and intelligence finally brought success. In 1898, the Curies isolated a new radioactive chemical element. In honor of Poland, Marie Curie's native land, the element was named polonium. Later that same year, the Curies isolated, from tons of pitchblende, a minute amount of another new element. That element, which they named radium, was over 300 000 times more radioactive than uranium.

REVIEW QUESTIONS

1 Explain how Thomson's model for the atom was satisfactory at the time it was proposed, since it explained all known facts about atomic structure.

2 As new information becomes available, models must be modified. Explain how Rutherford's model considered new information in describing the atom.

3 Prepare a short biographical sketch on each of the following scientists.

a. J. J. Thomson
b. Henri Becquerel
c. Madame Curie
d. Ernest Rutherford
e. Frederick Soddy
f. Hans Geiger

4 The modern measured value for e/m is 1.758796×10^8 coulomb per gram. Calculate the mass of an electron in grams. What is the ratio of an electron mass to the mass of a hydrogen atom? ($m_H = 1.6754 \times 10^{-24}$ g.) (The charge on an electron is 1.60×10^{-19} C/e.)

REFERENCES

Kendall, H. W., and W. H. Panofsky. "The Structure of the Proton and the Neutron." *Scientific American,* June 1971, p. 60.

Morrow, B. A. "On the Discovery of the Electron." *Journal of Chemical Education,* 1969, p. 584.

Zafiratos, C. D. "The Texture of the Nuclear Surface." *Scientific American,* October 1972, p. 108.

EXCURSION FOUR

The Nucleus: For Better or Worse?

As the world rapidly exhausts its fossil fuels, we must increase our use of other energy sources. We may run out of oil in the next hundred years. Therefore, in order to continue to run our hospitals, factories, schools, and homes, more of our energy must come from something besides petroleum. One source that many countries are developing is nuclear energy from nuclear reactors. Uranium is the fuel of a nuclear reactor. By causing the nucleus of the uranium to split into two smaller nuclei, large amounts of energy are released.

The release of nuclear energy is not the only way in which the atomic nucleus is used. Some nuclei undergo disintegration that is milder than the splitting into two parts of uranium. This milder disintegration is called **radioactivity.** Radioactive materials—those that disintegrate spontaneously—have been used in agricultural research to produce better crops, in chemical research to make many new products, in industry to perfect and control processes, in medicine to develop new drugs and treat many diseases, and in many other fields. Before discussing nuclear energy, let's study radioactivity in some detail.

THE DISCOVERY OF RADIOACTIVITY

A French scientist, Henri Becquerel, discovered that uranium is always emitting very penetrating "rays." Through the research of Becquerel and Pierre and Marie Curie in France, Ernest Rutherford in England, Hans Geiger in Germany, and other scientists, it was learned that a number of heavy elements emit such rays. Those elements are called radioactive elements.

The radioactive elements emit three types of rays. Those are called alpha (α), beta (β), and gamma (γ) rays. An alpha "ray" is really the same as the nucleus of a helium atom. It has an atomic number of 2 and a mass number of 4. A beta "ray" is identical with an electron. And a gamma ray is simply high-energy radiation—like light or X rays, but higher in energy. Excursion 3, What's in an Atom, is a detailed study of these and other investigations in radioactivity.

RADIOACTIVE DECAY

The removal of an alpha particle eliminates two positive charges and four mass numbers from an element. If the uranium isotope of mass 238 undergoes radioactive alpha decay, it must change from atomic number 92 (uranium) to 90 (thorium). The mass number must change from 238 to 234. The *nuclear* equation is as follows.

$$^{238}_{92}\text{U} \rightarrow {}^{234}_{90}\text{Th} + {}^{4}_{2}\text{He} \quad \text{(the alpha particle)}$$

Note that the mass numbers balance on each side of the equation ($238 \rightarrow 4 + 234$), as do the atomic numbers ($92 \rightarrow 2 + 90$). Compare the following equations dealing with alpha decay to be sure that the mass numbers and atomic numbers always balance.

$$^{252}_{98}\text{Cf} \rightarrow {}^{248}_{96}\text{Cm} + {}^{4}_{2}\text{He}$$

$$^{226}_{88}\text{Ra} \rightarrow {}^{222}_{86}\text{Rn} + {}^{4}_{2}\text{He}$$

$$^{212}_{84}\text{Po} \rightarrow {}^{208}_{82}\text{Pb} + {}^{4}_{2}\text{He}$$

The radioactive decay that produces a beta ray involves no change in the mass number. However, if a *negative electron* is emitted, the atomic number *increases* by one.

$$^{14}_{6}\text{C} \rightarrow {}^{0}_{-1}\beta + {}^{14}_{7}\text{N}$$

Note that the mass number balances on each side of the equation ($14 = 0 + 14$), as does the atomic number ($6 = -1 + 7$). Beta decay can occur for all elements.

$$^{3}_{1}\text{H} \rightarrow {}^{3}_{2}\text{He} + {}^{0}_{-1}\beta$$

$$^{24}_{11}\text{Na} \rightarrow {}^{24}\text{Mg} + {}^{0}_{-1}\beta$$

$$^{147}_{61}\text{Pm} \rightarrow {}^{147}_{62}\text{Sm} + {}^{0}_{-1}\beta$$

$$^{234}_{90}\text{Th} \rightarrow {}^{234}_{91}\text{Pa} + {}^{0}_{-1}\beta$$

Beta decay can also occur by the emission of *positive electrons* called **positrons.** When a *positron* (a positively charged particle with the same mass and magnitude of charge as an electron) is emitted, the atomic number *decreases* by one.

$$^{11}_{6}C \rightarrow ^{11}_{5}B + ^{0}_{+1}\beta$$

$$^{22}_{11}Na \rightarrow ^{22}_{10}Ne + ^{0}_{+1}\beta$$

$$^{140}_{59}Pr \rightarrow ^{140}_{58}Ce + ^{0}_{+1}\beta$$

Since gamma rays have neither charge nor mass, there is no change in atomic number or mass number with gamma decay. Gamma emission occurs when a nucleus changes from a higher to a lower energy level. Usually, gamma emission occurs immediately after alpha and beta decay.

RADIOACTIVE DECAY CHAINS

When a radioactive element decays, the new nucleus may also be radioactive. For example, $^{238}_{92}U$ decays to start a long series of successive decays. Eventually, a stable (nonradioactive) nucleus, $^{206}_{82}Pb$, is produced. The sequence of decay (α = alpha decay; β = beta decay) is shown in the following.

FIGURE E4–1 · *Uranium-238 to stable lead-206, a naturally occurring transformation series*

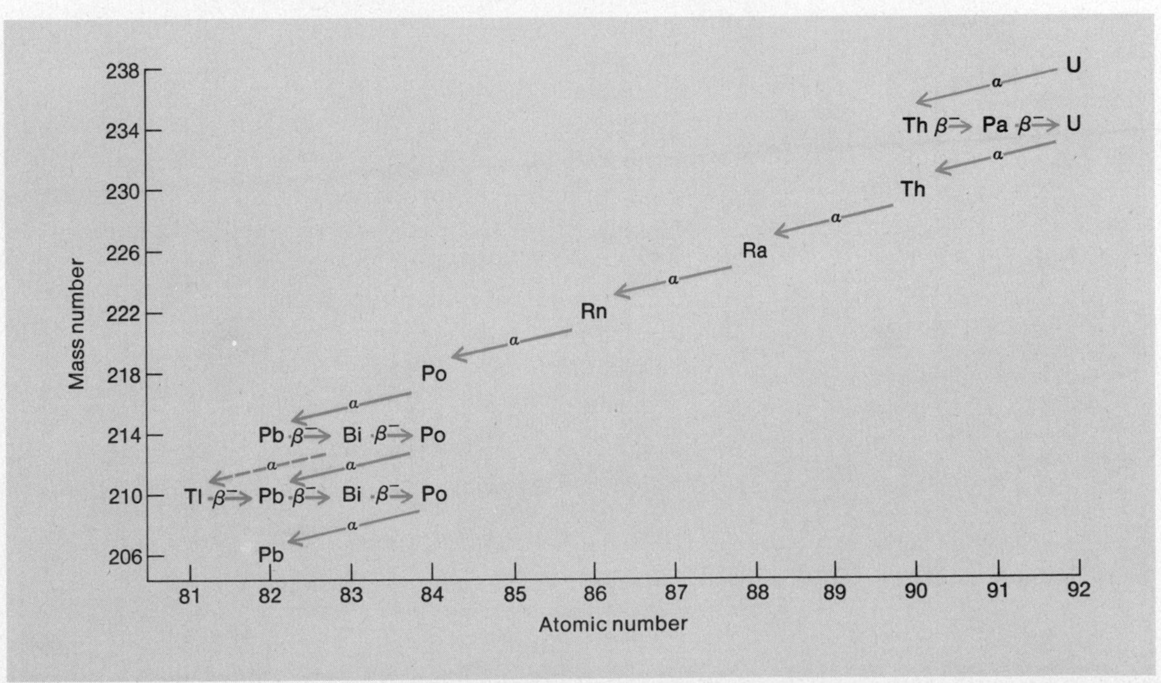

Radioactive nuclei undergo radioactive decay at different rates. Some nuclei decay so rapidly that all are decayed in a few seconds. Others decay so slowly that after billions of years, a large fraction remains unchanged. We define a radioactive **half-life** as the time necessary for 50 percent of the radioactive nuclei in a sample to decay. $^{238}_{92}U$ has a half-life of 4.5×10^9 years. Since that time is about the age of the earth, only about 50 percent of the $^{238}_{92}U$ that was present at the time of the birth of the earth is still here. The rest has decayed successively to Th, Ra, Rn, Po, Bi, and Pb.

RADIOACTIVE CLOCKS

We can use radioactive decay to measure the age of things. If we know how much radioactivity was present at a previous time, by comparing that amount with the rate of radioactivity now, we can calculate how many half-lives of a radioactive material have occurred. For example, $^{238}_{92}U$ has a half-life of 4.5×10^9 years and $^{235}_{92}U$ has a half-life of only 7.1×10^8 years. At present, we find that a uranium sample has 99.3 atoms of ^{238}U and 7 atoms of ^{235}U for every 1000 atoms. We assume that there was an equal number of atoms of $^{238}_{92}U$ and $^{235}_{92}U$ at the time of the formation of the uranium in our solar system. If that is correct, we can calculate that it requires 6×10^9 years to reach a ^{238}U-to-^{235}U ratio of 993 to 7. $^{238}_{92}U$ decays to $^{206}_{82}Pb$, while $^{235}_{92}U$ decays to $^{207}_{82}Pb$. The ratio of $^{206}_{82}Pb$ to $^{207}_{82}Pb$ in a mineral can be used to calculate the age of that mineral, assuming that the lead came from uranium decay. Another radioactive clock for geologic dating uses the decay of $^{87}_{37}Rb$ (half-life of 6×10^{10} years) to $^{87}_{38}Sr$. The amount of $^{87}_{38}Sr$ present in a mineral that contains $^{87}_{37}Rb$ measures how much decay has taken place.

Perhaps the most widely used radioactive clock is $^{14}_{6}C$. Neutrons in cosmic rays from the space continue to make $^{14}_{6}C$ in the earth's atmosphere by the following reaction.

$$^{14}_{7}N + ^{0}_{1}n \rightarrow ^{14}_{6}C + ^{1}_{1}H$$

The $^{14}_{6}C$ is radioactive by beta decay, with a half-life of 5300 years. The ratio of $^{14}_{6}C$ to $^{12}_{6}C$ (normal carbon) in the CO_2 of the air is constant. As long as an animal or a plant is alive, it continues to take in new carbon from the air. The $^{14}_{6}C$-to-$^{12}_{6}C$ ratio in living material is the same as that of the atmosphere. However, when the animal or plant dies, it stops taking in new carbon. As time passes, the ${}^{14}_{6}C$ decays, and the ${}^{14}_{6}C$-to-${}^{12}_{6}C$ ratio decreases. The exact ratio measures the time since the death of the animal or plant. Figure E4 – 2 shows the relationship between the ratio and the time that has gone by. Various materials that have been dated are also listed in Figure E4 – 2.

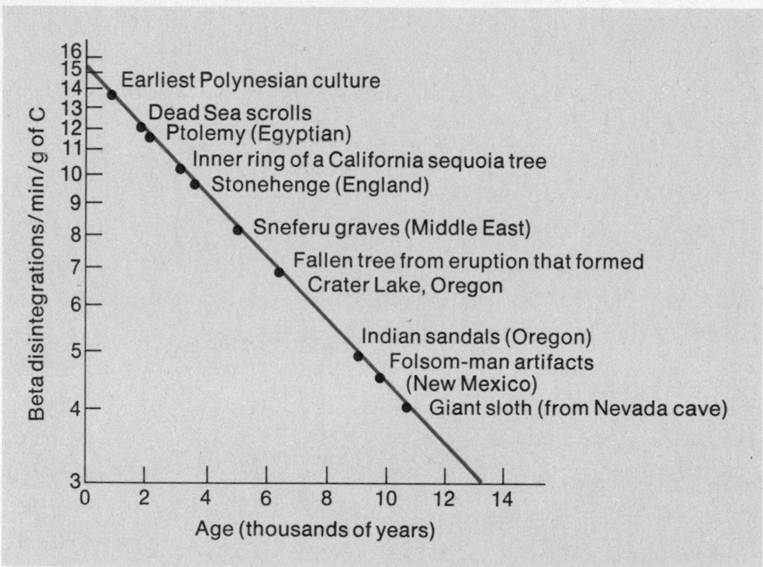

FIGURE E4–2 · *This graph names some archaeological objects dated by ${}^{14}_{6}C$ and shows their approximate age.*

By dating charcoal, pieces of rope, and other artifacts found in certain caves, it has been possible to show that the caves were inhabited by humans at least 12 000 years ago. In Africa, there is evidence of habitation of caves more than 43 000 years ago. Ancient biblical writings, such as the Dead Sea scrolls, were found in caves in Israel after World War II. Controversy arose as to whether those writings were from the time of Christ or were later fakes. Carbon-14 dating proved that the scrolls were about 1917 ± 200 years old.

WHY ARE SOME NUCLEI UNSTABLE?

We have discussed ${}^{14}_{6}C$, which is radioactive. That means it is an unstable nucleus and changes spontaneously to a more stable one, ${}^{14}_{7}N$. However, ${}^{12}_{6}C$ is stable and does not decay at all. Similarly, ${}^{23}_{11}Na$ is stable, but ${}^{22}_{11}Na$ decays by positron emission to ${}^{22}_{10}Ne$. ${}^{24}_{11}Na$ decays by electron emission to ${}^{24}_{12}Mg$. Some nuclei are stable and others are radioactive, or unstable. What do you think makes this so?

You already know that a nucleus is composed of neutrons and protons. The stability of a nucleus depends on its ratio of the neutrons to the protons. ${}^{12}_{6}C$ has six neutrons and six protons and, therefore, is stable. But ${}^{14}_{6}C$, with eight neutrons and six protons, is unstable, as is ${}^{11}_{6}C$, with five neutrons and six protons. So for carbon, nuclear stability is present when n/p (the ratio of neutrons to protons) is 6/6, or 1.00. For sodium, stability results when n/p is 12/11, or 1.10. ${}^{133}_{55}Cs$ is the only stable isotope of cesium. In that case, n/p is 78/55, or 1.40. ${}^{209}_{83}Bi$ is stable with n/p of 126/83, or 1.50. If there are more or less than 126 neutrons in a nucleus with 83 protons, that bismuth isotope is radioactive.

The lightest elements have stable nuclei when their n/p is equal to 1.00. As the atomic number increases, stability requires a larger increase in the number of neutrons and the n/p $>$ 1. But for any element, there is a small range of values of n/p for stability. An isotope with an n/p that is either smaller or greater than the stable n/p ratio is radioactive. Figure E4–3 is a plot of the relationship between the number of neutrons and the number of protons for stable nuclei.

FIGURE E4–3 · *This graph demonstrates the number of neutrons (A–Z) versus the number of protons (Z) for stable nuclei.*

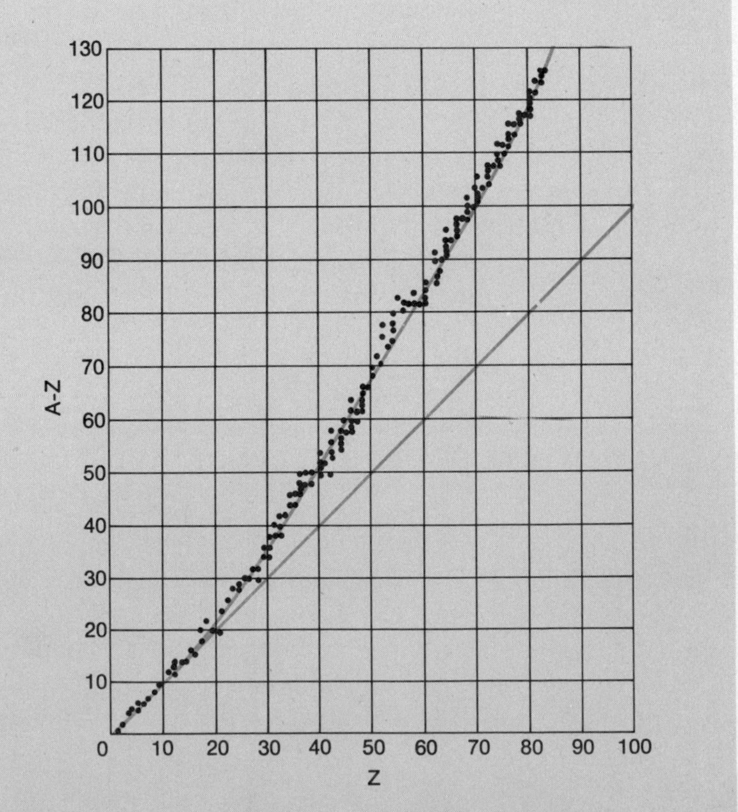

THE NUCLEAR BINDING ENERGY

When two chemical elements react to form a stable compound, energy is released. In fact, the greater the amount of energy released per mole, the more stable the compound. Similarly, if we could make nuclei by putting the neutrons and protons together simultaneously, energy would be released for stable nuclei. Actually, nuclei can only be made by adding another neutron, proton, or nucleus to a target nucleus. $^{14}_{6}C$ can be made by adding a neutron to $^{14}_{7}N$, with the simultaneous ejection of a proton. $^{24}_{11}Na$ can be made by adding a neutron to $^{23}_{11}Na$. $^{256}_{101}Md$ can be made by adding an alpha particle to $^{256}_{99}Es$, with the ejection of a neutron. $^{136}_{58}Ce$ can be made by the reaction of $^{124}_{50}Sn$ and $^{16}_{8}O$, or $^{128}_{52}Te$ and $^{12}_{6}C$, with the emission of four neutrons in both instances.

The energy released in the formation of a nucleus by putting neutrons and protons together cannot be measured directly. Imagine trying to make $^{136}_{58}Ce$ by putting 58 protons and 78 neutrons together simultaneously—in .001 of a millionth-millionth of a second! But we can add together the masses of 58 protons and 78 neutrons and compare that sum with the mass of $^{136}_{58}Ce$. When we compare the two masses, we find that the mass of $^{136}_{58}Ce$ is *less than* the mass of the protons and neutrons. The mass loss represents the energy that would be released if we were able to put the 58 protons and 78 neutrons together. (Remember, Einstein showed that the mass loss is equal to the energy released.)

The energy that is released if a nucleus could be made directly from neutrons and protons is called the **binding energy.** The larger the mass (A) of a nucleus, the larger the binding energy. However, the average binding energy—the binding energy ÷ (number of protons + number of neutrons)—is almost constant. The average binding energy only varies between six and nine MeV (million electric volts)* for most nuclei. Figure E4–4 shows the change in average binding energy as a function of the mass number. Note that although there is little variation in the BE/A above $A = 10$, the curve has a maximum for $A \sim 60$.

The maximum in the curve in Figure E4–4 is very important. It means that the nuclei around $A \sim 60$ are the most stable. If

*MeV = million electron volts. An energy unit such that 1 eV/atom = 23 kcal/mole. According to Einstein, 1 mass unit ≈ 931 MeV.

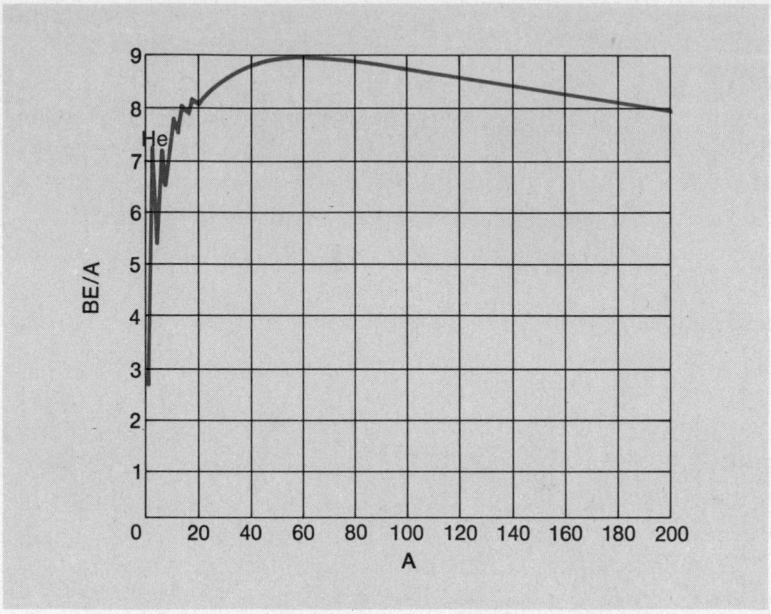

FIGURE E4–4 · *This graph shows the binding energy divided by the mass number plotted as a function of mass number.*

we break a heavy nucleus of $A \sim 240$ into two lighter nuclei, each one of $A \sim 120$, the BE/A value is increased. So splitting, or *fissioning*, heavy nuclei releases energy. Conversely, if we combine two light nuclei ($A < 10$) to become a heavier nucleus, energy is again released. So, as Figure E4–4 shows, nuclear *fission* of very heavy nuclei is an energy source. *Fusion* of very light nuclei can be an energy source, also. In an atomic bomb, the fission of uranium or plutonium provides its explosive energy. In a hydrogen bomb, the fusion of deuterium and lithium is the basis for the energy that is released.

NUCLEAR REACTORS

When a nucleus of $^{235}_{92}U$ is struck by a neutron, it undergoes fission into two smaller nuclei. Many nuclei are formed by fission—from $Z \sim 30$ to $Z \sim 62$. Let us assume that the uranium nucleus is split exactly in half. The reaction would be as follows.

$$^{235}_{92}U + ^{0}_{1}n \rightarrow 2\,^{117}_{46}Pd + 2\,^{0}_{1}n$$

The total binding energy of $^{235}_{92}U$ is about 1800 MeV, while the binding energy of each $^{117}_{46}Pd$ is about 1000 MeV. So, in the fission of $^{235}_{92}U$ to two $^{117}_{46}Pd$ nuclei, $2(1000) - 1800$, or 200, MeV of energy is released.

When scientists learned that more neutrons are emitted by a fissioning nucleus than are absorbed, they realized that it might be possible to have a self-sustaining *chain reaction*. In such a chain reaction, an initial reaction is multiplied in succeeding generations, without further external help. The first fission absorbs one neutron and releases two. The result is two fissions in the second step, four in the third, eight in the fourth, sixteen in the fifth, thirty-two in the sixth, and so on (Figure E4–5). Since fission occurs in a very short time, like 10^{-17} seconds, the multiplication occurs very rapidly. If allowed to proceed unimpeded, it results in an explosion, as in an atomic bomb. However, if it is possible to control the rate of fission once it reaches a certain level, then the energy that is released can be maintained at a controllable level for power use. Nuclear reactors operate by the control of the chain reaction of fission.

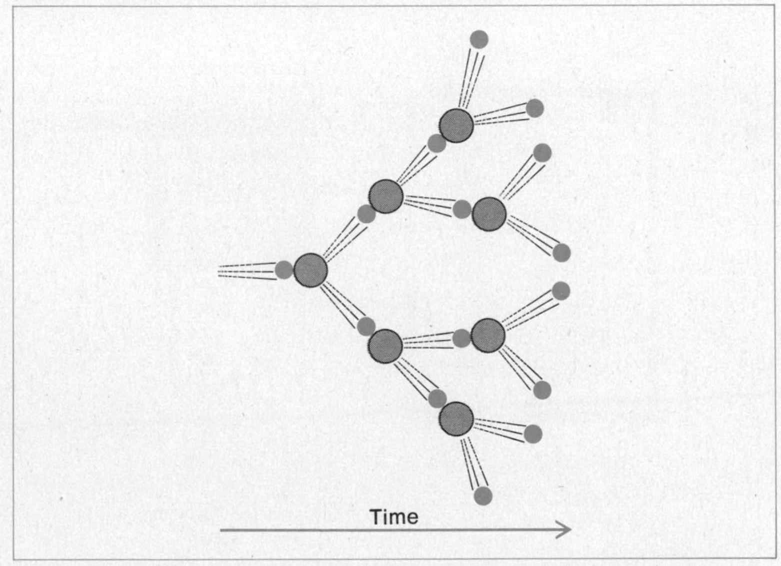

FIGURE E4–5 · *Fission chain reaction. First neutron fissions $^{235}U(O)$, releasing two neutrons. As these cause fission, four neutrons are released to produce more fission, and so forth.*

Although many different types of reactors are in operation around the world, they all have five basic components.

1. **Fuel.** *The fuel is either natural uranium or uranium enriched in $^{235}_{92}U$. In a few cases, $^{239}_{94}Pu$ is used as the fuel. Normally, the fuel is used in the form of rods enclosing thousands of small ceramic-coated pellets of uranium oxide.*
2. **Moderator.** *Graphite, water, and D_2O are the most common materials used to slow the fission neutrons down to that low energy at which they are most effective in causing further fission.*

3. **Control rods.** *Cadmium and boron are used to control the concentration of neutrons present in the reactor, since they have a great capacity for absorbing neutrons.*
4. **Coolant.** *The coolant conducts the heat away, to keep the temperature at a reasonable level. In power reactors, the coolant is the vehicle for the transfer of the fission energy to external use. H_2O, D_2O, air, or molten sodium is used as a coolant. In many reactors the same H_2O and D_2O serve as both moderator and coolant.*
5. **Shielding.** *Fission is accompanied by gamma ray emission as well as neutron emission. That, as well as the intense radioactivity of the fission products, requires thick layers of absorbent shielding. The shielding is usually water, concrete, or both. Figure E4–6 shows a schematic drawing of a nuclear reactor.*

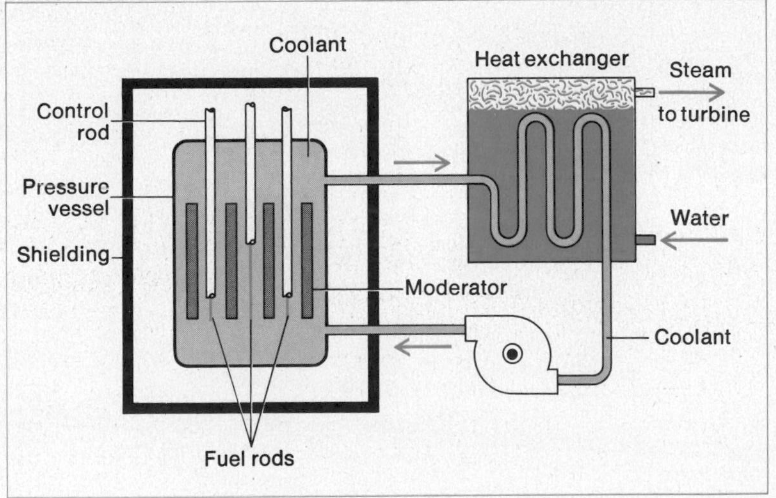

FIGURE E4–6 · *The nuclear reactor shown here uses a heat exchanger to produce the heat needed for the turbine engine to generate electricity.*

NUCLEAR ENERGY

We have already learned in Excursion 3 that a nuclear reaction releases a large amount of energy. In a nuclear reactor, that energy can be used to generate electricity. In many countries, nuclear power is supplying a growing percentage of national energy needs. Unfortunately, nuclear power has a price, since it results in the production of large quantities of intensely radioactive fission products. Those radioactive elements must be stored for many thousands of years, so that we can be certain there will be no escape of radioactivity into the environment. Such an escape results in undesirable, perhaps even disastrous, pollution. Intensive research to find the safest, most economical way to store the radioactive products is under way in many countries. When a satisfactory storage method is developed, nuclear energy can be exploited for the benefit of all people, with no hazard to present or future generations.

RADIOACTIVE TRACERS IN SCIENCE

Since the discovery of radioactivity, radioactive nuclei serving as "tracers" have been of immense value to science, agriculture, medicine, and industry. The first experiments with radioactive tracers were carried out in 1913 in Germany by G. de Hevesy and F. Paneth. They determined the solubility of lead salts by using one of the naturally occurring radioactive isotopes of lead. In 1935, de Hevesy and O. Chiewitz synthesized $^{32}_{15}P$ and used that tracer in biological studies.

FIGURE E4–7 · *A radioactive isotope*

When we use radioactive tracers, we assume that radioactive isotopes, such as $^{14}_{6}C$, are identical in chemical behavior to normal isotopes, such as $^{12}_{6}C$. In other words, the unstable nature of the radioactive atom does not change its chemical properties. Of course, when it decays, it becomes a different element. The radioactivity allows us to follow the behavior of an element in a reaction or in an industrial process.

The study of the reaction steps in the photosynthesis of carbohydrates from atmospheric CO_2 in the presence of light and chlorophyll is an outstanding example of the value of the tracer technique. The overall process, which must involve many steps, can be written as follows.

$$6CO_2 + 12H_2O \xrightarrow[\text{chlorophyll}]{\text{light}} C_6H_{12}O_6 + 6O_2 + 6H_2O$$

Using $^{14}_{6}C$, $^{32}_{15}P$ and $^{3}_{1}H$, M. Calvin and co-workers have been able to identify the intermediate steps involved in photosynthesis. Plants were placed in an atmosphere containing $^{14}_{6}C$-labeled CO_2 and irradiated with light. Photosynthesis was stopped by killing the plant and then separating as many as possible of the molecular components. The presence of radioactive carbon in a compound was used as proof that the compound was involved in the process of photosynthesis. Similarly, the involvement of phosphorus and hydrogen was determined

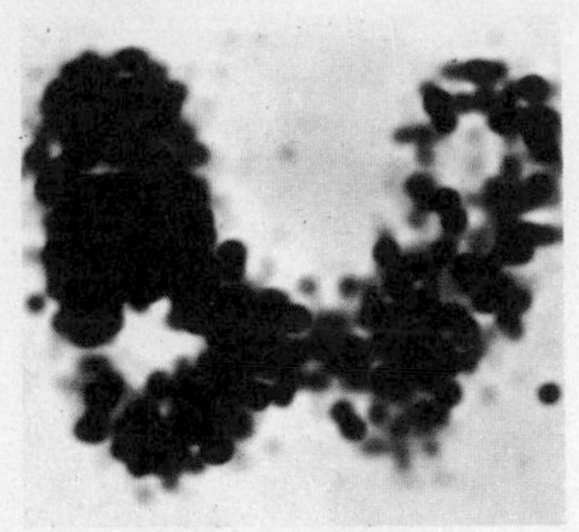

FIGURE E4–8 · *Iodine-131 radiation outlines a thyroid gland. The lighter, nonabsorbing areas are "trouble spots."*

through the detection of radioactive phosphorus and tritium in certain compounds. Radioactive tracers have also been used to measure equilibrium in chemical reactions, to determine the mechanism of a reaction, and to analyze materials for very small amounts of impurities. By inducing radioactivity through the reaction of stable nuclei with neutrons (*neutron activation analysis*), chemists can measure 10^{-9} of some impurities. Neutron activation analysis has been used to determine the authenticity of paintings, in criminology, in the analysis of lunar soil, and in many other ways.

RADIOACTIVE TRACERS IN MEDICINE

The largest single use of radionuclides is in medical science. It has been said that radioactive tracers have been as important to medicine as the discovery of the microscope.

If a radioactive compound, such as an amino acid, a vitamin, or a drug, is administered to a patient, the substance will be incorporated to varying degrees in different organs. The substance undergoes chemical exchange with other substances in the body. It is broken down and, finally, discharged from the body. The movement of radioactive atoms in the body can often be followed externally with instruments. Such studies give information about the relative concentration of radioactive elements and the time dependency of their distribution in different organs. The rate of incorporation and discharge of a radioactive substance in the body provides a measure of the metabolism of healthy and of sick tissues. Those data have considerable diagnostic value for physicians. For example, diseases of the blood-forming organs can be identified by the use of ${}^{59}_{26}Fe$ and those of the thyroid gland by the use of ${}^{131}_{53}I$. Radioactive tracers can also be used to measure the flow and amount of liquid volume in a biological system. For example, the amount of blood pumped by the heart per minute can be measured externally with scintillation detectors, following the injection of ${}^{59}_{26}Fe$ into the body. Simultaneously, an isotope-dilution analysis with ${}^{59}_{26}Fe$ can be used to measure the blood volume.

Such examples of the use of radioactive tracers, not only in medicine but also in general biology, agriculture, and industry, can cover many volumes. For example, industrial mixing, flow through a pipe, heterogeneous and homogeneous catalysis, wear, corrosion, and many other processes have all been studied using radioactive tracer techniques. It has been determined that industry has saved many hundreds of millions of dollars annually by the use of radioactivity.

REVIEW QUESTIONS

1 The most used radioactive clock is $^{14}_{6}C$. Describe other radioactive clocks, and discuss their use.
2 Explain why some atomic nuclei are stable, while others are not stable.
3 What is the relationship between the nuclear binding energy and the stability of nuclei?
4 How can a charged particle be artificially accelerated for use in promoting nuclear reactions?
5 Explain how radioactive isotopes are useful in the following areas.
  a. Archaeological dating
  b. Diagnosing disease
  c. Treating disease
  d. Industry

REFERENCES

Baranger, M., and R. A. Sorensen. "The Size and Shape of Atomic Nuclei." *Scientific American,* August 1969, p. 59.

Barish, B. C. "Experiments with Neutrino Beams." *Scientific American,* August 1973, p. 30.

Hahn, O. "Discovery of Fission." *Scientific American,* February 1958, p. 76.

Kendall, H. W., and W. Panofsky. "The Structure of the Proton and the Neutron." *Scientific American,* June 1971, p. 60.

Litke, A. M., and R. Wilson. "Electron-Positron Collisions." *Scientific American,* October 1973, p. 104.

Pasachoff, J. M., and W. A. Fowler. "Deuterium in the Universe." *Scientific American,* May 1974, p. 108.

Schramm, D. N. "The Age of the Elements." *Scientific American,* January 1974, p. 69.

Wiegand, C. E. "Exotic Atoms." *Scientific American,* November 1972, p. 102.

EXCURSION FIVE

Where and How Did It All Start?

Humans are different from other animals because they can speculate, reflect, and think abstractly. One of the earliest objects of such human activity must have been the stars. Millions of years ago, the first people stood upright and looked up to the heavens. The mystery of the stars has fascinated people since that time. The first mystery is, "How did it all begin?" The next obvious question is, "What's happening up there?" And now you may well ask, "And what does any of that have to do with our chemistry course?" In fact, it has everything to do with it, because "what's happening up there" is the formation of the chemical elements. Since there can be no chemistry without the elements, what is more important than their creation!?

In Chapter 3, we discussed briefly the abundances of the elements in the universe and on the earth. Ninety-one percent of all the atoms in the universe are hydrogen, the lightest element. Almost 9 percent are helium, the next lightest element. In fact, as the atomic numbers of the elements increase, the abundances decrease. That decrease is sharp at first—about a factor of 100 for every increase of ten in atomic number. However, after atomic number 30, the decrease is much less. For example, cadmium ($Z = 48$) is only ten times more abundant than mercury ($Z = 80$). Figure E5–1 shows the abundances of the elements as a function of their atomic numbers.

The pattern of abundances suggests that the simplest element, hydrogen, is the original material of our universe. All the other elements must have been synthesized at some time from hydrogen. The processes that made the lighter elements must have been similar, until about atomic number 30. The heavier elements must have been made in a different manner. Those conclusions are based on the different rates of

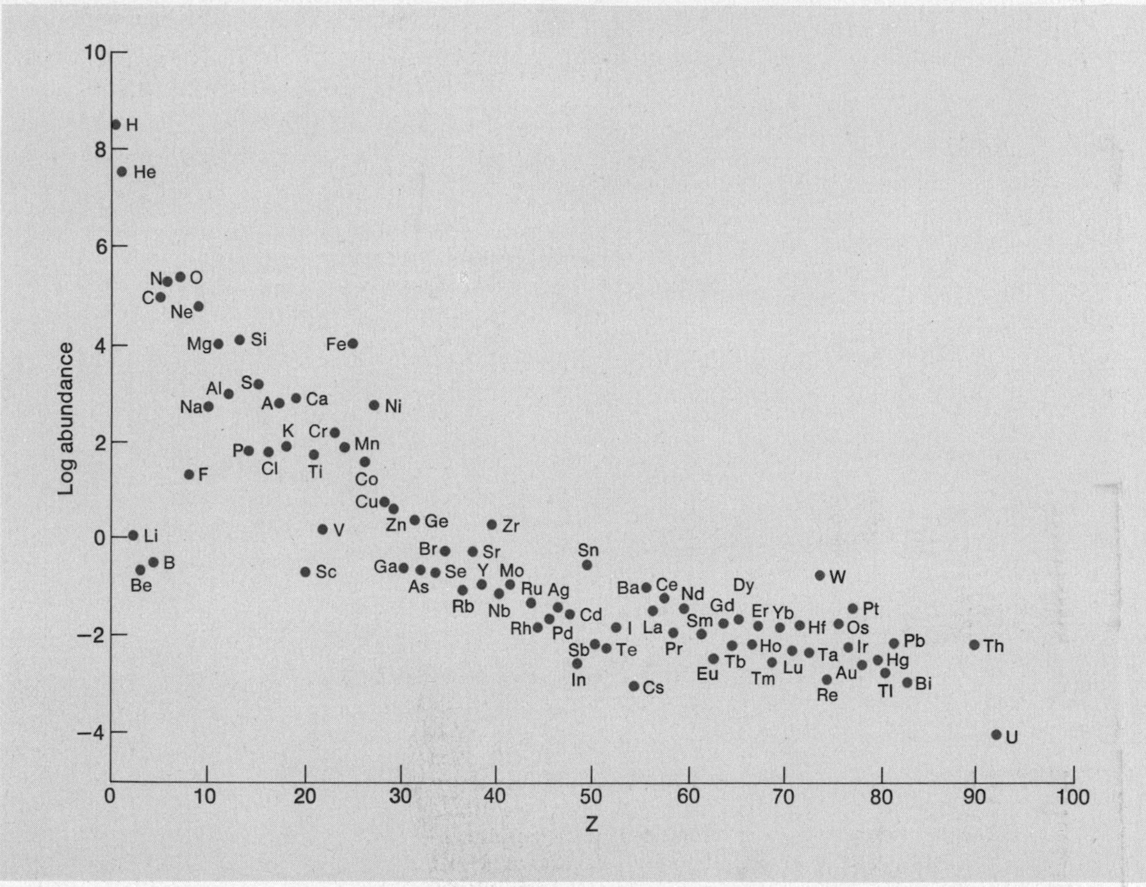

changes in abundance as a function of Z for the lighter and heavier elements and on the relative abundances of the stable isotopes of the elements.

FIGURE E5–1 · *Shown here are the cosmic abundances of the elements expressed as the logarithm of the number of atoms of the element per 10 000 atoms of silicon.*

THE BIG BANG

In the early 1930's, the American astronomer E. Hubble (1889–1953) proposed that all the galaxies of the universe are moving apart. Moreover, it can be calculated that the galaxies all started from the same place in space. It seems that sometime between seven and twenty billion years ago, all matter in the universe was packed together in a super, giant "star." The temperature in that primeval star was very, very high. As a result, any elements originally present were decomposed into protons and neutrons. So we can date everything in our universe from that time.

The matter in the primeval star was pulled closer together. That caused an increase in energy. Eventually, the energy became so great that the star exploded. Imagine an explosion of all the matter and energy of the universe! That explosion which began our universe is known as the "Big Bang."

FORMATION OF THE ELEMENTS

The neutrons and protons in the explosion of the Big Bang would be energetic enough to react.*

$$^{23}_{11}Na + ^{1}_{1}H \rightarrow ^{23}_{12}Mg + ^{1}_{0}n$$

The initial reaction would have been as follows.

$$^{1}_{1}H + ^{1}_{0}n \rightarrow ^{2}_{1}H$$

A proton ($^{1}_{1}H$) and a neutron ($^{1}_{0}n$) would combine to form a heavy isotope of hydrogen ($^{2}_{1}H$). That would have been followed by reactions such as the following.

$$^{2}_{1}H + ^{1}_{1}H = ^{3}_{2}He$$
$$^{3}_{2}He + ^{1}_{0}n = ^{4}_{2}He$$

However, the Big Bang could not have allowed the formation of the elements above He for many reasons. Moreover, we know that the elements are still being made in the stars.

ELEMENTS AND STARS

Chemical reactions are not sufficiently energetic to account for the energy that has been emitted by the stars during the billions of years that the universe has existed. However, nuclear reactions satisfactorily meet the requirements necessary for the release of large amounts of energy over a long period of time.

As a large mass of hydrogen in space begins to coalesce (unite) into a star, the increased gravitational attraction results

*Review the notation of nuclear reactions in Excursion 4 to understand the nuclear reactions that followed the Big Bang. $^{A}_{Z}X$ is used where X = elemental symbol, Z = atomic number (the number of protons), A = mass number (number of protons + number of neutrons). The total atomic number and total mass number must balance on each side of a nuclear equation (for example, atomic number: 11 + 1 = 12 + 0; mass number: 23 + 1 = 23 + 1).

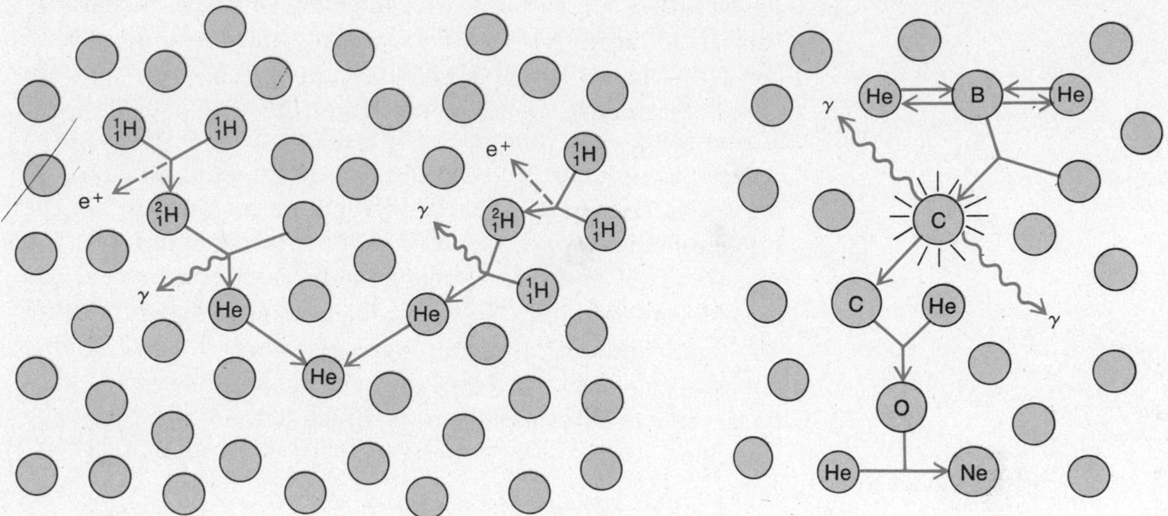

FIGURE E5–2 · *The illustration on the left shows hydrogen burning to form $^2_1$H, $^3_2$He, and $^4_2$He. The illustration on the right shows helium burning. An equilibrium is established between beryllium-8 and helium, which permits buildup of some beryllium; this then adds a helium-4 nucleus to form carbon-12. $^{16}_8$O, $^{20}_{10}$Ne, etc., can be synthesized from reactions of $^4_2$He on $^{12}_6$C, $^{16}_8$O, etc.*

in the conversion of potential energy into kinetic energy. As a result of the increased kinetic energy, the temperature of the hydrogen increases. When the temperature reaches about 2×10^6°C, the hydrogen atoms ($Z = 1$) begin to react to form helium ($Z = 2$), releasing very large amounts of energy, some in the form of light. After a star has used an appreciable supply of its hydrogen, it has a central core that is mostly helium and an outer region that is mostly hydrogen. The outer shell expands and the star becomes a "red giant."

Under such conditions, reactions can occur that form elements with a low atomic number. Such nuclear reactions are written as equations, quite similar to chemical equations. In writing equations for nuclear reactions, care must be taken that the total number of protons and of neutrons be conserved. Examples of the formation of elements in helium stars follow.

$$3\,^4_2\text{He} \rightarrow {}^{12}_6\text{C} + \text{Energy}$$
$$^{12}_6\text{C} + {}^4_2\text{He} \rightarrow {}^{16}_8\text{O} + \text{Energy}$$

The first of the nuclear reactions represents the transformation of three helium nuclei ($^4_2$He) into a single carbon nucleus ($^{12}_6$C).

The reaction occurs in two steps. The collision of two helium nuclei forms $^{8}_{4}Be$, which is very unstable. However, an equilibrium is established in the star. So there is a small amount of $^{8}_{4}Be$ present. A third $^{4}_{2}He$ combines with a $^{8}_{4}Be$ to form $^{12}_{6}C$ (Figure E5–2). In the second reaction, a helium nucleus coalesces with a carbon nucleus to produce oxygen ($^{16}_{8}O$).

After an interval of 10 to 100 million years, most of the helium is consumed. The gravitational attraction causes the heavier elements to concentrate in inner layers of the star. The remaining $^{1}_{1}H$ and $^{4}_{2}He$ concentrate in the outer layers. The inner layers are hotter, so the heavier elements begin to react. The temperature of the inner layers rises to 6×10^{8}°C. At that temperature, reactions involving ^{12}C predominate, and additional energy is released, as is illustrated in the following equations.

$$^{12}_{6}C + ^{12}_{6}C \rightarrow ^{24}_{12}Mg + \text{Energy}$$

$$^{12}_{6}C + ^{12}_{6}C \rightarrow ^{23}_{11}Na + ^{1}_{1}H + \text{Energy}$$

$$^{12}_{6}C + ^{12}_{6}C \rightarrow ^{23}_{12}Mg + ^{1}_{0}n + \text{Energy (n = neutron)}$$

$$^{12}_{6}C + ^{12}_{6}C \rightarrow ^{20}_{10}Ne + ^{4}_{2}He + \text{Energy}$$

Over thousands of years, reactions such as those, as well as others involving the neutrons, lead to the formation of elements with atomic numbers as high as those of iron and cobalt. The star concentrates the different elements in successive layers (Figure E5–3). The process does not seem capable of progress-

FIGURE E5–3 · *Shown here is a proposed scheme of a star as it appears at the end of burning to form elements between C and Fe.*

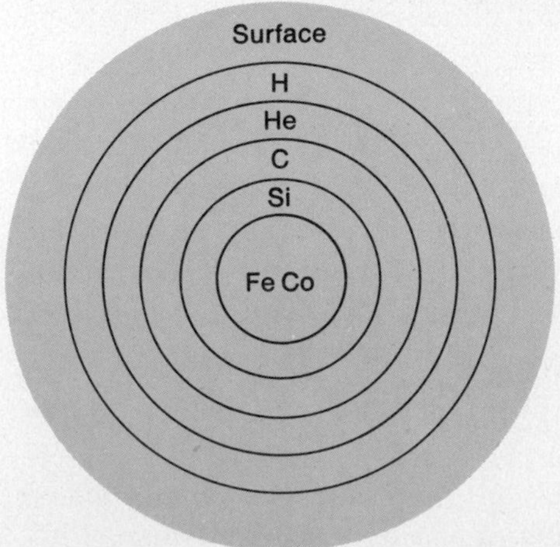

ing beyond that point, and, indeed, in some older stars the heavier elements are completely absent or are present only in very slight quantities.

It is believed some older stars have exploded (exploding stars are known as *novae* or *supernovae*) and "second-generation" stars have formed that include not only hydrogen but also some of the elemental debris from the explosion of the older stars.

FIGURE E5–4 · This is the supernova explosion of a star that reached maximum brightness in September, 1938 (top). Fourteen months later it faded (bottom). The heaviest elements are synthesized and blown into space.

The rather high abundance of heavy elements in our sun is evidence that it is a second-generation star. In such new stars, all the reactions described above proceed, but, in addition, there are reactions that form new heavy elements. Those reactions, which result primarily from the incorporation of neutrons into the nucleus and from radioactive decay, are illustrated in the next two equations.

$$^{100}_{44}\mathrm{Ru} + {}^{1}_{0}\mathrm{n} \rightarrow {}^{101}_{44}\mathrm{Ru} \xrightarrow{^{1}_{0}\mathrm{n}} {}^{102}_{44}\mathrm{Ru} \xrightarrow{^{1}_{0}\mathrm{n}} {}^{103}_{44}\mathrm{Ru}$$

$$^{103}_{44}\mathrm{Ru} \xrightarrow[\text{decay}]{\text{Radioactive}} {}^{103}_{45}\mathrm{Rh} \xrightarrow{^{1}_{0}\mathrm{n}} {}^{104}_{45}\mathrm{Rh} \xrightarrow[\text{decay}]{\text{Radioactive}} {}^{104}_{46}\mathrm{Pd}$$

That is a slow process—it is called the *s* process. It may take millions of years. The heaviest elements cannot be made in this way. It is believed they are made very quickly in the supernovae explosions of stars. The neutrons are added very *rapidly*. As a result, that is called the *r* process. Figure E5–4 is a picture of a supernova explosion in which heavy elements such as $_{92}$U and $_{98}$Cf must have been made.

THE ABUNDANCES OF ELEMENTS ON THE EARTH

The relative abundances of the elements on the earth are very different from their abundances in the sun. (See Tables 2-4 and 2-5 in Chapter 2.) The sun is very similar in composition to the universe. In contrast, the earth is almost devoid of $_1H$ and $_2He$, the two elements that make up 99.9 percent of all the atoms in the universe. Hydrogen and helium are very light gases. When the earth was formed, there must have been a lot of hydrogen and helium present. But the mass of the earth is too small to provide enough gravitational attraction for the very light atoms. So, over several billion years, the atoms of the lightest elements escaped into space. Since the mass of the moon is even less than that of the earth, the moon lost not only its hydrogen and helium, but also its nitrogen and oxygen.

We believe the Big Bang took place about twenty billion years ago. Our galaxy, the Milky Way, is probably fifteen billion years old. Our star, the sun, is much younger, about five to eight billion years old. And our earth is probably about the same age as our sun, five billion years old.

A number of facts indicate that the condensation of planetary matter took place approximately 4.5×10^9 years ago. At that time, the earth existed in a molten state that continued for about two billion years. The intense heat of the earth was the result of the decay of the radioactive elements in the planetary mass. Even today the earth's crust contains sufficient amounts of radioactive substances, such as uranium, thorium, and potassium (40 K), to account for half the heat given off from the earth (about 10^{-6} cal/cm^2). However, in contrast to the earth, smaller meteorites did not melt. It seems possible that even the moon did not go through a molten stage. If that is so, some of the rocks on the moon are much older than those on the earth. (This has been proven by tests done on some of the rocks collected during Apollo lunar expeditions.) As the radioactive decay decreased because of the decreasing amounts of uranium and potassium, the earth cooled. The first permanent solid crust was probably formed about three billion years ago. It is from that time that geologists can study the changes that have occurred on the earth's surface. (See Chapter 2, Tables 2-4 and 2-5, pages 32-33.)

Radiochemical investigations of meteorites and of minerals from the earth and the moon help scientists determine the age

FIGURE E5–5 · *The earth rising over the moon's surface*

of such materials and the temperature and pressure conditions that once existed. From those data, some reasonable conclusions can be drawn about the formation of the earth. However, a great deal of uncertainty still exists in such hypotheses. According to one model, the earth was formed at a relatively low temperature through the condensation of cosmic matter accumulated by gravitation. At the same time, that condensation led to the formation of the other planets, the moon, and the sun of our solar system. The combination of the gravitational and centrifugal forces of the rotating cloud of condensing matter may have led to the collection of the lighter elements in the center of the system (the sun). The elementary composition of the earth and the inner planets is quite different from that of the sun, which we believe is a better representation of the primary cosmic matter of our solar system. That is probably because those lighter elements were not attracted to the inner core of the condensing planetary matter. Instead, they were forced through the increasing radiation pressure of the primeval sun to the outer part of the evolving solar system. Thus, the earth became fairly poor with respect to the inert gases as well as hydrogen, ammonia, and methane. However, those gases are found in large amounts in the planets farther from our sun, such as Jupiter and Saturn.

One lesson that we learn as we study the chemistry of the solar system is that the particular properties of our earth are largely the result of many lucky circumstances. It is the right size, the right distance from the sun, and the right age to give us our temperature, climate, oxygen, water, and all other conditions suitable for life as we know it. All the other planets are too large or too small, too close to or too far away from the sun, and too hot or too cold to have any but a very primitive biology (if they have any at all).

THE SYNTHETIC ELEMENTS

Ninety elements have been found on the earth, some in extremely minute amounts and some in very large quantities. Two elements of average masses do not occur naturally on the earth—element 43, technetium, and element 61, promethium. Scientists have synthesized fourteen elements beyond the heaviest natural element, uranium. That gives us a total of 107 elements. The synthesis of the heavy elements is an active field of research at present. Let us study how some of those elements were made, as an example of modern research. You will understand the story much better if you have already read Excursion 3, "The Nucleus: For Better or Worse."

ANYONE CAN BE WRONG

The discovery of the neutron in 1932 provided scientists with a valuable tool for producing nuclear reactions. The neutron is uncharged and, therefore, when it approaches a nucleus, it experiences no repulsion, even though the nucleus has a positive charge. Consequently, neutrons of very low kinetic energy can easily strike nuclei, causing nuclear reactions. Enrico Fermi (1901–1954) and his co-workers in Rome realized that. They bombarded practically every known element with neutrons, which were liberated by bombarding beryllium with alpha particles from radium, to produce many new radioactive species.

A characteristic feature of radioactive nuclides (a nucleus of specific atomic mass and atomic number) produced by the capture of a neutron is decay by beta particle (high-energy electron) emission. That decay increases the atomic number by one.

$$^{75}_{33}\text{As} + {}^{1}_{0}n \rightarrow {}^{76}_{33}\text{As} \rightarrow {}^{76}_{34}\text{Se} + {}^{0}_{-1}\beta$$

In 1934, Fermi suggested that, via beta decay, elements with an atomic number greater than 92 could be made by bombarding uranium with neutrons. For example, Fermi's group found a new beta activity with a thirteen-minute half-life that could be separated from all the known elements heavier than lead, including uranium. They concluded that such radioactivity must stem from a new element heavier than uranium.

In Germany, Otto Hahn, Lise Meitner, and Fritz Strassmann confirmed that Fermi's radioactivity could not arise from any element between radium and uranium, and within the next few years, by using the same logic, those workers found a number of other radioactivities that they attributed to new transuranium elements. In fact, it seemed that four such elements had been made. Those four elements had chemical properties corresponding well with the properties of homologs of rhenium, osmium, gold, and platinum respectively. In 1938, a review article cited over ninety references supporting discovery of the four new elements. The most famous names in nuclear research were associated with those studies.

In 1938, however, Hahn and Strassmann began to have some doubts. Careful chemical experiments led them to realize that one of the "elements" that was made, when uranium was bombarded with neutrons, was barium. Since barium is an average-mass element ($Z = 56$), they concluded that it could only be formed by splitting uranium into two atoms. Hahn and Strassmann had discovered nuclear fission. So, they began a new era. The interpretation of the work between 1934 and 1939 on the transuranium elements was incorrect. The scientists had been making uranium by fission. Instead of studying elements with an atomic number greater than 92, they had been studying the average-mass elements made by fission. The story is useful, as it reminds scientists to be extremely careful in interpreting their results. Even the best scientists can and do make mistakes.

Enrico Fermi
(1901–1954, Italian) Among the most outstanding scientists in history, Fermi was one of the architects of the so-called atomic age. In 1939, he became professor of physics at Columbia University. Later he directed construction of the first nuclear reactor to achieve controlled nuclear fission. In 1938 Fermi won a Nobel prize for his earlier experimental and theoretical contributions in physics. Two days before his untimely death in late 1954, Fermi was awarded a special prize of $25 000.00 by the Atomic Energy Commission for his outstanding achievements in the fields of nuclear physics and chemistry. That prize is now awarded annually and has been named in honor of Fermi, as has been element 100, fermium.

NO MISTAKE THE NEXT TIME

E. M. McMillan at the University of California was interested in the newly discovered process of fission. He used a cyclotron to irradiate uranium in order to study the products of fission. Since nuclear fission is a very energetic reaction, the two atoms made by fission are quite energetic. But McMillan not only found energetic atoms. He also observed a radioactive substance with much less energy. He concluded correctly that he had discovered a true transuranium element. It was the first element beyond uranium in the periodic table, as Neptune is the next planet beyond Uranus in the solar system. To repeat that pattern, he named his new element neptunium.

Later in 1940, McMillan, with J. W. Kennedy, A. C. Wahl, and G. T. Seaborg, made the next transuranium element. They bombarded ${}^{238}_{92}U$ with deuterons, ${}^{2}_{1}H$, in a cyclotron to make ${}^{238}_{93}Np$.

$${}^{238}_{92}U + {}^{2}_{1}H \rightarrow {}^{238}_{93}Np + 2{}^{1}_{0}n$$

The ${}^{238}_{93}Np$ underwent radioactive beta decay to form ${}^{238}_{94}Pu$.

$${}^{238}_{93}Np \rightarrow {}^{238}_{94}Pu + {}^{0}_{-1}\beta$$

The new element was named plutonium, since it is the element after neptunium. (Pluto is the planet after Neptune.)

Albert Einstein
(1879–1955, German) Einstein was the greatest theoretical physicist of our century. In his later years, Einstein was a fervent advocate of nuclear disarmament. Element 99, einsteinium, was named in his honor.

SYNTHESIS IN A LITTLE BIG BANG

An interesting synthesis occurred in the explosion of the first major thermonuclear device by the United States. Late in 1952, that fusion device was exploded as part of the program to develop the hydrogen bomb. It was a tremendous explosion, throwing tons of coral, sand, and other debris into the air in its mushroom cloud. After that material fell back to the earth, scientists began to analyze it. Scientists at the University of California, at Argonne National Laboratory, and at Los Alamos Laboratory discovered two new synthetic elements. They named the new elements einsteinium ($Z = 99$) and fermium ($Z = 100$). Those elements were named after two great scientists. Albert Einstein was a great theoretical physicist. Enrico Fermi, although he was wrong about his transuranium elements, was right about so much else that he was one of the greatest nuclear physicists of the twentieth century.

How were the new elements made in the H-bomb type explosion? The fusion reaction in an H-bomb makes neutrons. The explosion was an unusually large one, so that unusually great numbers of neutrons were released. Uranium was present in the surrounding material. In the brief time—maybe 10^{-16} seconds—during the release of the neutrons and the vaporization of the whole device, some uranium atoms apparently captured as many as seventeen neutrons. The reaction would have been as follows.

$$^{238}_{92}U \xrightarrow{+n} {}^{239}_{92}U \xrightarrow{n} {}^{240}_{92}U \xrightarrow{n} {}^{241}_{92}U \rightarrow\rightarrow\rightarrow\rightarrow {}^{255}_{92}U$$

The uranium isotopes then changed to elements of a higher atomic number by radioactive beta decay.

$$^{255}_{92}U \xrightarrow[-1^e]{\beta} {}^{225}_{93}Np \xrightarrow[-1^e]{\beta} {}^{255}_{94}Pu \xrightarrow[1^e]{\beta} {}^{255}_{95}Am \xrightarrow[-1^e]{\beta} {}^{255}_{96}Cm \xrightarrow[-1^e]{\beta}$$

$$^{255}_{97}Bk \xrightarrow[-1^e]{\beta} {}^{255}_{98}Cf \xrightarrow[-1^e]{\beta} {}^{255}_{99}Es \xrightarrow[-1^e]{\beta} {}^{255}_{100}Fm$$

It is the same type of process that is believed to occur in supernovae to make the heavy elements by the *r* process.

THE NEW ELEMENTS AND CONTROVERSY

The transuranium elements can be made in a number of ways. The bombardment by neutrons, protons, deuterons, alpha particles, and heavy elements—such as $^{12}_{6}C$, $^{16}_{8}O$, $^{20}_{10}Ne$—is one method used to make transuranium elements. Table E5-1 lists some of the reactions. They are not the actual reactions used to make a particular element, but are examples of reactions.

TABLE E5–1 · Reactions Used to Synthesize Transuranium Elements

TARGET		PROJECTILE		PRODUCTS		
$^{238}_{92}U$	+	$^{2}_{1}H$	→	$^{238}_{93}Np$ (neptunium)	+	2^1_0n
$^{238}_{92}U$	+	$^{4}_{2}He$	→	$^{240}_{94}Pu$ (plutonium)	+	2^1_0n
$^{239}_{94}Pu$	+	$^{4}_{2}He$	→	$^{241}_{95}Am$ (americium)	+	$^1_1H + {}^1_0n$
$^{239}_{94}Pu$	+	$^{4}_{2}He$	→	$^{240}_{96}Cm$ (curium)	+	3^1_0n
$^{244}_{96}Cm$	+	$^{4}_{2}He$	→	$^{245}_{97}Bk$ (berkelium)	+	$^1_1H + 2^1_0n$
$^{238}_{92}U$	+	$^{12}_{6}C$	→	$^{245}_{98}Cf$ (californium)	+	5^1_0n
$^{238}_{92}U$	+	$^{14}_{7}N$	→	$^{247}_{99}Es$ (einsteinium)	+	5^1_0n
$^{238}_{92}U$	+	$^{16}_{8}O$	→	$^{250}_{100}Fm$ (fermium)	+	4^1_0n
$^{253}_{99}Es$	+	$^{4}_{2}He$	→	$^{256}_{101}Md$ (mendelevium)	+	0
$^{246}_{96}Cm$	+	$^{13}_{6}C$	→	$^{251}_{102}No$ (nobelium)	+	^1_0n
$^{252}_{98}Cf$	+	$^{10}_{5}B$	→	$^{257}_{103}Lr$ (lawrencium)	+	8^1_0n
a. $^{242}_{94}Pu$	+	$^{22}_{10}Ne$	→	$^{260}_{104}$eka-hafnium	+	4^1_0n
b. $^{249}_{98}Cf$	+	$^{12}_{6}C$	→	$^{257}_{104}$eka-hafnium	+	4^1_0n
c. $^{249}_{98}Cf$	+	$^{13}_{6}C$	→	$^{259}_{104}$eka-hafnium	+	3^1_0n
$^{243}_{95}Am$	+	$^{22}_{10}Ne$	→	$^{260}_{105}$eka-tantalum	+	5^1_0n
$^{249}_{98}Cf$	+	$^{18}_{8}O$	→	$^{263}_{106}$eka-tungsten	+	4^1_0n

The discoveries of elements 102, 104, 105, 106, and 107 have been surrounded by controversy. In the case of element 102, the initial discovery was claimed by a Swedish-British-American team in 1957. However, A. Ghiorso and his group in California showed that the claim was in error and, in 1958, successfully made element 102. The discovery of elements 104, 105, and 106 is claimed by Ghiorso and his co-workers and by Russian scientists, also. It is not certain who actually should be given credit for the initial synthesis in each case. The names suggested by the two groups for the elements are listed in Table E5–2.

TABLE E5–2 · The Most Recently Discovered Elements

ELEMENT	AMERICAN NAME	SOVIET NAME
104	rutherfordium	kurchatovium
105	hahnium	neilsbohrium
106	Not suggested	Not suggested
107	Not suggested	Not suggested
108	Not suggested	Not suggested

The same groups of Soviet and American scientists presently are seeking to synthesize element 108. All the synthetic elements are radioactive, with the rate of radioactive decay increasing rapidly with atomic number. For example, the half-life of $^{239}_{94}Pu$ is about 25 000 years, but already, by $Z = 98$ (Cf), it has decreased to a few years. Elements 105 and 106 have a half-life of a few seconds. The combination of increasing experimental difficulties and of decreasing half-lives makes the synthesis of heavier elements even more difficult. Although element 108 may be made in the next few years, it seems unlikely that attempts to make elements 109 and 110 will be successful for some time.

THE SUPERHEAVY ELEMENTS

It would seem there is a limitation of about 107 to 110 on the number of chemical elements. That is because of the electrostatic repulsion of the protons in the nucleus. That repulsion makes the nucleus unstable to radioactive decay. As the atomic number increases, the repulsion causes increasing instability. For the very heavy elements beyond uranium, the rate of radioactive decay by alpha emission increases rapidly with the atomic number. Also, the elements of a very high atomic number undergo spontaneous fission. The rate of fission decay increases even more rapidly than that of alpha decay. In fact, it is the radioactive decay by fission that sets a limit of about 108 on the synthesis of new elements.

About 1965, theoretical nuclear physicists calculated that there may be a change in the nuclear instability of elements with atomic numbers of 114 to 126. The neutrons and protons in the nuclei exist in shells, just as the electrons in atoms do. You know that filled electron shells make certain chemical elements very unreactive, or, in other words, very stable. Theoretical calculations indicated that the elements around $Z=114$ or around $Z = 126$ would have filled shells of protons and neutrons in the nucleus. The effect of the filled shells will make those nuclei more stable. In fact, some calculations predict that element 114 or element 126 may have a half-life of thousands, or even millions, of years. As a result, it seems there may be several elements between $Z = 112$ and $Z=128$ that are stable enough to synthesize. This region was given the name of *the island of stability* (Figure E5–6). It is even possible that some of these elements have enough stability to be present in nature.

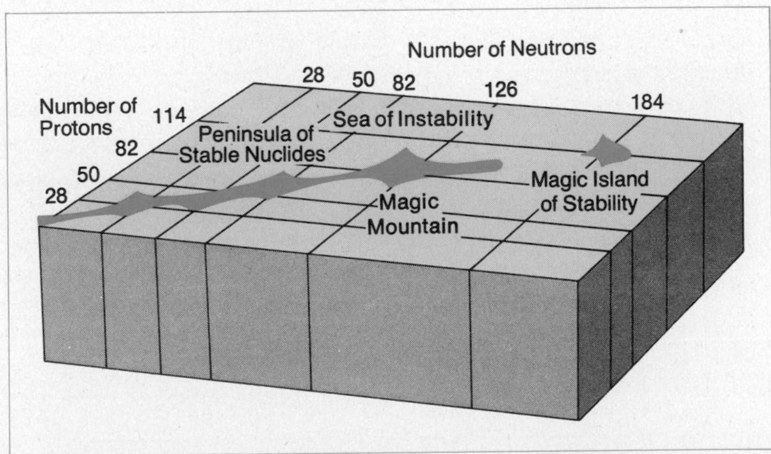

FIGURE E5–6 · *Nuclear stability is illustrated in a scheme that shows a peninsula of known elements and an island of predicted stability (nuclei around Z = 114 and N = 184) in a "sea of instability." Grid lines show numbers of protons and neutrons giving rise to exceptional stability. The most stable (called magic) regions on the mainland peninsula are represented by mountains or ridges.*

As a result of those predictions, scientists in many countries have begun a search for such elements in natural materials, such as ores and minerals. At the same time, they have begun to study ways to make them in the laboratory. Most attempts at synthesis have been very heavy projectiles, hoping to cause reactions such as those shown on the top of page 514.

Target		*Projectile*		*New element(?)*
$^{243}_{96}Cm$	+	$^{40}_{18}Ar$	→	114
$^{238}_{92}U$	+	$^{66}_{30}Zn$	→	122
$^{232}_{90}Th$	+	$^{84}_{36}Kr$	→	126
$^{232}_{90}Th$	+	$^{76}_{32}Ge$	→	122
$^{238}_{92}U$	+	$^{238}_{92}U$	→	Fission → 114 (as a fission product)

So far, all attempts to synthesize the superheavy elements in the island of stability have produced no positive results.

The search for such elements in nature has provided several exciting possibilities. E. Anders found the heavy xenon isotope $^{136}_{54}Xe$ in meteorites. It is believed the isotope came from the spontaneous fission decay of an element with an atomic number around 114.

Figure E5–7 is a periodic table with the superheavy elements placed in it, as based on their predicted chemical properties.

FIGURE E5–7 · *This illustration shows the periodic table with predicted superheavy elements.*

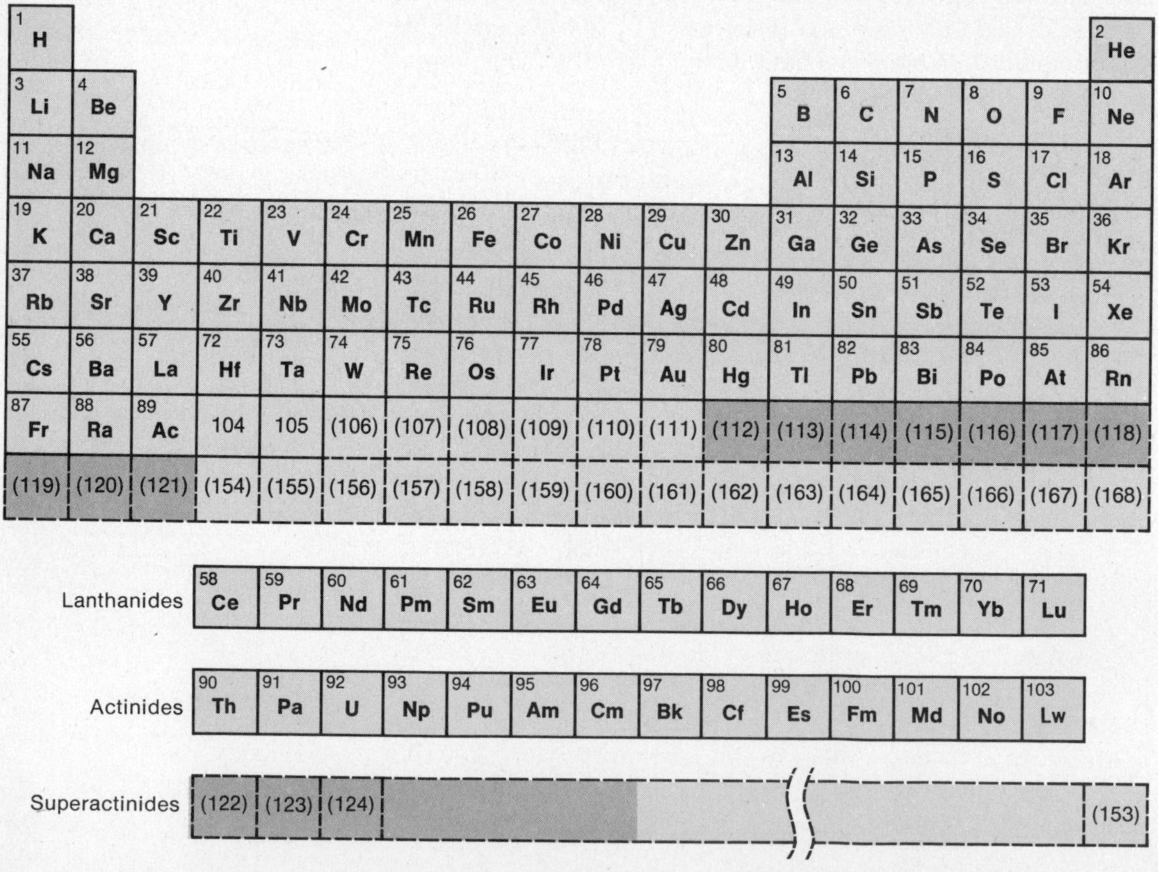

1 H																	2 He
3 Li	4 Be											5 B	6 C	7 N	8 O	9 F	10 Ne
11 Na	12 Mg											13 Al	14 Si	15 P	16 S	17 Cl	18 Ar
19 K	20 Ca	21 Sc	22 Ti	23 V	24 Cr	25 Mn	26 Fe	27 Co	28 Ni	29 Cu	30 Zn	31 Ga	32 Ge	33 As	34 Se	35 Br	36 Kr
37 Rb	38 Sr	39 Y	40 Zr	41 Nb	42 Mo	43 Tc	44 Ru	45 Rh	46 Pd	47 Ag	48 Cd	49 In	50 Sn	51 Sb	52 Te	53 I	54 Xe
55 Cs	56 Ba	57 La	72 Hf	73 Ta	74 W	75 Re	76 Os	77 Ir	78 Pt	79 Au	80 Hg	81 Tl	82 Pb	83 Bi	84 Po	85 At	86 Rn
87 Fr	88 Ra	89 Ac	104	105	(106)	(107)	(108)	(109)	(110)	(111)	(112)	(113)	(114)	(115)	(116)	(117)	(118)
(119)	(120)	(121)	(154)	(155)	(156)	(157)	(158)	(159)	(160)	(161)	(162)	(163)	(164)	(165)	(166)	(167)	(168)

Lanthanides	58 Ce	59 Pr	60 Nd	61 Pm	62 Sm	63 Eu	64 Gd	65 Tb	66 Dy	67 Ho	68 Er	69 Tm	70 Yb	71 Lu
Actinides	90 Th	91 Pa	92 U	93 Np	94 Pu	95 Am	96 Cm	97 Bk	98 Cf	99 Es	100 Fm	101 Md	102 No	103 Lw
Superactinides	(122)	(123)	(124)											(153)

REVIEW QUESTIONS

1 Write out the nuclear equations to show the difference between the s process and the r process.

2 Between 1969 and 1972, the United States sent six Apollo crews to the moon. What evidence was gathered by those explorers to help scientists better estimate the ages of the moon, the earth, and the universe?

If your school library does not have the reference material you need to answer the question, you can obtain free literature on the Apollo programs by writing to the following address.

Scientific and Technical Information Office
NASA
Washington, D.C. 20546

3 In 1976, the United States landed Viking I and Viking II on the surface of Mars. What information did those provide regarding the age of the universe?

4 Dr. Glenn Seaborg postulates the eventual existence of 200 or more elements. Describe the techniques for their synthesis that he envisions and discuss his theories.

Glenn Seaborg and J. L. Bloom. "The Synthetic Elements." *Scientific American.* April, 1969.

SUGGESTED READINGS

Keller, O. L. "Predicted Properties of Elements 113 and 114." *Chemistry*, November 1970, p. 8.

Lewis, John S. "The Chemistry of the Solar System." *Scientific American*, March 1974, p. 50.

Pasachoff, Jay M., and William A. Fowler. "Deuterium in the Universe." *Scientific American*, May 1974, p. 108.

Schramm, D. N. "The Age of the Elements." *Scientific American*, January 1974, p. 69.

Turner, Barry E. "Interstellar Molecules." *Scientific American*, March 1973, p. 50.

EXCURSION SIX

The Story of Element 101

The authors of a scientific textbook of chemistry are concerned with making certain that their book adequately teaches students the fundamentals of chemistry—for example, balancing equations, doing chemical calculations, and understanding the electronic structure of the atom. In doing that, the authors fail to reflect the personal excitement that a scientist feels in research. Many teachers and students have suggested that I use this excursion to describe my involvement in a particular research effort, that is, the discovery of element 101, mendelevium. Since that discovery in 1955, I have been involved in scientific research on many topics and have had equal excitement and pleasure for those efforts. Nevertheless, a story of the discovery of a new element seems to have a special interest for students, so it seems that a recounting of that experiment may be most suitable.

BEGINNINGS OF THE RESEARCH

In 1953, with a new Ph.D. degree from the University of Texas, I went to the Radiation Laboratory of the University of California at Berkeley. There I began post-graduate studies with Professor Glenn T. Seaborg. Professor Seaborg had received a Nobel prize in 1951 for his role in the discovery of the transuranium elements. The Radiation Laboratory at Berkeley was the world center of research in the new elements. I was particularly fortunate to have the opportunity to work with Professor Seaborg in radiochemistry. I knew that I would be working with people who were the very best in the world in that field. For the first six months, I kept quiet and worked as hard as possible so that no one would realize how very little I knew. Fortunately, Glenn Seaborg, as well as the other members of the new element research team, Albert Ghiorso, Stanley Thompson, and Bernard Harvey, were understanding and sympathetic. They did everything they could to increase my confidence, teach me all they knew about the new elements, and bring me up to date on their research.

The period of 1954–1955 was to be a particularly fruitful and busy one in the field of new element research. Several years earlier, the largest nuclear reactor had begun operation in Idaho. Ghiorso, Thompson, and Seaborg had initiated a program whereby samples of plutonium were placed in the reactor for long-term bombardment by the reactor neutrons. Over a period of several years, it was expected that the bombardment would cause the plutonium to be transmuted into heavier elements such as americium ($Z=95$), curium ($Z=96$), berkelium ($Z=97$), and californium ($Z=98$). About the same time, a rather unexpected event occurred when the first thermonuclear device was exploded by the United States in the Pacific. In the radioactive debris of that device, scientists at Berkeley, Argonne National Laboratory (outside Chicago), and Los Alamos Laboratory (in New Mexico) made several discoveries. The tremendous density of the neutrons generated at the moment of explosion had

FIGURE E6–1 · *This photograph of Dr. Stanley Thompson (left) and Dr. Glenn Seaborg (right) was taken in 1948 while the work on the discovery of elements 98 and 99 was in progress.*

served to transmute a portion of the uranium in the device into heavier elements, even up to element 100. That was unexpected, particularly since it meant the formation of two new elements, elements 99 (einsteinium) and 100 (fermium). Those elements had been discovered in connection with the explosion of a hydrogen bomb. But their discovery was classified as top secret, and no public disclosure was made at the time. Consequently, after I arrived at Berkeley, the group of scientists (Ghiorso, Thompson, and Harvey) that I joined were trying to remake elements 99 and 100 by methods that would permit their publication. In a sense, that was an easy task. The earlier discovery experiments had already provided the important data on the chemical and nuclear properties of the two elements. We were successful. The synthesis of element 99 was reported in December 1953. The synthesis of element 100 followed in February 1954. That allowed us to turn our attention to the more difficult task of making a new element, element 101.

PROBLEMS TO BE SOLVED

From the beginning, it was obvious that many problems would lie in our path in that research. First of all, the cyclotron with which we were working accelerated alpha particles ($^{4}_{2}He^{+2}$). Therefore, we could only add two charges to the target nucleus to make element 101. That meant that the lightest target element with which we could begin had to be einsteinium (element 99) by the following reaction.

$$^{253}_{99}Es + ^{4}_{2}He \rightarrow ^{256}101 + ^{1}_{0}n$$

Unfortunately, at the time we began to plan the experiment, there were only a few atoms of element 99 in existence. Also, those few atoms were in the plutonium sample that was being irradiated in the nuclear reactor in Idaho. We calculated that if we waited about a year, there would be about one billion atoms of element 99 in the reactor samples. We could then remove the sample and isolate the einsteinium to use as a target for our cyclotron bombardment. But the einsteinium that we made in the reactor has a half-life of only three weeks. That meant that a month after we removed it from the reactor, more than half of it would be gone. Therefore, we would have to do our experiments in a very short time period. Moreover, the billion atoms would be about a million times less than the smallest amount

FIGURE E6–2 · *This photograph shows the 60-inch cyclotron at the Radiation Laboratory of the University of California at Berkeley, in August 1939. The machine was the most powerful atom smasher in the world at that time. The machine was dismantled in June 1962, and the magnet was converted into a more modern machine.*

that can be seen even through a microscope. So, we would be faced with making a target out of an invisible and unweighable amount of material. Knowing all that, we could calculate the following. The cyclotron did not accelerate enough alpha particles per second to make any atoms of element 101, if we had only a billion atoms of einsteinium. That calculation is shown by the following equation.

$$N = N^1 \cdot P \cdot I \cdot t$$

where N = number of atoms of element 101,

N^1 = number of atoms of target Es $= 10^9$,

P = probability of reaction between an atom of Es and alpha particle $= 10^{-27}$,

I = number of alpha particles per second $= 10^{14}$,

t = length of bombardment time in seconds $= 10^4$ second, or about 3 hours

$$N = (10^9)\,(10^{-27})\,(10^{14})\,(10^4) = 1 \text{ atom Md/3 hours of bombardment}$$

We have 10^9 atoms of einsteinium. In order to make one atom of element 101 from 10^9 atoms of einsteinium in a reasonable time, or three hours of cyclotron bombardment, we would have to have an alpha beam of at least 10^{14} alpha particles per second. That was approximately 100 times greater than the alpha beam that the cyclotron was capable of producing. Even if we were able to modify the cyclotron to obtain enough alpha particles, it was obvious that we could not make more than a few atoms of element 101. Therefore, we also had to learn how to do chemistry that would separate those few atoms of element 101 very efficiently and very rapidly.

These then were our problems in 1954, when we began to plan the synthesis of element 101. First, we had to isolate a very small amount of einsteinium from plutonium. That would be done by bombarding plutonium in the reactor long enough to make about a billion atoms of Es. Second, we had to make the einsteinium atoms into a useful target for the cyclotron. Then the cyclotron had to be rebuilt and modified to produce a much more intense beam of alpha particles for our use. Finally, we had to develop new and faster chemical separations in order to purify the few atoms of element 101 that would be made.

Seaborg obtained the funds from the regents of the University of California for the modification of the cyclotron. Ghiorso began to work on the problem of how to bombard the invisible amount of Es in the cyclotron and how to detect and measure the radioactivity of the atoms of element 101. Harvey worked on the problem of how to make that amount into a target. Thompson and I concentrated our attention on developing new methods of fast separation to purify the target atoms of einsteinium from the plutonium. We also sought new methods for purifying the atoms of elements 101 that we might make from the cyclotron bombardment.

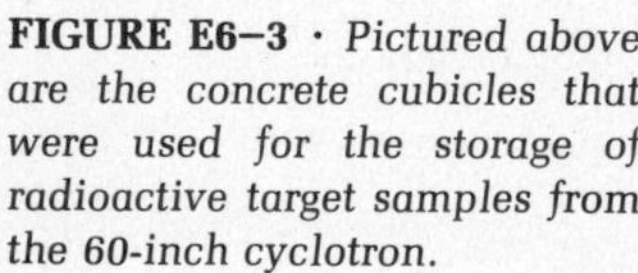

FIGURE E6–3 · *Pictured above are the concrete cubicles that were used for the storage of radioactive target samples from the 60-inch cyclotron.*

THE FIRST EXPERIMENTS

Those efforts took up much of our attention for eight or nine months. In September of 1954, we made our initial attempts to produce element 101. At that time, we believed the isotopes of element 101 that might be made would emit alpha particles. Consequently, Ghiorso designed a detection system to look for alpha radioactive decay. Also, he was responsible for proposing what was the most important aspect of the experimental design. We realized early that we would not be able to make a target of einsteinium and proceed in the normal fashion of irradiating it, dissolving it, and purifying the product element 101. In that procedure, the target material is recovered and made into a new target. Such procedure always results in a loss of 10–20 percent of the original material. Also, it may take almost a week before the new target is ready. We had neither enough target material to allow losses in the recovery and the refabrication, nor the time to spare because of the short half-life. Therefore, we realized that we would have to use our target over and over again.

Ghiorso remembered the following experiment done many years earlier by Lord Rutherford. In that experiment, Rutherford showed that when a target was struck by a beam of alpha particles, some of the atoms in the target were knocked forward. That can be compared to a billiard ball that is knocked forward when struck by the cue ball. As a result, Ghiorso proposed that we turn the target around and let the cyclotron beam go through the support foil to hit the target atoms on the backside of the foil. Then any target atoms that were struck by alpha particles to form an atom of element 101 would have enough momentum to be knocked out of the target. Those atoms would fly through space until they struck a solid object where they could be caught. Therefore, we put a thin gold foil in front of the target so that the atoms recoiling from the target would be caught on the foil. In that way, we would not have to dissolve the target to isolate our product atoms. They would all be on the "catcher" foil. Instead of dissolving the target atoms, we only had to dissolve the catcher foil and put it through separation chemistry.

Unfortunately, the September experiments proved to be negative. In several experiments, we failed to see any alpha-particle decay that we could ascribe to element 101. Everything else

FIGURE E6–4 · *The Lawrence Radiation Laboratory occupies a 120-acre tract in the hills overlooking the University of California campus. The large round building is the laboratory's Bevatron—one of the world's leading proton synchrotrons. The domed building to the right is the 184-inch cyclotron used for medical treatments, including cancer therapy.*

about the experiment seemed to be working well. But there simply seemed to be no atoms of element 101 made. We were able to do all the isolation chemistry that we needed within ten minutes after stopping the cyclotron bombardment. Therefore, we felt that the chemistry was not a problem.

The ten-minute time of isolation chemistry represented quite an achievement in itself. That is because the cyclotron was on the main campus of the University of California, and the Radiation Laboratory was on an adjacent hill. The routine was that Ghiorso would pull the catcher foil from the cyclotron as soon as it was shut off. He would give the foil to Harvey who would run about fifty yards and up a flight of steps to a little table that we had set up in a balcony of the cyclotron room. There I would take the foil, dissolve it quickly in aqua regia, and put that solution through a small column of anion-exchange resin. The gold of the foil, as well as some of the other radioactivities, would stick to the resin, and the transuranium elements would pass through. The eight or nine drops that we recovered from the column of ion-exchange resin were collected in a test tube. I would run out of the building with the tube and jump into Ghiorso's VW "bug" for a mad dash up the hill to the main chemistry laboratory of the Radiation Laboratory. We would do the experiments late at night so that traffic was not a problem. Also, the security police would clear the streets for us. Running from the car into the lab, I would give the sample to Thompson who proceeded to pass it through a bed of cation-exchange resin, in which the individual transuranium elements were isolated from one another. We would collect single drops of the solution from the bottom of the column on small flat disks of platinum. Those were dried, and the disks, which we calculated should contain the atoms of 101, were placed in the radiation counter. Figure E6–5 shows that chemistry.

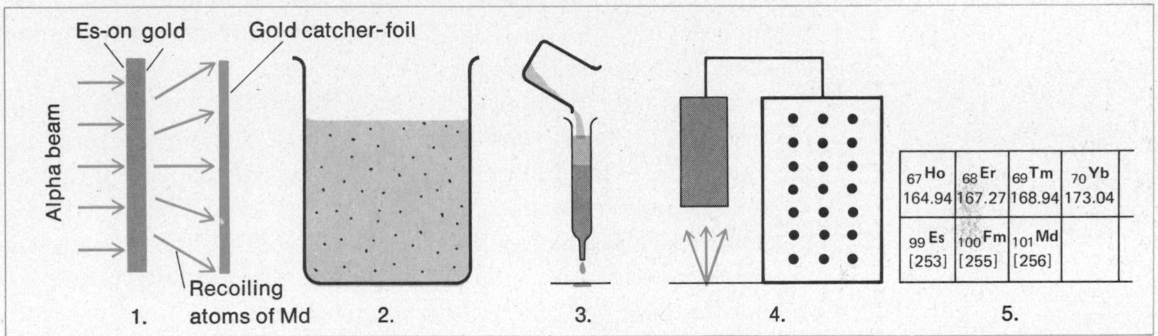

FIGURE E6–5 · *The steps involved in the formation and isolation of mendelevium: (1) Bombardment of Es^{254} with alpha particles, using the recoil technique. (2) Gold catcher foil dissolved in aqua regia. (3) Solution of Md(III) passed through both an anion-exchange resin and a cation-exchange resin column. (4) Fractions from the cation-exchange resin column counted. (5) Discovery of element 101 proved and mendelevium added to the periodic table.*

We failed to see any alpha-particle decay. However, one evening during an experiment, Ghiorso did notice that there was a very high-energy radioactive decay. It could not be the result of alpha particles, but could be the result of a form of radioactive decay known as spontaneous fission. In Excursion 3, "The Nucleus, For Better or Worse," we discuss fission induced by neutrons. However, in the heaviest elements, there is a natural tendency to undergo fission, just as there is a tendency to undergo alpha decay, beta decay, etc. The tendency to undergo spontaneous fission increases with the atomic number. Thus, because of the spontaneous fission, californium ($Z = 98$) and the heavier elements have half-lives of days, minutes, or even seconds.

Ghiorso suggested that we should try the experiment again. But instead of looking for alpha decay, we should look for spontaneous fission. He proposed that we *were* making atoms of elements 101. However, instead of those atoms undergoing alpha decay, they decayed by a process known as **electron capture.** In that process, they were converted to the element of the next lower atomic number. That element then underwent spontaneous fission. In that case, the synthesis and decay reactions would be as follows.

$$^{253}_{99}Es + ^{4}_{2}He \rightarrow ^{256}_{101}Md + ^{1}_{0}n \text{ E.C. } ^{256}_{100}Fm \xrightarrow{\text{Spontaneous Fission}}$$

THE DEFINITIVE EXPERIMENTS

We had to wait until February of 1955 before enough new einsteinium had been made in the reactor. We isolated about 10^9 atoms of Es and were ready to try again to make element 101 under the conditions proposed by Ghiorso. Every day for two weeks, we practiced the following routine. We entered the laboratory round lunchtime and spent the afternoon cleaning up from the night before. And we got ready for the cyclotron bombardments in the evening. We went home for dinner and returned to the lab about 7:30 or 8:00. About that time, the cyclotron would begin irradiating our targets. During the three or four hours of irradiation on the cyclotron, we made final preparations for the chemistry in the laboratory. Among other things, that involved making solutions and preparing the columns of ion-exchange resins. About midnight, the cyclotron irradiations ended. We quickly did the chemistry on the targets and put the samples in for counting. Afterward, we often sat around the laboratory until 3:00 or 4:00 A.M. discussing how things could be improved and, in general, reviewing the whole situation. Those were good times for us, as we enjoyed the work and the excitement of making something new. Obviously, our families were not very enthusiastic about the schedule. But the schedule allowed us to work with a minimum of interference with traffic and with other people around the lab. During the day, we would be visited constantly by other scientists in the lab, who wanted to know how everything was going.

FIGURE E6–6 · *This photograph shows the 16 million-electron-volt deuteron beam of the 60-inch cyclotron.*

Finally, we were ready for the big experiment. The target was irradiated for a total of nine hours in three-hour intervals. The catcher foils from the three targets were processed individually at the end of the three-hour irradiations and put into the counters. That occurred around midnight for that particular set of experiments. The counters were hooked up to a recorder so that the radioactive decay would show on the recorder as a large deflection on a chart. That allowed us to see how many radioactive decays would occur. And it allowed us to see at what time they would occur, since the distance between the deflections along the chart was a function of the time between events.

THE FIRE BELL INCIDENT

The night of the actual discovery experiment, not only were the four of us – Ghiorso, Thompson, Harvey, and myself – present, but also perhaps a half dozen other people, including the operators of the cyclotron, the technicians helping with the experiment, and people concerned with the radiation safety aspects. Our late hours had led us to set up a small cooking arrangement in one of the laboratories to prepare bacon and eggs before going home each morning. Since we were quite anxious to know if we had succeeded, we were reluctant to have the radioactive decay events occur without our knowledge while we were eating breakfast.

Ghiorso solved the problem by connecting the radiation counter to the fire alarm bell for the laboratory. Accordingly, soon after we started breakfast, the fire alarm bell went off. We all gave a loud enthusiastic cheer, since it meant that we had succeeded in synthesizing element 101. Ghiorso and Harvey raced down to the counting room to turn off the fire alarm bell. They also expressed their excitement by writing on the recorder chart connected to the counter. Bernie Harvey wrote "Hooray" on the chart beside the deflection, the first comment on the synthesis of element 101. When the fire alarm bell went off a second time, indicating that a second atom of 101 had decayed, Bernie wrote "Double Hooray," and after the next deflection, he wrote "Triple Hooray." The synthesis continued and other decays also occurred. But after the Triple Hooray, we knew that element 101 was definite, and we became somewhat more restrained in our enthusiasm. I was cleaning the laboratory from the experiments when Ghiorso and Harvey signed

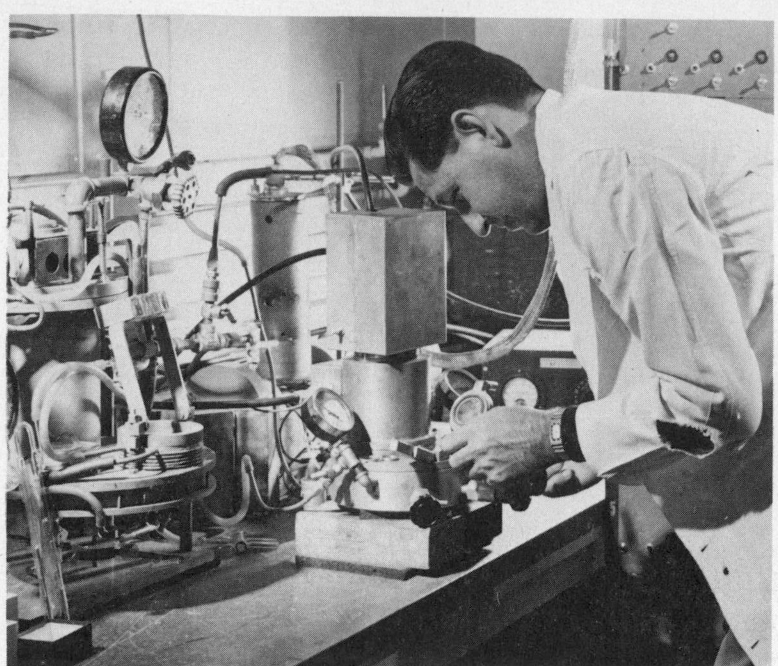

FIGURE E6–7 · *Dr. Albert Ghiorso is shown here with some of the equipment used in the discovery of elements 97–101. The photograph was taken in 1955.*

their names to the statement that this conclusively proved the identification of 101.

About 4:00 A.M., we all went home in a state of enthusiasm and excitement. I got very little sleep that morning. That isn't surprising, since participating in the discovery of a new element, which you know will be recorded in chemistry books as long as there are chemistry books, is a rather intoxicating experience for a twenty-seven-year-old post-graduate student just beginning his scientific career.

We had agreed to reassemble at the lab shortly after lunchtime the next day to begin to write a publication that we would send to the scientific journal *Physical Review* to inform the scientific world of our discovery. However, about 10:00 A.M., an event occurred while we were home sleeping that is still legend at the Radiation Laboratory. Ghiorso had unintentionally left the counter hooked to the fire alarm bell. A single atom, which should have decayed much sooner, fissioned that morning. It triggered the fire alarm bell, and since several thousand people at the Radiation Lab did not realize that the bell was hooked to the counter, they assumed that a fire had broken out. The laboratory operates with a volunteer fire force, and everyone in the lab is quite concerned with any fire, since there is so much radioactive material around. The result was a wild milling of people running up and down the hallways of the chemistry building looking for the fire. This state of affairs lasted for some fifteen or twenty minutes, until somebody traced the wire for the fire bell to the counter and learned the source of the "fire." The result of this incident was that E. O. Lawrence, the director of the laboratory and the man who had won a Nobel prize for the invention of the cyclotron, sent Glenn Seaborg, as the director of the chemistry division, an official note of congratulations on the discovery of element 101. He appended a statement saying it was official laboratory policy that even for so important an experiment as the discovery of a new element, fire alarm bells were not to be hooked to detectors.

During the many discussions when we used to sit around and talk about everything under the sun, including the experiments with which we were involved, we had decided that it would be appropriate to name the new element, which marked the beginning of the second hundred elements of the periodic table, after the man most responsible for the periodic table, Dmitri Mendeleev. That name was accepted by the International Union of Pure and Applied Chemistry (IUPAC), which made it official.

REVIEW QUESTIONS

1 The transuranic (synthetic) element plutonium is the subject of much discussion among the world's nations. Find out why this element may be so important.
2 The synthesis of new elements is done in particle accelerators. What is the principle behind such accelerators?
3 Helium was discovered on the sun before it was detected on the earth. How was this done?

REFERENCES

Maugh, T. H. II. "Element 106: Soviet and American Claim in Mutual Conflict." *Science*, 1974, p. 42.

Seaborg, G. T., and J. L. Bloom. "Fast Breeder Reactors." *Scientific American*, November 1970, pp. 13–21.

Seaborg, G. T., and J. L. Bloom. "The Synthetic Elements." *Scientific American*, April 1969, pp. 57–67.

Seaborg, G. T., and A. R. Fritsch. "Synthetic Elements III." *Scientific American*, April 1963, pp. 68–78.

EXCURSION SEVEN

What Is a Covalent Bond?

Stating that a covalent bond is a bond formed by two atoms sharing an electron pair does not tell why atoms share electrons. It is necessary to further study the nature of the covalent bond to learn why it is formed and why, once it has been formed, the bond holds atoms together in a molecule.

THE NATURE OF THE COVALENT BOND

For the purpose of discussing the nature of the covalent bond, let's consider two hydrogen atoms colliding to form the covalent molecule H_2. Each hydrogen atom consists of a one-proton nucleus and a single 1s orbital electron. (To minimize confusion, we'll refer to nucleus A and electron A of one atom, and nucleus B and electron B of the other atom.) The two atoms approach each other. In addition to the coulombic attractive force between each nucleus and its own electron, new coulombic *attractive* forces begin to operate. Those are the forces between nucleus A and electron B, and nucleus B and electron A. Furthermore, coulombic *repulsive* forces are experienced between the two electrons and between the two nuclei (Figure E7–1). Let's follow the course of the formation of a hydrogen molecule in terms of the energy involved.

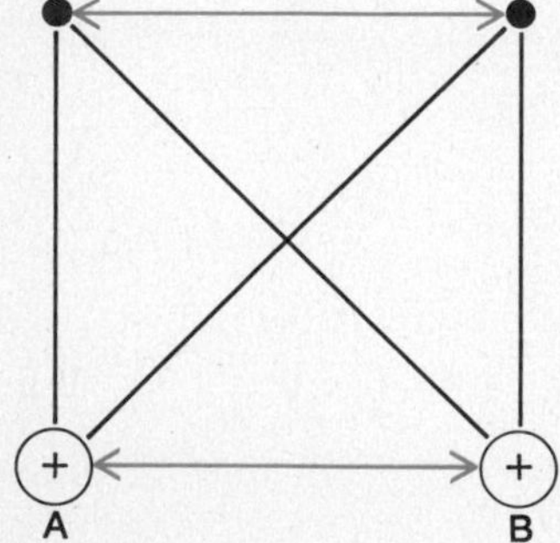

FIGURE E7–1 · *The coulombic forces of attraction and repulsion between two single-electron atoms are shown here.*

The two separated hydrogen atoms possess potential energy. As they approach each other, the atoms begin to be affected by the coulombic forces. Finally, a particular internuclear distance is reached at which the potential energy of the two-atom system reaches a minimum. At that distance, the attractive forces are exactly balanced by the repulsive forces, and a stable diatomic molecule has been formed. If the internuclear distance becomes smaller, the repulsive forces will predominate (Figure E7–2).

Let's summarize our picture of a covalent bond between any two nuclei. The charges of the two nuclei and their orbital electrons create both attractive and repulsive forces. At a certain internuclear distance, those forces are exactly balanced, and a stable molecule results. In the stable molecule, each nucleus exerts an attractive force on the bonding electrons. Consequently, the two electrons of the covalent bond are shared by the two atoms. When the process is considered in quantum mechanics, we find that there is a very high probability of finding the bonding pair of electrons between the two atoms. The higher the probability of finding the electrons between the two atoms, rather than elsewhere, the stronger is the bond. In other words, more energy is required to break the bond.

The force of attraction in a covalent bond is **electrostatic.** The two nuclei are held together by the high concentration of the negative charge of the shared pair of electrons between them. The theoretical description of covalent bonding is mathematically complex. But it describes the interaction in terms of the "exchange" attraction of the nuclei and the electron pair.

FIGURE E7–2 · *The potential electrical energy between two hydrogen atoms is shown in this graph. To what, do you think, does the distance 0.74A correspond?*

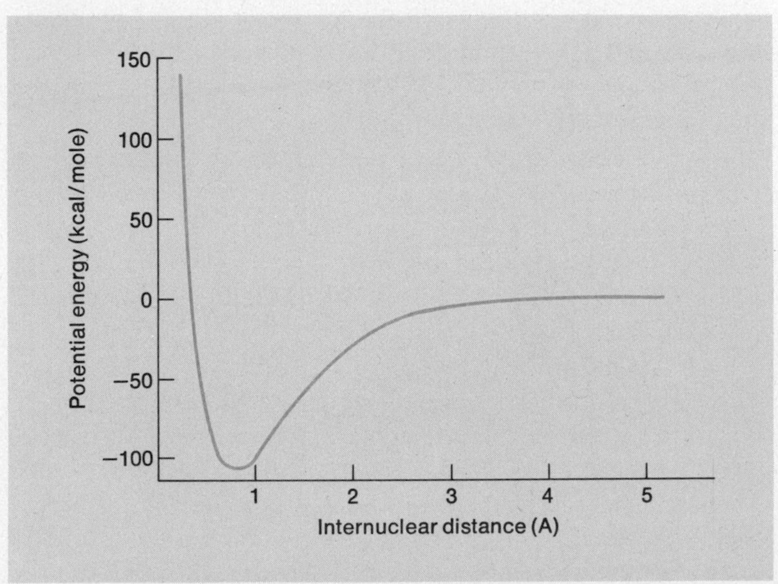

ORBITALS AND MULTIPLE BONDS

The quantum mechanical model has been quite successful in explaining multiple covalent bonding. Let us reconsider ethene, C_2H_4. Each carbon atom and the two hydrogen atoms surrounding each carbon atom are in a plane. By analogy to planar BF_3, we are led to believe sp^2 hybridization is present (see Chapter 11). The electron configuration for the carbon atom follows.

$$\frac{\uparrow\downarrow}{1s}\Big|\frac{\uparrow}{2sp^2}\ \frac{\uparrow}{2sp^2}\ \frac{\uparrow}{2sp^2}\Big|\frac{\uparrow}{2sp}$$

Ethene is bonded using the sp^2 orbitals in the structure. However, that does not account for the second bond between the carbon atoms. For that, the remaining $2p$ orbital must be used. The $2p$ orbital is perpendicular to the plane of the sp^2 orbitals. The $2p$ orbitals overlap side-to-side, so there is an overlap above and below the plane of the nuclei.

Bonds lying on a line between the two nuclei are termed *sigma* (σ) bonds. Molecules with single covalent bonds have only sigma bonds. Bonds formed from p orbitals that do not lie on the line between the two nuclei are termed *pi* (π) bonds. In a double bond, one bond is a sigma bond, and the second is a pi bond. Note that a pi bond has two areas of high electron probability, whereas a sigma bond has only one.

Nitrogen, N_2, is a molecule with a triple bond. The sigma bond is formed by the end-to-end overlap of two p orbitals. The two pi bonds are formed by the side-to-side overlap of the remaining perpendicular p orbitals.

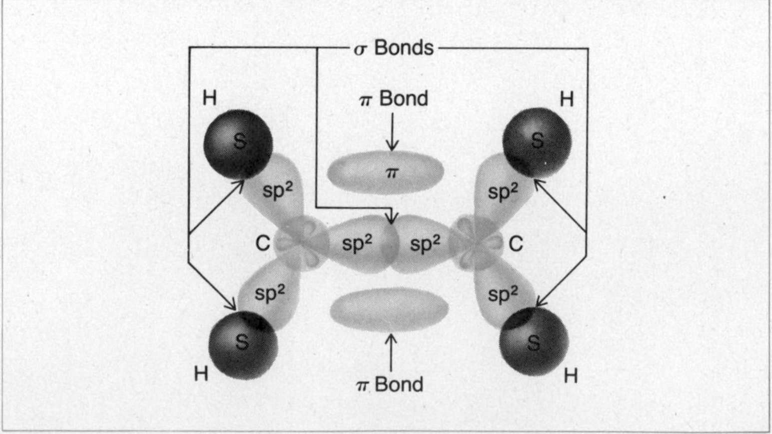

FIGURE E7–3 · *σ and π bonding in ethene, C_2H_4. The double bond consists of one σ and one π bond.*

REVIEW QUESTIONS

1 Using the following sketch of two helium atoms, show how repulsive forces outnumber attractive forces to prevent two helium atoms from forming a helium molecule.

⊖	⊖
++	++
⊖	⊖
He atom	He atom

2 Sketch a molecule of each of the following elements, showing sigma- and pi-bond formation.

a. H_2 (one sigma bond)
b. O_2 (one sigma bond and one pi bond)
c. N_2 (one sigma bond and two pi bonds)

3 Why can you have only *one* sigma bond between two atoms in a molecule?

4 The compound benzene (C_6H_6) has the following structure. Show how the formation of sigma and pi bonds between the carbon atoms can account for that structure.

```
        H
        C
      //  \
    HC      CH
    |       ||
    HC      CH
      \\  /
        C
        H
```

REFERENCES

Bent, H. A. "Ion-Packing Models of Covalent Compounds." *Journal of Chemical Education*, 1968, p. 768.

Christian, J. D. "Strengths of Chemical Bonds." *Journal of Chemical Education*, 1973, p. 176.

Drago, R. S. "A Criticism of the Valence-Shell Electron-Pair Repulsion." *Journal of Chemical Education*, 1973, p. 244.

Holliday, Leslie. "Early Views on Forces Between Atoms." *Scientific American*, May 1970, p. 116.

Luder, W. F. "The Electron-Repulsion Theory of the Chemical Bond." *Journal of Chemical Education*, 1967, p. 206.

Wall, A. C. "Chemistry by Computer." *Scientific American*, April 1970, p. 54.

EXCURSION EIGHT

Polymers and Plastics

An important property of carbon is its ability to form chains and rings of carbon atoms. This results in millions of different organic chemicals. It also means that carbon can form giant supermolecules. In this excursion we will study these giant molecules, known as **polymers.**

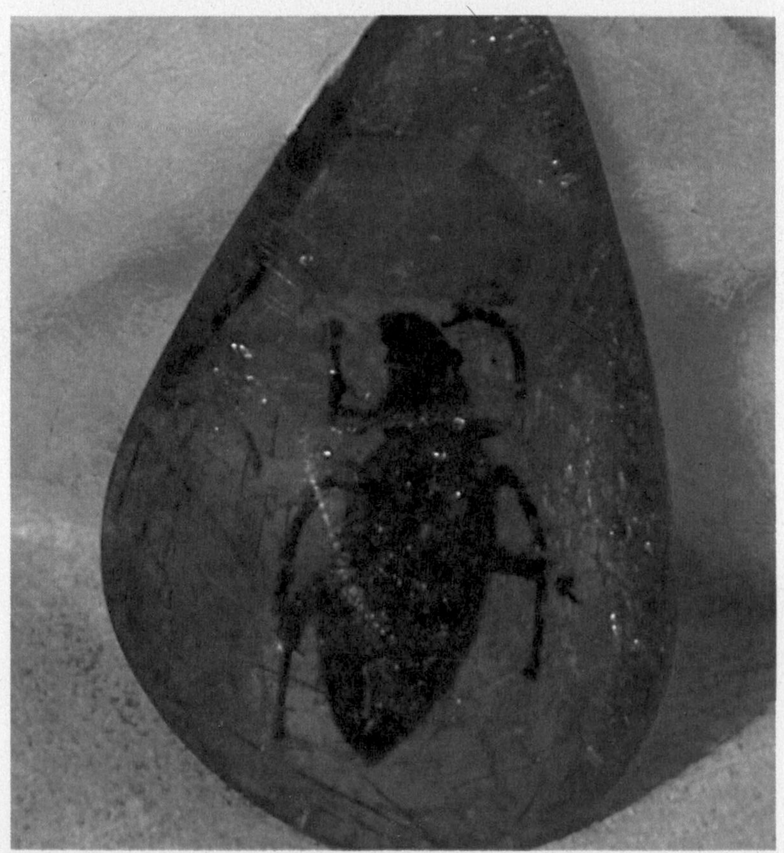

FIGURE E8–1 · *The insect in this picture is nearly 60 million years old. It was trapped in the sticky, natural resin (sap) produced by a coniferous tree. Eventually, organic molecules in the resin linked together, or polymerized. These giant molecules formed amber, which became a tomb for this fossil fly.*

MONOMERS

Polymer molecules consist of very large numbers of small molecular units linked together. These small units are called **monomers.** In some polymers, all the monomer units are identical. If the monomer units are not all alike, the substance is called a **copolymer.**

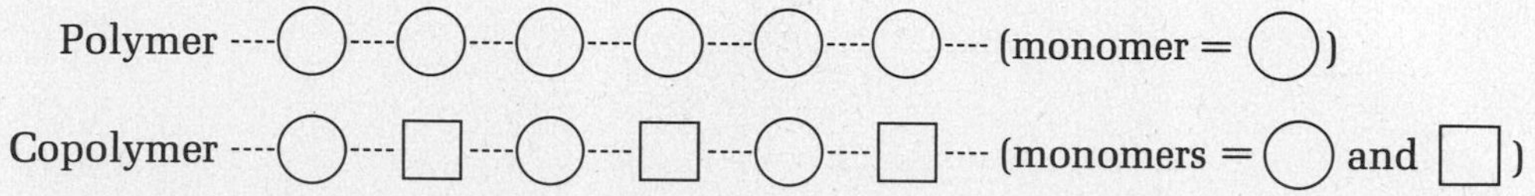

Polymer ----○----○----○----○----○----○---- (monomer = ○)

Copolymer ----○----□----○----□----○----□---- (monomers = ○ and □)

Polymers are common in nature. Since giant molecules are necessary to form strong structures, animal life depends on polymers. Our skin and other tissues, wool, leather, and hair are a few examples of animal polymers. Wood is mostly a polymer known as **cellulose.** Even the inorganic, mineral world needs the structural strength of polymers. However, in mountains and in clays, the polymer is not due to carbon chains as in living material. Instead of carbon, the mineral world depends on silicon to form its chains and rings.

ORGANIC POLYMERS

Let's briefly study the structure of some natural polymers. Cellulose is the structural material of plants.

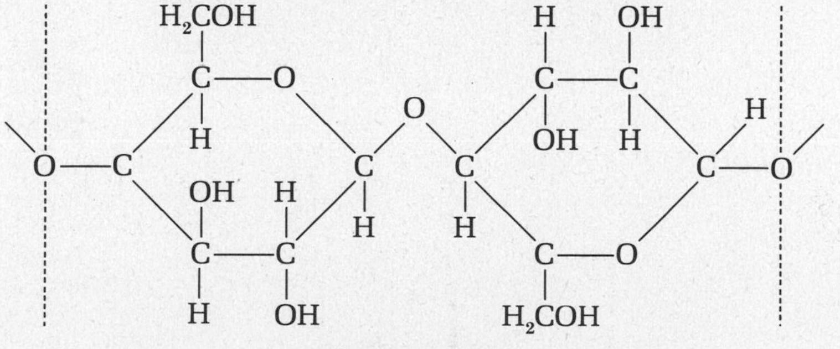

```
  :        H2COH                             H     OH          :
  :          |                               |     |           :
  :          C——O                            C——C              :
  :         /|    \            O            /|    |\        H  :
 \:       /  H      \        /   \        /  OH   H  \     /   :/
  O——C                 C            C                  C——O
  :     \   OH   H    /|            |\                /      :
  :       \ |    |  /  H            H  \            /        :
  :         C——C                         C——O                  :
  :         |    |                       |                     :
  :         H    OH                    H2COH                   :
```

Monomer unit

The polymer repeats this monomer pattern shown above in long chains. Starch is a polymer that is almost identical to cellulose except that some of the hydrogen atoms have a different orientation. Cotton is a polymer with cellulose structure,

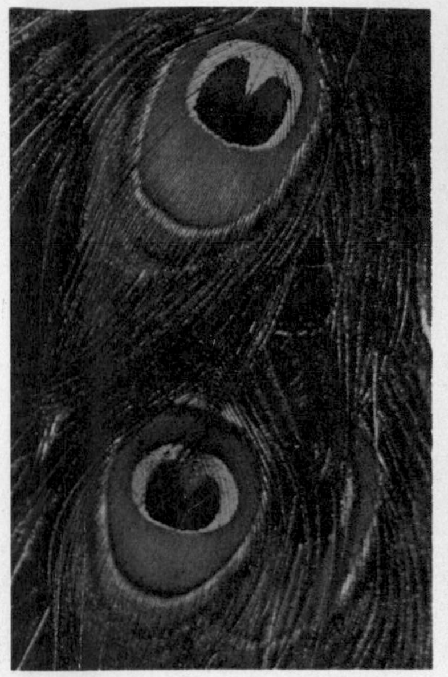

FIGURE E8–2 · *Keratin is an essential protein in animals. It accounts for the form and shape of many living organisms. Some examples of the structure and beauty created by keratin are the peacock's feathers and the toucan's beak. One example of fibroin, the basis of silk, is shown in the spider's web.*

as are the synthetic products rayon and cellophane. Acetate rayon is the cellulose polymer with an acetate, $—CH_2CO_2H$, added to each ring. Smokeless gunpowder is made of cellulose nitrate in which $—NO_3$ is always present on each ring.

Rubber is another natural polymer that has been important. Natural rubber has the following structure.

```
 ⎛—CH2         CH2—CH2          CH2—⎞
 ⎜     \      /       \        /    ⎟
 ⎜      C==C            C==C        ⎟
 ⎜     /    \          /    \       ⎟
 ⎝  CH3      H      CH3      H      ⎠m
```

In order to improve the ability of rubber to resume its shape after stretching, it is **vulcanized.** In vulcanization, sulfur is added to the rubber molecules. The sulfur atoms bond to carbon atoms in different chains by cross-links between the chains. These cross-links pull the chains back together after stretching.

```
          CH2—CH2             CH2
         /       \           /
     —C            C———————C
     / \          /|       |\
    H   S     H3C  S  CH3  H  S
       /           | /       /
     —C            C———————C
     / \          /         \
    H   CH2—CH2             CH3
```

Synthetic rubber has increasingly replaced natural rubber. The most common synthetic rubber is a copolymer of butadiene with styrene (SBR rubber). Synthetic rubber is cross-linked by vulcanization and is better and cheaper than natural rubber.

$$\underset{\text{Butadiene}}{H_2C{=}CH{-}CH{=}CH_2} + \underset{\text{Styrene}}{H_2C{=}CH{-}C_6H_5} \rightarrow \underset{\text{SBR rubber}}{\left(-CH_2{-}CH{=}CH{-}CH_2{-}CH_2{-}CH(C_6H_5)- \right)_m}$$

THE DISCOVERY OF SYNTHETIC POLYMERS

Although synthetic polymers are very much a part of everyday life, in the form of plastics, the plastics industry had a very slow beginning. Prior to 1868, synthetic changes in the structure of natural polymers were limited to a few processes such as the tanning of leather and the vulcanization of rubber. In 1868 an American printer, John Wesley Hyatt, was trying to develop a billiard ball that was not made of ivory. In his research, he treated pyroxylin with solid camphor. The result was Celluloid and the birth of the plastics industry.

The next advance was not made until 1909. In that year, Dr. Leo Hendrik Baekeland, a Belgian-born American, invented pheno-formaldehyde plastics. The first commercial phenolic was called Bakelite in Baekeland's honor. And it is still used today. From these beginnings, plastics have diversified into a whole range of types and uses.

THE STRUCTURE AND PROPERTIES OF POLYMERS

The properties of a polymer are a result of the structure and interaction of their molecular chains. Elasticity results because polymeric chains tend to slip past one another due to tension in the chain. The cross-linking between the chains keeps the chains from separating completely. Thus, cross-links limit the elasticity. The stronger are the hydrogen bonds (cross-links), the less is the elasticity. Natural rubber is quite elastic. But it is tacky and varies a great deal in elasticity due to temperature changes. As mentioned previously, heating natural rubber in the presence of sulfur forms sulfur bridges between the chains. This produces vulcanized rubber, which was discovered accidentally in 1839 by Charles Goodyear. Vulcanized rubber is less elastic but stronger and more easily molded than natural rubber.

As we mentioned, the stronger the hydrogen bond is, the less elasticity occurs. Many synthetic polymer fibers are cross-linked by strong hydrogen bonds. These bonds make the fibers strong but less elastic. However, it is possible to synthesize polymers that have cross-links in some regions and lack them in others. These are called "hard" and "soft" sections. The "hard" (cross-linked) sections make the fiber strong. The "soft" (non-cross-linked) sections give the fiber elasticity. Fibers containing these "hard" and "soft" sections are called **spandex fibers.** Their dual properties make them important in the clothing industry. Some examples of spandex fibers are Duraspan, Lycra, and Vyrene.

FIGURE E8–3 · *These rubber balls bounce to varying heights because they are composed of different polymers.*

POLYSTYRENE

As you learned earlier, styrene is used to form copolymers, as in synthetic rubber. Styrene also polymerizes itself to form a clear, colorless solid called **polystyrene.** This polymer is the plastic used in combs, toys, bowls, and other similar products. Styrene polymerization occurs when monomer styrene units attach to one another at the site of the double bonds.

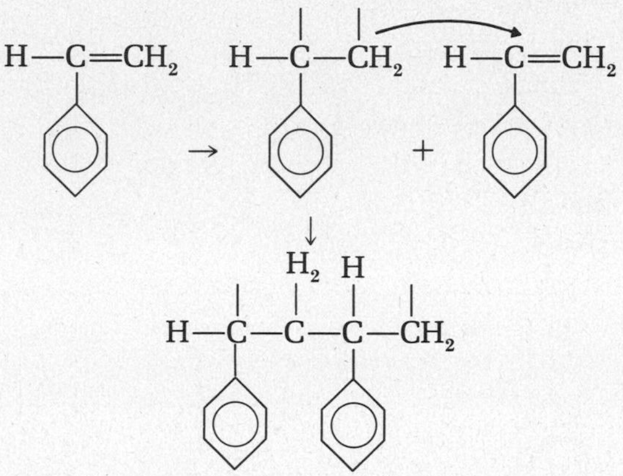

$$H{-}C{=}CH_2 \rightarrow H{-}\overset{|}{C}{-}\overset{|}{C}H_2 + H{-}C{=}CH_2$$

$$\downarrow$$

$$H{-}\overset{|}{C}{-}\overset{H_2}{\overset{|}{C}}{-}\overset{H}{\overset{|}{C}}{-}\overset{|}{C}H_2$$

Notice that when one styrene adds to another, the double bonds are broken but unused bonds are present.

(shown as $\overset{|}{C}$)

More styrene molecules add to these bonds. The process continues as the polymer forms a chain.

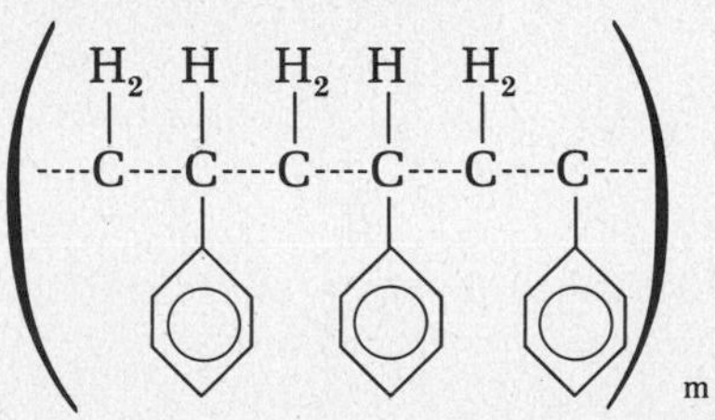

$$\left(\text{----}\overset{H_2}{\overset{|}{C}}\text{----}\overset{H}{\overset{|}{C}}\text{----}\overset{H_2}{\overset{|}{C}}\text{----}\overset{H}{\overset{|}{C}}\text{----}\overset{H_2}{\overset{|}{C}}\text{----}C\text{----} \right)_m$$

Polystyrene forms with chain lengths of 5500–6000 monomer units,

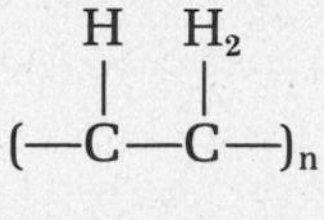

$$(\text{—}\overset{H}{\overset{|}{C}}\text{—}\overset{H_2}{\overset{|}{C}}\text{—})_n \text{ (where } n = 5500-6000\text{).}$$

One of the advantages of polystyrene is that it is a **thermoplastic.** Thermoplastic polymers can be melted and solidified,

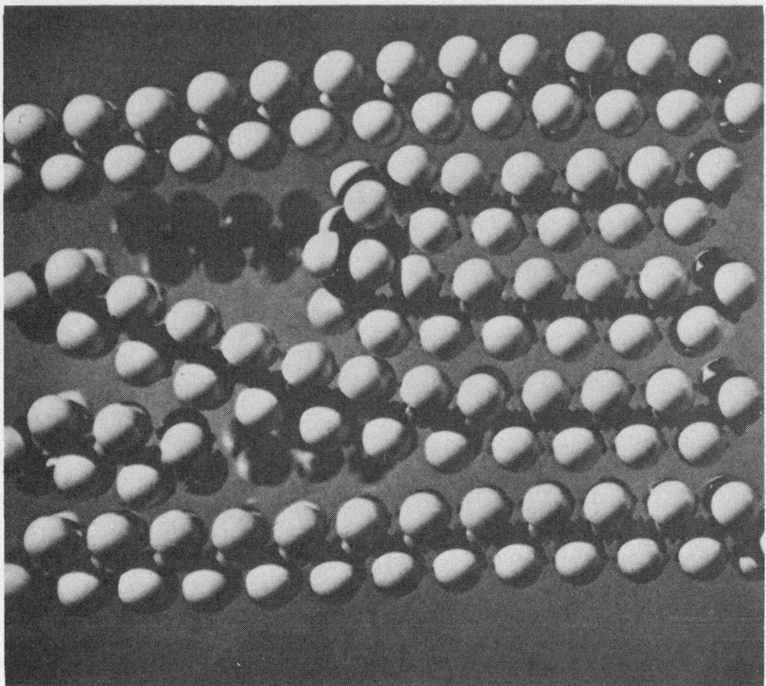

FIGURE E8–4 · *When ethylene molecules combine, they form chains of polyethylene. This formation of polyethylene is called polymerization. Note in this picture that almost no cross-linking or branching has occurred.*

then remelted. This process can be repeated over and over for thermoplastic polymers. However, **thermosetting plastics,** after hardening, cannot be remelted without being changed.

Polystyrene may be the most familiar plastic. It is most often found in the form of Styrofoam, which is used in ice chests, insulation, packing, and a variety of other uses.

Polystyrene is one example of a whole family of polymers. That family of polymers is related to the vinyl group,

$$\begin{array}{ccccc} & & H & & H \\ & & | & & | \\ R & — & C & = & C — H. \end{array}$$

In the general formula n may equal 100 000 or more.

$$\begin{array}{ccccc} & H & & R & \\ & | & & | & \\ (— & C & = & C & —)_n, \end{array}$$

The vinyl compounds polymerize, like styrene, through double bonds. Table E8–1 lists some of the vinyl polymers and their uses.

Vinyl plastic, actually called polyvinyl chloride or PVC, has replaced leather for upholstery. It is cheaper and wears as well as leather. Teflon is a very inert plastic. The fluoride atoms

TABLE E8–1 · Some Vinyl Polymers and Their Uses

MONOMER	POLYMER FORMULA	TRADE NAMES AND USES
$H_2C{=}CHCl$ vinyl chloride	$\left(-CH_2-CHCl-\right)_n$	Polyvinyl chloride (PVC), Geon (film, insulation, rainwear, floor tiles)
$H_2C{=}CH(C_6H_5)$ styrene	$\left(-CH_2-CH(C_6H_5)-\right)_n$	Polystyrene, Styrofoam (foam, molded articles)
$H_2C{=}CH-O-C(=O)-CH_3$ vinyl acetate	$\left(-CH_2-CH(O-C(=O)-CH_3)-\right)_n$	Polyvinyl acetate (PVA) (adhesives, latex paint, chewing gum)
$H_2C{=}CH-C{\equiv}N$ acrylonitrile	$\left(-CH_2-CH(C{\equiv}N)-\right)_n$	Acrilan, Orlon (fibers, rugs. clothing
$H_2C{=}CH-CH_3$ propene	$\left(-CH_2-CH(CH_3)-\right)_n$	Polypropylene, Polyolefin (fibers, molded articles, outdoor carpeting)
$F_2C{=}CF_2$ tetrafluoroethene	$\left(-CF_2-CF_2-\right)_n$	Teflon (nonstick coatings, bearings, gaskets)
$H_2C{=}C(CH_3)-C(=O)-O-CH_3$ methyl methacrylate	$\left(-CH_2-C(CH_3)(C(=O)-O-CH_3)-\right)_n$	Lucite, Plexiglas (transparent molded articles, windows, lamp globes)

in teflon make the polymer very inactive, because the C—F bonds are so strong. Lucite and plexiglass are thermoplastic polymers. Their chains have bulky groups attached to them. When the plastic is heated, the chains can slip and move with some freedom and we can bend the rod or sheet of plastic. However, when the plastic cools, the chains lose their freedom to slip around. There is not enough energy to let the bulky groups squeeze past one another. So the plastic keeps the new shape. We mentioned heating these plastics to shape and mold them. However, it should be noted that burning vinyl products should be done with extreme caution. The products of the decomposition of vinyl can be very dangerous.

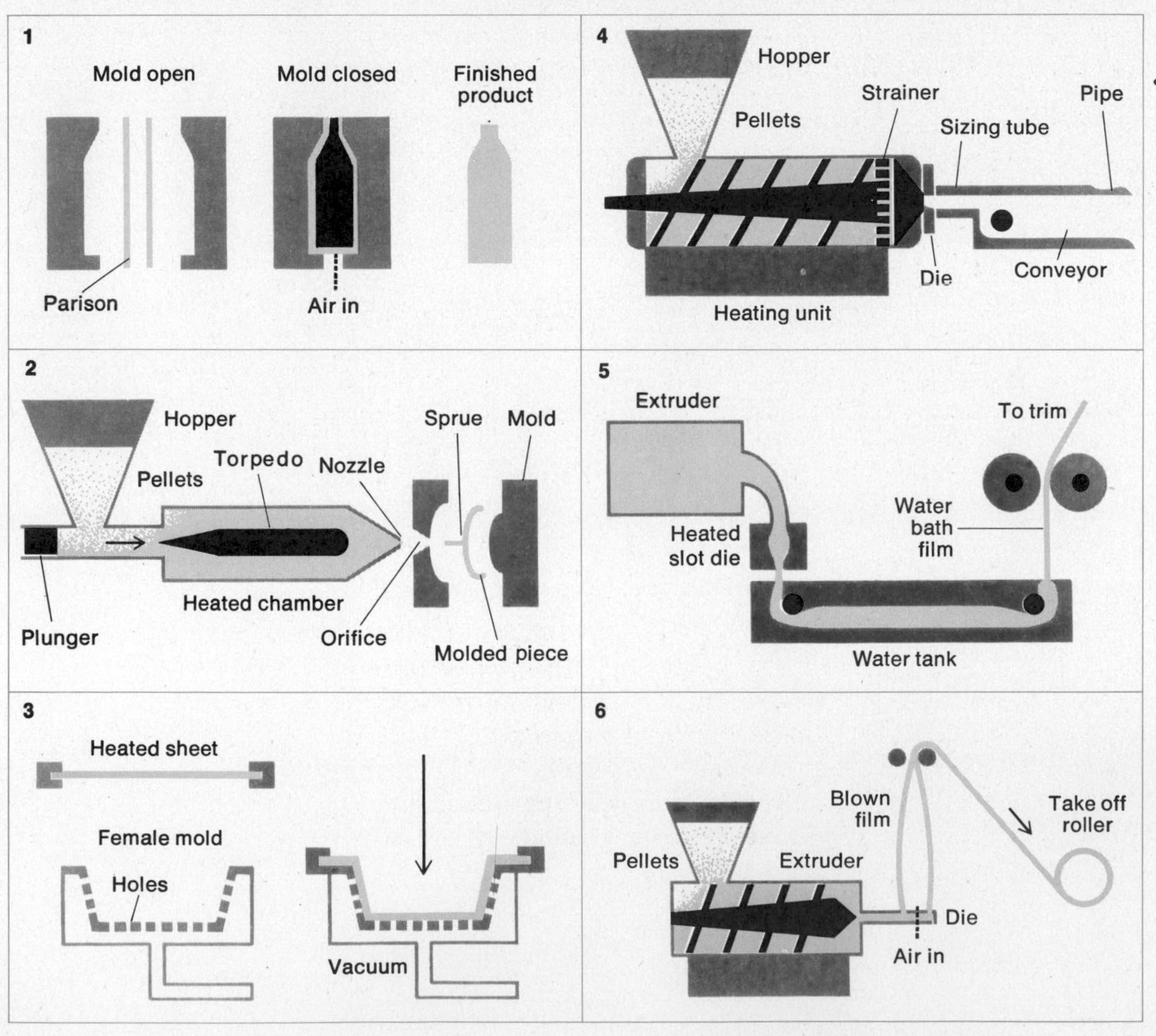

FIGURE E8–5 · *Methods of forming plastics are shown here. (1) Blow-molding—a heated plastic tube is enclosed in a mold and inflated. (2) Injection molding—raw pellets are heated and then forced into a cool mold. (3) Thermo-forming—heated plastic sheets are pulled against a mold. (4, 5, and 6) Extrusion process—molten plastic is fed through a die of some desired shape.*

NYLON AND DACRON

Some vinyl polymers are examples of **addition polymers,** in which monomer units *add* to each other. A second class of vinyl polymers are known as **condensation polymers.** Condensation polymers are formed by the reaction of monomer units with the elimination of water. Nylon is a condensation polymer. Nylon was discovered in 1930 by Dr. Wallace Hume Carothers. It was the first synthetic polymer derived from simple chemicals that could be spun into yarn. The discovery of other synthetic fibers followed. Those synthetic polymers have changed the clothing industry all over the world.

There is actually a family of nylons. One member of that family is Nylon-66, which is formed from adipic acid and hexamethylenediamine.

$$\underset{\text{Adipic acid}}{HO-\overset{O}{\overset{\|}{C}}-(CH_2)_4-\overset{O}{\overset{\|}{C}}-OH} + \underset{\text{Hexamethylenediamine}}{H_2N-(CH_2)_6-NH_2}$$

$$\downarrow$$

$$-\overset{O}{\overset{\|}{C}}-(CH_2)_4-\overset{O}{\overset{\|}{C}}-\underset{H}{\underset{|}{N}}-(CH_2)_6-\underset{H}{\underset{|}{N}}-\overset{O}{\overset{\|}{C}}-(CH_2)_4-\overset{O}{\overset{\|}{C}}-\underset{H}{\underset{|}{N}}-(CH_2)_6- + \text{water}$$

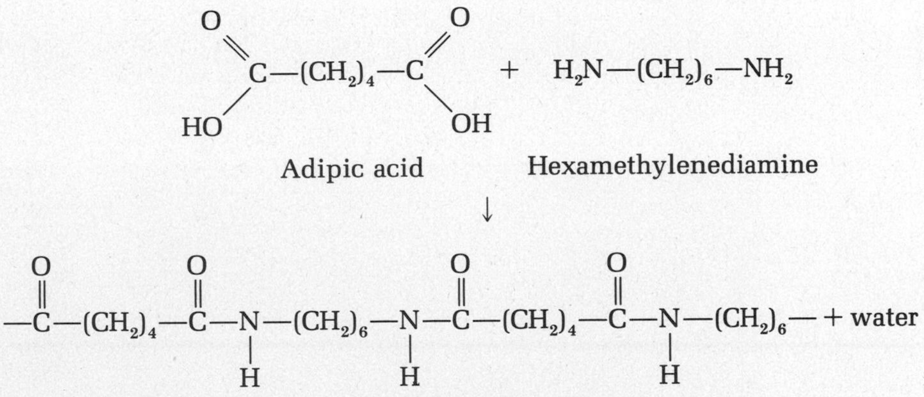

Nylon-66

Nylon is very strong. A nylon rope that has a 10-cm diameter can hold a 5000-kg load without breaking. The strength of nylon is due to hydrogen bond formation between the chains. Hydrogen bonds are strong enough to keep the chains together. But their strength does not make the nylon rigid.

Nylon is a polyamide, since it is formed by the reaction of carboxylic acid and an amine. Such a reaction forms an amide, a compound with a group.

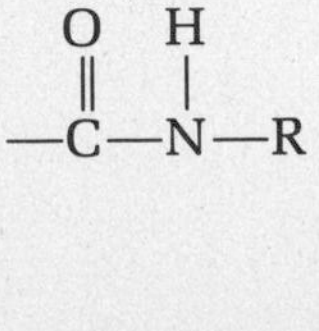

$$-\overset{O}{\overset{\|}{C}}-\overset{H}{\overset{|}{N}}-R$$

If the polymer is formed by condensation of an alcohol and an ester, a polyester is formed. Such compounds have the ester group.

$$\overset{\displaystyle O}{\overset{\|}{\text{—C}}}\text{—O—R.}$$

A very useful polyester polymer is obtained by condensing terephthalic acid and the ethylene glycol as follows.

$$\underset{\text{Terephthalic acid}}{\text{H—O—}\overset{\displaystyle O}{\overset{\|}{\text{C}}}\text{—}C_6H_4\text{—}\overset{\displaystyle O}{\overset{\|}{\text{C}}}\text{—OH}} + \underset{\text{Ethylene glycol}}{\text{H—O—}\overset{H_2}{\overset{|}{\text{C}}}\text{—}\overset{H_2}{\overset{|}{\text{C}}}\text{—OH}} \rightarrow$$

$$\underset{\text{Polyethyleneterephthalate}}{\text{—}\overset{H_2}{\overset{|}{\text{C}}}\text{—}\overset{O}{\overset{\|}{\text{C}}}\text{—}C_6H_4\text{—}\overset{O}{\overset{\|}{\text{C}}}\text{—O—}\overset{H_2}{\overset{|}{\text{C}}}\text{—}\overset{H_2}{\overset{|}{\text{C}}}\text{—O—}\overset{O}{\overset{\|}{\text{C}}}\text{—}C_6H_4\text{—}\overset{O}{\overset{\|}{\text{C}}}\text{—O—}\overset{H}{\overset{|}{\text{C}}}}$$

When this polymer is made into fibers it is called Dacron. But as a film rather than fibers, it is called Mylar.

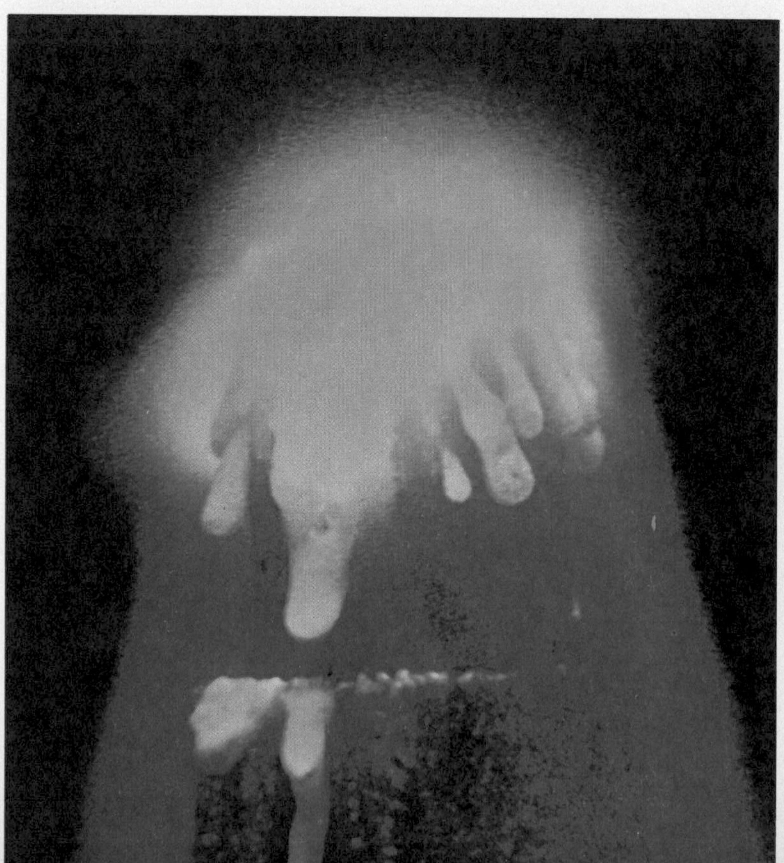

FIGURE E8–6 · *This is a photograph of a plastic nose cone designed for a space vehicle. The melting of the plastic protects the interior of the vehicle from the heat of re-entry.*

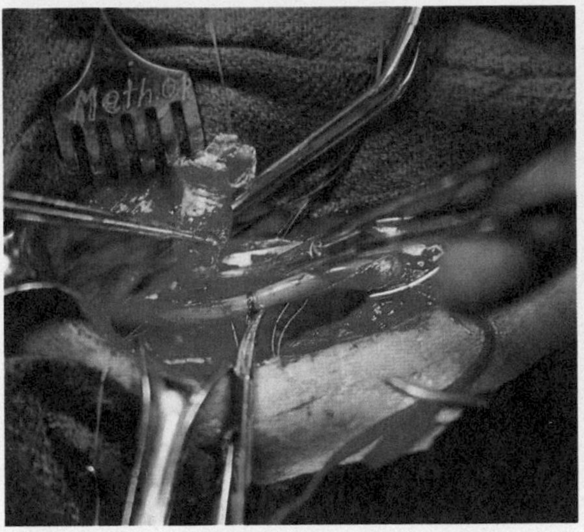

FIGURE E8–7 · *A plastic blood shunt (left) and Dacron patch (right) are used during an operation to remove fatty deposits from an artery wall.*

INORGANIC POLYMERS

The basic monomer unit of the inorganic polymers in nature is the anionic group SiO_4^{-2}. This group has a tetrahedral structure around the silicon atom.

Si

Polymers are formed by joining such tetrahedra at two corners of each to form negatively charged chains.

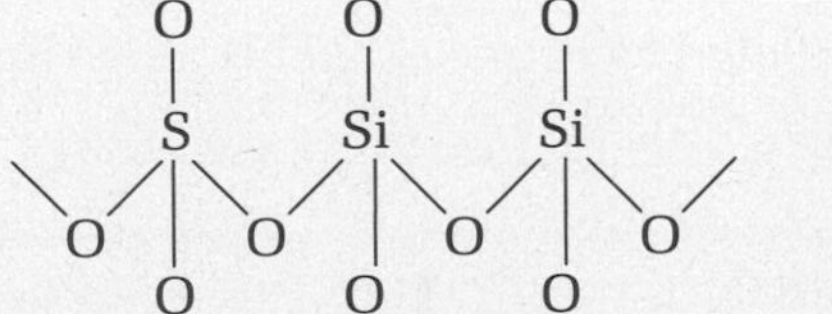

Silicate chain

Asbestos minerals used in fireproof insulation are composed of polymeric silicate chains. The chains have the general formula $(SiO_3)_n^{-2n}$ or $(Si_4O_{11})_n^{-6n}$. In asbestos, magnesium cations serve to neutralize the charge and hold the chains together in the fibers.

If a polymer has a structure in which each tetrahedron shares three oxygens, a two-dimensional sheet is formed. Mica and clays are examples of sheet silicates. Again, cations such as Al^{+3}, Fe^{+3}, Ca^{+2}, and Na^{+1} hold the negatively charged sheets together.

If all four oxygens of the SiO_4 tetrahedra are shared with other tetrahedra, the result is a three-dimensional network. Quartz and the feldspar minerals, which compose approximately 66% of the igneous rocks on the earth, are network silicates.

SILICONES

As with the organic polymers, chemists have learned to imitate the inorganic polymers in nature. They have synthesized new silicon polymers with useful properties. The backbone of organic polymers is a chain of C—C bonds. The silicon polymers, called **silicones,** have a backbone of Si—O—Si bonds. The general formula is as follows.

```
     O   R   O   R   O   R
   /   \ | /   \ | /   \ | /
        Si      Si      Si
        |       |       |
        R       R       R
```

The R groups in such chains are usually organic groups such as CH_3. Depending on the length of the —Si—O—Si chain, the silicones can be oils, greases, waxes, or solids. Silly Putty is a mixture of silicone and chalk.

The silicones can be cross-linked to form silicone rubbers. Silicone rubbers are used as sealants and gaskets in spacecraft, and in many other places where their resistance to extremes of temperature is valuable.

PROBLEMS WITH POLYMERS

As a result of technological progress in the polymer field, new and useful synthetics are continuously being discovered. Using the natural materials of the earth, millions of kilograms of plastics, fibers, and synthetic rubber are made each year. From clothing to housing, from medicine to space programs, synthetic polymers are adding to life. In every aspect of daily living we use plastics because they are better and cheaper than their natural counterparts. However, with every benefit, there is usually a problem. So it is with plastics. For example, since plastics are fairly inexpensive, we tend to use them once and then discard them. As a result, the volume of waste has increased enormously. The United States produces approximately 5 million kg of plastic waste each year. Some of this waste can be burned. But burning plastics can cause problems, too, as we mentioned earlier. For example, polyvinyl chloride (PVC) releases HCl when it burns. This HCl combines with water in the air or ground to form the very corrosive acid called hydrochloric acid. Also, small amounts of the deadly gas phosgene can form when PVC is burned. Burning Acrilan and Dacron can release the deadly gas HCN.

If we do not burn the polymer waste or reprocess it for reuse, it will be around a very long time. Most synthetic polymers are not biodegradable. They are not destroyed by nature. Chemists are trying to produce plastics that will degrade over a fairly short period of time. One approach is to make the plastics **photodegradable.** This type of plastic would be modified so that the energy from sunlight would cause them to fall apart. We must be successful in reprocessing most of the waste. Otherwise, imagine what the world will be like in a hundred years if we continue to make tens of millions of kilograms of nondegradable plastic waste each year!

REVIEW QUESTIONS

1 What is meant by the following terms?
   a. Vinyls
   b. Polymerization
   c. Vulcanized rubber
   d. Spandex fibers
   e. Polyester
   f. Copolymer

2 List some logical solutions for the pollution problems caused by synthetic polymers and their disposal.

REFERENCES

Bundy, F. P. "Superheated Materials." *Scientific American*, August 1974, p. 62–70.

Frazer, A. H. "High Temperature Plastics." *Scientific American*, July 1969, p. 96–100.

Mark, H. F. "The Nature of Polymeric Material." *Scientific American*, September 1967, p. 149–156.

Morton, M. "Polymers: Ten Years Later." *Chemistry*, October 1974, p. 11–14.

EXCURSION NINE

Thermodynamics, Progress, and Pollution

Thermodynamics, the science of energy, is important in every aspect of our lives, our physical world, even our universe. Thermodynamics was originally developed to aid in calculating the heat exchange in engines. However, in the second half of the nineteenth century, the principles of thermodynamics began to be applied to a broad spectrum of chemical and physical phenomena. Today, it is an indispensable tool of the scientist in every field. Although it has become one of the fundamental means of studying and describing nature from neutrinos (uncharged particles of zero mass) to neutron stars, all thermodynamics is based on only three laws. The three laws of thermodynamics are stated as follows.

1. *Energy can be neither created nor destroyed in a chemical change.*
2. *All systems tend to go to states of increased randomness.*
3. *In a crystal, a state of perfect order can exist only at absolute zero temperature.*

THE FIRST LAW: ENERGY CYCLES

The first law of thermodynamics is the Law of the Conservation of Energy. The Law of the Conservation of Energy states that the sum of matter and energy remains constant in a nuclear reaction. In a chemical reaction, within our ability to measure the mass and energy changes, we can state that the energy remains constant. The Law of the Conservation of Energy is also the basis of Hess's Law. For example, steam can be reduced by carbon as shown at the top of the next page.

$$H_2O(g) + C(s) \rightleftharpoons CO(g) + H_2(g)$$

To obtain the net equation above, we must write the equation for the formation of each compound. Then we add or subtract the equations to obtain a net equation.

$$2H_2(g) + O_2(g) = 2H_2O(g) \quad ; \quad \Delta H = 2 \times -57.8 \text{ kcal/mol}$$
$$2C + O_2 \rightleftharpoons 2CO \quad ; \quad \Delta H = 2 \times -26.4 \text{ kcal/mol}$$

$$2C + O_2 + 2H_2 + O_2 \rightleftharpoons 2CO + 2H_2O \quad ; \quad \Delta H = [-52.8] - [-115.6] \text{ kcal/mol}$$
$$2C + 2H_2O = 2CO + 2H_2 \quad ; \quad \Delta H = +62.8 \text{ kcal/mol}$$
$$C(g) + H_2O(g) = CO(g) + H_2(g) \quad ; \quad \Delta H = +31.4 \text{ kcal/mol}$$

We can expand the technique of Hess to energy cycles to calculate energies that cannot be measured directly. Suppose you wish to calculate the energy of interaction of Na^+ and Cl^- ions in crystalline NaCl. First, we devise a cycle in which we can use known energies for all but one section of the cycle. The interaction energy is called the **lattice energy,** denoted by $-\Delta H_l$. The lattice energy corresponds to the energy of separating Na^+ and Cl^- from the crystal into a gaseous state.

a. $NaCl(s) \rightleftharpoons Na^+(g) + Cl^-(g); -\Delta H_l = ?$

We know the enthalpy of solution of NaCl(s).

b. $NaCl(s) \rightleftharpoons Na^+(aq) + Cl^-(aq); \Delta H_s = -1.00$ kcal/mol

We can also find tables of hydration energies, ΔH_h, for the following reactions.

c. $Na^+(g) \rightarrow Na^+(aq); \Delta H_h(Na^+) = -95.0$ kcal/mol

d. $Cl^-(g) \rightarrow Cl^-(aq); \Delta H_h(Cl^-) = -90.0$ kcal/mol

If we subtract Step c and Step d from Step b, we have the following.

$$[-1] - [-95 + (-90)] = 184 \text{ kcal/mol}$$

So the lattice energy is 184 kcal/mol, or the amount of energy required to separate a mole of NaCl(s) into $Na^+(g)$ and $Cl^-(g)$.

That can be written in briefer fashion.

$$\begin{array}{ccccc} NaCl(s) & \xrightarrow{-\Delta H_l} & Na^+(g) & + & Cl^-(g) \\ & \searrow^{\Delta H_s} & \downarrow \Delta H_h(Na^+) & & \downarrow \Delta H_h(Cl^-) \\ & & Na^+(aq) & + & Cl^-(aq) \end{array}$$

This shorthand system is the reason that these reactions are called energy cycles.

The enthalpy of solution of $MgCl_2(s)$ is -55.0 kcal/mol; $\Delta H_h(Mg^{+2})$ is -456 kcal/mol.

$$\begin{array}{ccc} MgCl_2(s) & \xrightarrow{-\Delta H_l} & Mg^{+2}(g) \quad + 2\ Cl^-(g) \\ & \searrow^{\Delta H_s} & \downarrow \Delta H_h(Mg^{+2}) \quad \downarrow 2\Delta H_h(Cl^-) \\ & & Mg^{+2}(aq) + 2\ Cl^-(aq) \end{array}$$

Using the previous cycle, we calculate a value of 58.0 kcal/mol for $MgCl_2$. That is quite a bit larger than the value of NaCl, which is not surprising, as we expect a much stronger attraction between the dipositive Mg^{+2} ions and Cl^- than between unipositive Na^+ ions and Cl^-.

THE SECOND LAW: ENTROPY

The second law of thermodynamics was discussed briefly in Chapter 14, in which the concept of entropy was introduced. Entropy is a very fundamental concept, as it explains among other things the efficiency of energy conversion, the inevitability of pollution, the amount of useful work we can get from a chemical reaction, and the ultimate fate of the universe.

FIGURE E9–1 · *Animals such as these North American bighorn sheep will gather very closely in small groups near the warmest object they can find on a cold day. In this way, they transfer heat from one to another.*

As the second law states, all systems spontaneously become more random. If we wish to reverse that tendency and make a system more ordered, we must use energy to do so. We all know that heat flows spontaneously from a hot to a cold body. For example, a cold object warms to room temperature if it is left alone. A colder object never gets colder spontaneously in a warm room. However, in a refrigerator, we reverse the spontaneous process and lower the temperature. The reversal of the natural process costs energy—the electrical energy needed to run the refrigerator.

FREE ENERGY

In the Apollo spacecraft, $H_2(g)$ and $O_2(g)$ combined to form $H_2O(l)$ in an electrochemical battery. That battery provided both electrical energy for the spacecraft and drinking water for the astronauts. For the following reaction, the enthalpy of reaction, ΔH, is −68.3 kcal/mol.

$$2H_2(g) + O_2(g) = 2H_2O(l)$$

However, the maximum amount of electrical energy that can be obtained is −56.7 kcal/mol. The latter quantity—the maximum amount of energy that can be used to do mechanical, electrical, or some other form of work—defines for us the usefulness of any chemical system for doing work. It is the amount of the total energy, (the enthalpy), that is free for us to use. As a result, it is called the *free energy* and given the symbol G. The free-energy change in the $2H_2 + O_2 = 2H_2O$ reaction is −56.7 kcal/mol. The difference between the enthalpy change and the free-energy change of any reaction is the energy required to overcome the tendency to go to a state of disorder.

$$\Delta H - \Delta G = \text{Organization energy}$$

We have already associated entropy with the tendency to disorder. In Chapter 14, we also learned that the entropy change, ΔS, increases with temperature. So we can relate the organization energy with the temperature × entropy change.

$$\text{Organization energy} = \text{T}\Delta S$$

or

$$\Delta H - \Delta G = \text{T}\Delta S$$

$$\text{Total energy} - \text{Free energy} = \text{Organization energy}$$

More commonly, the relationship is written to give us the value of ΔG.

$$\Delta G = \Delta H - T\Delta S$$

Free energy = Total energy − Entropy energy

FREE ENERGY AND SPONTANEOUS REACTIONS

The equation above tells us which chemical reactions occur spontaneously—those with negative values of ΔG. The free-energy change is related to the equilibrium constant by the following equation.

$$\Delta G = -1.36 \log K$$

(where K is the equilibrium constant)

If $K > 1$, ΔG is negative, and the reaction can occur spontaneously. If $K < 1$, ΔG is positive, and the reverse reaction is the spontaneous direction for the system.

At equilibrium, there is no tendency toward further change. Since ΔG is the measure of the tendency to change, ΔG must equal zero at equilibrium.

$$\Delta H = T\Delta S$$

Let us calculate the entropy change for melting and for boiling. At 0°C, ice and water are in equilibrium.

$$T\Delta S_{(\text{melting})} = \Delta H_{(\text{melting})}$$

$$\Delta S_{(\text{melting})} = \frac{(80.0 \text{ kcal/g})(18.0 \text{ g})}{298°}$$

$$\Delta S_{(\text{melting})} = 4.80 \text{ kcal/mol/deg}$$

At 100°C, water and steam are in equilibrium.

$$T\Delta S_{(\text{boiling})} = \Delta H_{(\text{boiling})}$$

$$\Delta S_{(\text{boiling})} = \frac{(540 \text{ kcal/g})(18.0 \text{ g})}{298°}$$

$$\Delta S_{(\text{boiling})} = 32.6 \text{ kcal/mol/deg}$$

To go from the slightly disordered state of liquid water to the very disordered state of gaseous water involves about seven times as large an entropy change as to go from highly ordered ice to slightly disordered water.

THE SECOND LAW RESTATED

We can express the first law of thermodynamics in less scientific terms, *You can't win*. Since energy cannot be created, you can never increase the total amount of energy. So we cannot have a perpetual motion machine that, once started with the use of a certain amount of energy, will keep running without the addition of further energy.

In a similar way, we can restate the second law, *You can't break even*. Because of the natural tendency to increase entropy in any process, some energy is always degraded to "useless" energy. That means we cannot even have perpetual motion machines of a second type—that is, machines that produce work equal to the amount of energy put into the machine.

ENTROPY AND POLLUTION

The largest part of our electrical power comes from power plants in which heat from burning coal, gas, or oil is converted to electricity. This process is limited in its efficiency by the second law of thermodynamics by the following equation.

$$\text{Efficiency} = \frac{T_2 - T_1}{T_2} \times 100\%$$

FIGURE E9–2 · *Electrical energy is produced in power plants. Transformers transmit energy through power lines, such as those shown here.*

T_2 is the higher temperature of the hot water or gas released from burning the fuel. T_1 is the lower temperature to which the water or gas is cooled as it drives the dynamos of the power plant. Suppose a plant is designed to operate at an upper temperature of 900 K and a lower temperature of 300 K. Its maximum efficiency in converting the heat released from burning the fuel into electrical energy is as follows.

$$\text{Efficiency} = \frac{900 - 300}{900} \times 100\% = 67\%$$

It is unavoidable that the remaining heat energy will be lost to the environment as thermal pollution. There is no way to overcome the second law of thermodynamics. Even in the best designed, most efficient power plant, a portion of the heat produced cannot be converted to electricity. So there is quite simply no way to avoid thermal pollution in the production of electrical power.

Present fossil fuel plants operate at 60–65 percent efficiency. Nuclear power plants operate at a lower efficiency—about 45 percent. The higher temperature of a nuclear power plant is kept lower than that in a fossil fuel plant in order to provide an extra margin of operating safety. Consequently, the present nuclear plants produce more thermal pollution than do fossil fuel stations.

FIGURE E9–3 · *The steam produced as the hot water waste being eliminated enters the colder pond water is evidence that this plant is causing thermal pollution.*

THE SECOND LAW AND LIFE

Biological life represents very highly organized systems. Thus, evolution seems to be a violation of the second law of thermodynamics. In life, we have a constant reversal of entropy as simple foods are synthesized into more complex biological structures.

Entropy can be decreased, but only by the expenditure of energy. Life is a high-energy process, because of the need to overcome the natural tendency to disorder. Because we are alive, our awareness of life sometimes leads us to ignore how small a fraction of the matter in the world is involved in life. Only about one billionth of the mass of the earth is part of living organisms. Since life in our solar system seems restricted, at least to any significant level of abundance, to the earth, the percentage of living matter in the solar system is extremely minute, 10^{-13} percent. So perhaps we can view life as an improbable event that occurs. Even improbable events can occur, but only to a small degree. Drawing four aces in a poker hand is an improbable event, but it does occur if you play enough poker. However, even when an improbable event occurs, the second law is, in fact, still obeyed. Energy is used to reverse the natural tendency toward increased disorder.

THE THIRD LAW

We can restate the third law of thermodynamics in the following words, *Nothing is perfect*. Remember, the third law states that crystals have perfect order only at absolute zero temperature. The law includes all substances, as we expect everything to be crystalline at absolute zero. However, absolute zero temperature is an unobtainable goal. We can get closer and closer to absolute zero, but we can never get exactly to it. Temperatures as low as 10^{-7} K have been reached, but that is still not absolute zero. So no perfectly ordered crystals have been made. Everything in the world has some disorder—entropy.

Again, as with the first and second laws, our lives are affected daily by the third law. Every time you use your television, radio, a small calculator, or almost any other manufactured product, you are using directly or indirectly the product of our transistorized technology. Transistors, which have had perhaps the greatest technological impact of any new development in the last fifty years, are crystals whose very slight imperfections give them the property of *semiconductivity*. Semiconductivity is a direct consequence of the natural small imperfections in crystals of silicon, germanium, or other substances.

REVIEW QUESTIONS

1 Express in your own words the three laws of thermodynamics.
2 Define *entropy* and *enthalpy*.
3 Why is *G* refered to as "free energy"?
4 How is free energy related to organization energy?
5 What does entropy have to do with pollution?

REFERENCES

Bent, Henry. "The First Law: For Scientists, Citizens, Poets and Philosophers." *Journal of Chemical Education*. May 1973, p. 323.

Brown, S. C. *Count Rumford: Physicist Extraordinary*. Garden City, New York: Anchor Books, Doubleday & Co., Inc., 1962.

Clark, J. R. "Thermal Pollution and Aquatic Life." *Scientific American*. March 1969, p. 18.

Fowler, J. M. "Entering a New Energy Age." *The Science Teacher*. October 1975, p. 32.

Hutchinson, G. E. "The Biosphere." *Scientific American*. September 1970, p. 44.

Rogers, Donald W. "An Informal History of the First Law of Thermodynamics." *Chemistry*. December 1976, p. 11.

Starr, C. "Energy and Power." *Scientific American*. September 1971, p. 36.

EXCURSION TEN

How Do Reactions Go?

In Chapter 15, we discussed the fact that an increase of about 10.0°C doubles the reaction rate. We also learned that the rate of a reaction is proportional to the concentration of the reactants. For the general reaction $A + B = C + D$, the rate equation is expressed as the following.

$$\text{Rate } \alpha[A][B]$$

To make the equation an equality, a proportionality constant, k, must be included.

$$\text{Rate} = k[A][B]$$

The proportionality constant k is called the **reaction-rate constant.**

TEMPERATURE EFFECT ON REACTION RATE

The Swedish chemist Svante Arrhenius found that he could relate the effect of temperature and the reaction rate by the following expression.

$$\log k \; 1/T$$

When constants are included in the expression, it can be written as follows.

$$k = Ae^{-B/T}$$

T is the absolute temperature. The constant k is the reaction-rate constant. A and B are constants, and e is 2.7183 – the base number for natural logarithms. The equation describes the experimental relationship between k and T.

The constant B is usually associated with the energy barrier. The Arrhenius equation is frequently written as follows.

$$k = Ae^{-E_a/RT}$$

E_a is equal to ΔH_a. R is the universal gas law constant. Note that $PV = RT$, which relates temperature to energy units.

COLLISION THEORY OF REACTION RATES

In Chapter 15, we discovered that molecules must collide to react. Since Arrhenius's equation fits the experimental data so well, chemists have developed a theory involving collisions, which also results in an equation like that of Arrhenius's.

The first step in the theory is the assumption that molecules must collide to react. The number of collisions per second multiplied by the fraction of the collisions that result in a reaction is equal to the reaction rate. The number of collisions depends on the concentration of the reactants, the average diameter of the molecules of each reactant, the mass of the molecules, and the temperature of the reactants. This number, Z_{12} (the collision rate of molecules 1 and 2), can be calculated using the kinetic theory of gases.

To calculate the fraction of the collisions that result in a reaction, we must make two assumptions.

1. The energy of the collision must be greater than the activation energy, E_a.
2. Only the translational kinetic energy of the reactant molecules is considered in calculating the energy of collision.

In Chapter 15, we pointed out that the number of molecules with enough collisional energy to exceed E_a is related to the kinetic energy distribution (Figure 15–3). In that case, the fraction of reactant molecules with a kinetic energy greater than E_a can be calculated as follows.

$$\text{Fraction} = e^{-E_a/RT}$$

Now we can write the reaction-rate expression.

$$\text{Reaction rate} = \text{Collision rate} \times \begin{matrix}\text{Fraction of collisions}\\ \text{with } KE > E_a\end{matrix}$$

or

$$k = Z_{12} \times e^{-E_a/RT}$$

When the theory is tested in the laboratory, it is found that the experimental rates are very often much smaller than the equation predicts. To correct the theory, a third factor is included in the reaction rate. Unless molecules have the proper orientation in a collision, a reaction does not occur even with enough energy. The symbol *p* is used for the steric effect. The rate equation reads as follows.

Rate constant = Collision rate × Steric factor × Energy factor

or $$k = Z_{12} \times p \times e^{-E_a/RT}$$

At present, *p* cannot be calculated theoretically and is simply used as a correction to give agreement between theory and experiment.

THE TRANSITION STATE THEORY

The collision theory has been further developed by assuming that in a collision, a new species is formed temporarily, which then dissociates into the products. The reaction sequence would be as follows.

$$A + B \rightarrow AB \rightarrow C + D$$

The species AB contains the collisional energy as a high-energy intermediate. It is known as the **activated complex,** or the **transition state.**

The model of a chemical reaction in which there is an intermediate step, or the formation of an activated complex, is quite reasonable. When molecules collide, there must be a rearrangement of atoms to form new chemical bonds if products are to form from the reactants. Such rearrangement occurs in an activated complex. Both H_2Cl and HCl_2 represent activated complexes in the chain mechanism that forms HCl from H_2 and Cl_2. Since the activated-complex idea was first suggested, many such complexes have been observed. They are so short-lived, however, that direct observation is not possible in most reactions.

The activated-complex concept allows us to find a relationship between the thermodynamic and the kinetic properties of a reaction system. The key to such a relationship is that the enthalpy of activation, ΔH_a, is always endothermic. On the other hand, the enthalpy of the decomposition of the activated complex, ΔH_d, is always exothermic. The net enthalpy of the reaction, ΔH_r, is determined, therefore, by the difference between ΔH_a and ΔH_d.

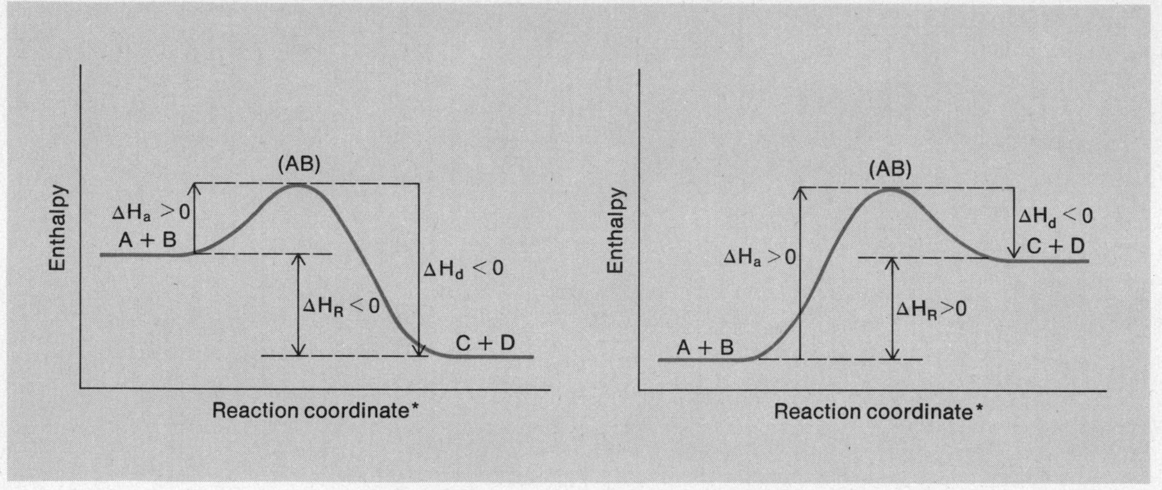

FIGURE E10–1 · *Enthalpy profile for an exothermic reaction (left); enthalpy profile for an endothermic reaction (right)*

Suppose the formation of the activated complex is treated as a normal reaction.

$$A + B = (AB)$$

Then the free energy of the formation of AB(ΔG_a), its enthalpy (ΔH_a), and the entropy (ΔS_a) are related as follows.

$$\Delta G_a = \Delta H_a - T\Delta S_a$$

ΔH_a is the enthalpy change representing the energy barrier to the reaction—E_a in the Arrhenius equation. ΔS is related to the configuration effect, or steric factor, *p*. A decrease in entropy means that the entropy of AB is less than that of the reactants. In that situation, the transition state represents a more organized situation than that associated with the separate reactants. If ΔS_a is positive, the activated complex must be loosely bonded compared with the reactants.

The relationships for the sequence A + B → AB → C + D are as follows.

$$\Delta G_r = \Delta G_d - \Delta G_a$$
$$\Delta H_r = \Delta H_d - \Delta H_a$$
$$\Delta S_r = \Delta S_d - \Delta S_a$$

The reaction-rate constant equation follows.

$$k = Z_{12} e^{+\Delta S_a/R} \times e^{-\Delta H_a/RT} = Z_{12} e^{-\Delta G_a/RT}$$

REACTION RATES AND EQUILIBRIUM

We have reached two conclusions from our study of chemical reactions and equilibrium. The first conclusion is that *the equilibrium state may be reached from either direction.* Second, if we examine the equilibrium concentrations of hydrogen, iodine, and hydrogen iodide at the same temperature, regardless of the initial nonequilibrium conditions, we discover that *they bear a constant mathematical relationship to each other.* From our kinetic interpretation of dynamic chemical equilibrium, and from our experimental knowledge of the kinetics of the opposing reactions that lead to the equilibrium state, we can deduce that relationship.

Recall that the experimentally determined rate law for the reaction between hydrogen and iodine, $H_2(g) + I_2(g) \rightleftarrows 2HI(g)$, is the following.

$$R_f = k_f[H_2][I_2]$$

R_f and k_f stand for the experimental rate and the reaction-rate law constant for the forward (f) direction of the reaction. The experimental rate law for the reverse (r) reaction, the decomposition of hydrogen iodide, follows.

$$R_r = k_r[HI]^2$$

At dynamic equilibrium, since there is no net change, the rates of the forward and reverse reactions are the same.

$$R_f = R_r$$

Substituting for R_f and R_r, we find the following.

$$k_f[H_2][I_2] = k_r[HI]^2$$

$[H_2]$, $[I_2]$, and $[HI]$ are the concentrations at equilibrium. By rearranging the equation, we have the following.

$$\frac{k_f}{k_r} = \frac{[HI]^2}{[H_2][I_2]}$$

Since k_f and k_r are constants, the division of k_f by k_r is also a constant, giving us the following equation.

$$K = \frac{[HI]^2}{[H_2][I_2]}$$

Again, the concentrations are those measured at equilibrium.

Dolphus E. Milligan
(1928–1973, American) Dr. Milligan's main research interest was in spectroscopic characterization of free radicals and reaction intermediates. These are short-lived and elusive structures which play important roles in chemical reactions. His techniques have led to the detection and identification of over fifty free radicals.

The expression is known as the **Law of Chemical Equilibrium** for the following reaction.

$$H_2 + I_2 \rightleftharpoons 2HI$$

K is called the **equilibrium constant.** Thus, by considering the kinetic properties of the system, we have arrived at a quantitative expression for the constant mathematical relationship that describes the composition of a system at chemical equilibrium. The relationship between the equilibrium constant and the reaction-rate constants can be valid only when the rate expression agrees with the stoichiometric chemical reaction.

REVIEW QUESTIONS

1 In terms of the collision theory, what effect would the following have on reaction rates?
   a. Temperature
   b. Concentration
   c. Pressure
2 How has the transition state theory modified the collision theory?
3 Show mathematically how reaction rates and equilibrium are related.
4 Why do we never include the concentration of water or the concentration of a solid in the equilibrium constant expression?

REFERENCES

Abbott, D. *An Introduction to Reaction Kinetics*. New York: Houghton Mifflin Co., 1968.

Haensel, V., and R. L. Burwell, Jr. "Catalysis." *Scientific American*, December 1971, p. 46.

Stevens, B. *Chemical Kinetics for General Students of Chemistry*, New York: Halstead Press, 1970.

Yole, G. R. "Dominoes and Activation Energy." *Chemistry*, October 1976, p. 8.

EXCURSION ELEVEN

Metals and Alloys

The emergence of people from the Stone Age was hastened by the discovery and utilization of bronze, a mixture of copper and tin. Because of bronze, more useful tools and ornaments could be made. And it was no longer necessary for people to use crude stone instruments for defense against their enemies.

The Bronze Age lasted until about 1500 B.C. At that time, ancient people began to develop iron for use as weapons and tools. Thus, the Iron Age began.

Modern civilization is totally dependent on the use of metals. The technology of the jet airplane and rocket has demanded the use of metals once considered only laboratory curiosities. For example, large amounts of titanium are used in the high-temperature components of jet engines and in the outer skins of supersonic fighter aircraft. Zirconium and beryllium alloys are widely used, also.

From the Bronze Age to the present Steel Age, we have primarily used metals in the form of alloys. An **alloy** is a solid solution of small amounts of one or more metals in a solvent metal. Those metals can dramatically change the properties of the solvent metal. The synthetic element plutonium is extremely hard in its pure form, which presents a problem in using it as a nuclear fuel. However, adding 1.00 percent aluminum to plutonium results in a soft alloy, which makes it possible for the plutonium to be shaped into rods, wires, and sheets.

WHICH ELEMENTS ARE METALS?

We can divide the chemical elements into two groups—metals and nonmetals. Approximately eighty elements can be classified as metals, although the degree to which they exhibit the chemical and physical properties of a metal varies. The eighty or so metallic elements can be further divided into four main groups within the periodic table (Figure E11–1).

1. *The pretransition elements, which include Groups I and II, as well as Al, Sc, and Y. These elements lose* s *electrons (plus one* p *electron for Al and one* d *electron for Sc and Y) to form ions of noble-gas electronic structures.*

2. *The posttransition elements, which include Groups III (except Al); Sn and Pb of Group IV, Sb and Bi of Group V, Po of Group VI, and Cu, Ag, Au, Zn, Cd, and Hg. All these elements have filled* d *subshells when they form ions in the oxidation state of their periodic group.*

3. *The transition elements have a partially filled* d *orbital.*

4. *The lanthanide and actinide elements, which have* f *orbitals involved in their electronic structure*

FIGURE E11–1 · *A broad classification of the elements in the periodic table demonstrates the four main groups of the metallic elements.*

Pre-transition metals
Transition metals
Post-transition metals
Lanthanides and actinides

H																	
Li	Be											B	C	N	O	F	Ne
Na	Mg											Al	Si	P	S	Cl	Ar
K	Ca	Sc	Ti	V	Cr	Mn	Fe	Co	Ni	Cu	Zn	Ga	Ge	As	Se	Br	Kr
Rb	Sr	Y	Zr	Nb	Mo	Tc	Ru	Rh	Pd	Ag	Cd	In	Sn	Sb	Te	I	Xe
Cs	Ba	†	Hf	Ta	W	Re	Os	Ir	Pt	Au	Hg	Tl	Pb	Bi	Po	At	Rn
Fr	Ra	‡	Rf	Ha													

†	La	Ce	Pr	Nd	Pm	Sm	Eu	Gd	Tb	Dy	Ho	Er	Tm	Yb	Lu
‡	Ac	Th	Pa	U	Np	Pu	Am	Cm	Bk	Cf	Es	Fm	Md	No	Lw

Many of these elements, such as aluminum, chromium, and iron, are familiar to us in their metallic state. We are unlikely to encounter many others in normal circumstances, as for example, the lanthanides. Other elements exist in such small amounts and for such brief periods of time that they have never been prepared in a metallic state. Examples are the synthetic, radioactive elements such as Fr, Fm, Md, No, and Lw. Many common commercial metals are not pure elements, but are in fact mixtures. Examples of commercial metals are brass, bronze, pewter, duraluminum, and steel.

PHYSICAL PROPERTIES OF METALS

All the elements classified as metals have certain properties in common. Those properties in some sense describe an ideal metal. Any real metal varies in the extent to which it possesses all the properties. The physical properties of an ideal metal are listed below.

1. **Malleability.** *A metal can be flattened into a very thin sheet, or foil. Gold is the most malleable metal and can be formed into a foil so thin that 300 000 sheets are necessary to make a pile ten centimeters thick—that means each sheet is less than 1000 atoms thick.*

2. **Ductility.** *A metal can be drawn into a wire. It is possible to draw platinum into a wire so fine that it cannot be seen by the unaided eye.*

3. **Electrical conductivity.** *A metal conducts electricity in its solid and liquid states. A nonmetal does not exhibit that type of electrical conductivity. The electrical conductance of a metal is much greater than that of an electrolytic solution. Also, in contrast to electrolytic conductance, metallic conductance decreases with an increase in temperature. Silver, copper, gold, and aluminum, in that order, have the highest conductance among the metals.*

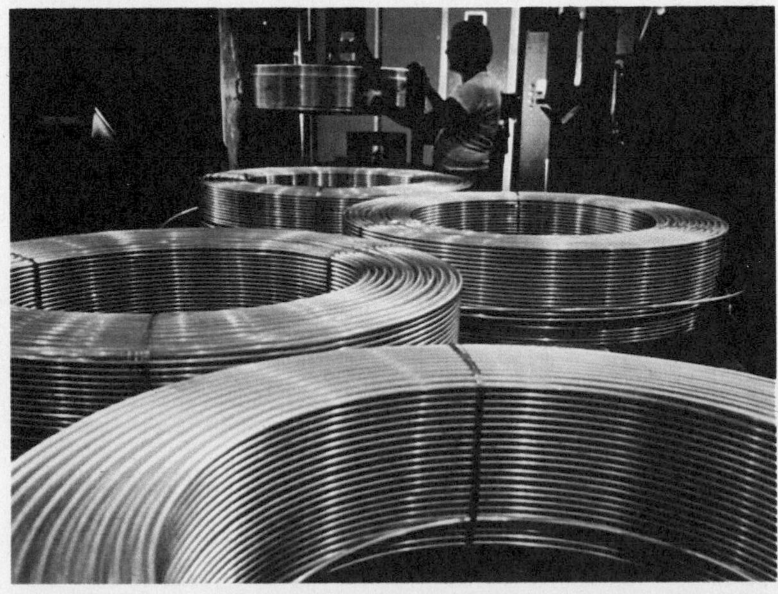

FIGURE E11–2 · *Aluminum is both malleable and ductile. Here, it is being drawn into aluminum tubing.*

FIGURE E11–3 · *Although Galena is a composite of various metals, it does show the high luster of metals even in their natural state. The most lustrous metals include gold, silver, aluminum, and chromium.*

4. **Heat conductivity.** *Like electrical conductivity, the conductivity of heat by a metal is large, but decreases as the temperature increases.*
5. **Luster.** *The metallic luster of gold, silver, aluminum, and chromium is familiar to all of us. It is less well-known that all metallic surfaces have this property. But the luster of many metals is obscured by a coating of oxide. Freshly cut iron has a typical metallic luster that quickly disappears in the air as rust forms. Any metal in a finely divided powder is black. Thus, the luster of a metal is associated with relatively large surface areas.*

While all metals share these physical properties to some extent, they also have many properties that vary greatly from one metal to another. The densities of metals range from very low, 0.53 g/cm^3 for Li, to very high, 22.5 g/cm^3 for Os. Their melting and boiling points also have a wide range. Mercury has a melting point of −39.0°C and is a liquid at room temperature. In contrast, the melting point of tungsten is 3380°C. Because its high melting point makes it very difficult to melt, tungsten is made into metallic rods by pressing the finely divided element in a mold and passing an electric discharge through the powder. This process, **sintering,** produces a hard material.

CHEMICAL PROPERTIES OF METALS

The list of chemical properties that metallic elements have in common is shorter than that of their common physical properties. The chemical properties are listed below.

1. **Cation formation.** *The most characteristic chemical property of a metal is the tendency to oxidize and form cations.*
2. **Basic oxides.** *The metal forms a nonvolatile oxide which is a basic anhydride—that is, when it is dissolved in water, the solution is basic.*

A MODEL OF THE METALLIC STATE

Let us consider which type of model of the metallic state is useful to explain the physical properties of a metal. The successful metallic model assumes that metal atoms exist as cations in a close-packed lattice. That lattice of cations can be expected to have a strong repulsion. Therefore, it is postulated that the electrons resulting from the ionization of the atoms are distributed throughout the lattice in such a manner as to overcome the mutual repulsion of the cations. In an ionic crystal, an alternation of cations and anions results in a stronger attraction than the total repulsion between anions and between cations. Similarly, the binding electrons in a metal must be in orbitals between the metallic cations in order to shield the cations from one another and produce a net attraction. The effect is to set up attractive forces between the electrons and the cations and to stabilize the structure. The binding electrons exist in orbitals associated with the total assembly of metal cations, rather than in orbitals associated with a single cation(ionic bond) or with pairs of atoms (localized covalent bond).

In such a model, the binding electrons belong to the crystal as a whole. Consequently, it is useful to think of a metallic structure as constructed according to this model of a lattice of close-packed cations floating in a "sea" of electrons, or bathed in a "gas" of electrons. It is the attraction between the large number of cations and the large number of electrons that constitutes metallic bonding.

THE EXPLANATION OF METALLIC PROPERTIES BY THE MODEL

In a metal, the cations are close-packed, but are not held rigidly in place by covalent bonds or by a surrounding array of bulky anions. Consequently, the cations in a metallic crystal have much greater freedom of movement than those in an ionic crystal or than atoms in a network solid. If a cation is moved closer to its neighboring cations, the latter are repelled by the increased coulombic repulsion. In effect, then, a moving cation creates its own pathway, since it pushes other cations out of its way by electrostatic repulsion. In contrast, when a cation is moved in an ionic crystal, the attraction to the anion serves to restrain the motion. The greater freedom of cations to be moved explains the malleability and ductility of a metal. The displacement of ions in a metal does not cause any decrease in the forces holding the crystal together. Therefore, the metal does not rupture. But the displacement of ions in an ionic crystal disrupts the forces holding the crystal together.

FIGURE E11–4 · *These structures illustrate the packing of atoms in metal crystals. (The structure on the left demonstrates cubic, and that on the right hexagonal, close packing.)*

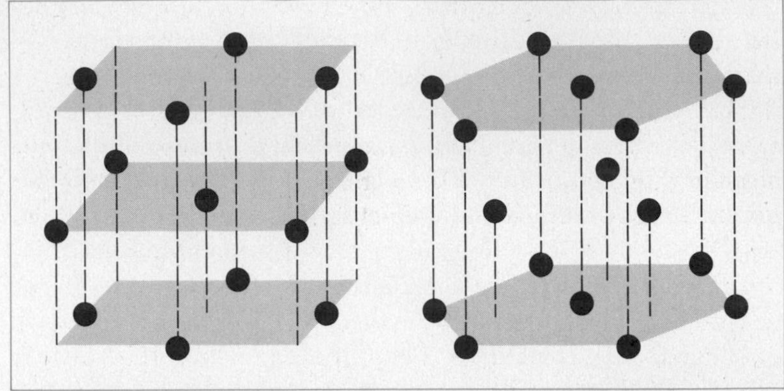

While the cations in a metallic lattice are relatively mobile, the electrons are much more so. Since the electrons exist in orbitals associated with the metal crystal as a whole, they are not restricted to any particular cation or group of cations. It is that freedom of electronic motion in a metal that gives a metal its high degree of electrical conductivity. The values of electrical conductivity in a metal are larger than the values of electrolytic conductivity in a solution. That is a direct result of the much greater ease of motion of electrons in a metal than of ions in a solution.

The "electron-gas" model also explains the high heat conductivity in a metal. Heat conductivity is accomplished in ionic or covalent solids by the transmission of small vibrations of the ions or atoms in their positions in the lattice. In a metal, however, heat energy is transported through the metal by the motion of the electrons. The movement of electrons is hindered by the vibrations of the lattice cations. Since the vibration increases as the temperature increases, the electronic motion decreases. As a result, both the electrical conductivity and the heat conductivity of metals, which depend on electronic mobility, decrease as the temperature increases.

Metallic luster can also be explained by the mobility of electrons. In their motion about the nucleus, the electrons behave as very small electric oscillators and are responsible for generating emitted light. Light striking a metallic surface is absorbed by loosely bonded electrons in the surface. Those electrons oscillate back and forth, and like any electric charge in motion, they emit radiant energy. As a result of absorption, and then emission, by the mobile, oscillating electrons, a metallic surface "reflects" light, thereby exhibiting the familiar metallic luster.

Gold and copper differ from other metals in the color of their luster. For all but these two metals, the total light energy absorbed is promptly re-emitted. Consequently, the reflected light of the metallic luster contains all wavelengths and is white light. In the case of gold and copper, all wavelengths are absorbed, but those in the blue-green end of the spectrum are not re-emitted. Since the reflected light lacks those wavelengths, it is reddish-gold. The photons of the blue-green portion of the spectrum cause excitation of the electrons in gold and copper to higher energy levels. The excitation energy is re-emitted as photons of a lower energy. Thus, the emitted wavelengths are longer than those of blue-green light.

ALLOTROPIC FORMS OF METALS

Metals form close-packed structures. However, since the cations are not held in place by bonds of a definite, fixed direction, it is common to find several allotropic forms of a metal. For example, plutonium is an unusual element, since it has six different allotropic forms—more than any other metal. Each form exists within a definite temperature range (Table E11–1).

TABLE E11–1 · Plutonium Allotropes

ALLOTROPE	CRYSTAL STRUCTURE	TRANSITION TEMPERATURE	DENSITY
α	Simple monoclinic	115°C	19.86 g/cm^3
β	Body-centered monoclinic	185°C	17.70 g/cm^3
γ	Face-centered orthorhombic	310°C	17.14 g/cm^3
δ	Face-centered cubic	452°C	15.92 g/cm^3
δ'	Body-centered tetragonal	480°C	16.00 g/cm^3
ϵ	Body-centered cubic	640°C(melts)	16.51 g/cm^3

The transition temperature is that temperature at which the transformation to a new allotropic modification takes place. For example, the β form of plutonium is stable from 185°C to 310°C. Above that temperature, the body-centered monoclinic form. Figure E11–5 shows the various crystal forms. A body-centered form has an additional atom inside its structure, while a face-centered form has additional atoms in the sides, or faces, of the structure (Figure E11–5).

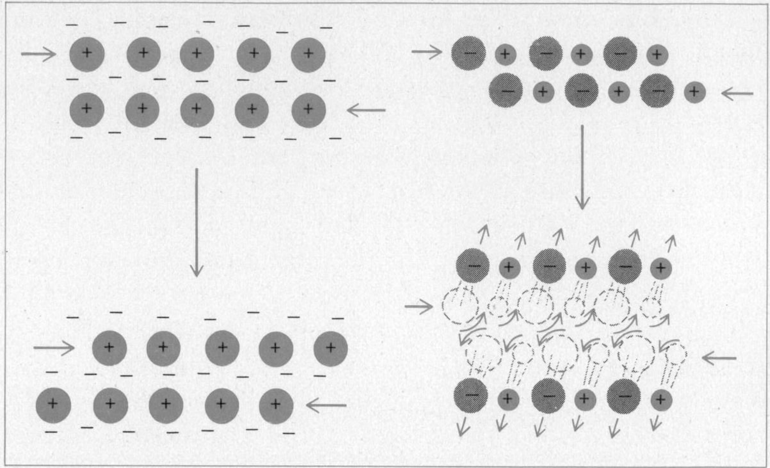

FIGURE E11–5 · *Ionic crystals (lower) are generally brittle. Metallic crystals (upper) are generally malleable and ductile. How do the models shown here account for those observed properties?*

An interesting story of uncertain validity involves the allotropes of tin. Gray tin is a nonmetallic form that is stable below 13.2℃. White tin is a metallic allotropic form with a simple cubic (ccp) structure. This soft, malleable, metallic-white tin converts slowly in cold climates to the hard, brittle, nonmetallic, allotrope, gray tin. This process is known as tin disease. That was supposedly a contributing factor to the debacle of the retreat of Napoleon's army in Russia in 1812, since the tin buttons used on the French uniforms crumbled because the cold weather converted them from white to gray tin.

HARDNESS IN METALS

Some metals, such as the alkali metals, are very soft and can be cut easily with a knife. Other metals, such as plutonium, are quite hard and brittle. The softness of the alkali metals can be explained by the relatively small number of electrons per atom available for metallic bonding in the crystal. There is a +1 cation lattice held together by an electronic bond of only one electron per cation, so the coulombic attraction forces are minimal. The relatively low boiling point of the soft metals is also consistent with this explanation.

The hard metals are found in the metallic groups that have a larger number of electrons involved in the electronic bonds.

In a hard metal, a lattice of multiply charged cations is immersed in a sea of electrons with three, four, or more electrons per cation. The coulombic attraction forces are much larger, exerting greater restraint on the distortion of the crystal structure.

ALLOYS

An alloy is a solid solution of metals. Some alloys are intermetallic solutions in which one metal is substituted randomly into the cation lattice of the host metal. Such substitutional solid solutions can form when the two metals have comparable radii and chemical natures. The number of electrons that each contributes to the metallic bond is also an important factor. If the difference in radii is too great, the substitution of one cation into the host cation lattice causes a strain, and the solubility is much less. Silver and gold have similar radii and chemical natures. As a result, they are mutually soluble in all proportions. In contrast, gold and cadmium have rather different radii and different chemical natures (the electronegativity difference between Au and Cd is 0.70, whereas between Au and Ag it is 0.40). Also, cadmium contributes two electrons per atom, whereas gold (or silver) contributes only one. As a result, cadmium dissolves in gold until a solution of 65.0 atom percent Au to 35.0 atom percent Cd results. The limiting value is for an alloy that retains the same structure as gold. Alloys of more than 35 atom percent cadmium content do form, but they have a different structure. That reflects the need for a readjustment of the metal lattice to accommodate the cadmium.

Metal solutions may also contain nonmetal atoms. Those solid solutions have a relatively small percentage of some element present in the holes of the close-packed lattice of metal cations. Hydrogen, carbon, and nitrogen atoms are common examples of such elements. Alloy formation is favored if the solute atoms are small, and if the cation lattice is open. Iron has a bond-centered cubic (bcc) structure up to a temperature at 906°C. At that temperature, it changes to a simple cubic (ccp) structure. Both structures can dissolve carbon to form steel. But the bcc structure can dissolve only 0.10 atom percent, whereas the ccp structure can dissolve 3.60 atom percent. The voids in the bcc have only 1.61 A between the center of the void and the centers of the surrounding iron atoms. However, in the ccp structure, the voids have 1.82 Å between the center of the void and the centers of the surrounding iron atoms. Thus, the carbon atom is less squeezed in the ccp structure. As long as the composition is below 8.70 atom percent carbon, the alloy is a steel and exhibits all the metallic properties of that substance. The higher the carbon content, the harder the steel. Above 8.70 atom percent carbon, however, the alloy becomes very hard and brittle. Then it is known as cast iron and can only be shaped by casting from the molten state.

Scientists and engineers have acquired a great amount of data about alloys. However, they have not yet developed a theory that satisfactorily describes why some alloys form and others do not, and that also explains the properties of alloys. As technology places more severe demands on the properties of alloys, the need for a satisfactory and more complete theory becomes greater.

CORROSION

One of the limitations of the utilization of metals and alloys is their tendency to corrode. Corrosion costs millions of dollars per year in the United States alone. **Corrosion** is the oxidation of a metal surface by water, air, CO_2, and other atmospheric oxidants. Before the full mechanism of metallic corrosion can be understood, its basic electrochemical nature must be discussed.

Oxidation-reduction occurs when there is a difference in potential between two metals surfaces. Thus, current can flow in a closed circuit. In the Cu – Zn Daniell battery described in Chapter 18, a copper electrode in a solution containing Cu^{+2} ions and a zinc electrode in contact with Zn^{+2} ions in solution are connected by a wire. A current flows spontaneously, oxidizing the zinc electrode and reducing $Cu^{+2}(aq)$ ions to metallic copper. Such a redox electrochemical reaction can occur whenever there is a potential difference and a path of current flow. Any small portion of a metal surface that is different from the bulk of the metal has a potential difference existing between it and the bulk metal. If an electrolytic solution (for example, a film of moisture with dissolved CO_2) covers the area including the bulk metal surface and the different portion of the metal, a localized electrochemical reaction can occur (Figure E11–7). Generally, the metal area that is different functions as an anode, and oxidative corrosion takes place. Impurities or stresses in the metal can cause sufficient differences in potential for corrosion to occur.

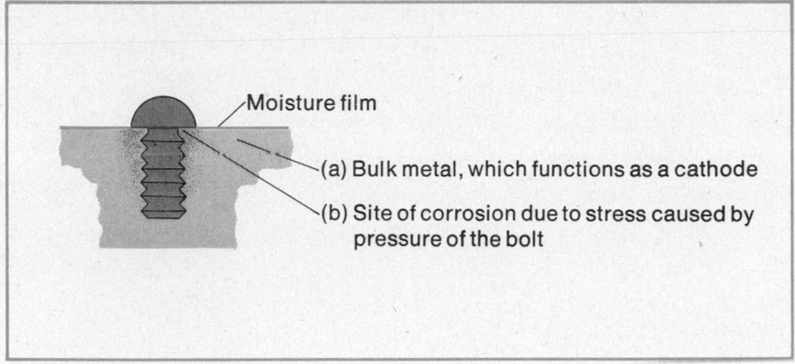

FIGURE E11–6 · *A metal under stress + air + moisture = corrosion.*

Corrosion can be prevented in a number of ways. One simple but effective method is to keep the metal surface free of moisture, oxygen, and carbon dioxide by a protective covering of paint. Methods that involve covering the metal with thin layers of noncorroding metal, such as chrome, zinc, or tin plating are based on the same concept. Zinc plating (galvanizing) has the advantage that if the protective plating is punctured, the zinc oxidizes rather than the underlying iron, because zinc has a higher oxidation potential. In contrast, since tin has a lower oxidation potential than iron, if tin plating is punctured, the iron corrodes even more rapidly than without the tin plate.

A different method of preventing corrosion is known as **cathodic protection.** This technique uses a metal of a lower reduction potential connected to the metal that is to be protected from corrosion. The protected metal functions as the cathode in the electrochemical reaction. The protecting metal oxidizes as the anode.

Magnesium is used extensively in the cathodic protection of buried iron pipelines, canal gates, water tanks, and ship hulls. Similarly, zinc is used to protect the bronze propeller shafts and rudders of small boats from corrosion by sea water.

The electrochemical properties of a corrosion-prone metal may be altered by the addition of small amounts of other elements to it. The resulting metal alloy is frequently more resistant to corrosion than the original metal. Stainless steel, an alloy of iron, is a familiar example.

FIGURE E11–7 · *Cathodes are being inserted in the ship's hull to protect against corrosion.*

From the aspect of the disposal of litter, it is unfortunate that aluminum cans have replaced tin cans. Aluminum has a rather high oxidation potential, yet it is quite inactive to corrosion. As corrosion proceeds on the metal surface, an impervious film of the corrosion product—usually hydrous oxide—forms and protects the underlying metal from further oxidation. In some cases, the oxide film does not adhere smoothly to the metallic surface, and the oxidizing agent continues to have access to the metal. The rapid oxidation of alkali and alkaline earth surfaces is a result of the lack of an adherent oxide coating. In such cases, the rate of oxidation is quite rapid. However, if the film adheres well to the surface and protects it, the rate of corrosion depends on the diffusion of metal atoms and/or oxygen through the film. That diffusion can be quite slow. The oxidation, or tarnishing, of silver and copper is an example of oxide-film formation that proceeds slowly by a diffusion of atoms through the growing film. For a few metals, oxidation ceases after only a very thin oxide film forms. The oxide film that forms to protect aluminum metal from further corrosion, is only twenty A thick at room temperature. For those thin films, the reaction rate depends not on diffusion of atoms through the oxide film, but rather on the transfer of metal atoms into interstitial positions in the film as cations. So the very durable, thin film of Al_2O_3 on aluminum metal protects it from further corrosion as effectively as a layer of paint. Thus, aluminum cans last for a very long time.

REVIEW QUESTIONS

1 Why is cesium, Cs, considered the most metallic element?

2 Show how the model for the metallic state, as described in this excursion, helps explain the following.
   a. Metallic luster
   b. Conductivity of electricity by metal
   c. Conductivity of heat by metal
   d. Formation of superconductors

3 Describe several ways to protect a metal from corrosion.

4 Explain why certain metals, like aluminum, do not rust.

5 The effort to explore space has resulted in the development of new applications for metals and new alloys. Describe some of these developments. (Use your school library for assistance.)

REFERENCES

Barnes, K. L. "Thermoluminescent Dating." *The Science Teacher,* October 1975, p. 18.

Battista, O. A. "Aluminum, Featherweight Champion of Metals." *Chemistry,* March 1969, p. 14.

——— "Copper, A Metal Known to Ancient Man." *Chemistry,* September 1969, p. 6.

Cook, N. C. "Metalling." *Scientific American,* August 1969, p. 38.

Ellington, G., et al. "The Carbon Chemistry of the Moon." *Scientific American,* October 1972, p. 80.

Lawless, J. G. et al. "Organic Matter in Meteorites." *Scientific American,* June 1972.

Page, T. "Puzzling Facts from Lunar Exploration." *The Science Teacher,* March 1973, p. 23.

Renfrow, C. "Carbon 14 and the Prehistory of Europe." *Scientific American,* October 1971, p. 63.

Slabaugh, W. H. "Corrosion." *Journal of Chemical Education,* April 1974, pp. 218–220.

Smith, Wayne L. "Corrosion." *Chemistry,* January–February 1976, p. 14; June 1976, p. 7; October 1976, p. 11.

Wentzel, D. G. "The Origin of the Stars and Elements." *The Science Teacher,* March 1973, p. 82.

EXCURSION TWELVE

Using Organic Chemicals

In Chapter 19, we studied the fundamentals of organic chemistry. In Excursion 12, we will discuss the properties and the uses of some organic compounds. We have learned that the chemical behavior of an organic compound is determined primarily by its functional group. We will use those functional groups as a convenient classification in our discussion of organic compounds.

THE HYDROCARBONS

Methane, CH_4, is the principal component of natural gas. However, natural gas also contains some ethane (C_2H_6), propane (C_3H_8), and butane (C_4H_{10}). Propane and butane are often used as bottled gas for heating and cooking. We learned in Chapter 19 that the process of cracking produces liquid hydrocarbon mixtures, such as naptha (C_4—C_6), gasoline (C_8—C_{10}), kerosene (C_{12}—C_{15}), fuel oil, and diesel oil (C_{15}—C_{18}). Lubricating oils and greases are hydrocarbons of sixteen or more carbons, while paraffin wax has compounds of twenty or more carbon atoms per molecule.

The principal aromatic hydrocarbon is benzene, C_6H_6, which is used to make a wide variety of other organic chemicals. Naphthalene is used in mothballs. Toluene reacts with nitro groups (NO_2) to make trinitrotoluene, the explosive TNT. Xylene can exist in three isomeric forms depending on whether the methyl groups are on adjacent carbons (ortho), on carbons separated by one carbon (meta), or on carbons separated by two carbons (para).

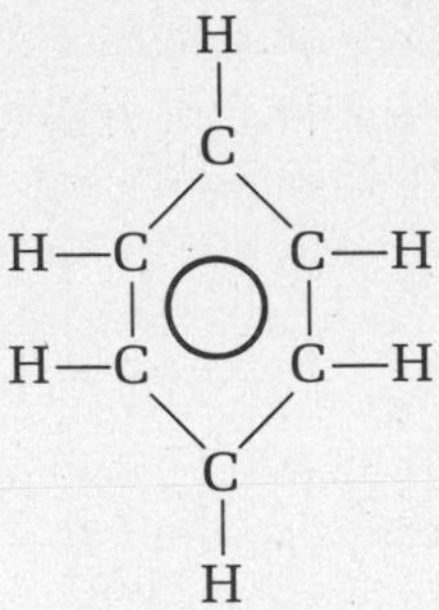

C_6H_6, benzene

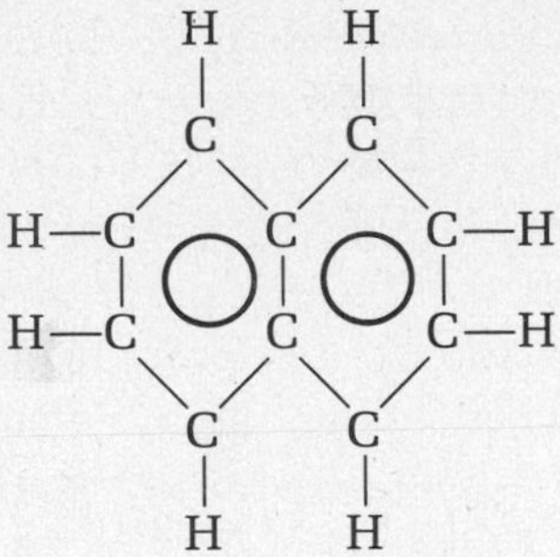

$C_{10}H_8$, naphthalene

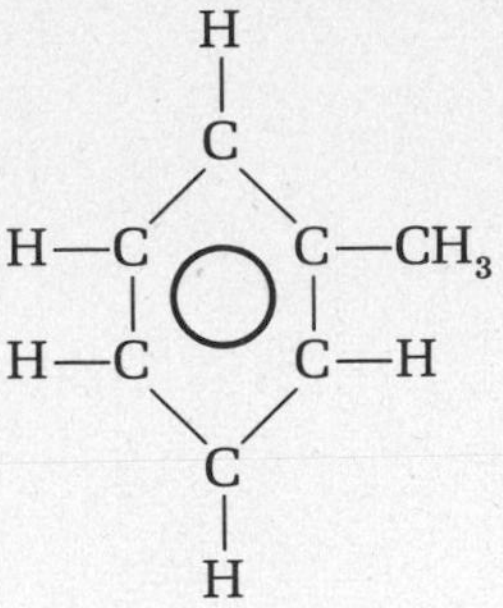

toluene

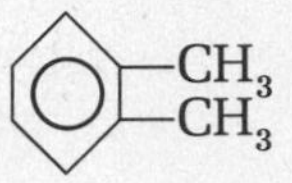

o-xylene
(mp = −29.0°C)

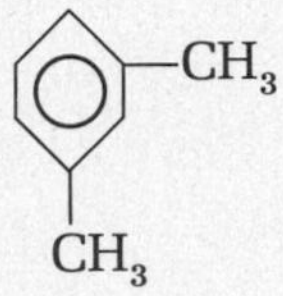

m-xylene
(mp = −47.4°C)

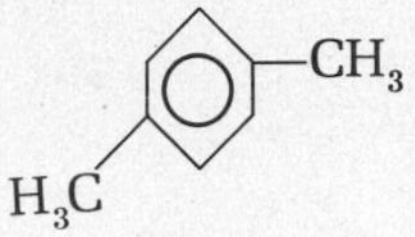

p-xylene
(mp = 13.4°C)

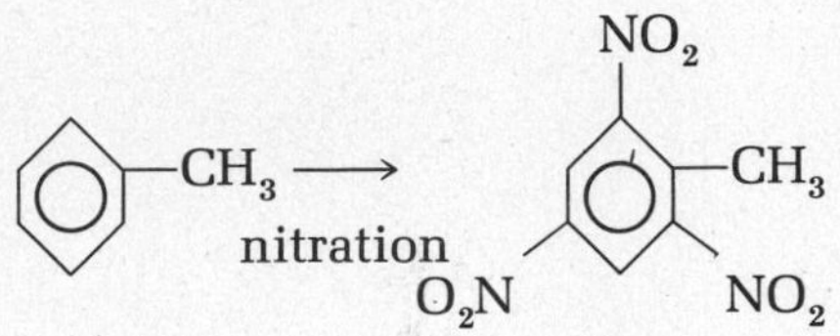

toluene → (nitration) TNT

ALCOHOLS

Alcohols with a lower molecular mass dissolve completely in water, as the hydroxl group forms hydrogen bonds to the H_2O molecules. Aqueous solutions of ethyl alcohol, C_2H_5OH, have been known since ancient times. The natural fermentation (oxidation) of sugar in grains or fruit converts the sugar to ethyl alcohol. The fermented liquids include wine, beer, whiskey, and brandy. Ethyl alcohol is also used as a solvent and in the synthesis of a number of industrial chemicals.

Methanol, CH_3OH, is known as wood alcohol. It used to be obtained by heating wood in a vacuum and distilling the methyl alcohol from the liquid that resulted. It is used to make formaldehyde, which is used in plastics, and other chemicals. Methanol is toxic and attacks the nervous system, causing blindness or, in larger amounts, death. It is added to ethyl alcohol to make it unfit to drink (denatured alcohol). Methanol is now made by the following reaction.

$$CO + 2H_2 \xrightarrow{\text{300 atm, 200°C}} CH_3OH$$

Methyl alcohol is easy to make and releases about 50 percent as much energy as the same amount of gasoline when it burns. It has been proposed as a fuel replacement for gasoline.

Isopropyl alcohol, i—C_3H_7OH, is used as rubbing alcohol, because it kills bacteria and cools the skin through evaporation. Ethylene glycol, $C_2H_4(OH)_2$, is used in "permanent" antifreeze. Like methyl alcohol (bp = 64.9°C), it is soluble in water and lowers the freezing point. Because of its higher boiling point (bp = 198°C), ethylene glycol is less volatile than methyl alcohol. Therefore, methyl alcohol is not as good an antifreeze, since it boils away over a period of time from the hot radiator fluid. Glycerol, or glycerin, is a trihydroxy alcohol that is used to make many drugs, cosmetics, and nitroglycerine.

isopropyl alcohol	ethylene glycol	glycerol	nitroglycerine
H	H	H	H
|	|	|	|
H—C—H	H—C—OH	H—C—OH	H—C—NO_2
|	|	|	|
H—C—OH	H—C—OH	H—C—OH	H—C—NO_2
|	|	|	|
H—C—H	H	H—C—OH	H—C—NO_2
|		|	|
H		H	H

CARBOXYLIC ACIDS

The simplest organic acid is formic acid, HCO_2H. Formic acid is the chemical injected into us by a bee or an insect sting. Formic acid causes burning and irritation, as our nerve ends react to the acidity of the chemical.* Acetic acid, CH_3CO_2H, is the active ingredient in vinegar and accounts for the sour taste of wine as it ages upon exposure to air. When it is exposed to air, the ethyl alcohol in wine oxidizes to become acetic acid. That oxidation is prevented in liquors of a higher alcohol content, because the bacteria that catalyze the oxidation reaction cannot live in such solutions.

Long-chain acids are known as fatty acids. Stearic acid, for example, has a chain of seventeen carbon atoms plus the acidic carboxylate groups, $C_{17}H_{35}CO_2H$. The long alkyl chain makes a fatty acid insoluble in water, but soluble in a nonpolar organic liquid. The sodium salt of stearic acid, sodium stearate —$C_{17}H_{25}CO_2Na$, is a good soap. Table E12 – 1 lists some fatty acids and their sources.

*****_The relation between an insect sting and formic acid is recognized in the French word for "ant"_ – fourmi.

TABLE E12–1 · Common Fatty Acids and Their Sources

NAME	FORMULA	TYPICAL SOURCE
Butyric	C_3H_7COOH	Butter
Caprylic	$C_7H_{15}COOH$	Coconuts
Palmitic	$C_{15}H_{31}COOH$	Palm oil
Palmitoleic	$C_{15}H_{29}COOH$	Milk
Stearic	$C_{17}H_{35}COOH$	Beef
Oleic	$C_{17}H_{33}COOH$	Olives, pork
Linoleic	$C_{17}H_{31}COOH$	Safflowers
Linolenic	$C_{17}H_{29}COOH$	Soybeans

SOAPS AND DETERGENTS

A soap dissolves the oily and greasy material that does not dissolve in water alone. A soap molecule has a long hydrocarbon chain that dissolves in oil or grease and a carboxylate end that dissolves in water. Soaps are normally soluble as sodium salts. But in "hard" water, which contains Ca^{+2} and Mg^{+2} ions, calcium and magnesium salts precipitate as the scum we often observe in sinks and bathtubs. To avoid that unpleasant precipitate, synthetic detergents have been developed to replace soap.

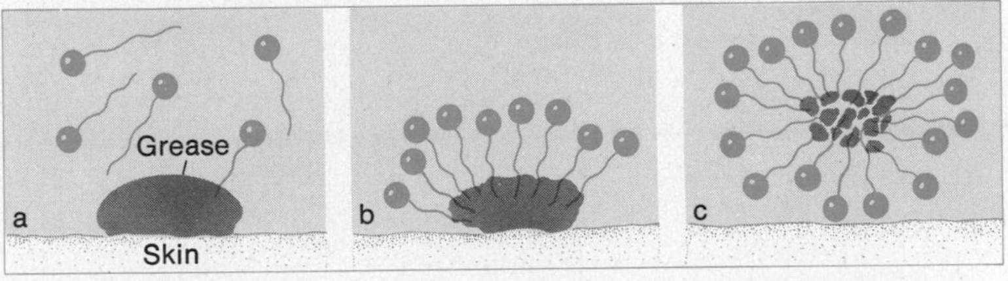

FIGURE 12–1 · *Soap molecules have an alkyl ($C_{17}H_{35}$) tail and a water-soluble ionized carboxylate end (CO_2). The soap molecules surround the grease spot, with their tails in the grease and their carboxylate end in the water. This results in the removal of the grease spot from the skin, so it can be dissolved in the water.*

A soap is a sodium salt of a fatty (carboxylic) acid. Detergents also have long alkyl chains to provide solubility in grease. However, the carboxylic acid groups, $-CO_2^-$, are replaced by sulfonic acid groups, $-SO_3^-$. A typical detergent has the following formula.

$$R-C_6H_4-SO_3^-\ Na^+ \qquad R = \text{alkyl group of } C_{12} \text{ to } C_{18} \text{ chain.}$$

Unfortunately, detergents are not readily destroyed by the bacteria in water. Therefore, the concentration of detergents increases in rivers and lakes. Biodegradable (substances that

FIGURE E12–2 · *Detergents are one of the major causes of water pollution today.*

can be destroyed by bacteria) detergents have now been developed. It seems that bacteria attack detergents with long straight alkyl chains, but not those with branched chains. So if only the straight-chain detergents are produced, the pollution problem caused by detergents can be solved.

ESTERS AND FATS

An ester is formed during the reaction between an alcohol and a carboxylic acid.

$$\underbrace{H_3C{-}C\begin{matrix}\diagup\!\!\!\!\!\!\!\;O\\ \diagdown OH\end{matrix}}_{\text{acid}} + \underbrace{H{-}O{-}C_2H_5}_{\text{alcohol}} \rightarrow \underbrace{H_3C{-}\overset{\overset{\displaystyle O}{\|}}{C}{-}O{-}C_2H_5}_{\text{ester}} + \underbrace{H_2O}_{\text{water}}$$

An ester usually has a very pleasant odor. Many of the aromas from flowers and fruits are the result of esters of low molecular weight, which are rather volatile. Table E12–2 lists some esters and their aromas. Esters of higher molecular weight are waxes, such as beeswax

$$(C_{30}H_{61}{-}O{-}\overset{\overset{\displaystyle O}{\|}}{C}{-}C_{25}H_{51}).$$

A fat is a naturally occurring ester containing an alcohol part, glycerol. Since glycerol has three alcohol groups, fats

TABLE E12–2 · **Formulas, Names, and Aromas of Some Esters**

ESTER	FORMULA	AROMA
Ethyl butyrate	$C_2H_5—O—C(=O)—C_3H_7$	Apricot
Octyl acetate	$C_8H_{17}—O—C(=O)—CH_3$	Orange
Isoamyl acetate	$H—C(CH_3)(CH_3)—C(H)(H)—C(H)(H)—O—C(=O)—CH_3$	Banana
Butyl butyrate	$C_4H_9—O—C(=O)—C_3H_7$	Pineapple
Methyl salicylate	$CH_3—O—C(=O)—C_6H_4—OH$	Wintergreen

have three fatty-acid segments connected to each glycerol segment. A fat can be decomposed by a process called **saponification.** During saponification, a base, such as NaOH, is boiled with the fat to produce glycerol and the sodium salt of the fatty acid. Soap is made by boiling fat with ash (basic).

$$\begin{array}{l} H_2C—O—\overset{O}{\overset{\|}{C}}—C_{17}H_{35} \\ H_2C—O—\overset{O}{\overset{\|}{C}}—C_{17}H_{35} \\ H_2C—O—\overset{O}{\overset{\|}{C}}—C_{17}H_{35} \end{array} + 3NaOH \rightarrow 3C_{17}H_{35}CO_2^-\ Na^+ + \begin{array}{l} H_2C—OH \\ H_2C—OH \\ H_2C—OH \end{array}$$

If only single bonds exist in the alkyl chain, the fat is solid and greasy. Such fat is called *saturated* fat. However, if there are some double bonds in the chain, the fat is often a liquid oil. A fat with double bonds is called *unsaturated*, since H_2 can be added to the fat at the double bonds. Generally, vegetable fats are oils, while animal fats are solid. A vegetable oil reacts with hydrogen to remove all its double bonds, making it a solid fat. That process is called *hydrogenation*. Oleomargarine is an example of a vegetable oil that is solidified by hydrogenation.

AMINES AND AMIDES

The amines are organic bases that react with carboxylic acid to form amides.

$$\mathrm{R{-}NH_2 + HO_2CR' \rightarrow R{-}\overset{\displaystyle H}{\overset{|}{N}}{-}\overset{\displaystyle O}{\overset{\|}{C}}{-}R' + H_2O}$$

$$\text{amine + acid} \rightarrow \text{amide} \qquad \text{+ water}$$

Amines have an unpleasant odor, like decaying meat. When animal protein decays, it forms amines that lead to the odor of rotting animal matter. Perhaps the best known amine is aniline, or aminobenzene.

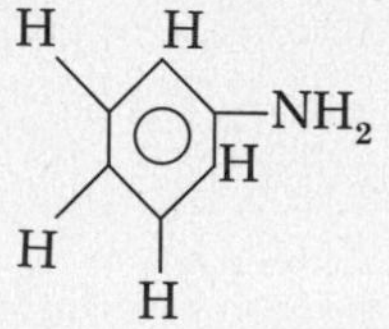

$$C_6H_5NH_2$$

Aniline is used in the manufacture of drugs, dyes, photographic developers, and other industrial products.

Perhaps the best known amide in the last twenty years has been lysergic acid diethylamide, or LSD, a hallucinogen.

$$\mathrm{C_{15}N_2H_{15}{-}\overset{\displaystyle O}{\overset{\|}{C}}{-}\overset{\displaystyle C_2H_5}{\overset{|}{N}}{-}C_2H_5}$$

The sulfa drugs that saved so many lives during World War II are also derivatives of aniline. Although antibiotics have replaced sulfa drugs as infection fighters in many diseases, sulfa drugs still have some specialized uses. For example, sulfa drugs are very effective in dealing with urinary tract infections. They are inexpensive, making them useful in veterinary medicine.

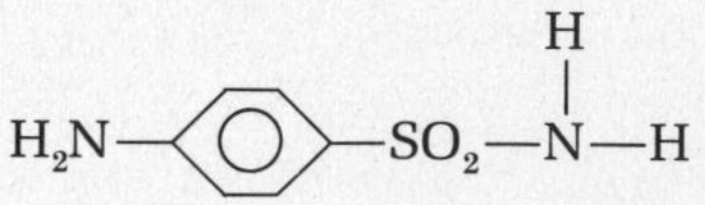

$$\mathrm{H_2N{-}C_6H_4{-}SO_2{-}\overset{\displaystyle H}{\overset{|}{N}}{-}H} \qquad \text{sulfanilamide}$$

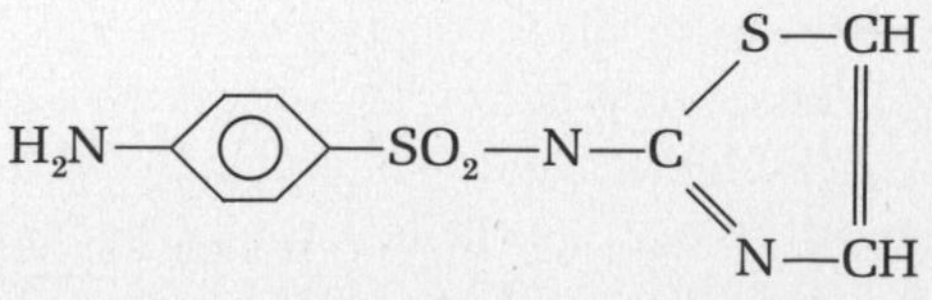

$$\mathrm{H_2N{-}C_6H_4{-}SO_2{-}N{-}C} \text{(thiazole ring: } \mathrm{S{-}CH{=}CH{-}N{=}C}\text{)} \qquad \text{sulfathiazole}$$

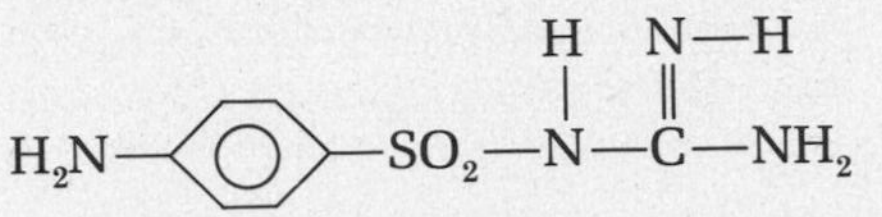

$$H_2N-C_6H_4-SO_2-N(H)-C(=N-H)-NH_2$$ sulfaguanidine

Sulfa drugs are all related to sulfanilamide, the structure of which resembles p-aminobenzoic acid.

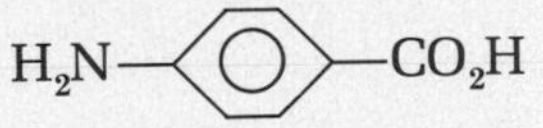

$$H_2N-C_6H_4-CO_2H$$

Bacteria normally use p-aminobenzoic acid to make the folic acid they need to live. Sulfa drugs replace p-aminobenzoic acid in the biochemical reactions in bacteria, but do not form folic acid. As a result, sulfa drugs cause the death of the bacteria.

Another aniline derivative is known as procaine. It is widely used as a local anesthetic, particularly when it has HCl added to it. With HCl, it is called novocaine.

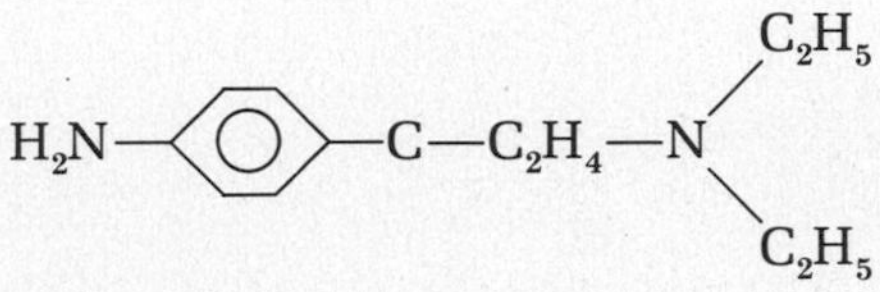

$$H_2N-C_6H_4-C-C_2H_4-N(C_2H_5)_2$$ procaine

$$Cl^-H_3{}^+N-C_6H_4-C-C_2H_4-N(C_2H_5)_2$$ novocaine

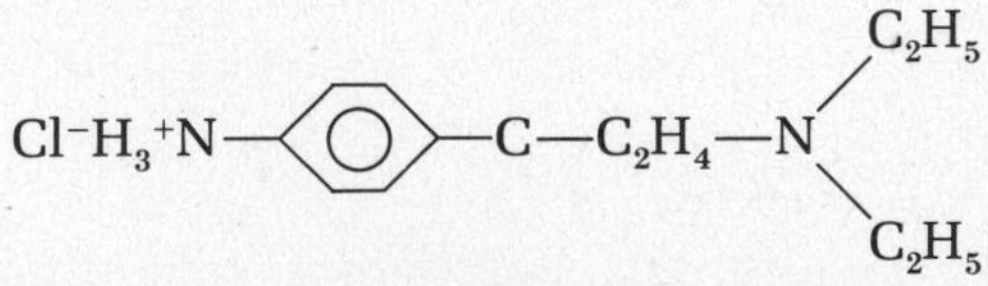

DRUGS

Perhaps the most commonly used medicine is aspirin. The chemical name for aspirin is acetylsalicylic acid. A related compound, salicylamide, has many of the analgesic properties of the acid, but has fewer of the side effects that aspirin causes in some people.

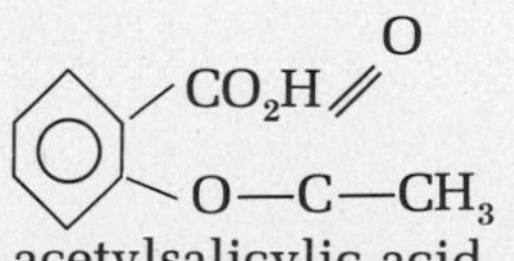

$$C_6H_4(CO_2H)(O-C(=O)-CH_3)$$
acetylsalicylic acid (aspirin)

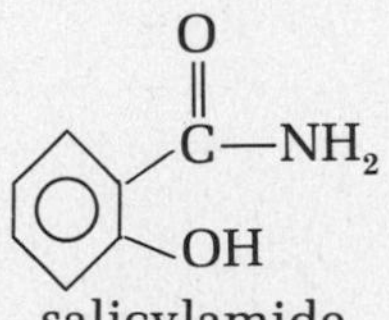

$$C_6H_4(C(=O)-NH_2)(OH)$$
salicylamide

Antibiotic drugs, such as penicillin and tetracycline, have saved millions of lives. Unfortunately, bacteria seem to be able to adjust to antibiotics. New strains of diseases are appearing

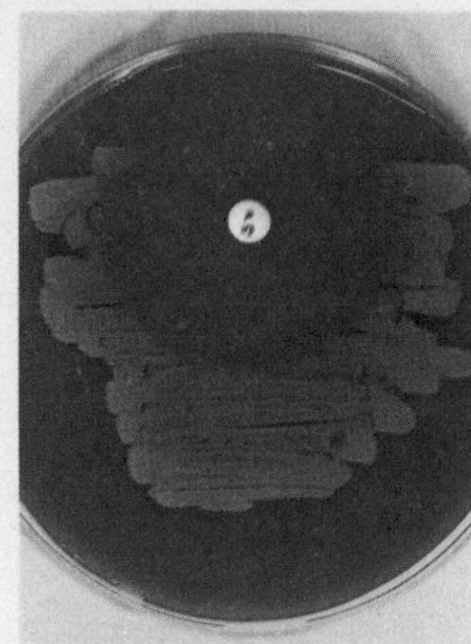

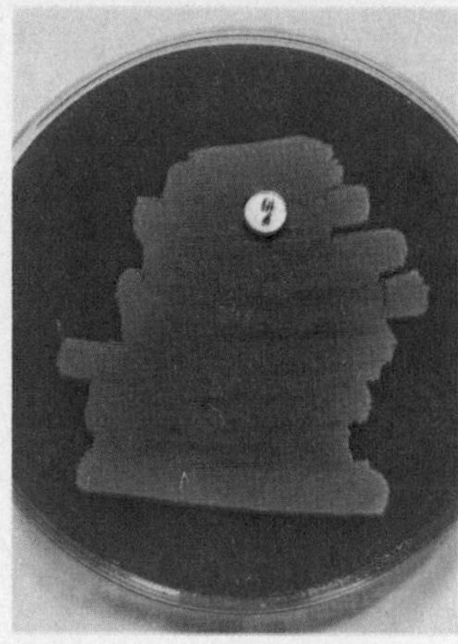

FIGURE E12–3 · *The picture above shows a bacterial strain that is being destroyed by penicillin. Note the clear area around the penicillin disk. In the lower picture, bacteria have developed a resistance to the penicillin.*

that are more resistant to present antibiotics. Consequently, it is a constant battle to develop new antibiotics to which the bacteria are not resistant.

The general structures of penicillin and tetracycline are as follows.

```
     O   H   H   H   S        CH3
     ‖   |   |   |  / \      /
R—C—N—C—C      C              penicillin
             |   |      |\
             C—N——C  CH3
             ‖          | \
             O          H  CO2
```

```
                                          CH3
                                         /
      CH3     OH  R2        H       N                tetracycline
 R1       \   /     \   /        |\
   \        C         C          C  CH3
                 H          H
                 |          |
                 C          C          C—OH
                 |          |          ‖
                 C          C          C—C—N—H
                            |             ‖   |
                            H             O   H
            C           C            C
            ‖           |            ‖
  OH        O           OH           O
```

Different types of penicillin and tetracycline have different R, R_1, and R_2 groups in their structure. The most commonly used penicillin is penicillin G, in which the structure of R is as follows.

H_3C–(benzene ring)–

Sedatives are narcotics that dull the senses and reduce pain. Opium is a mixture of narcotic compounds, of which the most important is morphine. Codeine is methyl morphine.

```
                 H
                /
          H   C      H
          |  /|\    /
      O—C  OH C
                  ‖
           C      CH
                 /
              C
          C
        /   \      H
       H     H      CH2—CH2—N—CH3
                             |
                             H
```

INSECTICIDES AND HERBICIDES

Organic chemicals have been developed to kill pests. Such chemicals are usually known as pesticides, but that general name covers many purposes. Pesticides are also called herbicides, if they destroy undesirable vegetation; insecticides, if they kill insects; germicides, if they kill germs; and fungicides, if they kill fungi.

In part, the tremendous increase in food production around the world is the result of the development of powerful pesticides. Perhaps the most famous insecticide is dichlorodiphenyl trichloroethane, or DDT.

Cl

H—C—CCl_3

Cl

FIGURE E12–4 · *With the aid of the helicopter blades, pesticides are forced through the foliage down to the ground.*

DDT is soluble in fat, but is not soluble in water. Because of its fat solubility, DDT is absorbed by the insect. It attacks the sensory organs, causing paralysis and death. Unfortunately, DDT becomes concentrated in fatty tissue. It is estimated that the use of DDT causes such pollution in the oceans that small fish may contain one part per million (ppm) DDT. Larger fish feed on the smaller fish, and DDT concentrates to ten ppm in the larger fish. Humans eat the larger fish and develop concentrations of ten ppm or more. We know very little about the long-term effects of such concentration in humans. Until more knowledge is accumulated through research, the use of DDT has been banned in the United States. Such bans mean increased crop damage, because of the inability to use such pesticides.

Excursion 12 has been a brief summary of a few of the uses of some organic compounds. Through such organic compounds, chemistry affects our lives every day. Our health, our food, our clothing, our housing, and our transportation are only a few of the areas affected. Some of the compounds we use are obtained from natural products; others are the product of chemical research.

REVIEW QUESTIONS

1 Explain the action of a detergent on grease.
2 Show a saponification reaction between a fat and a base.
3 Explain the difference between a saturated and an unsaturated fat. What is a polyunsaturated fat?
4 Show how amines and amides are used in the preparation of the following materials.
   a. Drugs
   b. Narcotics
   c. Insecticides
   d. Herbicides

REFERENCE

Jacobson, M., and M. Beroza. "Insect Attractants." *Scientific American Offprint* #189. August 1964.

Keller, Eugenia. "The DDT Story." *Chemistry*, February 1970, pp. 8–12.

Pratt, C. J. "Chemical Fertilizers." *Scientific American Offprint* #328. June 1965.

Williams, C. M. "Third Generation Pesticides." *Scientific American Offprint* #1078. July 1967.

EXCURSION THIRTEEN

Careers in Chemical Sciences

Some of you may become artists, accountants, sales representatives, teachers, lawyers, or journalists. These and many other occupations have little or no direct relationship to science. For you, this course in chemistry is a cultural exercise. Its primary good is the expansion of your understanding of the world and of the natural order of everything in it. But for others of you, this course has a more practical value. You will work in an area in which science is of direct importance. Perhaps you will be a physicist, a doctor, a geologist, an oceanographer, an astronaut, a nurse, an engineer, or even a chemist. In almost all the occupations related to modern technology, a basic knowledge of chemistry is necessary. In 1973, the American Chemical Society published a report on the role of chemistry in the future. It may be of interest to you to read about career possibilities listed in that article.

CHEMISTRY IN INDUSTRY

FOOD

Chemistry has already contributed enormously to the volume, variety, and efficiency at all stages from planting and growing to harvesting, processing, and distributing. In addition to further gains in farm productivity and in crop and livestock yields, we should expect:

1. Development of more formulated foods that increase consumer convenience, make diets more varied, and provide proper nutrition.

2. Enrichment of all basic foods with necessary nutrients, so that an adequate caloric intake would automatically provide adequate nutrition.

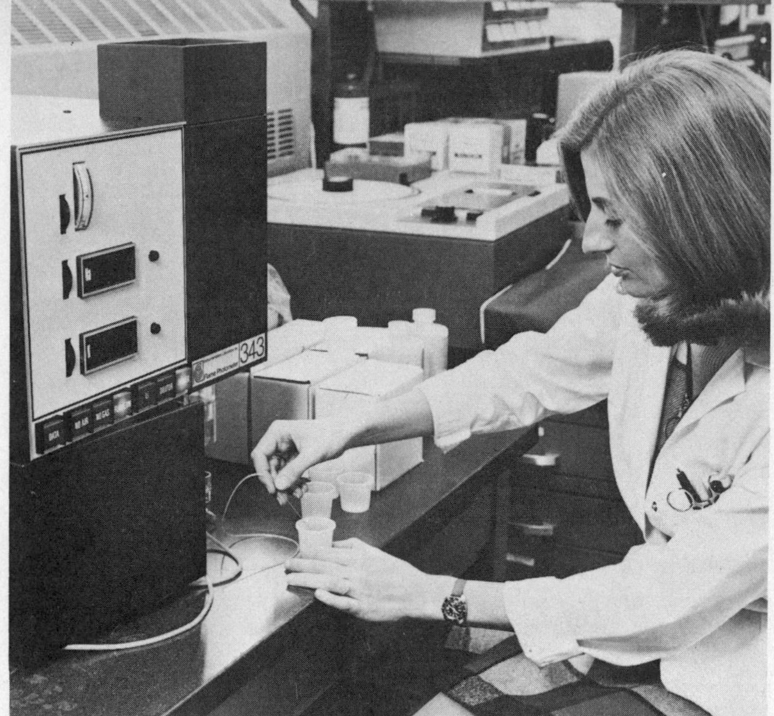

FIGURE E13–1 · *The correct concentrations of sodium (Na) and potassium (K) in the body are important to proper nerve and muscle function. The presence of these and other ions can be tested for by using a Flame Photometer. How do you think the ions are identified?*

3. Design of foods and diets for better control of diseases, such as the cardiac-related ones.
4. Foods especially developed for the very young and the very old and for persons with dietary problems.
5. Widening acceptance of meat analogs made of spun protein fibers impregnated with other ingredients.
6. Production of some feeds and foods from nonliving raw materials, such as petroleum, leading to reduced dependence on the biosphere.
7. Design of economical insecticides and herbicides that are highly specific as to target species and that degrade to ecologically acceptable residues within a reasonable time.

CLOTHING

Wardrobes are more varied and more easily cared for then ever, yet they account for a smaller share of the spending for personal consumption than in the past. Among future developments we may expect:
1. Even greater variety in the assortment of fabrics appropriate for work, home, and leisure through such techniques as chemical treatment of fibers and textiles and proper blending of natural and synthetic fibers.
2. Greater protection by chemical treatment against flammability, soiling, wrinkling, and deterioration by environmental and biological attack.

3. Easier maintenance of wardrobes and furnishings with quick, effective, and safe cleaning preparations.
4. Increases in the variety of disposable apparel and furnishings made of paper for one-time use in hospitals, factories, restaurants, and homes.

SHELTER

The kinds and versatility of structural materials and coatings will continue to increase. For example:
1. Plastics will continue to be substituted for metal, wood, and other conventional materials that may be more costly for similar service.
2. Improvements in steel, especially in production techniques but also in properties, will strengthen its competitive utility.
3. New paints and other coatings will be formulated to protect structures and equipment better against the environment and against fire.
4. Development of malleable, ductile glasses that yield rather than fracture under excessive load will open new applications as a material of construction for buildings and also for products and equipment.
5. Plastic fibers will be used to produce paper with superior dielectric properties, heat resistance, and flex and tensile strength.

HEALTH

The potential chemical contributions are enormous, and new opportunities will be afforded by:
1. Better understanding of how small molecules interact with the large ones that make up the genetic and enzymatic systems, leading among other results to the design of potent drugs having greater specificity.
2. Devising drug delivery systems in which products administered to patients find their ways, in the main, to the target tissues.
3. Manipulation of the body's immune responses for defense against viral diseases, perhaps including cancers.
4. Application of expanding knowledge about the newer hormones that will provide additional approaches to treating such ills as cardiovascular diseases, reproductive disorders, and degenerative processes.
5. Developing a basic biochemical understanding of addiction and devising better therapeutic measures of managing or curing it.

Percy Lavon Julian
(1899–1975, American) Among the many achievements of Dr. Julian were the synthesis of physostigmine, used in the treatment of glaucoma, the perfection of soya protein, which has applications in the paper industry, and research into the anti-fatigue drug pregnenolone. His accomplishments have been recognized in fields as varied as science, education, and humanism.

FIGURE E13–2 · *The increasing emphasis on environmental conservation has led to new developments in the treatment of sewage and waste water. In the photograph, the technician is determining the proper amounts of the chemicals needed to purify waste water. This is done by analyzing the suspended materials in the water.*

6. Intensified research on aging and the accompanying degenerative diseases, for which no cures now exist.

7. Enlargement of the variety of materials usable in medical engineering and prostheses and development of safe and specific immuno agents that will reduce the rejection rates for organ transplants.

8. More sensitive and earlier detection of the presence or onset of major killing diseases.

ENERGY

The country has become suddenly and increasingly aware of energy shortages. Chemistry will be involved in helping meet the increasing demand by the following means among others:

1. Coal gasification.

2. Greater use of such "clean" fuels as propane and hydrogen.

3. Methodical exploitation, when warranted by price competitiveness, of oil shale and tar sand reserves.

4. Heavier reliance on nuclear power and the eventual design and operation of practical breeder reactors.

5. More effective harnessing of solar and geothermal energy.

TRANSPORTATION AND COMMUNICATION

Chemistry is also destined to expand the scope of economic choice for satisfying private and social objectives. For example, it will contribute to:

1. Design of safer automobile tires, bodies, and windshields and of safer airplane interiors.

2. Provision of safer containers for long-distance shipping of toxic, explosive, and other hazardous substances.

3. Development of optical wave guides and laser beam communication to expand tremendously the number of communication channels available.

4. More compact and more economic microcircuits and memory units for telephone, TV, radio, and other communication equipment, computers, and other electronic applications.

5. Efficient data storage and retrieval systems based on microfilm and Microcards.

6. Improved recording media for sound and pictures and for their reproduction.

ECOLOGY

In helping to protect and recondition man's [human] physical environment, chemical science is bound to play a significant part. Included on the technical agenda are:

1. Better control of factory stack gases through recycling and through fuel improvement.

2. Greater attention to sewage treatment, the economic use of sludge, and the recovery of chemicals from effluents.

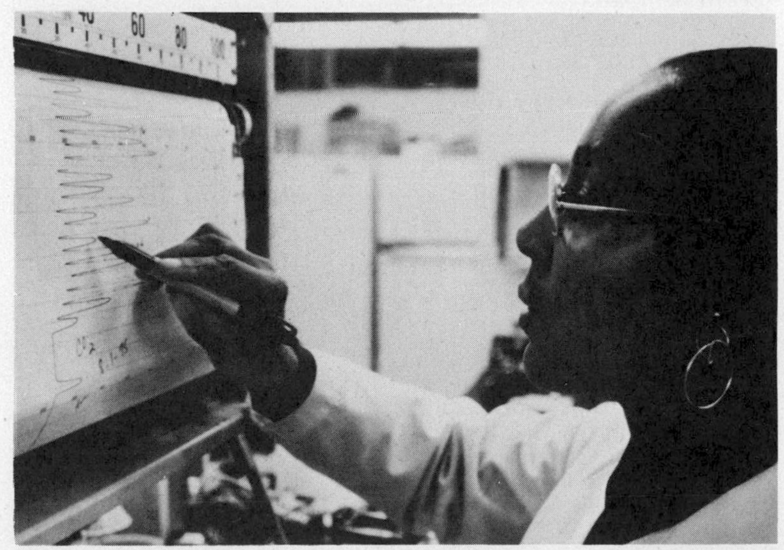

FIGURE E13–3 · *A medical technician analyzes the variations in the CO_2 content of a sample of blood. The breathing reflex is actually triggered when a certain level of CO_2 is reached.*

3. More systematic recovery and reuse of scrap paper, wood, plastics, and metals.
4. Possible replacement of phosphates in detergents with biodegradable alternatives.
5. Protection of water supplies from contamination by agricultural and other runoffs.
6. Quicker and more effective elimination of contaminations that do occur despite the best of control systems.

RESEARCH AND DEVELOPMENT (R AND D)

In addition to applied problems, we must maintain a vigorous research program in basic science. We are expanding our understanding of chemical bonding. As a result, our understanding of how to develop better plastics and better alloys expands. The more we learn about chemical energetics, the more likely we are to develop better solar cells, better batteries, and better energy sources.

As a society, we depend on science. It affects our daily lives in the technology of our food, health, materials, energy supply, and transportation. Science affects all human needs and activities. People trained in science are and will be needed in all these aspects of technology.

If you become a professional scientist, you are likely to be assigned to what most industrial concerns call their R and D department. Perhaps it would help you to anticipate what you might do. You can go about this by defining the terms research and development.

Research is used to describe the beginning studies of some problem. For example, you may start by investigating the properties of polymers. You can look at the synthesis of new organic compounds. The behavior of inorganic solids at very low temperatures might also be of interest. These studies could result in a new polymer that would have certain desirable properties. You might come up with a polymer that might be readily biodegradable. Or maybe the new organic compound might have promise as a useful drug. The inorganic compound might also be a good superconductor. Your research could proceed to a more detailed study of those particular materials. Your discovery could lead to better methods of synthesis. You might be able to test more thoroughly the biodegradability of the polymer. The physiological behavior of the drug and the electrical

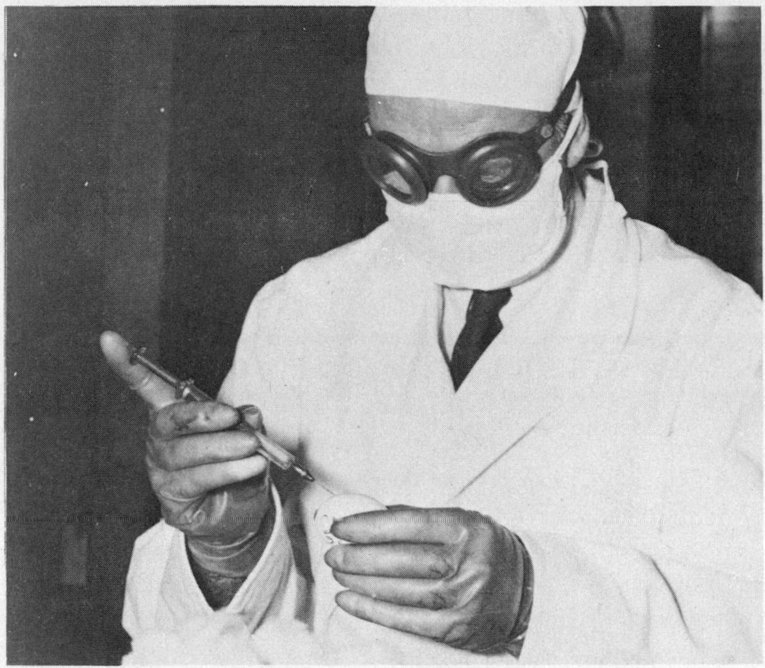

FIGURE E13–4 · *A researcher innoculates a chicken embryo with the sleeping sickness virus. This demonstrates one step in preparing a vaccine. Such vaccines have been used to treat many human and animal diseases.*

conductivity of the inorganic solid are some other possibilities. The research scientist is concerned primarily with a broad range of studies. The researcher looks at the more basic problems and the preliminary stages of assessing new materials for useful properties.

Your exact role in a research laboratory will depend on your experience. Normally, each project is headed by someone with a Ph.D. degree. Such a project leader will have several assistants with M.S. and B.S. degrees. These latter serve as technicians. They do much of the actual laboratory work under the planning and direction of the project leader.

Development is used to describe the phase between research and production. The work of the research laboratory leads to products that would seem to be useful. The development laboratory tries to solve the problems of producing these materials for the market. Development work is usually less fundamental in its approach than research. However, there is no sharp distinction between the two. The research group may continue their basic studies into the development stage. Also, many development groups discover new products and processes.

We should mention that an important role for the chemist lies in quality control. This is not R and D work. It involves constant measurement of the processes in a plant, using the techniques of analytical chemistry. You may be checking the yield or the purity of some product. Or you may be analyzing the level of pollution of the cooling water or of the smokestack emissions. This can be a challenging job, as the problems can vary daily. The entire plant operation can depend upon your analyses.

WHAT SHOULD YOU EXPECT OF A JOB?

Most people each have their own ambitions and priorities for a job. However, most people want a challenge from their work. People with a good scientific education want to employ it in doing something that seems useful. Also, they often want the opportunity to continue to grow as professional scientists. They can do this by periodically taking refresher courses. Another need, good physical working conditions, is usually not a problem today. The majority of laboratories—industrial, academic, and government—are modern, safe, and well-equipped. Salaries and fringe benefits are also usually satisfactory.

Lets look more fully at the first concerns. Are careers in science and technology likely to be challenging and satisfying? The brief list of areas in which chemistry has a role should convince you of the challenge. These areas will require R and D in industrial as well as government laboratories. Whether you would find satisfaction cannot be answered so easily. However, our society has so many problems that it would be an unusual person who would not find satisfaction in contributing to the solution of even one of those problems. Perhaps you can do so through a career in science and technology.

PRACTICE PROBLEMS

CHAPTER 3 · ATOMS AND MOLECULES

Sample Problem
How many moles of copper, Cu, are in a 222.39-g sample?

Solution:
Referring to Table 3–1 (p. 49), the relative atomic mass of copper is found.

$$\text{Relative atomic mass of Cu} = 63.54$$

Therefore, from our definition of mole we know that

$$1 \text{ mole Cu} = 63.54 \text{ g.}$$

Since we have 222.39 g of copper in our sample, the solution is

$$\frac{222.39 \text{ g}}{63.54 \text{ g/mole}} = 3.5 \text{ moles of Cu.}$$

Note In the following problems, all gases are considered to be at 0°C and 760 Torr, known as standard temperature and pressure, STP.

1. Calculate the mass of 1 mole of the following elements.

   Fe Ca Ni
   Al Hg Co

2. How many grams are there in .42 mole of sodium, Na?
3. How many moles of lead, Pb, are in a 134.68-g sample of this material?
4. Determine the number of moles in 90.8 g of neon, Ne.
5. Calculate the number of grams in 4.6 moles of silver, Ag.
6. How many grams are contained in a 1-mole sample of uranium, U?
7. Determine the number of moles of boron, B, in 356 g.
8. What volume will be occupied by 160 g of oxygen gas, O_2?
9. Determine the mass of 123.2 liters of nitrogen gas, N_2.
10. What volume will be occupied by 293.3 g of krypton gas, Kr?
11. Calculate the number of grams in 243 liters of argon gas, Ar.

CHAPTER 4 · FORMULAS AND CHEMICAL EQUATIONS

1. Calculate the mass of 1 mole of Na_3PO_4.
2. How many moles of PCl_3, phosphorus trichloride, are in 291 g of PCl_3?

3. If you have .086 mole of calcium oxide, CaO, how many grams do you have?
4. What is the mass of 1 mole of the compound Fe_2O_3?
5. How many moles of Mg_3N_2 would you have if you had 400 g?
6. Analysis of a compound shows that it contains 29.5% Ca, 23.6% S, and 47.1% of O. Calculate its simplest formula.
7. If you have 256 g of Al_2O_3, how many moles do you have?
8. Find the simplest formula of a compound if 2.676 g of the compound contain .732 g sodium, .440 g nitrogen, and 1.504 g oxygen.
9. Calculate the mass of 1 mole of each of the following compounds.

   a. H_2SO_4 **c.** $MgCl_2$ **e.** $CuSO_4$
   b. PbO **d.** Na_2CO_3 **f.** FeO

10. Determine the simplest formula for a compound containing 20% calcium and 80% bromine.
11. A certain compound is formed when 11.43 g of oxygen react with 8.87 g of phosphorus. Determine the simplest formula for this compound.
12. The molecular mass of a certain compound is 78.0. Analysis shows that the compound consists of 92.25% carbon and 7.75% hydrogen. Calculate the true (molecular) formula.
13. A compound contains 47% oxygen and 53% aluminum. Determine its simplest formula.
14. In the following reaction, 82.1 g of Fe are produced.
    ____ Fe_3O_4 + ____ CO → ____ Fe + ____ CO_2
    How many grams of CO_2 are produced?
15. How many grams of Zn are required to react completely with 11.2 g of HCl in the following reaction?
    ____ Zn + ____ HCl → ____ $ZnCl_2$ + ____ $H_2\uparrow$
16. Sodium reacts with water to form hydrogen gas.
    ____ Na + ____ H_2O → ____ NaOH + ____ $H_2\uparrow$
    a. Balance the equation.
    b. How many grams of sodium are required to produce .487 liter of H_2 (at STP)?
17. Magnesium burns in oxygen to form MgO.
    ____ Mg + ____ O_2 → ____ MgO
    a. Balance the equation.
    b. What volume of oxygen (at STP) is required to react completely with 217 g of Mg?
18. How many grams of potassium chlorate are needed to prepare 90.0 liters of oxygen in the following reaction?
    ____ $KClO_3$ → ____ KCl + ____ O_2
19. Ethene gas burns to form carbon dioxide and water.
    ____ C_2H_4 + ____ O_2 → CO_2 + ____ H_2O
    What volume (at STP) of ethene gas must be burned to produce 120 l of CO_2?
20. Hydrogen reacts with oxygen to produce water.
    $2H_2 + O_2 \rightarrow 2H_2O$
    If you have 85 liters of oxygen, what volume of hydrogen would be required for a complete reaction?

1. If you wish to triple the volume of a gas, by what factor must you decrease the pressure?
2. A 444-ml sample of oxygen gas exists at a pressure of 152 Torr. What volume will this gas occupy at standard pressure?
3. Determine the final volume of hydrogen gas if 176 liters is cooled from 273°C to 0°C with no change in pressure.
4. A 400-ml sample of Cl_2 is collected at a temperature of 273°C and 380 Torr. Calculate the volume of this gas at standard temperature and pressure.
5. A 48-ml sample of N_2 at 650 Torr and −173°C is heated to 727°C. The volume remains unchanged. Calculate the pressure at the new temperature.
6. A sample of ammonia gas occupies a volume of 155 ml at 25°C and a pressure of 760 Torr. If the temperature remains the same, but the pressure is increased to 1520 Torr, what will be the new volume occupied by the gas?
7. A sample of oxygen has a volume of 155 ml at 30°C and 760 Torr. In order for the gas to have a volume of 200 ml, to what must the pressure be changed?
8. At 20°C and 1 atm, a sample of helium has a volume of 1.00 liter. If the temperature is increased to 40°C, what volume will the gas occupy?
9. A sample of methane gas has a volume of 515 ml at 20°C and 1 atm. If the temperature is changed to 0°C and the pressure to 660 Torr, what will the new volume of the gas be?
10. 4.00 liters of krypton at a pressure of 760 Torr and a temperature of 293 K are changed by increasing pressure and temperature to 3 atm and 439 K. What is the new volume?
11. There is a mixture of methane and ethane in a closed container. There are twice as many moles of methane as ethane. The partial pressure of the methane is 40 Torr. What is the total pressure in the container?
12. A gas occupies a volume of 200 ml at 0°C and 760 Torr. What volume will it occupy at 100°C and 760 Torr?
13. At what temperature will 150 liters of hydrogen at 12°C and 750 Torr occupy a volume of 200 liters at a pressure of 730 Torr?
14. The volume of a gas is 400 ml at 12°C and 750 Torr. What will it occupy at 40°C and 720 Torr?
15. If you have 2.71 moles of oxygen gas at STP, what volume of oxygen would you have?
16. If you had 18.3 liters of oxygen at STP, how many moles of oxygen would you have?
17. At 20°C, a sample of neon gas has a volume of 400 liters. If the volume is decreased by half, and the pressure stays the same, what will the new temperature be?
18. If the temperature of a sample of ammonia gas is 0°C, and the temperature is changed so that the gas volume doubles, what is the new temperature of the gas?

19. A balloon is partially filled at a temperature of 293 K and a pressure of 750 Torr to occupy 0.75 liter. At a pressure of 755 Torr, the volume will be 2.0 liters, which will stretch the balloon, causing it to burst. At what temperature will the balloon burst?
20. What is the volume of a gas at 800 Torr and 40°C if its volume at 720 Torr and 288 K is 6.84 liters?

CHAPTER 6 · LIQUIDS AND SOLIDS

1. How many calories are required to increase the temperature of 90.0 ml of water from 20°C to 40°C? (Note: 1 g of H_2O = 1 ml of H_2O)
2. Upon heating, 500 ml of water increased in temperature from 27°C to 85°C. How many calories of heat were involved?
3. The molar heat capacity of iron (Fe) is 6.49. How much heat would be required to increase the temperature of 111.68 g of Fe by 10°C?
4. If 13.45 g of Al metal at 100°C cools to room temperature, 27°C, how much heat is evolved?
5. How much heat is required to convert 5 moles of ice, at −10°C, to steam at 110°C?

CHAPTER 7 · CHEMICAL PERIODICITY

1. Name the following compounds.

a. $NaHSO_4$	h. $CuSO_3$	o. $NH_4C_2H_3O_2$	v. $Ba(NO_3)_2$
b. NaH_2PO_4	i. $CoSO_4$	p. NH_4ClO_3	w. $Al(OH)_3$
c. K_2HPO_4	j. $Pb_3(PO_4)_2$	q. $CaSO_3$	x. $(NH_4)_2S$
d. $NaHCO_3$	k. Cu_2SO_4	r. $(NH_4)_2CO_3$	y. Na_2SO_4
e. $Fe_2(SO_4)_3$	l. $Cr_2(SO_3)_3$	s. Ag_2CrO_4	z. $BaCO_3$
f. $Hg_2(ClO_3)_2$	m. $Cr(OH)_2$	t. $Fe(C_2H_3O_2)_2$	
g. $MnSO_4$	n. $NaNO_3$	u. $AlPO_4$	

2. Write formulas for the following compounds.

a. Silver carbonate	m. Copper (II) chlorate
b. Sodium bromide	n. Cobalt (III) sulfate
c. Ammonium dichromate	o. Copper (II) phosphate
d. Lithium nitrate	p. Zinc nitrate
e. Ammonium carbonate	q. Silver oxide
f. Potassium chlorate	r. Iron (III) oxide
g. Sodium nitrite	s. Ammonium sulfide
h. Calcium sulfate	t. Mercury (I) sulfide
i. Mercury (I) sulfate	u. Aluminum chlorate
j. Tin (IV) nitrate	v. Copper (I) carbonate
k. Mercury (I) nitrite	w. Lead (II) acetate
l. Iron (II) hydroxide	x. Chromium (III) sulfite

CHAPTER 8 · THE MODERN ATOM

1. The mass number, A, for bromine is 81. If there are 46 neutrons in the Br atom, what is the atomic number, Z?
2. Mn has 30 neutrons and Z = 25. What is A for Mn?
3. Calcium has 20 neutrons in its nucleus and A = 40. What is Z?
4. The gold (Au) nucleus contains 79 protons and has A = 197. How many neutrons are in the Au nucleus?
5. Arsenic has Z = 33 and A = 75. How many neutrons are in an As nucleus?
6. Argon has 22 neutrons and A = 40. How many electrons does argon have?
7. The element silicon has three isotopes, ^{28}Si, ^{29}Si, and ^{30}Si. The following chart shows the abundance and mass of each isotope. Calculate the atomic mass of silicon (to four significant figures).

Isotope	*Abundance*	*Mass (amu)*
^{28}Si	92.21%	27.97693
^{29}Si	4.70%	28.97649
^{30}Si	3.09%	29.97376

8. There are two isotopes of Ga, gallium, ^{69}Ga and ^{71}Ga. The abundance of ^{69}Ga is 60.16% and its mass is 68.9257. The abundance of ^{71}Ga is 39.84% and its mass is 70.9249. Calculate the atomic mass of gallium (to four significant figures).
9. What is the atomic mass (A) for bromine (Br) if the abundance and mass of its two isotopes are as follows.
   ^{79}Br 50.537% and 78.9183
   ^{81}Br 49.460% and 80.9163
10. From the following information, determine the atomic mass of strontium (Sr).

Isotope	*Abundance*	*Mass (amu)*
^{84}Sr	0.560%	83.9134
^{86}Sr	9.870%	85.9094
^{87}Sr	7.035%	86.9089
^{88}Sr	82.535%	87.9056

CHAPTER 9 · ELECTRON ORBITALS AND CHEMICAL BEHAVIOR

Refer to the periodic table in answering problems 1–4.

1. Determine the electron configurations for silver, Ag, and gold, Au.
2. The discovery of element 106 is in dispute between the United States and the Soviet Union. Determine the electron configuration of this new element. Is it most likely to have the properties of a metal, a reactive gas, or an inert gas?
3. Life on the earth is based on the element carbon, C. Scientists sometimes speculate on the possibility of life based on the element silicon. Compare the electron configurations of these two elements. Why do you think scientists might believe in the possibility of silicon-based life?

4. If radioactive strontium, Sr, atomic number 38, is absorbed by the body, it will become part of the skeleton. It can cause damage over a period of time. Its position in the periodic table is just below calcium, Ca. How might a scientist have suspected that strontium would become part of the skeleton without doing an experiment? By checking the periodic table, determine another element that, if absorbed, might become part of the skeletal system.

CHAPTER 10 · CHEMICAL BONDING

1. By analysis of electron configurations, determine the probable formulas for compounds of the following ionically bonded elements.
   a. Magnesium (Mg, atomic number 12) and chlorine (Cl, atomic number 17)
   b. Lithium (Li, atomic number 3) and bromine (Br, atomic number 35)
   c. Calcium (Ca, atomic number 20) and fluorine (F, atomic number 9)
2. By analysis of dot structures, determine the probable formulas for compounds of the following covalently bonded elements.
   a. Aluminum (Al, atomic number 13) and chlorine (Cl, atomic number 17)
   b. Hydrogen (H, atomic number 1) and sulfur (S, atomic number 16)
3. By referring to Table 10–6, determine if the following compounds are strongly ionic, mainly covalent, or intermediate.
   a. Na_2O d. KI
   b. $AlBr_3$ e. CS_2
   c. SrF_2 f. LiCl

CHAPTER 13 · CHEMICAL ENERGY

1. Are the following reactions endothermic or exothermic?
   a. $NH_3(g) + \frac{5}{4}O_2(g) \rightarrow NO(g) + \frac{3}{2}H_2O(g) \quad \Delta H = -54.1$ kcal
   b. $H_2O(l) + SO_3(l) \rightarrow H_2SO_4(l) + 20.92$ kcal
   c. 399 kcal $+ Al_2O_3(s) \rightarrow 2Al(s) + \frac{3}{2}O_2(g)$
2. Assume the following three steps to produce the overall reaction $NH_3(g) + \frac{5}{4}O_2(g) \rightarrow NO(g) + \frac{3}{2}H_2O(g)$.
   (1) $\frac{1}{2}N_2(g) + \frac{1}{2}O_2(g) \rightarrow NO(g)$
   (2) $\frac{1}{2}N_2(g) + \frac{3}{2}H_2(g) \rightarrow NH_3(g)$
   (3) $H_2(g) + \frac{1}{2}O_2(g) \rightarrow H_2O(g)$
   a. Determine ΔH for each reaction.
   b. Calculate ΔH for the overall reaction.
3. Calculate ΔH for the formation of 1 mole of CO(g), given the following reactions:
   a. $C(s) + O_2(g) \rightarrow CO_2(g) \quad \Delta H = -94.0$ kcal
   b. $CO(g) + \frac{1}{2}O_2(g) \rightarrow CO_2(g) \quad \Delta H = -67.6$ kcal
4. Calculate ΔH for this reaction:
   $NO(g) + \frac{1}{2}O_2(g) \rightarrow NO_2(g)$

5. Hexane, C_6H_{14}, has a $\Delta H_f = -39.96$ kcal/mol. Hexane burns according to this reaction:
$2C_6H_{14}(l) + 19O_2(g) \rightarrow 12CO_2(g) + 14H_2O(l)$
Determine the ΔH for the reaction.

CHAPTER 14 · ENERGY AND EQUILIBRIUM

1. Write an equilibrium constant for the following reactions.
   a. $N_2O_4(g) \rightleftharpoons 2NO_2(g)$
   b. $CaCO_3(s) \rightleftharpoons CaO(s) + CO_2(g)$
   c. $H_2(g) + Fe_3O_4(s) \rightleftharpoons Fe(s) + H_2O(g)$
   d. $NO_2(g) + H_2(g) \rightleftharpoons NH_3(g) + H_2O(g)$
2. N_2O_4 decomposes, under certain conditions, to NO_2. Determine K if 0.324 mole of N_2O_4 produces 1.85×10^{-3} moles of NO_2 at equilibrium.
3. Under other conditions, at equilibrium, 0.129 mole of N_2O_4 and 1.17×10^{-3} mole of NO_2 were found in solution. Calculate the equilibrium constant.
4. The following data were collected, showing concentration of reactants and products at equilibrium. Calculate K.
   $2HI(s) \rightarrow H_2(l) + I_2(g)$
   HI = 1.27×10^{-2} mole/liter; $H_2 = 5.62 \times 10^{-3}$ mole/liter; $I_2 = 5.94 \times 10^{-4}$ mole/liter
5. At equilibrium, *K* for the decomposition of HI(g) was found to be 1.07×10^{-5}. The concentration of HI(g) was found to be 0.129. Calculate the concentration of $I_2(g)$ at equilibrium. (All concentrations are in moles/liter.)
6. Under different conditions, HI(g) produced .112 mole/liter of $H_2(g)$. At equilibrium, *K* for the reaction is 2.07×10^{-6}.
   a. What concentration of $I_2(g)$ is present at equilibrium?
   b. Determine the concentration of HI(g) at equilibrium.

The next three problems also involve this reaction:

$$2HI(g) \rightleftharpoons H_2(g) + I_2(g)$$

In each problem, calculate the missing concentration or constant at equilbrium.

	2HI(g)	⇌	$H_2(g)$	+	$I_2(g)$	K
7.	1.78		0.172		0.406	x
8.	x		0.242		0.242	0.217
9.	0.78		0.112		x	2.06×10^{-2}

10. At equilibrium, HI was found to be 22.3% dissociated. Calculate K.

CHAPTER 16 · WATER AND IONIC SOLUTIONS

1. How much KBr would you weigh to make 1 liter of 1 molar KBr solution?
2. If you evaporated 250 ml of a 3.5 molar solution of NaCl, how much NaCl would you recover?

3. 500 ml of a solution of NaOH contains 10.0 g of NaOH. Calculate the molarity of the solution.
4. How much NaOH must be used to prepare 2 liters of a 2.0 molar solution.
5. A chemist has 4.0 g of $AgNO_3$ and needs to prepare 2.0 liters of a 0.01 M solution. Will there be enough $AgNO_3$? If so, will there be any left over?
6. A solution contains 85.5 g of $C_{12}H_{22}O_{11}$ (sucrose) in a liter of solution. Calculate the molarity of the sugar solution.
7. If you have 200 ml of a 0.125 M solution of KNO_3, what mass of KNO_3 is present?
8. A chemist needs to prepare a 1.5 molar solution of H_2SO_4, but has only 49 g of the acid. How many ml can be prepared?
9. 50.0 g of ethylene glycol ($C_2H_6O_2$), better known as "antifreeze," is placed in a radiator containing 2.0 liters of water. How much will this lower the freezing point of the water?
10. How much will the freezing point of water be lowered if 57 g of sucrose ($C_{12}H_{22}O_{11}$) is added to 100 ml of water?
11. What is the freezing point of a 6.0 molal solution of KBr? (Note: $KBr \rightleftharpoons K^+ + Br^-$).
12. Calculate the boiling point of a 2.5 molal solution of glucose.
13. When 720 g of dextrose is dissolved in a liter of water, the solution boils at 102.08°C. Calculate the molecular mass of dextrose.
14. The solubility of $BaSO_4$ is 3.87×10^{-5}. Calculate K_{sp} for $BaSO_4$.
15. From Table 16-1, calculate the solubility of the following compounds.
    a. PbS   b. AgCl   c. ZnS

CHAPTER 17 · ACIDS AND BASES

1. What is the pH of a .01 molar solution of HNO_3?
2. What is the pOH for a .01 M HNO_3 solution?
3. If a solution has $[H^+]$ of 10^{-6}, is the solution acidic, or basic?
4. A solution of HCl has a pH of 5.0. What is the $[H^+]$?
5. Calculate the pH and pOH for a solution that contains 10^{-4} mole of H^+ per liter.
6. What is the pOH and pH of a solution of .001 M NaOH?
7. The pH of a solution containing 10^{-5} mole of OH^- per liter is 9.0. What is the pOH?
8. Calculate the pH and pOH for a solution containing 0.0001 mole of H^+ per liter.
9. What is the $[H^+]$ for a solution with pH=3?
10. A solution has pOH=12. Calculate the H^+.
11. Calculate the pH and pOH for the following solutions.
    a. 1.0×10^{-4} M HCl
    b. 1.0×10^{-3} M NaOH
    c. 0.10 M H_2S
    d. 3.00 M NaOH
    e. 1.00×10^{-6} M HCl

CHAPTER 18 · OXIDATION AND REDUCTION

1. Assign an oxidation number to each element in the following compounds.
   a. Li_2SO_4
   b. O_2
   c. H_2Te
   d. SF_4
   e. H_2SO_4
2. In the following reactions, indicate which elements are *oxidized*, and which are *reduced*, (if any).
   a. $Cu + 2Ag^+ \rightarrow Cu^{+2} + 2Ag$
   b. $Zn + Cu^{+2} \rightarrow Zn^{+2} + Cu$
   c. $Fe_3O_4 + 4H_2 \rightarrow 3Fe + 4H_2O$
   d. $CaCO_3 \rightarrow CaO + CO_2$
   e. $2KClO_3 \rightarrow 2KCl + 3O_2$
   f. $NH_4NO_2 \rightarrow N_2 + 2H_2O$
   g. $MnO_2 + 4HCl \rightarrow MnCl_2 + Cl_2 + 2H_2O$
3. Balance the following oxidation-reduction reactions (H^+ and H_2O may need to be added to the reaction).
   a. ____ Al + ____ $H^+ \rightarrow$ ____ Al^{+3} + ____ $H_2\uparrow$
   b. ____ Fe^{+2} + ____ MnO_4^- + ____ $H^+ \rightarrow$ ____ $Mn^{+2} + Fe^{+3}$ + ____ H_2O
   c. ____ Cu + ____ SO_4^{-2} + ____ $H^+ \rightarrow Cu^{+2}$ + ____ SO_2 + ____ H_2O
   d. ____ H^+ + ____ Br^- + ____ $BrO_3^- \rightarrow Br_2 + H_2O$
   e. ____ H^+ + ____ Ag + ____ $NO_3^- \rightarrow$ ____ Ag^+ + ____ NO_2 + ____ H_2O
   f. $I_2(s)$ + ____ $OH^- \rightarrow$ ____ I^- + ____ IO_3^- + ____ H_2O
   g. ____ H^+ + ____ H_2S + ____ $Cr_2O_7^{-2} \rightarrow$ ____ S_8 + ____ Cr^{+3} + ____ H_2O
   h. ____ Zn + ____ H^+ + ____ $NO_3^- \rightarrow$ ____ Zn^{+2} + ____ NH_4^+ + ____ H_2O
4. The half-cell reaction for $Cd \rightleftharpoons Cd^{+2} + 2e^-$ has $E = 0.403$ volt. Will cadmium reduce Cu^{+2}?
5. Calculate E° for the following reactions.
   a. $Cu + Ag^+ \rightarrow Cu^{+2} + Ag$
   b. $Zn + Cu^{+2} \rightarrow Zn^{+2} + Cu$
   c. $Cl_2 + Sn^{+2} \rightarrow Cl^- + Sn^{+4}$
   d. $Br_2 + I^- \rightarrow Br^- + I_2$
   e. $Cr + Ni^{+2} \rightarrow Cr^{+3} + Ni$
   f. $Al + H^+ \rightarrow Al^{+3} + H_2$
   g. $Hg + Hg^{+2} \rightarrow Hg_2^{+2}$
6. Indicate whether the following reactions will have a positive potential, or a negative potential.
   a. $Ni + Cu^{+2} \rightarrow Ni^{+2} + Cu$
   b. $Cu + H^+ \rightarrow Cu^{+2} + H_2$
   c. $Mn + Co^{+2} \rightarrow Mn^{+2} + Co$
   d. $Zn^{+2} + Pb \rightarrow Zn + Pb^{+2}$

APPENDIX

APPENDIX 1 · THE INTERNATIONAL (METRIC) SYSTEM

The system of measurement used in science, and throughout most of the world, is commonly known as the metric system. It was originated in France about 1790 and there have been several versions since then. The most recent updating of the system was done at an international conference in 1960. Some of the older units are still commonly used, even though they are not officially a part of the most modern revision of the system.

The metric system is used in science because it is easier to work with than any other system. It is a decimal system and, therefore, conversions are made by multiplying or dividing by the appropriate power of ten.

The standard units of the metric system are these:

PROPERTY	UNIT	SYMBOL
length	meter	m
mass	kilogram	kg
time	second	s

The meter was originally defined as 1/10 000 000 of the distance between the North Pole and the equator along the surface of the earth. Since this distance is still not known exactly, the meter was redefined as the distance between two marks on a platinum-iridium bar kept at the International Bureau of Weights and Measures in France. However, it is difficult to duplicate this measurement. Therefore, the meter is now defined as 1 650 763.73 times the wavelength of the orange-red spectral line emitted by krypton-86. This standard can be reproduced in laboratories all over the world.

The kilogram standard is a platinum-iridium cylinder, also at the International Bureau in France. All secondary standards for the kilogram are calibrated against this standard. The original unit of mass was the gram, defined as the mass of 1 cubic centimeter of pure water at 3.98°C. The gram is now defined as 1/1000 of the standard kilogram, which, for all practical purposes, gives a result identical to the earlier definition.

The second is defined in terms of the precession frequency of a cesium-133 nucleus. The value of such exact standards may not be apparent to you. The accuracy obtained in a high school laboratory does not require such precise definitions. However, in measurements concerning atoms and molecules, or the path of a rocket in space, extreme accuracy is needed and exact standards are very important.

Prefixes are used to indicate multiples and submultiples of the standard units. Following is a list of prefixes most commonly used.

giga (G) $= 10^9$	deci (d) $= 10^{-1}$	micro (μ) $= 10^{-6}$
mega (M) $= 10^6$	centi (c) $= 10^{-2}$	nano (n) $= 10^{-9}$
kilo (k) $= 10^3$	milli (m) $= 10^{-3}$	pico (p) $= 10^{-12}$

Examples of units that are derived from the basic units:

area (length^2) = square centimeters (cm^2), square meters (m^2);
volume (length^3) = cubic centimeters (cm^3), cubic meters (m^3);
density (mass/volume) = grams/cubic centimeter (g/cm^3)

The following list gives conversions for the units that would be most often encountered in chemistry.

Length
1 meter (m) = 100 centimeters (cm) = 1000 millimeters (mm)
1 kilometer (km) = 1000 m

Mass
1 kilogram (kg) = 1000 grams (g)
1 g = 1000 milligrams (mg)

Volume
1 cubic decimeter (dm^3) = 1 liter (l)*
1 cubic centimeter (cm^3) = 1 milliliter (ml)*
1 l = 1000 ml*

Many other units, such as the newton (N) for force and the joule (J) for energy, are derived from the basic units. These are important in physics and more advanced chemistry courses.

APPENDIX 2 · SCIENTIFIC NOTATION

Very large and very small numbers are hard to work with, and they take up much space when written. There are no names for extremely large or small numbers, and it is very easy to lose a decimal place or a zero and not even realize it. Scientists and others have overcome these difficulties by using scientific notation (or powers-of-ten notation) to express these numbers.

From your math studies you know that our number system has a base of 10. Thus, any number can be expressed as a decimal value, equal to or greater than 1 but less than 10, times 10 raised to some power. For example:

$$900 = 9 \times 100 = 9 \times (10 \times 10) = 9 \times 10^2$$
$$80 = 8 \times 10 = 8 \times 10^1$$
$$\begin{aligned} 3\,450\,000 &= 3.45 \times 1\,000\,000 \\ &= 3.45 \times (10 \times 10 \times 10 \times 10 \times 10 \times 10) \\ &= 3.45 \times 10^6 \end{aligned}$$

*Officially, the liter is not a unit in the revised system. However, it is used often and, for the purposes of this book, the relationships shown can be considered equalities.

When a number is less than one, the number can be expressed in a similar way.

$$0.06 = 6 \times \frac{1}{100}$$

$$= 6 \times \frac{1}{10 \times 10} = 6 \times \frac{1}{10^2}$$

In bringing the 10 into the numerator, the sign of the exponent changes. Thus:

$$\frac{1}{10^2} = 10^{-2}$$

Therefore:

$$6 \times \frac{1}{10^2} = 6 \times 10^{-2}$$

Another example is the following.

$$0.000093 = 9.3 \times \frac{1}{100\,000}$$

$$= 9.3 \times \frac{1}{10 \times 10 \times 10 \times 10 \times 10}$$

$$= 9.3 \times \frac{1}{10^5} = 9.3 \times 10^{-5}$$

As shown by these examples, proper scientific notation has one place at the left of the decimal point. All other significant figures are at the right of the decimal point.

Until you become proficient, the easiest method for converting decimal notation to scientific notation is to count the number of places the decimal point must be moved to leave one place at the left.

Moving the decimal point to the left raises 10 to the power equal to the number of places moved. For example, translating 7 000 to scientific notation requires moving the decimal three places to the left. Thus, $7\,000 = 7.00 \times 10^3$. Other examples of this process are: $94\,000 = 9.4 \times 10^4$ (decimal point moves four places to left) and $3\,830\,000\,000 = 3.83 \times 10^9$ (decimal point moves nine places to left).

When the decimal point is moved to the right, the power to which 10 is raised is numerically equal to the number of places moved, but it has a negative value. For example:

$$0.00700 = 7.00 \times 10^{-3}$$

(Decimal point moves three places to right.)

$$0.0000580 = 5.80 \times 10^{-5}$$

(Decimal point moves five places to right.)

$$0.0000000000432 = 4.32 \times 10^{-11}$$

(Decimal point moves eleven places to right.)

The advantage of stating that a gram of hydrogen gas contains 6.023×10^{23} atoms rather than 602 300 000 000 000 000 000 000 atoms is obvious. The 6.023×10^{23} is easier to write and easier to say, and there is no chance of losing or gaining zeros.

Not only is 6.023×10^{23} easier to handle, but it is a better statement of the facts than the 24-place number. We are not really sure of the exact number of atoms in 1 gram of hydrogen gas. The 6.023×10^{23} indicates that we are sure of the 6, the 0, and the 2. The 3 is an uncertain, doubtful figure. However, in the 24-place number, the first twenty-three places are written as if they are exact numbers and we are unsure of only the last zero. Scientific accuracy demands that we use 6.023×10^{23}; this particular value is not known accurately to twenty-four places.

To convert scientific notation to decimal form, the reverse of the procedure above can be used. Move the decimal point the number of places indicated by the exponent of 10. Negative exponents indicate numbers less than one. Thus:

$$3.00 \times 10^{2} = 300$$
$$6.9 \times 10^{-3} = 0.0069$$

APPENDIX 3 · UNIT ANALYSIS

To scientists, numbers are important. Without measured data they cannot do their work. But units are equal in importance to numbers. It does no good to say that an item has a mass of seven. Seven what? Seven g? Seven kg? Seven mg? The unit tells as much as the number. One without the other says nothing.

Units can be used to help solve problems. Just as numbers can be multiplied and divided, so can units. Thus:

$$\frac{50.0\ \text{cm}}{\cancel{\text{sec}}} \times 3.00\ \cancel{\text{sec}} = 150\ \text{cm}$$

Suppose you wanted to calculate the concentration of a particular solution. In 350.0 milliliters of solution, there is 0.700 mole of a solute. You are not sure what to do with the numbers, but you know that concentration is expressed in moles per liter. If the units are moles per liter, then the concentration must be the mole value divided by the liter value. Thus:

$$\text{Concentration} = \frac{0.700\ \text{mol}}{0.350\ \text{l}} = 2.00\ \text{mol/l}$$

Again, suppose you wish to determine the volume (V) of a sample of gas. You know that the temperature (T) is 300 K, the pressure (P) is 1.50 atmospheres, and the sample contains 0.500 mole (n) of the gas. The gas constant, R, equals 0.080 liter-atmospheres/mole-K.

If you remember the formula $PV = nRT$, there is no difficulty. If you don't remember it, you can still work the problem. The unit in the answer (volume) is liters. How can you arrange the other values, the knowns, to arrive at liters as the answer?

$$\text{liters} = \frac{\text{liter-}\cancel{\text{atm}}}{\cancel{\text{mole-K}}} \times \frac{\cancel{(\text{moles})(\text{K})}}{\cancel{\text{atm}}}$$

Using the units to help solve the problem means that you do not have to clutter up your mind with memorized formulas for every operation. Also, because units, like numbers, can be manipulated, many time- and labor-consuming steps can be saved by first doing a unit analysis and then following the same scheme for the numerical portion of the problem.

What is the density of carbon, calculated from the following information?

$$\text{Atomic volume}_C = 5.30\ \text{cm}^3/\text{mol}$$
$$\text{Mass}_C = 1.99 \times 10^{-23}\ \text{g/atom}$$
$$1\ \text{mol of C atoms} = 6.02 \times 10^{23}\ \text{atoms/mol}$$

The units of density are mass per volume—that is, in the units of our problem, g/cm^3. By arranging the given units so that they will form the required answer, we arrive at the solution for the problem.

$$\text{g/cm}^3 = \frac{\text{g/atom} \times \text{atoms/mol of atoms}}{\text{cm}^3\text{/mol of atoms}}$$
$$= \frac{\text{g}}{\cancel{\text{atom}}} \times \frac{\cancel{\text{atoms}}}{\cancel{\text{mol of atoms}}} \times \frac{\cancel{\text{mol of atoms}}}{\text{cm}^3}$$
$$= \text{g/cm}^3$$

Now put in the numbers that go with the corresponding units.

$$\text{Density of C} = 1.99 \times 10^{-23}\ \text{g}/\cancel{\text{atom}} \times 6.02 \times 10^{23}\ \cancel{\text{atoms/mol}} \times \frac{1}{5.30}\ \cancel{\text{mol}}/\text{cm}^3 = 2.26\ \text{g/cm}^3$$

APPENDIX 4 · EXPONENTS

Values raised to an exponent or power are frequently found in science. A number written as 6^3 means $6 \times 6 \times 6$. That is, the base number 6 has been multiplied by itself three times (not 6×3 but $6 \times 6 \times 6$). Thus:

$$x^4 = x \cdot x \cdot x \cdot x$$
$$9^8 = (9)(9)(9)(9)(9)(9)(9)(9)$$
$$10^2 = 10 \times 10$$

The symbol for multiplication can be × or · or (). All three are acceptable and are used interchangeably.

There are only two rules to use when working with exponents—one for multiplication and the other for division.

Multiplication is accomplished by addition of the exponents. The numbers to be multiplied must be the same base. For example:

$$(x^4)(x^2) = x^6 \qquad 9^3 \times 9^5 = 9^8 \qquad 2^3 \times 2^9 = 2^{12}$$

Division involves subtraction of the exponents. Thus:

$$x^4 \div x^3 = \frac{x^4}{x^3} = x^1 = x \qquad a^{10} \div a^4 = \frac{a^{10}}{a^4} = a^6 \qquad 9^3 \div 9^3 = \frac{9^3}{9^3} = 9^0 = 1$$

From this last example, we can see that any number raised to the 0 power equals 1.

Sometimes negative exponents are found. To remove the minus sign from the exponent, invert the base and the exponent. For example:

$$2^{-2} = \frac{1}{2^2} \qquad \frac{1}{x^{-3}} = x^3 \qquad 9^{-7} = \frac{1}{9^7}$$

$$(a^4)(a^{-3}) = a^1$$

$$= a^4 \cdot \frac{1}{a^3} = \frac{a^4}{a^3} = a^1 \qquad \frac{a^7}{a^{-3}} = a^{10} = a^7 \div a^{-3} = a^7 \div \frac{1}{a^3} = a^7 \times a^3 = a^{10}$$

APPENDIX 5 · PROPORTION

Many of the problems scientists are concerned with involve proportions. A proportion exists when the variation in one value is related to the variation in some other measurement.

The distance an automobile travels is related to the amount of time it is in motion. For any increase in time, there is an increase in distance covered. Thus, the distance is directly proportional to the time. In mathematical terms:

$$d \propto t$$

The symbol $\propto$ is read "is directly proportional to." To convert $d \propto t$ into an equation, that is, to replace $\propto$ with $=$, we put in a proportionality constant. The constant is usually symbolized as k. It will be different for different relationships. Thus:

$$d = kt$$

This now reads "the distance traveled is equal to a constant (the velocity) times the time during which the vehicle is moving." A direct proportion can also be stated as

$$\frac{d}{t} = k.$$

The ratio of the two values is a constant.

The relationship between the volume of a fixed weight of a gas and its temperature is a direct proportion (provided the pressure stays constant). When a gas is heated, it expands; when cooled, it contracts. Thus:

$$V \propto T \text{ or } V = kT \text{ or } \frac{V}{T} = k$$

Some properties are related in an inverse manner. That is, as one increases, the other decreases. The pressure on a gas is related to the volume of the gas in this way. (This is true as long as the temperature does not change.)

The harder a gas is squeezed (P increases), the less space it takes up (V decreases). Thus:

$$P \propto \frac{1}{V}$$

Using a proportionality constant k^1, then:

$$P = k^1\left(\frac{1}{V}\right) = \frac{k^1}{V}$$

or

$$PV = k^1$$

An indirect or inverse proportion exists when the product of the two variables is a constant. An example of an inverse proportion is the number of equal pieces cut from a pie and the size of each piece. When more pieces are cut, each piece is smaller. But the number of pieces multiplied by the size of each slice is always equal to the whole pie.

Other proportionalities, which are not direct or indirect, also occur. For example:

Area of a square $\propto$ (side^2)	$A \propto s^2$
Volume of a cube $\propto$ (side^3)	$V \propto s^3$
Kinetic energy of a gas molecule $\propto \sqrt{\text{Temperature}}$	$KE \propto T^{1/2}$

Sometimes it is easier to see the relationship between two properties when they are graphed. The changes in one compared with the changes in the other can be shown by plotting points on a graph. One of the properties is the vertical axis (ordinate); the other is the horizontal axis (abscissa).

The following table contains pressure and temperature data for a sample of gas (volume kept constant).

Pressure (atm)	*Temperature (K)*
1	122
2	244
3	366
4	488
5	610

The graph shows that there is a steady rise in P with a rise in T. The slope of the line

$$\left(\text{slope} = \frac{\text{changes in } P}{\text{changes in } T}\right) \text{ is } \frac{1}{122} \text{ atm/K (Fig. 1).}$$

Figure 1

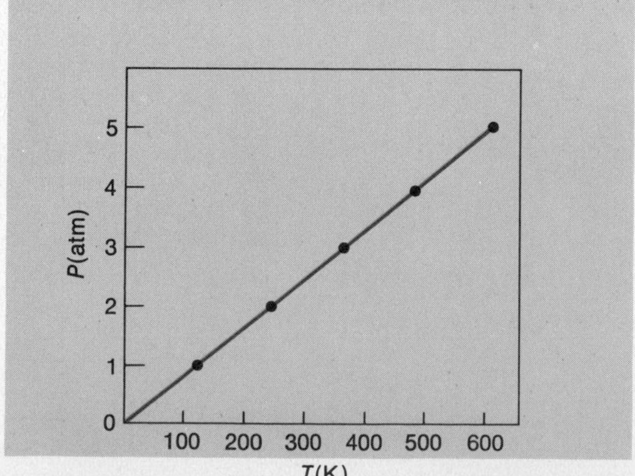

Generalized to any set of variables, such as x and y, the x values are plotted along the abscissa; and the y values, on the ordinate. The slope of the line through the points or the graph relates the two properties. Slope (m) $= \frac{\Delta y}{\Delta x}$. Because the properties have units, the slope will have units. For example, if y is in meters and x is in seconds, then the slope will be in meters per second.

Not all graphs give straight lines. If the graph is a straight line going up to the right, then a direct proportion has been shown. (See *P-T* graph.) If the graph is a curve, then something other than a direct relationship has been shown. A pressure-volume graph looks like Figure 2.

Figure 2

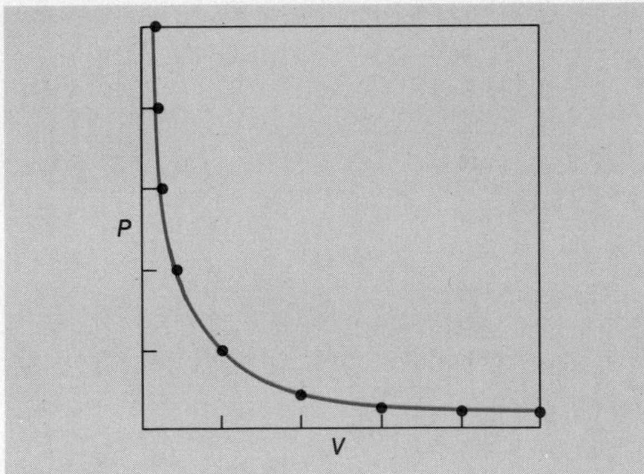

GLOSSARY

In order to learn the correct use of these terms refer to the pages that are shown by **boldface** numerals in the Index.

absolute zero The hypothetical lowest possible temperature, equal to -273°C or 0 K. It is thought that substances at this temperature have no molecular motion and no thermal energy.

acid A substance that donates a proton (acts as an electron-pair acceptor) in a chemical reaction.

acid radicals Stable groups of atoms that behave like nonmetal combinations in chemical compounds.

activated complex Highly unstable structures that last for only about 10^{-13} second, and serve as intermediate complexes in reaction mechanisms.

activation energy The minimum amount of energy required to break chemical bonds and initiate a chemical reaction.

addition polymers Large molecules formed by the combination of two or more smaller molecules (monomers), with no water or other by-product given off.

addition reactions Reactions of unsaturated hydrocarbons in which an atom is added to each carbon where a double bond is located.

aggregates Clusters or groups of ions or atoms, as found in crystalline solids.

alchemy A precursor of chemistry developed in ancient Egypt and practiced in the Middle Ages and the Renaissance. Alchemists searched for the philosopher's stone and an elixir of life.

alicyclic A class of organic compounds that contain carbon and hydrogen atoms joined to form one or more rings.

aliphatic Any organic compound of hydrogen and carbon characterized by a chain of the carbon atoms; three subgroups of such compounds are alkanes, alkenes, and alkynes.

allotropic forms Different forms of the same element that have different properties due to differences in bonding.

alloy A solid solution composed of two or more metals, or of a metal or metals with a nonmetal.

amino acids The fundamental structural units of proteins; they are carboxylic (fatty) acids in which one hydrogen atom has been replaced by an amine group.

amphoteric Having both acidic and basic characteristics.

anions Negatively charged ions, which move toward the anode during electrolysis.

apoenzyme The protein component that with a coenzyme forms a complete enzyme.

aromatic Of or pertaining to any organic compound containing an unsaturated ring of carbon atoms.

atom The smallest particle of an element which has all the properties of that element and which can enter into a chemical combination.

atomic mass unit A unit of atomic mass equal to one twelfth of the mass of a carbon-12 atom.

binary compounds Compounds that contain only two elements; they may contain two or more atoms.

binding energy The energy needed to break down a molecule, an atom, or a nucleus into its constituent particles.

biochemistry The integrated science that deals with the chemistry of living matter; life processes are studied on the molecular level.

buffer solutions Solutions that have been selected or prepared to minimize changes in the hydrogen ion concentration that would otherwise have occurred as a result of chemical change.

calorie The amount of energy necessary to increase the temperature of one gram of water by one degree Celsius (1.00°C), specifically from 14.5°C to 15.5°C, at a constant pressure of one atmosphere.

calorimeter constant The amount of heat energy necessary to cause a rise in temperature of 1.00°C for the calorimeter itself.

carbohydrates A group of organic compounds with the general formula $C_x(H_2O)_y$; includes sugars, starch, glycogen, cellulose, etc.

carboxyl group The radical $COOH^-$ contained in organic compounds, combining a carbonyl and a hydroxide group.

chain mechanism Basically the same thing as a reaction mechanism, using slightly more descriptive terminology. The analogy formed is that a sequence of reactions occurs like links in a chain.

chain-breaking steps Reactions that eliminate free radicals from the system.

chain-initiating step The first reaction in a chain mechanism.

chain-propagating steps Reactions that continue to produce free radicals.

chemical activity The most basic chemical property of the elements, that being the ability to take part in a chemical reaction.

chemical change A transformation of substances from one form to another with the absorption or liberation of energy.

chemical equation The symbolic language used to describe a chemical reaction, showing the number of atoms and molecules of the reactants and the proportional amounts of the products resulting from the reaction.

chemical kinetics The branch of physical chemistry that deals with the mechanisms and rates of chemical reactions.

chemical nomenclature The naming of chemical compounds.

chemical reaction A chemical change, where the transformation of one or more components into new substance(s) occurs, accompained by an energy change.

chemistry The study of the composition and properties of various forms of matter and their transformations.

colligative properties The properties of a solution that are determined by the number of particles of solute present.

colloidal suspension An intimate mixture of two substances, one of which, called the disperse phase (or colloid), is uniformly distributed as finely divided particles through the second substance, called the dispersion medium (or dispersing medium). *See* sol and gel.

combustion A rapid oxidation that is accompanied by the generation of heat and often light.

compound A substance composed of two or more simpler substances united in definite proportions and assuming properties different from the composing substances.

conceptual definition A definition that uses all possible observed facts to infer what is happening on a microscopic level.

condensation Transformation from a gas to a liquid.

condensation polymers Large molecules formed from the combination of two or more smaller molecules (monomers), with the elimination of water, alcohol, or similar byproduct.

conductance A measure of the ability of a solution to conduct electricity.

conjugate acid-base pair An acid and a base related by the ability of the acid to generate the base by loss of a proton.

coordinate covalent bond A covalent bond in which one atom donates both of the electrons to be shared.

copolymer A compound of high molecular weight produced by polymerizing two or more different monomers together.

corrosion The slow destruction of materials by the chemical action of the environment, as distinct from mechanical action.

covalent bond A chemical bond in which electrons are shared between the outer orbitals of the atoms that form the bond.

covalent crystal A crystal held together by covalent bonds.

cracking A very important reaction involving the breaking of a hydrocarbon chain by a combination of high temperature and high pressure; much of our gasoline is produced mainly by this process.

critical pressure The pressure of a vapor at its critical temperature necessary for liquefaction of the vapor to occur.

critical temperature The highest temperature at which the liquefaction of a gas can occur; the vapor and liquid densities of a substance are equal at this point.

crystal lattice An arrangement in space of isolated points in a regular pattern, showing the positions of atoms, molecules, or ions in the structure of a crystal.

diatomic molecule A molecule consisting of two atoms.

dipole-dipole forces Intermolecular forces that occur in molecules having permanent dipoles.

dipole moment The product of the magnitude of either charge in a dipole and the distance between the charges.

dipoles Molecules that have a slight positive charge at one end and a slight negative charge at the other end.

dispersion forces Intermolecular forces that exist between molecules that have no permanent dipoles; they arise from the interaction of the electrons and the nuclei of atoms or molecules that are close together.

distillation The separation of a substance by vaporizing the desired volatile components and then condensing them to the liquid state.

dualistic The idea that electrons, or matter in general, have both a particle and a wave nature.

ductility The property of a material characterized by the ability to be drawn into a wire or otherwise undergo deformation without breaking.

dynamic state A state in which change is occurring in both directions but at an equal rate, as in equilibrium.

electrical conductivity The property of a material that allows it to conduct the flow of electricity.

electron configuration The orbital and spin arrangement of an atom's electrons, specifying the quantum numbers of the atom's electrons in a given state.

electron shells The collection of all the electron states in an atom that have a given principal quantum number.

electronegativity A relative measure of the electron-attracting power of an atom involved in a chemical bond. Fluorine, oxygen, and nitrogen are the three most electronegative elements.

electrons Minute elementary particles that have a negative charge and exist independently or as components of atoms outside the nuclei.

element A primary substance that cannot be decomposed into simpler substances by ordinary chemical methods; a substance of which all the atoms have the same atomic number.

energy The capacity to do work, or to overcome resistance.

enthalpy The energy content of a system under constant pressure, designated by the symbol H.

enthalpy of formation The enthalpy of a reaction in which a compound is formed from its elements.

entropy The measure of the randomness or disorder of a system, designated by the symbol S.

enzymes A group of catalytic proteins that are produced by living cells and that regulate chemical reactions within the cells without themselves being altered or destroyed.

equilibrium system A system that has reached a steady state; it is microscopically dynamic and macroscopically static.

evaporation The conversion of a liquid to a vapor by the addition of latent heat.

excited state Any energy level of a physical system (usually referring to an atom) that has higher energy than the ground state.

exothermic reaction A reaction that releases energy.

formula A notation utilizing chemical symbols and numbers to indicate the chemical composition of a compound.

free radicals Atoms or diatomic or polyatomic molecules that possess at least one unpaired electron.

gamma radiation Electromagnetic energy of a short wave length and high energy.

gas A state of matter having no definite shape or definite volume; the molecules in a gas have high kinetic energy, and the attractive forces between the molecules are weak.

gel The semisolid colloidal state, having little Brownian movement (as opposed to a sol).

geometric isomerism A type of isomerism in which the isomers contain atoms attached to each other in the same order and with the same bonds, but with different spatial, or geometric, relationships.

ground state The lowest energy level of a particle or a system of particles (atom).

groups The vertical rows of elements in the periodic table.

half-life The rate of decay of radioactive materials; that period of time in which half of a given number of atoms in the material disintegrate.

heat capacity The amount of heat energy needed to raise a system one degree in temperature in a specified way, usually at constant pressure or constant volume.

heat of combustion The amount of heat released in the oxidation of one mole of a substance at constant pressure, or constant volume.

heterogeneous In reference to a mixture, composed of dissimilar or unlike parts unevenly distributed throughout the mixture.

heterogeneous catalyst A catalyst that is not in the same physical state as the reactants.

homogeneous In reference to a mixture, composed of similar or identical parts evenly distributed throughout the mixture.

homogeneous catalyst A catalyst that is in the same physical state as the reactants.

hybrid orbital A molecular orbital which is a linear combination of two or more orbitals of comparable energy (such as 2s and 2p orbitals). It is concentrated along a certain direction in space and participates in the formation of a directed valence bond (a bond formed between the electrons of two or more atoms).

hydration The chemical union of molecular water with the molecules or units of another chemical species into a complex molecule.

hydrogen bond A weak intermolecular bond between a hydrogen atom that is covalently bonded to a strongly electronegative atom (usually oxygen, nitrogen, or fluorine) and a strongly electronegative atom of another molecule.

hydrolysis In aqueous solutions of electrolytes, the reactions of cations with water to produce a weak base or of anions with water to form a weak acid.

hydronium ion H_3O^+, a proton combined with a molecule of water (a hydrated H^+ ion); found in pure water and in all aqueous solutions.

immiscible Pertaining to substances that will not mix with each other, usually liquids such as oil and water.

intermediate bonding A type of chemical union that is an intermediate between ionic bonding and covalent bonding; electrons are still shared between two atoms, but not equally.

intermolecular forces Forces that exist between two molecules.

ion An atom that has lost or gained one or more electrons and consequently is left with a positive or negative electric charge.

ionic bond A chemical bond in which electrons from the outer orbitals of one atom are transferred to the outer orbitals of a second atom.

ionic crystal A crystal in which the lattice-site occupants are ions (charged particles) held together primarily by their electrostatic attraction.

ionization energy The amount of energy necessary to remove the electron in the highest orbital from a gaseous atom or ion in its ground state.

ionize To separate into ions.

isomers Compounds having the same molecular formula but different molecular structures, and different properties.

isotopes Atoms of the same element that have the same chemical properties but different atomic mass numbers, due to different numbers of neutrons.

kilocalorie A unit of heat energy equal to 1000 calories; abbreviated kcal.

kinetic energy The energy that a body possesses because of its motion. It may be defined according to the following formula: $KE = \frac{1}{2}mv^2$.

Lewis electron-dot structures A type of notation chemists use to portray the bonding in covalent molecules, using chemical symbols, dots for the valence electrons, and a dash for a pair of shared electrons.

liquid A state of matter with a definite volume that takes the shape of its container.

mass The quantity of matter in a body; a measure of a body's inertia.

mass number The sum of the number of protons and neutrons in the nucleus of an atom, represented by the symbol A.

metallic crystal One of the four classes of crystalline solids.

miscible Referring to substances (usually liquids) that are mutually soluble; that is, they will dissolve in each other.

mixture A substance composed of two or more substances that are not chemically combined and that can be separated by physical means.

molality Concentration given as the number of moles of solute in a kilogram of solvent; indicated by *m*.

molar gas volume The volume that one mole of any gas will occupy under standard conditions of temperature and pressure. It is equal to 22.4 liters.

molar heat capacity The amount of heat energy required to increase the temperature of one mole of a substance by 1.00°C.

molar heat of fusion The energy required to melt one mole of a solid at its melting point.

molarity Measure of the number of moles of solute dissolved in one liter of solution; it is indicated by *M*, preceded by a number to show solute concentration.

mole The molecular or atomic mass of a substance expressed in grams.

molecular crystal A solid consisting of a lattice array of molecules bound by weak van der Waals forces.

molecular mass The sum of the atomic masses of all the atoms in a molecule.

molecule The smallest component of a substance that retains the properties of the substance.

monatomic Composed of one atom.

monomers Simple molecules that are capable of combining with a number of like or unlike molecules to form a polymer.

neutralization reaction An acid reacting with a base to form a salt and water.

neutrons Elementary particles that have approximately the same mass as protons but lack electric charge.

nonelectrolyte A substance in a solution that does not exhibit electrical conductance.

nucleons A collective name for protons and neutrons.

nucleus The central, positively charged, dense portion of the atom, constituting the main mass of the atom and determining the location of the protons and neutrons.

operational definition A definition that is based on experimental observations and describes what one can measure on a macroscopic level.

orbital The energy level that an electron occupies, described by a combination of the first quantum number (n) and the second quantum number (l).

organic Of chemical compounds, based on carbon chains or rings and also containing hydrogen with or without oxygen, nitrogen, or other elements.

oxidation A chemical reaction that involves the loss of electrons, that is, in which the positive valence of a compound or radical is increased.

oxidation number The number of electrons to be added (or subtracted) from an atom in a combined state to convert it to elemental form.

oxidizing agent A compound that gives up oxygen easily, removes hydrogen from a compound, or attracts negative electrons.

periodic law The properties of the elements and their compounds are periodic functions of their atomic numbers.

periodic table A systematic arrangement of the elements in order of their atomic numbers, which shows similar properties of families of elements.

periods The horizontal rows of elements in the periodic table.

physical change An alteration that does not produce any difference in the basic identity of a substance in terms of its fundamental properties.

polar covalent bond A bond in which a pair of electrons is shared in common between two atoms, but the pair is held more closely by one of the atoms.

polyunsaturated Of or pertaining to a class of fats of animal or plant origin (especially plant oils) whose molecules consist of carbon chains with many double bonds.

potential energy Stored energy; the energy that a body has by virtue of its position or configuration.

primary structure The linear sequence of amino acids in a protein molecule.

proton acceptors The definition of bases according to the Brönsted-Lowry theory.

proton donors The definition of acids according to the Brönsted-Lowry theory.

protons Elementary particles that are fundamental constituents of all atomic nuclei, each having a positive charge.

radioactivity The emission of alpha or beta particles or gamma rays by nuclei, resulting in spontaneous transmutation.

reactants The molecules that act with one another to produce a new set of molecules (products). They are written on the left-hand side of the arrows in a chemical equation.

reaction mechanism The sequence of separate steps involved in a chemical reaction.

reducing agent A compound that brings about reduction in a chemical reaction by reacting with oxygen or by increasing its valence as a result of electron interchange.

reduction Chemical process that is the opposite of oxidation, involving the removal of oxygen from a compound or the lowering of the valence of a combined element by the addition of an electron.

reduction-oxidation (redox) reaction An oxidizing chemical change, where an element's positive valence is increased (electron loss), accompanied by a simultaneous reduction of an associated element (electron gain).

relative atomic mass The mass of one atom of an element relative to the mass of one atom of carbon.

relative molecular mass The mass of one molecule of a compound relative to the mass of one atom of carbon.

saturated A solution that contains enough of a dissolved solid, liquid, or gas so that no more will dissolve into the solution at a given temperature and pressure.

secondary structure The spatial configuration of the amino acid chain; a common secondary structure is a helix.

simple covalent bond A covalent bond in which the electrons are shared evenly between the two atoms.

sol A free-flowing colloidal state consisting of a suitable dispersion medium, which may be gas, liquid or solid, and the colloidal substance (the disperse phase), which is distributed throughout the dispersion medium.

solid A state of matter that has a definite shape and volume.

solubility The ability of a substance to form a solution with another substance. Also, the solution concentration at the saturation point.

solute The substance dissolved in a solvent.

solvent That part of a solution that is present in the largest amount, or the compound that is normally liquid in the pure state (as for solutions of solids or gases in liquids).

specific heat The number of calories required to raise the temperature of one gram of a substance one degree Celsius; it is by convention 1.0° for water.

stationary states Various energy states an atom may occupy without emitting electromagnetic radiation.

strong acids Acids that dissociate completely or nearly completely in aqueous solution.

structural isomers Two or more compounds that are composed of the same number and types of atoms but differ in structural arrangement, and therefore have different physical and chemical properties.

sublimation The process whereby a solid changes directly to the gaseous state, without going through the liquid phase.

supersaturated Referring to a solution that contains more solute than is needed to cause saturation.

symbol A letter or combination of letters that represents an element.

ternary compound A compound that contains three elements.

tertiary structure A description of how the amino acid chain is bent and folded back on itself to form a convoluted globular structure.

tetrahedron (tetrahedral) An isometric crystal form in cubic crystals, in the shape of a four-faced polyhedron, each face of which is an equilateral triangle.

unsaturated hydrocarbons A class of hydrocarbons that have at least one double or triple carbon-carbon bond that is not in an aromatic ring.

valence The combining capacity of an element in a compound, as measured by the number of bonds to other atoms that one atom of the given element forms upon chemical combination.

valence electron An electron in the highest electron energy shell that is occupied in a certain element.

valence shell The electrons that form the outermost shell of an atom; that part of the atom which is involved in chemical reactions.

vapor A gas at a temperature below the critical temperature, so that it can be liquefied by increasing the pressure, without lowering the temperature.

vapor pressure The pressure exerted by a vapor when liquid and vapor are in equilibrium with each other.

weak acids Acids that dissociate to only a limited extent in aqueous solution.

INDEX

CREDITS

Cover: John Carnevale for Silver Burdett
Unit Divider illustration: William Schmidt
Text art: Eric Hieber (except as noted)

Other sources for the illustrations are listed below. Some have been abbreviated as follows: E.R. Degginger for Silver Burdett (E.R.D. for S.B.); Silver Burdett photo (S.B.). ii–iii: NASA.

Chapter 1 p. X: Fisher Collection, Fisher Scientific Company. p. 2: Courtesy of the American Museum of Natural History. p. 3: map by David Lindroth. p. 4: Historical Pictures Service. p. 5: Fisher Collection, Fisher Scientific Company. p. 6: Manso, Courtesy The Prado Museum, Spain. p. 8: S.J. Krasemann-Peter Arnold. p. 9: S.B. p. 10: E.R.D. for S.B. p. 13: U.S. Energy Research & Development Administration. p. 15: Courtesy Bethlehem Steel. p. 16: E.R.D. for S.B. p. 17: (T.) The Bettmann Archive; (B.) S.B. p. 18–19: S.B. p. 20: Harry Hamlin-Photo Trends.

Chapter 2 p. 24: Copyright by the California Institute of Technology and Carnegie Institution of Washington. p. 26: Peter Gregg for Silver Burdett. p. 28: Brown Brothers. p. 31: NASA. p. 36: E.R.D. for S.B. p. 39: U.S. Energy Research & Development Administration.

Chapter 3 p. 42: Bell Laboratories. p. 44: The Bettmann Archive. p. 45: (R.) Culver Pictures; (L.) Brown Brothers. p. 47: The Bettmann Archive. p. 48: National Bureau of Standards. p. 51: (T.) S.B.; (B.) E.R.D. for S.B. p. 52: art by Earl Kvam. p. 53: S.B.

Chapter 4 p. 60: Lothar Roth. p. 63: art by Earl Kvam. p. 67: E.R.D. for S.B. p. 69: art by Earl Kvam. p. 79: The Bettmann Archive.

Chapter 5 p. 84: National Center for Atmospheric Research (NCAR), Boulder, Colorado. p. 85: art by Earl Kvam. p. 86: (B.) S.B.; (T.) art by Earl Kvam. p. 90: National Center for Atmospheric Research (NCAR), Boulder, Colorado. p. 95: New York Daily News. p. 101: Jonathon Rawle-Stock Boston.

Chapter 6 p. 108: Zübli-Photo Trends. p. 113: Imagery. p. 119: Courtesy of Professor M.J. Buerger, Massachusetts Institute of Technology. p. 121: John Running-Stock Boston. p. 129: art by Earl Kvam. p. 130: E.R.D. for S.B. p. 131: art by Earl Kvam.

Chapter 7 p. 134: S.B. p. 136: E.R.D. for S.B. p. 137: Bell Laboratories. p. 138: (L.) The Bettmann Archive; (R.) Historical Pictures Service. p. 139: (T.) Argonne National Laboratory Photo; (B.) NASA. p. 140: American Gas Association. p. 141: Argonne National Laboratory Photo. p. 142: Photographed at "Let There Be Neon Gallery," 451 West Broadway, New York City, photo by Linda Lindroth-Peter Arnold. p. 150: E.R.D. for S.B. p. 153: S.B. p. 155: Manfred Kage-Peter Arnold. p. 156: The Bettmann Archive.

Chapter 8 p. 164: Belgian National Tourist Office. p. 166: Dr. Albert V. Crewe. p. 167: W.R. Grace & Co. p. 168: Brown Brothers. p. 173: Brookhaven National Laboratory. p. 176: Brown Brothers. p. 177: Jean-Claude LeJeune-Stock Boston. p. 182: Courtesy of Bausch & Lomb, Inc. p. 184: Harvey Lloyd-Peter Arnold.

Chapter 9 p. 190: John Weiss for Editorial Photo Service.

Chapter 10 p. 212: Shostal Associates. p. 224: I. Fankuchen, Late Professor at the Polytechnic Institute of Brooklyn. p. 227: art by Earl Kvam. p. 229: Brown Brothers. p. 232: Floyd Clark, California Institute of Technology. p. 236: art by Earl Kvam.

Chapter 11 p. 240: Edward Lettau-Peter Arnold. p. 242–245: art by Earl Kvam. p. 248–250: art by Earl Kvam.

Chapter 12 p. 256: Manfred Kage-Peter Arnold.

Chapter 13 p. 272: S.B. p. 274: Werner H. Müller-Peter Arnold. p. 275: Exxon Company, USA. p. 286: Pennsylvania Power & Light Company. p. 287: NASA.

Chapter 14 p. 290: Frank Siteman-Stock Boston. p. 292–293: E.R.D. for S.B. p. 304: John Running-Stock Boston.

Chapter 15 p. 308: James V. Elmore-Peter Arnold. p. 311–312: S.B.

Chapter 16 p. 326: Richard Weiss-Peter Arnold. p. 328: Jim Holland-Stock Boston. p. 332: Camera Press London-Photo Trends. p. 333: John Zoiner-Peter Arnold. p. 334: S.B. p. 344: Brown Brothers. p. 347: no credit.

Chapter 17 p. 352: Ernst Haas. p. 355–371: S.B.

Chapter 18 p. 374: Imagery. p. 376–394: S.B. p. 396: Brown Brothers.

Chapter 19 p. 402: Werner H. Müller-Peter Arnold. p. 408: Courtesy Mount Holyoke College. p. 420: S.B.

Chapter 20 p. 424: Manfred Kage-Peter Arnold. p. 426: Photo Trends. p. 427: The Bettmann Archive. p. 428: Schwarz Bioresearch, Inc. p. 431: American Chemical Society. p. 436: © Alfred T. Lamme, 1974-Camera M.D. Studios, Inc. p. 443: NASA. p. 444–445: art by Earl Kvam. p. 446: S.B. p. 446: art by Earl Kvam. p. 448–449: E.R.D. for S.B. p. 456: The Bettmann Archive.

Excursion 1 p. 463: Bergakademie Freiberg. p. 464: International Minerals & Chemical Corporation. p. 465: Ben Schnall. p. 467: Oberlin College Library. p. 468–470: The Bettmann Archive.

Excursion 2 p. 473: S.B.

Excursion 3 p. 478: Photo Trends. p. 480: art by Earl Kvam. p. 481: (B.)—482: art by Earl Kvam. p. 485: Brown Brothers.

Excursion 4 p. 497: Brookhaven National Laboratory. p. 498: Picker X-ray Corporation.

Excursion 5 p. 505: Mt. Wilson & Palomar Observatories. p. 507: NASA. p. 509–510: Brown Brothers.

Excursion 6 p. 517–526: University of California Lawrence Berkeley Laboratory.

Excursion 8 p. 532: Courtesy of Professor F.M. Carpenter, Harvard University. p. 534: (L.) R. Van Nostrand-National Audubon Society; (M.) Carl Rettenmeyer; (R.) E. Guthrie, The American Museum of Natural History. p. 536–538: Molecular models and bouncing spheres provided by Prof. M. Goodman, Polytechnic Institute of Brooklyn, and photographed by Henry Groskinsky for Silver Burdett. p. 540: Phillips Petroleum Company. p. 542: AVCO-Everett Research Laboratory, a Division of AVCO Corporation. p. 543: Albert Fenn for Time.

Excursion 9 p. 548: Grant Heilman. p. 551: Harald Sund. p. 552: Ellis Herwig-Stock Boston.

Excursion 10 p. 559: National Bureau of Standards.

Excursion 11 p. 563: Photri-Photo Research International. p. 564: S.B. p. 572: Dow Chemical Company.

Excursion 12 p. 578: Photo Trends. p. 582: © Carroll H. Weiss, RBP, 1974, Camera M.D. Studios, Inc. p. 583: Public Relations, Bell Helicopter (a Textron Company).

Excursion 13 p. 586: Warner Lambert Research Institute. p. 587: Diamond Shamrock Chemical Company/ Julian Research Institute. p. 588–589: W.R. Grace & Company. p. 591: U.S.D.A. photograph by Peter Killian.

3 4 5 6 7 8 9 10—**RMcN**—83 82 81 80 79

PERIODS	GROUPS I	II				TRANSITION ELEMENTS			
1	1 1.00797 H Hydrogen								
2	3 6.939 Li Lithium	4 9.0122 Be Beryllium							
3	11 22.9898 Na Sodium	12 24.312 Mg Magnesium							
4	19 39.102 K Potassium	20 40.08 Ca Calcium	21 44.956 Sc Scandium	22 47.90 Ti Titanium	23 50.942 V Vanadium	24 51.996 Cr Chromium	25 54.9380 Mn Manganese	26 55.847 Fe Iron	27 58.9332 Co Cobalt
5	37 85.47 Rb Rubidium	38 87.62 Sr Strontium	39 88.905 Y Yttrium	40 91.22 Zr Zirconium	41 92.906 Nb Niobium	42 95.94 Mo Molybdenum	43 (99)* Tc Technetium	44 101.07 Ru Ruthenium	45 102.905 Rh Rhodium
6	55 132.905 Cs Cesium	56 137.34 Ba Barium	57 138.91 La Lanthanum †	72 178.49 Hf Hafnium	73 180.948 Ta Tantalum	74 183.85 W Tungsten	75 186.2 Re Rhenium	76 190.2 Os Osmium	77 192.2 Ir Iridium
7	87 (223)* Fr Francium	88 (226)* Ra Radium	89 (227)* Ac Actinium ‡	104 (259)* Rf ** Rutherfordium	105 Ha Hahnium**	106***	107***	108***	

† LANTHANIDE SERIES	58 140.12 Ce Cerium	59 140.907 Pr Praseodymium	60 144.24 Nd Neodymium	61 (147)* Pm Promethium	62 150.35 Sm Samarium	63 151.96 Eu Europium	64 157.25 Gd Gadolinium	65 158.924 Tb Terbium
‡ ACTINIDE SERIES	90 232.038 Th Thorium	91 (231)* Pa Protactinium	92 238.03 U Uranium	93 (237)* Np Neptunium	94 (242)* Pu Plutonium	95 (243)* Am Americium	96 (247)* Cm Curium	97 (247)* Bk Berkelium

*Atomic masses appearing in parentheses are those of the most stable known isotopes.

**Names are unofficial.